THE ARDEN SHAKESPEARE

GENERAL EDITORS:
RICHARD PROUDFOOT, ANN THOMPSON
and DAVID SCOTT KASTAN

KING RICHARD III

THE ARDEN SHAKESPEARE

THE ARDEN EDITION OF THE
WORKS OF WILLIAM SHAKESPEARE

KING RICHARD III

Edited by
ANTONY HAMMOND

LONDON AND NEW YORK

The general editors of the Arden Shakespeare have been

First Series
W. J. Craig (1899–1906) and R. H. Case (1909–44)

Second Series
Una Ellis-Fermor (1946–58), Harold F. Brooks (1952–82),
Harold Jenkins (1958–82) and Brian Morris (1975–82)

Third Series
Richard Proudfoot, Ann Thompson and
David Scott Kastan

This edition of *King Richard III*, by Antony Hammond,
first published in 1981 by
Methuen & Co. Ltd
Reprinted twice
Reprinted 1987

Reprinted 1988, 1990, 1992, 1994 by
Routledge
11 New Fetter Lane, London EC4P 4EE
29 West 35th Street, New York, NY 10001

Typeset by Western Printing Services Ltd, Bristol
Printed in Great Britain by
Western Printing Services Ltd, Bristol (hardbound)
Printed in England by Clays Ltd, St Ives plc
Cased edition bound by Hunter & Foulis Ltd

British Library Cataloguing in Publication Data

Shakespeare, William
King Richard III.—(The Arden Shakespeare)
I. Title   II. Hammond, Antony   III. Series
822'.3   PR 2821

ISBN 0 416 17970 3
ISBN 0 415 02694 6 Pbk

TO
HAROLD BROOKS

CONTENTS

ACKNOWLEDGEMENTS

My work on this edition began in September 1973, but owes immensely to the twenty or more years of gathering materials which Professor Harold Brooks had spent on the play, the fruits of which he made over to me in their entirety. Any misapprehension or misuse of these materials is of course mine alone, but they have enriched the edition beyond any short description. I owe to Harold Brooks many other debts, for his kindness and encouragement, and for the detailed advice without which this work would be far more imperfect. I dedicate it to him in heartfelt gratitude.

I have received help from more kind and wise people in completing my work than any man has a right to. I must especially thank the other two General Editors, and, in addition, Professors William J. Cameron, University of Western Ontario; Richard Morton, Ronald Vince, James King, Douglas Duncan and Thomas Cain, all of McMaster University. Then there are many North Library friends, especially David Paisey and Ian Willison, and a number of my co-workers there, including Samuel Schoenbaum and Paul Korshin, who must be mentioned. I have had helpful advice from many people, including Mac Jackson of the University of Auckland, Kristian Smidt, Marvin Spevack, Fredson Bowers and John Tobin.

I must thank the staff of the British Library (Reference Division), the Bodleian Library, and the Huntington Library for their willing help, and register a debt of gratitude to the Canada Council for their award of research grants and a Leave Fellowship; I have also received invaluable research grants from McMaster University. I am grateful for the great help given me by Doreen DelVecchio, and my research assistants, Margaret Duff, Jennifer Taylor and Robert Young. I have also had much help from my students, especially my graduate class: Barbara Brown, Cynthia Eland, Barbara Pankhurst and James Penistan. Finally, let me thank my wife and children for their help, their patience and forbearance, during the edition's preparation.

Hamilton, Ontario

ABBREVIATIONS AND REFERENCES

The abbreviated titles of Shakespeare's works are those in C. T. Onions, *A Shakespeare Glossary*, 2nd edn, 1919. Passages quoted or cited are from the *Riverside Shakespeare*, ed. G. Blakemore Evans (Boston, 1974). Passages quoted from old-spelling texts, with the exception of quotations from the early editions of *Richard III*, have been modified in the usual way by replacing the long s with the short, and by regularizing the typographical conventions of u and v, i and j. In the collation $Qq = Q1–Q6$ inclusive. Variants in $Q7–8$ and $F2–4$ are not routinely collated.

I. EDITIONS

Q1	*The Tragedy of King Richard the third* . . . Printed by Valentine Sims, for Andrew Wise . . . 1597 [First Quarto. Copy used: British Library, Huth 47. Facsimile ed. W. W. Greg, Shakespeare Quarto Facsimiles No. 12, Oxford, 1959.]
Q2	—— . . . Printed by Thomas Creede, for Andrew Wise . . . 1598 [Second Quarto].
Q3	—— . . . Printed by Thomas Creede, for Andrew Wise . . . 1602 [Third Quarto].
Q4	—— . . . Printed for Thomas Creede, and are to be sold by Mathew Lawe . . . 1605 [Fourth Quarto].
Q5	—— . . . Printed by Thomas Creede, and are to be sold by Mathew Lawe . . . 1612 [Fifth Quarto].
Q6	—— . . . Printed by Thomas Purfoot, and are to be sold by Mathew Law . . . 1622 [Sixth Quarto].
Q7	—— . . . Printed by Iohn Norton, and are to be sold by Mathew Law . . . 1629 [Seventh Quarto].
Q8	—— . . . Printed by Iohn Norton . . . 1634 [Eighth Quarto].
F	*Mr. William Shakespeares Comedies, Histories & Tragedies.* 1623 [First Folio. Copy used: British Library C.39. k. 15. Facsimile: *The Norton Facsimile*, prepared by Charlton Hinman, New York, 1968].
F2	—— 1632 [Second Folio].
F3	—— . . . The third Impression, 1664 [Third Folio].
F4	—— . . . The fourth Edition, 1685 [Fourth Folio].
Rowe	*The Works of Mr. William Shakespear* . . . *Revis'd and Corrected by N. Rowe Esq.*, 1709 [Rowe[2], a 2nd edn, 1709].
Rowe[3]	—— 1714.
Pope	*The Works of Shakespear* . . . *Collected and Corrected* . . . *by Mr. Pope*, 1723.
Theobald	*The Works of Shakespeare* . . . *Collated with the Oldest Copies, and Corrected; With Notes* . . . *By Mr. Theobald*, 1733.

Hanmer	*The Works of Shakespear . . . Carefully Revised and Corrected by the former Editions* [ed. Thomas Hanmer], Oxford, 1744.
Warburton	*The Works of Shakespear. The Genuine Text . . . settled . . . By Mr. Pope and Mr. Warburton,* 1747.
Johnson	*The Plays of William Shakespeare . . . To which are added Notes by Sam. Johnson,* 1765.
Capell	*Mr. William Shakespeare his Comedies, Histories, and Tragedies* [ed. Edward Capell, 1768].
Rann	*The Dramatic Works of Shakespeare . . . with notes by Joseph Rann,* Oxford, 1787.
Malone	*The Plays and Poems of William Shakespeare . . . with . . . notes by Edmond Malone,* 1790.
Steevens	*The Plays of William Shakespeare . . . The Fourth Edition* [ed. George Steevens], 1793.
Singer	*The Dramatic Works of William Shakespeare. With notes . . . by Samuel Weller Singer,* 1826.
Knight	*The Pictorial Edition of the Works of Shakspere. Edited by Charles Knight,* 1839–1842.
Collier	*The Works of William Shakespeare . . . with . . . notes . . . by J. Payne Collier,* 1842 etc.
Dyce	*The Works of William Shakespeare. The Text revised by the Rev. Alexander Dyce,* 1857.
White	*The Works of William Shakespeare ed. R. G. White,* Boston, 1865–57–61.
Camb.	*The Works of William Shakespeare. Edited by W. G. Clark, J. Glover, and W. A. Wright,* Cambridge and London, 1863–6 (The Cambridge Shakespeare).
Keightley	*The Plays and Poems of William Shakespeare. Edited by Thomas Keightley,* 1865.
Marshall	*The Henry Irving Shakespeare: The Works of William Shakespeare, edited by Henry Irving and F. A. Marshall,* 1887–90.
Craig	*The Oxford Shakespeare: The Complete Works . . . ed. . . . W. J. Craig,* Oxford, 1892.
Thompson	*The Tragedy of King Richard the Third Edited by A. Hamilton Thompson* (Arden Shakespeare), 1907.
Variorum	*The Tragedy of Richard the Third . . . Edited by Horace Howard Furness* (New Variorum Edition of Shakespeare), Philadelphia, 1908.
Alexander	*William Shakespeare: the Complete Works, ed. Peter Alexander,* London and Glasgow, 1951.
NCS	*Richard III. Ed. John Dover Wilson,* Cambridge, 1954 (The New Cambridge Shakespeare).
Eccles	*The Tragedy of Richard the Third, ed. Mark Eccles,* New York, 1964 (Signet Classic Shakespeare).
NPS	*King Richard the Third, ed. E. A. J. Honigmann,* 1968 (New Penguin Shakespeare).
Evans	*The Riverside Shakespeare, textual editor G. Blakemore Evans,* Boston, 1974.

2. OTHER WORKS

Abbott	E. A. Abbott, *A Shakespearian Grammar,* 1966 (1870).
Alcazar	George Peele, *The Battell of Alcazar,* 1594 (Greg 127).

Andria	The *Andria*, in *Terence with an English Translation* (by John Sargeaunt), 1912 (Loeb edn).
Appius and Virginia	*A new Tragicall Comedie of Apius and Virginia*, 1575 (Greg 65).
Arcadia	Sir Philip Sidney, *The Countesse of Pembroke's Arcadia*, in *Prose Works of Sir Philip Sidney*, ed. Albert Feuillerat, Cambridge, 1963.
Arden of Faversham	*The Tragedy of Master Arden of Faversham*, 1592 (ed. M. L. Wine (The Revels Plays), 1973).
Astrophel and Stella	In *The Poems of Sir Philip Sidney*, ed. William A. Ringler Jr, Oxford, 1962.
Baldwin	T. W. Baldwin, *William Shakspere's Small Latine & Lesse Greeke*, 2 vols, Urbana, 1944.
BCP	*The Booke of Common Prayer and Administration of the Sacraments*. Edn used: printed by Christopher Barker [1585].
Bible	Books of the Bible are referred to by their usual abbreviations. Edn used: *The Bible Translated According to the Ebrew and Greeke*, printed by Christopher Barker, 1583 (Geneva Bible).
Boas	F. S. Boas, *University Drama in the Tudor Age*, Oxford, 1914.
Bullough	Geoffrey Bullough, *Narrative and Dramatic Sources of Shakespeare;* vol. II, 1958; vol. III, 1960.
Campaspe	John Lyly, *A moste excellent Comedie of Alexander, Campaspe and Diogenes*, 1584 (Greg 84).
Carter	T. Carter, *Shakespeare and Holy Scripture*, New York, 1905.
Chambers	E. K. Chambers, *William Shakespeare: a study of facts and problems*, 2 vols, Oxford, 1930.
Chambers, *Elizabethan Stage*	E. K. Chambers, *The Elizabethan Stage*, 4 vols, Oxford, 1923.
Churchill	George B. Churchill, *Richard the Third up to Shakespeare*, Berlin, Palaestra x, 1900.
Cowden-Clarke	C. Cowden-Clarke, *Shakespeare's Characters*, 1863.
Cromwell	*The True Chronicle Historie . . . of Thomas Lord Cromwell*, 1602 (Greg 189).
Daniel	P. A. Daniel, Introduction to William Griggs's facsimile of *Richard III* Q1 [1885].
Darius	*A Pretie new Enterlude . . . of King Darius*, 1565 (Greg 40).
Douce	Francis Douce, *Illustrations of Shakespeare*, 1807.
Edward III	*The Raigne of King Edward the Third*, 1596 (Greg 140).
Franz	Wilhelm Franz, *Die Sprache Shakespeares in vers und prosa*, Halle/Saale, 1939.
Frye	Roland M. Frye, *Shakespeare and Christian Doctrine*, Princeton, 1963.
Golding's Ovid	*Shakespeare's Ovid: being Arthur Golding's Translation of the Metamorphoses*, ed. W. H. D. Rouse, 1961.
Greg	W. W. Greg, *A Bibliography of the English Printed Drama to the Restoration*, 4 vols, 1939–59.
Greg, *Ed. Prob.*	W. W. Greg, *The Editorial Problem in Shakespeare*, 3rd edn, Oxford, 1954.
Greg, *S.F.F.*	W. W. Greg, *The Shakespeare First Folio*, Oxford, 1955.
Hall	Edward Hall: *The Union of the Two Noble and Illustrate Famelies of Lancastre and York*, 1548. Note: the three

books of Hall's chronicle which contain Richard's story are referred to by abbreviation of their titles: *Edward IV* (which concludes a foliation sequence), *Edward V* and *Richard III* (which are consecutively foliated).

Hanham   Alison Hanham, *Richard III and his Early Historians*, Oxford, 1975.

Heath   Benjamin Heath, *A Revisal of Shakespear's Text*, 1765.

Hinman   Charlton Hinman, *The Printing and Proof-Reading of the First Folio of Shakespeare*, 2 vols, Oxford, 1963.

Holinshed   Raphael Holinshed, *The Firste [&c] Volume of the Chronicles of Englande*, 2nd edn, 1587. (The second edn was that used by Shakespeare.)

Homilies   *Certaine Sermons or Homilies Appoynted to be Read in Churches*, 1574 (*STC* 13654), etc.

Honigmann   E. A. J. Honigmann, 'The Text of *Richard III*', *Theatre Research* 7 (1965), 48–55.

Honigmann,   E. A. J. Honigmann, *The Stability of Shakespeare's Text*, Stability   1965.

Impacyente Poverte   *A newe Interlude of Impacyente poverte*, 1560 (Greg 30).

Jahrbuch   *Jahrbuch der Deutschen Shakespeare-Gesellschaft.*

James IV   Robert Greene, *The Scottish Historie of Iames the Fourth*, 1598 (ed. Norman Sanders (The Revels Plays), 1970).

Jones   Emrys Jones, *The Origins of Shakespeare*, Oxford, 1977.

Kinnear   Benjamin Gott Kinnear, *Cruces Shakespearianae*, 1883.

Krappe   A. H. Krappe, 'Shakespeare Notes', *Anglia* 52 (1928), 174–82.

Law   R. A. Law, '*Richard the Third*, Act I, Scene 4', *PMLA* 27:2 (1912), 117–41.

Leir   *The True Chronicle History of King Leir*, 1605 (Greg 213).

Lyly   See *Campaspe* and *Sapho and Phao.*

Marlowe   *The Complete Works of Christopher Marlowe*, ed. Fredson Bowers, 2 vols, Cambridge, 1973. Marlowe's plays are referred to by their usual abbreviated titles.

Mirror   *The Mirror for Magistrates*, ed. Lily B. Campbell, Cambridge, 1938.

More   Sir Thomas More, *The History of King Richard the Third*, ed. Richard S. Sylvester (*The Complete Works of St. Thomas More*, vol. 2), New Haven, 1963.

Nice Wanton   *A Preaty Interlude called, Nice Wanton*, 1560 (Greg 31).

Noble   Richmond Noble, *Shakespeare's Biblical Knowledge*, 1935.

OED   *Oxford English Dictionary*, 13 vols, Oxford, 1933.

Parts Added   *Parts Added to the Mirror for Magistrates*, ed. Lily B. Campbell, Cambridge, 1946.

Patrick   David Lyall Patrick, *The Textual History of Richard III*, Stanford, 1936.

Pickersgill   E. H. Pickersgill, 'On the Quarto and Folio of *Richard III*', *Shakespeare Society Transactions*, 1875–6.

Prior   Moody E. Prior, *The Drama of Power*, Evanston, 1973.

Promos   George Whetstone, *The Right Excellent and Famous Historye, of Promos and Cassandra*, 2 parts, 1578 (Greg 73–4).

Reese   M. M. Reese, *The Cease of Majesty: a study of Shakespeare's history plays*, 2nd edn, 1968.

Ross   Charles Ross, *Richard III*, 1981.

Rossiter   A. P. Rossiter, 'The Structure of *Richard the Third*', *DUJ* 31 (1938), 44–75.

Sapho and Phao   John Lyly, *Sapho and Phao*, 1584 (Greg 82).

Schmidt   Alexander Schmidt, *Shakespeare Lexicon*, 3rd edn, New York, 1968 (1902).

Selimus   *The First Part of the Tragicall Raigne of Selimus*, 1594 (Greg 130).

Seneca   Lucius Annaeus Seneca, *Seneca's Tragedies with an English Translation* (by F. J. Miller), 2 vols, 1917 (Loeb edn; the plays are referred to by their usual abbreviated titles).

Smidt   Kristian Smidt, *Iniurious Impostors and Richard III*, Oslo, 1964.

Smidt, *Memorial Transmission*   Kristian Smidt, *Memorial Transmission and Quarto Copy in Richard III*, Oslo, 1970.

Solyman and Perseda *The Tragedye of Solyman and Perseda*, [n.d.; Stationers' Register, 20 November 1592,] (Greg 109).

Spanish Tragedy   Thomas Kyd, *The Spanish Tragedy* (ed. Philip Edwards (The Revels Plays), 1959).

Spedding   J. Spedding, 'On the Quarto and Folio of *Richard III*', *Shakespeare Society Transactions*, 1875–6.

Spenser   References to both *The Shepheardes Calender* and *The Faerie Queene* are to Edmund Spenser, *Poetical Works*, ed. J. C. Smith and E. de Selincourt, 1912.

Spivack   Bernard Spivack, *Shakespeare and the Allegory of Evil*, New York, 1958.

STC   A. W. Pollard and G. R. Redgrave, *A Short-Title Catalogue of Books Printed in England . . . 1475–1640*, 1926. Revised edn, vol. 2 only (I–Z), 1976.

Tilley   Morris Palmer Tilley, *A Dictionary of Proverbs in England in the Sixteenth and Seventeenth Centuries*, Ann Arbor, 1950.

Triall of Treasure   *A New and Mery Enterlude, Called the Triall of Treasure*, 1567 (Greg 49).

Vergil   *P[olydorus] Vergilii . . . Anglicae Historiae libri XXVI*, Basle, 1534.

Walker   Alice Walker, *Textual Problems of the First Folio*, Cambridge, 1953.

Walton   James K. Walton, *The Copy for the Folio Text of Richard III*, Auckland, 1955.

Whitaker   Virgil K. Whitaker, *Shakespeare's Use of Learning*, San Marino, 1953.

Wounds of Civil War Thomas Lodge, *The Wounds of Civil War*, ed. J. W. Houppert (Regents Renaissance Drama series), 1969.

3. PERIODICALS

DUJ   *Durham University Journal.*

ELH   *Journal of English Literary History.*

ELN   *English Language Notes.*

Eng.S.   *English Studies.*

JEPG   *Journal of English and Germanic Philology.*

MLN	Modern Language Notes.
MLR	Modern Language Review.
N&Q	Notes and Queries.
PBSA	Papers of the Bibliographical Society of America.
PMLA	Publications of the Modern Language Association of America.
RES	Review of English Studies.
SB	Studies in Bibliography.
SNL	Shakespeare Newsletter.
Sh.S.	Shakespeare Survey.
SP	Studies in Philology.
SQ	Shakespeare Quarterly.
TLS	The Times Literary Supplement.

INTRODUCTION

I. PUBLICATION

Richard III was entered on the Stationers' Register by Andrew Wise on 20 October 1597. The title-page of the First Quarto (hereafter Q1) declares it to have been printed by Valentine Simmes, for Andrew Wise; it is dated 1597.[1] In fact, Simmes printed only the first seven gatherings of the book; the remaining five were worked in the shop of Peter Short. Subsequently, the play was reprinted in new editions in 1598, 1602, 1605, 1612, 1622, 1629 and 1634. Of these quartos Q2–Q5 were printed by Thomas Creede, Q6 by Thomas Purfoot, Q7–8 by John Norton. The copyright was transferred to Matthew Law on 25 June 1603; there seems to have been nothing irregular at any point in the publication history of the quarto version of the play.

In 1623 the work was included in the First Folio edition of Shakespeare's plays (hereafter F) where it occupies leaves q5^r–t2^v, pp. 173–204 of the section devoted to the Histories. Further details concerning the printing of both Q1 and F will be found subsequently in this introduction. The essential fact, however, is that Q1 and F each preserves a distinctly different version of the play. The following parts of the introduction are directed principally towards describing and accounting for this fact.

2. THE TEXT

THE TWO TEXTS

The editors of the famous Cambridge Shakespeare, Clark and Wright, declared, 'The respective origin and authority of the first Quarto and first Folio texts of *Richard III*. is perhaps the most difficult question which presents itself to an editor of Shakespeare'.[2] In the century or so since this judgement was

---

1. Five copies survive of Q1: the Huth (British Library), Malone (Bodleian), Devonshire (Huntington), Folger, and Elizabethan Club (Yale) copies, the last fragmentary.
2. *The Works of William Shakespeare* (1864), v.xvi.

made, information and theories concerning the text have burgeoned, but a definitive solution is still to seek. The difficulties arise basically from the need to reach an understanding of the nature and relationship of the two texts of the play, to account for the number and kind of differences between the work as represented by the Quarto tradition and by the Folio.

It is not easy briefly to summarize the nature of these differences. The Folio (F) text is longer: it includes some fifty passages of varying length collectively amounting to rather more than two hundred lines which do not appear in the Quarto version (Q). These passages range from single words or phrases to complete lines, and to longer passages of several lines together, the longest being over fifty lines. In Q there are twenty-seven passages not present in F: most of these are very much shorter, and they amount in total to only some thirty-seven lines: there is among them one quite extensive passage, however.[1] In addition, those parts of the play which are substantially the same in each text still manifest great differences. There are literally hundreds of variants in the text, frequently taking the form of transposition of words and phrases within speeches, the movement of words and phrases from one speech to another, the extensive use of synonyms and other kinds of near-equivalent expression, changes in tense, number and other grammatical variations, and other, less readily definable changes, which sometimes hardly affect the meaning at all. Some characters are omitted, or their parts changed with others in Q: the Messenger's part is given to Dorset in II.iv; Dorset and Rivers are omitted entirely from II.ii. The stage-directions differ too, those of Q usually being less complete than those of F. Finally, there are literally thousands of differences in spelling, punctuation, the use of capitals and italics and so on, not only between Q and F generally, but from quarto to quarto as well.

These differences must be accounted for by assuming that the manuscript which was printer's copy for Q1 was different from that used to prepare copy for F. Since neither manuscript is extant, it is possible to infer their nature only from the evidence provided by Q and F; the problem is exacerbated by the long line of quartos between Q1 and F. When printer's copy for F was prepared, the manuscript supplied by the company was collated against a quarto (or quartos), with the result that some errors from the Q tradition found their way into the F text. Argument

---

1. The 'clock' passage (IV.ii.97–116 of this edn): it is difficult to give precise figures for the number of lines since many are metrically defective, or only part-lines.

has raged over which quarto or quartos were involved,[1] but it is fairly clear that it was not Q1. It is not difficult to demonstrate that each succeeding quarto was set in type from its predecessor (with the minor exception that although three gatherings of Q5 were set from Q4, the rest employed Q3 as copy); this is shown by the progressive increase of error through the series. Thus, all quartos save the first are derivative texts without independent authority, and any readings in F that originate in a derivative Q may be normally presumed to be errors.

QI AND PATRICK'S THEORY OF MEMORIAL RECONSTRUCTION

Because the text of Q1 reveals no obvious signs that the manuscript was defective or surreptitious, or indeed anything other than an ordinary theatrical document, it has proved difficult to reach agreement on the nature of the manuscript sold to Wise in 1597. It was for a long time held that Q must preserve at least a version of the play as revised by Shakespeare. This proposition is however difficult to maintain since Q is in many ways patently inferior to F—less regular metrically, less grammatically correct, often manifestly less verbally effective. Yet it does contain material which is not in F, and which must be accounted for.

Modern discussion of the copy for Q begins effectively with Patrick's monograph.[2] Following upon the earlier work of Greg[3] and Alexander[4] in the tradition of textual scholarship incepted by Pollard, Patrick sought to show that the 1597 Q was a 'bad quarto', based upon a memorial reconstruction of the play as performed. His arguments won almost total assent, and for twenty years it was assumed that the problem of *Richard III* was solved. In support of his case, he brings in several classes of evidence. First there is what he calls 'shifting': the transposition of words and phrases, usually within the line. He lists sixty-four simple instances of this, and a further three of a more elaborate nature. Most of these are uninformative: there is no way in which one can argue, for instance, that at II.ii.59 Q's 'Edward, and Clarence' is patently wrong, while F's 'Clarence and Edward' is inherently right. However, there are examples which are more interesting.

1. See below, pp. 32–41; it has long been accepted that III.i.1–165 and v.iii.49–end of play were printed from Q3 with a minimum of alteration.
2. D. L. Patrick, *The Textual History of Richard III* (Stanford, 1936).
3. W. W. Greg, *Two Elizabethan Stage Abridgements* (Oxford, 1922).
4. Peter Alexander, *Shakespeare's Henry VI and Richard III* (Cambridge, 1929).

A simple one occurs at I. iv. 3, which reads in Q, 'So full of vgly sights, of gastly dreames', and in F, 'So full of fearefull Dreames, of vgly sights'. Apart from the variant fearefull/gastly, there is not much to choose between the two versions: F is perhaps a little more natural, but Q is not self-evidently wrong. However, in l. 23 where F has 'What sights of vgly death within mine eyes', Q reads 'What vgly sights of death within my eies'. Here it is very persuasive that the transposition occurred because the phrase 'vgly sights' had lodged in the actor's mind from l. 3.

Patrick goes on to consider instances of anticipation and recollection, and the strongest evidence in support of the memorial theory is to be found in some of the examples he adduces here. In III. ii. 8–10, the scene before Hastings's house (an unusually troubled scene, textually), F reads:

> *Mess.* First, he commends him to your Noble selfe.
> *Hast.* What then?
> *Mess.* Then certifies your Lordship, that this Night
>   He dreamt, the Bore had rased off his Helme:

In Q we find:

> *Mess.* First he commends him to your noble Lordship.
> *Hast.* And then. *Mes.* And then he sends you word.
>   He dreamt to night the beare had raste his helme: . . .

Apart from the misprint of 'beare' for 'boare' (not corrected, incidentally, until Q6!) it is easy here to agree with Patrick that the likeliest explanation of this variant is that the messenger replaced 'selfe' in his first line with 'Lordship' from his next; which, when he reached it, he felt obliged to vary in turn, this time by a clumsy repetition of Hastings's question. This example is typical of many variations which seem, because of their obvious clumsiness, their quality of improvisation, unlikely to have originated with the author.

Another, perhaps even clearer, example is found in III. v. Buckingham has three speeches, which read in F as follows:

> Which since you come too late of our intent,
> Yet witnesse what you heare we did intend:
> And so, my good Lord Maior, we bid farwell. [ll. 69–71]

> Were for my selfe: and so, my Lord, adue. [l. 97]

> Looke for the Newes that the Guild-Hall affoords. [l. 102]

These appear in Q in the following form:

But since you come too late of our intents—
Yet witnesse what we did intend, and so my Lord adue.

Were for my selfe.

What news Guildhall affordeth, and so my Lord farewell.

Here, it is hard to avoid the conclusion that the phrase 'you heare' (which is vital to the sense) was inadvertently dropped by the actor from l. 70, and the second half of l. 97 used instead to fill the line out to an enormous fourteener. When l. 97 arrives, the actor cannot think what to do, and simply stops short; finally in l. 102 the lost 'farewell' is recovered and put to use. The value of this particular example lies in its hardly being possible to conceive of the Q version arising by any agency other than faulty memory. And Q is obviously corrupted out of F: it would be impossible to suppose Q here a draft of F (much less a revision).

Only one clear case of memorial contamination is needed, provided it is clear and unequivocal, to oblige us to suspect its potential effects throughout the text. These examples are among the strongest that Patrick cites, and it is hard indeed to think of any alternative explanation for them. However, as the question is of the utmost importance to the establishment of the text of the play, another example may be given to support the case, one whose significance Patrick overlooked. The character Brakenbury puts in an appearance at intervals throughout the play—in i.i, i.iv especially—and his name is included in the list of those slain at Bosworth. In iv.i there is a part for the 'Lieutenant of the Tower'; it was Capell who recognized that this, too, was meant to be Brakenbury. Proof is to be found in the text. Lines 27–8 of iv.i read in F:

> No, Madame, no; I may not leaue it so:
> I am bound by Oath, and therefore pardon me.

The Q version of this is:

> I doe beseech your graces all to pardon me:
> *I* am bound by oath, I may not doe it.

We have, however, heard one of these lines before: at i.i.84 both texts read:

> I beseech your Graces both to pardon me

Moreover, lower down, l. 103 begins in F 'I do beseech your Grace/to pardon me' (Q: 'I beseech your Grace to pardon me').

The speaker here is Brakenbury, and it is hard indeed to resist the obvious conclusion that in Act IV he recalled his lines from Act I.

A further class of variant which Patrick considers is substitution of various kinds: there are synonyms (such as avenged/revenged, murder/slaughter), changes in number (water/waters) or in tense (did I enjoy/have I enjoyed) or in terms of address (my gracious/ noble Lord), the introduction of exclamations or interjections such as 'O', 'Why', 'Tush' and so on (and the omission of some present in F), and various other kinds of change in enormous number. It is, finally, the sheer quantity of variation which tells most heavily in favour of Patrick's theory. He lists, for instance, over two hundred cases of synonymous substitution, over seventy cases of change in number, nearly a hundred of various kinds of paraphrase. It is hard to argue that a consciously revising author would have introduced such sweeping changes into the texture of his work without altering it in more fundamental ways; by the same token it is hard to find rational grounds for discriminating between such alternatives as speak/say, kept/held, yet/but, Peers/ Lords, fruit/fruits, hand/hands and so on. Any convincing theory of the text must find an explanation for these: neither conscious revision, nor careless copying nor any other of the usual explanations for variation in reading are sufficient to account for the sheer number and relative insignificance of these variants.

There is, besides, an additional very telling point in favour of Patrick's theory. The amount of variation is not constant: it varies from scene to scene, and from character to character. In general terms, there is more of this minor variation in Acts III and IV than elsewhere, and, as Patrick has shown, the part of the Duke of Buckingham is more prone to variation than others. Buckingham regularly transposes words, alters phrasing, substitutes one word for another, changes the metre, and is prone to intrusive exclamations. It adds up to a portrait of an actor who got the gist of his part but was shaky in points of detail. By contrast, Richard's part is relatively free from such variation (especially in view of its sheer length), as is the Earl of Richmond's. Other parts which are poorly remembered include those of the various messengers, and some of the women's parts. The minor roles, generally, are less accurate than the major parts, presumably because they were doubled, and in any event would not have remained in the same hired man's hands for ever.

Patrick concludes by surveying the material which appears only in F and only in Q. This amounts to some fifty passages of varying

length in F, and twenty-one generally short ones in Q.[1] Seven of
the F-only passages (I.ii.159–70; I.iv.69–72; I.iv.247–57;
III.vii.143–52; IV.i.97–103; IV.iv.222–35; IV.iv.288–342) and one
of the Q-only (IV.ii.97–116) are long enough to be considered
separately as either theatrical cuts or deliberate additions. They
are discussed individually in Appendices I and II. Of the thirty
longish passages remaining which appear in F only, compositor's
error may be held to account for seven; some other accidental
kind of omission (perhaps a copyist's mistake) is likely in another
seven or so, while fifteen at least seem most plausibly to have
originated with the actor. It is significant that, of these, seven are
found in Buckingham's part.

Two of the most convincing examples are these: in III.i.169 ff.
Buckingham is speaking; in Q he says:

> Well then no more but this:
> Go gentle Catesby, and as it were a farre off,
> Sound thou Lo: Hastings, how he stands affected
> Vnto our purpose, if he be willing,
> Encourage him, and shew him all our reasons:
> If he be leaden, icie, cold, vnwilling. . . .

Even without comparing this with F, it looks corrupt: apart from
the first line, with only six syllables, the rhythm is poor in the
second and especially the fourth lines, and the repetition of
willing/unwilling hardly euphonious. At first glance the F version
looks longer, but little better:

> Well, then, no more but this:
> Goe gentle *Catesby*, and as it were farre off,
> Sound thou Lord *Hastings*,
> How he doth stand affected to our purpose,
> And summon him to morrow to the Tower,
> To sit about the Coronation.
> If thou do'st finde him tractable to vs,
> Encourage him, and tell him all our reasons:
> If he be leaden, ycie, cold, vnwilling . . .

However, the first three lines should be printed as two: this forme
was set in F by Compositor A; there is no special reason to think
he was trying to spread the text (indeed, the conjugate r1^v has
many signs of an over-full page), but it is possible that he was
influenced by the appearance of his copy, derived from the Q
text: he was more prone to follow copy literally than Compositor

---

1. There are actually twenty-seven; Patrick overlooks a few in his survey.

B. Apart from this, two lines have disappeared altogether from Q, and in the third the actor has evidently remembered 'unwilling', but forgotten 'tractable', with the unfortunate results evident in the Q text.

The other example is found in iv.iv.274–8, where F reads:

> Therefore present to her, as sometime *Margaret*
> Did to thy Father, steept in Rutlands blood,
> A hand-kercheefe, which say to her did dreyne
> The purple sappe from her sweet Brothers body,
> And bid her wipe her weeping eyes withall.

Q's version is this:

> Therefore present to her as sometimes Margaret
> Did to thy father, a handkercher steept in Rutlands bloud,
> And bid her drie her weeping eies therewith,

Patrick argues that this is a classic case of memorial lapse, resulting in transposed (and more colloquial) order, with a consequent unmetrical line, the commoner form 'handkercher' and a synonym for 'withall' as well as a chunk missing from the text: a real chapter of accidents.

As for the passages unique to Q, eight are attributable to accidental omission by the F corrector or compositor. A couple are accounted for by the excision of profanity, thirteen are probably gag, and three seem to reflect a change made for theatrical reasons.[1] Of these last, the most interesting case is at iii.iii S.D. The stage-direction in F is very informative: '*Enter Sir Richard Ratcliffe, with Halberds, carrying the Nobles to death at Pomfret.*' However, the location is not mentioned in the text until l. 9, nor is anyone immediately named except Ratcliffe. One might speculate that the opening of the scene was found to be ineffective on stage, perhaps because the characters involved are not as familiar to the audience as those elsewhere in the Act. Q's unique opening line for Ratcliffe, 'Come bring foorth the prisoners', while not metrical, may have been added to clarify the dramatic situation. There seems to be a practical advantage in retaining it, and no major reason for its exclusion.[2] Another suggestive alteration is found at iv.iv.135 S.D., where F's 'The Trumpet sounds' becomes in Q 'I heare his drum', another alteration made perhaps for theatrical reasons.

---

1. The only long Q-only passage, iv.ii.97–116, is discussed in Appendix I.
2. Among modern editions, the conservative Riverside includes the line whereas the more adventurous NPS and NCS, curiously, do not.

This brings us to the end of the survey of Patrick's principal argument. The strongest examples have been selected here, those which most clearly find an explanation in the memorial theory, and which are least tractable to other solutions. It should not be assumed that all of Patrick's argument is equally strong; indeed, it is much easier to accept that the text was memorially reproduced than it is to adopt his second thesis, namely that the Q version is a deliberate simplification of the play produced for provincial touring. It is undoubtedly true that the Chamberlain's Men were in the provinces in August and September of 1597, following the *Isle of Dogs* affair; they visited Kent (Faversham, Rye, Dover) and subsequently went to the west (Marlborough, Bath, Bristol).[1]

One of the signs of provincial adaptation one would expect to find is the reduction of the cast to as small a number as practicable by the omission of hired men, and in Q Dorset and Rivers are omitted from II.ii; the Keeper in I.iv is eliminated, and his lines given to Brakenbury.[2] Dorset takes the Messenger's part in II.iv; the Archbishop of York and the Cardinal in II.iv and III.i respectively are telescoped into a single prelate. Catesby substitutes for Ratcliffe and Lovell in III.iv and v and in IV.ii, and for Surrey in v.iii. Ratcliffe replaces the Sheriff in v.i. In addition to these substitutions, a number of minor roles are eliminated: the 'neece Plantagenet' of IV.i; Sir William Brandon, the Earl of Oxford and Sir Walter Herbert in Act v; and the ghost-persons, Woodeville and Scales, of II.i.[3] Collectively, these curtailments led Patrick to suppose that a simplified version of the play underlay Q. The difficulties entailed on this view are reviewed in the next section.

Nor is Patrick convincing on the means, namely that the actors dictated their parts to a scribe who took them down in shorthand, whereby the report was produced.[4] Greg, in his review of Patrick,[5] proposed the view which has been universally

---

1. The records are reprinted in E. K. Chambers, *William Shakespeare: a Study of Facts and Problems* (Oxford, 1930), II, p. 321. For the suppression of *The Isle of Dogs*, see his *Elizabethan Stage* (Oxford, 1923), III, pp. 453–5.

2. The F S.D. *Enter Clarence and Keeper* was a stop-press correction on r2ʳ: that is, the direction was supplied during proofing. There is no exit-direction for the Keeper.

3. See below, pp. 17–18 for the explanation of this omission.

4. G. I. Duthie, in *Elizabethan Shorthand, and the First Quarto of King Lear* (Oxford, 1949), demonstrated that shorthand was not then an adequate means of recording a play in performance.

5. *The Library*, 4th series, 19:1 (1938), pp. 118–20.

accepted since, namely that the text was collaboratively prepared by the company in order to replace a missing prompt-book.

Greg assumed the Chamberlain's Men produced the reconstruction. The only other possibility, urged by Cairncross[1] and Wentersdorf[2] is that Q1 of *Richard III*, like the bad quartos of *2* and *3 Henry VI* (*The First Part of the Contention* and *The True Tragedie of Richard Duke of York*), was a product of the 'rump' of Pembroke's Men, made for provincial use following their disappearance from London towards the end of 1592. Cairncross lists some examples of mutual recollection between the plays (some rather lame), but, so far as *Richard III* goes, this only proves that some of the actors who reconstructed it also played in the *Henry VI* plays. If indeed Pembroke's began life as an offshoot of the Admiral's/Strange's Men for whom the First Tetralogy was probably written,[3] then it is hardly surprising that such recollections should occur. There must have been a considerable traffic, especially of hired men, between the companies in the crisis years of 1593-4. The objections to the Pembroke theory are first the enormous qualitative difference between Q1 of *Richard III* (which is remarkably accurate) and the other two (which are very bad indeed), and secondly that it is unlikely that the powerful Chamberlain's Men would as late as 1597 have tamely allowed the publication of a piracy of one of their popular plays, with their own name on the title-page. Hence, for all the inherent oddity of a company's reconstructing its own prompt-book, it seems on balance that the Chamberlain's Men is the only probable source for the copy of *Richard III* Q1.

WAS Q BASED ON A PROMPT-BOOK?

Since Patrick wrote, only one scholar has sought to overset his findings: this is Kristian Smidt, of Oslo, who has published two monographs on the text of *Richard III*,[4] as well as an immensely useful and highly accurate parallel-text edition of the play.[5] In

1. A. S. Cairncross, 'Pembroke's Men and some Shakespearian piracies', *SQ* 11 (1960), pp. 335-49.

2. Karl P. Wentersdorf, 'The Repertory and size of Pembroke's Company', *Theatre Annual* 33 (1977), pp. 71-85; '*Richard III* (Q1) and the Pembroke "Bad" Quartos', *ELN* 14 (June 1977), pp. 257-64.

3. See below, pp. 54-7, 61-2.

4. Kristian Smidt, *Iniurious Impostors and Richard III* (Oslo, 1964); and his *Memorial Transmission and Quarto Copy in Richard III: a Reassessment* (Oslo, 1970).

5. *The Tragedy of King Richard the Third: Parallel Texts of the First Quarto and the First Folio with Variants of the Early Quartos* (Oslo, 1969).

his first monograph he attacks Patrick's conclusions, that Q is a
reported text of an acted version of the play, and argues instead
that Q is a revision. To be sure, one of the weaknesses of Patrick's
case was that it was necessary to see every change from F as an
error, and therefore (one would assume) inferior in a literary as
well as a textual sense. Smidt's revaluation arose from his feeling
that a number of the Q readings are arguably superior in the
literary sense to what is in F, and that Patrick's classing of them
as corruptions must be wrong.

It would be neither possible nor fruitful to attempt yet another
evaluation of this argument. The method itself is subjective and
impressionistic, and so will never of itself lead to universal agreement. For all that Smidt keeps finding Q variants 'preferable'
where Patrick saw in them only error, Smidt is unable to reach a
credible theory to account for the multitudinous minor variants
between the texts. In any event, in his later monograph he partially retracts, and allows a memorial link of some kind to be
present in Q, so that it is not necessary to pursue this side of the
case further.

The second question is much more relevant. Does Q indeed
preserve a version of the play as acted in the provinces? First, is
it necessary to abandon the notion that the Q text as it stands
could have been used as a prompt-book? Consider such stage-
directions as '*Enter the Lords to Councell*' [III.iv S.D.]; '*Enter Glocest.
with others*' [II.ii.100 S.D.]; '*The Trumpets sound, Enter Richard
crownd, Buckingham, Catesby with other Nobles*' [IV.ii S.D.]; '*Enter
Buckingham to execution*' [v.i S.D.]. These, and others, in Q all have
the quality of vagueness or 'permissiveness' which Greg, Chambers and others identify as characteristic of authorial, rather than
prompt, directions. In many cases, directions to enter for major
speaking characters are omitted (as in v.i, where in Q Ratcliffe
conducts Buckingham's execution; and in II.ii where Buckingham
is not named in the direction). In addition, there are many incomplete or omitted directions, especially for exits.

In his *Dramatic Documents* Greg complains of scholars who
generalize about the characteristics of prompt-books without
having sufficiently examined the surviving examples.[1] A survey
of the directions in the prompt-books transcribed by Greg reveals
that in many cases prompters allowed authorial 'permissive'
directions to stand. In *The Second Maiden's Tragedy* we find that
on fol. 48ª the book-keeper or prompter himself has changed the

1. W. W. Greg, *Dramatic Documents from the Elizabethan Playhouses* (Oxford,
1931), commentary, p. 189.

original directions to the vague 'Enter Soldiers'.[1] *The Two Noble Ladies* is authorial fair copy, annotated by the book-keeper; to a direction on fol. 233(10)[a] calling for 'soldiers' is added 'Tay. Gib: Stage k',[2] which usefully makes it clear that the stage-keepers could be called upon to act mute parts.

The playhouse scribe known as 'Jhon'[3] wrote a direction in *The Honest Man's Fortune* which is interestingly vague: 'Wthin: Clashing of weapons: Some crying downe wth theire weapons: then Enter Longauile: Dubois: their swords drawne: 3: or: 4 Drawers betwene em' (fol. 12[a]).[4] This manuscript was submitted to Herbert in replacement of a lost prompt-book: that is, it was an old play, of which 'Jhon' made a copy for the Master's perusal. There is no doubt that 'Jhon' could have tidied up such directions if he had been minded, and no doubt that in this instance he allowed the author's vague direction to stand. Greg calls the manuscript of Massinger's *Believe as you List* 'the most important document we possess for the study of contemporary prompting';[5] it is autograph, carefully prepared for the stage by 'Jhon' to adapt the directions to the prompter's needs (which was not invariably the case). Indeed, 'Jhon' went as far as 'making adjustments in the minor parts, clearing up a confusion of the author's, and further adapting them to the exigencies of the cast'.[6] If 'Jhon' could do this in 1625, there is no reason to assume that the book-keeper of thirty years previously could not do the same upon occasion. Yet even the meticulous 'Jhon' allowed such indeterminacies as 'Attendants', 'Garde', and 'Soldiers' to stand.

In *The Shakespeare First Folio*, Greg declares that the hand of the author was that usually responsible for vague or permissive directions, but also that where such groups have been defined previously, or by the action, the book-keeper would allow the vague direction to stand. Greg notes a number of permissive directions in Shakespearean plays which are believed to be derived from prompt-copy, and concludes, 'It is little use arguing that indefinite and optional directions must have been cleared up in the prompt-book when we have reason to suppose that in fact they were often left standing.'[7] It is worth underlining that Greg himself saw nothing inherently impossible in the supposition that Q was a reconstructed prompt-book.

1. Ibid., p. 267.   2. Ibid., p. 277.
3. Identified by Johan Gerritsen, in his edn of *The Honest Man's Fortune* (Groningen, Djakarta, 1952, pp. xxi–xxii), as Edward Knight.
4. Ibid., p. 291.   5. Ibid., p. 296.   6. Ibid., p. 294.
7. W. W. Greg, *The Shakespeare First Folio* (Oxford, 1955), p. 137.

Smidt's case against Q's being a prompt-book is based chiefly on inconsistency of speech-prefixes,[1] the unsatisfactory stage-directions as noted above, and the general quality of vagueness Q exhibits over details of staging. It has other features which seem ill-adapted to prompt use, such as the apparent confusion over Stanley/Derby. The play actually conflated two Stanleys: Lord Thomas and Sir William; it was the former who after the battle of Bosworth was created Earl of Derby. In the play this character is referred to as Derby in stage-directions, speech-prefixes and dialogue in I.iii; thereafter he is always Stanley in dialogue in both Q and F; in stage-directions and speech-prefixes he is Stanley in III.ii; Derby in III.v, IV.v, and v; in IV.ii and IV.iv stage-directions and speech-prefixes he is Derby in Q and Stanley in F. Smidt makes much of these inconsistencies,[2] but it must be remembered that Lord Thomas's descendant, Ferdinando, Lord Strange, was the fifth Earl of Derby, and the master of Strange's Men. The names of Derby and Stanley were so closely associated with each other in the world of the theatre that no ambiguity would be likely to arise from their interchange in use.[3]

There are, besides these, some directions one would think more characteristic of authorial foul papers than of prompt-copy: two such instances are the directions at III.ii.96 S.D. and v.iii.313 S.D.: 'Enter Hastin. a Purssuant' and 'His Oration to his army'. The first of these preserves from the Chronicles the coincidence that Hastings's interlocutor bore the same name as himself; both are curiously literary features to be found in a work of memorial reconstruction intended for use as a prompt-book.

Smidt challenges Patrick's view that numerous changes in Q were made to fit the play for performance by a restricted company during provincial tour. There are three variables which need to be assessed: the length of the play, the number of actors available, and the possibility of adaptation caused by the lack of heavy properties or stage furnishings when on tour. As for length, Q is about 200 lines shorter than F, but is still a very long play: the F text, in Hinman's through-line-numbering, totals 3887 lines, longer than any play of Shakespeare's save Hamlet.[4] Whether long

1. Richard is Glo. until IV.ii, after which he is King, but in the ghost-scene he is sometimes Ri., while Richmond is Rich. usually, once Ri. (as was Rivers in I. iii). These are hardly significant.

2. Iniurious, pp. 23–4; Memorial Transmission, p. 12.

3. Lewis Mott (Todd Memorial Vols, Columbia U.P., 1930, II, pp. 41–4) thought, rather improbably, that a political compliment to the family was intended.

4. The text of the present edition runs to 3596 lines of dialogue.

plays were cut specially for provincial tour, we simply do not know. Most of what is said about provincial performances is inferred from the characteristics of bad quartos, and as we are trying to define the characteristics of this particular quarto, the danger of circular argument is evident.

One passage in *Richard III*, at least, looks like a cut made to shorten a scene: this is the 55 lines omitted at IV.iv.288–342. No proposal made in favour of any other theory is anywhere near as plausible as the obvious one, that these lines were cut to abridge an excessively lengthy scene. 'We must be brief,' says Richard at the end of the previous scene, 'when traitors brave the field'; yet far from being brief, he collogues with his mother for some 66 lines, and then debates with Elizabeth for another 257. It is hard not to feel that in this instance Shakespeare's youthful judgement erred, and that the decision to abridge, while it cost some pretty rhetoric, aids the dramatic pace of the Act. We cannot, therefore, argue that the cut was made especially for touring. Much the same objection can be made to the other passages which might represent theatrical cuts, none of which are long enough in any event to make very much difference to the total performance time. These are discussed below in Appendix 1.

It must always have been difficult to cast *Richard III*, in view of its very large number of speaking parts, not to mention the need for a fair number of supernumeraries. The lesser parts must inevitably have been doubled: the extent to which this may have been undertaken is discussed below, in the section '*Richard III* in performance'. However, a number of changes in the text seem to have been made for the purpose of accommodating the play to the performers, and these must now be examined. In I.iv, Clarence recites the account of his dream to an anonymous 'Keeper' in F, who, having listened to Clarence, disappears from the scene (and the play) without an exit direction, after l. 75. Brakenbury enters, makes a moralistic speech, disputes briefly with the murderers, and withdraws. In Q the 'Keeper' disappears, and it is Brakenbury who is made the confidant of Clarence's conscience-smitten nightmare. Some slight adjustment of the text is made to accommodate this sudden elevation of the Keeper's status: Clarence now calls him 'gentle Keeper', and refers to him by name: 'O Brokenbury'. These alterations prove that a genuine change in the dramatis personae was made (rather than that the Keeper in F was really meant to be Brakenbury all the time). Patrick believes that this change represents an attempt by the company to economize on the number of actors required (and it is true that the Keeper is eliminated from the play),[1] but it could equally well represent, as Smidt suggests,[2] Shakespeare's deliberate decision to tighten up the scene, to give Clarence a more appropriate audience, and to provide motivation for Brakenbury's speech, ll. 76–83.

The most notable examples of alteration of the text to save actors are found in the crowded battle scene in Act v. Thus at v.iii.22 F reads 'Sir *William Brandon*, you shall beare my Standard:', which becomes in Q 'Where is Sir William Brandon, he shall beare my standerd'. In addition, the next three lines, in which Richmond speaks to the Earl of Oxford, Brandon and Sir Walter Herbert, are omitted from Q, whose stage-direction is the ultra-vague 'Enter Richmond with the Lordes, &c.' In fact the only speaking part left beside Richmond's is that of Sir Walter Blunt. These shifts, to which may be added the omission of the Earl of Surrey from Richard's side, were surely occasioned by shortage of actors in this very crowded episode.[3] Whether the substitutions were made for the regular performances, or instituted for a provincial tour, is not evident: the question is complicated by the fact that for a goodly portion of this Act the collation of Q copy with the F manuscript was of the sketchiest nature;[4] after l. 49 of v.iii, the stage-directions of F derive chiefly from Q, so that we have no independent test of their completeness.

A far less obvious instance of the alteration of parts occurs in ii.ii, from which Rivers and Dorset are eliminated in Q. Patrick suggests this was done for reasons of economy; Smidt very reasonably replies that as the characters are not omitted from the play, but merely from this single scene, it is hard to see what economy this could represent. Perhaps they were needed as the anonymous citizens in the next scene, and did not have time to effect the costume changes. Yet if there were enough actors to play the Bosworth scene, there were spare actors at this point to play the citizens.[5] It is all rather puzzling. So is the substitution of Dorset for the Messenger in ii.iv: none of the Messenger's lines are adapted to the different rank and status of Dorset, and neither mother nor son acknowledges the other apart from the replacement of 'Lord' in l. 48 by 'Lady', perhaps an improvised attempt

1. Patrick, p. 21.
2. *Iniurious*, p. 21.
3. See further details below, '*Richard III* in performance', pp. 64–5.
4. See below, pp. 40–1.
5. See further details below, '*Richard III* in performance', pp. 62–5.

to make Dorset react to Elizabeth's presence. Again, the reason for the substitution does not evidently appear: there should have been ample hired men available for the anonymous part of the Messenger. Yet quite clearly the change must have been made to accommodate a theatrical need which we cannot now determine.

In the same scene, Q replaces the Archbishop of York with the Cardinal of III.i (the Archbishop of Canterbury). Here a confusion in the sources has added to the problem. Holinshed, following More, mistakenly telescopes the two prelates into one: Archbishop Rotherham of York.[1] However, if (as is argued below in the section on sources, pp. 79–80) Hall rather than Holinshed was the primary source of the play, then Shakespeare would have been aware that it was Rotherham who illegally gave the Great Seal to the Queen (ll. 70–1), and Thomas Bourchier, Cardinal of San Ciriaco and Archbishop of Canterbury, who persuaded her to deliver Prince Edward from sanctuary.[2] The question is whether Shakespeare intended to distinguish the two prelates at any point, and if so, whether he subsequently changed his mind. Patrick's view that the Q version is an adaptation of F to save a bulky costume is rather more plausible than Smidt's that the change was made for dramatic effectiveness (Richard persuading the Cardinal to reverse his judgement;[3] it is actually Buckingham, not Richard, who persuades the Cardinal). The likely conclusion, then, is that Shakespeare did indeed intend the two bishops, as we read in F, but that he or another decided to eliminate one of them, probably for costuming reasons.

These changes represent modifications which seem to be based on practical expediency rather than on their dramatic desirability, and so perhaps bring us close to the kind of thing that might have happened to a text to enable it to be performed on tour. Another change shares both qualities: in III.iv, Ratcliffe and Lovell are replaced in Q by Catesby. Catesby also takes over Ratcliffe's part in III.v and IV.iii; Ratcliffe himself does duty for the Sheriff in v.i; Lovell is eliminated from Q by this, and there are other internal rearrangements. Now, Catesby and Ratcliffe as it were play Rosencrantz and Guildenstern to Richard throughout the play: a pair of tools or stooges whose duty is to be available to their master, and whose characters are in no way distinctive. If one replaces the other, it can thus only be for a specific theatrical or dramatic reason.

1. Holinshed, p. 716.
2. See Appendix III, pp. 346–8.   3. *Iniurious*, p. 21

Not all the changes are readily explicable, but it is hard not to feel that the reason for the change in III.iv was that as Ratcliffe had in the immediately preceding scene been executing the Queen's kindred at Pomfret, it was an affront to verisimilitude to have him perform the same office for Hastings the same day in London. The question is, who made the substitution, and when? The complications arising from the change are imperfectly resolved in the next scene in Q, where l. 17, 'Catesby ouerlooke the wals', stands in Q though Catesby does not enter for another three lines. In any event there is another, slighter problem: a good deal of stress was laid on the matter of the divided Council in III.ii, one of Hastings's points being that, as he and Stanley would be at the one and Catesby, his 'servant', would be at the other, there was nothing to fear. Catesby now must be at the same Council as Hastings, and nothing is said about the change. Nor is anything made of the fact that it is now Catesby, Hastings's trusted associate, who is placed in charge of his patron's execution. Smidt is particularly impressed by this latter point, remarking 'That [Catesby] should betray his former master and be the one to put him to death, as in the Quarto, makes the general conflict of loyalty and treachery in this play all the more poignant'.[1] However, this desire to elevate Catesby into a Judas is ineffective without some addition to the text which would make Hastings, or Catesby, or both, react to the irony of the situation. But there is nothing. We must therefore consider the possibility that as Shakespeare, in locating Ratcliffe in two places at once had (not uncharacteristically) blundered, and as the change to replace Ratcliffe with Catesby was not carried through consistently, nor with any awareness of the dramatic possibilities thus opened, the alteration was made by the book-keeper, or some other individual associated with the company, rather than the author.

There are other variants between F and Q which might fall into this category. For example, in II.i.66–7 ff., F reads

> Of you and you, Lord Riuers and of Dorset,
> That all without desert haue frown'd on me:
> Of you Lord Wooduill, and Lord Scales of you.

Of this passage it was observed by Furness that Shakespeare had been misled by a sentence in Hall: 'The gouernaunce of this younge Prince was committed too Antony Wooduile erle Ryuers and lord Scales, brother to the quene.'[2] Earlier in the play

1. *Iniurious*, p. 100. See also note to III.ii.21.
2. Hall, *Edward V*, fol. v^r.

Shakespeare had revealed that he knew that Anthony Woodeville
was Rivers's name; Scales was one of his titles. It is the sort of
trifling slip one is really surprised to find so seldom. In Q, however—

> Of you Lo: Riuers, and Lord Gray of you,
> That all without desert haue frownd on me

—the third line is omitted. This correction can certainly not be
regarded as coincidental, nor the product of an actor's faulty
memory (though the change of Dorset to Grey may be); nor need
it have originated with the author. It is the sort of correction that
an alert book-keeper might very easily, and very properly, make.

In II.iv, ll. 1–2 in F read:

> Last night I heard they lay at Stony Stratford,
> And at Northampton they do rest to night:

while Q has:

> Last night I heare they lay at Northampton,
> At Stonistratford will they be to night.

At first glance here Q is right and F wrong, for Stony Stratford is
nearer London than Northampton. But as Pickersgill observed,[1]
F is closer to the sources, which relate how Richard caused the
Prince's party to backtrack. For some reason Shakespeare decided against explaining this in his original text, which left an
apparent error or contradiction in the Archbishop's speech. No
doubt at a later date someone, perhaps the prompter, noticed the
apparent mistake, and 'corrected' it, at some cost to the metre.
The original historical point had by then presumably slipped
everyone's mind. However, the identification of the Pursuivant
in III.ii by name as Hastings in Q (l. 92), since it introduces a
potential ambiguity into the scene, surely goes beyond prompter's
meddling, and must originate with the author.

None of these alterations can be considered as relating to a
provincial tour: they could have been made at any time after the
play was put into rehearsal. Some changes in Q sound-effects are
a little more possible as touring alterations. We have already
noticed that at IV.iv. 135 S.D. F's 'The Trumpet sounds' becomes
in Q '*I* heare his drum'; at l. 151, Richard calls in both texts for
trumpets and drums to silence the clamour of the women; in Q
only the trumpets respond. Then, at l. 180, Richard's demand for

---

1. *Shakespeare Society Transactions*, 1875–6, p. 90.

the drum to strike is omitted from Q. One may speculate that the drum was not available for use on-stage: off-stage drumming is needed or at least alluded to at III. v. 16, IV. iv. 151, v. iii. 338 S.D. (the direction, in F only, is '*Drum afarre off*'), and perhaps at v. iii. 270, where Richmond calls for trumpets and drums to sound, but there is no indication that the musicians are on stage. It seems fair to conclude that at some point the company lacked a drum to be taken on stage, and was obliged to improvise back-stage; it is also persuasive that such a circumstance would be most likely to occur during a tour.

It is a meagre harvest of evidence to support the theory of memorial reconstruction occasioned by the loss of the prompt-book during a tour. *Richard III* is not a play which depends on heavy properties or particularly elaborate staging. Henry VI's bier, some 'rotten' armour (and some less rotten, for Bosworth), and the tents for the battle scene,[1] together with the musical instruments, are all the large properties needed. There must be provision for playing 'aloft' for III. vii; there are other scenes which could benefit from the use of an upper level, but none in which it is imperative; there is no need for a trapdoor. From this it may be seen that, length and large cast aside, *Richard III* would have been quite an easy play to tour. The cast substitutions we have noticed in II. ii and II. iv have the quality of improvisation which one might expect of a provincial tour, as to some extent have the rearrangements in Catesby's and Ratcliffe's parts (though that is less evident); finally there is the elimination of the stage drum, noted above, and perhaps the saving of one bishop's costume. It would be rash indeed to declare on the basis of these scraps of information that Q had been adapted to provincial needs.

In conclusion, then, the evidence concerning the nature of the manuscript underlying Q is inconclusive. There are strong reasons for believing it to have been produced by an act of collective memorial reconstruction involving virtually the entire company. That this consequently preserves aspects of the play as emended for performance (i.e. after the author delivered his copy to the company) is not to be doubted: both serious alterations and casual improvisations must therefore appear in Q as well as a huge number of greater and lesser actors' errors. Not enough evidence exists to enable one to say that it represents the play as performed on provincial tour, though there is nothing that makes

1. For a discussion of the tents, see below, '*Richard III* in performance', pp. 65–6.

it impossible. The directions are often very vague for prompt use, to be sure.[1] But the actual manuscript sold to Wise may have been the version as it was written down during the reconstruction, from which a tidier copy was made for the prompter. This would allow us at least to account for the less-than-precise quality of the stage-directions, though we must still presume that the real prompt-copy was for some reason unavailable in order to account for the fact of the memorial reconstruction.

The Quarto remains a document of primary importance in the textual history of *Richard III*, despite its ambiguous origins. Not only does it preserve evidence of the ways in which the play was adapted to performance by cutting and by book-keeper's alterations, but it also reveals, among its corruptions and mistakes, a layer of changes to the text which by any reasonable estimate must derive from Shakespeare. It must be regarded as a substantive text, and its readings carefully evaluated in any modern edition. There is one other intriguing possibility which warrants mention. If indeed the entire company partici-pated in the reconstruction, or at least the principal actors and most of the hired men (and it is hard to account for the excellence of the report otherwise), then it must be remembered that one member of this group was none other than William Shakespeare. It is, of course, impossible to say certainly that he participated, and if he did we cannot know what part or parts he played. Yet in the circumstances we find ourselves looking for evidence whether or not he was in any way involved. The evidence that he was not is the persistence of verbal errors, which—for all that they are numerous—are not however so severe that it is possible to declare that the author would have insisted on their correction. As for positive signs of his presence, we may note the unusual directions such as '*His Oration to his army*' (v.iii.313), which are exceptionally hard to account for by any usual theory of memorial reconstruction. It is not impossible that these simply record an authorial remark made during reconstruction and written into the text by the scribe. This possibility is not advanced as a definite theory, and no feature of the present edition is derived from the idea. But no other account of the 'literary' or 'authorial' features found in Q is at all convincing either.

To summarize, then, the evidence supporting the memorial theory of Q is too strong to be rejected. The various unusual features of Q may be largely accounted for by supposing that the

1. Another potential cause of the inadequacy of the stage-directions is dis-cussed below, p. 27.

reconstruction was made by the co-operative efforts of most of the company in the absence of the official prompt-book, perhaps during a provincial tour (that of 1597 is a possible candidate). The company involved was almost certainly the Chamberlain's Men, whose familiarity with the text results in a reconstruction of quite surprising accuracy, though it is necessarily unreliable in point of detail.

THE PRINTING OF Q

The preceding discussion of the nature of the manuscript underlying Q was all based on deduction and inference, drawn from the physical evidence of the Q text. It must be remembered, however, that the processes by which a manuscript was translated into a printed book have a bearing on this evidence. The actions of compositors, proof-readers and to a lesser extent the press-men themselves may leave their mark upon the printed version in such a way as to confuse the trail for the scholar in search of the characteristics of the manuscript. Our investigation of the type-setting of the play is made more difficult by the fact, mentioned previously, that *Richard III* Q1 was produced by two different printers: the first seven gatherings (sheets A–G) in the shop of Valentine Simmes, the remaining five (sheets H–M) in the shop of Peter Short. Short is not named on the title-page, but the evidence is clear: the actual types used in *Richard III* have been found in other books by the two printers. Simmes used the same fount to print *Richard II* a little before; Short used his fount for *1 Henry IV* early in the next year; and the same two type-founts have been identified in a number of other books.

Why the printing was thus divided, we do not know. Peter Blayney, who has studied the work of the Snowdon/Okes shop, finds that nearly a third of the books produced therein were shared: in the period 1606–9 only two printers did not share work.[1] In view of this, we must accept that there is no reason to think Simmes's and Short's collaboration in 1597 other than commonplace.

The two printers did not use identical methods, however. It can be shown that the gatherings of *Richard III* set by Peter Short were set by formes (a not unusual method, the chief advantage of which is to save type). If a book is set seriatim, page by page, any single individual piece of type cannot be used more than once in a gathering. If, therefore, we find a distinctive piece of type

1. *PBSA* (1973), pp. 437–42.

occurring in both inner and outer forme of the same gathering, the inescapable inference is that the gathering was set by formes: that after its use in the inner forme, the piece of type was distributed back into the case, and set again thence in the outer forme. There are several instances of this happening in Short's portion of the book.[1] And the reason for this proceeding is found immediately one examines the type. The fount used is quite clean —it makes a sharper, clearer impression than that used by Simmes—but is quite spectacularly short of certain letters (in technical phrase, out of sorts). There is a great lack of capital letters, particularly T and I, which sends the compositor to the italic case for substitutes. Most pages show some signs of these shifts: on I1^r, for instance, capital T runs out half-way down; on I2^v the compositor has three to begin with, then runs out again until two-thirds of the way down the page, when a further supply becomes available. From this it may be inferred that the compositor interspersed his setting with stretches of distribution, a slower proceeding, but inevitable in view of the shortages. Some curious shifts were resorted to: the use of a double-o ligature,[2] or the employment of wrong-fount letters.[3]

The fount which Valentine Simmes used was, by contrast, old and rather battered, but well-stocked. A single skeleton-forme was used, and the pages were set seriatim, not by formes. From the fact that Short did set by formes, we may deduce one significant conclusion: that the manuscript copy was sufficiently clear and clean to enable it to be 'cast-off', that is, measured so that the compositor would know where to begin each page to make the patchwork fit together. Gatherings H–M are fairly neatly set out, with none of the grosser signs of either 'stretched' copy or of over-full pages. The only exception to this is the placing of entrance directions. In gathering H, entrances are regularly placed in the right-hand part of the line, in the same position as exit directions (unless the direction is too long to be thus fitted in). In some places this practice has resulted in a very tight line: iv.ii.84 in Greg's facsimile reads: '*K ng* Shal we heare from thee *Tirrel* ere we sleep? Enter Buc.*' This line, which occurs only in Q,

---

1. See Greg's facsimile (Shakespeare Quarto Facsimiles No. 12, Oxford, 1959), L1^r, l. 535, the o in 'Milford'; cf. L2^r, l. 10, the first o in 'bosomes'. K3^r, l. 385, the capital W in 'Which'; cf. K4^r, l. 461, the same letter in 'Why'; H1^r, l. 79, the damaged y in 'souerainty', which recurs on H2^r, l. 154 in the second 'my'. There are others; one would have sufficed.

2. I2^v, l. 45; H1^v, l. 124.

3. For instance the wrong-fount capital Y at H2^v, ll. 214–15 or the half-cap. E on I3^r, l. 29.

is absolutely full-measure. The first centred direction where there is no necessity for it to have a line of its own is on I2^r; thereafter the proportion of same-line entrances falls sharply; there are none after gathering K. This gives a strong impression of a compositor saving lines at first, and then relaxing as it became clear there was space to hand. By contrast Simmes's compositor set same-line and separate-line entrances with a fine impartiality, as for example on E3^r.

THE COMPOSITORS OF QI

Both Simmes and Short were very active in the printing of plays by Shakespeare and others in this period; Simmes and his compositors especially were major influences on dramatic publication during Shakespeare's maturity. Clearly, it would be desirable to know more about the men who set type for these printers. Much of the recent work on them has been done by Alan Craven.[1] Short produced two other plays with Shakespearean associations at something near the date of *Richard III*, which also use the same type-face: the *True Tragedy* of 1595 and the two quartos of *1 Henry IV* of 1598. MacD. P. Jackson, of the University of Auckland, is also working on his compositors at present, and has been kind enough to allow me to make use of his results. These show that two compositors, whom he calls X and Y, worked on gatherings H–M. Although they spelled in much the same way (though X preferred 'do' and 'Catesby', and used more commas generally than Y, who tended to prefer 'doe' and 'Catesbie') they differed in two significant practices. X did not usually set a space after a comma, and never set one before a question mark; Y frequently did both. These practices enable it to be determined that X set the first half of gatherings H, I and K, and the second halves of L and M, while Y set the remainder. As these gatherings were set by formes, one man would have set first 1^v and 2^r while the other worked at 3^v and 4^r, to complete the inner forme; then they would have set 1^r and 2^v, and 3^r and 4^v respectively, thus finishing the outer forme.

While Jackson's researches have established that this was the normal pattern, there are anomalies in the setting which are not fully accounted for. Consider, for instance, the use of a period after a speech-prefix. *King* (used alone, i.e. not as in *King Ri.*) has

---

1. There are articles in *SB* (1973), pp. 37–60 and (1979), pp. 186–97, and *PBSA* (1974), pp. 361–72 on Simmes, and in *PBSA* (1971), pp. 393–7 on Short.

no period following it on H4^v, I1^v, I4^v, K1^v (with one exception), K2^v, M2^v and M3^r. On the other hand, it is followed by a period on I1^r, I2^r, I2^v, K1^r, K3^r, K3^v, K4^r (with two exceptions), K4^v, L1^r, L2^r, L2^v, L3^r (with one exception), M1^r (with one exception), M2^r (with one exception). It must be added that the inking of punctuation of this quarto is not good, and some of the exceptions noted above may simply not have inked. Yet the pattern is curious: the most interesting page is K2^r, where the prefix is stopped four times, then unstopped five times.

It is hard to make anything positive of this evidence: we must either suppose the men were simply erratic in their treatment of this typographical convention, or that there were *four* compositors at work on these few gatherings, which seems extravagant. As we have seen, type was in short supply, and it is to be expected that the compositors would have helped each other whenever they had time, by distributing, imposing, or even setting a few lines. This makes it very hard (especially in view of the similarity of their spelling habits) to deduce anything solid about their influence on the text.

The results of a study of Simmes's compositor are more informative. Craven identifies as 'Compositor A' the workman in Simmes's shop who set the sheets of the *Richard III* Q1, and reports that this man also set the quartos of *Much Ado* and *2 Henry IV*, and the first quartos of *Hamlet*, and (most significantly) *Richard II* noted above. His most characteristic feature is that he regularly does not use a period after a full word in a speech-prefix; other aspects of his treatment of stage-directions and exit-directions can be recognized. He also has a number of spelling preferences: 'heart' against 'hart'; 'yong', but 'tongue'; 'eie'; 'here' against 'heere' in a proportion of more than 2:1, 'do' against 'doe' in the proportion 3:1, and so on.[1] *Richard II* (which was set by formes) was divided between two compositors, A and S: S prefers most of A's spellings, but always stops speech-prefixes; A in this play shows a fondness for abbreviating names and titles in dialogue, 'Lo:' for 'Lord' being a particularly common one. The significance of this is that while some compositorial habits remain fixed, others change over a period of time, and under the influence of different kinds of copy. *Richard II* is nearest to *Richard III* in date of the books Craven alleges were set by A, and thus may well reveal most clearly A's habits at that time. Although Craven is confident that the two books were set by A, the characteristic feature of unstopped

1. Craven, *SB*, loc. cit.

speech-prefixes hardly occurs in *Richard III*.[1] Craven accounts for this by appealing to the general sense of crowding of space in this quarto; there is something in this, but it is hardly a complete answer. Consider B1^v–B2^r, a pair of pages with many incomplete lines, on which *Lady* is twenty-one times abridged to *La*. It is hard to see how much space was saved by abbreviating *King* to *Kin.*, as is done on D3^v–E1^r, for example. Generally in Simmes's part of the quarto the speech-prefixes are limited wherever possible to three or four letters, including the period. This practice is quite unlike that of *Richard II*.

Spelling tests are a little more helpful: Craven counts heart 28/ hart 3; eie 17/eye 4; do 2/doe 60; go 32/goe 0; bloud 30/blood 0; heere 30/here 3. These spelling preferences are certainly close to those he has identified in other work attributed to A. But some other habits in *Richard III* are less characteristic: A elsewhere shows a preference for -nesse suffixes over -nes, and is inclined to double the e as in hee, wee, shee, etc. to assist in justification; he also tends not to capitalize titles, such as prince, lord, etc. In *Richard III* such titles are usually capitalized; A uses -nes suffixes 17 times to 8 of -nesse; the doubled e is hard to find as there is so little prose in the play; but in what there is it does not occur. And there are other preferences which hardly equate with those found elsewhere for this workman. However, the practice of abbreviating names and titles is strongly present. It is, indeed, one of the most characteristic features of the typesetting of *Richard III*: Lord is abbreviated no fewer than 73 times to Lo: (cf. 12 in *Richard II*). Craven's conclusion is that it is more plausible to suppose that *Richard III* was set by A than that Simmes had a fourth compositor who shared many of A's preferences. We do not know how many compositors Simmes was employing in 1597, but the weight of the evidence suggests a cautious acceptance of Craven's theory, pending computerized analysis of *all* Simmes books printed in this period (not just the dramatic quartos).

If we accept that the case for Simmes's workman being Compositor A is fairly strong, it is worth enquiring into his habits and practices. Again, Alan Craven has explored this question. The Second Quarto of *Richard II* was set entirely by Compositor A: his reliability can thus be assessed against the First Quarto. Craven finds he created 146 variants in dialogue and 9 in stage-

---

1. In gatherings A–G there are only four examples of unabridged unstopped prefixes: *Ambo* on E2^r, *Lady* twice on B1^r and *Gray* on B3^v. There is also *Ambo* as a catchword on E2^r.

directions, an alteration on average every 17 lines. These variants may be defined as follows: 63 substitutions, 30 omissions, 14 interpolations, 25 literals, 8 transpositions, 9 sophistications and 6 corrections. It will be remarked at once how similar these categories are to the evidences of memorial contamination discussed above (pp. 3–7). The cause of this is surely the compositor's attempting to hold more of his copy in his mind than he could manage: the results make sense, but often are not precisely what his copy read. It is, then, very precisely, a form of memorial corruption which we are discussing.

Now, Craven's results are based on the setting of a reprint from printed copy. It is not legitimate to translate these into expectations of what a compositor will do when setting from manuscript. If, however, he behaved in something like the same way, we might expect to find as many as a hundred readings introduced by the compositor, in his proportionately shorter work in *Richard III*. Many of them would not be self-evidently wrong, and so (without the copy) would be virtually unidentifiable as errors. However, some of these corruptions would leave signs, such as disturbance of metre, dittography, 'catching', repetition and so on; but many of these of course are characteristic of the errors of actors, and so in a memorial text would not be identifiable as compositorial. The implication of this is to suggest the strong possibility that a goodly proportion of 'memorial' errors in Q may originate with the compositor rather than the actors, whose standard of accuracy is therefore seen to be higher than Patrick and others assumed.

The other implication is that a new element of unreliability has entered the Q text. If a Q reading originated in the theatre, there was at least the chance that even if it was not of the author's writing, it might have received at least his tacit sanction. Compositorial errors of course have no such element of doubt about them, and must be weeded out, if they can be identified. Nothing extreme seems to have happened in *Richard III* (though the cautious might like to remember the unique-to-Q 'clock scene'),[1] but there are signs of the compositor's corrupting the text. We cannot of course identify the errors in *Richard III* which Simmes

1. Compare the conclusion of *Titus Andronicus*, which Blakemore Evans rightly calls 'a sobering situation for those concerned with the authenticity of Shakespeare's text' (*Riverside Shakespeare*, p. 1051). Q2 of this play, the earliest text until the discovery of Q1 in 1904, was set from a damaged copy of Q1; no attempt was made in the printing house to obtain a correct text: the deficiencies were supplied by sheer guesswork, which amounted to someone in the printing house's writing four lines of his own for Aaron.

A may be presumed to have made since his copy is not extant. But examples of what a compositor *may* do are afforded by later quartos in the stemma.

An example is found in 1.iv, where l. 230 in F reads ' 'Tis he that sends vs to destroy you heere'. In Q1 we find 'Tis he hath sent vs hither now to slaughter thee'; the variant is caused by the actor's recollection of l. 211. However, Q2 reads 'murder' for 'slaughter', which by a curious accident produces an even closer repetition of l. 211. The compositor could hardly have misread his (printed) copy; there is no graphic resemblance between 'slaughter' and 'murder' to mislead him: the probability is that he, like the actor, was influenced by recollection of l. 211. This then is a clear case of compositorial memorial contamination: fortunately it occurs in a derivative quarto and so has no direct bearing on the text. Another example in the same scene occurs at l. 39, where F reads 'find', and Q1–2 'feeke'. In Q3 this is metamorphosed to 'keepe', which, for all that it makes nonsense of the line, was happily followed by subsequent Qq compositors. If such misreadings of printed copy can occur, we must be very cautious in rejecting as impossible even the most outrageous misreadings of manuscript copy.

One of Compositor A's habits which leads to trouble on more than one occasion is his practice of abbreviating 'Lord' to 'Lo:'. Act I, sc. ii provides us with the best example: the first line reads in Q 'Set downe set downe your honourable lo'; the word 'lo' here is a typographical accident for 'load'. The compositor of Q2, knowing Q1's habits, expanded the word without thinking to 'lord', and tried to make sense of the line by altering 'Set' to 'Sit' (but forgot to complete the transmogrification by changing 'your' to 'you'). Q3 reverted to 'Set', but confirmed the lord by capitalizing him, thus changing the individual nominated back to Henry. This chain of error is a useful, and typical, example of the inventiveness of compositors, and of their reluctance to check copy. So far, however, all these instances are of compositor error in the derivative quartos, where, as Patrick noticed, the proportion of such lapses declines sharply.[1]

The likeliest examples of Q1's compositor interfering with the text are found in the stage-directions. We have already discussed these above in terms of their inadequacy for prompter's directions. It is now worth considering whether, at least in Simmes's part of the book, some of their deficiencies may have originated with the compositor. It has been noted that in this book the

1. Patrick, p. 70.

compositor liked to abbreviate speech-prefixes; this tendency may be observed also in stage-directions. The most extreme example is III.i.150: '*Exeunt Prin.Yor.Hast.Dors.manet.Rich.Buck.*' In this instance the compositor has in fact managed to mention every significant name.

But what ought we to make of the direction to II.iv: '*Enter Cardinall, Dutches of Yorke, Quee. young Yorke*'? There are at least three redundant letters in this direction which could have been omitted to save the odd abbreviation of 'Queen': the refusal to do so suggests that the man preferred to take things as easily as possible with directions. This being so, consider III.iv.58, where in F Richard comes storming back into the Council followed by Buckingham. In Q the direction is simply '*Enter Glocester*'. It is scarcely possible that Buckingham could have been omitted from the scene for any practical theatrical purpose; it is equally hard to find a persuasive reason on dramatic grounds why he might have been eliminated. We might then wonder if the compositor set Richard's name in full, then, rather than change it when he realized he lacked room for Buckingham, simply left the latter out. Similar doubts arise in II.i, where the initial direction in Q reads '*Enter King,Queene,Hastings,Ryuers,Dorcet,&c.*' Did the *&c* stand in the copy, or was it Compositor A's way of not setting a second line of directions (or resetting the existing line) to allow for the not unimportant presence of Buckingham? Later, in II.ii.100, we find in Q the direction '*Enter Glocest. with others*' squeezed on to two lines in the right-hand margin. The 'others' again include Buckingham, who has an important speaking part; once more one wonders if the abbreviation might not have originated with the compositor. If these cases are probable, then why may not other directions which are abridged in Q (such as III.iv's initial direction, or that of III.v) have originated at least in part with Compositor A? The case, it seems, is quite a strong one.

The other process likely to have a bearing on the final text is proof-reading. Practices varied in the period, but it is fair to say that a cheap play quarto would be hardly likely to receive rigorous proofing, and that it was relatively unusual for copy to be consulted at the proof stage, and that uncorrected sheets which had already been printed would not be destroyed. These expectations are met in the *Richard III* QI.[1] The five surviving copies of

---

1. Alan Craven has made a study of the proof-reading of the Shakespearean plays printed by Valentine Simmes. His conclusions agree with those presented here: *Richard III* is revealed to have been less carefully proofed than most. See *PBSA* (1974), pp. 361-72.

Q1 (including the incomplete Malone and fragmentary Elizabethan Club copies) reveal signs of proof-correction. Greg provides a list of variants on p. vi of his Oxford facsimile of the Quarto.[1] Most of these variants are, as he says, to be ascribed to bad inking, broken or dirty type, rather than to an actual alteration of the setting. There are only two corrections which did require resetting: on D3^v, l. 5 of Greg's facsimile (II.i.5) reads 'from heauen' in the Huth (BL) and Devonshire copies; it is corrected to 'to heauen' in the others. L2^r, l. 10 in Greg (V.iii.10) reads 'greatest' in the Devonshire, 'vtmost' in the rest.[2]

Of these two substantive variants, the first hardly required the consultation of copy: 'And now in peace my soule shall part from heauen' is fairly obviously wrong, and within the scope of the corrector's common sense. The Act V variant is a more complex one. In F the line reads 'Six or seuen thousand is their vtmost power'; the uncorrected Q1 has 'Sixe or seuen thousand is their greatest number'. 'Number' for 'power' is probably an actor's slip, one of the synonymous variants discussed above, and probably an echo of l. 9, 'the number of the Traitors' (F reading). However, 'greatest' was not an actor's, but a compositor's synonym, which did not stand in his copy. The line makes adequate sense as set, and therefore, for 'vtmost' to have been recovered, the copy must have been consulted, in this forme at least, by the corrector. It is worth remarking the later consequences of the compositor's version: Q2 by chance was set from the uncorrected version at this point, and so preserves the error, and is in turn followed by the remainder of the derivative Qq.

There is one other possible place where a stop-press correction of importance was made in Q1. In I.i, ll. 101–2 are not present in Q1: they are there, however, in Q2, and subsequent Qq. The only reasonable explanations for this are either that the compositor of Q2 occasionally consulted the manuscript of the play, or else that at this point (the outer forme of A) he was setting from a corrected copy of Q1, no example of which survives today. Since there is no real evidence to suggest that Q2 used the manuscript anywhere else in the play (and in view of the unlikeliness of such a proceeding anyway) it seems more probable that the second alternative is correct. In conclusion, then, we may say that as a result of this

1. Surprisingly, this list is very inaccurate. He believed, for instance, that there were three unique variants in the Devonshire copy, but was mistaken; there are numerous other errors.

2. Greg, extraordinarily, overlooks this, the one significant stop-press correction in the book.

investigation of the composition and proofing of Q, certain of its weaker features, including unreliability of stage-directions, and memorial variants, may well have been introduced by Simmes's compositor. Those portions printed by Peter Short are perhaps somewhat more reliable.

After this long and somewhat scholastic study of how many compositors can dance on the tail of a thin-space, we may survey the remaining quartos much more succinctly. Q2–Q5 all derive from the shop of Thomas Creede; Q6 was set in Thomas Purfoot's shop, the last quarto before F. Each successive quarto was set from its predecessor, save that, as Greg has shown,[1] sheets C and E–M of Q5 were printed from a copy of Q3. However, his belief that both Q4 and Q5 were set up from the same 'file copy' in Creede's office can be shown to be incorrect. In III.vii, l. 115 reads in Q1 'Else wherefore breath I in a Christian land?'. The Kemble copy of Q3 (in the Huntington Library, which Greg did not examine) uniquely has an uncorrected state of this forme, outer H, in which the line begins 'Els wherefore'. The proof-reader caught this, and in all other copies the phrase reads 'Else wherfore': the corrector was reluctant to reset and rejustify the line, so he merely transferred the redundant mute e from the second word. Q5 was set from a corrected copy of Q3, and retains its rather odd spelling; Q4, however, must have been set from an uncorrected copy since it retains the version originally set.

Act IV, sc. i, l. 35 reads in Q1 'May haue some scope to beate, or else I sound'. Q2 by oversight dropped the pronoun, reading 'else sound', in which it was followed by Q3's compositor. Once again, the error was noticed by the proof-reader and changed, so that Q5 and its derivative, Q6, are correct. And once again, Q4 follows the uncorrected forme (this line is also in the outer forme of H) and so reproduces the error. The chance of survival of uncorrected formes is not enormously high. There are numerous Q4-only variants and errors in (roughly) Act IV of the play; since Q4 is generally unadventurous, it is probable that at this point also the Q4 compositor was working from an uncorrected forme or formes in Q3, no copy of which has survived.[2] The general impression left by the quartos is quite clear: the two which introduce most variants are Q3 and Q6. Q2 follows Q1

1. *The Library*, 4th series, 17:1 (1936), pp. 88–97.
2. See IV. iv. 153 and elsewhere in the apparatus.

very closely; Q4 and Q5 have little distinctive character. Q6, however, is the product of a new printer, and introduces a fine new crop of errors.

These impressions are relevant since it has long been accepted that F was set from a copy or copies of a quarto, collated against a manuscript. The best proof of this is found at i.iii.234 and iv.iv.364. In the first of these, the interjected line '*Rich.* Ha?' is printed on the same line as the preceding '*Marg.* Richard?' in both Qq and F, instead of on a line of its own (as is normal F practice); in the second a line present in Q1 but missing in Q2–5 is inserted from the manuscript, but inserted in the wrong place. As Alice Walker says,

> A marginal addition in a manuscript might have been misplaced when the manuscript came to be printed, but it is not very likely that the line lost in printing Q2, and therefore missing from its successors, should have coincided with a line inserted in the manuscript. The explanation must be that the line was written in the margin of one of the derivative quartos used as Folio copy and that either the collator failed to make clear where it was to be inserted or that the compositor was careless in incorporating it in the Folio text.[1]

There are other lineation problems, especially the crux at i.iv.247–57, which seem to originate in misplaced insertions in quarto copy. In addition, there are errors shared by Q and F throughout the text which indicate dependence: these are usually matters of lineation or stage-directions (such as v.iii.67) but there are occasional errors in readings (i.ii.32).

Not all such errors will be visible and obvious, of course: the spectre arises, to haunt the editor, of a large class of unperceived errors which were taken over into F from its Q source, errors which make sense, and so are not susceptible to elimination. Alice Walker has addressed herself to this problem of contamination, and attempted to make an estimate of the concealed errors in *Richard III*. We can determine how many errors introduced in Q2–6 escaped correction in F: the collator restored a Q1 reading corrupted in Q2–6 on some 300 occasions (dialogue variants only). A further 44 readings found in Q6 (which Miss Walker believes was copy for F) escaped correction, which suggests that the collator missed about one in every eight errors. Since he corrected about 1200 readings which originated in Q1, if the proportion

1. Alice Walker, *Textual Problems of the First Folio* (Cambridge, 1953), pp. 14–15.

holds, then some 170 readings common to Q and F are erroneous. Miss Walker admits this is a maximum figure, but still feels we should expect something like 110 to 140 such errors in fact.[1] In practice, about ten errors common to Q and F are corrected by most editors; she believes another twenty corrections can be safely made, which still leaves over a hundred concealed errors in the final text. Most of these will be of a trivial kind, to be sure. The only edition to attempt large-scale emendation as a result of this kind of thinking is the New Cambridge. For reasons discussed below, pp. 50-1, the present editor, while agreeing in principle with Miss Walker's calculations, finds the practical application of them a much riskier business than she.[2]

WAS Q6 THE COPY FOR F?

The first serious attempt to solve the question of which quarto or quartos F was printed from was undertaken by P. A. Daniel, in his introduction to the Griggs facsimile of Q1. Using the collations of the Cambridge Shakespeare, he found 435 cases where the six pre-F quartos disagreed among themselves. Of these, he culled a list of 72 'doubtful or erroneous readings imported into the F. text'.[3] And his demonstration is as follows:

> Out of my list of 72 doubtful or erroneous readings I find that the F. shares
>
> 10 with Q1, two exclusively;
> 19 with Q2, none exclusively;
> 53 with Q3, one exclusively;
> 54 with Q4, one exclusively;
> 52 with Q5, one exclusively;
> 56 with Q6, twelve exclusively.[4]

This certainly looks, on the face of it, a very pretty demonstration of the conclusion that Q6 was the copy for F. Daniel goes further, and says that he can find no evidence to suggest that Q3 was copy, though he is unconvincing in his discussion of III.i.123.[5] Other

1. This entire summary is based on Walker's survey, ch. 2.
2. Walker assumes, without good reason, a constant proportion between manifest and latent errors—and latent error is by definition unrecognizable.
3. Daniel. p. vii. He nowhere prints this list.
4. Ibid.
5. In Q3 this reads 'I would that I might thanke you as as you call me' and F takes over this obvious dittography. It is perhaps the single most conclusive demonstration of Q3's influence on the F text (ibid., pp. vii-viii).

investigators had come to a different conclusion: Koppel and Schmidt both observed that in two passages, III.i. 1–165, and v.iii. 49–end of play, F was printed with little alteration from Q3, and lacks any influence from the Q4–6 series.[1] This has long been generally admitted, and the debate is concerned with the remaining five-sixths of the play.

Daniel went on to examine the readings, rather than rely entirely on statistics, and of the twelve errors exclusive to Q6 and F, two must be noted here for the bearing they have on later discussion. At III.v. 74 Q1–5 read 'There at your meetst aduantage of the time'; Q6 reads 'meetest', thus producing an eleven-syllable line. F 'corrects' this, not by dropping the superfluous syllable from 'meetest', but by eliminating the prefix from 'advantage'. The other is at IV.iv.534, where Q1 reads 'Is colder tidings, yet they must be told'. Q6, perhaps catching the word from l. 532, prints 'newes' instead of 'tidings';[2] F (noticing the bad rhythm, one assumes) inserts 'but' before 'yet' to make up the line. Both of these conjectural corrections of Q6-only errors appear to support Daniel's case for very strong dependence of F on Q6.

WAS Q3 THE COPY?

Since Daniel's time there has been only one scholar who has set out to challenge his results. This is J. K. Walton, who has published a monograph,[3] several articles and a book[4] urging the thesis that Q3 was the only quarto collated with the manuscript in the preparation of copy for F. Mr Walton writes forcefully, but rebarbatively; it is hoped his argument is here correctly represented (he claims Bowers has misunderstood him).[5] Essentially he seeks to present three arguments: that the statistical and logical basis of Daniel's method was wrong, that it is essential to classify variants according to whether they are definite errors or not, and that the collator who prepared the F copy was grossly uneven in his performance.

1. R. Koppel, *Textkritische Studien über Shakespeares 'Richard III' und 'King Lear'* (Dresden, 1877); A. Schmidt, 'Quartos und Folio von *Richard III*', *Jahrbuch der Deutschen Shakespeare-Gesellschaft* 15 (1880), 301–24.

2. Fredson Bowers notes (*SQ* 10 (1959), p. 544) that compositorial error will not explain the F readings as line 532 was set by A, and line 534 by B.

3. *The Copy for the Folio Text of Richard III* (Auckland, 1955); hereafter *Copy*.

4. *The Quarto Copy for the First Folio of Shakespeare* (Dublin, 1971); hereafter *Quarto*.

5. *Quarto*, appendix B.

Taking these in turn, the first point is perhaps the least controversial. Daniel reached his large count of 'doubtful or erroneous' readings common to Q6 and F only because Q6 was last in the series. He treated the quartos as if they were polygenous texts, radiating from a single archetype (as is usual with manuscripts) rather than the monogenous chain they actually are (as is normal with printed texts) in which each exemplar is dependent upon the preceding one. In such circumstances, errors once created tend to be carried on to the next item in the chain, which reduces the number of unique variants in any one example to a vanishingly small quantity. If (purely as an experiment) we examine Q7 and Q8, we find that the errors in Q6 which Daniel described as exclusive to that quarto are largely carried on to the later quartos. If we take Q7 (but not Q8) into account, as Greg noticed,[1] we find seventeen exclusive agreements between F and it; if we take Q8 we find it shares ten exclusive agreements with F. 'Since F can be in no way dependent on quartos respectively six and eleven years younger than itself, these figures show the worthlessness of the evidence that has been supposed to prove [F's] dependence on Q6.'[2] Walton backtracks to the earlier quartos, and finds that Q3 is the latest quarto with sufficient distinctive variants—twenty-two in number—in which F concurs; these he maintains provide strong evidence that Q3 was copy for F throughout.

The argument is partially correct, in that Daniel's criterion of exclusiveness was false. Its weakness is that it in turn depends on statistical arguments of doubtful validity. However, Walton seeks to avoid this trap by attempting to draw a distinction between definite errors and what he calls 'indifferent variants'. This latter term has caused a good deal of discontent among scholars; Walton means by it a 'variant which has a meaning similar to the meaning of the reading it replaces',[3] or, more precisely, a variant in a text where the tradition has been contaminated, which may be an error or may equally well be a correction; since the difference between the two readings is so slight, one has no basis for declaring for the one or the other. Now such variants are common in editorial experience, especially in a play like *Richard III*, so liberally supplied with minor variation, thanks to the actors' memories. These variants are not a matter of indifference, however, but rather of ignorance; it is not that the readings cannot

1. Review of *Copy*, *The Library*, 5th series, 11:2 (1956), p. 126.
2. Ibid.; there is no convincing evidence to suggest that F was consulted in the composition of Q7 and Q8.
3. *Quarto*, p. 64.

be discriminated, but that we lack the information wherewith to discriminate between them. Variants range from palpable errors at the one extreme, through a variety of probable and possible error into a grey area where uncertainty reigns. Walton is asking the impossible in attempting to distinguish into a mere two classes all such variants: certainly he is forfeiting the chance of scholarly consensus.

Of the twenty-two agreements he finds between Q3 and F he declares that nine are errors, and thirteen are indifferent variants, while the twelve agreements between Q6 and F are, he maintains, all indifferent. To say this is not to say enough, for it is so far still a statistical argument only, and his figures have been challenged by other investigators.[1] The alternatives are to mount a massive, computerized attack on the accidentals of all the quartos (which no one has attempted) or to attempt to evaluate the readings, the substantive variants, which occur. Walton follows this second line of enquiry, without carrying entire conviction.

Space precludes a complete examination of the thirty-four Q3 and Q6 variants in question (many are commented on in the notes of this edition), but it will be necessary to notice the most crucial examples. The questions to be settled here are not issues of probability, but rather issues of fact: is there any conclusive evidence that F used Q3 (outside of the Act III and Act V passages where everyone agrees it was copy), or Q6? Is there any proof that either quarto was *not* used? Walton's thesis is that Q6 was not used, so his first task is to explain the occurrence of the Q6/F agreements. To do so, he is obliged to assert that in I.iv.13 'There' and 'thence', in I.iv.262 'Heauen' and 'heauens', and in IV.iv.507 'ye' and 'you', for instance, are 'indifferent'. It seems quite clear, however, that if one were so minded, one could find a distinct difference between the specifically Christian oath 'by Heaven' and the far vaguer colloquialism 'by heavens'. The other examples, and some not here quoted, are susceptible to the same objections. In any event, we must still be provided with a mechanism to account for the presence of these readings in both F and Q6. Walton's mechanism is coincidence: he argues that, in 'indifferent' matters, a certain number of coincidental agreements will occur in any resetting. That is to say, in the example given above, the compositor of Q6 happened to set 'ye' instead of 'you' at IV.iv.507; and so, independently of Q6, did the F compositor. That this does happen cannot be denied, but it becomes hard to

---

1. Walker, p. 44; Bowers, p. 542. Smidt lists a large number; *Iniurious*, appendices 1–3.

argue for such coincidence when the reading is plainly awry, and it is on this basis that Walton attempts to distinguish true errors from 'indifferent' variants.

The further complication exists in F of the readings cited above (p. 33), where it certainly looks as if F is trying to put a Q6 error right. On these, Walton must speak for himself: of the variant at III.v.74 he remarks, 'It is at least as easy to suppose that the collator of the quarto used as copy for F corrected the Q1–5 "meetst advantage", which may easily have been an actor's corruption, to the right reading "meetest vantage", as it is to suppose that the F reading arose as a result of conjectural emendation of the Q6 reading'.[1] We are to believe, then, the Q6 compositor made the change from 'meetst' to 'meetest' and that by coincidence it happened to be correct, that the Q1 compositor made two errors (or the actor reporting the text did) which the F finally got right. Walton may find this as easy to suppose as that F conjecturally emended Q6, but it is difficult to agree with him. Another example occurs at III.v.65, where Q1–5 read 'cause', Q6 has 'ease' and F 'case'. Now 'cause' and 'case' can mean the same thing (OED case *sb*.[1]6=cause *sb*.8), and it is thus possible, as Walton avers, that F is right here. But most commentators agree that Q6's erroneous reading looks so much like a simple misprint for 'case' that the F corrector or compositor surely just changed the letter without checking.[2]

Even weaker is his treatment of the variant in IV.iv, quoted on p. 33. Of this he enquires,

Can we be sure in a a play of which repetition is the outstanding characteristic of its general style, repetition of words and phrases just as much as repetition of lines and whole scenes, that the F 'Newes' in line [534] is incorrect? Can we also be sure that the Q1–5 reading 'tidings' does not originate in a 'recollection' of IV.i.35–37? Here the F version reads:

> Or else I swoone with this dead-killing newes.
> *Anne.* Despightfull tidings, O vnpleasing newes.

Line 37, 'Despightfull tidings, O vnpleasing newes.', is omitted from the quartos, and has thus all the authority of a passage peculiar to F.[3]

To this it may be returned that it is hard to see how 'tidings' in IV.iv can be a recollection of a line which does not occur in the Q version of the play, the one being recollected (especially when the

1. *Copy*, pp. 26–7.   2 Ibid., p. 26.   3. Ibid., p. 27.

speaker in IV.iv was certainly not on stage in IV.i). Walton has been unable to improve on this explanation, though he has been attacked for it,[1] and it remains the weakest feature of his case. To conclude, Walton has certainly been unable to prove that Q6 was not used as copy (though he has undoubtedly damaged Daniel's supposed demonstration that it was).

Let us turn now to his attempt to prove that Q3 was the copy throughout. We can ignore any variants which are 'indifferent' in Walton's terms: he counted twenty-two agreements, thirteen of which he conceded to be indifferent. Nine 'definite' errors thus originate in Q3 which occur also in F. However, it must be pointed out that seven of these nine also occur in Q6 (as do all but one of the 'indifferent' variants) and so *could* have entered F from that source. If we are seeking proof positive, we must find, as Bowers pointed out, errors which occur in Q3 and F only. As the chain is monogenous, and errors tend to be carried over into the next in the series, the number of these will be vanishingly small: as Bowers puts it, 'These conditions are so stringent as to remove almost all possibility that agreement of readings alone could ever prove that Q3 served as copy for the Folio.'[2] Let us be clear: what has been said is not that Q3 could not have been copy: rather that the evidence Walton has brought forward is not sufficient to *prove* that it was copy throughout. The two readings shared by Q3 and F and not by Q6 are III.v.107, where they read 'manner person' (Q4 also reads thus) while the other quartos have 'man[n]er of person', and IV.iv.423, where they read 'I bury' (Q3 'burie') against Q1-2's 'I buried' and Q4-6's 'Ile burie'.

Of the first of these, it ought to be remarked that 'manner person' is perfectly good English (see OED Manner *sb*.9), and that Q1's 'manner of person' stretches an already long line. Yet the agreement of Q3 and F is unusual, and the reading may be an error. The alternative, that F is right and Q3 a coincidental correction, is not at all impossible—there are, as we shall see, examples in the play. As for the second, the chance of coincidental correction is even higher: the present used for the future is a not uncommon piece of Shakespearean grammar, and should not be rejected even though 'I'll bury' is what we would now expect. Q1's version is patently mistaken; the Q4 reading a probable sophistication. So it has been assumed in this text, but that does not of course rule out the possibility that both Q3 readings are errors. It is a nice decision, either way—and all that could be

1. e.g. A. S. Cairncross, *The Library*, 5th series, 13:3 (1957), pp. 189–90.
2. Bowers, 'The Copy for the Folio *Richard III*', *SQ* 10 (1959), p. 542.

claimed, even if it were conceded that Walton was right, is that at these two specific points Q3 was copy.

Another line of argument which Walton produces in support of his case is evidence from spelling. He finds altogether nine places where the F compositor has used Q3's spelling of a word when his own usual preferred form is to be found in Q6. This sort of evidence can be very persuasive, but the fundamental objection remains that Walton examined only fifteen words throughout the play: a complete spelling analysis (which could in practice only be done by computer) might reveal more, or less, than this select evidence.[1] And while the allocation of pages to compositors in F *Richard III* is quite stable,[2] it is always possible, as Hinman sagely observed, that although an F page was set by one compositor, another may have taken over for a few lines, thereby producing anomalous spellings, and unsettling our carefully-drawn chains of inference.[3]

One final example will be discussed to reveal how uncertain this entire business of evaluating copy through readings can be. In I.iii the speech-prefixes cause some difficulty, especially at l. 309, where Queen Elizabeth should be the speaker. The prefix is *Qu.* in Q1-5, *Hast.* in Q6, and *Mar.* in F. Queen Margaret in fact left the stage six lines earlier; l. 309 is Elizabeth's first line since l. 240, and one may speculate that the Q6 compositor, having forgotten her existence, but feeling that l. 309 wouldn't do for Margaret, supplied Hastings for the line, *faute de mieux*: he was followed by the compositors of Q7 and Q8 without question. Subsequently, F3 proposed Derby as speaker of the line, and Rowe nominated Dorset, a pretty chain of error; Malone restored it to Elizabeth. But how did Margaret get into F? Walton has it that Compositor B saw the prefix *Qu.* in Q3, and, also having forgotten Elizabeth, and with less scruple than Q6, simply set *Mar.*, his usual form for Margaret. It is equally possible[4] that the corrector, producing copy for F, saw *Hast.* in Q6 and changed it, from the manuscript, to 'Queen' or some such form, and that B, seeing this, followed the chain of incorrect reasoning already described. So far as proof concerning copy goes, this example offers nothing, neither way, as Osric has it.

1. Bowers (ibid., pp. 543-4) has pointed out the shortcomings in Walton's method. Smidt has investigated in some greater detail, with different results; see his *Memorial Transmission*, pp. 60-3, 73-5.

2. See below, pp. 44-5.

3. Charlton Hinman, *The Printing and Proof-Reading of the First Folio of Shakespeare* (Oxford, 1963), II, p. 120.

4. As Smidt noted *Memorial Transmission*, p. 63.

We thus certainly lack proof that Q3 was throughout copy for F, but in the absence of such proof we can still find reasons for believing that it rather than Q6 was copy, for much of the time—certainly for more than the Acts III and V portions universally conceded to have been set from it. Yet we cannot eliminate Q6 either. The three 'conjectural corrections' discussed above, where F amends a Q6 reading, do not amount to proof positive either, but the balance of probabilities supports the interpretation argued here, that at those points Q6 was copy. And if it was copy at some points, unless there was some specific reason for its being used there only (which there is not), common sense suggests that it was used elsewhere. It is true that there are many more places in F where a Q3 error is accepted into the text than there are similar contributions from Q6. Perhaps it would be more accurate to put this the other way: that F manages to avoid a large number of Q6 errors while accepting rather more of those originating in Q3. The question thus remains open, after all the arguing: only a computerized investigation of accidentals remains as a potential tool to investigate further. It is not possible from study of the readings to assign in detail which parts of F derive from which quarto. The most that can be said to console the reader is that it matters very little, in practice, in a modernized text. A couple of readings would be changed if we could prove that Q3 rather than Q6 was copy, such as 'manner person' and 'I bury', but by and large the text would be unchanged. The opinion of this editor is that both quartos were used, in a way to be suggested a little later.

Coincidental correction (the compositor of a derivative quarto hitting on the right reading without manuscript authority) has been mentioned. The evidence for this is quite good: not counting the examples already discussed, let us look at five more. At II.ii.25 Q1 reads 'in my', where 'on my' is necessary. It is found in F, but also in Q2–6, the compositor of Q2 having made the correct deduction. At III.ii.91 Q1 correctly reads 'hats', with which F concurs. This time Q2 made a mistake, and set the singular 'hat', in which mistake Q3–5 followed him. Q6, however, restored 'hats'. At III.v.26 all Qq save Q4 wrongly read 'this'; Q4 shares with F the correct reading, 'the'. At IV.ii.79 the mistake, 'is it', is shared by Q1–2 and Q6; Q3 found the right reading, 'it is', and was followed by Q4–5; F confirms it. Finally, IV.iv.260 contains 'thou love' correctly in Q1, 'thou' in Q2–5, and the correct reading again in Q6 and F. From these examples it can be seen that coincidental correction is a not uncommon occurrence. Examples have been given of F agreeing with Q3 and

Q6 and with neither, so as to eliminate the possibility that F is merely following copy. The existence of undeniable cases of coincidental correction supports Walton's general position, though it does not make his explanation of (say) IV.iv.534 any more convincing.

One further element in his discussion remains to be examined. If Q3 was indeed the copy for much of the time, why is it that some F passages (in III.i and V.iii) were set from Q3 with almost no correction? The pre-Walton explanation of this was that the quarto copy was Q6, corrected against an authoritative manuscript—but a manuscript which had lacunae which had been repaired by patching in pages torn from a copy of Q3. This, in outline, is the theory which has grown up around Daniel's thesis, and was accepted (with minor variations) by Greg and Walker. Perhaps the strongest objection to the theory is that the passages (III.i.1–166 and V.iii.50–end of play) do not correspond with complete pages in Q3. Act III, sc. i begins half-way down a page (E4^r), and l. 166 is one line from the bottom of F2^r. Line 50 of V.iii is one line from the top of L2^r. However, as Walton remarks, the postulate of a damaged manuscript was created merely to account for the presence of Q3 passages in an otherwise Q6-derived text. If we prefer to think that both Q3 and Q6 were used in preparing F copy, the need for such an hypothesis disappears. We are still left with the need to explain the virtual cessation of collating activity in these two passages.

Walton begins by observing that there are other parts of the play where collation was slight, especially in I.i, a point previously made by Walker. He goes on to attempt to analyse the differences statistically, an attempt which looks impressive, but is invalid, because based on too small a sample: the inclusion or omission of a single item at one point causes a percentage figure to change from 67 per cent to 71 per cent.[1] The drift of his argument is that the collation varied in efficiency throughout the play, a conclusion one may accept while rejecting the detail of the method.[2] His opinion, then, is that the collator was simply quite spectacularly inefficient in the Act III and V passages. He points out that some corrections were in fact made there, generally in the stage-directions and speech-prefixes. One important change in the dialogue is found at V.iii.222 where the word 'eavesdropper'

---

1. *Quarto*, p. 265.
2. Note, for instance, that the standard of correction fluctuates in I.ii, rising sharply after l. 255, near the end of the scene; or that early in I.iii the standard is high.

passed through some strange metamorphoses of spelling (see collation). Q3's form was 'ewse-dropper'; F reverts to the rather unusual form found in Q1, 'Ease-dropper'. This version was already old-fashioned (see OED) and so is not likely to be a Compositor B 'modernization'. The natural inference is that the manuscript was consulted at this point at least. There are a fair number of other verbal variants which may have originated with the F collator rather than with the compositor.[1]

Walton believes that at this point in the play the idle corrector merely checked the stage-directions, and occasionally noticed errors in the adjacent dialogue. He is unable to reconcile convincingly this image of unconcern with the collation which at other points in the play is so painstakingly meticulous, and he prefers to reject, for not very persuasive reasons, Greg's common-sense solution that more than one scribe was working on the preparation of F copy.[2] Perhaps one was armed with a copy of Q3, and the other with a Q6, and they divided the play up between them, with Jaggard finally being supplied with disbound, mixed Q copy. Nor is there any ground for believing that the preparation of F copy was supervised by anyone that we might call an 'editor'. There are no features of F which require for their explanation agents other than scribes, compositors and the proof-reader. For this reason the term 'corrector' has been used throughout this introduction to describe the scribe or scribes who prepared copy for F.

F COPY: WAS IT A TRANSCRIPT?

So far the presumption has been followed that F copy was a quarto or quartos, collated against a manuscript. It seems the obvious explanation of how errors in the derivative quartos find themselves in F: but it is not, perhaps, the only explanation. It is true that the sheer quantity of annotation and correction which would have had to be inserted into the margins of the Q copy would have presented great obstacles to the compositors.[3] The possibility remains that a manuscript transcript was made from Q3/Q6, and corrected from the authoritative theatrical manu-script. It is difficult to see the rationale for such a proceeding, as the theatrical manuscript was already available, and if a tran-script was wanted, the reason for bothering with the quartos does not evidently appear.

1. See *Copy*, pp. 108–20 for a list and discussion.
2. In his review of Walton, *Copy*, in *The Library*, 5th series, 11:2 (1956), p. 126.
3. See Smidt, *Iniurious*, pp. 204–5, for an illustration.

However, there is a slight possibility that, odd as it seems, this was what was done. MacD. P. Jackson has allowed me the use of an unpublished article in which he explores this matter. The starting point is William Kable's article on the Pavier Quartos,[1] in which the habits of Compositor B when setting from printed copy were investigated. Kable's results showed that certain of B's spellings reflect his copy at a rate of better than 80 per cent. Jackson examined these 'copy-reflecting spellings' in B's share of *Richard III* and found the agreements as follows: Q1, 45 per cent; Q3, 61 per cent; Q6, 62 per cent. In the Act v Q3 passage, however, the agreement rate rises to 81 per cent: if this portion of the play is omitted, the general agreement rate drops to 57 per cent with Q3 and 61 per cent with Q6—in other words, far below the rate Kable's investigations would lead us to expect. It must be emphasized that this study is a preliminary one only, but it does support to some extent the idea that Compositor B was setting from manuscript rather than directly from the quartos.

THE F MANUSCRIPT

It used to be widely accepted that the manuscript used for colla-tion against the quartos was the theatre's prompt-copy, but Alice Walker objected that the stage-directions were inadequate for prompt use: speaking parts are omitted from directions (e.g. Catesby at III.vii.93, Hastings and Dorset in I.iii) while silent characters are included: Norfolk in III.iv, Ratcliffe and Lovell in IV.ii, for instance. Act III, sc. iii's direction, *Enter Sir Richard Ratcliffe, with Halberds, carrying the Nobles to death at Pomfret*, is 'insufficiently explicit for a prompt-book', while descriptive direc-tions, such as *She looks scornfully at him* (I.ii.174), 'suggest an author thinking of production rather than a book-keeper concerned in regulating a performance'.[2] Although these arguments are not conclusive, Greg was persuaded by them. We must, to be fair, recall that—as has already been noted—book-keepers did not necessarily eliminate authorial directions when preparing their copy, nor were vague directions inevitably made specific, provided that the speakers were named in the dialogue.[3] The directions in F are as good as those in any of the surviving prompt-books, and are sufficient to allow the play to be performed, with very little in

1. William Kable, 'Compositor B, the Pavier Quartos, and Copy-Spellings', *SB* 21 (1968), pp. 131–62.
2. Summarized and quoted from *Textual Problems*, p. 18.
3. Discussed above, pp. 11–13.

the way of correction or addition except in Act v, where dependence on Q copy has left the battle scene short of directions.

A feature of F which suggests that the manuscript had passed through some process of preparation for the stage is the expurgation of oaths. The celebrated Statute to Restrain Abuses (3 Jac. 1., c.21) was aimed at eliminating profanity from the stage, not from books. That F was purged in accordance with the provisions of this Act is quite clear, though the work was done (as was not unusual) in a haphazard manner. The most important of these changes occurs at iii.vii.218, where Buckingham's exasperated line, 'Come Citizens, zounds ile intreat no more', is purged of its oath: this costs us in consequence Richard's elegant piece of hypocrisy, 'O do not sweare my Lord of Buckingham', which was dropped entirely from the F text. 'Zounds' was much misliked; it is eliminated from the scene of Clarence's murder; but oaths by God and Heaven are often left alone, perhaps on the grounds that they are intended as prayers rather than mere cussing; perhaps because the expurgator, like Walton's collator, was lazy. There may be places in the text where no trace of an expurgation survives: a probable example occurs at iv.iv.400 (q.v.). The implication of this is that at some time after the 1606 Act was passed, someone went through the manuscript (perhaps rather carelessly) to purge it of profanity. Walker holds the opinion that such tinkering as appears in the F texts was 'editorial in inspiration'.[1]

However, there are features of the manuscript which seem hardly consistent with prompt-book use. Perhaps the plainest of these is the presence in F of passages which to a greater or lesser degree seem to have been deliberately cut from the performed version of which the Q text is our record. It is possible (but not very likely) that some of these were later additions, but it cannot be believed that anyone would have wanted the second wooing scene longer.[2]

The most plausible explanation is to assume that the manuscript was what is termed the author's 'foul papers' (defined by

1. Walker, p. 31. Greg (*Shakespeare First Folio*, p. 152) observes that there is evidence that there existed, 'some time before 1628, a purely literary tradition of expurgation', which may have affected F. 'It follows, therefore, that the presence or absence of profanity cannot be regarded as affording altogether reliable evidence respecting the nature and date of the manuscript that served as copy for a printed text.' However, the evidence to which he refers is almost exclusively late in the Caroline period. All that need be said is that, whoever did the expurgation of *Richard III*, it does not affect the probability that the manuscript was foul papers.

2. See above, pp. 13–14, and Appendix 1.

Bowers as the author's final complete draft of the play) which the
company had retained as insurance against the loss of the prompt-
book. Certain it is that Shakespearean foul papers survived to be
used in the printing of other plays in the First Folio; the permissive and descriptive directions which bothered Walker thus
would be perfectly at home. There is, then, every reason to think
the manuscript authoritative, but pre-theatrical: the omission
from it of the very stageworthy 'clock' scene in iv. ii is enough to
confirm that it must pre-date the version of the play as performed,
and as reported in Q.

THE PRINTING OF F

The account which follows is deeply indebted to the late Professor
Charlton Hinman's massive study of the printing of the First
Folio.[1] *Richard III* occupies part of quires q–t in the Histories
section of the volume. There was a hiatus during the printing:
when quire s was complete, and the play still in v. iii, work was
suspended; the section on the tragedies was begun, and the
completion of *Richard III* had to wait until somewhat later. It was
then resumed and completed without further delay.[2]

The work of composition was divided between the two workmen known as Compositors A and B, whose spelling preferences
and general work habits are by now tolerably well known. A was
more likely to follow copy accurately than B, but perhaps more
prone to certain literal errors. A set r1^v, r5^v, r6^{r-v}, s1^r-s3^v and
s6^{r-v}; B set q5^r-q6^v, r1^r, r2^r-r5^r, s4^r-s5^v and t1^r-t2^v. That is, of
the thirty-two pages in question, B set twenty and A twelve.

Of these thirty-two pages, there is evidence of proof-correction
in only six. Most of the corrections entailed the elimination of
purely technical errors such as inking spaces (q6^{r-v}, t1^v). There are

1. Charlton Hinman, *The Printing and Proof-Reading of the First Folio of
Shakespeare*, 2 vols (Oxford, 1963).
2. Hinman observes (II, 523) that the delay evidently arose from the non-
availability of copy for *Henry VIII*, rather than any difficulty over *Richard III*.
This delay ought not to be confused with that described in the now-exploded
theory of E. E. Willoughby (*The Printing of the First Folio of Shakespeare*, Oxford,
1932) that the printing of F was subject to extended delay, a theory referred to
by many authorities (such as Greg, Walker and Walton) in their published
work. Walker indeed made it the centre of her argument concerning F copy
for *Richard III*. Hinman's more rigorous study has completely overset Willoughby's theory (see *Printing*, I, 334–65). It now seems clear that the Histories
were printed between January and March of 1623, with the exception of the
conclusion of *Richard III*, and *Henry VIII*, which were completed between April
and July of that year.

a number of places where a true correction has been made: 'off' instead of 'oft' and 'want' instead of 'went' on s6ᵛ, as well as the correction of obvious misprints: 'necke' replaces 'neeke' on the same page. None of these implies reference to copy, with the possible exception of two corrections on r2ʳ. The first of these is the change of a speech-prefix from *Riu.* to *Ric.*, the second supplies the direction for I.iv: *Enter Clarence and Keeper.* Hinman believes that both of these could readily be deduced from the dialogue, but it is certainly not impossible that the proof-reader just checked the copy to make sure the entrance direction was complete.[1]

Although *Richard III* is almost entirely verse (prose presents much greater difficulties), the casting-off of the copy was not faultless. Note, for example, I.ii.39, 50, 83–4, 95–6, 103, 104: these single or double lines are arranged in F to make two or three lines each, a characteristic of 'stretched' copy, filling up what would otherwise be a gap at the end of a quire: they all occur on the last page of the inner forme of gathering q. It looks as if the trouble was not entirely solved by this expedient, since on r1ʳ we also find four lines printed as eight. Both of these pages were set by compositor B who, as has been remarked, had a high-handed way of dealing with problems. Another example of his carelessness can be identified in II.iii.43, where F reads 'Pursuing', and Q (correctly) 'Ensuing'. F's reading is an error. It is the first word on r5ʳ, and the correct reading is present as the catchword on r4ᵛ. Both of these pages were set by B, who must have misremembered the word, and set 'Pursuing' without checking his copy. It must therefore be classed as a memorial error, but one originating with the compositor, rather than the scribe. No doubt B left many other errors of a like nature in the F text without any sign of their presence to alert the editor.

THE 'STABILITY' OF THE TEXT

Thus far we have traced as best we may the origin of the two texts of *Richard III*, and the processes by which they were translated into print. One further element remains to be considered, in connection with the lost manuscripts. Reasons have been given above for thinking that the manuscript that lay behind F was foul papers. However, in his 1954 Rosenbach lectures Fredson Bowers challenged the customary view that a dramatist would supply the company with foul papers, from which the book-keeper would transcribe a copy for theatrical use. On the con-

---

1. Hinman, I, pp. 276–8 gives a complete account of the press variants.

trary, Bowers showed that it was normal practice for an author to write out a fair copy for sale to the theatre.[1] The evidence gleaned from the practices of other dramatists cannot, of course, be automatically applied to Shakespeare. Yet at the time of his writing *Richard III* he was not a sharer in the company, and there is no reason to think that his practice would have differed significantly from that of his contemporaries. It is thus quite possible that Shakespeare himself wrote out a fair copy of the text of *Richard III* to submit to the company. If so, whether he kept the foul papers himself until later or handed them in with the fair copy cannot now be determined.

Bowers, like most scholars, assumes that any such authorial fair copy would contain no variants from the foul papers that were not deliberate and significant: that is, that the author either copied exactly or else consciously revised. However, Ernst Honigmann in a major contribution to textual studies challenged this assumption.[2] He argued (that which common sense and one's own experience confirms) that when writing something out an author, especially a fluent author such as Shakespeare was universally acknowledged to be, does not have the sacred respect for his original that a later copyist or editor might have. Besides the odd deliberate and considered change, we would expect to find minor variants, changes of tense and number, slight re-phrasings, use of synonyms, and other lesser variations which the author makes, *currente calamo* in the process of copying, on the instinctive basis that they read better, not to mention the ordinary slips to which any scribe is liable. These changes can hardly be called revisions, in that the next time the author made a copy he might very well revert to the original reading, or introduce another variant in turn. Yet they do cast a shadow of uncertainty, or as Honigmann has it, instability, over the text.

Honigmann attempts to assess the degree of instability we may expect to find in Shakespeare by comparing his probable be-haviour with that of other fluent authors for whom some manu-scripts survive, and by examining some extant examples of 'instability'. For our purposes the most telling comparison is that with Middleton's *A Game at Chess*, for which we have two partially complete holograph manuscripts; examination of these certainly bears out the presence of these minor variants. We find 'hiddest' in the one, 'hiddenst' in the other; 'smoothest' and 'Secretst'; 'I am' and 'I'me'; 'spoke' and 'spake'. These variants are

1. Fredson Bowers, *On Editing Shakespeare* (Charlottesville, 1966), ch. 1.
2. E. A. J. Honigmann, *The Stability of Shakespeare's Text* (1965).

similar to the kind of thing found in *Richard III*, cited by Patrick as examples of actors' variation, and discussed above (pp. 3–8). We have already (pp. 25–8) found that the compositor's poor memory may have been the cause of some of these variants: if indeed Shakespeare did write the play out again, it now appears possible that some at least of them may have originated with him.

If we have two authorial versions of a line, which is to be preferred? The first thoughts, or the later? One cannot assume that all such changes introduced by the author in this way will necessarily be for the better. We may agree that 'adders' is a better, more consistent, more effective word than 'wolves' at I.ii.19, but we may also suppose that occasionally in the course of his copying Shakespeare may have made the odd deliberate improvement (cf. III.i.193 for another example). The entire 'clock' scene in IV.ii may be put down to such an action. However, these are the exception, rather than the rule: most Q-only passages cannot be seen to be such clear improvements that we can confidently adopt them. Besides, we have already examined (pp. 16–18) a number of Q-only features which seem to point to the work undertaken by the book-keeper and/or prompter, rather than the author, in fitting the work for the stage.

There are other variants, however, so far hard to account for, which are aptly accounted for by this concept of 'instability'. Consider I.iv.85, which in Q reads 'In Gods name what are you?'. Clarence later (I.iv.155) has the line 'In Gods name, what art thou?', and to explain the earlier variant Patrick proposed an actor's anticipation. But by the time Clarence speaks his line, Brakenbury has long been off-stage: it is a rather desperate expedient to imagine that he overheard the line by chance and either liked it so well that he imported it into his own speech, or substituted it through some subconscious association.[1] Another most illuminating example is found at I.iv.47 and II.ii.46. The first of these reads in both texts 'Vnto the Kingdome of perpetuall Night'; the second in F reads 'To his new Kingdome of nere-changing night', in Q 'To his new kingdome of perpetuall rest'. Once again, the chance of contamination from the actors is small, since the relevant persons were not on stage to hear the other line spoken. It is far more persuasive that the group of words 'rest', 'night', 'perpetual' and 'ne'er-changing' formed an association in Shakespeare's mind, which led to their reshuffling in II.ii. In both

---

1. Harold Brooks thinks the odds of something like this happening may sometimes be better than the editor is prepared to admit.

these examples, and many more in the play, it could well be the author, rather than the actor, who anticipates or recollects his own work. To these grosser variants might be added a goodly proportion of the lesser ones, especially some of the puzzling variants in commonplace words, such as 'methoughts/methought' and 'waters/water', both also from I.iv. There is, of course, no way of separating these satisfactorily from the actors' variants which they so closely resemble, nor any certain way of preferring one to the other even if we could. The chance that such fine detail of the play's linguistic texture would survive memorial reconstruction is not very strong; neither would any such survivals be likely to be identifiable. However, the possibility that some of the Q/F variants may be authorial alternatives means that one must take the Q readings seriously, and individually, in constructing a modern edition.

Honigmann has also written an article on the text of *Richard III*,[1] in which he remarks that Q on several occasions more exactly reproduces the source than F. The most important examples occur in III.ii: the name of Hastings the Pursuivant, and some associated dialogue. There are other less persuasive ones elsewhere in Acts III and IV. Some of them are very insignificant, and in others F seems to have altered the source for the sake of the metre. But some do indeed suggest that Q's accuracy is not to be lightly dismissed; again, this suggests the possibility that two holograph versions of the play existed, and that Shakespeare had looked again at the Chronicles between writing the foul papers and producing his postulated fair copy.

SUMMARY

The judgement of Clark and Wright now being vindicated, and this survey of the complex web which scholarship has woven about the text of *Richard III* being at an end, 'tis time to arm and give direction: or at least to summarize the conclusions reached, and to spell out the ways in which these have influenced the present edition. The F text is based on the collation of a manuscript which was probably the author's foul papers with a mixture of Q3 and Q6. Probably two collators were at work, one on the earlier quarto, and the other using a copy of the later. The evidence that has been brought into play in an attempt to determine which quarto was used is so far inconclusive: Q3 was

1. *Theatre Research* 7:1 (1965), pp. 48–55.

certainly used in Act III and Act V, and probably elsewhere, but the evidence that Q6 was used in some parts of the play has not been overset. Nor is it certain that annotated Q was the form of copy supplied: against the probability of printed copy must be set some slight evidence that a manuscript transcript may have been made.

The evidence that Q originates in a memorial reconstruction has survived the challenges made against it. When allowance is made for compositorial corruption, the reconstruction appears extraordinarily good, an even better job than Patrick thought. Shakespeare could well have been among the people involved in this collective reconstruction, and his personal touch certainly seems present in some aspects of the Q text. Behind the actors' memories lies the prompt-book of the play, prepared from a fair copy probably written by Shakespeare himself, and preserving changes made by Shakespeare and the book-keeper to fit the play to the stage. The F, being based as it seems on foul papers, misses a good deal of this practical material, but because no memorial link is involved, it is generally a much more reliable guide to Shakespeare's text.

If we are concerned to recover Shakespeare's intentions, we ought to give a careful degree of consideration to alterations introduced into the prompt-book, whether by Shakespeare himself, or (if we can accurately distinguish) by another. We must weigh carefully the chances: that an alteration was made with Shakespeare's assent, willingly or grudgingly, or that an alteration was made against his desires. This weighing is not easily or reliably done. In the present edition, the elimination of the ghost-parts of Woodeville and Scales has been accepted; the revision of II.iv.1–2 has not. A more complex case is that of the exchange of Catesby for Ratcliffe in III.iv: the alteration is attractive, but to make it workable there would have to be editorial intervention in III.v which would go beyond the limit of simple correction of error. Another testing case is IV.iv.288–342: it is hard to believe that this part of the play was ever performed. But it might have been, and it would be exceeding the warrant of the facts to print it in square brackets or as an appendix.

Who is the author of the play? 'Shakespeare', we reply. But to distinguish between 'Shakespeare' the solitary artist, scribbling in his garret (as it were), and 'Shakespeare' as the complex of author/book-keeper/actor/prompter and others who actually created the play in the sense of a living performance on the stage is to find oneself on one side or other of a philosophical issue concerning the nature of artistic creativity.[1] Each position has its justification; the attempt at a middle ground can also be defended intellectually; it is the position which has been adopted for this edition.

THE PRESENT EDITION

Much recent textual theory assumes that an 'old-spelling' edition is being prepared.[2] This aspect of the theory has only incidental bearing on the production of a modernized edition such as the Arden. The principle that one chooses the copy-text on the basis of its superior accidentals does not apply to a modernized edition in which most accidental features, especially spelling and punctuation, are altered.

Both the Quarto and Folio texts of *Richard III* are substantive texts, in that, except in so far as F used Q copy to print from, neither is derived from the other: each contains unique material and depends upon a different manuscript. F's authority, however, is much higher, as it is uncontaminated by a memorial link.[3] In accordance with the textual theory outlined in the previous section, this edition is based upon F, as the text of higher authority. However, every reading in which Q differs from F must be evaluated, since any such difference may originate with Shakespeare, or perhaps have his sanction. To be sure, most such variants are actors' or compositors' errors, and will be rejected; but if there is reason to think the Q reading represents an authoritative later stage of the text than what is in F, it has been accepted into this edition.[4] A problem still remains: the immense number of readings where either there are no rational grounds for seeing one as preferable to the other, or where there is reasonable doubt that the Q version has authority. 'What dreadful

1. Cf. M. C. Bradbrook, 'Shakespeare and his collaborators', in *Shakespeare* (1971), p. 28: 'All drama, being an art of performance, is collaborative.'

2. The classic theory was developed in Greg's 'A Rationale of Copy-Text', *SB* 3 (1950), pp. 19–36.

3. Bowers remarks that even a bad quarto must be regarded as substantive 'in so far as it gives some notion of the performance of the play . . . and may reflect differences due to stages in the play's revision, theatrical or authorial. That is, a bad quarto must go back to a report of the prompt-book version of the play and so may differ authentically in some details from a good text that represents the dramatist's original working papers.' ('McKerrow, Greg, and "Substantive Edition"', *The Library*, 5th series, 33:2 (1978), p. 105.) This description accords exactly with the view of Q and F *Richard III* adopted here.

4. Such readings must be more than 'preferable' in a literary sense. The most difficult of such choices was II.iv.65 (q.v.).

noise of water/waters in mine ears' (I.iv.22), or the numerous my lord/my liege variants are simple examples of the dozens which occur in the play.[1] These variants do not affect the meaning of the line in any way that can be discriminated by an editor. They are thus hardly 'substantive' in Greg's sense, and could be said to approach the condition of 'accidentals'.[2] When editorial judgement is thus rendered helpless, the principle followed in this edition has been to follow F, as the text of higher authority.

This amounts to a declaration of conservatism as a policy, which runs counter to Walker's statement that 'conservatism in the editing of this play is no virtue'.[3] Her view was espoused by Dover Wilson, whose New Cambridge edition introduced around sixty emendations, some from earlier editors, some for the first time.[4] Of these, only three have been admitted into the present edition, though two others are differently emended. Most of them seek to improve erratic metre, but the general metrical pattern of the play remains irregular even when all such improvements are admitted. Others attempt to recover readings where Wilson believes F and Q to be in agreement in error. This is a risky business, and despite the attractiveness of many of the proposed readings, this edition has eschewed them, following rather Ernst Honigmann's principle, that it is 'an editor's worst offence to campaign against any reading that might be Shakespeare's'.[5]

Punctuation and spelling are modernized and normalized in this edition.[6] We have passed safely through the period when scholars believed that the pointing of F was Shakespeare's, and the subsequent period when it was held that, while not Shakespeare's, at least the punctuation of early editions was rhetorical in intent, and thus served the function of a sort of stage-directions, indicating to the actor how to speak the lines. Elizabethan punctuation, especially of dramatic texts, varied immensely from author to author, scribe to scribe, compositor to compositor. If, as seems probable, the pages in Hand D in *The Book of Sir Thomas*

1. Patrick gives a lengthy list, pp. 94–6.

2. The rigid distinction between substantives and accidentals is now in the process of revaluation; see for instance David Foxon, *The Library*, 5th series, 33:2 (1978), pp. 119–24, or (an analogous problem) William J. Cameron, *Poems on Affairs of State*, v (New Haven, 1971), p. 529.

3. Walker, p. 25.

4. List in NCS, pp. 156–8.

5. *Stability*, p. 171.

6. The most comprehensive survey of the principles involved is Stanley Wells, *Modernizing Shakespeare's Spelling* (Oxford, 1979). Although this edition was completed before Wells's work was published, its practice coincides very closely with his views.

More are in Shakespeare's autograph,[1] and if these pages represent anything like his normal habits of writing, then it can be inferred that Shakespearean manuscripts were virtually innocent of punctuation—and would one really want an unpunctuated *Richard III*? The manuscript underlying Q1 was not, as we have seen, holograph, yet there are reasons for thinking its punctuation was similarly slight. Certainly the scheme of punctuation in Q1 is random and haphazard: some of Simmes's compositor's punctuation is positively malign (see Clarence's dream in Greg's facsimile for an instance); Short's workmen punctuate more extensively, though not much more gracefully or intelligibly, than Simmes's.

The Folio, as befits a major book, is much more scrupulously punctuated both for rhetorical sense and for grammar. There is no reason to think that its underlying manuscript was any fuller in these respects: rather, the practices of Compositors A and B were both more modern (the book is later than Q1 by twenty-six crucial years) and more careful than those of their predecessors. While there is a greater chance of copy-spellings surviving into print than there is of copy-punctuation, it is as well to remember Trevor Howard-Hill's caveat: all spellings in the printed text are compositorial.[2] There can thus be no more reason for preferring F's punctuation to that of any other text than there would be for retaining its spellings.

It should not be mistakenly inferred from this that the editor regards punctuation as relatively unimportant. On the contrary, it frequently calls for great delicacy, especially in scenes where conventions of rhetoric, unfamiliar to the modern reader, can only be clarified by the limited tools of punctuation. A good case is IV.iv.243 ff., the second wooing scene. The editor expresses his general acknowledgement to Peter Alexander's lucidly pointed version of the play, which has been a great influence at testing moments, and to Harold Jenkins, whose advice has been invaluable. The present edition is sparing in its use of the exclamation mark, often used as a sort of editorial nudge at the reader. It has been kept for a few passages of particularly overbearing rhetoric, but elsewhere largely eschewed.

More capitalization has been retained than many modern

1. See *Shakespeare's Hand in the Play of Sir Thomas More* (Cambridge, 1923). The general impression among most Shakespeareans today is a cautious acceptance of the identification; for a recent (not very persuasive) attempt to refute it, see Paul Ramsey, *PBSA* (1977), pp. 333–46.

2. See 'Spelling and the Bibliographer', *The Library*, 5th series, 18:1 (1963), pp. 1–28, especially the fifth principle.

editions employ. It seemed useful to distinguish between the theological state of grace, and the Grace which is a duke's form of address. Heaven in a deliberate Christian sense has been distinguished where the distinction was clear from heaven or heavens in the merely ejaculatory. The individual who is King or Queen has been distinguished from the office of king and queen. And, rather more specifically, personified abstractions like Vice or grim-visag'd War have been capitalized to emphasize their link with the morality drama.

A modern spelling has been used if one exists,[1] though defeat has had sometimes to be conceded, as with 'Iwis', a word which simply does not exist in modern English. Words used in an unfamiliar sense, as well as obsolete words, are glossed in the commentary. In accordance with Walker's suggestion, these references usually merely cite the appropriate entry in the *Oxford English Dictionary*.[2] Occasionally some parallel is given where a specific point needs to be made.

The treatment of stage-directions needs a word of explanation. We have already noticed that while the F stage-directions are quite full, though not always as precise as desirable, they fail us badly in Act V. It seems silly to present a text that cannot be acted, so without going to the extremes advocated by Dover Wilson of extending directions to bring the play to life from the printed page for the reader,[3] fairly extensive additions (indicated by square brackets) have been made to the directions in Act V to supply the minimum to make the play actable on the kind of stage for which it was written.

Throughout, all concordance references and data are taken from the one-volume *Harvard Concordance to Shakespeare*;[4] as this is based on G. Blakemore Evans's Riverside Shakespeare, that text has been used for all quotations from Shakespeare's other works in the commentary. Besides theatrical and linguistic notes, the commentary includes textual and historical notes (for which the editor is much indebted to the excellent notes of A. Hamilton Thompson, the editor of the original Arden volume), notes on source material, and the occasional literary observation.

---

1. At the General Editors' request, 'corse' has been retained rather than modernizing to 'corpse'.
2. 'Principles of Annotation', *SB* 9 (1957), pp. 95–105.
3. 'On Editing Shakespeare' in John Garrett (ed.), *Talking of Shakespeare* (1959), pp. 231–57.
4. Ed. Marvin Spevack (Cambridge, Mass., 1973).

3. DATE

Discussion of the date of *Richard III* almost immediately becomes discussion of the date of *Henry VI*: as Dover Wilson remarked, 'Shakespeare had obviously begun *Richard III* in mind, if not on paper, when writing the soliloquy at *3 Henry VI*, 3.2.124ff.'[1] It is true that *Richard III* is a single entity, an artistic unity; it is also true that its genesis at least is intimately related to the trilogy which preceded it, and that its composition may properly be regarded as part of the single creative impulse which engendered the entire first tetralogy of history plays.[2]

Unfortunately, the date of the *Henry VI* cycle is not easily established. The evidence is discussed in detail in A. S. Cairncross's editions in this series, but a summary of it must be made here. Henslowe's *Diary* records a performance of a new play called 'harey the vj' by Lord Strange's Men on 3 March 1591/2;[3] this play was repeated fourteen (or thirteen[4]) times before the closing of the theatres on 23 June, and netted Henslowe about £30. This would imply a total audience of perhaps 22,000 spectators,[5] which agrees adequately with the remark of Nashe that Talbot's death had been wept over by 'ten thousand spectators at least (at severall times)';[6] if, that is, the play to which Nashe refers and 'harey the vj' are the same play.

The case for their identification has recently been re-examined by Hanspeter Born.[7] He argues that Nashe's reference is unmistakably to the Shakespeare play, and that it would be an odd coincidence for there to have been two plays on the subject which were both enormously popular. Besides, if F. P. Wilson's identification of the dedicatee ('Amynthas') of *Pierce Penilesse* with Lord Strange is correct,[8] and in view of the praise Nashe expends on

---

1. NCS, p. ix n.   2. See below, 'The play'.

3. *Henslowe's Diary*, ed. R. A. Foakes and R. T. Rickert (Cambridge, 1961), p. 16. Henslowe is using old-style dating so the year appears as 1591 in his manuscript.

4. A play called *harey of cornwell* was also in the repertory at the time; on 16 March 1591/2, 'harey' was performed but Henslowe omits to say which.

5. Based on Alfred Harbage's calculations (*Shakespeare's Audience*, New York, 1941, ch. 2). It was, obviously, a successful play. One revival is noted, 3 January 1593/4.

6. Nashe, *Pierce Penilesse*, in *Works*, ed. McKerrow, rev. F. P. Wilson (Oxford, 1958), I.212.

7. Hanspeter Born, 'The Date of 2, 3 Henry VI', *SQ* 25:3 (1974), pp. 323–34.

8. F. P. Wilson, *A Supplement to McKerrow's Edition of Nashe* (Oxford, 1958), pp. 15–16.

Alleyn, Strange's principal actor, 'it is quite incredible that Nashe should have sung the praises of a *Henry VI* play performed by a rival company and at the same time have totally ignored the showpiece of the company whose leading actor he glorifies and to whose patron he wished to ingratiate himself'.[1] It is, perhaps, not incredible; but it is decidedly unlikely. What evidence is there to suggest that 'harey the vj' is not *1 Henry VI*?

First, there is the problem that there are echoes of the *Henry* trilogy in other works which can be dated earlier than 1592. Indeed, there seems to be an echo of *Richard III* in *The Troublesome Raigne of King John*: 'Set downe, set downe the load not worth your pain'[2] is remarkably close to Anne's 'Set down, set down your honourable load' (1.ii.1), and this play was published in 1591. It is probably of earlier composition: Chambers refers to it as being 'of the Armada period',[3] and as no one would think *Richard III* could be as early as that, it looks at first as though Shakespeare recollected the line from *Troublesome Raigne*, rather than the other way about. However, it is possible that *Troublesome Raigne* is (despite the early date) later than *Richard III*: if so, the anonymous dramatist was echoing Shakespeare (see below, pp. 93–5).

One of the problems is that the company who performed 'harey the vj' was Strange's, and while of course Shakespeare later became a member and sharer in Strange's/Chamberlain's, there is no evidence other than this title to associate his name with them before 1594. And we know that *2* and *3 Henry VI* belonged to Pembroke's, not Strange's, Men. It is possible, as Schoenbaum remarks, that Shakespeare freelanced at first, like many of his contemporaries.[4] Nor is it unlikely, as Chambers remarked, that Pembroke's originated as an offshoot of Strange's in the second part of 1592;[5] if so, Born's suggestion that *2* and *3 Henry VI* were originally intended for Strange's but in the formation of the new company were 'hived off' to the new one, becomes more plausible.[6] And it is certainly not possible to identify Shakespeare with any other company.[7]

1. Born, op. cit., p. 324.   2. *2 Troublesome Raigne*, vi.1 (D2ᵛ).
3. *Elizabethan Stage*, IV, p. 24.
4. *Shakespeare, a Documentary Life* (Oxford, 1975), p. 125.
5. Chambers, I, p. 49. The notion is strengthened by Mary Edmond, 'Pembroke's Men', *RES* (1974), pp. 129–36.   6. Born, op. cit., p. 333.
7. Both Cairncross ('Pembroke's Men') and Wentersdorf ('Repertory') attempted to show that *Richard III* was a Pembroke's play. (See above, p. 10, and notes 1 and 2.) But there is simply no real evidence of that company's existence before 1592. If, then, Pembroke's did perform *Richard III* along with

The other piece of external evidence with a bearing on the question is Greene's famous attack on Shakespeare, published in his *Groats-worth of Witte*: Greene died on 3 September 1592, and since he parodies a line from *3 Henry VI* therein, it is a reasonable inference that the play was known before the closing of the theatres on 23 June. This makes life very difficult, for there is no mention of the later parts of *Henry VI* in Henslowe's *Diary*, and it is reasonable to wonder if in any case there would have been time to stage the entire trilogy between 3 March (the date of 'harey the vj' as a new play) and 23 June. What are the alternatives? That, contrary to what might seem reasonable, Part 1 was written after the later parts? This notion has been effectively rejected, but the arguments are too complex to summarize here.[1] That the marginal note 'ne' which Henslowe appended to the 3 March performance might mean something other than 'brand new'? Foakes and Rickert in their edition of the *Diary* suggest it might mean 'newly licensed by the Master of the Revels'.[2]

Born rejects this, arguing that Greene had heard the parodied line while attending a rehearsal, and included it in his attack in anticipation that the theatres would reopen in the autumn.[3] This is intolerably speculative. His comparison with Greene's anticipation of the publication of *Pierce Penilesse* will not satisfy, since Nashe's book must have been in preparation long before its publication, and what Greene burlesqued was nothing less memorable than the title itself. It would have been optimistic indeed of Greene to select a single phrase from *3 Henry VI* as the target for his satire before the play had been performed: he couldn't have known it would be popular or the line unusually memorable; there is no point in satire unless its object can be recognized. Born does not refer to Foakes and Rickert's theory, but the hypothesis that 'harey the vj' was 'new' only in some special sense seems the only one to enable the evidence to be reconciled. Allison Gaw has shown that every play produced by Strange's during the period in question which goes back to earlier ownership by another company can be traced from the Queen's or Admiral's repertory, but this does not, of course, rule out *1 Henry VI*'s being a special case.[4] At any rate, it is not possible to recon-

---

2 and *3 Henry VI* (which is not, in fact, proven), it could scarcely have been their play originally.

1. See A. S. Cairncross's Arden editions.

2. p. xxx.   3. Born, op. cit., p. 325.

4. Allison Gaw, *The Origin and Development of 1 Henry VI* (Los Angeles, 1926), p. 22.

cile all these conflicting items of evidence perfectly. On the whole, the likeliest explanation is that 'harey the vj' is Shakespeare's play, but that it was not new—rather, newly licensed—when Henslowe acquired it in March 1592, and that the composition of the work may date back two years or more.

Another reason for believing this to be the correct interpretation is to be found in the complex relationship between the play and Marlowe's *Edward II*. It seems evident that Marlowe in his work was influenced by *Henry VI*: to be sure, the dating of Marlowe's plays is an even more perilous venture than that of Shakespeare's, but the time-span in question is shorter, and few would assert that the *Henry VI* cycle postdates *Edward II*. We find in Marlowe's play material which was also used in *Henry VI*, material which was taken from his source by Shakespeare, but which does not appear in the source of *Edward II*. It is distinctly unlikely that Marlowe should have consulted an irrelevant part of the chronicles for this: the best inference then is that he absorbed it from the Shakespearean works.[1]

This much may be easily accepted. That Marlowe was also Shakespeare's debtor in the connections between *Richard III* and *Edward II* requires more careful demonstration. That there is a link is not in doubt: there are over ninety places where the phraseology of the two plays has something in common, apart from similarities in theme or situation. Clearly, it would be impossible to descant on all of these; many of the echoes anyway are of phrases whose origins may be proverbial, or traceable to a common ancestor, or merely coincidental. But these explanations will not do for all. Let us consider some examples. Richard, in his opening soliloquy, complains, 'I . . . have no delight to pass away the time,/Unless to spy my shadow in the sun' (I.i.24–6); Richard, now a private man, in peacetime notices the deformity of his shadow. Edward, in prison, muses, 'But what are kings, when regiment is gone,/But perfect shadowes in a sun-shine day?' (V.i.26–7)—lines whose thought, as well as whose words, seem to grow out of Richard's image. Another of the lines in the opening soliloquy, 'And all the clouds that lour'd upon our house' (l. 3) seems to be recalled by Edward's 'O day! . . . O my starres!/Why do you lowre unkindly on a king?' (IV.vii.61–3).[2] There is something of a parallel situation, with some verbal echoes, between

1. See A. S. Cairncross's editions.
2. Cf. *Solyman and Perseda*, v.iv.82–3: 'Ah heavens, that hitherto have smilde on me / Why doe you so unkindly lowre on Solyman?' The uncertain dating of this play makes the echo unavailable as evidence.

Clarence in I.iv and Edward, before and after his capture, while Richard's prior urging of his villains, warning them that 'Clarence . . . May move your hearts to pity, if you mark him', and the Second Murderer's reply, 'Tut, tut, my lord: we will not stand to prate', etc. (I.iii.348–52) are echoed by the exchange between Mortimer and Lightborne:

> *Mortimer.* But at his lookes *Lightborne* thou wilt relent.
> *Lightborne.* Relent, ha, ha, I use much to relent. (v.iv.26–7)

The language Clarence used to urge his murderers to repent (I.iv.246–7) is also perhaps echoed by this interchange.

The Prince's expressed desire, in III.i, for more uncles to meet him, and Richard's polite refusal to supply him with any, resembles:

> *King.*   My lord, he is my unkle, and shall live.
> *Mortimer.* My lord, he is your enemie, and shall die. (v.iv.91–2)

In the same scene, Richard's scornful aside, 'So wise so young, they say, do never live long (III.i.79) is recalled in Queen Isabella's lines, 'A boye, this towardnes makes thy mother feare/Thou art not markt to many daies on earth' (III.i.79–80). Later, Elizabeth's apostrophe to the Tower (IV.i.98–100) is recalled by Mortimer's lines, 'can ragged stonie walles/Immure thy vertue that aspires to heaven?' (III.i.256–7), where the key repeated words are 'stones', 'immur'd', 'walls', and 'ragged'. The parting of Rivers, Vaughan and Grey in III.iii resembles that between Edward, Spencer and Baldock in IV.vii, ll. 72 ff., especially the line 'In heaven wee may, in earth never shall wee meete' (80); compare III.iii.26. 'Insulting tyranny begins to jut', complains Queen Elizabeth at II.iv.51; 'And *Midas* like he jets it in the court' grumbles Mortimer (I.iv.408). The base-born quality of Gaveston excites Mortimer to use Richard's contemptuous term 'jack' (I.iii.53, IV.ii.114): 'I have not seene a dapper jack so briske' (I.iv.412). 'Peace, Master Marquess: you are malapert' snarls Margaret at Dorset (I.iii.255); Mortimer declares, 'But this I scorne, that one so baselie borne,/Should by his soveraignes favour grow so pert' (I.iv.403–4). Another passage where the two authors share abusive language is in the orations of Richmond and of Isabella and Mortimer (*Richard III*, v.iii.238ff.; *Edward II*, IV.iv.1 ff.). To some extent this is a consequence of their subject matter, as each claims to be acting under divine sanction, and each abuses the other side for their spoliation of the land; but the verbal parallels are quite strong.

These are a few of a very large number of examples, many of which are not of any special account. For they do not, by their very nature, define the direction of the borrowing. If, however, we could demonstrate plausibly just one case where it was clear that *Edward II* borrowed from *Richard III* rather than the other way about, all these echoes would become available as evidence to imply the importance of that association.

Harold Brooks has made such a demonstration, and the following summary is based upon his work.[1] Again, the evidence derives from passages in *Edward II* which have no source 'unless in some account of Richard's usurpation'.[2] Some of these of course Marlowe could have obtained from Holinshed, or from the original of the *True Tragedy of Richard III*, or from the *Mirror for Magistrates*, which Marlowe knew.[3] These parallels aside, it also seems clear that Marlowe knew Shakespeare's play. Mortimer, describing how he became Protector, says:

> They thrust upon me the Protectorship,
> And sue to me for that that I desire,
> While at the councell table, grave enough,
> And not unlike a bashfull puretaine,
> First I complaine of imbecilitie,
> Saying it is, *onus quam gravissimum*,
> Till being interrupted by my friends,
> *Suscepi* that *provinciam* as they terme it,
> And to conclude, I am Protector now. (v.iv.56–63)

This is effectually a précis of the practice of Richard and Buckingham in iii.v and vii. Brooks comments, 'The mock Puritan Richard exists, I believe, nowhere but in Shakespeare's *Richard III*, where, for example, he plays the saint with the help of Scripture maxims, claims the unworldly innocence of a new-born infant, and thanks his God for his humility.'[4] To be sure, Richard had long been known as 'a deepe dissimuler' (the phrase is More's)

1. Harold Brooks, 'Marlowe and early Shakespeare', in *Christopher Marlowe*, Mermaid Critical Commentaries, ed. Brian Morris (1968), especially pp. 72–9.

2. Brooks, p. 72.

3. Marlowe's most striking borrowing from the *Mirror* is from the poem 'Shore's Wife', ll. 139–40 of which read: 'They brake the boowes and shakte the tree by sleyght, / And bent the wand that might have growen ful streight.' Cf. *Doctor Faustus*, Epilogue. This is doubly interesting since it demonstrates that Marlowe knew at least one of the poems in the *Mirror* dealing with *Richard III*.

4. Brooks, p. 73.

and the characteristic trick of disguising vicious behaviour with a colour of religion was a literary commonplace:

> Religions cloake some one to vyce doth chuse,
> And maketh god protectour of his cryme.

This is from the poem on Hastings in *The Mirror for Magistrates*,[1] and there are many similar expressions in the volume, and similar behaviour on the part of vicious characters elsewhere. But the quality of sanctimonious puritanical hypocrisy was Richard's unique contribution: 'O, do not swear, my lord of Buckingham!' (III.vii.219) is the most amusing of several false pieties.

Any alternative explanation of the appearance of this character trait in Mortimer is too complicated to be plausible. One settles on the inference that Marlowe derived it from *Richard III*. The probability thus shown may be strengthened by other evidence. For example, Marlowe makes use of images which he had found in Shakespeare's tetralogy. When Edward resigns the throne he thinks of his son as 'a lambe, encompassed by Woolves' (v.i.41); in *3 Henry VI* we find 'The trembling lamb environed with wolves' (I.i.242), an image which in turn suggested the lines in *Richard III*:

> Wilt Thou, O God, fly from such gentle lambs,
> And throw them in the entrails of the wolf? (IV.iv.22–3)

Imagery of the hierarchy of birds and trees is used in both *3 Henry VI* and *Richard III*:

> Thus yields the cedar to the axe's edge,
> Whose arms gave shelter to the princely eagle . . .
> (*3H6*, v.ii.11–12)

> Our aery buildeth in the cedar's top . . . (*R3*, I.iii.264)

Mortimer, in *Edward II*, produces a 'device' of the cedar, the eagle, and the canker:

> A loftie Cedar tree faire flourishing,
> On whose top-branches Kinglie Eagles pearch. (II.ii.16–17)

Collectively, then, the case is strong that the first tetralogy was in existence by the time Marlowe came to write *Edward II*, and the many verbal connections between the plays indicate that Marlowe was Shakespeare's debtor. Although *Edward II* was printed in

---

1. ll. 374–5, *Mirror*, p. 282.

1594, Marlowe was dead on 30 May 1593. If—as I believe —*Doctor Faustus* was his last play,[1] *Edward II* must predate that work; in any event, as Pembroke's Men (who are said on the title-page to have acted it) disappeared into the provinces in the latter part of 1592, early 1592 seems as late as is plausible for its composition. *Richard III* thus seems likely to have been written in 1591.

Another reason for dating *Richard III* relatively early is found in *Pierce Penilesse*, where Nashe refers to 'cunning drifts ouer-guylded with outward holinesse'[2] in the course of his defence of plays. It is not impossible that Nashe had some other work in mind, but the most obvious illustration of this behaviour is, again, *Richard III*. *Pierce* was entered on 8 August 1592, with the implication that *Richard III* was a known play before the closure of the theatres in June of that year.

To conclude, it seems that despite some problems concerning the company of players responsible, Shakespeare's first tetralogy was begun by 1590 and concluded with *Richard III* probably late in 1591. How *1 Henry VI* came to be performed on its own by Strange's Men in 1592 we do not know, but it is possible that the other parts, including *Richard*, were also intended for performance but prevented by the stoppage of playing in June. Certainly this chronology accounts for more data and causes fewer difficulties than that entailed upon Born's hypothesis, which would mean that *Richard III* could not have been performed in London until the summer of 1594.

4. *RICHARD III* IN PERFORMANCE

As has been made clear, we do not know for what company *Richard III* was written, nor the precise date of either its composition or its première. We know from the title-pages of their Bad Quartos that *2* and *3 Henry VI* were performed by Pembroke's, but we have no evidence of the existence of that company before autumn 1592. It is therefore hard to avoid the conclusion

1. The evidence on dating is most fully detailed in Greg's parallel text edn of the play (Oxford, 1950), pp. 5–10. Bowers, in his edn of the *Works*, cautiously concurs (II, pp. 123–4). But see H. Jenkins, *MLR* 46 (1951), pp. 85–6.

2. *Pierce Penilesse*, p. 213: the phrase 'I began to complaine in this sort: Why ist damnation to dispair and die' may be an echo of Act v. Note that Nashe also used the phrase 'to poyson the growth of glory by giving it nought but the puddle water of penury to drinke' (p. 179), which recalls Edward II's humilia-tion ('choake your soveraigne with puddle water', v.iii.30 and 37 S.D.). This helps to confirm the dating of *Edward II* as early 1592 at the latest.

that despite the absence of mention of him, Shakespeare was associated with the Admiral's/Strange's conglomerate until that year. Certainly the size of cast demanded especially for *Richard III* and *Titus Andronicus* implies a large company. A fair assumption, then, is that *Richard III* was originally performed by this company, perhaps late in 1591. The alternative, discussed above, is that it was written while Shakespeare was associated with Pembroke's Men, and if this was so, its first performance would have been in the provinces, and it could not have been regularly given in London until the summer of 1594, by which time Shakespeare's permanent association with Strange's had begun. This is one of the questions which do not admit of answers, only a weighing of probabilities: for the reasons adduced previously, a première with the Admiral's seems more likely.

We have also noticed that *Richard III* must inevitably have been difficult to cast.[1] The problem is the Bosworth scene, in which we find many characters who have not hitherto appeared, and in which several characters reappear as ghosts. There is also an obvious need for supernumeraries as soldiers, but some of these could have been supplied by the stage-keepers.[2] Elsewhere the demands on manpower are not so severe. Yet there are altogether fifty-two speaking parts, three more named but mute parts, and an indefinite number of supernumeraries required: it is clear that even the largest Elizabethan company would have had to double extensively to perform the work.

William A. Ringler, Jr has published an article in which he declares that all of Shakespeare's pre-Globe plays can be performed with a cast of sixteen including boys.[3] For *Richard* he specifies seventeen mutes, but does not tell us how he arrived at the figure, nor does he provide a doubling chart to support his statement. Wentersdorf[4] gives a doubling chart which shows that the Q version of *Richard III can* be played with eleven actors and four boys, but he makes no allowance for supernumeraries and requires some doublings which are both inartistic and unlikely (e.g. the Duke of Buckingham and the Duke of Norfolk, or Clarence and Ratcliffe). Let us assume that boys played only women's or children's parts as a rule.[5] If Anne doubles Margaret,

1. See above, pp. 14–17.   2. See above, p. 12.
3. 'The number of actors in Shakespeare's early plays', in G. E. Bentley, ed., *The Seventeenth-Century Stage* (Chicago, 1968), pp. 110–34. He excepts *Titus* and *Two Gentlemen*.
4. Wentersdorf, 'Repertory', p. 80.
5. Smidt (*Iniurious*, p. 206) imagined that Richmond could pair with the Duchess of York, an apparently preposterous notion: yet in 1808 a Mrs Maples

and the Duchess of York doubles Prince Edward, while the smallest member of the company is the pert Duke of York, Clarence's daughter, and the Page, the usual four boys will suffice (even then Anne/Margaret will also have to be Clarence's son in his single appearance in II.ii). The omission of the 'neece Plantagenet' from IV.i in Q thus cannot be an actor economy, since a boy was available.

As for the rest, we can probably assume that the players of Richard and Buckingham would not have doubled: their parts are too long, and they are too much in the audience's eye to do so convincingly. The other characters regularly on stage are Stanley, Catesby, and Ratcliffe. If these doubled, they could do so convincingly only in mute parts: perhaps Stanley and Ratcliffe could by donning cassocks conveniently become the mute bishops Shaa and Penker who accompany Richard at his devotions in III.vii. Any two of them could, beneath a shroud and the disguised voice apt to the supernatural, represent the ghosts of the elder Prince Edward and King Henry VI, who appear at Bosworth.

Among the other major parts, Clarence could perhaps double the Mayor. Clarence's manner and style are very individual, so it would be necessary to pair him with a totally different part to carry conviction, and the semi-comic Mayor is the best possibility. Perhaps he could also be a mute helmeted soldier in Bosworth, only needing to shroud himself to become Clarence's ghost in that scene. Similarly, Hastings could serve in a mute soldier's role in Act V without compromising his strong part in the middle of the play. Dorset could pair adequately with Richmond, with change of costume and wig.[1] This gives a total of four boys and eight actors so far; probably the sharers would have taken these parts: even if they disliked doubling,[2] filling in mute roles was perhaps not too much to ask in this complex cast.

---

actually doubled the parts of Richmond and Queen Elizabeth in a provincial performance.

1. Note the correction necessary at v.iii.18 S.D., where F has 'Dorset', a copyist's error for 'Herbert'.

2. As W. J. Lawrence (*Pre-Restoration Stage Studies*, Cambridge, Mass., 1927) and A. C. Sprague (*The Doubling of Parts in Shakespeare's Plays*, 1966) declare. This does not seem to have been an absolute rule, however. See also David Bevington, *From Mankind to Marlowe* (Cambridge, Mass., 1962): his ch. vii deals with doubling patterns in the 1580s and 1590s; he usefully disposes of T. W. Baldwin's odd views (in *The Organization and Personnel of the Shakespearean Company*, Princeton, 1927), and re-examines the evidence for the pre-Shakespearean drama.

The distribution of minor parts may now be undertaken. Rivers, Brakenbury, Bishop Morton, the Scrivener, a messenger, the Sheriff and Herbert could all be undertaken by one actor; a similar complex pattern of small parts fills up another seven actors' available time, allowing a reasonable number to be available as halberdiers, gentlemen, citizens, etc. As a rule, exit followed by immediate re-entry was avoided at the time, but every rule has its exceptions, and a fairly strong case is noted at III.iv.1. Similarly, in v.iii, we may assume a fluidity of identity as men-at-arms become ghosts, in order to keep the cast within bounds. The numbers involved are discussed in the commentary, but a summary here may be useful.

In v.ii Richmond enters, accompanied by Oxford, Herbert and Blunt, and undoubtedly a supernumerary or two dressed as men-at-arms. Act v, sc. iii begins with a similar scouting party on Richard's side: the King, accompanied by Surrey and Norfolk, and perhaps three soldiers to pitch the tent. Ratcliffe is also specified, though he remains mute. They exit, and the stage is now empty save for the tent; Richmond and his party (now augmented by Sir William Brandon) arrive, again accompanied by tent-pitching soldiers. There is thus no opportunity for doubling among these attendant lords. They then withdraw; some leave, but some go into Richmond's tent (which may have been so arranged as to permit them to exit therefrom unobtrusively). Catesby now comes on with Richard and his entourage, so—even if the same three men acted as soldiers and tent-raisers for both sides—we have a minimum of ten actors and three supernumeraries already, none of whom can be doubled.

Richard remains alone as night falls, guarded (l. 77). While he rests, Stanley, an eleventh character, confers with Richmond: it would not be out of the question for Stanley to have doubled one of the other minor lords such as Surrey or Norfolk; but they draw enough attention to themselves, and Stanley is so important in this part of the play as to make the doubling undesirable. Now the ghosts appear, singly, except for the two princes and the group of Rivers, Vaughan and Grey; it is scarcely possible that any one actor represented more than one ghost. In any case, the characters of Clarence, Buckingham and Hastings were so strongly presented in the play that their ghosts would surely have to be represented by the same actors who played them living. But the ghosts of Vaughan, Rivers and Grey would have to be taken by the actors who have previously been Herbert, Oxford and Blunt. This should present no great difficulties: all that is required is a shroud draped over the costume, and a ghostly voice, as they announce their identities at once.

Altogether, eighteen actors are required in the scene, and one of the boys is unused. The only way of reducing this is that taken by Q: the elimination of Brandon. Q also replaces Surrey with Catesby, thus perhaps avoiding that bad doubling of Surrey and Stanley. The Q version can thus be done with eighteen players, or seventeen if Richmond is not allowed a guard. This, however, argues a degree of exactitude which a practical theatrical company would be wise to avoid: it seems improbable that a company would so cast its repertory that if one hired man fell ill the play could not be performed. It thus seems reasonable to suggest that, while *Richard III* can indeed be played by a cast as small as has been demonstrated, in practice probably about twenty players were involved, with, no doubt, some mute help from the stage-keepers.[1] It is also worth noting that *Richard III* has no part for a clown, and Kemp therefore, though available, would presumably not have been used in its performance.

We have already noted that *Richard III* is not a play which depends heavily on properties, so that while it is expensive in terms of manpower, it is otherwise suitable for a touring production. About the only necessary properties seem to be the pair of tents. Some debate has been published on this issue. R. J. Fusillo has suggested that the audience was supposed to imagine the tents, the actors curling up to sleep before the tiring-house doors.[2] His argument is based on Reynolds's study of staging at the Red Bull, but Reynolds gives no warrant for such a drastic presumption of imaginative powers on the audience's part; indeed, he assumed that tents would in fact have been used.[3] Although Fusillo received some support from Richard Hosley,[4] Albert Weiner rightly protested that Richard's very explicit instructions for the raising of the tent could hardly be glossed over. His contention, however, that only one tent was used, with both generals making Cox-and-Box use of it,[5] provokes the danger of the ludicrous, and is anyway potentially perplexing.

It seems preferable to assume that Richard's soldiers did indeed

1. See Chambers, *Elizabethan Stage*, i, p. 79: 'We hear of the stage-keeper, the tireman, and the book-keeper or prompter . . . probably all, except the book-keeper, were available upon occasion to take minor parts.'

2. 'Tents on Bosworth Field', *SQ* 6 (1955), pp. 193–4.

3. G. F. Reynolds, *The Staging of Elizabethan Plays at the Red Bull Theater 1605–1625* (New York, 1940), pp. 42–8, 77.

4. 'More about "Tents" on Bosworth Field', *SQ* 7 (1962), pp. 458–9.

5. 'Two tents in *Richard III*?' *SQ* 13 (1962), pp. 258–60.

pitch his tent, and that when Richmond requests the lords to withdraw into his tent, it is a different tent, pitched for the occasion. There is no shortage of space for the two tents: a pair of circular pavilioned tents 9 feet in diameter would together occupy about 127 square feet; the probable dimensions of the Theatre's stage were 43 by 27 feet,[1] an area of 1161 square feet, of which the two tents would occupy only 11 per cent. Besides, as is noted in the commentary, the ghosts almost certainly used the entrance-doors, which could not therefore be blocked by the sleeping leaders.[2]

The other problem to be faced in connection with early performance of *Richard III* is its length: would a play as long as *Richard* ever have been performed in its entirety, or would it always have been cut? Reasons have been given above for thinking that some of the omissions from the Q text represent theatrical cuts, but we have no certain way of knowing whether they were made at the time of the initial production, or later, or for a specific reason such as the postulated provincial tour of 1597. The complete F text of the play is about 3600 dialogue lines long. While it is true that there is very little dumb-show or ceremonial action to delay the performance, and no music that requires appreciable time to perform, it would take at least two and three-quarter hours, and perhaps half an hour longer.[3] There are sufficient surviving references to plays of the period taking three hours to perform[4] to enable us to think that *Richard III*, while long, was not impossibly long. There is thus no cause for us to reject the notion that it could have been performed in its entirety: a swiftly-paced play about the celebrated national villain, with very little non-verbal material to delay the action, might well have been something of a special case.[5]

1. Based on the dimensions of the Fortune, whose contract specified a stage itself based on that of the Globe. As the Globe was built of the timbers of the Theatre, it is a reasonable inference that all three stages were approximately equal in dimensions.

2. Chambers confirms the regular use of tents: *Elizabethan Stage*, III, pp. 53–4 and n., p. 106 and n.

3. The shorter time is calculated on an average speaking rate of not more than 200 words a minute, and a performance rate of not more than 22 lines a minute. It would be hard to keep up such a rate: if one slowed down by a fifth (17 lines a minute) it would take 211 minutes to speak the dialogue. Most modern performances go much slower still.

4. See Chambers, II, p. 543 n. 2.

5. Alfred Hart's dogmatic and intemperate view that all plays over c.2500 lines were subject to gross cutting is unsupported by evidence or common sense. See his *Shakespeare and the Homilies* (Melbourne, 1934), pp. 77–153. For a more

This, then, is as much as can be surmised about the initial performance of *Richard III*. Its subsequent history is more easily traced. We can infer its popularity on the stage both from the impressively large number of published editions before 1640, and from the relative frequency of allusions to the work. The earliest of these date from 1598, when Meres published his *Palladis Tamia*, and Marston, in his *Scourge of Villanie*, was the first of many to have found 'A horse! A horse! My kingdom for a horse!' a line eminently apt for parody.[1] The most celebrated early allusion to the play occurs in John Manningham's diary, and is worth quoting in full, as it is also one of the earliest surviving anecdotes about the dramatist.

> *13 March 1601/2* . . . Upon a tyme when Burbidge played Rich. 3. there was a citizen greue soe farr in liking with him, that before shee went from the play shee appointed him to come that night unto hir by the name of Ri: the 3. Shakespeare overhearing their conclusion went before, was intertained, and at his game ere Burbidge came. Then message being brought that Rich. the 3.[d] was at the dore, Shakespeare caused returne to be made that William the Conqueror was before Rich. the 3.[2]

Common saloon-bar witticism though this is, it attests to the continuing popularity of the play in the early seventeenth century.[3] The first author to express hostility towards Shakespeare's interpretation of the last Plantagenet was Sir William Cornwallis,[4] who thereby initiated a long line of enthusiasts who see in the dramatist's work a sinister Tudor plot to blacken their hero. Many other authors of the Jacobean and Caroline period allude to the play, but there are also specific references to performances.

A *Richard the Third* was performed at the Red Bull theatre, as a prologue and epilogue by Heywood reveal.[5] This could have been another play, of course. The performance given at court on 16

---

reasonable view, note Greg's opinion (*SFF*, p. 147) that 'plays differed considerably in length and performances in duration'. The recent uncut yet highly popular and successful *Hamlet* by the National Theatre (1975) should give theorizers pause in their belief that the longest plays could never have been performed in their entirety.

1. Both quoted in *The Shakspere Allusion-Book* (Oxford, 1932), I, pp. 46 and 54 respectively.

2. Harleian MS. 5353 fol. 29[v], quoted from Chambers, II, p. 212.

3. There were several references, beside Manningham's, to the popularity and effectiveness of Burbage in the title-role: see, for instance, *The Return from Parnassus* (quoted Chambers, II, p. 201) or Corbet's epigram, written in 1621, in his *Iter Boreale* (quoted NCS, p. xlvii).

4. *Shakspere Allusion-Book*, I, 85. 5. Reynolds, op. cit., p. 21.

November 1633, however, was unquestionably of Shakespeare's play.[1] There seems therefore to be no reason to suppose that the play did not remain in the King's Men's repertory until the closing of the theatres. After the Restoration, the play was assigned to the King's Company and occasionally performed. There is a prologue dating from 1672 written for it,[2] and a cast-list survives (written into a copy of the 1634 Quarto) dating from about 1690.[3] This reveals that the best-known portrayer of villains on the Restoration stage, Sandford, took the part of Richard, while Betterton contented himself with Edward IV. Clarence was played by Kynaston, and Buckingham by Williams; Mrs Barry played Queen Elizabeth, and Mrs Bracegirdle, Anne.

In 1700 Colley Cibber staged and published his adaptation of the play. Initially this was performed without the first Act (in which Richard murders Henry VI), perhaps because of official fears that it might arouse sympathy for the exiled King James,[4] but later the Act was included. Cibber's version swept the original from the boards with complete effectiveness, and remained the usual performed version of the play until the end of the nineteenth century. It is much shorter than Shakespeare's, running to some 2050 lines, nearly half of which are Shakespeare's (some from other history plays) and the remainder Cibber's own; with a praiseworthy attempt at honesty, his lines are set in roman type to distinguish them from Shakespeare's, which are italicized. However, the 'Shakespearean' lines are frequently altered, while not a few lines printed in roman are actually Shakespeare's. Many characters are omitted entirely: Clarence, Edward IV, Margaret and Hastings among the major roles. Altogether the fifty-seven characters of Shakespeare's play are reduced to thirty-one, many of whom are now mute, or nearly so: Dorset and Rivers, for instance. There is still a need for a sizeable number of supernumeraries, but the worst problems of doubling are eliminated; Sprague believes the long continuance of the Cibber version was in part owing to its relative ease of performance.[5] Another reason was beyond doubt the emphasis placed by Cibber on the title-role: some 815 lines are Richard's, or 40 per cent of the total: in Shakespeare's play Richard has some 1150 lines, but that represents only a little over

1. Listed in Sir Henry Herbert's records, ed. J. Q. Adams (1917), p. 53.
2. See W. Van Lennep, *The London Stage* (Carbondale, 1965), i, p. 188.
3. Originally reported by J. G. McManaway, *TLS*, 27 June 1935.
4. So Cibber believed; see his preface to the play.
5. Sprague, *Doubling of Parts*, p. 30.

31 per cent. Besides, Cibber's Richard dominates the stage more: he does not enter until after l. 250, but thereafter is scarcely off the stage. The part is an egomaniac's delight.[1]

It seems hardly worth the space to detail the changes Cibber made, or the various burglaries from other Shakespearean texts he imported into his *Richard*.[2] Its general characteristics are swiftly identified. Pathos is, predictably, increased: the murder of the princes occurs on-stage, so that we may have a good cry at their expense; motivation is constantly made explicit: Cibber is like a bad lecturer, constantly over-explaining and repeating himself for fear of being misunderstood; Richard's valour is insisted on: he is portrayed as a potentially good man turned to evil, and there is nothing left of the ordained nemesis one finds in Shakespeare. Richmond sums him up thus:

> Farewel, *Richard*, and from thy dreadful end
> May future Kings from Tyranny be warn'd;
> Had thy aspiring Soul but stir'd in Vertue
> With half the Spirit it has dar'd in Evil,
> How might thy Fame have grac'd our *English* Annals:
> But as thou art, how fair a Page thou'st blotted. (p. 55)

One of the most fearful things about Shakespeare's Richard is that there is never a sufficient explanation for the evil he commits; Cibber's Richard is all too patently obvious. The following speech will suffice to demonstrate this, and serve as example of Cibber's Pegasus. It takes place after Richard and Buckingham have formed their schemes as in III.v of Shakespeare.

> How many frightful stops wou'd Conscience make
> In some soft heads to undertake like me:
> —Come; this Conscience is a convenient Scarecrow,
> It Guards the fruit which Priests and Wisemen tast,
> Who never set it up to fright themselves:
> They know 'tis rags, and gather in the face on't,
> While half-starv'd shallow Daws thro Fear are honest.
> Why were Laws made, but that we're Rogues by Nature?
> Conscience! 'tis our Coin, we live by parting with it,
> And he thrives best that has the most to spare:
> The protesting Lover buys hope with it,
> And the deluded Virgin short liv'd pleasure.

1. A point made with great relish by Bernard Shaw (*Our Theatres in the Nineties*, 1932, p. 288).
2. NCS lists these, pp. xlviii–xlix.

Old gray beards cram their Avarice with it,
Your Lank-jaw'd hungry Judge will dine upon't,
And hang the Guiltless rather than eat his Mutton cold.
The Crown'd Head quits it for Despotick sway,
The stubborn People for unaw'd Rebellion:
There's not a Slave but has his share of Villain;
Why then shall after Ages think my deeds
Inhumane? Since my worst are but Ambition:
    Ev'n all Mankind to some lov'd Ills incline,
    Great Men chuse Greater Sins—Ambition's mine.

(pp. 24-5)

The best that can be said of this is that it contains an echo of Hobbes and anticipates a famous couplet of Pope's. As Sprague sums up: Cibber's version 'does best when it keeps to surfaces and shallows'; it is 'an opportunist version, cunning, prosaic and vulgar'.[1]

Cibber himself was not a great success in the part: a contemporary unkindly described his performance as 'the distorted *Heavings* of an *unjointed Caterpillar*',[2] but bad as he was he launched the play. It was left to Garrick to make it immensely successful: so successful, in fact, that, despite the protests of Lamb and Hazlitt, the emendation survived the various half-hearted nineteenth-century attempts at restoration. It would serve no useful purpose to detail here these performances of Cibber; the curious will find information in the New Cambridge Shakespeare. It is rather interesting to see in what direction the productions tended. The nineteenth century was the time of elaborate scenery, archaeological and sartorial 'historical accuracy': it produced such grotesques as Charles Kean's production at the Princess Theatre in 1857, of which a contemporary critic remarked, 'the painter, the tailor and the upholsterer are Mr. Kean's interpreters of Shakespeare'.[3] The play-bill gives a cast of 121, with a funeral procession of monks with torches, priests with a golden cross, 59 banner-men and so on; a coronation scene of equal dimensions was introduced to match. An army of 58, all dressed in historically exact costumes, followed Richard. But Cibber pure was the text, defended as 'rather a condensation than an alteration'.[4] This farrago ran only nineteen nights, and was not repeated, but the

1. A. C. Sprague, *Shakespeare's Histories: Plays for the Stage* (1964), p. 124.
2. Aaron Hill in *The Prompter*, no. 3, 19 November 1734.
3. Quoted in Alice Wood, *The Stage History of Shakespeare's King Richard the Third* (New York, 1909), p. 127.
4. Ibid., p. 128.

tradition of grotesquely massive productions survived: Sprague describes an actor in 1920 protesting at the curtailment, in a Barrymore production, of the funeral train for Henry VI from its former size of 70 or 80 people.[1]

The elimination of Cibber from the theatre began effectively with Irving's production of 1877: 'thenceforth, use of the alteration was to be exceptional and a little furtive'.[2] Yet Sprague saw a performance of Cibber's version in Boston in 1930, proving again that theatre is the most conservative of the arts. Irving should not be credited with more than is his due, however. His version of the text is worthy of examination: its chief feature is a series of positively brutal cuts. Even Richard's part is butchered: for example the soliloquy at the end of I.ii is cut, as is much of I.iii. All the conversation between Clarence and his murderers is omitted, as are large sections of II.i and all of II.ii except for a passage inserted in II.iii which itself is cut to a dozen lines, incongruously given to Hastings, Buckingham, Richard, Stanley and Brakenbury. A part of III.v is attached to III.i; III.iii is omitted, and the remainder of III.v attached to III.vii and grossly abridged. So it continues, with such features as the reduction of the ghosts at Bosworth to five, who speak only to Richard; the play ends on Richard's last line. It comes altogether to only about 2000 lines, sorely jumbled: in fact, it reads remarkably like a bad quarto—not a 'good' bad quarto, like that of *Richard III*, but a really bad one, like those of *Romeo* or *Hamlet*. So despite Irving's preenings in the preface on his 'successful restoration of the text', the work is just another arrogant actor's botch, save that the raw materials were all Shakespeare's rather than Cibber's.

Richard III has become a more common item in the repertory as the twentieth century has progressed, perhaps because of our increasing unhappy awareness of the significance of dictators to our times. But the great watershed in the play's theatrical history is the appearance of Laurence Olivier's brilliantly-acted film. The total previous audience for the play would have been numbered in the thousands. After the film, the number must be reckoned in the millions—our collective awareness of the play as performed will never be the same again.[3] For a film is not strictly a performance of the play: in its very permanence, its being exactly the same every time it is seen, it establishes a theatrical text for the

1. *Shakespeare's Histories*, p. 138.   2. Ibid., p. 131.
3. This is not the place to attempt an analysis of the film. Readers are referred to Roger Manvell, *Shakespeare and the Film* (1971) and Jack J. Jorgens, *Shakespeare on Film* (Bloomington, 1977) for helpful discussions.

play, much as an editor establishes a reading text. The influence of the film thus is of a different kind from that of any stage performance, however successful: the film is an experience which is repeatable. For these reasons it is regrettable that Olivier elected to perform a bastardized text, beginning with a chunk of *3 Henry VI* and including scraps of Cibber, but excluding a great deal, most notably Queen Margaret. Posterity deserved better of Sir Laurence, and it is worth noting that the film's main effect on subsequent stage productions has been mainly a negative one.[1]

Some modern productions suffer from the director's treating the script 'as the work of an incompetent dramatist for a primitive stage to be converted into a better play by the director, more relevant to the times and to the bored audience'.[2] On the other hand, some recent productions have been very good, and Bill Alexander's, for the RSC in 1984, was wonderful: gloriously imaginative and intelligent, as was Antony Sher's brilliant realization of Richard in it.

A final note on performance might well consist of an expression of the editor's opinion on presentation. The producer will of course make his own decisions, but it seems reasonable at least to proffer some advice. *Richard III* is a long play, but because of its nature, its highly ritualized character, it is not easy to cut.[3] If abridgement must be made, it is best to follow the guidance of Q in the first instance, and omit the passages discussed in Appendix 1. If the play is still too long, it is suggested (with great diffidence) that the following could perhaps be sacrificed: II.i.95–130; II.ii.1–33 and 47–88; IV.iii.1–22; IV.iv.82–115; IV.v. This amounts to some 180 lines, which with the Q omissions, brings the total down to about 3200. Another twenty or thirty lines could be removed from Buckingham's and Richard's oratory in III.vii, but more extensive cuts than that cannot fail to damage the play's internal structure, its patterns of imagery, rhetoric and tone, and its moral and historical fabric. The element of ritual is crucial to the work, and should not be eschewed in favour of naturalistic action, especially in the battle scene, where balletic rather than realistic action suits better the sacrificial nature of the

1. An example of a superficial kind: in the distinguished production of the play at Stratford, Ontario, in 1977, Brian Bedford delivered the famous demand for a horse *pianissimo*, for no reason one could think of other than that Olivier had done so *con tutta forza*.

2. Kenneth Muir, 'Was Shakespeare really incompetent?' *SNL* 39:4 (1979), p. 30.

3. In particular, abridgement of the rhetorical structures amounts to tampering with the play's architecture. See below, 'The play', pp. 114 ff.

elimination of Richard from the world. More commentary than this would be impertinent as well as fruitless; this much may prove helpful.

5. SOURCES

Discussion of the sources of *Richard III* entails the consideration of a number of delicately interlocked issues, rather more complex a problem than is presented by many plays. Four chief objects of enquiry may be identified. First, there is the nature of the source of the factual historical material which is implied in the very concept of a 'history play'. This presents no great problem: Shakespeare's primary sources for his plays on English history were the chronicles of Hall and Holinshed, to which I shall return in due course.

The second issue is the source of the particular emphasis or colour Shakespeare laid on these historical materials. We should not be surprised if Shakespeare accepted bald statements of historical fact from his chronicle sources; it is not so self-evident that a mind like his would have been contented with the interpretation of history found in these books. Much of the published debate on the history plays since Tillyard's pioneering work[1] has focused on this very question. Was there a 'Tudor myth' expressed in Hall and Holinshed, and others, and was Shakespeare dramatizing this myth, and if so, was he a believer in it? These questions have been argued with a good deal of vigour recently,[2] and are of special significance in *Richard III*, since a sizeable body of public thought holds that Shakespeare created this play as a tool (or, more moderately, a victim) of Tudor propaganda against the maligned Last Plantagenet. Clearly, this has ceased to be a question of source, and has become a matter of literary and dramatic intention more appropriate to a critical than an historical investigation.

The third issue is to determine what other materials from Shakespeare's reading were incorporated into the play: materials which do not themselves relate to *Richard III* but which Shakespeare found apt for inclusion in the work. Or, in other words, what are the sources for the episodes in the play which cannot be traced to the chronicle material: Clarence's dream, the wailing Queens, and so on?

The fourth issue is the question of the relationship between

1. E. M. W. Tillyard, *Shakespeare's History Plays* (1944).
2. See below, pp. 107–19, for a treatment of the topic.

Shakespeare's play and other, earlier works (whether dramatic or otherwise) on the same subject: Legge's *Ricardus Tertius*[1] and the anonymous *True Tragedie*[2] or the *Mirror for Magistrates*.[3] Another related question is that of what general influence was felt by Shakespeare from his most important contemporaries. For *Richard III* this boils down in practice to evaluating his relationship with Marlowe, though other possible influences require consideration.

Again, this leads into literary criticism and away from purely factual considerations. So does the entire conception of the 'history play' as a genre: necessarily much that might well come into the present section is thus to be found in the subsequent one, 'The play'. However, best treated here is another question which impinges on literary judgement, the issue of what Shakespeare elected to omit from his sources of historical material; the negative can be as relevant in consideration of sources as the positive.

Let us, before examining these four kinds of source in detail, look at the whole matter of 'sources' in another way. Today, anyone writing a play which sought to give dramatic form to an historical episode from the relatively recent past would almost certainly preface the writing by careful research, comparison of primary and secondary sources if he had a conscience, and consideration of various points of view about the subject. This approach we are now accustomed to; we find it hard to think of circumstances in which not only might it not have been followed, but in which it could not be followed. Those who criticize Shakespeare's 'biased' portrait of Richard tend to do so from such unconscious assumptions.

Even if we leave for later consideration the question of the morality of Shakespeare's practice, it must be observed that if he had attempted consciously to contrast his historical sources, he would have wasted most of his labour. For all the sources available to Shakespeare about Richard III were interlinked, More's *History*[4] being incorporated into Grafton,[5] and Hall, who incorporated Vergil,[6] and who was in turn incorporated by

1. Unpublished (various MSS extant) until 1844 by the Shakespeare Society.

2. *The True Tragedie of Richard the Third* Q, 1594 (Greg 126). Ed. W. W. Greg, Malone Society (1929).

3. Ed. Lily B. Campbell (Cambridge, 1938).

4. Sir Thomas More, *The History of King Richard the thirde*, ed. Richard S. Sylvester, *Complete Works*, vol. 2 (New Haven, 1963).

5. Richard Grafton, *A Chronicle at Large* (1569).

6. *Polydori Vergilii Urbinatis Anglicae Historiae* (Basle, 1534).

Harding,[1] Stow,[2] and of course Holinshed. Naturally, there are differences between these works, but the process of redaction would leave a dramatist in search of variety of information or of emphasis very little to go on. His only alternatives lay in other literary forms: the poems of *The Mirror for Magistrates*; the *Ricardus Tertius* of Legge, and perhaps the *True Tragedie*. However, none of these would help significantly, since they too are based on the same chronicle material. The truly early sources: the Crowland Chronicle,[3] or Mancini's diary,[4] for instance, were not available in published form, much less the various letters and government documents bearing on the time and subsequently unearthed by patient researchers.[5]

There is no reason to suppose that Shakespeare found these limitations irksome; they may seem to us so, for the reasons described above, but the Elizabethan concept of history was both more didactic and aesthetic, and less circumscribed by a regard for precise detail, than our own. To reduce this to a sentence or two, we may say that in this particular instance Shakespeare's 'source' was the account of Richard which not only supplied him with the bulk of his information, but which fixed in his mind a tone, a general approach, towards the subject. This source was Sir Thomas More's *History*; for the rest, we shall find that other materials surface regularly and vividly enough in the play to describe them as minor sources, but they do not combine the first and second classes of source in the way More's work does. In this book we find the Richard of the play: a witty villain, described in ironical terms by the author. Shakespeare modifies More in two ways: by adding to him (More ends his account with Buckingham's flight), and by omitting materials he included. But he is true to the tone of the book: his emphases are More's, though they are modified by the technique of dramatization. What this means in practice is (as Aristotle observed of poetic art) that Shakespeare universalizes the historical detail. He does not falsify, but he makes general what in More is sometimes more specific, by use of the materials available to the dramatist in the 1590s: Seneca, the tradition of the Vice, the Machiavel, and so

1. John Hardyng, *Chronicle* (1543).

2. John Stow, *The Chronicles of England* (1580).

3. B.L. MS. Cotton Otho. B.XIII; Bodleian MS. Corpus Christi Coll. B.208.

4. Dominico Mancini, *de Occupatione Regni Anglie per Riccardum Tercium libellus*, MS. Lille Bibliothèque Municipale.

5. Mancini's work was first described by C. A. J. Armstrong (letter to *The Times*, 26 May 1934).

on. He thereby remains true both to the drama and to the concept of history as he and More understood it. It is true that he invents more villainies for Richard than More (or anyone else), but this is compatible with this view of history—that the fact is less important as such than the moral truth, the detail less important than the general principle: More and Shakespeare both set out to present a tyrannical monster. The modern scholar might say that More's *History* is more witty and ironic fiction than history, and that Shakespeare's play shares this characteristic. However, the notion that anything not strictly factual must be regarded as fiction is a modern one; neither author would have thought of the genres as incompatible. More, though presenting his history wittily and ironically, undoubtedly believed himself to be writing history, of a kind he and his contemporaries would have recognized.

Our search, then, ends in More. With the accuracy and reliability of More's interpretation we are not directly concerned. All that need be said on this issue is that contemporary sources collectively give the impression that at the time Richard was regarded as a dangerously unscrupulous usurper, who had almost certainly had Prince Edward and his brother privily murdered after executing Rivers, Hastings and the others with only the poorest colour of legality; that he probably poisoned his wife, and that he had intended to marry his niece had public opinion and the advice of his closest counsellors Catesby and Ratcliffe not dissuaded him. He was not thought to have been responsible for Clarence's death: Queen Elizabeth and her relatives were held to blame for that. He was generally conceded to be a brave and effective soldier. These early opinions have recently been re-examined and their justness confirmed by Hanham;[1] the details of the growth of the legend of the monster-Richard are to be found in the invaluable survey by Churchill.[2] However, the notion—a minority view since the early seventeenth century but popularized recently by Kendall[3] and others—that 'Tudor historians' collectively plotted to blacken Richard's character (and by implication to whitewash the Tudor usurpation) is not well-founded: almost all the things said about Richard in subsequent chronicles were common gossip in his own time or shortly thereafter. This, of course, does not mean that gossip was reliable, then

1. Alison Hanham, *Richard III and his Early Historians* (Oxford, 1975). See also Charles Ross's excellent biography, *Richard III* (1981).
2. George B. Churchill, *Richard III up to Shakespeare* (Berlin, 1900).
3. Paul M. Kendall, *Richard the Third* (1955).

any more than now. It is also true, as Churchill's survey shows, that subsequent accounts tend to accrete all the individual charges of villainy, no doubt on the principle that, if one bad thing were true, others must also be so.[1]

What is clear, however, is that Shakespeare was writing in a tradition, and that he was not the originator of that tradition. It is More who gave the tradition the decisive turn which surely attracted Shakespeare's attention: that this villain was witty. More's irony is far cooler and less theatrical than Shakespeare's,[2] but it is still clear. He is at his dryest and most ironical in the account of the public spectacle by which Buckingham and Richard stage-managed the demand for Richard's accession; for instance, in his description of the citizenry's response to all the oratory:

the people departed, talkyng diversly of the matter every man as his fantasye gave hym. But muche they talked and marveiled of the maner of this dealing, that the matter was on both partes made so straunge, as though neither had ever communed with other thereof before, when that themself wel wist there was no man so dul that heard them, but he perceived wel inough, y^t all the matter was made betwene them. Howbeit somme excused that agayne, and sayde all must be done in good order though. And menne must sommetime for the manner sake not bee a knowen what they knowe. For at the consecracion of a bishop, every man woteth well by the paying for his bulles, y^t he purposeth to be one, & though he paye for nothing elles. And yet must he bee twise asked whyther he will be bishop or no, and he muste twyse say naye, and at the third tyme take it as compelled there unto by his owne wyll. And in a stage play all the people know right wel, that he that playeth the sowdayne is percase a sowter. Yet if one can so lyttle good, to shewe out of seasonne what acquaintance he hath with him, and calle him by his owne name whyle he standeth in his magestie, one of his tormentors might hap to breake his head, and worthy for marring of the play. And so they said that these matters bee

1. A similar progression can be observed in Richard's portraiture, as the excellent exhibition at the National Portrait Gallery in 1973 showed (catalogue by Pamela Tudor-Craig). Progressively, the portraits reveal greater deformity and unpleasantness of visage: compare catalogue no. 26 (the progenitor of the series) with nos 35 and 37, late descendants.

2. Hanham, whose approach is in general admirably balanced, overstates badly the comic and what she calls the theatrical content of More's *History*, attempting to force upon the work a terminology of drama that did not exist when More wrote—see her pp. 177–85.

Kynges games, as it were stage playes, and for the more part plaied upon scafoldes.[1]

This passage has been chosen partly because Shakespeare did not elect to use it, and it can therefore be seen more clearly than by the reflected light of a speech from the play; partly because in it More shows his fondness for the theatrical metaphor (which Shakespeare must surely have found entertaining and profitable), and partly for its dry irony, concluding with a pun so good it is surprising that Shakespeare made only limited use of it.[2]

More, of course, was not the inventor of the factual material as he was of the tone of his book. Fortunately the absurd notion that he was not even the author, that the *History* was the work of John Morton, Bishop of Ely (and a character in the play, as well as More's patron) has long been abandoned in responsible academic circles.[3] Hanham's recent study shows that More used Fabyan, or one of his sources, and the *Great Chronicle*, but that his chief source was Polydore Vergil.[4] Vergil's basic text for the Richard III story seems to have been an analogue of the original version of the Crowland Chronicle[5]—one of the best sources extant.

The conclusion which seems apparent then is that More, like Shakespeare, used the sources available to him in a fairly responsible way. True, he challenged none of the charges against Richard, but rather set out to present his tyrant in a satiric light, maximizing his villainy, but treating it always with irony and detachment, fictionalizing the details in the tradition of Renaissance historians, who in turn were influenced by their classical predecessors. This process of imposing form upon history results in what are to us areas of vagueness. As Hanham observes,

> It is hard to know whether their dissimulating and timorous villain owes his being to authentic reports of the historical King Richard . . . just as it is difficult to tell whether their manifestations of Richard's tormented conscience depend on genuine information or a sense of what was proper to a bad man.[6]

This attitude of ambiguity is one we must expect to find, and do find, in Shakespeare's play.

1. More, pp. 80–1.   2. iv.iv.242–3. But cf. Jones, p. 215.
3. Hanham, pp. 163–74.   4. Ibid.   5. Ibid.
6. Ibid., p. 194. More goes out of his way to appear judicious and responsible. For instance, writing of the deaths of the Princes, he refers his account to what 'I have learned of them that muche knewe and litle cause had to lye' (Hall, *Richard III*, fol. xxviii^r). But Hanham regards these and other like assertions as part of More's Lucianic irony. Harold Brooks observes that they are the criteria he would apply to evidence given in court.

The net effect of this discussion of More has been to say all that can be usefully said at this point about the second class of source materials outlined above. Of the first class of sources, it has already been said that Shakespeare read More not in the collected edition of the *Works* published by Rastell in 1557,[1] but in Hall's chronicle. In this the text differs markedly from that found in the *Works*, and it must be recalled that a Latin version of the *History* exists also. Readers who bore with patience the long section on the text of the play in this introduction will not wish to be belaboured with the equally complex problems surrounding the texts of More's *History*. A very full statement of the questions is made in the introduction to the Yale edition,[2] and a shorter but cogent argument is presented by Hanham in her appendix;[3] the Yale edition also has a full textual collation.

There is no doubt whatever that Shakespeare knew Holinshed, in the edition of 1587; the question is, did he use Hall also? Edleen Begg successfully argues that he did.[4] Zeefeld[5] has added to this evidence the useful point that Hall, rather than Holinshed, seems to have been Shakespeare's source for Margaret's oratory in *Henry VI*: Holinshed tends to abridge the rhetoric, and he plays down Margaret's role as a spokeswoman for the general historical thesis. Of course, Shakespeare altered Margaret's character after the battle of Barnet to accord with his later treatment of her. Yet there are also details which come exclusively from Holinshed, such as the bleeding of Henry's body in Richard's presence (I.ii.55), or the fear of the physicians for Edward (I.i.137). The most striking of these are the lines which relate to Richard's visit to Exeter, and his finding an omen in the homophone Richmond/Rugemount. This occurs in IV.ii.101–5, in the passage unique to Q. A final, most specific, proof of use of Holinshed is V.iii.325, where the reading 'mother's' derives from a misprint in the 1587 Holinshed; Hall correctly gives 'brothers'. Passages unique to Hall include the misidentification of Rivers at II.i.66 and the tale of Burdet the merchant (III.v.75–8). Often the two texts are so close as to prohibit determining which was used; a fair conclusion would be that Shakespeare had both to hand, but that, as

1. *STC*. 18076.
2. pp. xvii–liv.
3. Hanham and Sylvester (*Complete Works*, 1963) do not agree on all points.
4. 'Shakespeare's debt to Halle and Holinshed in *Richard III*', *SP* 32:2 (1935), pp. 189–96.
5. W. Gordon Zeefeld, 'The Influence of Hall on Shakespeare's English Historical Plays', *ELH* 3:4 (1936), pp. 317–53.

Begg has suggested, Hall was the primary source and Holinshed used chiefly for additional details.

Let us now consider the third issue, of the sources of materials in the play which do not derive from More, Hall or Holinshed. The chief such scenes are the bravura wooing of Anne (I.ii), Clarence's dream (I.iv), the scenes of the wailing Queens (II.ii and IV.iv chiefly) and the second wooing scene (IV.iv). Fortunately, Harold Brooks has recently published exhaustive examinations of these scenes,[1] and it will only be necessary to summarize his conclusions here. The first of his papers deals with Clarence's dream, an episode entirely without warrant in the chronicle accounts. The three parallels nearest in time and place to Shakespeare are Sackville's Induction to the tragedy of Buckingham in the *Mirror for Magistrates*,[2] the narrative of Andrea's ghost in the first scene of *The Spanish Tragedy*, and, from Golding's Ovid, Juno's descent into Hades (in Book IV). We can be certain that Shakespeare was familiar with these, but to them Brooks has added a large number of suggestive parallels from Seneca's plays; especially the *Hercules Furens*, but also the *Hippolytus*, the *Medea*, the *Hercules Oetaeus*, the *Agamemnon*, and the *Thyestes*; besides this there are echoes from the pseudo-Senecan *Octavia*. The more significant details of these echoes are noted in the commentary.

A second major influence on the scene is that of Spenser; the first three books of his *Faerie Queene* were in print by 1590, and available to Shakespeare. From Book II, Shakespeare used the Cave of Mammon episode for the connection between Hades and treasure, and the visit of Guyon to the Bower of Bliss suggested aspects of the terror of Clarence's dream. Spenser also links the treasure and the journey to Hades with sea and underwater imagery. Brooks concludes, 'The investigator's impression is of a molten confluence of influences fusing together at a high temperature and pressure of creative imagination, to yield the most eloquent poetry in the play.'[3]

The eclectic nature of Shakespeare's creative processes is further documented in the second of Brooks's articles, in which he considers the profound influence of Seneca on the wooing of Anne, and on the scenes of the wailing Queens. As far as the latter are concerned, the most influential work is the *Troades*, all

1. Harold F. Brooks, '*Richard III*: antecedents of Clarence's Dream', *Sh.S.* 32 (1979), pp. 145–50 and '*Richard III*: unhistorical amplifications: the women's scenes and Seneca', *MLR* 75 (October 1980), pp. 721–37.

2. pp. 298 ff. (All references to the *Mirror* are to Campbell's edn.)

3. Brooks, 'Clarence's Dream', p. 150. See also Jones, p. 208.

of whose four female parts find analogues in Shakespeare which were not implied in the chronicles.[1] Queen Margaret's unhistorical appearance in *Richard III* may be justified by appeal to dramatic construction and theme, but the importance of the Duchess of York seems to owe nothing to the English sources. Hecuba in Seneca's play is, like the Duchess, an ancestral figure, whose ominous giving birth to Paris resulted in a son who inflicted calamity upon her own family and disaster upon the nation. In the same way, parallels can be seen between the roles of Queen Elizabeth and Andromache, Anne and Polyxena, and even between Margaret and Helen—not in looks, one hastens to add— but in the sense that both are outsiders: hostile, hated, yet victims along with the others. Details of these borrowings will be found in the commentary, but it needs to be emphasized here that Shakespeare was influenced by more than verbal expressions: he seems to have found the situation of the women in defeated Troy and Ricardian England to have had elements in common.

Turning next to Anne's wooing, Brooks remarks on the way in which the chronicle data inevitably led Shakespeare to include the scene. With the known facts of Anne's parentage and betrothal, and the other known fact that she married Richard, comes the conclusion that at some point she must have been persuaded to accommodate herself to him. We also know (via Hall) that Richard was believed to have laid temporarily successful suit to Queen Elizabeth for her daughter's hand. As Brooks observes, 'that brazen proposal would assure Shakespeare that the courtship of Anne in its breath-taking impudence was thoroughly in keeping with Richard's character as history recorded it'.[2] He was thereby enabled to employ his favoured dramatic structural device of creating two scenes in which the later matches the earlier, with significant variation in the details and a different conclusion. The facts of Henry's funeral were also known via the chronicles: Shakespeare's one bold invention was in making Anne Henry's chief mourner and in bringing Richard in to interrupt the event.

In determining on a style for the scene, Shakespeare returned to Seneca, specifically to the wooing of Megara by Lycus in the *Hercules Furens*, adding the incident to the offered sword from the *Hippolytus*; there are also recollections of the *Hercules Oetaeus* and the *Medea*. A final confirmation of the influence is provided by

1. Geoffrey Bullough (*Narrative and Dramatic Sources of Shakespeare*, III, *Earlier English History Plays*, 1966), had previously noted, in general terms, the *Troades* parallel, and that of Lycus and Megara in the *Hercules Furens*.

2. Brooks, 'Women's scenes', p. 728.

Shakespeare's use of Senecal stichomythia in half-lines in the scene. This does not complete the account of the influence of the Latin dramatist on the play: for example, Richard's soliloquy in v. iii owes much to the *Hippolytus* and to the *Phoenissae*. These things Brooks seems to have demonstrated conclusively, with his usual large learning and sound judgement. His opinion that Shakespeare was recalling the Latin, rather than the Heywood translations, casts another interesting light on Shakespeare's linguistic capacities, though on this point the demonstration amounts to a strong probability rather than complete proof.

Let us continue by investigating the fourth kind of source material before attempting to summarize. Of the extant potential sources, the three most likely are Legge's Latin play, the *True Tragedie*, and the *Mirror*. Of these, it is possible to dismiss the *Ricardus Tertius* from consideration. This long play, written about 1579, was not printed (though from the number of surviving manuscripts it seems to have circulated quite widely), and there is no record of a London production (Legge was Master of Caius College at Cambridge). The few similarities in situation between it and *Richard III* may be attributed either to the sharing of the two plays in their basic chronicle sources, or to the influence of Seneca. Legge set out deliberately to write a Senecan tragedy of nemesis, and in view of Shakespeare's close contact with Seneca, just discussed, it is hardly surprising that there should be parallels. They are all, however, sterile: there are no signs of creative recognition in Shakespeare of material present in Legge. We may conclude the resemblances to have been accidental.[1]

In Peele's *The Battle of Alcazar* we find the lines:

> *Moore.* A horse, a horse, villain a horse
> That I may take the river straight and flie.
> *Boy.* Here is a horse my Lord. (ll. 1413–15)

The quarto of this play was published in 1594, but it is generally agreed that its date of composition cannot be later than 1589. Peele is perhaps recalling the phrase in Hall describing Richard at Bosworth, that when the battle was clearly going adversely, 'they brought to hym a swyfte and a lyght horse to convey hym awaie',[2] but if so he gave it a new and vigorous turn. In the *True Tragedie* we find the exchange developed:

---

1. Bullough, III, pp. 234–7, argues the possibilities in a more favourable light, but underestimates the direct influence of Seneca on Shakespeare. He also prints some excerpts (III, pp. 306–12).

2. Hall, *Richard III*, fol. lviii^r.

King. A horse, a horse, a fresh horse.
Page. A flie, my Lord, and save your life.
King. Flie villaine, looke I as tho I would flie . . .

(ll. 1985-7).

This version is obviously closer to the famous lines in *Richard III* than either Peele or Hall. Is it safe to assume that Shakespeare was the debtor?

Alas, no: the text of *True Tragedie* is contaminated. What we have is a palimpsest of the original work, with reporter's (and perhaps actors') additions, very much garbled in transmission. The text is abominably lineated and punctuated: vast passages of prose could be rearranged into intelligible blank verse, and in places vestiges of fourteeners can be found. It is clear that trying to find reliable evidence from such a document is akin to building a house on quicksand. The very lines which strike one as reminiscent of *Richard III* may be precisely that: copyist's or performer's recollections of the Shakespeare play, which had no place in the original text.

This aside, the plays are very dissimilar. *Pace* Bullough[1] the curious thing about the *True Tragedie* is how little of it is about Richard. He does not appear until l. 342 (a sixth of the play already by then over) and is present only in scenes iv, vii, viii, x, xiv, xvii and xviii, some of which are very short. The focus is often on events which Shakespeare chose to ignore, such as the humbling of Mistress Shore, and the historical perspective is a great deal simpler than Shakespeare's. Kenneth Muir has protested against Bullough's speculation that Shakespeare deliberately refrained from dramatizing the material included by the author of the *True Tragedie*;[2] in any event, we have seen (p. 56) that there is good reason for believing that *Richard III* was in existence before Greene published his attack on Shakespeare, who thus would have no reasons for undue sensitivity on the subject of plagiarism.

A reasonable conclusion would be that the surreptitious publication of the *True Tragedie* was an attempt to make capital out of the success of Shakespeare's play; that the original of which the printed version is a defective copy may have been quite early, but survived long enough in repertory for Shakespeare to have seen

---

1. Bullough, III, p. 237; also Churchill, p. 398.
2. Bullough, III, p. 239; cf. Kenneth Muir, *The Sources of Shakespeare's Plays* (1977), p. 35.

it.[1] Certainly, at some point, he read or heard it: l. 1872, 'The sckreeking Raven sits croking for revenge' is parodied by Hamlet as a jibe at the players. But there is no reason to think that Shakespeare was directly influenced by the work in the composition of his *Richard III*. The parallels and similarities noted by Dover Wilson and Bullough,[2] where they are not the result of memorial contamination, can be attributed to the influence on both Shakespeare and the *True Tragedie* of the much more significant *Mirror for Magistrates*.[3]

This famous collection owes its existence to the authors' desire to combine the medieval *speculum principis* and *de casibus* traditions with material culled from English history. The chief source was Hall; the first edition, containing nineteen 'tragedies', was printed in 1559 (it had been prepared for printing in Mary's time, but was 'stayed'). In 1563 a second part appeared, and the collections were further modified and extended at various dates, chiefly 1571 and 1578. In 1587 a new rearrangement appeared which also included some Scots stories: these were taken from a manuscript owned by Holinshed, and a link between these two great historical sources is thus made. From some echoes from this material, we may conclude that Shakespeare was acquainted with the 1587 edition, though he may well have had the book in an earlier version previously.[4]

Some of the poems in the collection attained a degree of

---

1. A play called 'Buckingham' was part of Sussex's repertory in 1593/4. Chambers (*Elizabethan Stage*, II, pp. 130, 202, 217) believes this was either Shakespeare's *Richard III* or an ur-version of *Henry VIII*. It is not impossible that it was a version of the *True Tragedie*. It is hard to think that *Richard III* could ever have been known by any other title.

2. NCS, pp. xxviii–xxxii; Bullough, III, pp. 237–40.

3. It should be remarked that Dover Wilson's view of the relative importance of the *True Tragedie* and the *Mirror* (*SQ* 3 (1952), pp. 299–306) has been reversed by these more exhaustive investigations.

4. Two apparent echoes of 1587 poems may be noted here. The joke about the 'high account' Richard and Buckingham make of Hastings ('For they account his head upon the Bridge', III.ii.68–9) and Queen Elizabeth's wry rejoinder to Richard's promise of 'advancement' for her children ('Up to some scaffold, there to lose their heads', IV.iv.243) were both perhaps partially suggested by these lines: first, from 'Sigebert': 'I hopte to have preferment for my deede, / I was preferde, and hangde al save the head'; secondly, from 'Galba': 'This was the guerdon of my hawty pride / To have mine head thus wise extold aloft: / Thus I the geynes of hasty climing tride'. (Both quoted from L. Campbell's edn of *Parts Added to the Mirror for Magistrates* (Cambridge, 1946), pp. 462 and 325 respectively.) Lady Anne's description of Henry VI's body as a 'poor key-cold Figure of a holy King' (I.ii.5) is anticipated by this line from 'Nennius': 'in performance, waxe as Key full colde' (*Mirror*, p. 208).

notoriety, if not fame, such as Churchyard's on Mistress Shore; others show genuine poetic distinction, such as Sackville's Induction to Buckingham's tragedy. Their authors collectively share an attitude towards history adopted from Hall, and given point by Calvin. Lily Campbell observes the significance of the key word, *magistrate*, which to Calvin signified the divine election of the ruler and his delegated divine authority.[1] 'Against the tyrant, God permits the rebel to rage and war to threaten, conscience torments him, his kingdom may be taken from him, and by God's doom an ignominious death awaits him.'[2] The tragedies were chosen more for their instructional value than for their historical importance, while the concept of tragedy remains firmly at the level of a just punishment for sin, a punishment which emphasizes divine providence.

Whatever the level of belief in the moral potential and power of history revealed by Hall or Holinshed or other chroniclers, it is clear that the *Mirror* is a principled and didactic work. For the first time in English the teaching of political ethics is assumed in it by the poet rather than the historian, and it cannot be doubted that this approach suggested possible uses of historical themes to the dramatists who read the work, Shakespeare included. For *Richard III*, Shakespeare seems to have made particular use of the tragedies of Clarence, Hastings, and Shore's Wife. He also (obviously) had read those on Richard III, Edward IV, Rivers, and Buckingham, but, for reasons to be discussed presently, made less use of them—in fact, he seems not to have found anything in the Edward IV poem for this play. Some passages from the more generally influential sections of these poems are printed in Appendix III. However, it would be wrong to leave the subject without a few examples which show the ways in which the poems refine upon concepts in Hall that Shakespeare develops further.

For example, in the story of Clarence's death, we find both Hall and More agreeing that he was drowned in a malmsey-butt.[3] The *Mirror* gives this version (Clarence is speaking):

> Howbeit they bound me whether I would or no.
> And in a butte of Malmesey standing by,
> Newe Christned me, because I should not crie.

(ll. 369–71)

This grim jest appealed to Shakespeare, who not only alludes to

1. Calvin, *Institution of Christian Religion* (1561), fol. 161, quoted *Mirror*, p. 52.
2. *Mirror*, p. 52.
3. See Appendix III, pp. 341 and 342.

Christian rituals in the murder scene,[1] but borrows the joke itself: in 1.i, when Clarence complains he is being sent to the Tower because his name is George, Richard returns:

> Alack, my lord, that fault is none of yours:
> He should for that commit your godfathers.
> O, belike his Majesty hath some intent
> That you should be new-christen'd in the Tower.
>
> (ll. 47–50)

This notion is made by Richard to grow naturally out of the quip about the godfathers, but to an audience familiar with the oft-told tale of Clarence's vinous fate, it would come as another of the ironical prophecies Richard is free with at this point in the play. Clearly, the line in the *Mirror* suggested a good deal. Also particularly important in the 'Clarence' tragedy are the clear association of Richard and the guilt of Clarence's murder (in Hall the final responsibility is not determined) and the use of the rhyming prophecy about 'G', ll. 181–2, which suggested to Shakespeare the facetious treatment Clarence accords the prophecy in 1.i. The prophecy is in Hall and Holinshed; the rhyme, obviously, is not.

The connection between Sackville's Induction and Clarence's dream has already been mentioned; it will suffice to quote some relevant lines here. Sackville speaks with Sorrow, who takes him to the underworld, Avernus:

> A deadly gulfe where nought but rubbishe growes,
> With fowle blacke swelth in thickned lumpes that lyes
>
> Choakt with the pestilent savour that aryse.
> Hither we cum, whence forth we still dyd pace,
> In dreadful feare amid the dreadfull place.
>
> (ll. 211–12, 215–17)

There they find characters both allegorical and historical until they come to Acheron,

> a lothsome lake to tell
> That boyles and bubs up swelth as blacke as hell.
> Where grisly Charon at theyr fixed tide
> Stil ferreies ghostes unto the farder side, ...
>
> (ll. 480–3)

where they meet with Buckingham. It is an effective evocation of

---

1. See below, p. 112.

a semi-classical Hades, with many lines and phrases that recall Clarence's words.

In the tragedy of 'Buckingham' itself, we find a close parallel to the proverbial observation that Richard is 'So far in blood, that sin will pluck on sin; / Tear-falling pity dwells not in this eye'. Buckingham recalls:

> Yet when I sawe mischiefe on mischiefe fall,
> So diepe in blud, to murder prynce and all,
>
> Alas, it could not move him any jote.
> Ne make him once to rue or wet his iye. . . .
>
> (ll. 347–8, 358–9)

The significant thing is that the proverbial concept is being used here by Sackville at the same point (the murder of the princes) as in the play, and it is likely that it provoked Shakespeare's lines, especially as both aspects of Shakespeare's image occur so close together in the *Mirror*.[1]

Of the two, Shakespeare seems to have found the 'Clarence' poem the more useful; in the 'Buckingham' a great deal of emphasis is placed by Sackville on the treachery of Banister (as it was also by Hall), material which Shakespeare decided to omit: the theme of disloyalty is scarcely glanced at in *Richard III*. The manner of Buckingham's curses may have suggested something of Margaret's style, especially in the way the curses foreshadow the actual punishments wreaked on Banister and his sons. However, the emphasis found in More, Hall and Sackville's poem on Buckingham's motivation did not appeal to Shakespeare, who deliberately leaves his Buckingham an enigma.[2]

Seagar's poem on Richard III (a dull, lame piece of verse)[3] suggested nothing to Shakespeare for his theme or general treatment of the subject, but none the less contains lines which are echoed in the play: 'The wolves at hand were ready to devoure / The silly lambes in bed' (ll. 99–100; cf. iv.iv.22–3); 'But what thing may suffice unto the bloudy man, / The more he bathes in

1. See iv.ii.63–4.

2. Hanham (p. 163) asks, 'What were Buckingham's motives in first supporting, then opposing Richard? (Plainly More did not know and would have liked to.)' Stephen Gresham (*SNL* 39, February 1979, p. 2) remarks that Sackville 'focusses in large part on the complex relationship between Richard and Buckingham'. See also Ross's discussion of this, pp. 113–15.

3. Baldwin's subsequent prose piece observes that 'it was thought not vehement ynough'. As for the deficiencies of metre, someone took the theory of decorum to an amusing extreme by retorting that as Richard's life lacked measure, so ought any poem about him.

bloud, the bloudier he is alway' (ll. 120–1; cf. iv.ii.63–5). There are others, which however are more obviously dependent on More/Hall, and so probably entered the play from that source.

The poem on Rivers has a number of echoes: those of high degree hate climbers because such cannot be contented 'with any state, till tyme he apprehend / The highest top: for thereto clymbers tende' (ll. 305–6; cf. i.iii); of Richard: 'outwardly he wrought our state to founder, / Where inwardly he mynded nought save murder' (ll. 335–6; cf. i.ii.101–2); Richard's 'clokyng flattery' and 'depe dissimulacion' are alluded to (ll. 332, 537); at his death Rivers admits 'In parte I graunt I well deserved thys' (l. 575) and comments 'Thus dyed we gyltles' (l. 568; cf. iii.iii.14–17). Perhaps the most telling parallel with 'Rivers' comes from the stress on illegal condemnation:

> proces heard we none,
> No cause alleged, no Judge, nor yet accuser,
> No quest empaneled passed us upon. (ll. 568–70)

In his poem in the *Mirror* Clarence laments that he was 'accused without cause', that he lacked a 'proces', his 'quest' was unjust, and he suffered from 'false accusers'. But these words are scattered (ll. 167–8, 352, 355) whereas in 'Rivers' the key term 'Judge' appears, and the concept of false justice groups the ideas together. This, then, no doubt reinforced the 'Clarence' material to give us i.iv.171–4:

> What is my offence?
> Where is the evidence that doth accuse me?
> What lawful quest have giv'n their verdict up
> Unto the frowning judge? . . .

Shakespeare obviously read the poem, as these lines suggest, but he made no use of its substance. Rivers bleats at length about unjust wedlock, which is not even relevant to the poem, and complains at equal length about the mechanism of his arrest, which Shakespeare ignored. The cause of his alienation of Margaret which Shakespeare uses (see iii.iii.15–17) does not receive mention in the poem.

The two remaining poems relevant to the play are those of 'Hastings' and 'Shore's Wife'. It is true that Shore's wife makes no appearance in the play, but her invisible presence is quite important in the middle acts,[1] and there is no doubt that Shake-

---

1. A possible reason for Shakespeare's omission of her is discussed below, pp. 96–7.

speare read Churchyard's poem on her. It is a fine rhetorical complaint against the fickleness of Fortune, couched in appropriate language: with Sackville's 'Buckingham', it is the best thing in the book. Some of its phrases perhaps reinforced the Senecal style of the laments of the Queens; note in particular 'Oh wicked wombe that such yll fruite did beare' (ll. 318; cf. IV.i.79 and IV.iv.47-8, among other instances); there are also these lines:

> Oh darke deceyt with paynted face for showe,
> Oh poysoned baite that makes us egre styll,
> Oh fayned frende deceyving people so (ll. 22-4).

Here the subject is Fortune, but Shakespeare, in borrowing the lines, applies them to Richard, and makes the speaker Lady Anne (as at IV.i.79 and in I.ii), and they apply in general to Richard's character of a hypocritical mocking puritan. Again, as in the poem on Buckingham, Shakespeare seems to have been stimulated by the rhetoric while eschewing the content.

Finally, the 'Hastings' poem: here direct influence is difficult to demonstrate, because this section of the play is very closely dependent on More's story of Hastings's death, which was also the source for Dolman's poem. However, two echoes from the poem are undoubtedly present in the play: Hastings's claim 'my chamber England was' is repeated in Richard's line 'Welcome, sweet Prince, to London, to your chamber' (III.i.1; 'Hastings', l. 91). More significantly, Hastings refers to those who 'whyle on earth they walke [are] disguysed devyls, / Sworne foes of vertue, factours for all evylls', a concept applied by Margaret to Richard in IV.iv.71-3:

> Richard yet lives, hell's black intelligencer:
> Only reserved their factor, to buy souls
> And send them thither.

She applies this to Richard's function as scourge of God (a phrase Shakespeare elected not to use in *Richard III*). We also find some characteristic images in the poem which indicate Shakespeare's familiarity with it: 'Hopest thou to cloake thy covert mischief wrought? / Thy conscience, Catyf, shall proclayme thy thought' (ll. 265-6; cf. I.iii.336-8; V.iii.199-200); 'Feare the kyte, / Whoe soareth aloft, whyle frogge and mouse do fyght / In civill Combatt' (ll. 307-9; cf. I.i.132-3); 'Marke gods just judgements, punishyng synne by synne. / And slyppery state wherin aloft we swymme' (ll. 633-4; cf. the general tone of acknowledgement of pride and guilt in Hastings's final speech, III.iv. 80 ff.). Richard's nature as a mock-religious dissembler is emphasized, as in ll. 374–5, already noted,[1] and also in l. 572: 'Suche cloakes they use, that seek to clowd theyr synne'. The phrase 'depe dissemblers' (l. 421) is also reiterated from More/Hall. The poem catches much of the quality with which Shakespeare invests his Hastings scenes, stressing the man's irrational good humour (as in III.ii and the first part of III.iv), the ominous meeting with the priest and the pursuivant Hastings (included by More as an afterthought), and laying less stress on Catesby's treachery than does More (Dolman rather emphasizes Hastings's affection for him: Shakespeare plays the whole betrayal down). We may safely conclude that Shakespeare quarried a good deal from the *Mirror*, using it selectively, but to a far greater degree in this play than has hitherto been recognized.

As for the relationships between Shakespeare and his contemporaries in the theatre, the most important is clearly that with Marlowe. It is also extremely difficult to be precise about it, the uncertain dating of half a dozen relevant works being the principal obstacle to firm conclusions. It can nevertheless be asserted that there is ample evidence of interchange of ideas as well as of specific verbal properties between the two dramatists. In *Richard III* Shakespeare recalls at least one line from Marlowe's first major play, *1 Tamburlaine*:

> I glorie in the curses of my foes,
> Having the power from the Emperiall heaven,
> To turn them al upon their proper heades.
>
> (IV.iv. 29–31)

This may be compared with Buckingham's lines,

> That high All-seer which I dallied with
> Hath turn'd my feigned prayer on my head,
> And given in earnest what I begg'd in jest.
>
> (v.i. 20–2)

The application is entirely different: Tamburlaine is vaunting, Buckingham is penitent. But the association of divine power with the effect of cursing, together with the closeness of the language, suggests a deliberate recall by Shakespeare. We also find in *Richard* a formula which occupies an important place in what is widely accepted as Marlowe's last play, *Doctor Faustus*: the

1. See p. 60.

refrain of the ghosts at Bosworth, 'despair and die', is adapted to Marlowe's line: 'Damned art thou Faustus, damned, despaire and die' (v.i., l. 1725). The theological concept of despair occupies a large place in the last acts of both plays.

As M. C. Bradbrook observed, Richard III is the most Marlovian of Shakespeare's heroes, combining 'the scepticism of Machiavel with the diabolic sadism of Barabas'.[1] As one might expect, there are echoes of The Jew of Malta in Richard III, but they are usually echoes of situation and character rather than language. Of course, the most celebrated such echo occurs outside the play, in 3 Henry VI, where Richard declares himself able to 'set the murtherous Machevil to school' (III.ii.193), a clear allusion to the prologue of the Jew. But in Richard III we find Shakespeare making use of Barabas's form of self-incriminating monologue, in which the villain who conceals his nature from the other characters invites the audience to share his delight in his villainies, an invitation that the audience in turn responds to in a more complex way than the villain anticipates. The revelling in vicious, malicious behaviour is of course shared not only by Richard and Barabas, but by all characters who owe their origins in part to the tradition of the Vice.[2] But Richard and Barabas stand closer together than any others.

In the Henry VI plays, Richard's desire for the crown arose from motives Tamburlaine would have understood:

> Therefore to arms! And, father, do but think
> How sweet a thing it is to wear a crown,
> Within whose circuit is Elysium,
> And all that poets feign of bliss and joy.
>
> (3H6, I.ii.28–31)

As the prize becomes an object of his own desires, his motivation becomes less evident, until in Richard III it is as obscure and contradictory as that of Barabas: this in both plays is an isolating factor which separates the protagonist from his environment. But Richard's ambition remains earthbound, in so far as it is ever articulated.[3] Unlike Marlowe's star-flaming heroes, he always says he wants something concrete: the crown, Lady Anne, to secure his position (later in the play). The hints of a set of un-

---

1. English Dramatic Form (1965), p. 55.

2. See Bernard Spivack, Shakespeare and the Allegory of Evil (New York, 1958). This question is discussed in detail in the next section (pp. 99 ff.).

3. A similar point was made by Nicholas Brooke, 'Marlowe as provocative agent in Shakespeare's early plays', Sh. S. 14 (1961), p. 37.

spoken motivations are kept in careful check by Shakespeare,[1] but we are left with an impression of a man who dares not really know himself: his one moment of introspection at Bosworth is swept away before the need for action. Isolation is not of course unique to Barabas and Richard: Hieronimo is forced into a terrible isolation which so distracts him it costs him his sanity, and the same pattern is followed in *Titus Andronicus*. Only Richard and Barabas, however, so consistently deceive themselves in their isolation.

A lesser influence is felt on *Richard III* from *2 Tamburlaine*, where some of Richard's scornful imagery in his opening soliloquy is anticipated:

> they are too dainty for the wars.
> Their fingers made to quaver on a Lute,
> Their armes to hang about a Ladies necke:
> Their legs to dance and caper in the aire: . . .

(I.iii.28–31)

As for the other plays, we have already considered *Edward II*, and concluded that it postdates *Richard III*. It is impossible to date *The Massacre at Paris* with any certainty: the best indication is Henslowe's 'ne' entry in 3 January 1593. If this does indeed mean that the play was new at the time, then Marlowe was Shakespeare's debtor for the parallels. In particular, the speech of the Guise in ii.91–165 seems a version, adapted to the circumstances, of Richard's opening soliloquy,[2] and there are echoes from other parts of the play as well, as for example at xix.931 ff., where the villains' speech recalls that of the murderers in Shakespeare's I.iv. Perhaps these parallels and echoes are no more than we should expect in view of the nature of Elizabethan dramaturgy,[3] but the plain fact is that, apart from some influence of Kyd, there is very little in the extant drama of the time apart from Marlowe which stimulated Shakespeare in *Richard III*.

As for Kyd, we have already remarked upon the relevance of the prologue of *The Spanish Tragedy* to Clarence's dream. Note, for example,

---

1. We must have a care in attempting 'psychological' interpretations of Richard's behaviour. Most such attempts conclude by being mawkish and inaccurate. This issue is discussed further in the next section.

2. See also F. P. Wilson, *Marlowe and the Early Shakespeare* (Oxford, 1953), p. 89.

3. See M. C. Bradbrook, *Themes and Conventions of Elizabethan Tragedy* (Cambridge, 1935), pp. 78 ff.

Then was the ferryman of hell content
To pass me over to the slimy strond
That leads to fell Avernus' ugly waves:

Where bloody furies shakes their whips of steel

And perjur'd wights scalded in boiling lead,
And all foul sins with torments overwhelm'd.

(I.i.27–9, 65, 70–1)

There are other echoes: the letter Hieronimo reads in III.vii contains the phrase 'That you would labour my delivery' (l. 33; cf. I.iv.236) and further examples are noted in the commentary. There can be no doubt that Shakespeare knew Kyd's play; it is harder to see it as a powerful intellectual influence on *Richard III*, in the way that it surely was on *Titus Andronicus*.

What emphasis should be placed upon the occasional echoes of other literary and dramatic works in *Richard III* is an open question. On the one hand they reveal something of the range and variety of Shakespeare's reading; on the other hand none of them seems truly significant, in the way in which Seneca, Spenser and Marlowe were significant. For example, there are some definite echoes from Whetstone's *Promos and Cassandra*,[1] of which the following affords a good example:

    thy bytter plaintes bestowe
To hasten lyngring death . . .

Condole with me whose heavy sighs the pangs of death do
sho[w]e

My brother slaine, my husband ah, at poynt to lose his head,
Why lyve I then unhappy wench my succors being dead?

(Quoted Bullough, II, pp. 510–11)

This may be compared with II.ii.41, 43, 57–8, 76. In Lodge's *Wounds of Civil War*[2] we find 'Dispatch! . . . / For sore I long to see the traitors's head' (v.i.110, 115; cf. III.iv.96–7). This play was not published until 1594, but had certainly been written some years earlier: Houppert nominates either 1586–7 or 1589. Either way, it would have been available to Shakespeare. There are several apparently significant connections between *Richard III*

1. *The Right Excellent Historye of Promos and Cassandra* (1578); Greg, 73–4.
2. Q 1594, Greg 122; ed. J. W. Houppert, Regents Renaissance Drama series (1969).

and *The Troublesome Raigne of King John*: one has already been alluded to,[1] but a more extended one occurs in Part II, vi. 4–11:

> The world hath wearied me, and I have wearied it:
> It loathes I live, I live, and loath my self.
> Who pities me? to whom have I been kinde?
> But to a few; a few will pity me.
> Why dye I not? Death scornes so vilde a pray
> Why live I not, life hates so sad a prize.
> I sue to both to be retaynd of either,
> But both are deafe; I can be heard of neither.
>
> (sig. D2ᵛ–D3ʳ)

Clearly, this bears a close resemblance to Richard's soliloquy on the eve of Bosworth. As the play was in print in 1591, there is no physical obstacle to Shakespeare's being the debtor. However, Harold Brooks remarks,

> I believe that not only the Bad Quarto, dated 1591 in the imprints of its two parts, but also the original play of which it is a version, *is* later than *Richard III*. Memorial contamination by the actors, or reminiscence by the anonymous dramatist, are the likeliest explanations of the parallel passages. . . . Since, however, they do not produce symptoms of corruption in the text of *Troublesome Raigne*, the dramatist is more probably responsible for them than the actors. That the debt is his, not Shakespeare's, is suggested particularly by [passages] where Shakespeare has a source in what he drew on for his play[2] . . . while *Troublesome Raigne* has no source unless Shakespeare is one. The fragmentary parallels in John's speech of despair . . . are surely echoes of Richard's soliloquy . . . rather than contributors to it. . . . In the other parallels noted, the phrase comes as a rule from a more memorable context in *Richard III* than in *Troublesome Raigne*.[3]

This demonstration cannot readily be refuted; it implies a date for *Richard* earlier in 1591 than has been suggested yet, but one may remember that it was not out of the question for a book published as late as March 1592 to have the date 1591 correctly

---

1. See p. 55 above.
2. The best example is at the end of Part 1: John exclaims, 'What lives he? Then sweete hope come home agen, / Chase hence despaire, the purveyer for hell' (G4ᵛ); compare Margaret's 'Richard yet lives, hell's black intelligencer: / Only reserv'd their factor . . .' (IV. iv. 71–2).
3. Brooks, 'Women's scenes', p. 722, n.2.

on the title-page. As for other similar works, a number of parallels are noted in the commentary. Those with most connections with *Richard III* are *King Leir*[1] (a probable source; see notes to I. iv); *Arden of Faversham*,[2] *Edward III*,[3] *Thomas Lord Cromwell*,[4] and, interestingly, Lyly's *Campaspe*.[5] This play, at any rate, was earlier than *Richard*, and the link between it and the opening soliloquy seems clear. We may conclude this section then by glancing at it. The associative imagery, linking the clamour of war with the soft rites of peace, is used several times by Lyly in the course of the work, but this passage is perhaps the most significant:

> Is the warlike sound of drumme and trumpe turned to the soft noyse of lire and lute, the neighing of barbed steedes, whose loudnes filled the ayre with terrour, and whose breathes dimmed the sunne with smoake, converted to delicate tunes and amorous glaunces? . . . Remember *Alexander* thou haste a campe to governe, not a chamber, fall not from the armour of *Mars* to the armes of *Venus*, from the fiery assaults of warre, to the maidenly skirmishes of love. . . . (II. ii; B4^{r-v})

Campaspe, then, must be added to the list of works which coalesced in Shakespeare's imagination at the time of *Richard III*. Harold Brooks sums this up admirably:

> More than any other of Shakespeare's plays, *Richard III* is his contribution to that phase in the development of the Elizabethan drama in which the neo-classical and the popular native traditions were brought together. . . . [The prominent Senecan elements are] made to combine with the native dramatic heritage. . . . In so far as the play is a tragedy, it is tragedy of the medieval *casus* type. Primarily it is a drama of history, moralised according to the Tudor political idea of the providentially-ordered process that brought Richmond and his successors to the throne. . . . The play exemplifies, moreover, in an early form, the extraordinary synthesizing power of Shakespeare's creative gift. . . . Its strands from Seneca are woven into a fabric which comes from the chronicles and *The Mirror for Magistrates* . . . with further colour from moral and Tudor interpretations of history and politics such as were embodied in some Interludes.

1. *The True Chronicle History of King Leir* (1605), Greg 213.
2. *The Lamentable and True Tragedie of M. Arden of Feversham* (1592), Greg 107.
3. *The Raigne of King Edward the Third* (1596), Greg 140.
4. *The True Chronicle History of Thomas Lord Cromwell* (1602), Greg 189.
5. John Lyly, *A Moste Excellent Comedie of Alexander, Campaspe and Diogenes* (1584), Greg 84; ed. W. W. Greg, Malone Society (1933).

> Richard himself is modelled . . . on the Vice of the Interludes; and on the Senecan criminal hero. He has affinities, too, with the Machiavels, Kyd's Lorenzo and Marlowe's Barabas. The play has Kyd's combination of the neo-classical and the popular; but with poetry beyond Kyd's range, and akin to Marlowe's. . . . Yet the range of its eclecticism is not the most remarkable feature of *Richard III*. More remarkable still is its harmonisation of elements so variously derived.[1]

This seems to summarize the subject of the sources perfectly, though some of the points mentioned will be discussed in the subsequent section.

One final issue for this section is Shakespeare's excisions and omissions. We have seen that More gave him the image of a demonic villain in Richard, and Hall stressed the workings of providential justice. These essential features of the legend were preserved and made dramatic by Shakespeare to a far greater extent than was contrived by the authors of *The Mirror for Magistrates* or the *True Tragedie*. Yet in some respects he went against the pattern of the legends, and certainly gave them a different shape. He and the chronicles are closest in the fall of Hastings, a neatly encapsulated image of the fate of the ordinarily ambitious and unscrupulous in an age dominated by an arch-villain. He deliberately reduced in importance the falls of the Queen's kindred and Buckingham, and—as has already been noted—eliminated from his material the theme of perfidy and betrayal which bulks so large in Hall especially. Instead he chose to strengthen the theme of nemesis by the introduction of Margaret.

Perhaps the reason for this choice was that he did not want any great pity diverted to Richard's victims: it was important to see them suffering what Margaret at any rate thought was justice in their falls. Clarence's end is terrifying—but in the play we do not see Clarence committing evil; the hypocrisy and the villainy are reserved for those who suffer later. The emotional climaxes of the play are thus in i.iv and v.iii; in the middle acts we are more concerned to see the absorbing game of strategy being played before us than distressed for the individuals who suffer. In pursuit of this decision, Shakespeare eliminated almost everything that could give rise to genuine pathos: the wailing of the Queens is so formalized it seems more ritual than real. Even the murder of the princes is resolutely banished off-stage, and reported in a rather

---

1. Brooks, 'Women's scenes', pp. 734-7. Cf. Jones, p. 206.

stiff recitation.[1] Surprisingly, in a play so full of deaths, only one death occurs on-stage, and that is Richard's: even Clarence, though wounded on-stage, meets his famous end in the malmsey-butt 'off'; none of the other victims dies before our eyes, and the death of Anne happens so casually, almost as an afterthought, that it could easily be overlooked by an inattentive spectator. The juicy moral episode of Mistress Shore is chastely banished from Shakespeare's play; her penitence and humiliation would be totally out of place in a play where penance and humiliation are so resolutely restrained. It is thus clear that, far from being a play of indiscriminate bloodshed and powerful passions, it is really a very controlled work, in which material not germane to the theme as Shakespeare perceived it was rigorously excluded. It is to the identification of this theme that we must now turn.

6. THE PLAY

Published criticism has done indifferent justice to *Richard III*. Many works discuss it only as a twig on the tree of 'Shakespeare's histories'; others suffer from what Nicholas Brooke condemns, a sort of teleological fallacy, seeing the earlier work merely as prototype or prelude to the achievements of the 'great tragedies' to come.[2] It is thus perhaps worth beginning with Schiller's remark that *Richard III* is 'one of the noblest tragedies I know. . . . No Shakespearean play has so much reminded me of Greek tragedy.'[3] An unusual judgement; but one undoubtedly worth considering, especially since nobility is not a quality normally found in the play. As for its Grecian characteristics, it is worth remembering that A. P. Rossiter too saw in its blend of political and moral themes something akin to Aeschylus.[4]

The structure of the play is highly organized and formal, in a way that reveals its debt to its Senecan models. The protasis has to resume a great deal of material from the *Henry VI* cycle at the same time as preparing the audience for the new material and emphases of the present play. Shakespeare uses a most regular 'rising action' to deal with both this and the ensuing epitasis as Richard progressively surmounts the obstacles in his path. These

1. John Tobin has recently pointed out what seem to be some parallels with Apuleius' *The Golden Ass* in this speech. See his 'Shakespeare and Apuleius', *N&Q*, April 1978, p. 121. It also has an Ovidian quality in its juxtaposition of lyrical description with horrible action.

2. In his *Shakespeare's Early Tragedies* (1968), Introduction.

3. Quoted in G. Steiner, *The Death of Tragedy* (New York, 1961), p. 158.

4. *DUJ* 31 (1938), p. 72.

are chiefly the existence of his brothers and their children, and the presence of a powerful party under Queen Elizabeth (the Lancastrians are by now a spent force). The climax, however, occurs at the elimination of a relatively unimportant third party: Lord Hastings, whose equivocal stance makes his a representative figure of the moral decay into which English politics has fallen.

The catastasis consists of Richard's actual gaining of the throne at the very moment when his own nature and the efforts of others have begun the process that will unseat him. The catastrophe is spread leisurely upon the field of Bosworth, a much more elaborately prepared and symbolically significant event than any of the battles (even Wakefield and Towton) in the *Henry VI* plays. In it, the violence and treachery which had been the ruling characteristics of the country since the accession of Henry VI are expiated in ritual acts of retribution and reconciliation.

Perhaps also from Seneca, by way of Kyd and Marlowe, comes the single action and tone of the play. There is no sub-plot; there is precious little comic relief, save Richard's own diabolical humour. It is an unusually chaste play so far as sensational action is concerned: although it adapts many elements from the revenge drama and the 'tragedy of blood', there is very little action on-stage that is physically shocking. Clarence is stabbed (but dragged off-stage to be drowned), but this and Richard's death are the only on-stage acts of violence. Many potentially gruesome or shocking events are reported to us, the most obvious being the death of the princes. But Hastings, Grey, Vaughan, Rivers, Anne, Buckingham and King Edward all meet their ends off-stage. Such resolute avoidance of violence in a play about so famous a violent man can hardly be accidental.

Certainly the revenge element is stressed. Anne prays for vengeance in i.ii; Margaret dominates i.iii with her appalling litany of revenge; it is cried upon Richard by the wailing Queens in iv.i and iv, and finally threatened upon him by the ghosts in v.iii. Revenge is not only threatened; it falls—upon those who grimly acknowledge their guilt at the time of their execution. Again, Hastings is the most important of these, but the theme is strongly present in Clarence's fearful dream and anguished end, and elsewhere. 'Guilt' is a word that occurs more often in *Richard III* than in any other play by Shakespeare. Both the Lancastrians and the Yorkists are guilty: the moral abdication of Henry VI leads to the dominance of Margaret in the later stages of the Wars of the Roses; her violence and brutality are referred to by others in i.iii, though she shows no awareness of her part in the collective blood-guilt. The Yorkists in turn provoked civil war; Edward broke his oaths, as did Clarence: they are a generation nurtured in violence whose individual repentances do not suffice to heal the cancer of usurpation, civil disorder and self-seeking.

Shakespeare makes use of a number of conventions extant in the drama of his time to reinforce the sense of a ritual expiation of collective guilt that the play develops: for instance, the extensive use of omens and portents. Clarence's dream is the most extended of these, but the unexpected reappearance of Margaret as a modern kind of Fury ('foul wrinkled witch') is another. Omens beset the Princes as they go to the Tower, and are thick to the point of embarrassment about the obtuse Hastings. The Citizens of II.iv are full of dark forebodings, and those in III.vii make something eloquent out of their fearful silence. Richard too finds himself prey to omens, even as far-fetched as the resemblance in sound between 'Richmond' and 'Rougemont'; at last all these signs coalesce into the fearsome parade of the dead during his sleep in v.iii. Many of these are in the sources, especially those concerning Hastings;[1] but they are woven by Shakespeare into a web of numinous threats which strengthen the ritual seriousness of the play.

For all the contemporaneity of Shakespeare's dramatic construction, the play owes an even greater debt to the heritage of the morality drama. This is true in small matters as in great: one might note the emblematic use made of simultaneous staging at Bosworth, for instance;[2] Richard's dialogue with himself before the battle;[3] the allusions to the wheel of fortune and other elements of the *de casibus* tragedy, which becomes intermingled with the morality in the early Elizabethan period. 'O momentary grace of mortal men' laments Hastings, and the phrase sums up a world of influence from the earlier drama upon which Shakespeare has drawn.

The most momentous use he makes of his dramatic heritage is in the characterization of Richard himself. Shakespeare rejected the obvious choice of representing him merely as a ranting tyrant, and, following up the hints found in More, wrote for Richard a

1. See Appendix III, especially pp. 351–3.

2. See Madeleine Doran, *Endeavors of Art* (Madison, 1954), p. 287; she also refers (p. 114) to the way form is given to chronicle drama by its borrowing from morality structure.

3. 'Precisely in the tradition of the morality drama' notes Bernard Spivack, *Shakespeare and the Allegory of Evil* (New York, 1958), p. 378, comparing with *Appius and Virginia*, ll. 501–8.

part developed from the morality play Vice.[1] A word of background may be useful: in the earlier moralities the several vices which afflict mankind were individually personified; in the mid-sixteenth century a single representative figure of evil came to be called 'the Vice', who 'acquired distinctive theatrical personality and status far beyond the allegorical features'.[2] Happé identifies Avarice in *Respublica* as the first Vice to fulfil all functions characteristic of the type. He is 'homiletic showman, intriguer extraordinary, and master of dramatic ceremonies';[3] his method is always deceit and guile; his purpose the 'translating into vivid dramatic image the habitual self-deception or blindness of mankind to the real nature of the temptations to which it succumbs'.[4] He displays the 'trick of tears and laughter. His weeping feigns his affection and concern for his victim; his laughter, for the benefit of the audience, declares the triumph of his subtle fraud and his scorn for the puny virtue of humanity.'[5] Yet he attracts the audience's attention and even sympathy, both by embodying its own destructive and anti-authoritarian impulses,[6] and by engaging the audience in a conspiratorial relationship with him, a relationship strengthened as the plays explored increasingly secular themes and were presented in aesthetic rather than in homiletic form.

Clearly, the Vice offered opportunities for the actor on a much broader scale than did the characterization of most Tudor plays, and thus became in a sense the 'star' part, no doubt an eagerly awaited feature of the performance. Happé finds the Vice's greatest popularity occurred between 1550 and 1580, after which the increasing sophistication of plot and character in the professional drama led to a diminution of his importance. Yet later dramatists still employed recognizable derivatives of the Vice for specific dramatic purposes. Marlowe's Barabas, Villuppo in *The Spanish Tragedy*, Piero in *Antonio's Revenge* and others sometimes have Vice-like characteristics (Mephostophilis in *Doctor Faustus* does not); but it is Shakespeare who found the figure particularly useful. Falstaff is compared to the Vice, Iniquity, by Hal;[7] Aaron the Moor, Iago and Don John share the Vice's features. So, clearly, does Richard III.

Of the sixty-odd characteristics of the 'formal Vice' listed by Happé, the following can be recognized in the Richard of Shake-

---

1. The ensuing account is deeply indebted to Spivack, op. cit., and Peter Happé's London Ph.D. thesis, *The Vice 1350–1605* (1966).

2. Spivack, p. 135.   3. Ibid., p. 151.   4. Ibid., p. 157.
5. Ibid., pp. 161–2.   6. Happé, p. 83.   7. *1H4*, II.iv.453–4.

speare's play: the use of an alias, strange appearance, use of asides, discussion of plans with the audience, disguise, long avoidance, but ultimate suffering of punishment, moral commentary, importance of name, and reluctance concerning it,[1] self-explanation in soliloquy, satirical functions which include an attack on women, and various signs of depravity such as boasting and conceit, enjoyment of power, immoral sexuality. Of the Vice's familiar modes of expression we find impertinence, logic-chopping, use of oaths and proverbs, and the self-betraying slip of the tongue. Let us take the last as example: in i.i Richard makes merry with Clarence over Mistress Shore and the Queen, while pretending to Brakenbury that he is not (ll. 90–102). Compare, from *Triall of Treasure* (D4ᵛ):

> *Inclination.* I may say to you she hath an ilfavoured favour.
> *Luste.* What saiest thou?
> *Inc.* I saye she is loving and of gentle behaviour.

This 'moralizing two meanings in one word' is reminiscent of the most celebrated passage of the kind in the play, in iii.i:

> *Rich.* So wise so young, they say, do never live long.
> *Prince.* What say you, uncle?
> *Rich.* I say, without characters fame lives long.
>
> (ll. 79–81)

A closely similar episode occurs in *Impacyente Poverte* (D1ᵛ):

> *Prosperyte.* Then let us go our waye
> I syt on thornes tyll I come ther
> *Envye.* That shall make your thyrste full bare
> *Pros.* What wyll it do?
> *Envye.* I say we shall have good chere
> When we come there.

Clearly, the Vice formed in Shakespeare's mind the natural theatrical mode of expressing inordinate evil, evil which springs from a context of decayed public morality, evil which has no satisfactory rational explanation. For, ultimately, Richard's motives are no more intelligible than Iago's: there is a superficial plausibility, but that is not enough. Bacon does as well as anyone in explaining those aspects of Richard which are explicable in terms of cause and effect. He observes in his essay 'Of Deformity',

> *Deformed Persons* are commonly even with Nature: For as Nature hath done ill by them; So doe they by Nature: Being

---

1. Richard sought to avoid the ill-starred name of Gloucester: *3H6*, ii.vi. 106–7.

for the most part, (as the Scripture saith) *void of Naturall Affection*; And so they have their Revenge of Nature . . . all *Deformed Persons* are extreme Bold . . . it stirreth in them Industry . . . to watch and observe the Weaknesse of Others . . . And it layeth their Competitours and Emulatours asleepe; As never beleeving, they should be in possibility of advancement, till they see them in Possession . . . in a great Wit, *Deformity* is an Advantage to Rising . . . they will, if they be of Spirit, seeke to free themselves from Scorne; Which must be, either by Vertue, or Malice.[1]

This is such a good description of Richard's behaviour that one wonders if he was in Bacon's mind as he penned it (though it is more likely he was thinking of Cecil). He adds, in his essay 'Of Ambition' a further useful gloss on Richard's behaviour:

Ambition is like *Choler*; Which is an Humour, that maketh Men Active, Earnest, Full of Alacritie, and Stirring, if it be not stopped. But if it be stopped, and cannot have his Way, it becommeth Adust, and thereby Maligne and Venomous. So *Ambitious Men* . . . if they be check't in their desires, they become secretly discontent. . . .[2]

All these observations are true, and have been made of Richard since by various critics. But they are not a complete account; they do not describe the wholly irrational aspects of Richard's behaviour: the evil that the other characters react to in varying degrees of fright and horror. Such evil is also characteristic of the devil, and Richard is called 'devil' often enough in the play; at various points (e.g. IV. iv. 419) he seems to accept the identification.[3] His behaviour is as relentlessly anti-Christian as he can manage, his favourite device being 'With odd old ends stol'n forth of Holy Writ, / [To] seem a saint, when most I play the devil' (I. iii. 337–8). He determinedly inverts all Christian values: he hates his fellow man (but 'Alack, I love myself'); he is an entirely accomplished hypocrite; he is brutal, vicious, egocentric, cruel and unnatural, conceited, blasphemous: the perfect example of the anti-Christ.

Yet he has become King, and dares to call himself 'the Lord's anointed' (IV. iv. 151). His moral perversity afflicts now, not only

1. *The Essayes . . . of Francis Lo. Vervlam*, World's Classics edn (1937), pp. 179–80.
2. Ibid., p. 154.
3. It should be noted that the Vice, though diabolical in his interests and behaviour, is not actually intended to be a representation of Satan or Lucifer.

family and friends, but the entire nation. Thus his Vice-like, anti-Christ qualities are linked with those of another familiar medieval horror: the Scourge of God.[1] The fact of bad, tyrannical kings had to be reconciled with the rule of a benevolent Deity; some scriptural references (e.g. *Isaiah*, x. 5–15, where Assyria is called the rod of God's wrath raised against the sins of Israel) and some classical (in Plutarch and Plotinus) combine to create the concept of the 'flagellum dei'. This is the ruler whose personal wickedness (freely chosen) yet makes his actions a means of expressing the divine will, by chastising and mortifying a sinful people; the chastisement done, the scourge is in turn destroyed. Famous scourges remarked on in literature included Herod and Nero, but the most celebrated theatrical example in Shakespeare's time was of course Tamburlaine.

The concept was also available in the sources of *Richard III*; More, as we have just noted, knew it; Holinshed (of King John) refers to 'the generall scourge wherewith the people were afflicted';[2] and Shakespeare himself makes use of the term in the *Henry VI* plays (most appositely in *2H6* where Margaret is called 'England's bloody scourge', v. i. 118). The actual term is not applied to Richard in the play (though he fits the part precisely), but it is clearly implied in the attacks made upon him by Anne (i. ii) and Margaret (i. iii and iv. iv), especially in her description of him as 'hell's black intelligencer, / Only reserv'd their factor, to buy souls / And send them thither'. Most significantly, Richmond appeals to the concept in v. i and, especially, in his oration in v. iii, where he stresses Richard's tyranny, that Richard 'hath ever been God's enemy', and that the act of deposing him is divinely sanctioned. In his final speech in v. v Richmond refers to the long madness that has scarred England, and which has now been brought to an end by the removal of Richard, its final manifestation.

1. For instance, from the *Ancrene Riwle*: 'reflect, that whosoever harmeth thee, . . . is God's rod: and that God beats thee with him, and chasteneth, as a father doth his dear child, with the rod. . . . But, let him not think well of himself because he is God's rod. For, as the father, when he hath sufficiently beaten his child, and well chastised him, casteth the rod into the fire . . . so, the Father of Heaven, when he, by means of a bad man or woman, hath beaten his dear child for his good, casteth the rod, that is the bad man, into the fire of hell.' (trs. James Morton, Camden Soc. (1853), p. 185.) More knew this, either directly or at second hand from sermons: there is a closely parallel passage in his *Apologye* (1533).

2. Holinshed, p. 173/2. Also in *Parts Added*: 'Sigebert', ll. 292–3 (p. 461), or 'Lady Ebbe', ll. 29, 31 (p. 466).

Richard, then, is much more than a realistic character with intelligible motivation: his origins lie in recognizable dramatic and political archetypes; he is the representative of the Arch-enemy, whose function as political anti-Christ is expressed in a conventional theatrical idiom. Into this mixture derived from medieval models is added a more modern ingredient: the Machiavel. Derived originally from misrepresentation of Innocent Gentillet's massive remonstrance against Machiavelli,[1] the stage-Machiavel was already a familiar figure in 1591. There are Machiavels in *The Spanish Tragedy*, but the most recent and stimulating example was, of course, in *The Jew of Malta* ('Machivel' himself speaks the prologue to the play). The essential qualities of the Machiavel coincided nicely with those of the Vice: he was ambitious, cruel, morally depraved to the point of seeing immorality as something virtuous, sinister, treacherous, guileful, anti-religious, criminal from choice. The Machiavel brings some new language (Spivack remarks that 'policy' is the new word that replaces the Vice's 'gear') and some new style: horseplay, lewd jesting and coarseness are replaced by relative gravity and political interest, while the allegorical emphasis gives way to 'the moral image of a formidable, if depraved, human nature, drawn from history and dramatized by the method of naturalistic art'.[2] Richard identifies himself as a Machiavel in *3H6*, especially in III.ii.193, where he declares he can 'set the murtherous Machevil to school', and in *Richard III* his 'plots, inductions dangerous' are the stock-in-trade of the ambitious Machiavel, as is his playing off of one side against the other (e.g. in I.iii).

It is all very well to identify the ideas and concepts which lie behind Shakespeare's Richard; it is quite another thing to account for the amazing vitality and theatrical success of the result: *Richard III* without the Usurper is a prospect even harder to contemplate than *Hamlet* without the Prince. To be sure, there was at the time a wave of creative interest in the concept of the criminal hero, a fertile field planted with Seneca (especially the *Thyestes* and the *Agamemnon*) which grew such crops as *Tamburlaine*, the *Jew*, the Guise in Marlowe's *Massacre at Paris* and other, less successful, strains. None, however, has had the theatrical longevity, nor the audience appeal of Richard; never have the elements described above been combined into so persuasive and attractive a consequence as Richard III. Partly, as we have seen,

1. *Discours, sur les moyens de bien govverner . . . un Royaume . . . contre Nicolas Machiauel* (Paris, 1576). No English translation was published until 1602.
2. Spivack, p. 393.

Shakespeare was guided by the characterization in his source, but the result is still entirely his own.

To some extent it is a matter of strategy: Richard is more likeable than the other characters in the play, just as Don Giovanni (who goes to hell) is more attractive than the gaggle of dolts who seek to tame or destroy him (and who do not). Shakespeare paves the way carefully: he has Richard announce his evil intentions immediately to us in such a way that we are almost persuaded that they are a reasonable response to his personal problems—deformed, ugly, out of work[1]—and then shows him developing them with rare grace and skill. First Clarence is taken in by the blend of brotherly affection, hostility towards the Queen and Mistress Shore, indignation at Edward's shabby treatment and so on (all most skilfully feigned); then Lady Anne serves as an object lesson of Richard's power to dominate even those implacably his enemies. He succeeds with Lady Anne because he is cleverer than she (as indicated by his superior command of rhetoric), but also because he is immensely attractive.

This attractiveness is not, perhaps, physical—but Richard's deformity is too easily accepted at face value. He himself uses it as an excuse; yet when it suits him he can have the superiority of his appearance adduced in support of his claim to the throne (in III.vii). His opponents criticize his appearance unmercifully, yet one feels their reaction is rather to the evil within him; the deformity is an outward and visible sign of his inward spiritual gracelessness.[2] His attractiveness lies chiefly in his ability to make us admire him, even while our better natures know perfectly well that what he is doing is monstrous. In this he shares something with Aaron, but not with Don John or Iago, who are by no means sympathetic. He also shares this quality with Falstaff; but Falstaff is neither as successful in his ambitions, nor as evil, as Richard, who—even at his most diabolical—remains interesting, magnetic. It is not only that he has immense self-confidence (so have other,

---

1. Bacon puts this idea (of course) more gracefully: 'Deformed Persons, and Eunuches, and Old Men, and Bastards, are *Envious*: For he that cannot possibly mend his owne case, will doe what he can to impaire anothers.' ('Of Envy', *Essayes*, p. 33.)

2. Robert Ornstein, in *A Kingdom for a Stage* (Cambridge, Mass., 1972) remarks apropos of this subject that Richard is hardly tormented by the deformity 'which he describes with such humour and sweet reasonableness' (p. 67). Jorgens, commenting on Olivier's Richard, observes, 'physically, he is good-looking, having a Byronic attractiveness, limp and all, and is extremely mobile compared to the static characters around him. . . . His list to one side . . . shows him askew in a world in which he does not belong' (op. cit., p. 143).

lesser characters such as Hastings and Buckingham, neither of whom is at all likeable). We admire his discernment of character, his address and fertility of resource, the command of his temper, his versatility, the 'alacrity' whose loss he laments on the eve of Bosworth, and his unquestioned courage and military prowess.

It is worth noting these qualities, since otherwise it is hard to see why at the end of the play there is some sense of tragic loss at Richard's death. To be sure, he is no conventional Aristotelian hero 'much like ourselves'; not at all a Macbeth. In *Richard III* we do not participate in the agony of a man's loss of his soul; Richard, true to his dramatic origins, is committed to evil at the beginning of the play. Whatever was potentially good in him is already subverted to the drive of will[1] and power, the Machiavel's immense belief in his *virtù*, his superiority to the rest of mankind[2] —that belief in power and ability which later finds re-expression in Raskolnikov's theories, or in Nietzsche's *Übermensch*. Marlowe, at this time, created his superb megalomaniacs whose dedication to the belief that might is right leads at last to the terrifying discovery of their own inadequacy. The revelation of the superman's vulnerability is not part of Shakespeare's scheme, whose villain-hero either remains enigmatic like Iago and Aaron or, if the iron enters his soul, shows himself glumly defiant, stoical, always a man of action, preferring to go down with guns blazing rather than endure the harsher light of self-revaluation.[3] Nothing becomes Richard in the play so well as his death, as he dares an opposite to every danger, and seeks Richmond (the doubtless wisely, but unheroically, disguised Richmond) in the throat of death. It is the only action in the play which reminds us of Richard's early achievements as a warrior—and so in an unexpected way it brings another wheel full circle and allows us to sense, at the end, the greatness of Richard's daring, whilst we are simultaneously relieved that the dare is safely over.

Richard himself has his doubts, beginning in IV.ii, and coming to a head in the soliloquy after the ghost scene, as to the wisdom of his actions. One of the most celebrated antecedents for an

1. See A. W. Fields's valuable article, 'The Shakespearean self-author', *South Central Bulletin* 34 (1974), pp. 150–6, for an examination of the destructive effect of wrong acts of will.

2. See W. A. Armstrong, 'The Influence of Seneca and Machiavelli on the Elizabethan tyrant', *RES* 24 (1948), pp. 19–35.

3. See T. S. Eliot, 'Shakespeare and the Stoicism of Seneca', in *Selected Essays*, 3rd edn (1951), pp. 126–40. W. A. Armstrong, 'The Elizabethan conception of the tyrant', *RES* 22 (1946), pp. 161–81 usefully re-expresses these concepts in detail.

inner dialogue of this kind is Christ's agony in the garden of Gethsemane.[1] This is enough to re-establish a proper perspective, to prevent sympathies from being excessively engaged. Richard's hesitation before drinking the cup he has chosen is part of his role as anti-Christ; for us to accept him in this role we must perceive him as both comic and callous (or the mind would revolt at the sacrifice) yet also sufficiently serious for us to see his acts as important. Richard's is the one act of sacrifice needed to redeem England from her accumulated sins (as Richmond's final soliloquy makes clear); it restores England to grace. The anti-Christ takes the sins of the world on his shoulders not for altruistic, but for selfish reasons; he does not offer himself as ransom, but is pushed, fighting and shouting, to his fate. It is an awe-inspiring concept. It can be an overwhelming one, theatrically, as Evil and Good— personified, as if in a morality play, in Richard and Richmond —face each other on the bare stage in v.iv.

The theology of *Richard III* has not been spoken well of by critics, especially such intelligent and influential writers as Rossiter and Brooke, by whom it has been called 'repulsive' or worse;[2] they object that it seems to present a crude concept of retributive justice, derived from such minor thinkers as Hall.[3] England collectively was guilty of permitting the Lancastrian usurpation; this guilt must be purged by a series of blood-lettings, culminating in the scourge of Richard, against whose career the warnings and threats of Margaret can be seen as the expression of a fearsome Nemesis awaiting its time. It would be foolish to deny that there is a structure like this implied in the play;[4] but it would be a grave mistake to imagine that it is *all* the play is about, or that it is a complete statement of the theology implied.

That theology, the political theology of the Renaissance, is a subtler creation. It owes its origins to St Augustine's *Civitas Dei*, in which the saint solved a notable paradox cleverly by observing,

1. There are, of course, many other models, from Ovid, through the medieval tradition, to *The Spanish Tragedy*. This by no means reduces the importance of the Gospel prototype, which would have been familiar to all.

2. A. P. Rossiter, *Angel with Horns* (1961), pp. 1–22, and Nicholas Brooke in 'Reflecting Gems and Dead Bones', *Crit.Quart.* 7 (1965), pp. 123–34, who uses the term 'repulsive'.

3. This is the view of Tillyard (*Shakespeare's History Plays*, 1944) and M. M. Reese (*The Cease of Majesty*, 2nd edn, 1968), among others; it has been challenged by Ornstein (op. cit., pp. 18–20), who rightly points out that Hall's emphasis lies far more on reconciliation than on retribution.

4. Richard Moulton pointed this out long ago, in his influential *Shakespeare as a Dramatic Artist* (Oxford, 1893).

apropos of providential intervention in worldly affairs, that if all punishment were delayed to the Day of Judgement, there would be no visible sign of providence in the world, and men would lose their faith. On the other hand, if all offences were punished immediately, there would be no need for the Last Judgement— yet that has been promised; it will come, and some judgements at least must be suspended until then. This rational explanation of the worldly success of evil men qualified and balanced the effect of the relevant Biblical texts, of which the most important was Christ's remark to Pilate: 'Thou couldest have no power at all against mee, except it were given thee from above' (John, xix. 11). Other important texts were, 'It must needes bee that offences shall come, but woe bee to that man, by whome the offence commeth' (Matt., xviii. 7); 'Vengeance is mine: I will repay saith the Lord' (Rom., xii. 19); and 'The Lord is slow to anger . . . but . . . visiting the wickedness of the fathers upon the children' (Num., xiv. 18).

The wherewithal was there, if Shakespeare had chosen, to write the crude play of vengeful retribution Margaret imagines she is acting in. Offences certainly had come, in England in the fifteenth century. One can see in the anxious Citizens of ii.iii, the silent Londoners of iii.vii, or even the cynical Scrivener of iii.vi, a collective awareness of the corruption of the national life, the decay of society towards chaos.[1] Yet there is also, by contrast with the *Henry VI* plays, a sense of narrowing scope in this decay. No rebellious element, inflamed by a Jack Cade, spreads the social disorder to the entire populace; on the contrary, while the people wait, silently, for the end of the nightmare, the handful of titled rogues play out the last act to their mutual destruction. There is a realistic element to this: as Prior says, 'Richard is a product not only of nature but of the times, that for a Richard to come into being and flourish both must cooperate . . . the deformities which he owed to his prodigious birth were shaped and disciplined for his evil mission by the vicious and fiercely cruel world of strife into which he was born.'[2]

But 'il teatro e la vita non son la stessa cosa': the way Shakespeare has chosen to dramatize the pattern of history he has imagined is not by any means simply realistic. As we have seen, he sought in the remnants of the earlier drama for means by

---

1. Bacon says, 'when Discords, and Quarrells, and Factions, are carried openly, and audaciously; it is a Signe, the Reverence of Government is lost' ('Of Seditions and Troubles', *Essayes*, p. 58).
2. Moody E. Prior, *The Drama of Power* (Evanston, 1973), p. 301.

which to characterize Richard; he borrowed from such highly formalized sources as Seneca and the *Mirror*. He invests his play in an aura of ritual or myth to make a drama of sin and expiation in which ordinary everyday responses must be modified before they apply. Tillyard remarked of *Richard III* that it can have 'the solemnity we associate . . . with the Dionysia at Athens and the Wagner festival at Bayreuth'[1] and if ordinary responses will not do for *Parsifal* or the *Ring* (and they will not) then neither will they for *Richard*.

Tillyard also observes that where others' sins breed more sins in turn, 'Richard's are so vast they are absorptive, not contagious'.[2] Shakespeare enables us to keep our distance from Richard by investing him with inhuman qualities, the semidiabolical characteristics of the Vice—yet at the same time,

> Like most ironists, Richard secures the audience 'on his side' and yet involves us even further when (again like most ironists) he betrays our trust, and turns out to be way beyond us, leaving us embarrassed as Baudelaire did: 'Vous! hypocrite lecteur: mon semblable! mon frère!' Our condemnation of evil is involved in our recognition of our brotherhood with it.[3]

Theologically, it is not God who condemns Richard to suffer for the nation's ills. It is Richard who elects to become an anti-Christ, whose free choice of evil is also (by the familiar Christian paradox) the means by which God brings about good. The sympathy we feel for Richard is on account of his expressing some of our own less admirable attitudes openly, and this enables us to participate imaginatively in his fall, as the fall of a wretched human being. Yet we are also so distanced by ritual that the intervention of Richmond can seem wholly right, and the final response a sigh of relief that the horror and grief are over.

The other characters of the play must contribute to both its realistic and its ritual levels. Margaret, for instance, is almost entirely ritual: a crazed figure of impotence brought back from the past to represent the brutal, un-Christian, Old Testament concepts of retributive justice which Richmond effectively negates with his New Testament of forgiveness and reconciliation. Moody Prior rightly warns us against the *post hoc, propter hoc* interpretation of Margaret and her curses:

> The belief of these characters in a divine justice is entirely self-serving, without an ethical base. . . . for these people, living in a

1. Tillyard, p. 200.   2. Ibid.
3. Brooke, 'Reflecting gems', p. 130.

frightful and disordered world, belief in the operation of a divine retributive justice provides a sense of moral order ... but it keeps alive the urge for private vengeance and relieves them of a feeling of responsibility for wrongs suffered by others.[1]

Especially, Margaret's smug satisfaction at the deaths of the Princes can only 'produce dislike for her and all the others who insist on identifying the fulfilment of their ugly wishes with the moral order of the universe'.[2] Margaret's curses come true, not because she utters them, but because in the circumstances their fulfilment is entirely probable. Many things happen in the play which are not foretold by her (she has no inkling of Richmond's importance) and some things which she prophesies do not come true (Elizabeth is not left childless, for instance). Margaret is morally myopic: she can see the injuries done her, and resent them, but cannot recognize her own criminal actions. It is one of the most shocking things in the play that Queen Elizabeth joins in her incantatory cursing in iv.iv—far more distressing than the moot issue of whether or not Richard persuaded her to allow him to pay suit to her daughter.

It has often been remarked that all the characters in the play (except for the Princes and Richmond) are at least partly guilty. This is so: we saw that Anne succumbs to Richard's wooing partly because he is attractive, but she would not have fallen so readily into such a terrible mistake if she too had not been corrupt. The scene opens with her dreadful curses: Richard is right when he twits her that she knows no charity. Yet Anne, like Elizabeth, is characterized in a more realistic manner than Margaret or the Duchess. She and Edward's Queen, for all their rhetoric, are believable as women. The others are mere monotones of complaint, and again it is alarming that the real and the surreal should blend so effectively in their quartets of grief and hate in Act iv. And it is worth remembering that the motives for their behaviour, when examined, are no more rational than Richard's.

Neither are those of Buckingham and Hastings, yet the latter is characterized particularly realistically, from the abundant material in More and the *Mirror*—to the point that an audience can become exasperated by his wilful blindness. He, like Buckingham, rejoices in 'the false security of the politician who deceives himself into thinking that there can be a limited liability in

1. Prior, p. 51.
2. Ibid., p. 52. J. Wilders (*The Lost Garden*, 1978, p. 57) notes Margaret's attribution of her own barbarism to God.

crime',[1] an error Richard never makes.[2] Many other characters in the play are represented carefully on the realistic (though not the profound) level, such as Stanley, whose unattractive trimming enables him to weather the storms successfully,[3] or the seemingly ineffective clergy—the two Archbishops and the Bishop of Ely—or the young Duke of York, who may be innocent, but is a most thoroughly dislikeable brat.

There are also others in the play whose purposes are more symbolic or ritual. In such a class fall the various representatives of the people, and the curious Murderers, who begin as a comic turn but adapt into theologically literate debaters in the argument with Clarence. On a realistic level, this is absurd; emotionally, the scene never jars if well performed. Of the other characters whose function is both ritual and realistic, Clarence and Richmond are the most important. Richmond has regularly had a bad press, critics finding him boring, stuffy, predictable and unbearably righteous. On the realistic level, these objections have some force. On the ritualistic, they are irrelevant; he is presented, as Prior remarks, in an apolitical light, purely as a saviour;[4] 'in its context the lifelessness of the character shows how seriously Shakespeare took him', says Reese.[5] He steps into a prepared role: Margaret, the incarnation of the wrong sort of vengeance, disappears, leaving the place vacant for the minister of God's justice. Yet he must fight a battle, and go through all the military and political preparations. His is perhaps the most difficult part in the play to bring off successfully on stage.

Clarence, by contrast, is a 'gift' part. Into his dream Shakespeare poured the most impassioned, lyrically active verse in the play. Most other characters are assigned a single tone of voice, but apart from Richard Clarence alone is allowed the span of the poet's abilities. His suffering, fear, guilt and death make a powerful impression early in the play; they serve to remind us that Richard's schemes are not played out upon mere puppets, but men and women whose agony of spirit and body can be intense. We have just been through the long scene of Margaret's curses, a scene not devoid of power, but one infused with a ritual, abstract quality—a little like a chess game—especially as the crimes for

1. John Palmer, *Political and Comic Characters of Shakespeare* (1962), p. 90.

2. Cf. iv. ii. 63–5; v. iii. 312–14.

3. Andrew Gurr's attempt ('*Richard III* and the democratic process', *Essays in Criticism* 24 (1974), pp. 39–47) to show Stanley as a significant moral and political force in the play seems decidedly far-fetched.

4. Prior, p. 45.

5. Reese, p. 212.

which Margaret is howling for vengeance have not occurred within the play.

Clarence's scene breaks in upon all this with the force of a terrible shock: it is, perhaps, the most emotional experience in the play. He confesses to guilt; again it is something that happened before the play began, but *his* suffering is fearfully immediate. He thus serves as a balance in the audience's mind for its assent to Richard's cleverness. We have been taken in, incited to admire Richard (partly because his opponents are a tedious lot) and now we are made to recognize the human cost of that assent. It is a salutary experience, whose force recurs in Act v as we see Richard in the throes of his dream and death, the only other act of violence committed on-stage. But in addition, Clarence's death serves as the occasion for a debate on the issue of political morality, of guilt and vengeance; when the Murderers force Clarence to justify his behaviour, much of contemporary theory on private and public action is laid open. And finally, it is not entirely fanciful to see a grotesque parody of the Eucharist taking place in the scene at the behest of the anti-Christ Richard, the significance of which again becomes clear in the final scene. Clarence is 'made a sop' of, a human host soaked in wine, by murderers who call him a 'bloody minister', debate of theology, and make comparisons of their acts with those of Pilate. Clarence's death is thus an anticipation of the sacrifice of the anti-Christ at the end; but Clarence here is merely victim, not agent: his death hurts, but cannot help. [1]

Characterization is one, but only one, of the means Shakespeare employs to develop his ritual dramatization of history. Another is that which, since Brecht, we have learned to call alienation, or the *Verfremdungseffekt*. Any play in which a character addresses the audience directly will have something of this quality by its lending a dialectical rather than a realistic quality to the work, but in *Richard III* it is emphasized. There can be few plays peopled by such a determined collection of role-players as this: we cannot help becoming aware that we are watching a play about people who are playing parts, well or badly. The best treatment of this aspect of the play is by Van Laan, whose survey of the range of the subject is indispensable. [2] 'The hero's play-acting forms the only real subject of at least the first three acts' of *Richard III*, he

1. In remarking on the power of Clarence's scene, one must not overlook Shakespeare's resolute avoidance of either violent or tender scenes in the play generally; for instance his deliberate avoidance of the possibilities offered by Elizabeth's defence of her son in sanctuary (recounted at length by More) or the famous penitence of Mistress Shore.

2. Thomas F. Van Laan, *Role-Playing in Shakespeare* (Toronto, 1978).

declares,[1] and while he exaggerates—Clarence at least, and Margaret, cannot be so lightly dismissed—there is an element of truth in the observation. Richard's role is 'the villain'; 'the idea that a character's primary activity consists of role-playing . . . that, in fact, he thereby gains an identity'[2] seems indeed to be what Richard is saying in his opening soliloquy. 'Proving a villain . . . also involves carrying out all the activities traditionally associated with the villain in drama: such as oppressing the weak and helpless, undermining the efforts of the hero [i.e. Edward IV] and constantly devising and executing crimes of an increasingly hideous nature.'[3] Richard stages a variety of little playlets in the first three acts in ostensible support of his attainment of the crown; but in reality his goal is rather 'not what the show may accomplish but the show itself';[4] like Iago he plumes up his will by knavery, demonstrating his versatility while his opponents tediously stick to their single roles. Van Laan wittily calls i.iii.328 Richard's 'highly favourable review of a good performance'.[5] Perhaps *ars gratia artis* should have been Richard's motto, too.

The ending of the play is brought about and made acceptable by the change in Act IV. Richard, who has hitherto played the villain excellently, now proves but indifferent in the role of King: he is nervous, preoccupied, makes mistakes and loses control (neatly represented by Shakespeare in the form of an actor's forgetting his lines, as at IV. iv. 452–5).[6] His revival, as Van Laan puts it, of *The Wooing of Anne* in IV.iv is a failure, owing to the recalcitrance of his new leading lady, Queen Elizabeth. So now Richard must go on to enact *The Fall of the King*, which he does with something of his old panache. Obviously, this is an incomplete account of the play, but it brings a valuable insight into its nature.[7]

One of Richard's most characteristic scenes is III.v, where he instructs Buckingham to play 'the deep tragedian', and the two perform a little farce for the credulous Mayor's benefit. In III.vii, Richard is affronted that the citizens did not enjoy and applaud the performance by Buckingham of the monodrama *Richard Should Be King* (one suspects Buckingham wasn't as good as he thought he was, a common delusion amongst actors). It is easy to

1. Ibid., p. 72.   2. Ibid., pp. 137–8.   3. Ibid., p. 139.
4. Ibid., p. 141.   5. Ibid.   6. See also Jones, p. 218.
7. Peter Ure, in 'Character and role from *Richard III* to *Hamlet*', in his collection of essays, *Elizabethan and Jacobean Drama* (Liverpool, 1974), pp. 22–43, presents a similar, though less elaborate, reading of this aspect of the play.

see virtually any scene in the play as one of role-playing, even those of the saintly Richmond, who is—seriously, and devoutly, to be sure—playing the role of England's saviour. This stress on actors playing at being people who are playing roles adds up to a formidable alienation effect, which in turn lessens the realistic, and strengthens the dialectical, ritualistic qualities of the play.

The language in which the work is conveyed is obviously another important ingredient in determining its nature. *Richard III* has long been recognized as the play of Shakespeare's which most depends upon the deployment of formal rhetoric.[1] This formality has the effect of marmorealizing the scenes into 'a wall of stone music', a rigid, formalized kind of structure into which Richard's protean mutability strikes with the force of a mason's hammer. Brooke rightly remarks that the play is 'a work of outstanding technical virtuosity',[2] and investigates the ways in which linguistic forms parallel the dramatic and thematic structures: for instance the contrasts between the formality of the wailing Queens and Richard's off-hand casualness: 'Chop off his head.' Irony is omnipresent in the play, verbal as well as dramatic irony; 'its cumulative effect is to present the personages as existing in a state of total and terrible uncertainty'.[3]

Rhetoric can be an instrument of characterization: witness Buckingham, whose orotund platitudes conceal the shallowness of his insight. Ironies can multiply as words crack under the strain of perpetual misuse; 'god', 'grace' and 'lord' are used more frequently in *Richard III* than in any other of Shakespeare's plays, but so are 'murder', 'hell' and 'hate', 'kill' and 'blood'. Richard's habitual duplicities, and Margaret's constant misuse, devalue the name of God, make heaven a hell, unsettle the linguistic foundations of morality. Elizabeth scornfully points out that Richard's actions belie his noble words (IV.iv.369–97), yet drama is built on language: in Richard's world, the very nature of reality is unstable. In such a world, fictions may appear as solid as facts: the sun will not rise at Bosworth; omens and prophecies are as real as the history that everyone has perverted for their selfish ends. A

1. On this subject, see especially Sister Miriam Joseph, *Shakespeare's Use of the Arts of Language* (New York, 1947) and Brian Vickers, 'Shakespeare's use of rhetoric' in *A New Companion to Shakespeare Studies* (Cambridge, 1971). Also useful are Robert Paul Dunn, '*A Crooked Figure*': the Functions of the Tropes and Similes in Shakespeare's History Plays, Ph.D. thesis, Univ. Wisconsin (1970); David Riggs, *Shakespeare's Heroical Histories* (Cambridge, Mass., 1971), especially ch. 2; R. F. Hill, 'The composition of *Titus Andronicus*', *Sh.S.* 10, pp. 64–8.

2. Brooke, 'Reflecting gems', p. 123.

3. Rossiter, *Angel with Horns*, p. 6.

pursuivant named Hastings pops up from nowhere to confront
Lord Hastings on his unwitting journey to execution. Margaret
suddenly appears from banishment: the oddity is scarcely remarked upon. The words that seem so frozen in their formal
rhetorical patterns end by being paradoxically all the more elusive.

That things are not what they seem is reinforced by the imagery.
The characteristic images of the natural world, disordered by
men's actions which (for instance) the Citizens express in II.iii, the
kind of normative imagery which John Danby has demonstrated
lies centrally in Shakespeare's mind,[1] are used by Richard for his
own purposes. The other characters retort by locating their
imagery for Richard in the most loathsome and despised elements
of nature; he is a toad, a snake, a bottled spider and so on; he is a
wolf ravening among the lambs (an inversion of the usual image
of the king as shepherd to his flock, with its figural overtones). It
ought to be stressed that there is no sign of immaturity in the
language of the play. Shakespeare achieves any effect he desires
with remarkable subtlety and precision. This is so whether the
idiom is the naturalistic dialogue of I.i, for instance, or the rich
blend of literary archetypes into Clarence's dream, or the formal
laments and complaints—arias, ensembles, fugues of grief and
lamentation—or the blend of military realism and ominous ritual
drama at Bosworth. He is master of all. There can be no doubt
that, both in grasp of structure and in command of language,
Richard III represents a great advance on the *Henry VI* trilogy,
itself an achievement of no mean order.

This brings up the question of the relationship of the play to
the rest of what is called the 'first tetralogy'. The origins of the
history play as a genre have been studied by Irving Ribner and
F. P. Wilson;[2] there seems to be no reason to dissent from Wilson's
view that Shakespeare was the effective originator of the English
history play.[3] And it is certainly worth remarking that he seems
to have elected to launch his career as a dramatist by an unusually
bold venture: a linked series of four plays—as if Wagner had
begun his career with the *Ring* cycle. To be sure, *Richard III* is not
necessarily implied by *1 Henry VI* as the conclusion of the series,

1. *Shakespeare's Doctrine of Nature* (1949). Charles Forker also stresses the
importance of the natural world as a source of imagery, but muddies the waters
by using 'pastoral' as a term to describe this kind of image: 'Shakespeare's
chronicle plays as historical-pastoral', *Shakespeare Studies* I (1965), pp. 85–104.

2. Irving Ribner, *The English History Play in the Age of Shakespeare*, rev. edn
(1965); F. P. Wilson, *Marlowe and the Early Shakespeare* (Oxford, 1953).

3. M. C. Bradbrook's attempt, in *The Living Monument* (Cambridge, 1976),
to contradict this view is not at all persuasive.

but it becomes the inevitable termination as the series develops. And the subject chosen was not (as might have been expected) a cheerfully patriotic one: it is not famous victories, but rather tragical doings on which Shakespeare turned the first light of his dramatic imagination. David Riggs has remarked that Shakespeare's 'choice of the one epoch that could be fully known by the Elizabethan historian finally limited him to a single way of knowing it',[1] but this is not so. The very fullness of the information available, together with the fact that debate on the nature of the subject's duty, the morality of politics, the attitudes that could be taken towards rebellion was lively, rather seems to have stimulated Shakespeare to a vast dramatic exploration of these themes in the context of a history with which everyone was familiar, yet which was sufficiently remote to admit of personal opinion and judgement.

There are many thematic and historical connections between the *Henry* trilogy and *Richard III*. The series begins with a sense of loss: Henry V is the great absent character at the beginning. *Richard III* ends with a great gain, the new hero who will restore the golden age. Villainy is endemic in the corrupt land: in *1 Henry VI* Winchester acts the part of an ineffectual Richard; he prefigures the final monster that is bred by civil dissensions. The death of Talbot is an emblem of the suffering of England, just as Clarence at last is an emblem of the suffering of the guilty individual. The wooing of Lady Grey by Edward (a performance commented on unfavourably by Richard at the time) becomes a model for his much better-staged encounter with Lady Anne.

There are connections of a much more direct kind: there is material in *Richard III* which is barely understandable without some familiarity with *Henry VI*—the closeness of Richard and Clarence, for instance, or the upstart nature of Queen Elizabeth and her friends. It is a base and costly match that Edward makes —the brothers' enmity is justified, though Shakespeare gives Elizabeth little of the pride of which they accuse her, and for which there was ample justification in the sources. The 'bright angel' who confronts Clarence in Hades, the lamented Prince Edward, Henry VI's son, is central to *Richard III* as the focus of Anne's and Margaret's grief—yet unless we know *3 Henry VI* we shall not know that his death was undertaken by York's sons Edward, Clarence and Richard together. In *Richard III* Richard alone is blamed for it. There is no trace of Richard's abominable character in *2 Henry VI*: he merely seems the most warlike of the three valiant brothers. His Machiavel's ambitions surface in

1. Riggs, op. cit., p. 28.

Part III, but there is little sign of his development as a Vice in that play. It certainly seems that a growth and development occurred to Shakespeare as the tetralogy progressed; the growth of his dramatic abilities, and the material itself, suggested the way in which the work would be concluded in the fourth play.

Certainly, anything but a slavish dependence upon the emphases of the chronicles is the determining factor. As Prior observes, for instance, Richard's death is not degraded as it is in the chronicles, in the *Mirror* and the *True Tragedie* (though Shakespeare does not go so far as to allow him a dying speech). The solution to the problem of disorder and tyranny proposed by the play is not political; rather 'a public myth about the succession' is deployed.[1] A. L. French has rightly argued that the context of *Henry VI* is essential to *Richard III*, since otherwise Richard's villainy escapes from artistic control: 'the play as a whole gets reduced to a comédie noire, or a hilarious melodrama, or something between the two'.[2] It is true that the inability to take the 'public myth' seriously (which French himself falls victim to) is a grave weakness in many critical treatments of *Richard III*. Especially at this distance in time, now that the issues are cold, it is easier to distort *Richard*'s balance in the absence of the *Henry VI* trilogy.

That Shakespeare wrote the plays in a single creative phase seems likely, especially in view of the early date for *Richard III* argued here. That they were performed as a cycle at the time cannot now be shown, though it seems likely enough. That *Richard III* became detached from the other plays and has led a long and successful independent theatrical life is undeniable. It is for this reason that it is necessary to consider the play on its own, as a complete aesthetic experience; to do so, data from the Richard who appears in the *Henry VI* plays should not normally be admitted into critical consideration. That Richard says 'I am myself alone' in *3 Henry VI* has no direct bearing on the crux at v.iii.184, unless we can unequivocally determine that Shakespeare intended *Richard III* never to be played without *Henry VI*— and of course we cannot. This is not to say that there is no sense of unity in the tetralogy; only that *Richard III* is a proven independent aesthetic success. In the same way, while Wagner's *Ring* is a single work, its members (especially *Die Walküre*) can successfully be played on their own.

The thematic concerns at issue go beyond *Richard III*, beyond

1. Prior, p. 136.
2. 'The world of Richard III', *Shakespeare Studies* 5 (1968), p. 25.

the first tetralogy into the second, indeed recur throughout Shakespeare's life-work. The concept of history, the providential, theocentric history expounded by writers from Augustine to Hooker via Aquinas, was under attack by the Machiavellian, individualistic attitudes spawned by the Renaissance and Reformation. In response, princes evolved the doctrine of their divine status, to rebel against which was to rebel against God. This attitude is entirely characteristic of the new times of the Reformation and of the nation-state. Historiography and historical drama in the sixteenth century are an expression of this new philosophy of politics, which made the immediate past visible in a new and interesting light.[1] The 'chronicle' or 'history' play, ('a play drawn from a chronicle source which we know that at least a large part of the audience accepted as factual' which 'appears to fulfil what we know the Elizabethans considered to be the legitimate purposes of history'[2]) is an expression of that interest. Was political life under the direct control of providence? If so, how was this manifested?[3] If history was indeed providential, how ought one to react to tyrants?[4] How ought one to react to our current rulers, the Tudors?

Since E. M. W. Tillyard's pioneering work, debate has proliferated on the question of whether there was a 'Tudor myth', and if so who was responsible for it, and whether or no Shakespeare himself believed in it to the extent that he would write no fewer than eight, or nine, plays in support of it, as Tillyard supposed.[5] Part of the difficulty, as Prior has shown, is that our reconstruction of the intellectual climate of the time is collected from all sorts of sources; it is an artificial construction which probably bears little resemblance to how any particular person saw things at the time. And he goes on to warn us that, 'the grander and more inclusive the unifying idea which the critic applies to these eight plays, the more likely it is that the individual play will lose some of its individuality and distinctiveness by being subsumed within the framework of the whole'.[6] He remarks of the five plays *Richard III–Henry V* for instance that each 'is concerned

1. Ribner has a valuable appendix where these matters are discussed at length.
2. Ribner, p. 25.
3. The best treatment is in C. A. Patrides, *The Phoenix and the Ladder* (Berkeley, 1964).
4. A good summary of opinion is found in Prior, pp. 122 ff.
5. Ornstein, especially, finds this hard to believe (*A Kingdom for a Stage*, p. 3). Harold Jenkins provides an excellent summary of earlier opinion in 'Shakespeare's History Plays: 1900–1950', *Sh. S.* 6 (1953), pp. 1–15.
6. Prior, p. 7.

with a particular problem of kingship in relation to legitimacy, authority, and the exercise and influence of sovereign power'.[1] Each play evolved its own dramatic form in order to be an appropriate vehicle for the theme.

It is in such an aesthetic context that Shakespeare's interpretation of the fifteenth century is best regarded. Nothing is more belittling or misleading than to see him as parroting 'Tudor propaganda'. The very word, with its connotations so powerfully influenced by events of the past fifty years, cannot but mislead. As we have seen, Richard in the play is constantly mistreating the language in the way that modern propagandists, whether political or commercial, understand so well. But it is Richard's propaganda, not the Tudors', that is thus expressed. The semi-official volume of *Sermons and Homilies* is the nearest thing in the period to an attempt by government to influence the minds of the people through words; and its tone is rather that of an eager attempt to be rational than the duplicity we associate with propaganda.

We must also firmly resist the tendency in some published criticism[2] to see Shakespeare not as a dramatist, but as a somewhat unorthodox political scientist. His plays are not personal exhortations to virtue, calm explorations of current trends or vehicles of popular education. They are plays: he found in the events of history and their interpretation a way of representing dynamic human conflict in the theatre.

Richard was a demon of the past who needed regular exorcism. Shakespeare made his version of that exorcism an occasion for the interpretation of history on the level of providential ritual. There is in this exactly the nobility and the Grecian seriousness which Schiller found in the play: the *Oresteia* also dramatizes (among other things) the supersession of the blood feud by public justice, a rule of law. When the jokes are over, the arguments ended, the victims dead and the battle done, there is achieved in *Richard III* a profound sense of a great episode concluded, and a great opportunity beginning. These feelings are the achievement of art, not of political theory nor of history. And already at this early stage of his career Shakespeare created, through his art, a reality which triumphantly survives its time:

> As 'twere retail'd to all posterity,
> Even to the general all-ending day.

1. Ibid., p. 8.
2. In Ribner, and in Lily B. Campbell, *Shakespeare's Histories* (San Marino, 1947) among others.

KING RICHARD III

DRAMATIS PERSONÆ

RICHARD, *Duke of Gloucester, later King Richard III.*
THE DUKE OF CLARENCE, *his brother (later, his Ghost).*
SIR ROBERT BRAKENBURY, *Lieutenant of the Tower.*
LORD HASTINGS, *the Lord Chamberlain (later, his Ghost).*
LADY ANNE, *widow of Edward, Prince of Wales (later, her Ghost).*
TRESSEL
BERKELEY } *Gentlemen attending Lady Anne.*
A Halberdier.
A Gentleman.
QUEEN ELIZABETH, *wife of King Edward IV.*
LORD RIVERS, *her brother* } *(later, their Ghosts).*
LORD GREY
THE MARQUESS OF DORSET } *her sons.*
THE DUKE OF BUCKINGHAM *(later, his Ghost).*
STANLEY, THE EARL OF DERBY.
QUEEN MARGARET, *widow of King Henry VI.*
SIR WILLIAM CATESBY.
Two Murderers.
The Keeper of the Tower.
KING EDWARD IV.
SIR RICHARD RATCLIFFE.
THE DUCHESS OF YORK, *mother of Richard, Edward IV, and Clarence.*
Boy
Girl } *Clarence's children.*
Three Citizens.
ARCHBISHOP OF YORK.
THE DUKE OF YORK, *younger son of King Edward IV (later, his Ghost).*
A Messenger.
PRINCE EDWARD, *Prince of Wales, elder son of King Edward IV (later, his Ghost).*
LORD CARDINAL BOURCHIER, *Archbishop of Canterbury.*
Lord Mayor of London.
A Messenger.
HASTINGS, *a Pursuivant.*
A Priest.

SIR THOMAS VAUGHAN.
THE BISHOP OF ELY, *John Morton*.
THE DUKE OF NORFOLK.
LORD LOVELL.
A Scrivener.
Two Bishops (Shaa and Penker).
A Page.
SIR JAMES TYRREL.
Four Messengers.
CHRISTOPHER URSWICK, *a Priest.*
Sheriff of Wiltshire.
THE EARL OF RICHMOND, *afterwards King Henry VII.*
THE EARL OF OXFORD.
SIR JAMES BLUNT.
SIR WALTER HERBERT.
THE EARL OF SURREY.
SIR WILLIAM BRANDON.
Ghost of EDWARD, *Prince of Wales, son of Henry VI.*
Ghost of KING HENRY VI.
A Messenger.

Guards, Halberdiers, Gentlemen, Lords, Citizens, Attendants, Soldiers.

RICHARD THE THIRD

ACT I

SCENE I

Enter RICHARD, *Duke of Gloucester, solus.*

Rich. Now is the winter of our discontent
Made glorious summer by this son of York;
And all the clouds that lour'd upon our House
In the deep bosom of the ocean buried.
Now are our brows bound with victorious wreaths,   5
Our bruised arms hung up for monuments,
Our stern alarums chang'd to merry meetings,
Our dreadful marches to delightful measures.

ACT I

Scene 1

ACT I SCENE I] *As* F *(Actus Primus. Scaena Prima.)*; *not in Qq.*   S.D. *Gloucester*]
F,Qq (Gloster/Q2,F; Glocester/Q1,3-5).   1. of our] *F,Q1-2;* of *Q3-6.*   2. son]
F,Qq (subst.); sun *Rowe.*   7. alarums] *F,Q2-6;* alarmes *Q1.*   8. measures]
F,Q1-3; pleasures *Q4-6.*

1. *winter*] Cf. *Astrophel and Stella* (69,
l. 7ff: 'Gone is the winter of my
miserie, / My spring appeares . . .' The
entire image is almost proverbial:
Krappe cites Claudian, *de Bello
Gothico* (ed. T. Birt, Berlin 1892,
p. 265): 'Hic celer effecit, bruma ne
longior una / Esset hiems rerum,
primis sed mensibus aestas / Temper-
iem caelo pariter belloque referret'.
Historically, Edward re-entered London on 21 May 1471, the same day
that Henry VI's body was brought
through London from the Tower (see
sc. ii).

2. *son*] Despite *QF* concurrence in
the spelling, virtually all eds (though

not Evans) have followed Rowe's
emendation 'sun' to give point to the
pun: Edward IV assumed the device
of a sun as his emblem in consequence
of the vision of three suns which
appeared to him during the battle of
Mortimer's Cross (see *3H6*, II.i.21–
40).

3. *House*] of York.

6. *bruised arms*] Cf. *Lucr.*, l. 110.

8–13.] The images here of martial
music and activity in contrast with
amorous music and peace-time behaviour are suggested in Lyly's
Campaspe, especially II.ii. See Introduction, pp. 95–6. Also cf. *Ven.*, ll.
103–8.

Grim-visag'd War hath smooth'd his wrinkled front:
And now, instead of mounting barbed steeds   10
To fright the souls of fearful adversaries,
He capers nimbly in a lady's chamber,
To the lascivious pleasing of a lute.
But I, that am not shap'd for sportive tricks,
Nor made to court an amorous looking-glass;   15
I, that am rudely stamp'd, and want love's majesty
To strut before a wanton ambling nymph:
I, that am curtail'd of this fair proportion,
Cheated of feature by dissembling Nature,
Deform'd, unfinish'd, sent before my time   20
Into this breathing world scarce half made up—
And that so lamely and unfashionable
That dogs bark at me, as I halt by them—
Why, I, in this weak piping time of peace,
Have no delight to pass away the time,   25
Unless to spy my shadow in the sun,

13. lute] *F;* loue *Qq.*   14. shap'd for] *F;* shapte for *Q1–3;* sharpe for *Q4–5;* sharpe of *Q6.*   15. Nor] *F,Q1,3–6;* Not *Q2.*   21. scarce half] *F,Q1–2;* halfe *Q3–6.*   26. spy] *Qq;* see *F.*

9. *Grim-visag'd War*] Cf. Sackville's Induction to 'Buckingham', ll. 386–7: 'Warre . . . With visage grym' (*Mirror,* p. 311).

10. *barbed*] armed for war: OED barbed *ppl.a.*[2]

12–13. *capers . . . lute*] Cf. *2 Tamburlaine,* I.iii.28–31: '. . . they are too dainty for the wars. / Their fingers made to quaver on a Lute, / Their armes to hang about a Ladies necke: / Their legs to dance and caper in the aire'.

14. *sportive tricks*] sexual games. See OED sportive *a.2.*

18. *proportion*] This word introduces a chain of images continued in 'dissembling Nature', 'unfinish'd', 'unfashionable', and 'deformity' which depend on the Elizabethan concept of harmony in Nature expressing fitness and aptness to the divine plan. Richard's lack of proper proportions, that is his irregularity

of appearance, his ugliness, his deformity, are outward and visible signs of the disharmony and viciousness of his spirit. Very plausibly, he presents them as the *causes* of his villainy, but we ought not to be fooled. See also Introduction, pp. 101–6.

20.] Cf. *3H6,* v.vi.51.

22. *lamely and unfashionable*] Idiom of the extended suffix. See Abbott §397.

24. *piping*] OED *ppl.a.*1b: Characterized by piping, the music of the pastoral pipe (in contrast to martial music), citing this example. A musical thread of metaphor runs through the speech, including besides this, the pleasing of the lute, and the grisly descant that Richard will sing to such harmonies.

26. *spy*] NCS rightly says that 'spy' 'gives just the sense of stealthy observation which the context de-

And descant on mine own deformity.
And therefore, since I cannot prove a lover
To entertain these fair well-spoken days,
I am determined to prove a villain,   30
And hate the idle pleasures of these days.
Plots have I laid, inductions dangerous,
By drunken prophecies, libels, and dreams,
To set my brother Clarence and the King
In deadly hate, the one against the other: 35
And if King Edward be as true and just
As I am subtle, false, and treacherous,
This day should Clarence closely be mew'd up
About a prophecy, which says that 'G'
Of Edward's heirs the murderer shall be—   40
Dive, thoughts, down to my soul: here Clarence comes.

Enter CLARENCE *and* BRAKENBURY, *with a guard of* Men.

Brother, good day; what means this armed guard

40. murderer] *F,Q 3–6* (murtherer); murtherers *Q 1–2.*   41.] *As F; . . .* my
soule/Heere *Qq.*   41. S.D. *and Brakenbury*] *F; not in Qq.*   with a guard of
Men] *Qq; guarded / F.*   42. day] *F;* dayes *Qq.*

mands' (p. 153); it also offers a
mechanism for the appearance of
'see' in F: if the p in 'spie' were
omitted by the compositor, the
proof-corrector would be likely to
think 'sie' a misprint for 'see'.
Against this, it must be noted that
Hinman found no press-corrections
in this forme, and that the omission
of the p is not a very likely compositorial error. It is perhaps more
probable that a genuine variant
existed in the MS., and if so we may
concur with NCS in thinking 'spy' a
worthwhile authorial change. See
also I.i.133.

27. *descant*] enlarge upon a theme:
OED *v.* 2, by figurative extension
from meaning 1, to sing a melody
against a fixed harmony.

30. *determined*] Richard means he is
resolved, has made up his mind, to
be a villain. But, as D. S. Berkeley
(*SQ* 14 (1963), pp. 483–4) points out,

the verb can be read in the passive
voice, implying that Richard's role
has been determined by providence.
OED determine *v.* III.14b. See also
Jennifer Strauss, '*Determined to prove a
villain*: Character, action and irony
in *Richard III*', *Komos* 1 (1967), pp.
115–20.

32. *inductions*] OED 3c: the initial
step in any undertaking (citing this
line).

38. *mew'd up*] confined: a term
from hawking: OED mew *v.*² 3b.
Cf. l.132.

39–40.] See ll. 55–9.

41. S.D. *Brakenbury*] Sir Robert
Brakenbury was not appointed Constable of the Tower until 1483, five
years after Clarence's death. He was
killed at Bosworth (v.v.14).

42. *Brother* . . .] Cf. Atreus' hypocritical greeting to his brother:
Seneca, *Thyestes*, ll. 508–9.

That waits upon your Grace?

Cla.   His Majesty,
Tend'ring my person's safety, hath appointed
This conduct to convey me to the Tower.   45

Rich. Upon what cause?

Cla.   Because my name is George.

Rich. Alack, my lord, that fault is none of yours:
He should for that commit your godfathers.
O, belike his Majesty hath some intent
That you should be new-christen'd in the Tower.   50
But what's the matter, Clarence, may I know?

Cla. Yea, Richard, when I know: for I protest
As yet I do not. But, as I can learn,
He hearkens after prophecies and dreams,
And from the cross-row plucks the letter G;   55
And says a wizard told him that by 'G'
His issue disinherited should be.
And for my name of George begins with G,
It follows in his thought that I am he.
These, as I learn, and such like toys as these,   60
Have mov'd his Highness to commit me now.

43–5.] *As Pope; . . . grace? / His . . . appointed / This . . . tower.* Qq; *. . . Grace? / His . . . safety, / Hath . . . Tower* F.   44. Tend'ring] *F; tendering* Qq.   45. the Tower] Qq; *th'Tower* F.   46.] *As Var. '93; . . . cause? / Because F,Qq.*   48. godfathers] *F,Q1–3; good fathers Q4–6.*   50. should be] *F; shalbe Q1; shall be Q2–6.*   51. what's] *F; whats Q1–2; what is Q3–6.*   52. I know] *F,Q1–5; I doe know Q6.*   for] Qq; *but* F.   59. follows] *F,Q1–4,6; fellowes Q5.*   61. Have] Qq; *Hath* F.

44. *Tend'ring*] being solicitous of. From OED tender *v.*² 3a.

45. *the Tower*] F's 'th'Tower' is unmetrical, caused by the short measure of the F composing-stick, and the compositor's evident desire to avoid a turn-under.

48–50.] See Introduction, pp. 85–6.

52. *for*] F 'but' may have been caught by the compositor from the following line.

54. *prophecies*] Cf. *1 Tamburlaine*, I.i.41: 'misled by dreaming prophesies'.

55–9.] Cf. *Mirror*, 'Clarence', ll. 181–4: 'A prophecy was found,

which sayd a G, / Of Edwardes children should destruccion be. / Me to be G, because my name was George / My brother thought, and therfore did me hate.'

55. *cross-row*] See OED: the alphabet, so called because formerly the Maltese cross was prefixed to it.

60. *toys*] trifles: OED toy *sb.4*.

61. *Have*] Third-person plural in -th, such as F's 'Hath', is to be found elsewhere in Shakespeare: see Franz, §156; this leads NCS to retain the F form as do Evans and NPS. Franz does not cite this example, and in any event the Q reading, followed here,

Rich. Why, this it is, when men are rul'd by women:
   'Tis not the King that sends you to the Tower;
   My Lady Grey, his wife, Clarence, 'tis she
   That tempers him to this extremity.   65
   Was it not she, and that good man of worship,
   Anthony Woodeville, her brother there,
   That made him send Lord Hastings to the Tower,
   From whence this present day he is deliver'd?
   We are not safe, Clarence, we are not safe!   70
Cla. By heaven, I think there is no man secure,
   But the Queen's kindred, and night-walking heralds
   That trudge betwixt the King and Mistress Shore.

---

65. tempers] *Q1*; tempts *Q2,4–6,F*; temps *Q3*.   extremity] *Qq*; harsh extremity *F*.   67. Woodeville] *Capell*; Wooduile *Qq*; Woodeulle *F*.   71. secure] *F*; is securde *Q1–3*; securde *Q4–6* (*subst.*)

---

has the advantage of not looking incorrect in a modernized text.

64. *Lady Grey*] For Edward's impolitic and passionate infatuation with Elizabeth Grey, see *3H6*, III.ii ff. Her first husband, Sir John Grey, was killed at the battle of St Albans in 1461. Although not a commoner by birth (her father was Sir Richard Woodville, Earl Rivers) her rank was hardly equal to the King's, and the hostility his preference for her occasioned in his brothers is a powerful motivating force which spills over from *3H6* into *R3*. This hostility is a strong undercurrent throughout the present scene, marked by Richard's contemptuous use of her first married name here.

65. *tempers*] Q1 is patently correct; the image is developed from *Mirror*, 'Clarence', ll.341–2: 'This made [Richard] plye the while the waxe was soft, / To find a meane to bring me to an ende' (p. 232); the meaning is to control, direct, guide, or govern: OED *v.*II.7. Q2's error 'tempts' was taken over into the subsequent Qq; the irregular metre thus exposed led F to mend by adding 'harsh' to 'extremity', thus making plausible sense of the line and persuading

Rowe, Capell, Malone, and others to follow it.

67. *Woodeville*] F's 'Woodeulle' is a bungled attempt to indicate that the name is pronounced as a trisyllable. Anthony Woodeville, Earl Rivers, was born in *c.*1442 and executed in 1483.

71. *secure*] The additional verb of the Q reading seems intrusive, though it is retained by Evans; NCS prefers Capell's 'There's no man is secure'.

72. *night-walking*] Slang for thievery. See *John*, I.i.172, and Honigmann's note in the New Arden edn. OED does not record 'night-walker' = prostitute until 1670, though of course it may have been in use earlier.

73. *Mistress Shore*] This lady, the most famous absentee from the dramatis personæ in the play, was actually named Elizabeth. (See Nicolas Barker, *Etoniana*, No. 125, and *TLS*, 7 July, 1972.) She was daughter of John Lambert, mercer, and sheriff of London in 1460–1; she married William Shore but petitioned for annulment of the marriage on the grounds of his impotence. She subsequently married Thomas Lynom

Heard you not what an humble suppliant
Lord Hastings was to her, for his delivery?   75

Rich. Humbly complaining to her deity
Got my Lord Chamberlain his liberty.
I'll tell you what: I think it is our way,
If we will keep in favour with the King,
To be her men, and wear her livery.   80
The jealous o'er-worn widow and herself,
Since that our brother dubb'd them gentlewomen,
Are mighty gossips in our monarchy.

Brak. I beseech your Graces both to pardon me:
His Majesty hath straitly given in charge   85

---

74. you] *F;* ye *Qq.*   75. was to her, for his] *Qq;* was, for her *F;* was, for his
F4, Rowe.   76. Humbly] *F,Q1–4;* Humble *Q5–6.*   83. our] *F;* this *Qq.*
84. I beseech] *F,Qq;* I beg *Pope;* Beseech *Dyce.*

(Richard III's solicitor-general) and survived until about 1527. Her scandalous life made her a favourite subject of moralistic literary treatments, which (as noted in the Introduction, pp. 96–7) Shakespeare elected to omit and ignore.

75. *was to her, for his*] F's 'was, for her' is inadequate: if 'delivery of himself' is to be understood, the phrase is perplexing — indeed, comically ambiguous — for stage use. It is more likely to be an error; most rightly prefer the extra-metrical, but intelligible, Q version.

77. *Lord Chamberlain*] William Hastings was elevated to the barony and to this position in 1461.

80. *her*] Mistress Shore's. Naturally, she had no livery, so the comment is another jibe at Edward's propensity for low-born women.

81. *widow*] i.e. Queen Elizabeth; 'herself' is Mistress Shore.

82. *that*] As a conjunctional affix: see Abbott §287.

dubb'd] Parodistic, in reference to the ceremony of knighthood. The tone throughout the scene is strongly misogynistic.

83. *gossips*] Rather obscure. Perhaps used in the sense 'godparents'

(OED *sb.* 1a) in view of the joke about Clarence's being new-christen'd in the Tower (l. 50): the Queen and Elizabeth Shore are seen as the monstrous new godparents who send the people they sponsor to a hideous baptism in the Tower. But if so Clarence could not be expected to understand the joke; nor is it possible to take the word in its other common sense of crony (OED *sb.*2.) since Richard rightly remarks that the Queen was jealous of Mistress Shore. Perhaps OED sense 3 is most apt: one who delights in idle talk, a tattler. The idle chatter of the Queen and Mistress Shore has the serious effect of the imprisonment of important men.

our] F's reading is probably right, since Richard and Clarence habitually think of themselves as participators in the Yorkist monarchy. Richard in particular is already casting his toils about the throne, and has begun to regard it with a proprietorial eye. An ironical emphasis: 'our brother' (l. 82) / 'our monarchy' is to be inferred.

84. *I beseech*] Dyce's emendation, adopted by NCS, has nothing beyond an over-precise concern with metre to recommend it.

That no man shall have private conference—
Of what degree soever—with his brother.
Rich. Even so; and please your worship, Brakenbury,
You may partake of any thing we say.
We speak no treason, man: we say the King   90
Is wise and virtuous, and his noble Queen
Well struck in years, fair, and not jealous.
We say that Shore's wife hath a pretty foot,
A cherry lip, a bonny eye, a passing pleasing tongue,
And that the Queen's kindred are made gentlefolks.   95
How say you, sir? Can you deny all this?
Brak. With this, my lord, myself have nought to do.
Rich. Naught with Mistress Shore? I tell thee, fellow,
He that doth naught with her (excepting one)
Were best to do it secretly, alone.   100

87. his] *Qq;* your *F.*   92. jealous] *Qq;* iealious *F.*   95. kindred] *F,Qq;*
kin *Marshall.*   97. nought] *F,Q 1,6;* naught *Q 2–5.*   98–100.] *As Qq;* . . .
Shore? / . . . her / . . . alone. *F.*   98. Naught with] *This edn; conj. H. F.
Brooks (privately);* Naught to do with *F,Qq.*   100. to] *F;* he *Qq.*

87. *degree*] rank. Brakenbury is politely explaining that his orders allow of no exceptions, not even for the Duke of Gloucester.

his] No bibliographical reason exists for preferring the Q reading here: only the feeling that 'his brother' preserves the official sense of the King's command appositely in Brakenbury's mouth.

92. *Well struck*] Normally = advanced in age (see OED stricken A. *pa.pple.*). Yet here Richard makes the phrase imply something like 'mature without being elderly', and in fact Queen Elizabeth was aged about 46 at Edward's death. As Thompson remarked, 'All Richard's remarks are coloured by insinuation' in this passage; indeed they are informed by witty malice.

jealous] NCS observes that the metre requires a trisyllable; and it is true that the word was often so pronounced, and sometimes so spelled, but it is a point of doubtful weight in

a passage abounding in irregular metre.

95. *kindred*] NCS adopts Marshall's emendation, again out of over-scrupulous care for metre.

97. *nought*] Richard's play on nought (= nothing) / naught (= naughty) is indicated by the spelling in F, though of course it requires a different exposition on stage to make the pun clear. Hall (*Edward V*, fol. xviʳ) observes Mistress Shore was 'naught of her body'.

98–104.] One of the most difficult passages, textually, in the early part of the play. The disturbance of the rhythm and the unmetrical lines make it imperative to emend. The form here was suggested by Harold Brooks, who points out that the suggestion of rhyme in ll. 99–100 is evidence that the lines are verse. It is not impossible however to speculate that the persistent growth of vulgarity in Richard's manner during the colloquy with Brakenbury has

Brak. What one, my lord?

Rich. Her husband, knave! Wouldst thou betray me?

Brak. I do beseech your Grace to pardon me, and withal
　　Forbear your conference with the noble Duke.

Cla. We know thy charge, Brakenbury, and will obey.　105

Rich. We are the Queen's abjects, and must obey.
　　Brother, farewell. I will unto the King,
　　And whatso'er you will employ me in—
　　Were it to call King Edward's widow 'sister'—
　　I will perform it to enfranchise you.　　　　　110
　　Meantime, this deep disgrace in brotherhood
　　Touches me deeper than you can imagine.

[Embraces Clarence, weeping.]

Cla. I know it pleaseth neither of us well.

Rich. Well, your imprisonment shall not be long:
　　I will deliver you, or else lie for you.　　　115
　　Meantime, have patience.

101-2.] *Q2–6,F; not in Q1.*   103-4.] *As Capell; . . . Grace / . . . forbeare /
. . . Duke. F; . . . forbeare / . . . Duke. Qq.*   103. and withal] *F,Qq; and to
Pope; not in NCS.*   108. whatso'er] *F;* whatsoeuer *Qq.*   112. deeper] *F,Qq;*
nearer *NCS.*   112. S.D.] *This edn; not in F,Qq.*   115. or else] *F;* or *Qq;*
else *NCS.*

finally dropped this passage into
prose. There is no sign of any attempt
to 'stretch' the copy to fill the forme
in F, so it must be concluded that the
difficulties of the passage arose in the
copy.

106. *abjects*] A neologism from
abjection (OED 2) to parallel
'subjects'. Cf. *Campaspe*, I.i.93–4:
'not be as abjects of warre but as
subjects of Alexander'; here however
the word has a different sense (OED
abject B. *sb.*); cf. also *H8*, I.i.127,
where the phrase 'abject object'
occurs. Clearly, Richard implies that
the State exists in abject submission
to the Queen.

109. *widow*] i.e. the widow Edward
married. To raise her mentally to the
status of sister(-in-law) is represented
by Richard as a superhuman feat of
patience and humility.

112. *deeper*] NCS holds that this
word echoes 'deep' in l. 111 and thus,
suspecting it to be a contamination,
replaces it with a commoner Shakespearean idiom. The repetition does
not seem so obviously erroneous as to
warrant the emendation.

112. S.D.] Instructions for Richard's behaviour here are to be found
in I.iv.234–6, sufficiently specific, and
in character, to require an introduced
prescriptive direction. The ability to
provide crocodile tears on demand is
a characteristic of the Vice: see
Spivack, pp. 397–8. Cf. I.ii.157 and
Introduction, p. 100.

115. *lie for*] Carefully ambiguous:
to Clarence it means 'take your place';
Richard of course means 'tell lies
about you'. Equivocation is the chief
characteristic of the Vice. See
III.i.83 and Introduction, pp. 99–101.

Cla.   I must, perforce. Farewell.
                  Exeunt Clarence [, *Brakenbury and guard*].
Rich. Go, tread the path that thou shalt ne'er return;
        Simple, plain Clarence, I do love thee so
        That I will shortly send thy soul to Heaven—
        If Heaven will take the present at our hands.   120
        But who comes here? The new-deliver'd Hastings?

                  Enter LORD HASTINGS.

Hast. Good time of day unto my gracious lord.
Rich. As much unto my good Lord Chamberlain:
        Well are you welcome to the open air.
        How hath your lordship brook'd imprisonment?   125
Hast. With patience, noble lord, as prisoners must;
        But I shall live, my lord, to give them thanks
        That were the cause of my imprisonment.
Rich. No doubt, no doubt; and so shall Clarence too:
        For they that were your enemies are his,   130
        And have prevail'd as much on him, as you.
Hast. More pity that the eagles should be mew'd,
        While kites and buzzards prey at liberty.
Rich. What news abroad?

116. S.D.] *Capell; Exit Clar*/ *F,Qq.*   117. ne'er] *F;* nere *Q1,3–6;* neare *Q2.*
121. new-deliver'd] *Pope;* new deliuered *F,Qq.*   124. the] *Q1–2;* this *Q–6,3F.*
132. eagles] *F;* Eagle *Qq.*   133. While] *Qq;* Whiles *F.*   kites] *F,Qq* (keihts
Q1; kights *Q2*).   buzzards] *F,Qq* (Buzards *F;* bussards *Q1–2;* buzars *Q3–5*).
prey] *Qq;* play *F.*

116. *patience . . . perforce*] Proverbial:
see Tilley P111. Frequently used at
this time: see (for instance) *Spanish
Tragedy,* III.ix.12–13; *I Tamburlaine,*
I.ii.259.

130. *enemies*] Richard's strategy
throughout the first two acts is to
align associates to himself by insinuating that the Queen and her relatives
are their common enemies.

132. *eagles*] The discussion concerns
both Hastings and Clarence, so the
plural is correct.

mew'd] See l. 38.

133. *prey*] The Q reading is clearly
correct, and the F surely is the result
of a compositor's error. NCS, p. 153,

advances the theory of an error compounded by mistaken proofing, but
there are no press-corrections in this
forme, and a simple misreading on
the compositor's part is a more
plausible explanation.

134–43.] Mary Gross, *PBSA* (1977),
74–5, would assign l. 134 to Hastings, ll. 135–7 to Richard, l. 138 to
Hastings, ll. 139–40 to Richard,
ll. 141–2 to Hastings, l. 143 to Richard.
This on the grounds that Hastings,
new-deliver'd from prison, is in a
worse position than Richard to
know these things (and that Saint
Paul is Richard's usual oath, *q.v.* l.
138 n.). She overlooks that Richard is

Hast. No news so bad abroad, as this at home: 135
 The King is sickly, weak and melancholy,
 And his physicians fear him mightily.
Rich. Now by Saint John, that news is bad indeed.
 O, he hath kept an evil diet long,
 And over-much consum'd his royal person: 140
 'Tis very grievous to be thought upon.
 Where is he, in his bed?
Hast. He is.
Rich. Go you before, and I will follow you.   *Exit Hastings.*
 He cannot live, I hope, and must not die   145
 Till George be pack'd with post-horse up to Heaven.
 I'll in to urge his hatred more to Clarence,
 With lies well-steel'd with weighty arguments;
 And if I fail not in my deep intent,
 Clarence hath not another day to live: 150
 Which done, God take King Edward to his mercy,
 And leave the world for me to bustle in.
 For then I'll marry Warwick's youngest daughter—

138. Saint John] *F* (S. Iohn); Saint Paul *Qq.* that] *F;* this *Qq* 142.
Where] *F;* What *Qq.*

playing his usual role of innocent/ ignorant bystander here, which he also plays to great effect in 1.iii. Besides, re-arranging the lines costs us the utterly Vice-like irony of 138–41. Gross offers no plausible mechanism to account for the compound error, nor does she acknowledge the oddity that the F corrector should have changed two substantive readings (John, Where) in the passage while not noticing that the Q speech-prefixes were wrong. The argument is far too weak to carry conviction.

137. *fear him*] Preposition omitted after some transitive verbs (= fear for him): Abbott §200. That his doctors despaired of his recovery is a point made about Edward in Holinshed (see p. 708/2), but not in Hall.

138. *Saint John*] As various eds have remarked, Q gives Richard his habitual oath, and yet is for that reason suspect: it is the sort of

memorial error even a good actor is prone to.

140. *consum'd*] Richard is here playing his role of puritan (see Introduction, pp. 59–60); the reference is to Edward's sexual excesses.

142. *Where*] Q's version makes the line into an exclamation: 'What! is he in his bed!'; F's is a request for information more in line with the questions Richard has been asking Hastings, and with the implications of l.144 ensuing.

146. *post-horse*] Cf. *Leir:* 'Why, he must go along with you to heaven . . . he must needs ride Poste' [F4ʳ]. Possibly an allusion to the ascent of Elijah is intended: 2 Kings, ii.11.

152. *bustle*] Richard's animation, his fondness for vigorous activity, is central to his nature.

153. *Warwick*] the Earl of Warwick, the 'King-maker'. Anne Neville was the younger of two daughters (in

What though I kill'd her husband and her father?
The readiest way to make the wench amends   155
Is to become her husband, and her father:
The which will I, not all so much for love
As for another secret close intent,
By marrying her which I must reach unto.
But yet I run before my horse to market: 160
Clarence still breathes, Edward still lives and reigns;
When they are gone, then must I count my gains.   *Exit.*

SCENE II

Enter the corse of HENRY THE SIXTH *with* Halberds *to guard it,*
LADY ANNE *being the mourner* [, *attended by* TRESSEL, BERKELEY
and other Gentlemen].

Anne. Set down, set down your honourable load
(If honour may be shrouded in a hearse)

Scene 11

SCENE II] *Capell; Scena Secunda | F; not in Qq.*   S.D.] *Enter the Coarse of Henrie
the sixt with Halberds to guard it, Lady Anne being the Mourner| F; Enter Lady Anne
with the hearse of Harry the 6 | Qq.*   1. Set . . . set] *F,Q1,3–6;* Sit . . . sit *Q2.*
load] *F;* lo *Q1;* lord *Q2–6 (subst.)*

3H6 she is wrongly called the eldest
daughter) and in fact she was never
married to Prince Edward, Henry
VI's son, though she was betrothed
to him in 1470.

154. *husband, and her father*] See
previous note: Prince Edward was
not her husband, and Richard was
not solely responsible for his death
(see *3H6*, v.v); 'father' means
father-in-law, i.e. Henry VI.

157–8.] Richard's motives here are
as obscure as his successor Iago's. Cf.
Oth., II.i.291 ff.: 'Now I do love her
too, / Not out of absolute lust (though
peradventure / I stand accomptant
for as great a sin), / But partly led to
diet my revenge . . .' See also Introduction, p. 101.

160. *I run . . . market*] Proverbial:
Tilley M649.

Scene 11

S.D.] Capell usefully added 'born
in an open Coffin, and slenderly
attended' to 'Henry the Sixth'. Like
Ophelia, Henry is being awarded
only maimed rites, and interred, if
not in hugger-mugger, then with as
little official remark as possible, and
Lady Anne is defying censure by her
public display of grief. Sprague has
remarked that in the 19th and early
20th centuries the scene was so far
misunderstood as to be turned into
an immense ceremonial, with a
funeral procession numbering 70 or
80 (see Introduction, pp. 70–1). This
would make the ensuing wooing-
scene absurd instead of merely outrageous: Richard elects to woo Lady
Anne in public, but not in the context

Whilst I awhile obsequiously lament
Th'untimely fall of virtuous Lancaster.
Poor key-cold Figure of a holy king,   5
Pale ashes of the House of Lancaster,
Thou bloodless remnant of that royal blood:
Be it lawful that I invocate thy ghost
To hear the lamentations of poor Anne,
Wife to thy Edward, to thy slaughter'd son,   10
Stabb'd by the selfsame hand that made these wounds.
Lo, in these windows that let forth thy life
I pour the helpless balm of my poor eyes.
O, cursed be the hand that made these holes;
Cursed the heart that had the heart to do it;   15

5. key-cold] *F,Q6;* kei-cold *Q1–5.*   11. hand] *F;* hands *Qq.*   wounds] *F;* holes *Qq.*   12. these] *F;* those *Qq.*   13. pour] *all edns;* powre *F,Q1–5;* poure *Q6.*   14. O, cursed ... holes] *F;* Curst ... fatall holes *Qq.*   these] *F,Q1–2;* the *Q3–6.*   15. Cursed] *F;* Curst be *Qq.*

of a vast procession. Q's word 'hearse' does not imply a wheeled conveyance, but a litter with a coffin. F's 'Halberds' is expanded by some eds to 'Gentlemen with halberds', but gentlemen wore swords, and did not carry halberds. Tressel and Berkeley are named by Anne at l. 225, but, as they do not carry the litter, it may be assumed that four other gentlemen (addressed by Richard as 'sirs' in l. 229) are needed as pall-bearers; the halberdiers, encumbered with their weapons, could hardly carry the bier. Thus the total procession could not number less than about nine including Lady Anne; this seems about right.

3. *obsequiously*] in the manner of a mourner: OED b, citing this example.

4. *virtuous Lancaster*] One meaning is Henry VI, whose piety was a by-word. But Anne also identifies with the fall of the House of Lancaster, from her close association with it.

5. *key-cold*] Proverbial: Tilley K23. Recently used in *Parts Added*, 'Nennius', l. 63: 'in performance, waxe

as key full colde' (p. 208). Used again in *Lucr.*, l. 1774.

Figure] Capitalized to suggest the link with the theory of Figuralism, as discussed by Auerbach, *Mimesis* (Princeton, 1953), *passim.* See Introduction, p. 102. Also see OED figure *sb.*II.12.

8. *lawful*] Whitaker, p. 80: 'Anne is using contemporary controversy between Protestants and Catholics over the invocation of saints as a way to call Henry a saint, and the implied Protestant reluctance only heightens the compulsion suggested and therefore the compliment.' See Article 22 in the *BCP.*

11. *hand*] It is Richard who is being cursed, so F's singular is correct.

wounds] Q's 'holes' is caught from l.14.

14. *cursed*] The rather more formal disyllable of F more aptly suits the context of Lady Anne's ritual curse than Q's blunter monosyllable, especially when that requires an additional adjective ('fatall') and verb ('be') to sustain the metre.

Cursed the blood that let this blood from hence.
More direful hap betide that hated wretch
That makes us wretched by the death of thee
Than I can wish to adders, spiders, toads,
Or any creeping venom'd thing that lives.   20
If ever he have child, abortive be it:
Prodigious, and untimely brought to light,
Whose ugly and unnatural aspect
May fright the hopeful mother at the view,
And that be heir to his unhappiness.   25
If ever he have wife, let her be made ⌐
More miserable by the death of him ⌐

16.] F; *not in* Qq.   19. adders] Qq; Wolues, to F.   25.] F; *not in* Qq
26. made] F,Q1-5; mad: Q6.   27. More] F; As Qq.

16.] The omission from Q of this
line is most readily explained as eye-
skip on the compositor's part. Walker
(p. 32) conjectures that the line
should have preceded l.15 but that
the compositor misread the signs and
inserted it in the wrong place. From a
rhetorical point of view this scarcely
seems sufficiently self-evident to justify
emendation.

17. *hap*] OED sb.[1] 1: chance or
fortune.

18. *thee*] Henry VI.

19. *adders*] Opinion has been
divided among eds here, since both
Q and F versions are satisfactory.
On the whole there is a feeling that
while Q is preferable from a literary
standpoint, F, as the text of higher
authority, ought to be retained.
Could 'adders' have originated with
an actor? Possibly, but if so it would
have been a deliberate change rather
than a memorial slip. Is it rather one
of the signs that the Q version is
based on a later state of the play than
the F, that Shakespeare himself
altered the word? Very likely, in
view of *Cym.*, IV.ii.90-1: 'Were it
Toad, or Adder, Spider, / 'Twould
move me sooner'. That both words
originated in Shakespeare's mind is
suggested by *3H6*, I.iv.111-12: 'She-
wolf of France, but worse than wolves

of France, / Whose tongue more
poisons than the adder's tooth!' If
both are Shakespearean, then 'adders'
is preferable from a literary, and,
arguably, from a textual, point of
view. (See also Introduction, pp.
47-8.)

21. *abortive*] None of the senses in
OED quite match the intention, but
see abortion 3: the imperfect offspring of an untimely birth, or any
dwarfed or misshapen product of
generation. This sense is confirmed
by the next two lines.

22. *Prodigious*] portending evil
because abnormal or monstrous in
appearance (a blend of OED senses
1 and 2).

23. *unnatural aspect*] Continues the
imagery of portents of the previous
two lines. Unwittingly(?) Anne is
describing Richard's own birth: see
the references at IV.iv.163 ff. and
elsewhere.

25.] Patrick (p. 107) observes that
this line must have been omitted by
the actor's oversight, since it has the
key function of returning the focus
of the curse to Richard. It means:
'let this monstrous birth be the sole
consequence of Richard's evil-doing'
(OED unhappiness 2).

27-8. *More . . . Than*] See Appendix
II.

Than I am made by my young lord, and thee.
Come now towards Chertsey with your holy load,
Taken from Paul's to be interred there;   30
And still, as you are weary of the weight,
Rest you, while I lament King Henry's corse.

Enter RICHARD.

Rich. Stay, you that bear the corse, and set it down.
Anne. What black magician conjures up this fiend
    To stop devoted charitable deeds?   35
Rich. Villains! set down the corse or by Saint Paul
    I'll make a corse of him that disobeys!
Halberdier. My lord, stand back and let the coffin pass.
Rich. Unmanner'd dog, stand thou when I command!
    Advance thy halberd higher than my breast,   40
    Or by Saint Paul I'll strike thee to my foot,
    And spurn upon thee, beggar, for thy boldness.
Anne. What, do you tremble? Are you all afraid?
    Alas, I blame you not, for you are mortal,
    And mortal eyes cannot endure the devil.   45
    Avaunt, thou dreadful minister of hell!
    Thou hadst but power over his mortal body:
    His soul thou canst not have; therefore begone.
Rich. Sweet saint, for charity be not so curst.

28. Than] *F;* As *Qq.*   young] *F;* poore *Qq.*   29. Chertsey] *F,Q 1–5;*
Chertley *Q 6.*   31. weary] *F,Q 1–2;* awearie *Q 3;* a wearie *Q 4–6.*   the]
Qq; this *F.*   32. while] *Pope;* whiles *F,Qq.*   32. S.D.] *F; Enter Glocester Qq.*
36. Villains] *F;* Villaine *Qq.*   38. *Halberdier*] *This edn; Gent./Qq,F.*   My
lord,] *F,Q 1–5; not in Q 6.*   39.] *As Qq;* . . . Dogge, / Stand'st *F.*   stand]
Qq; stand'st *F.*   46. dreadful] *F,Q 1–5;* fearefull *Q 6.*

    29. *Chertsey*] On the Thames, near
Staines, site of a famous abbey.

    31. *the*] There seems no need for
F's demonstrative 'this'; perhaps a
compositor-error. The line is a little
obscure anyway; 'Still' means constantly (Abbott §69): i.e. whenever
you are tired, rest again.

    38. *Halberdier*] It seems clear that
the speaker of this line is the same as
the man Richard retorts upon: if so,
he is carrying a halberd, and is not
one of the gentlemen with the coffin.

    43–5.] Cf. Seneca, *Hercules Furens*,
ll. 269 ff.: 'quo reccidistis? tremitis
ignavum exulem, / suis carentem
finibus, nostris gravem'.

    46. *minister of hell*] This is the first
time of many in the play when
Richard's diabolical associations are
emphasized. Cf. IV.iv. 71–3 for the
most specific instance.

    47–8.] Cf. Matthew, x. 28 (Noble
p. 131].

    49. *curst*] The usual meaning of
'shrewish' (OED *ppl.a.*4) is present,

Anne. Foul devil, for God's sake hence, and trouble us not;   50
  For thou hast made the happy earth thy hell,
  Fill'd it with cursing cries and deep exclaims.
  If thou delight to view thy heinous deeds,
  Behold this pattern of thy butcheries.
  O gentlemen! See, see dead Henry's wounds   55
  Open their congeal'd mouths and bleed afresh.
  Blush, blush, thou lump of foul deformity,
  For 'tis thy presence that exhales this blood
  From cold and empty veins where no blood dwells:
  Thy deed inhuman and unnatural   60
  Provokes this deluge most unnatural.
  O God! which this blood mad'st, revenge his death;
  O earth! which this blood drink'st, revenge his death;
  Either heav'n with lightning strike the murderer dead,
  Or earth gape open wide and eat him quick,   65
  As thou dost swallow up this good King's blood
  Which his hell-govern'd arm hath butchered.
Rich. Lady, you know no rules of charity,
  Which renders good for bad, blessings for curses.
Anne. Villain, thou know'st no law of God nor man.   70

50.] *As Qq; . . .* Diuell, / For *F.*   60. deed] *Qq;* Deeds *F.*   66. dost] *F;*
doest *Q 1-5;* didst *Q 6.*   70. no] *Qq;* nor *F.*

but Richard is also manipulating the
contrast between a 'saint' who
'curses', thereby being damned (OED
3).
  54. *pattern*] OED *sb.*6: a signal
example.
  55-6.] Cf. *Spanish Tragedy,* II.v.53-
4: 'Seest thou those wounds that yet
are bleeding fresh? / I'll not entomb
them till I have reveng'd'. The
bleeding of wounds in the presence
of the murderer was a well-established
piece of folklore; in this instance the
immediate source was Holinshed,
p. 691/1: the body 'in presence of the
beholders did bleed'. Churchill (p.
19) notes that the original source was
the Warkworth Chronicle.
  58. *exhales*] causes to flow: OED
*v.*² 1b, citing this line.
  63. *earth! which this blood drink'st*]

Cf. Genesis, iv.11 (Noble, p. 131).
Also cf. *Arden of Faversham,* sc. xvi,
4-6 (where the incident of the bleeding of the body in the presence of
murderers is not in the sources).
  65.] Various Biblical parallels are
noted by Noble, p 131, but cf.
especially *3H6,* I.i.161: 'May that
ground gape, and swallow me alive'.
Also cf. *Leir* [F3ᵛ]: 'Swear not by
hell; for that stands gaping wide, /
To swallow thee, and if thou do this
deed'.
  68-9.] Proverbial: Tilley G318, but
also probably echoed from Seneca,
Hercules Furens, ll. 362-5: 'si aeterna
semper odia mortales gerant / nec
coeptus umquam cedat ex animis
furor, / . . . / nihil relinquent bella'.
Also cf. Matthew v. 44.
  70. *no*] F's 'nor' is acceptable

No beast so fierce but knows some touch of pity.

Rich. But I know none, and therefore am no beast.

Anne. O wonderful, when devils tell the truth!

Rich. More wonderful, when angels are so angry.

    Vouchsafe, divine perfection of a woman,   75
    Of these supposed crimes, to give me leave,
    By circumstance, but to acquit myself.

Anne. Vouchsafe, diffus'd infection of a man,
    Of these known evils, but to give me leave,
    By circumstance, t'accuse thy cursed self.   80

Rich. Fairer than tongue can name thee, let me have
    Some patient leisure to excuse myself.

Anne. Fouler than heart can think thee, thou canst make
    No excuse current but to hang thyself.

Rich. By such despair I should accuse myself.   85

---

73. truth] *F,Q 2–6;* troth *Q 1.*   76. crimes] *F;* euils *Qq.*   78. a man] *Qq;*
man *F.*   79. Of] *F;* For *Qq.*   80. t'accuse] *This edn, conj. Spedding;* to
curse *Qq,F.*   83–4.] *As Qq; . . .* thee, / Thou *. . .* currant, / But *F.*

grammar, though less vehement; but it may be compositorial dittography.

71–3.] The argument here may be paraphrased: Lady Anne says that even beasts feel pity; Richard retorts (rather weakly) that this means he must be a man rather than a beast, since he does not feel pity; Lady Anne neatly caps him by implying that he must therefore be neither man nor beast, but devil.

73. *truth*] Q1's 'troth', preferred by Evans, was in 1590 not a variant reading but merely a variant spelling. The entire phrase is proverbial: Tilley D266.

76. *crimes*] The entire passage, ll. 76–80, has caused difficulty, but forms a clear rhetorical pattern. Richard offers to defend himself in legal manner ('circumstance' = circumstantially, detail by detail) against the crimes Anne alleges against him. She neatly retorts in moral and religious terms that his evils—known, not merely supposed— may be denounced against him in equal but more crushing detail.

Spedding's conjecture 'accuse' keeps the legal imagery in play. The Q1 compositor perhaps repeated 'evils' in place of 'crimes' from l. 79 (or it may have been a reporter's error) and also misread the MS. as 'to curse'.

78. *diffus'd*] spread abroad, dispersed: OED *ppl.a.*II.2. Anne sees Richard as a pestilence whose effects are spreading across England.

80. *t'accuse*] See above, l. 76 n.

84. *current*] genuine, authentic: OED *a.*5.

85. *despair*] A most important term in the play, not satisfactorily defined in its technical, theological sense in OED. It means the state in which one loses all hope of being worthy of divine forgiveness, a state so degraded that its automatic concomitant was suicide. The most celebrated close parallel in the drama is *Doctor Faustus*, v.i., l. 1725 ff., but even more important is its use later in *R3:* at v.iii.201, and in the preceding curses of the ghosts. A very full description of the state is to be found

Anne. And by despairing shalt thou stand excus'd
      For doing worthy vengeance on thyself
      That didst unworthy slaughter upon others.
Rich. Say that I slew them not?
Anne. Then say they were not slain: 90
      But dead they are, and, devilish slave, by thee.
Rich. I did not kill your husband.
Anne. Why then he is alive.
Rich. Nay he is dead, and slain by Edward's hand.
Anne. In thy foul throat thou liest: Queen Margaret saw   95
      Thy murd'rous falchion smoking in his blood,
      The which thou once didst bend against her breast,
      But that thy brothers beat aside the point.
Rich. I was provoked by her sland'rous tongue,
      That laid their guilt upon my guiltless shoulders.   100
Anne. Thou wast provoked by thy bloody mind,
      That never dream'st on aught but butcheries.
      Didst thou not kill this King?
Rich.   I grant ye, yea.
Anne. Dost grant me, hedgehog! Then God grant me too

---

86. shalt] *F;* shouldst *Qq.*   88. That] *F;* Which *Qq.*   90.] *F;* Why then
they are not dead, *Qq.*   94. hand] *Qq;* hands *F.*   95–6.] *As Qq;* . . .
Ly'st, / Queene . . . saw / Thy *F.*   96. murd'rous] *F;* bloudy *Qq.*   97.
didst] *F,Q 1,3–6;* did *Q 2.*   98. brothers] *F,Q 1–2;* brother *Q 3–6.*   99.
sland'rous] *F;* slaunderous *Qq (subst.).*   102. That . . . dream'st] *F;* Which
. . . dreamt *Qq.*   103.] *As Qq;* . . . King? / *Rich.* / *F.*   ye, yea] *NPS,*
conj. Ritson; ye *F;* yea *Q 1–2;* yee *Q 3–6.*   104.] *As Qq;* . . . Hedge-hogge, /
Then *F.*

in *Pilgrim's Progress* (Oxford, 1960,
pp. 34–5).

90.] Q's version of the line represents probable corruption by both
actor-reporter and compositor, the
latter supplying 'Why then' by eye-
skip from l. 93, and the former 'dead'
by anticipation of the next line.

94. *hand*] By analogy with l. 11 of
this scene, the singular is preferred.

95. *In . . . liest*] Proverbial: Tilley
T268.

96. *murd'rous falchion*] Q's reading
'bloudy' indicates that the word was
much in the actor's mind at this
point—thrice in two speeches. A

falchion (originally a technical name
for a certain kind of sword) by this
time meant a sword of any kind: see
OED. For the death of Prince
Edward, see *3H6,* v.v; in fact
Edward IV there struck the first
blow, and Clarence was also involved.

103. *ye, yea*] Neither Q's 'I grant
yea' nor F's 'I grant ye' seems quite
right, especially metrically; the Q 3–6
reading 'yee' may further have confused the compositor or corrector. It
seems clear that both words are
required.

104. *hedgehog*] A derisory reference
to Richard's crest, the boar.

Thou mayst be damned for that wicked deed.   105
O he was gentle, mild, and virtuous.

Rich. The better for the King of Heaven that hath him.

Anne. He is in Heaven, where thou shalt never come.

Rich. Let him thank me that holp to send him thither,
For he was fitter for that place than earth.   110

Anne. And thou unfit for any place but hell.

Rich. Yes, one place else, if you will hear me name it.

Anne. Some dungeon?

Rich. Your bed-chamber.

Anne. Ill rest betide the chamber where thou liest.   115

Rich. So will it, madam, till I lie with you.

Anne. I hope so!

Rich. I know so. But, gentle Lady Anne,
To leave this keen encounter of our wits,
And fall something into a slower method: 120
Is not the causer of the timeless deaths
Of these Plantagenets, Henry and Edward,
As blameful as the executioner?

---

107. better] *F;* fitter *Qq.*   112. you] *F,Q 1–2,6;* ye *Q 3–5.*   119. keen]
F,Q 1; kinde *Q 2–6 (subst.).*   120. something] *F;* somewhat *Qq.*   121. time-
less] *F,Q 1–3,5–6;* teem-lesse *Q 4.*

---

107. *better*] Patrick observed (p. 48) that the Q reading 'fitter' was an actor's anticipation of l. 110. Smidt's objection that l. 108 is tautological is answered by noting that he mistook the emphasis: Edward is, indeed, in Heaven. However, the matter is complicated by a close parallel from *Leir:* 'You are the fitter for the King of heaven' [F3ʳ] and 'to send us both to heaven, / Where, as I thinke, you never meane to come' [I4ʳ]. Law has demonstrated adequately that a connexion between *Leir* and *R3* exists, but in this instance that connexion may be via the actors rather than the dramatists. *Per.,* IV.i. 10, reads 'The fitter then the gods should have her'. However, on the other side, it is not possible to see l.110 as being in error and the repetition of 'fitter' seems clumsy; on the

whole it is preferable to stay with the F reading. Whitaker reminds us that Luke, ix. 62, in the A.V. reads 'fit for the kingdom of God', but all 16th-century Bibles read 'apt to'. Is it conceivable that one of the A.V. translators recollected the phrase from a theatrical visit in his nonage? And if so, the irony is cosmic that what he recollected seems to be an actor's error!

116. *till I lie with you*] Cf. Seneca, *Hercules Furens,* ll. 348–9: 'non equidem reor / fore ut recuset ac meos spernat toros'.

121. *causer*] The -er suffix to noun or verb used to signify a masculine agent: Abbott §443.

timeless] untimely, occurring prematurely: OED *a.* 1. Cf. Marlowe, *Massacre,* I.ii.46: 'And brought by murder to their timeles ends'.

Anne. Thou wast the cause, and most accurs'd effect.

Rich. Your beauty was the cause of that effect: 125
    Your beauty, that did haunt me in my sleep
    To undertake the death of all the world,
    So I might live one hour in your sweet bosom.

Anne. If I thought that, I tell thee, homicide,
    These nails should rend that beauty from my cheeks.

Rich. These eyes could not endure that beauty's wrack;   131
    You should not blemish it if I stood by.
    As all the world is cheered by the sun,
    So I by that; it is my day, my life.

Anne. Black night o'ershade thy day, and death thy life.   135

Rich. Curse not thyself, fair creature; thou art both.

Anne. I would I were, to be reveng'd on thee.

Rich. It is a quarrel most unnatural,
    To be reveng'd on him that loveth thee.

Anne. It is a quarrel just and reasonable,   140

124. wast] *F; art Qq.*   126. that] *F;* which *Qq.*   128. live one] *F;* rest one
Q 1–4; rest that *Q 5–6.*   130. rend] *Qq;* rent *F.*   my] *F,Q 1–5;* their *Q 6.*
131. not ... that] *F;* neuer ... sweet *Qq.*   132. it] *F;* them *Qq.*   133. sun]
F,Q 3–6; sonne *Q 1–2.*   135. o'ershade] *F* (ore-shade); ouershade *Q 1–5;*
ouershad *Q 6.*   136.] *As Qq; ...* Creature, / Thou *F.*   139. thee] *F;* you
Qq.

124. *effect*] Walker, with NCS, would read 'of that accursed effect', on the grounds that the line as it stands 'is clearly corrupt'. *Pace* their authority, the corruption is not clear at all: since Warburton most eds have understood 'effect' to mean 'effecter': 'executioner' (Warburton), 'effecter' (Capell), 'agent' (Marshall), etc. (OED sense 5 comes close to this.) The fact that Richard immediately uses the word in reply in its modern sense of result or consequence should hardly surprise us in a scene in which rhetorical play on words, paranomasia of all kinds, is the life of the dialogue. Lady Anne is simply saying, in response to Richard's insinuation that the responsibility for Henry's and Edward's deaths could be divided, that, on the contrary, he was both the cause and the executioner.

128. *live*] The correctness of the F verb is proved by the antithesis made with the previous line: 'To undertake the death . . . So I might live'.

129 ff.] There is a resemblance between Anne's horror-stricken reaction to Richard's claims and Hippolytus' to Phaedra's advances in Seneca's *Hippolytus*, ll. 682–4.

130.] Cf. Marlowe, *Massacre*, I.ii.102: 'Ile either rend it with my nayles to naught'.

133.] A sonneteer's cliché, most happily expressed in *Astrophel and Stella*: '*Stella*'s eyes, wont to give me my day (89); 'faire you my Sunne' (91); other examples in 96, 97, 98.

135–7.] Cf. Seneca, *Hercules Furens*, ll. 427–8, Megara's retort 'Aut tuam mortem aut meam', in particular.

140. *reasonable*] Walker conjectures 'natural', 'because the rules of the game require Anne to counter his

To be reveng'd on him that kill'd my husband.

Rich. He that bereft thee, lady, of thy husband,
Did it to help thee to a better husband.

Anne. His better doth not breathe upon the earth.

Rich. He lives that loves thee better than he could.   145

Anne. Name him.

Rich.   Plantagenet.

Anne.   Why that was he.

Rich. The selfsame name, but one of better nature.

Anne. Where is he?

Rich.   Here.   *Spits at him.*
Why dost thou spit at me?

Anne. Would it were mortal poison, for thy sake.

Rich. Never came poison from so sweet a place.   150

Anne. Never hung poison on a fouler toad.
Out of my sight! Thou dost infect mine eyes.

Rich. Thine eyes, sweet lady, have infected mine.

Anne. Would they were basilisks, to strike thee dead.

Rich. I would they were, that I might die at once;   155
For now they kill me with a living death.
Those eyes of thine from mine have drawn salt tears,

---

141. kill'd] *F;* slew *Qq.*   142. thee] *Qq;* the *F.*   145. He] *F;* Go to, he
Qq.   146.] *As Steevens; . . .* him / Plantagenet. / Why *F; . . .* Plantagenet. /
Why *Qq.*   148.] *As Steevens; . . .* he? / Heere: / Why *Qq,F.*   148. S.D.]
F; Shee spitteth at him Qq.   152. mine] *F;* my *Qq.*   156. they] *F,Q1–4,6;*
thy *Q5.*

"unnatural"' (NCS, p. 176). Only
if the 'rules' are interpreted very
mechanically is there any such
requirement.

145. *He*] Q's 'Go to' is an uncommon instance of actor's padding in
Richard's part, which is freer than
most from these hypermetrical excre-
sences.

146. *Plantagenet*] A name that
echoes like an incantation throughout
the First Tetralogy. Geoffrey, Count
of Anjou and Maine, wore as his
badge a sprig of broom (*planta
genista*) from which he derived his
surname. His son became Henry II
of England, and so the ancestor
of both the Houses of York and

Lancaster.

148. S.D. *spit*] An action to avert
the influence of the 'evil eye'; see also
Tilley V28.

150–3.] Cf. *Arcadia*, I.i.13: 'there
were mine eyes infected, and at your
mouth did I drinke my poison. Yet
alas so sweete was it unto me . . .'
(p. 85).

151. *toad*] Cf. Tilley T360.

152. *eyes*] Cf. Tilley E246.

154. *basilisks*] the mythical creatures
whose gaze is mortal. Cf. *3H6*,
III.ii.187, where Richard proposes to
'slay more gazers than the basilisk'.
Also proverbial: Tilley B99.

157–68.] Cf. Seneca, *Hercules
Oetaeus*, ll. 1265–72.

Sham'd their aspects with store of childish drops;
These eyes, which never shed remorseful tear,
No, when my father York and Edward wept   160
To hear the piteous moan that Rutland made
When black-fac'd Clifford shook his sword at him;
Nor when thy warlike father, like a child
Told the sad story of my father's death,
And twenty times made pause to sob and weep,   165
That all the standers-by had wet their cheeks
Like trees bedash'd with rain. In that sad time
My manly eyes did scorn an humble tear;
And what these sorrows could not thence exhale,
Thy beauty hath, and made them blind with weeping.
I never sued to friend nor enemy: 171
My tongue could never learn sweet smoothing word;
But now thy beauty is propos'd my fee,
My proud heart sues, and prompts my tongue to speak.

She looks scornfully at him.

Teach not thy lip such scorn; for it was made   175
For kissing, lady, not for such contempt.
If thy revengeful heart cannot forgive,
Lo here I lend thee this sharp-pointed sword,
Which if thou please to hide in this true breast,

---

158. aspects] *F;* aspect *Qq.*   159–70.] *F; not in Qq.*   171. friend] *F,Q 1–5;* friends *Q6.*   172. smoothing] *F;* soothing *Qq.*   word] *F;* words *Qq.*   174. S.D.] *F; not in Qq.*   175. lip] *F;* lips *Qq.*   it was] *F;* they were *Qq.*   179. this true] *F,Q 1–2,4–6;* true this *Q3.*   breast] *F;* bosome *Qq.*

158 ff.] For Richard's stoic refusal to weep, see also *3H6*, II.i.79–86.

159–70.] For the omission of this passage from Q, see Appendix I.

159. *shed remorseful*] Omission of indefinite article following 'never' before a noun clause: Abbott §84.

166. *That*] 'So' before 'that' frequently omitted: Abbott §283.

169. *exhale*] See l. 58n.

170. *made . . . weeping*] Cf. *Tit.*, II.iv.52–3; III.i.268–9; v.iii.49.

172. *smoothing*] Cf. *Tit.*, v.ii.140: 'smooth and speak him fair'.

173. *now*] 'that' omitted after 'now': Abbott §284.

173–4. *fee . . . sues*] The imagery is from legal practice.

178–82.] Whitaker (p. 66) remarked the parallel between this passage and Seneca's *Hippolytus*, ll. 616 and 1176–77 (see also Boas, pp. 126–31), and it is re-used in *Tit.*, IV.i.81–2 and II.i.135. Another Senecan parallel is to be found in *Hercules Oetaeus*, ll. 1000–1, 1015, which in the Heywood translation read 'my breast lies bare unto my hand. Stryke, I thy gylt forgeve, . . . Th'offence I did was ment in love'.

179. *this true*] Q3's 'true this' is the first of a number of curious inversions

And let the soul forth that adoreth thee,   180
I lay it naked to the deadly stroke,
And humbly beg the death upon my knee.
            [*Kneels;*] *he lays his breast open, she offers*
                        at [*it*] *with his sword.*
Nay, do not pause, for I did kill King Henry—
But 'twas thy beauty that provoked me.
Nay, now dispatch: 'twas I that stabb'd young   185
    Edward—
But 'twas thy heavenly face that set me on.
                                    She falls the sword.
Take up the sword again, or take up me.
Anne. Arise, dissembler; though I wish thy death,   [*He rises.*]
    I will not be thy executioner.
Rich. Then bid me kill myself, and I will do it.   190
Anne. I have already.
Rich.   That was in thy rage:

181. the] *F,Q1–5;* thy *Q6.*   182. S.D.] *F;* not in *Qq.*   183. for I did kill
King Henry] *F;* twas I that kild your husband *Qq.*   185. stabb'd young
Edward] *F;* kild King Henry *Qq.*   186. S.D. She falls] *F;* Here she lets fall /
Qq.   188. S.D.] *This edn;* not in *Qq,F.*   189. thy] *F;* the *Qq.*   191.] *As
Steevens; . . .* already. / *Rich.* That *F,Qq (subst.).*   That] *F;* Tush that *Qq.*
thy] *F,Q1–2;* the *Q3–6.*

in the next few lines: see ll. 195, 199, 203. Some of these make sense: l. 199's Q3 variant 'Then never man was true' has a natural turn to it which caused the F corrector to overlook it, and so it turns up in some later editions. However, F corrects Q2's 'thou shalt' in l. 195 which survived all the other Q compositors, and 'I shall' in l. 203. The inference is that correction was being made quite conscientiously at this point: see also the corrections made at ll. 181, 189, 191, 193, 208, 209, 215. There are still some curious oversights, e.g. ll. 206, 229.

180 ff.] Cf. *Arcadia,* I.iii.3: 'in her hands the balance of his life or death did stand. I who am readie to lie under your feete . . . to loose my life at your least commandment' (pp. 368–70).

182. *the death*] 'Death after judicial sentence' (Thompson).

182. S.D.] A direction for Richard to kneel is required; Capell thought to insert it at l. 177, but later eds have not followed him. A direction to rise must also be supplied, and the logical point is at Anne's command, l. 188. The entire business with the sword was undoubtedly suggested by the almost exactly parallel directions implied in Seneca's *Hippolytus* at ll. 710–14.

183–5.] Q inverts the order of the two statements, and the inferiority of the Q version is revealed by its flat repetition of 'twas I that kild'. We may assume this error to have arisen with the actor.

191. *That*] Q's 'Tush that' is another of the rare intrusive expletives in Richard's part.

Speak it again, and even with the word,
This hand, which for thy love did kill thy love,
Shall for thy love kill a far truer love:
To both their deaths shalt thou be accessary.   195

Anne. I would I knew thy heart.

Rich. 'Tis figur'd in my tongue.

Anne. I fear me both are false.

Rich. Then never was man true.

Anne. Well, well, put up your sword.   200

Rich. Say then my peace is made.

Anne. That shalt thou know hereafter.

Rich. But shall I live in hope?

Anne. All men, I hope, live so.

Rich. Vouchsafe to wear this ring.   205

Anne. To take is not to give.

Rich. Look how my ring encompasseth thy finger:
Even so thy breast encloseth my poor heart;
Wear both of them, for both of them are thine.
And if thy poor devoted servant may   210
But beg one favour at thy gracious hand,
Thou dost confirm his happiness for ever.

Anne. What is it?

193. This] *F;* That *Qq.*   195. shalt thou] *F,Q 1;* thou thalt *Q 2–6.*   199. was man] *Q 1–2;* man was *Q 3–6,F.*   202. shalt thou] *F;* shall you *Qq.* 203. shall I] *F,Q 1;* I shall *Q 2–6.*   205. *Rich.*] *Qq (Glo.); not in F.*   Vouchsafe] *F,Q 2–6;* Voutsafe *Q 1.*   206.] *Qq; not in F.*   207. my] *F;* this *Qq.* 208. my] *F,Q 1–4;* me *Q 5–6.*   209. Wear] *F,Q 1–3 (subst.);* Were *Q 4–6.* 210. devoted] *F,Q 1; not in Q 2–6.*   servant] *F;* suppliant *Qq.*

195. *shalt thou*] See l. 179 n.

196 ff.] This passage of sticho-mythia in half-lines is one of the most important evidences of Senecan in-fluence on the play. See Introduction, pp. 80–2.

199. *was man*] See l. 179 n.

200.] Reese (p. 281) remarks that Anne is overcome by Richard's verbal dexterity much as Hubert is by Arthur's in *John*, iv.i.

203. *shall I*] See l. 179 n.

205.] The omission from F of the speech-prefix, and the whole of the subsequent line, is put down by Walker (p. 32) to Compositor B's

negligence. It is hard to conceive that the line was not in the F MS. so some error in the printing-house must be assumed. NCS points out that the episode is a parody of the marriage-service in the *BCP.*

208. *breast . . . heart*] Cf. *Ven.*, 580–2; *LLL*, v.ii.816; *Sonn.* 22, ll. 5–7.

210. *servant*] Q's 'suppliant' is perfectly acceptable, and has been preferred by many eds including Johnson and Camb. However, the F term has a technical meaning in the Petrarchan tradition of *cortesia*, which Richard is employing at this juncture.

Rich. That it may please you leave these sad designs
  To him that hath most cause to be a mourner,   215
  And presently repair to Crosby Place,
  Where, after I have solemnly interr'd
  At Chertsey Monastery this noble King,
  And wet his grave with my repentant tears,
  I will with all expedient duty see you.   220
  For divers unknown reasons, I beseech you
  Grant me this boon.
Anne. With all my heart, and much it joys me too,
  To see you are become so penitent.
  Tressel and Berkeley, go along with me.   225
Rich. Bid me farewell.
Anne.   'Tis more than you deserve;
  But since you teach me how to flatter you,
  Imagine I have said farewell already.
      Exeunt [Tressel and Berkeley] with Anne.
Rich. Sirs, take up the corse.
Gent. Towards Chertsey, noble lord?   230
Rich. No, to Whitefriars; there attend my coming.
    Exeunt [Gentlemen and Halberds with] corse.
  Was ever woman in this humour woo'd?
  Was ever woman in this humour won?
  I'll have her, but I will not keep her long.

---

214. may] *F;* would *Qq.* you] *F;* thee *Qq.* 215. most] *F;* more *Qq.*
216. Place] *Qq* (place); House *F.* 225. Berkeley] *F,Q 1–2* (Barkley), *Camb.;*
Bartley *Q 3–6* (*subst.*). 226.] *As Steevens; . . . farewell. |* 'Tis *F,Qq.* 228. S.D.
Tressel and Berkeley] As Knight; two|F, not in *Qq.* 229.] *Qq; not in F.* 230.
Gent.] F; Ser. | Qq. 231. S.D. *Gentlemen and Halberds with] This edn;* not in *F;*
Exeunt. manet *Gl. | Qq.*

214. *leave*] 'To' omitted in infinitive: Abbott §349.

216. *Place*] So named in More; both 'Place' and 'House' were current.

229.] The omission of this line from *F* may arise simply from the compositor's oversight, since it follows an emended stage-direction.

230. *Gent.*] For reasons noted before (i.ii. S.D. n) it is clear that Richard is addressing the gentlemen-pall-bearers, not the halberdiers; so *F*'s speech-prefix is correct.

231. *Whitefriars*] A probable error: Hall does not specify, but Holinshed (p. 691/1) says the body was taken to Blackfriars — plausible enough if it was to be taken by water to Chertsey. Whitefriars, the Carmelite priory, did not abut on the river.

232–3. *Was . . . won*] A stock formula (Tilley W681); cf. *Tit.,* ii. i. 82–3; *1H6,* v. iii. 78–9.

What, I that kill'd her husband and his father: 235
To take her in her heart's extremest hate,
With curses in her mouth, tears in her eyes,
The bleeding witness of her hatred by,
Having God, her conscience, and these bars against
    me—
And I, no friends to back my suit at all   240
But the plain devil and dissembling looks—
And yet to win her, all the world to nothing!
Ha!
Hath she forgot already that brave prince,
Edward, her lord, whom I, some three months since, 245
Stabb'd in my angry mood at Tewkesbury?
A sweeter and a lovelier gentleman,
Fram'd in the prodigality of Nature,
Young, valiant, wise, and no doubt right royal,
The spacious world cannot again afford.   250

235. his] *F,Q 1–2;* her *Q 3–6.*   236. hate] *F,Q 1;* heate *Q 2–6.*   238. her]
Qq; my *F.*   240. no friends] *F;* nothing *Qq.*   at all] *Q 1–2;* withall *Q 3–*
6,F.   243.] *F; in l. 242 Qq.*   246. Tewkesbury] *F;* Tewxbery *Qq.*

235–6. *I . . . hate*] Cf. Seneca,
Hercules Furens, ll. 372–3, 380–1:
'Egone ut parentis sanguine aspersam
manum / fratrumque gemina caede
contingam . . . / una res superest
mihi / fratre ac parente carior, regno
ac lare—/ odium tui'. Also cf. *LLL,*
III.i.174 ff. (Berowne's speech on the
absurdity of his being in love).
  235. *his*] Her father was of course
Warwick the King-maker.
  236. *To take her*] Infinitive indefinitely used: Abbott §356.
  238. *her*] A disputed point: Rowe,
Pope, Hanmer, and Collier among
the earliest eds and, more recently,
NCS, NPS, Evans, and Eccles prefer
the F reading. The point at issue
however is not Richard's hatred, but
that Anne's 'extremest hate', with its
still-bleeding witness of her impreca-
tions (Henry's corpse) lying by, has
been changed to mildness. Richard
does *not* hate these people: he despises
them, makes use of them, and kills

them, but in contempt, not in hatred.
The Q reading is thus on all counts
preferable; the F mistake may be
attributed to Compositor B's inattention.
  240. *no . . . all*] A partial correction
in F succeeded in replacing Q's
'nothing' with the obviously right
'no friends', but overlooked 'withall'
that crept into the text via Q3.
  243. *Ha!*] Surely rightly given a
line to itself in F.
  246. *Tewkesbury*] In Q1 this is three
timeś 'Teuxbery', once (here) 'Tewxbery', and once, in Peter Short's
section of the play, 'Teukesburie'. The
variants more likely arise from
technical issues in the printing-shop
than from copy-spellings: there was
no ſb ligature: the kern of the f would
foul the ascender of the b. Thus
either the small s had to be used (as
by Short) or the word would have to
be respelled, which seems to have
been Simmes's preference.

And will she yet debase her eyes on me,
That cropp'd the golden prime of this sweet prince,
And made her widow to a woeful bed?
On me, whose all not equals Edward's moiety?
On me, that halts and am misshapen thus?   255
My dukedom to a beggarly denier,
I do mistake my person all this while!
Upon my life, she finds—although I cannot—
Myself to be a marvellous proper man.
I'll be at charges for a looking-glass,   260
And entertain a score or two of tailors
To study fashions to adorn my body:
Since I am crept in favour with myself,
I will maintain it with some little cost.
But first I'll turn yon fellow in his grave,   265
And then return, lamenting, to my love.
Shine out, fair sun, till I have bought a glass,
That I may see my shadow as I pass.   *Exit.*

251. debase] *Qq;* abase *F.*   255. halts] *F;* halt *Qq.*   misshapen] *F;*
vishapen *Qq.*   256. to] *F,Q 1–4;* to be *Q 5–6.*   261. a] *F;* some *Qq.*
262. adorn] *F,Q 1–2;* adore *Q 3–6.*   264. some] *F,Q 1–2;* a *Q 3–6.*   265.
yon] *F,Q 1–3;* you *Q 4–6.*   267. out] *F,Q 1–5;* our *Q 6.*

251. *debase*] The superiority of the
Q reading here is confirmed by the
next line with its contrasting metal-
lurgical image of Edward's 'golden
prime'. To be sure, 'abase' could
convey the same meaning (OED *v.* 3),
and since the reading is unlikely to
have originated with the compositor,
we may assume that the more current
verb was substituted (let us presume,
by Shakespeare) for the less common
alternative.

254. *moiety*] half. All Richard's
comparisons here are of course
entirely ironical.
256. *denier*] OED [3] 1. Originally
the twelfth of a sou, in common 16th-
century use for any small sum. Cf.
with Richard's later, greater wager
of his kingdom for a horse.
259. *marvellous*] Adjective used as
adverb: Abbott §1.
265. *in*] 'In' used with verbs of
motion: Abbott §159.

SCENE III

Enter QUEEN [ELIZABETH], LORD RIVERS, LORD GREY
[*and the* MARQUESS OF DORSET].

Riv. Have patience, Madam, there's no doubt his Majesty
Will soon recover his accustom'd health.

Grey. In that you brook it ill, it makes him worse;
Therefore, for God's sake entertain good comfort,
And cheer his Grace with quick and merry eyes.   5

Eliz. If he were dead, what would betide on me?

Grey. No other harm but loss of such a lord.

Eliz. The loss of such a lord includes all harms.

Grey. The heavens have bless'd you with a goodly son
To be your comforter when he is gone.   10

Eliz. Ah, he is young, and his minority
Is put unto the trust of Richard Gloucester,

Scene III

SCENE III] *Capell; Scena Tertia* | *F; not in Qq.*   S.D.] *As Hanmer; Enter the
Queene Mother, Lord Riuers, and Lord Gray.* | *F; Enter Queene, Lord Riuers, Gray.* | *Qq
(subst.).*   3. it ill,] *F,Q2–6;* it, ill *Q1.*   5. with quick] *F,Q2–6;* quick *Q1.*
eyes] *F;* words *Qq.*   6. on] *F;* of *Qq.*   *Line repeated in F, not in Qq.*
7. *Grey*] *F; Ry* | *Q1; Ri* | *Q2–6.*   8. harms] *F;* harme *Qq.*   11. Ah] *F;*
Oh *Qq.*   12. Richard Gloucester] *F (subst.);* Rich. Glocester *Qq.*

Scene III

S.D. *Dorset*] Although Dorset does
not speak until l. 186, there is no
natural later place for him to make an
entry. Capell brings him on with
Richard and Hastings at l. 41, and
has been followed by numerous eds
including Thompson and—obscured
by a misprint—NCS. It is, however,
dramatically unlikely to find Dorset
making a third with his enemies
Richard and Hastings, and the long
silence must therefore perforce be
accepted. Cf. Menelaus in *Troil.*,
I. iii.

3. *it ill*] The significance of this and
the next variant ('with quick', l. 5)
is that the reading here accepted as
correct enters F via Q2. In neither

case is it necessary to assume Q2's
correction depended on examination
of the MS.

6.] The repetition of this line in F
was an inadvertent error: it occurs at
the foot of one page and the head of
the next.

betide on] become of: OED betide
v. 2 (citing this example).

7. *Grey*] Q gives the line to Rivers,
presumably to provide him with
something to say, but the conversation
between Grey and the Queen is
coherent as F presents it, and ought
not to be divided.

12. *Richard*] Q's 'Rich.' does not,
of course, imply that the name was
abbreviated in speech; it merely
shows Simmes's compositor's reluctance to set more than is absolutely

A man that loves not me, nor none of you.

Riv. Is it concluded he shall be Protector?

Eliz. It is determin'd, not concluded yet;   15
But so it must be, if the King miscarry.

Enter BUCKINGHAM *and* [STANLEY *Earl of*] *Derby.*

Grey. Here come the lords of Buckingham and Derby.

Buck. Good time of day unto your royal Grace.

Stan. God make your Majesty joyful, as you have been.

Eliz. The Countess Richmond, good my lord of Derby,   20
To your good prayer will scarcely say Amen;
Yet, Derby, notwithstanding she's your wife,
And loves not me, be you, good lord, assur'd
I hate not you for her proud arrogance.

Stan. I do beseech you, either not believe   25
The envious slanders of her false accusers,
Or if she be accus'd on true report,
Bear with her weakness, which I think proceeds
From wayward sickness, and no grounded malice.

---

14. Is it] *F,Q 1–5;* It is *Q 6.*   16. S.D. *F (Enter Buckingham and Derby); Enter*
Buck. Darby / *Qq.*   17. come . . . lords] *Q 1–2;* comes . . . Lords *Q 3–6;*
comes . . . Lord *F.*   21. prayer] *F;* praiers *Qq (subst.).*   24. arrogance]
F,Q 1–2; arrogancie *Q 3–6.*   25. do] *F,Q 1–2 (subst.); not in Q 3–6.*   26. false]
F,Q 1–2; not in Q 3–6.   27. on] *F;* in *Qq.*

necessary (the line is nowhere near
full measure).

14–15.] For the actual dating of
Richard's establishment as Protector,
and the attempts of the Queen's
faction to prevent it, see Hanham,
pp. 5–6. Though Edward died on 9
April, Hanham argues that the
documents referring to Richard as
Protector before 4 May are in fact
misdated.)

16. *miscarry*] meet with one's death:
OED *v.*1.

16. S.D. *Stanley, Earl of Derby*] This
form is used in stage-directions
throughout this edn for clarity.
Stanley was not made Earl of Derby
until after Bosworth; after this scene
Shakespeare generally uses 'Stanley'

(invariably in the dialogue). See
Introduction, p. 13.

17. *come . . . lords*] A typical
example of mistaken correction in
F: Q3's corrupt 'comes' was noted
by either the corrector or the compositor, and 'lords' reduced to the
singular, making correct grammar,
but nonsense.

20. *Countess Richmond*] Margaret,
daughter of John Beaufort, first Duke
of Somerset. After the death of her
first husband, Edmund Tudor, Earl
of Richmond, half-brother to Henry
VI, she married first Sir Henry
Stafford, and subsequently Stanley
(Malone).

29. *grounded*] firmly fixed or established: OED *ppl.a.*1 1.

Riv. Saw you the King today, my lord of Derby?   30
Stan. But now the Duke of Buckingham and I
    Are come from visiting his Majesty.
Eliz. What likelihood of his amendment, lords?
Buck. Madam, good hope; his Grace speaks cheerfully.
Eliz. God grant him health. Did you confer with him?   35
Buck. Ay, madam; he desires to make atonement
    Between the Duke of Gloucester and your brothers,
    And between them and my Lord Chamberlain;
    And sent to warn them to his royal presence.
Eliz. Would all were well—but that will never be;   40
    I fear our happiness is at the height.

       Enter RICHARD [*and* HASTINGS].

Rich. They do me wrong, and I will not endure it!
    Who is it that complains unto the King
    That I, forsooth, am stern, and love them not?
    By holy Paul, they love his Grace but lightly   45
    That fill his ears with such dissentious rumours.
    Because I cannot flatter, and look fair,

---

30. *Riv.*] *Qq; Qu. | F.*   of Derby] *F,Q 1–5 (subst.);* Darby *Q6.*   32. Are
come] *F;* Came *Qq.*   33. What] *F,Q 3–6;* With *Q 1–2.*   34. speaks] *F,Q 1–
2,4–6;* speaketh *Q 3.*   36. Ay, Madam] *F;* Madame we did *Qq.*   to make]
F,Q 1–3,5–6; make *Q 4.*   37. Between] *F;* Betwixt *Qq.*   38. between] *F;*
betwixt *Qq.*   39. to his] *F,Q 1–5;* ot his *Q6;* of his *Q 7–8.*   41. height] *F;*
highest *Qq.*   41. S.D.] *As Hanmer; Enter Richard. | F; Enter Glocester. | Qq.*
43. is it] *F;* are they *Qq.*   44. and] *F,Q 1–5; not in Q6.*   45. holy] *F,Q 1–
5;* wholy *Q6.*   47. look] *F;* speake *Qq.*

---

30. *Riv.*] In F, this line is given to
the Queen, which is possible: however,
as Smidt (p. 88) says, the introduction of a new topic into the strained
conversation might come more naturally from a third party, and Rivers
is an apt candidate for the line. The
F assignment may then be an error.

  33. *amendment*] recovery: OED 4.

  36. *Ay, madam*] Q's 'Madame we
did' commences the series of unmetrical variants in Buckingham's
part which is one of the most convincing evidences for the memorial
phase of the Q text. See Introduction,
p. 6.

atonement] reconciliation: OED 2.

  37. *your brothers*] How many
brothers had Elizabeth Woodeville?
In the play, only one: Rivers. However, here and elsewhere Grey is
implied to be her brother, a mistake
shared by the *True Tragedie;* the
Mirror gets it right in the title of
Rivers's tragedy (p. 245), and at l.
522, so the error did not originate
there. See also l. 67 n. (Actually,
Elizabeth did have other brothers,
but they do not appear in the play.)

  47. *look fair*] Richard's deceptive
looks are discussed at length:
III. iv. 9–12, 48–57.

Smile in men's faces, smooth, deceive and cog,
Duck with French nods and apish courtesy,
I must be held a rancorous enemy.   50
Cannot a plain man live and think no harm,
But thus his simple truth must be abus'd
With silken, sly, insinuating Jacks?
Grey. To who in all this presence speaks your Grace?
Rich. To thee, that hast nor honesty nor grace.   55
When have I injur'd thee? When done thee wrong?
Or thee? Or thee? Or any of your faction?
A plague upon you all! His royal Grace
(Whom God preserve better than you would wish)
Cannot be quiet scarce a breathing while   60
But you must trouble him with lewd complaints.
Eliz. Brother of Gloucester, you mistake the matter:
The King, on his own royal disposition,
And not provok'd by any suitor else,
Aiming, belike, at your interior hatred,   65

---

52. his simple] *F,Q 1–4;* in simple *Q5;* in simpla *Q6.*   53. With] *F;* By *Qq.*
54. *Grey.*] *F;* Ry. / *Q1;* Ri. / *Q2–6.*   who] *F;* whom *Q1–5;* home *Q6.*
all] *F,Q 1–5; not in Q6.*   55. hast nor] *F,Q 1–3,5–6;* hast not *Q4.*   58. Grace]
F; person *Qq.*   63. on] *F;* of *Qq.*

48.] Cf. 'The Blacksmith', l. 146: 'Can carde and dyse, both cogge and foyst at fare' (*Mirror*, p. 407). Cog: OED *v.*³ 3: to employ fraud or deceit. Smooth: cf. 1.ii.172.

49.] Cf. *LLL*, v.ii.324; *John*, v.ii.131. The association of affected manners with foreign models is also a theme in *Rom.*: note II.iv.26–45. The mimicry of the ape, imitating forms of behaviour while ignorant of their meaning, is implied in 'apish courtesy', a sub-human practice. Cf. Dekker's *Seven Deadly Sinnes of London*: the fifth sin is apishness: 'counterfetting or imitation' (Thompson).

53. *With*] Q's 'By' is in accord with modern grammatical expectations, but Schmidt, II. 1382/2, defines With: 'Lastly, denoting an external agency, by which an effect is produced, and which is usually—and at

present exclusively—expressed by the prepos. by.' Q's usage may then be an actor's unconscious normalization.

silken] As a metaphor for ingratiating, flattering behaviour by deceitful people: see OED *a.*II.7.

Jacks] A contemptuous term for individuals of the working-class: hence, someone ill-bred or badly mannered: OED *sb.*¹ I.2.

55. *nor . . . grace*] Richard declares that Grey has neither honesty (in the sense in which he has been claiming it for himself) nor grace in the theological sense (as opposed to the courtesy title for a duke which Grey has just used).

61. *lewd*] foolish, ill-mannered: OED 4.

62. *Brother*] brother-in-law. Cf. Richard's contempt at the concept of calling Elizabeth 'sister', I.i.109.

That in your outward action shows itself
Against my children, brothers, and myself,
Makes him to send, that he may learn the ground
Of your ill will, and thereby to remove it.

Rich. I cannot tell; the world is grown so bad   70
That wrens make prey where eagles dare not perch.
Since every Jack became a gentleman
There's many a gentle person made a jack.

Eliz. Come, come: we know your meaning, brother
Gloucester.

66. That] *F; Which Qq.*   action] *F; actions Qq.*   67. children, brothers]
F; kindred, brother Qq (subst.).   68–9.] *As Pope;* Makes him to send that
thereby he may gather / The ground of your ill will and to remoue it. *Qq*
(grounds *Q6*); Makes him to send, that he may learne the ground. / *F (l. 69
not in F).*   71. make] *F,Q1–2;* may *Q3–6.*   72. Jack] *Qq;* Iaeke *F.*

66. *action*] F's singular is correct;
the word is in contrast: outward
action versus interior hatred, l. 65.

67. *children*] Smidt (p. 97) says that
the children in question cannot be
the princes Edward and York (but
why not?); there are other references
(II.iii.28; III.vii.183) to the Queen's
sons by her former marriage with
Grey. In the play her relatives are
represented by Rivers, Dorset, and
Grey: Rivers is clearly her brother
and Dorset her son; Grey's status is
ambiguous. References at III.i.12
and IV.iv.93–4 seem to imply he is a
brother; see also l. 37 of this scene.
Margaret curses Rivers, Dorset, and
Hastings, yet her curse is recalled by
Grey in his execution-scene as
having been uttered against himself
as well as Rivers and Hastings. It
seems evident that there was an area
of uncertainty in Shakespeare's mind
concerning the precise relationships
within the group of the 'Queen's
kindred'. Smidt's notion that 'children' was deliberately altered in Q to
'kindred' in order to avoid the
implication that Elizabeth had adult
sons implies a more precise awareness
of this issue in the author's mind than
the facts seem to warrant.

68–9.] Q's version of these two
lines is obviously garbled, and F's
correction incomplete. Most eds
follow Pope's neat emendation, which
retains the F line and most of Q's
words. It is true that this still leaves
the Queen's speech ungrammatical:
the subject of 'makes' is in fact 'the
King', and the implication is that it
is the King's awareness of Richard's
hatred that 'makes' him send for the
nobles. See also Abbott §376 for a
similar interpretation.

70–3.] Like a good Machiavel,
Richard makes whatever use he
wishes of popular opinions, whether
or no he himself believes in them.
Here he alludes to the common
doctrine of order and hierarchy: the
world has been thrown out of kilter
by the unnatural ennobling of the
Woodeville faction; the world of
nature reflects this inversion of
values (cf. *Mac.*, II.iv.10–13). The
consequence is the inversion of the
social hierarchy, with 'Jacks' (see
l. 53) taking the place of gentlemen
and vice versa. In l. 73 'jack' means
not only the lower-class person meant
before, but the 'jack' in the game of
bowls (OED *sb.*[1] II.18), knocked
about by the other balls. In l. 72, F's

<blockquote>
You envy my advancement, and my friends'.   75
God grant we never may have need of you.
</blockquote>

Rich. Meantime, God grants that we have need of you:
<blockquote>
Our brother is imprison'd by your means,
Myself disgrac'd, and the nobility
Held in contempt, while great promotions   80
Are daily given to ennoble those
That scarce some two days since were worth a noble.
</blockquote>

Eliz. By Him that rais'd me to this careful height
<blockquote>
From that contented hap which I enjoy'd,
I never did incense his Majesty   85
Against the Duke of Clarence, but have been
An earnest advocate to plead for him.
My lord, you do me shameful injury,
Falsely to draw me in these vile suspects.
</blockquote>

Rich. You may deny that you were not the mean   90
<blockquote>
Of my Lord Hastings' late imprisonment.
</blockquote>

Riv. She may, my lord, for—

Rich. She may, Lord Rivers; why, who knows not so?
<blockquote>
She may do more, sir, than denying that:
She may help you to many fair preferments,   95
And then deny her aiding hand therein,
And lay those honours on your high desert.
</blockquote>

---

75. my advancement] *F,Q1;* mine aduancement *Q2–6.*   77. grants] *F,Q1–2;* grant *Q3–6.*   we] *Qq;* I *F.*   80. while great] *F;* whilst many faire *Qq.*   90. mean] *F;* cause *Qq.*   92. lord, for—] *F;* Lord. *Qq.*   97. desert] *F;* deserts *Qq.*

'Iaeke' is simply a foul-case error. See also Tilley J3.

77. *we*] Q's 'royal plural' is in keeping with Richard's habitual assumption of that status well before he is made King; cf. 'Our brother' in the next line. It is delicately ambiguous—Richard *may* of course mean his and Edward's brother, but the concealed assumption of monarchy is highly characteristic.

81–2. *ennoble . . . noble*] Great promotions are given to those who were scarcely worth a noble (the coin worth a third or half of a pound, OED *B.*2). Richard's puns are all characteristic of the Vice.

83. *careful*] i.e. full of care.

84. *hap*] fortune, i.e. the contented state in which I was.

89. *in . . . suspects*] into these vile suspicions of yours. For 'suspects' see OED suspect *sb.*[1] 1e, citing this example.

90. *mean*] means, agent, cause: OED *sb.*[2] II.10a. For the intensified negative in this line, see Abbott §406.

92. *lord, for—*] F is obviously right here, as Richard runs verbal rings around Rivers, interrupting him before his laboured defence of the Queen can even begin.

What may she not? She may—ay, marry may she—
Riv. What, marry may she?
Rich. What marry may she? Marry with a king;   100
　　　A bachelor, and a handsome stripling too:
　　　Iwis, your grandam had a worser match.
Eliz. My lord of Gloucester, I have too long borne
　　　Your blunt upbraidings and your bitter scoffs;
　　　By heaven, I will acquaint his Majesty   105
　　　Of those gross taunts that oft I have endur'd.

Enter old QUEEN MARGARET.

　　　I had rather be a country servant maid,
　　　Than a great queen, with this condition,
　　　To be so baited, scorn'd, and stormed at:
　　　Small joy have I in being England's queen.   110
Marg. [*Aside*] And lessen'd be that small, God I beseech
　　　Him:
　　　Thy honour, state, and seat is due to me.
Rich. What, threat you me with telling of the King?

98. ay] *F* (I); yea *Qq.*   101. and a] *F;* a *Qq.*   102. Iwis] *Q1-3,6;* I wis
Q4-5,F.   a worser] *F,Q1-2,6;* aworser *Q3-4;* worser *Q5.*   106. Of] *F;*
With *Qq.*   that oft I] *F;* I often *Qq*   106. S.D.] *This edn; after l. 109 Qq;*
after l. 110 F.   109. so baited . . . stormed] *F;* thus taunted . . . baited *Qq.*
111, 118, 126, 134, 137, 143, 155. *Aside.*] *As NCS; not in F,Qq.*   111. Him]
F; thee *Qq.*   113. of] *F,Q1,3-5;* , or *Q2; not in Q6.*

101. *and a*] The middle syllable of
'bachelor' is elided.

102. *Iwis*] Linguistically, the Q
form is more correct: the word is an
adverb rather than a verb with
subject: see OED B. It means
'certainly'; cf. German 'gewiß'.

106. S.D.] Margaret must enter in
time to hear l. 110; it seemed preferable to move her entrance back to
the previous full-stop so that she
might be seen to comprehend the gist
of Elizabeth's hyperbole. In other
words, she enters, and pauses near
the door upon seeing the dispute in
progress on the forestage.

108. *with . . . condition*] Probably
suggested by Edward's defence of his
marriage as represented by Hall, from
More: 'I would not bee a kyng with
that condicion to forbeare mine awne

libertie in choyse of mine awne
mariage' (*Edward V*, fol. [xix]r).

109. *baited . . . stormed*] Patrick
(p. 36) argues that Q's version is an
actor's transposition, the more or less
synonymous 'taunted' replacing
'stormed', and the two words transposed in the line. It is not necessarily
obvious that this is so: although
Patrick remarks 'the colloquial and
rather incorrect "baited at" is
hardly the original reading', OED
bate *v.*[1] 46 records it in 1579 and
1607. Smidt (p. 40) suggests 'taunts'
in l. 106 as the source of the Q verb.
A sounder objection to the Q reading
is that 'taunted' is a synonym for
'baited' in this sense, whereas the F
line achieves an appropriate rhetorical
crescendo.

Tell him, and spare not: look what I have said
I will avouch't in presence of the King: 115
I dare adventure to be sent to th'Tower;
'Tis time to speak: my pains are quite forgot.

Marg. [*Aside*] Out, devil! I remember them too well:
Thou kill'dst my husband Henry in the Tower,
And Edward, my poor son, at Tewkesbury.   120

Rich. Ere you were queen, ay, or your husband king,
I was a pack-horse in his great affairs;
A weeder-out of his proud adversaries;
A liberal rewarder of his friends:
To royalize his blood, I spent mine own.   125

Marg. [*Aside*] Ay, and much better blood than his, or thine.

Rich. In all which time, you and your husband Grey
Were factious for the House of Lancaster:
And Rivers, so were you. Was not your husband

114.] *Qq; not in F.*   115. avouch't] *F;* auouch *Qq.*   116.] *F; not in Qq.*
117.] *As Qq;* ... speake, / My *F.*   my] *F,Q 1–5;* when *Q 6.*   118.] *As Qq;*
... Diuell, / I *F.*   remember] *Qq;* do remember *F.*   119. kill'dst] *F;*
slewest *Qq.*   121. *As Qq;* ... Queene, / I *F.*   ay] *F* (I); yea *Qq.*   or]
F,Qq; of *Q 2* (*Trinity Coll. copy*).   125. spent] *F;* spilt *Qq.*   126.] *As Qq;*
... blood / Then *F.*

114.] Omitted from F surely by
some oversight of the corrector's,
though NCS classes it as 'doubtful ...
because not essential to the context'
(p. 146).

116.] Omitted from Q; it is hard
to think the line was ever intended
to be absent, as the touch of Richard's
daring to be sent to the Tower, when
he is the effective dispatcher to that
place, is too ironically apt to have
been missed except by oversight;
whether of actor or printer it is
impossible to say, though there is no
obvious reason why a compositor
should miss it. Adventure means 'run
the risk of', OED *v.*1.5, citing this
example.

117. *pains*] Richard uses the word
in the sense of labour or efforts (OED
sb.[1] 6); the trouble he went to for
Edward's sake, which he enlarges on

at ll. 121 ff. Margaret, in the next
line, uses Richard's own trick of
double meaning: to her Richard's
pains are the agonies he inflicted on
her and hers.

118. *remember*] Q's version is
metrically correct, and so may be
slightly preferable. NCS remarks that
'devil' is usually monosyllabic in
Shakespeare, but a glance at the
concordance reveals that over half
the instances in the verse of this play
at least are unmistakably disyllabic.

121. *or*] The correction of the
compositor's error 'of' does not
imply reference to copy.

125. *spent*] i.e., tired, or exhausted:
OED 5c. (OED wrongly cites this
line under 6: to suffer the loss of
(blood, life, etc.)); Q is also wrong,
since Richard was not wounded in
the Wars.

In Margaret's battle at Saint Albans slain?   130
Let me put in your minds, if you forget,
What you have been ere this, and what you are;
Withal, what I have been, and what I am.

Marg. [*Aside*] A murd'rous villain, and so still thou art.

Rich. Poor Clarence did forsake his father Warwick,   135
    Ay, and forswore himself—which Jesu pardon—

Marg. [*Aside*] Which God revenge.

Rich. To fight on Edward's party for the crown:
    And for his meed, poor lord, he is mew'd up.
    I would to God my heart were flint, like Edward's,   140
    Or Edward's soft and pitiful, like mine.
    I am too childish-foolish for this world.

Marg. [*Aside*] Hie thee to hell for shame, and leave this
        world,
    Thou cacodemon: there thy kingdom is.

Riv. My lord of Gloucester, in those busy days   145
    Which here you urge to prove us enemies,
    We follow'd then our lord, our sovereign king:
    So should we you, if you should be our king.

Rich. If I should be? I had rather be a pedlar!
    Far be it from my heart, the thought thereof.   150

Eliz. As little joy, my lord, as you suppose
    You should enjoy, were you this country's king:

131. minds] *F,Q 1–4* (*subst.*); minde *Q 5*; mind *Q 6*.   you] *F*; yours *Qq*.
132. this] *F*; now *Qq*.   142. childish-foolish] *Theobald*; childish, foolish *Q 1–
2*; childish foolish *Q 3–6,F*.   143. this] *F*; the *Qq*.   147. sovereign] *F*;
lawfull *Qq*.   148. you, if] *F,Q 1–5*; now, if *Q 6*.   149. If I] *F,Q 1–5*; If *Q 6*.
150. thereof] *F*; of it *Qq*.   151. *Eliz.*] *F,Q 1–2* (*Qu.*); *Q.M.* | *Q 3–4*; *Qu.
Nar.* | *Q 5*; *Qu. Mar.* | *Q 6*.

130. *slain*] In 1461, Grey was
indeed killed in this battle. Richard
perhaps implies that Margaret was
responsible for the battle: see *3H6*
generally for Margaret's active prose-
cution of the military effort against
York. The Second Battle of St
Albans of 1461 is not represented in
that play, however (though Warwick
gives an account of it, II.i.111–37);
it is also true that 'battle' can mean a
body of troops in battle-array (OED
*sb.*II.8).

135. *Clarence . . . Warwick*] Clarence
married Isabel Neville, Warwick's
elder daughter (Lady Anne's sister);
for his betrayal of Warwick, see
I.iv, and *3H6* v.i.

139. *meed*] reward, recompense:
OED *sb.*1.

mew'd] See I.i.38.

144. *cacodemon*] an evil spirit:
OED 1.

151. *Eliz.*] The error in the later
quartos arose no doubt through
compositorial inattention.

As little joy you may suppose in me
That I enjoy, being the Queen thereof.
Marg. [*Aside*] Ay, little joy enjoys the Queen thereof: 155
For I am she, and altogether joyless.
I can no longer hold me patient!
[*Coming forward*] Hear me, you wrangling pirates, that
    fall out
In sharing that which you have pill'd from me:
Which of you trembles not, that looks on me?   160
If not that I am Queen you bow like subjects,
Yet that by you depos'd you quake like rebels.
Ah, gentle villain! do not turn away.
Rich. Foul wrinkled witch, what mak'st thou in my sight?
Marg. But repetition of what thou hast marr'd: 165
That will I make, before I let thee go.
Rich. Wert thou not banished on pain of death?

153. you may] *F*; may you *Qq*.   155. Ay,] *This edn*; A *Qq,F*; As *Heath*;
And *White*.   157. S.D.] *This edn, after Capell; not in F,Qq*.   159. sharing]
F,Q1; sharing out *Q2–6*.   160. looks] *F,Q1–4*; looke *Q5–6*.   161. am]*F*;
being *Qq*.   162. by you] *F,Q1–2,5–6*; byou *Q3*; by on *Q4*.   163. Ah] *F*;
O *Qq*.   167–9.] *F; not in Qq*.

155. *Ay*] QqF 'A' is hard to accept
as correct, though many eds have
printed it. 'As' has the advantage of
following repetitively the phrases of
Elizabeth; Walker thought it was
needed for the rhetoric (NCS, p.
181). On the contrary, something
stronger is needed for the rhetoric,
since Margaret is not merely parallel-
ing, but capping, Elizabeth's studied
lament. White's 'And' is on the right
lines, but 'Ay' has the advantage of
being even stronger and more
consciously ironical, while needing
only one letter more than is in F. It
is true that the F compositors usually
print 'I' for 'Ay', but this may be
more their habit than reflection of
what is in the copy: see the Yea/I
variants in ll. 98, 121, 126. It seems
possible that the compositor of Q1
mistook the MS., and for some
reason the error was not corrected
when F copy was prepared.

159. *pill'd*] pillaged, taken by
violence: OED pill *v.*[1] 1.3, citing this
line.

161–2.] 'The construction is somewhat involved and confusing. "You
all tremble as you look on me, if not
because, as subjects, you bow in awe
of me, your queen, at any rate
because, as rebels, you quake before
me, the sovereign whom you have
deposed." The sense is easy to see,
and hard to express' (Thompson).

164.] Cf. Marlowe's *Dido*, III.ii.25:
'Avaunt old witch and trouble not
my wits'.

165. *repetition*] recital, narration:
OED 1.3, citing this example.

167–9.] Omitted from Q; no
mechanism in the printing-house is
probable as an explanation. Patrick
comments: 'It is not unusual to find
in the quarto text the omission of a
question and answer when they are
interposed between consecutive parts

Marg. I was, but I do find more pain in banishment
       Than death can yield me here by my abode.
       A husband and a son thou ow'st to me;   170
       And thou a kingdom; all of you, allegiance.
       This sorrow that I have by right is yours;
       And all the pleasures you usurp are mine.
Rich. The curse my noble father laid on thee
       When thou didst crown his warlike brows with paper,
       And with thy scorns drew'st rivers from his eyes,   176
       And then to dry them, gav'st the Duke a clout
       Steep'd in the faultless blood of pretty Rutland—
       His curses then, from bitterness of soul
       Denounc'd against thee, are all fall'n upon thee,   180
       And God, not we, hath plagu'd thy bloody deed.
Eliz. So just is God, to right the innocent.
Hast. O, 'twas the foulest deed to slay that babe,
       And the most merciless, that e'er was heard of.
Riv. Tyrants themselves wept when it was reported.   185
Dors. No man but prophesied revenge for it.

---

170. to] *F,Q 1–5;* vnto *Q 6.*   172. This] *F;* The *Qq.*   173. are] *F,Q 1–2;* is
Q 3–6.   174. my] *F,Q 1–5;* me *Q 6.*   176. scorns] *F;* scorne *Qq.*   178.
faultless] *F,Q 1–2; not in Q 3–6.*   180. all] *F,Q 1–2; not in Q 3–6.*   184. e'er]
F; euer *Qq.*

---

of a speech' (p. 108), conjecturing
that an actor's omission is as likely
an explanation as that Shakespeare
had the afterthought for F of explaining the presence of an unhistorical
character in the play. Smidt, in
contrast, taking up a point made first
by Malone, finds it odd that the
banishment should be mentioned at
all if Margaret is allowed to remain
at liberty (p. 107). Perhaps the
rather lame explanation was deliberately dropped; yet Margaret's function in the play is not governed by
naturalistic criteria. See Introduction,
pp. 109–10.

   174. *curse*] See *3H6,* I.iv.111 ff.,
esp. ll. 164–6 for the curse itself.
   178. *faultless . . . Rutland*] The
murder of Rutland, already alluded

to in I.ii.160–2, occurs in *3H6,*
I.iii. In both plays, infanticide provokes almost universal horror and
revulsion (only Richard and Margaret
are not thus affected); it serves to
mark the turning-point of the action
for the guilty parties in both plays,
as a crime which alienates their
supporters.
   182.] Cf. *Cromwell,* II.iii.64: 'How
just is God to right the innocent'.
   183. *babe*] Shakespeare, following
Hall, believed Rutland to be 12 at the
time of his death (he was actually 17).
'Babe' is often used of quite old children, as in Act IV where the two
princes (aged respectively 13 and 11)
are so described, not only by their
mother, but by Tyrrel (IV.iii.9).

Buck. Northumberland, then present, wept to see it.
Marg. What? Were you snarling all before I came,
　　　Ready to catch each other by the throat,
　　　And turn you all your hatred now on me?　　　　190
　　　Did York's dread curse prevail so much with heaven
　　　That Henry's death, my lovely Edward's death,
　　　Their kingdom's loss, my woeful banishment,
　　　Should all but answer for that peevish brat?
　　　Can curses pierce the clouds and enter heaven?　195
　　　Why then, give way, dull clouds, to my quick curses:
　　　Though not by war, by surfeit die your King,
　　　As ours by murder, to make him a king.
　　　Edward thy son, that now is Prince of Wales,
　　　For Edward my son, that was Prince of Wales,　200
　　　Die in his youth, by like untimely violence.
　　　Thyself, a queen, for me that was a queen,
　　　Outlive thy glory like my wretched self:
　　　Long may'st thou live to wail thy children's death,
　　　And see another, as I see thee now,　　　　　205

190. all . . . now] *F,Q 1*; now . . . all *Q 2-6*.   194. Should] *F*; Could *Qq*.
197. Though] *F*; If *Qq*.   198. ours] *F,Q 1-2*; our *Q 3,5-6*; out *Q 4*.   199.
that] *F*; which *Qq*.   200. my] *Qq*; our *F*.   that] *F*; which *Qq*.   201.
violence] *F,Q 1-5*; violences *Q 6*.   204. death] *F*; losse *Qq*.

187. *Northumberland*] See *3H6*,
I. iv. 169-71.

190. *all . . . now*] A probable actor's
transposition in Q.

195.] Cf. Marlowe, *Jew*, III. ii. 33:
'And with my prayers pierce th'im-
partiall heavens'.

196. *quick*] full of vigour and energy,
swift-acting: OED A. III. 19c.

197.] Cf. *Mirror*, 'Clarence', ll.
337-8: 'For though the king within a
while had died, / As nedes he must, he
surfayted so oft' (p. 233).

Though] There is a considerable
difference in meaning between Q and
F: in F Margaret assumes the
Yorkists to be victorious, but that an
ignominious death may yet strike
Edward; Q leaves the issue open. F
is right: Margaret's sense of defeat

in battle informs her entire jeremiad.

197-209.] Something of the sweep
of Margaret's curse is found in
Marlowe's *Dido*, II. i. 233-7: '*Achilles*
sonne, remember what I was, /
Father of fiftie sonnes, but they are
slaine, / Lord of my fortune, but my
fortunes turnd, / King of this
Citie, but my *Troy* is fired, / And
now am neither father, Lord, nor
King.'

200. *my*] Q's version here seems
marginally preferable for the sake of
the sonic antitheses: 'your King /
ours; thy son / my son'. But the
retention of the royal plural would
also be entirely characteristic of
Margaret.

204. *death*] Q's vaguer 'losse' is
surely wrong.

Deck'd in thy rights, as thou art stall'd in mine;
Long die thy happy days before thy death,
And after many lengthen'd hours of grief,
Die neither mother, wife, nor England's Queen.
Rivers and Dorset, you were standers-by,   210
And so wast thou, Lord Hastings, when my son
Was stabb'd with bloody daggers. God, I pray Him,
That none of you may live his natural age,
But by some unlook'd accident cut off.

Rich. Have done thy charm, thou hateful wither'd hag.   215
Marg. And leave out thee? Stay, dog, for thou shalt hear me.

If heaven have any grievous plague in store
Exceeding those that I can wish upon thee,
O, let them keep it till thy sins be ripe,
And then hurl down their indignation   220
On thee, the troubler of the poor world's peace.
The worm of conscience still begnaw thy soul;
Thy friends suspect for traitors while thou liv'st,
And take deep traitors for thy dearest friends;
No sleep close up that deadly eye of thine,   225
Unless it be while some tormenting dream
Affrights thee with a hell of ugly devils.
Thou elvish-mark'd, abortive, rooting hog,

206. rights] *F,Q1;* glorie *Q2–6 (subst.).*   211. wast] *F,Q1–2;* was *Q3–6.*
213. his] *F;* your *Qq.*   216. thee] *F,Q3–6;* the *Q1–2.*   223. while] *F,Q1–*
5*;* whilst *Q6.*   liv'st] *F;* liuest *Qq.*   224. for thy] *F,Q1–3,5–6;* forth, *Q4.*
226. while] *F;* whilest *Q1–5;* whilst *Q6.*

206. *rights*] There can be no doubt
that Q2's 'glorie' is erroneous (if it
were held to be a correction, copy
would have had to be consulted, of
which there is no firm evidence
whatever). It is possible that the
compositor's eye picked up the word
from l. 203.

stall'd] OED *v.*[1] II.7: to induct
formally into a seat of rule or dignity,
to enthrone (citing this line).

212. *God . . . Him*] Insertion of a
pronoun after a proper name as the
subject or object: Abbott §243.

214. *But . . . unlook'd*] but be by
some unlooked-for accident, etc. See
also Abbott §§385, 294.

216. *thee*] Q1–2's 'the' is not a
variant reading, just a variant
spelling. See also l. 234.

219. *them*] The inhabitants of
heaven. Margaret's theology is, as
usual, sub-Christian.

222. *still*] constantly (as at i.ii.31).

223. *friends*] Confusion of friends
and foes was a common mark of the
disintegration of personality. Cf. in
Parts Added, 'Rudacke', l. 60: 'Our
fauners deemde faythfull, and frend-
shippe a foe' (p. 256); or 'Carassus',
l. 326: 'Fearing my fall, my friends I
deemd my foes' (p. 409).

228. *elvish-mark'd, abortive*] marked
by the elves as of their kind, i.e.

Thou that wast seal'd in thy nativity
The slave of Nature, and the son of hell;   230
Thou slander of thy heavy mother's womb,
Thou loathed issue of thy father's loins,
Thou rag of honour, thou detested—

Rich. Margaret!
Marg.   Richard!
Rich.   Ha?
Marg.   I call thee not.
Rich. I cry thee mercy then, for I did think   235
That thou hadst call'd me all these bitter names.
Marg. Why so I did, but look'd for no reply.
O, let me make the period to my curse!
Rich. 'Tis done by me, and ends in 'Margaret'.
Eliz. Thus have you breath'd your curse against yourself.
Marg. Poor painted queen, vain flourish of my fortune: 241
Why strew'st thou sugar on that bottled spider,
Whose deadly web ensnareth thee about?
Fool, fool; thou whet'st a knife to kill thyself.
The day will come that thou shalt wish for me   245
To help thee curse this poisonous bunch-back'd toad.

231. heavy mother's] *F;* mothers heauy *Qq.*   233. detested—] *F;* detested,
&c. *Qq.*   234.] *As Steevens; Rich.* Margaret. | *Q.M.* . . . Ha. | I *F,Qq (subst.).*
thee] *F,Q 1–5;* the *Q6.*   235. I . . . mercy then] *F;* Then I . . . mercy *Qq.*
did think] *F;* had thought *Qq.*   236. That] *F,Q 1; not in Q2–6.*   237. look'd]
F; lookt *Q 1–5;* looke *Q6.*   245. day] *F;* time *Qq.*   that] *F,Q 1;* when
Q2–6.   246. this] *F;* that *Qq.*   poisonous] *F,Q 1 (subst.);* poisoned *Q2–6*
(subst.).

spiteful, peevish. For abortive, see
I. ii. 21.

hog] An allusion to Richard's
badge, the white boar.

230. *slave of Nature*] Whitaker (p.
79) quotes art. 9 of the Thirty-Nine
Articles, and comments: 'he is in
bondage to the sin which is man's
fallen nature and by which he is a
"son of hell" until redeemed by the
grace of God'.

231. *heavy mother's*] Most commentators quoted in the Variorum, and
Smidt more recently, feel that 'heavy'
more aptly qualifies 'womb' than
'mother'. But it is being used in the

sense of sad or grieved (OED *a.*[1]
VII. 27), and so F is correct.

240.] Proverbial: Tilley C924.

241. *painted . . . flourish*] Imagery
from painting: Elizabeth is only
painted, i.e. not a real queen; a
mere decoration (flourish) or false
ornament upon reality, that is, upon
Margaret, who still believes her
'fortune' is to be Queen of England.

242. *bottled*] resembling a bottle,
protuberant, swollen: hence, by
association, hunch-backed: OED
ppl.a. 1. Swollen with venom is also
clearly implied.

246. *poisonous*] Q2's variant may

Hast. False-boding woman, end thy frantic curse,
　　Lest to thy harm thou move our patience.
Marg. Foul shame upon you, you have all mov'd mine.
Riv. Were you well serv'd, you would be taught your duty.
Marg. To serve me well, you all should do me duty:　　251
　　Teach me to be your queen, and you my subjects.
　　O, serve me well, and teach yourselves that duty.
Dors. Dispute not with her; she is lunatic.
Marg. Peace, Master Marquess: you are malapert;　　255
　　Your fire-new stamp of honour is scarce current.
　　O, that your young nobility could judge
　　What 'twere to lose it and be miserable.
　　They that stand high have many blasts to shake them,
　　And if they fall, they dash themselves to pieces.　　260
Rich. Good counsel, marry! Learn it, learn it, Marquess.
Dors. It touches you, my lord, as much as me.
Rich. Ay, and much more; but I was born so high:
　　Our aery buildeth in the cedar's top,
　　And dallies with the wind, and scorns the sun.　　265
Marg. And turns the sun to shade, alas, alas!
　　Witness my son, now in the shade of death,
　　Whose bright out-shining beams thy cloudy wrath

---

259. blasts] *F,Q2–6;* blast *Q1.*　　262. touches] *F;* toucheth *Qq.*　　267. son]
Q1; sonne *Q2–4,F;* sunne *Q5–6.*

have arisen from an attempt to make
the rhythm more obviously correct.
Or it may be a simple error.

255. *malapert*] impudent.

256. *fire-new stamp*] Imagery from
coining: the new rank of Dorset has
just been coined from molten metal;
it is scarcely current coin.

259–60.] The perils of over-
ambition expressed in the image of
climbing high are one of the great
Elizabethan commonplaces. See
Tilley S823 and (for instance)
Arden of Faversham, sc. viii, 15–18;
from the *Mirror,* 'Shore's Wife', ll.
241–53; 'Humfrey Duke of Glocester',
ll. 1–4; from *Parts Added,* 'Alurede',
ll. 10–14; 'Guidericus', ll. 320–2;
'Carassus', ll. 241–2; 'Porrex' (first

version), ll. 149–54, etc. Note also
Seneca, *Agamemnon,* ll. 83–6, 90–6.

264–5.] See Introduction, p. 60
for the bearing of these lines on
Marlowe's *Edward II.* The vaunt is
unusual for Richard, but it continues
the imagery introduced by Margaret.
Also cf. *3H6,* II.i.91, v.ii.12; *John,*
v.ii.149; Noble reminds us of Ezekiel,
xvii.3. An aery is the nest of an eagle.

266–7. *sun . . . son*] Margaret
appropriates Richard's pun from
I.i.2; the compositors of Q5–6 seem
to have been bemused thereby, but
F reverts to the earlier form; in a
modernized text the distinction must
be carefully made.

268–9.] Cf. Marlowe, *Jew,* I.ii.193–
4: 'And henceforth wish for an

Hath in eternal darkness folded up.

Your aery buildeth in our aery's nest;   270
O God, that seest it, do not suffer it:
As it is won with blood, lost be it so.

Buck. Peace, peace, for shame, if not for charity.

Marg. Urge neither charity nor shame to me:
Uncharitably with me have you dealt,   275
And shamefully my hopes by you are butcher'd.
My charity is outrage, life my shame;
And in that shame, still live my sorrows' rage.

Buck. Have done, have done!

Marg. O princely Buckingham, I'll kiss thy hand   280
In sign of league and amity with thee:
Now fair befall thee and thy noble House;
Thy garments are not spotted with our blood,
Nor thou within the compass of my curse.

Buck. Nor no-one here: for curses never pass   285
The lips of those that breathe them in the air.

---

272. is] *F;* was *Qq.*   273. *Buck.*] *Qq,F; Gloucester. | NCS, conj. Walker.*
Peace, peace] *F;* Haue done *Qq.*   276. my hopes by you] *F;* by you my
hopes *Qq.*   278. that] *F;* my *Qq.*   still] *F,Q1–5;* shall *Q6.*   279. Have
done, have done] *F;* Haue done *Qq.*   280. *Marg.*] *F (subst.); Q.M. | Q1–2;
Q.Mar. | Q3–4; Q.Mary. | Q5–6 (subst.).*   princely] *F,Q1–3,5–6;* pricely *Q4.*
I'll] *F;* I will *Qq.*   282. noble] *F;* Princely *Qq.*   286. those] *F,Q1–5;*
them *Q6.*

---

eternall night, / That clouds of
darkenesse may inclose my flesh'.

272.] Cf. *Genesis,* ix.6, and
Matthew, xxvi.52 (Noble).

is] A form of past tense.

273. *Buck.*] W. S. Walker (quoted,
Variorum, p. 105) queried the attribution of this speech; Alice Walker
proposed assigning it to Richard, and
was followed by NCS on the grounds
that ll. 274–6 and 280–4 cannot be
said to the same person. No doubt;
Margaret, in her first speech, hears
the words of l. 273 but does not
attend to the speaker; rather she
snatches two words from the line
that she can fling again at her
tormentors. 'You' in ll. 275–6 is
surely plural—she is at bay, snarling

at the group. When Buckingham
reiterates his plea she turns to him
and answers him in gentler fashion.
There is no need for amendment,
especially in view of the fact that one
of l. 279's 'have dones' migrated in
Q to l. 273: a clear indication that
both were spoken by the same actor.

280. *Marg.*] F's corrector was alert
enough to purge the hypothetical
'Queen Mary'—if indeed he was
using Q6 copy here.

princely] Henry Stafford, the Duke
of the play, was a descendant of
Thomas, Duke of Gloucester, youngest
son of Edward III, so the epithet is
apt enough.

284. *compass . . . curse*] Also found
in *Tit.,* v.i.126.

Marg. I will not think but they ascend the sky,
　　And there awake God's gentle sleeping peace.
　　O Buckingham, take heed of yonder dog!
　　Look when he fawns, he bites; and when he bites　　290
　　His venom tooth will rankle to the death.
　　Have not to do with him; beware of him;
　　Sin, death, and hell have set their marks on him,
　　And all their ministers attend on him.
Rich. What doth she say, my lord of Buckingham?　　295
Buck. Nothing that I respect, my gracious lord.
Marg. What, dost thou scorn me for my gentle counsel,
　　And soothe the devil that I warn thee from?
　　O, but remember this another day
　　When he shall split thy very heart with sorrow,　　300
　　And say, poor Margaret was a prophetess.
　　Live, each of you, the subjects to his hate,
　　And he to yours, and all of you to God's.　　　　*Exit.*
Buck. My hair doth stand on end to hear her curses.

287. I will not think] *F;* Ile not beleeue *Qq.*　　289. take heed] *F;* beware *Qq.*
291. rankle] *F,Q2–6;* rackle *Q1.*　　to the] *F;* thee to *Qq.*　　297.] *As Qq;*
. . . me / For *F.*　　298. soothe] *F,Q1–5 (subst.);* soothd *Q6.*　　302. to] *F;*
of *Qq.*　　303. yours] *F;* your *Q1–2;* you *Q3–6.*　　304. *Buck.*] *F; Hast. | Qq.*

287. *ascend the sky*] Cf. *Parts Added*, p. 286, 'Varianus', ll. 23–4.

288. *awake . . . peace*] For the arousing of God, cf. Psalms, xliv. 23 and lxxviii. 65.

289–90.] Cf. Marlowe, *Jew*, II. iii. 20–1: 'We Jewes can fawne like Spaniels when we please; / And when we grin we bite'. See N. Brooke, *Sh.S.*, 14, p. 37. His contention that Shakespeare intended the audience to recollect Barabas and his villainy from this echo is speculative. The concept was anyway proverbial: Tilley C732.

291. *venom*] venomous (regularly used as an adjective: OED B). Though not literally venomous, a mad dog's bite will cause a wound to 'rankle', with equivalent result.

rankle] inflict a festering wound: OED *v.*2. Q1's 'rackle' is simply a compositorial oversight.

293. *marks*] As have the elves: Richard bears ample warning signs of his nature from the malignant powers.

302. *to*] Margaret envisions her enemies, not subjects *of* Richard's enthroned hatred, but subjected *to* his hate, a thought pursued in the next line.

304. *Buck.*] Whose hair stood on end? (Or 'an end' as F has it—a mere lexical difference.) Most eds have preferred Q's Hastings, including Thompson and NCS. In recent years Eccles, Evans, and NPS have supported Buckingham. Smidt observes (p. 17) that Buckingham is not impressionable, because he has just told Richard he does not respect Margaret's warning. However, this was obviously said just to avoid repeating Margaret's accusations to Richard, and as the previous 30 lines

Riv. And so doth mine; I muse why she's at liberty.   305
Rich. I cannot blame her: by God's holy mother,
    She hath had too much wrong; and I repent
    My part thereof that I have done to her.
Eliz. I never did her any, to my knowledge.
Rich. Yet you have all the vantage of her wrong.   310
    I was too hot to do somebody good
    That is too cold in thinking of it now;
    Marry, as for Clarence, he is well repaid:
    He is frank'd up to fatting for his pains.
    God pardon them that are the cause thereof.   315
Riv. A virtuous and a Christian-like conclusion,
    To pray for them that have done scathe to us.
Rich. So do I ever—(*Speaks to himself*) being well advis'd;
    For had I curs'd now, I had curs'd myself.

Enter CATESBY.

Cat. Madam, his Majesty doth call for you,   320
    And for your Grace, and you my gracious lords.

305. muse why] *F;* wonder *Qq.*   308. to her] *F; not in Qq.*   309. *Eliz.*]
Q 1–5 (*Qu.*)*; Hast. | Q 6; Mar. | F.*   310. Yet . . . her] *F;* But . . . this *Qq.*
315. thereof] *F;* of it *Qq.*   318. S.D.] *F; not in Qq.*   319. S.D.] *F; not in*
Qq.   321. you] *Qq;* yours *F.*   gracious lords] *Alexander;* noble Lo: *Q 1–*
2; noble Lord *Q 3–6;* gracious Lord *F.*

have comprised a kind of duet between Margaret and Buckingham,
during which he found himself
increasingly implicated in her complaints, and as he tried to prevent
her cursing with some vehemence, it
is not inherently improbable that he
should express his unease once she left.
    314. *frank'd*] shut up in a pen or
sty to fatten: see OED *sb.*[2] and *v.*[1]
    317. *scathe*] harm, injury: OED 2b.
    318. S.D., 319. S.D.] Omitted
from Q presumably through the
compositor's dislike of stage-directions: see Introduction, pp. 27–8.
    320–1.] This pair of lines has
occasioned much difficulty. Q1's
version, 'for your Grace, and you my
noble Lo:', is acceptable provided we
recall that 'Lo:' can be an abbrevia-

tion for 'Lords' as well as 'Lord' (cf.
I.ii. 1 for another accident arising
from the same contraction). Q3 in
expanding it made the error of
putting it into the singular, and this
form gets into F despite the corrector's
substitution of 'gracious' for 'noble'.
A further difficulty was noted by
Spedding, p. 61, who observed that
as there are two dukes present, both
of whom should be addressed as
'your Grace', and as II.i makes it
clear that Edward wants both of
them, it is necessary to decide to whom
Catesby's lines are addressed. Presumably, it is Richard (who is of
superior degree to Buckingham, and
is of greater dramatic importance).
Buckingham here must be included
with the collective 'lords'.

Eliz. Catesby, I come. Lords, will you go with me?
Riv. We wait upon your Grace.   *Exeunt all but Richard.*
Rich. I do the wrong, and first begin to brawl:
    The secret mischiefs that I set abroach   325
    I lay unto the grievous charge of others.
    Clarence, whom I, indeed, have cast in darkness,
    I do beweep to many simple gulls,
    Namely to Derby, Hastings, Buckingham;
    And tell them 'tis the Queen and her allies   330
    That stir the King against the Duke my brother.
    Now they believe it, and withal whet me
    To be reveng'd on Rivers, Dorset, Grey.
    But then I sigh, and, with a piece of Scripture,
    Tell them that God bids us do good for evil: 335
    And thus I clothe my naked villainy
    With odd old ends stol'n forth of Holy Writ,

322. I . . . me] *F;* we . . . vs *Qq.*   323. We wait upon] *F;* Madame we will
attend *Qq (subst.).*   323. S.D.] *F (Gloster); Exeunt man. Ri. | Qq (subst.).*
324. begin] *F;* began *Qq.*   325. mischiefs] *F,Q1–2;* mischiefe *Q3–6.*
327. whom] *Qq (subst.);* who *F.*   cast] *F;* laid *Qq.*   329. Derby, Hastings]
F; Hastings, Darby *Qq.*   330. tell them 'tis] *F;* say it is *Qq.*   332. it] *F;*
me *Qq.*   333. Dorset] *F;* Vaughan *Qq.*   334. I sigh] *F,Q1–2,4;* sigh *Q3,
5–6.*   335. do] *F,Q1–4;* to do *Q5–6 (subst.).*   337. odd old] *F;* old odde
Qq (subst.).   forth] *F;* out *Qq.*

324.] Proverbial: Tilley C579.

325. *abroach*] afoot, abroad: OED *adv.*2.

327. *whom*] Both forms 'who' and 'whom' were acceptable in the accusative: in a modernized text there is advantage in preferring the more correct form.

cast] Q 'laid' may be an actor's echo from the previous line. The F verb has an authentically Biblical ring (cf. Matthew, viii.12) and thus more accurately reflects Richard's blasphemous state of mind.

328. *gulls*] simpletons, credulous fools: OED *sb.*[3]

333. *Dorset*] It is Vaughan who is executed along with Rivers and Grey in III.iii, and the likeliest explanation of his appearance here in Q is an actor's or book-keeper's gesture towards consistency. Dorset is by far the more important figure among the

Queen's allies, and the more likely to be in Richard's mind at this point in the play.

335.] Proverbial (Tilley G318) as well as scriptural (Matthew, v. 44; Luke, vi.27, among numerous others —see Noble, p. 132).

336. *clothe . . . villainy*] Cf. Erasmus, letter to Abbot of St Bertin (1514) tr. L. K. Born, p. 19: 'there are princes who first decide what they want and then look out for a title with which to cloak their proceedings'.

337. *odd old ends*] The Q inversion of the phrase may be merely fortuitous. 'Ends' are tags, or commonplaces (Thompson); they are old, since they are scriptural; they are odd because they are a random assortment. They are also scraps of cloth (OED *sb.*1.15) which carries on the metaphor of the previous line.

And seem a saint, when most I play the devil.

Enter two Murderers.

But soft, here come my executioners.
How now, my hardy, stout, resolved mates;   340
Are you now going to dispatch this thing?
1 M. We are, my lord, and come to have the warrant,
That we may be admitted where he is.
Rich. Well thought upon; I have it here about me.
When you have done, repair to Crosby Place—   345
But sirs, be sudden in the execution,
Withal obdurate: do not hear him plead;
For Clarence is well-spoken, and perhaps
May move your hearts to pity, if you mark him.
2 M. Tut, tut, my lord: we will not stand to prate.   350
Talkers are no good doers; be assur'd
We go to use our hands, and not our tongues.
Rich. Your eyes drop millstones, when fools' eyes fall tears.
I like you, lads: about your business straight.
Go, go, dispatch.
Both.   We will, my noble lord. *Exeunt.*   355

338. S.D.] *F;   Enter Executioners. | Qq.*   339. come] *F,Q1;* comes *Q2–6.*
341. you] *F,Q1–2;* ye *Q3–6.*   now] *F,Q1–5;* not *Q6.*   thing] *F;*
deede *Qq.*   342. *1 M.] Capell; Vil. | F; Execu. | Qq (subst.).*   344. Well]
F; It was well *Qq.*   350. *2 M.] This edn; Vil. | F; Exec. | Qq (subst.).*
Tut, tut] *F;* Tush feare not *Qq.*   352. go] *F;* come *Qq.*   353. fall] *F;*
drop *Qq.*   354. straight] *F; not in Qq.*   355.] *F (. . . dispatch. | Vil.);*
not in Qq.   Both.] This edn;/Vil. | F.   355. S.D.] *Qq (after l. 354); not*
in F.

338.] Cf. 'Edmund Duke of Somerset', l. 285: 'A saynt in showe, in
proofe is found a fende' (*Mirror*, p.
400).

342, 350, 355.] Virtually all eds
allocate all three speeches to the
First Murderer. There seems to be
no reason to leave the Second silent,
and some slight advantage may be
gained from distinguishing the man
who declares he will not prate from
the man who instantly decides to
reason with Clarence (i.iv.152).

Hence the speeches have been
divided between the two in this edn;
the last line is a characteristic duet
(cf. i.iv.163), a mumbled response
of agreement.

350. *we . . . prate*] Proverbial:
Tilley T64.

353. *millstones*] Proverbial: Tilley
M967; also cf. Whetstone's *Promos*,
p. 453: 'I have eyes will looke into a
Mylstone'.

fall] drop, let fall.

SCENE IV

Enter CLARENCE *and* KEEPER.

Keep. Why looks your Grace so heavily today?
Cla. O, I have pass'd a miserable night,
So full of fearful dreams, of ugly sights,
That, as I am a Christian faithful man,
I would not spend another such a night   5
Though 'twere to buy a world of happy days,
So full of dismal terror was the time.
Keep. What was your dream, my lord? I pray you tell me.
Cla. Methoughts that I had broken from the Tower,
And was embark'd to cross to Burgundy;   10
And in my company my brother Gloucester,

Scene IV

SCENE IV] *Capell; Scena Quarta | F; not in Qq.* S.D.] *F; Enter Clarence,
Brokenbury | Qq.* 1. *Keep.*] *F; Brok. (subst.) Qq [throughout].* 3. fearful
dreams . . . ugly sights] *F; vgly sights . . . gastly dreames Qq.* 8. my lord?
I pray . . . me] *F; I long to heare . . . it Qq.* 9. Methoughts] *F,Q1–3 (Me
thoughts); Me thought Q4–6.* 9–10.] *F; Me thoughts I was imbarkt for
Burgundy, Qq (subst.).*

Scene IV

S.D.] for Q's substitution of
Brakenbury for the Keeper in this
scene, see Introduction, pp. 14–15.

2.] For the Senecan, Ovidian, and
Spenserian inspiration and derivation
of Clarence's Dream, see Introduction, p. 80, and especially Harold
F. Brooks, '*Richard III*: Antecedents
of Clarence's Dream', *Sh.S.*, 32 (1979),
pp. 145–50.

2–3.] Cf. 'Seneca', *Octavia*, l. 712 ff.
There is also probably an echo from
More of the account of Stanley's
dream (Hall, *Edward V*, fol. xiv^v): 'he
had a fearfull dreame . . . [which]
made such a fearfull impression in hys
harte'. Also cf. *Leir*: 'I had a short
nap, but so full of dread, / As much
amazeth me to think thereof. . . . I
pray, my Lord, what was the effect
of it?' [F1^v].

5. *a*] Used pleonastically: Abbott
§85.

9, 24, 58. *Methoughts*] NCS's view
that this is an actor's form is unintelligible. There is no evidence that F
is memorially contaminated.

9–10.] The absence from Q of the
information that Clarence, in his
dream, was still aware of his incar-
ceration is very hard to explain. His
imprisonment clearly began Clarence's mind on its journey towards
an awareness of his own guilt, a
journey paralleled by the image of
the dream-journey. Yet he is aware
of Richard's part in his imprisonment only unconsciously (ll. 18–20).
These two lines seem crucial to the
development of the scene and
Clarence's state of mind: either an
actor's or a copyist's oversight must
be invoked to account for their
omission from Q.

Who from my cabin tempted me to walk
Upon the hatches: thence we look'd toward England,
And cited up a thousand heavy times,
During the wars of York and Lancaster,   15
That had befall'n us. As we pac'd along
Upon the giddy footing of the hatches,
Methought that Gloucester stumbled, and in falling,
Struck me (that thought to stay him) overboard,
Into the tumbling billows of the main.   20
O Lord! Methought what pain it was to drown:
What dreadful noise of waters in my ears;
What sights of ugly death within my eyes!
Methoughts I saw a thousand fearful wrecks;
Ten thousand men that fishes gnaw'd upon;   25
Wedges of gold, great anchors, heaps of pearl,
Inestimable stones, unvalu'd jewels,
All scatter'd in the bottom of the sea.
Some lay in dead men's skulls, and in the holes
Where eyes did once inhabit, there were crept—   30
As 'twere in scorn of eyes—reflecting gems,

13. thence] *Q 1–5*; there *Q6,F.*   toward] *F,Q 1–5*; towards *Q6.*   14. heavy]
F; fearefull *Qq.*   18. falling] *F*; stumbling *Qq.*   21. O] *F*; Lord, *Qq.*
22. waters] *Q 1–5*; water *Q6,F.*   my] *Q 1*; mine *Q 2–6,F.*   23. sights of
ugly] *F*; ugly sights of *Qq.*   my] *Q 1*; mine *Q 2–6,F.*   24. Methoughts] *F*;
Me thought *Qq.*   25. Ten] *Qq*; A *F.*   26. anchors] *F,Qq*; ingots *NCS*;
ingowes *conj. Kinnear.*   28.] *F*; *not in Qq.*   29. the] *F*; those *Qq.*

13–18.] Cf. Golding's Ovid, III.
792–9.
　13. *thence*] F correction is distinctly
uneven in this passage: here a Q6
error is taken over, but in the same
line Q6's 'towards' is corrected.
　21–3.] Cf. 'Seneca', *Octavia*, ll.
343–7. Messalina, expecting to drown,
exclaims that this is the nemesis for
her murderous crimes (she is going
to her wronged husband's ghost).
　22, 23. *my*] F's 'mine' (more
normal before a vowel, and certainly
more euphonious) entered via Q2's
normalization and thus is without
authority.
　25. *Ten*] Q has the rhetorical edge
here, and has been preferred by Camb.

among other eds. F's repetition of 'a
thousand' is plausible as a compositor's error.
　26. *anchors*] See Appendix II.
　27. *unvalu'd*] of inestimable value:
OED 1.
　28.] Omitted from Q: Smidt (p.
70), noting the repetition of 'bottom'
and 'scatter'd' in ll. 32–3, believed
the omission was deliberate. Many
eds since Pope have dropped the line,
but in recent times it has been included, and the rhetorical rhythm
of the passage is improved by its
presence. It is equally plausible that
its omission from Q should have
arisen from compositor's inattention.
See also ll. 36–7.

That woo'd the slimy bottom of the deep,
And mock'd the dead bones that lay scatter'd by.

Keep. Had you such leisure in the time of death
To gaze upon these secrets of the deep?   35

Cla. Methought I had; and often did I strive
To yield the ghost, but still the envious flood
Stopp'd in my soul, and would not let it forth
To find the empty, vast, and wand'ring air,
But smother'd it within my panting bulk,   40
Which almost burst to belch it in the sea.

Keep. Awak'd you not in this sore agony?

Cla. No, no; my dream was lengthen'd after life.
O, then began the tempest to my soul:
I pass'd, methought, the melancholy flood,   45
With that sour ferryman which poets write of,
Unto the kingdom of perpetual night.

32. That] *F;* Which *Qq.*   woo'd] *F,Q 1–4 (subst.);* wade *Q 5–6.*   35. these]
F; the *Qq.*   36–7. and . . . ghost,] *F; not in Qq.*   37. but] *F;* for *Qq.*
38. Stopp'd] *F;* Kept *Qq.*   39. find] *F;* seeke *Q 1–2;* keepe *Q 3–6.*   41.
Which] *Qq;* Who *F.*   42. in] *F;* with *Qq.*   43. No, no] *F;* O no *Qq.*
44. to] *F,Q 1–5;* of *Q 6.*   45. I] *F;* Who *Qq.*   46. sour] *F;* grim *Qq.*

32. *slimy bottom*] Cf. *Spanish Tragedy,* I.i.28 and III.xiii.115.

36–8.] Cf. *2 Tamburlaine,* IV.ii.34–5: 'Making a passage for my troubled soule, / Which beates against this prison to get out'; also 'watery wilderness', l. 30. The idea of the soul struggling to escape from the body is a commonplace; 'yield the ghost' is perhaps a recollection of Matthew, xxvii.50.

36–7.] The omission in Q of a clause, and the alteration of the conjunction to make what remains intelligible, suggests deliberate alteration in the text, and avoids a somewhat awkward image at the cost of spoiling the antithesis. The change is more likely to have originated with the actor than with the poet or the compositor.

44. *tempest . . . soul*] Cf. *1 Tamburlaine,* III.ii.86–7: 'That sent a tempest to my daunted thoughtes, / And

makes my soule devine her overthrow'.

45. *melancholy flood*] Cf. Seneca, *Agamemnon,* l. 12, 'tristes lacus', and *Hercules Oetaeus,* l. 1950, 'vada trista'.

46. *sour*] Slightly more appropriate to the common conception of Charon than Q's 'grim'. The actor seems to have treated the text of the dream with some freedom, and this is probably his substitution. Cf. Seneca, *Hercules Furens,* ll. 771, 764, 'dirus Charon . . . aspectu horridus', and *1 Tamburlaine,* V.i.246: 'the ugly Ferriman'.

poets] Most notably Vergil and Dante, but also Sackville, in his Induction to 'Buckingham' in the *Mirror.* See Introduction, pp. 86–7.

47. *kingdom . . . night*] An epic phrase; cf. *Edward III*: 'Leaving no hope to us but sullen darke, / And eielesse terror of all ending night' [H1ᵛ–2ʳ]. Also cf. *Spanish Tragedy,*

The first that there did greet my stranger-soul
Was my great father-in-law, renowned Warwick,
Who spake aloud, 'What scourge for perjury   50
Can this dark monarchy afford false Clarence?'
And so he vanish'd. Then came wand'ring by
A shadow like an angel, with bright hair
Dabbled in blood; and he shriek'd out aloud,
'Clarence is come: false, fleeting, perjur'd Clarence,   55
That stabb'd me in the field by Tewkesbury!
Seize on him, Furies! Take him unto torment!'
With that, methoughts, a legion of foul fiends
Environ'd me, and howled in mine ears
Such hideous cries, that with the very noise   60
I trembling wak'd, and for a season after
Could not believe but that I was in hell,
Such terrible impression made my dream.

Keep. No marvel, lord, though it affrighted you;
    I am afraid, methinks, to hear you tell it.   65

Cla. Ah, Keeper, Keeper, I have done these things,

50. spake] *F;* cried *Qq.*   53. with] *F;* in *Qq.*   54. shriek'd] *F;* squakt *Q1;*
squeakt *Q2–6 (subst.).*   57. unto] *F;* to your *Qq.*   torment] *F;* torments
Qq.   58. methoughts] *Q1;* me thought *Q2–6,F.*   59. me] *F;* me about *Qq.*
63. my] *F;* the *Qq.*   64. lord] *F;* my Lo: *Qq (subst.).*   65. am afraid,
methinks] *F;* promise you, I am afraid *Qq.*   66. Ah, Keeper, Keeper] *F;* O
Brokenbury *Qq.*   these] *F;* those *Qq.*

1.i.56: 'Through dreadful shades of
ever-glooming night'. Note, further,
Seneca, *Hippolytus,* l. 221, 'nocte
perpetua domum', and *Oedipus,* l.
393, 'noctis aeternae plagis'.

  50. *spake*] Q 'cried' is preferred by
many eds. Perhaps a contrast of tone
was desired between the voice of
Warwick and that of Prince Edward,
but the actor felt the more emphatic
'cried' sounded better.

  51. *this dark monarchy*] Many Senecan
sources, including *Hercules Furens,* l.
707, *Hercules Oetaeus,* ll. 558–60, 938.

  53. *shadow*] The ghost of Prince
Edward. For the entire phrase, cf.
Seneca, *Medea,* ll. 963 ff.

  54. *shriek'd*] Q's 'squakt' means, as
Q2 etc. have it, 'squeakt'; the verb

'to squawk' is not found until the
19th century. Although Thompson
and others have followed Q here,
reminding us that ghosts were often
described as having thin, squeaking
voices (cf. *Caes.,* II.ii.24; *Ham.,*
I.i.116, etc.—though in *Caes.* they
shriek as well as squeal), the context
makes the word absurd: to squeak
Edward's thunderous denunciation
is impossible.

  55. *fleeting*] fickle, vacillating: OED
*ppl.a.*2.

  57–9.] Cf. *Spanish Tragedy,* I.i.65,
70–1. The original source is perhaps
Medea, ll. 965 ff; but see also *Hercules
Furens,* ll. 86 ff. and 100.

  58. *legion*] See Noble, pp. 132 and
273.

That now give evidence against my soul,
For Edward's sake: and see how he requites me.
O God, if my deep prayers cannot appease Thee,
But Thou wilt be aveng'd on my misdeeds,   70
Yet execute Thy wrath in me alone;
O spare my guiltless wife and my poor children.
Keeper, I prithee sit by me awhile:
My soul is heavy, and I fain would sleep.

Keep. I will, my lord; God give your Grace good rest.   75

Enter BRAKENBURY *the Lieutenant.*

Brak. Sorrow breaks seasons and reposing hours,
Makes the night morning, and the noontide night.
Princes have but their titles for their glories,
An outward honour for an inward toil;
And for unfelt imaginations   80
They often feel a world of restless cares:
So that between their titles, and low name,
There's nothing differs but the outward fame.

Enter the two Murderers.

1 M. Ho, who's here?

Brak. What would'st thou, fellow? And how cam'st thou
hither?   85

67. That now give] *F;* Which now beare *Qq.*   69–72.] *F; not in Qq.*
73.] *F;* I pray thee gentle keeper stay by me, *Qq.*   75. S.D.] *F; not in Qq.*
76. Brak.] *As F; speaker continues, Qq.*   breaks] *F,Q2–6;* breake *Q1.*   80.
imaginations] *F;* imagination *Qq.*   82. between] *F;* betwixt *Qq.*   their]
F,Q1–2; your *Q3–6.*   name] *F;* names *Qq.*   83. S.D.] *As F;* The murtherers enter *Qq.*   84.] *F; not in Qq.*   85.] What would'st thou, fellow?]
F; In Gods name what are you, *Qq.*   cam'st] *F;* came *Qq.*

69–72.] See Appendix I.

73. *Keeper*] Q's emendation 'gentle
keeper' is made to correspond with
the merging of that role and Bracken-
bury's.

74.] Cf. Matthew, xxvi. 38.

76.] It is odd, as Harold Brooks
remarked privately, that this monologue should not be a soliloquy, and
that Brakenbury should voice his suspicions with the Keeper for a witness.

76–7.] See Job, xvii. 11–12.

80. *unfelt imaginations*] i.e. those
satisfactions it is imagined princes
enjoy, but which they do not actually
feel.

84 ff.] The prose scene ensuing
reveals a greater degree of variation
between Q and F than most of the
text. The probable explanation is the
survival of gag in Q. Hence F has
been followed fairly rigorously with a
few specific exceptions (e.g. l. 120).

85. *What would'st thou, fellow?*]

2 M. I would speak with Clarence, and I came hither on
          my legs.
Brak. What, so brief?
1 M. 'Tis better, sir, than to be tedious. Let him see our
          commission, and talk no more.   [*Brakenbury*] *reads.*   90
Brak. I am in this commanded to deliver
          The noble Duke of Clarence to your hands.
          I will not reason what is meant hereby,
          Because I will be guiltless from the meaning.
          There lies the Duke asleep; and there the keys.   95
          I'll to the King, and signify to him
          That thus I have resign'd to you my charge.
1 M. You may, sir; 'tis a point of wisdom. Fare you well.
                                   Exeunt Brakenbury [and Keeper].
2 M. What, shall I stab him as he sleeps?

86. *2 M.*] *F; Execu. | Qq (subst.).*   88. What] *F;* Yea, are you *Q 1–2;* Yea,
are ye *Q 3–6.*   89. *1 M.*] *F;* 2 Exe. | *Qq (subst.).*   'Tis] *F;* O sir, it is *Qq.*
better, sir] *F;* better *Qq.*   than to be] *F;* to be briefe then *Q 1–2;* be briefe
then *Q 3–6.*   Let him see] *F;* Shew him *Qq.*   90. and talk] *F;* talke *Qq.*
90. S.D.] *F; He readeth it. Qq.*   93. hereby] *F,Q 1–2;* thereby *Q 3–6.*   94.
from] *F;* of *Qq.*   95.] *F;* Here are the keies, there sits the Duke a sleepe, *Qq*
(subst.).   96. the King . . . signify to him] *F;* his Maiesty . . . certifie his
Grace *Qq (subst.).*   97. to you my charge] *F;* my charge to you *Q 1–2;* my
place to you *Q 3–6.*   98. *1 M.*] *F; Exe. | Qq.*   You may, sir; 'tis] *F;* Doe
so, it is *Qq.*   Fare you well.] *F; not in Qq.*   98. S.D.] *F (Exit) after l.96;*
not in Qq.   99. I] *Q 1–2;* we *Q 3–6,F.*

Patrick (p. 50) regards the Q version
of this as derived by anticipation
from l. 155; Smidt (p. 54) also points
out the similarity of Q l. 162 (*q.v.*).
The parallel situations, of someone
suddenly becoming aware of the
presence of two unprepossessing persons, evidently evoked in Shakespeare's mind a group of similar
verbal responses. It is likely that
some of the variation then may have
arisen in the manuscripts. Cf. *R2*,
v.v.69, for an almost identical line
in a similar situation.
          86. *2 M.*] Malone, followed by
almost all eds (but not NPS) gives
l. 86 to the First Murderer and l. 89
to the Second, on the grounds (in

the words of NCS) that l. 86 'clearly
belongs to the man who spoke l. 84.'
As the murderers enter together and
act in a choric way at this point, the
necessity for emendation does not
evidently appear.
          86–7. *came . . . legs*] Proverbial:
Tilley L191.
          89.] Surely proverbial, though not
listed in Tilley.
          95–7.] Cf. 'Richard', ll. 85–6:
'The keyes he rendered, but partaker
would not be / Of that flagitious
facte' (*Mirror*, p. 363).
          99 ff.] The scene is obviously prose,
and so almost all edns print it.
          99.] Cf. *Leir*, 'Now could I stab
them bravely, while they sleepe' [F1r].

1 M. No: he'll say 'twas done cowardly, when he wakes.   100

2 M. Why, he shall never wake until the great Judgement Day.

1 M. Why, then he'll say we stabbed him sleeping.

2 M. The urging of that word, 'Judgement', hath bred a kind of remorse in me.   105

1 M. What, art thou afraid?

2 M. Not to kill him—having a warrant—but to be damned for killing him, from the which no warrant can defend me.

1 M. I thought thou hadst been resolute.   110

2 M. So I am—to let him live.

1 M. I'll back to the Duke of Gloucester, and tell him so.

2 M. Nay, I prithee stay a little: I hope this passionate humour of mine will change. It was wont to hold me but while one tells twenty.   115

1 M. How dost thou feel thyself now?

2 M. Some certain dregs of conscience are yet within me.

1 M. Remember our reward, when the deed's done.

2 M. Zounds, he dies! I had forgot the reward.   120

100. he'll] *F;* then he will *Qq.*   100–52. *As prose, this edn; as verse, Qq; ll. 107–15 as verse, otherwise prose, F.*   101. Why] *F;* When he wakes, / Why foole *Qq.* until the great] *F;* till the *Qq.*   103. he'll] *F;* he will *Qq.*   107. warrant] *F;* warrant for it *Qq.*   108. the which] *F;* which *Qq.*   109. me] *F;* vs *Qq.* 110–11.] *F; not in Qq.*   112. I'll back . . . and tell] *F;* Backe . . . tell *Qq.* 113. Nay, I] *F;* I *Qq.*   prithee] *F;* pray thee *Qq.*   little] *F;* while *Qq.* 113–14. this passionate humour of mine] *F;* my holy humor *Qq.*   114. It was] *F;* twas *Qq.*   115. tells twenty] *F;* would tel xx *Qq.*   117. Some] *F;* Faith some *Qq.*   119. deed's] *F;* deede is *Qq.*   120. Zounds] *Qq;* Come *F.*

101–2.] Cf. *Leir*, 'And thou shalt never wake untill doomes day' [F3r].

110–11.] Smidt (p. 108) regards l. 111 as 'out of character' and supposes the omission thereof from Q deliberate, for this reason. The argument is unconvincing, since the very point at issue is the momentary wavering of the Second Murderer. In any event, these minor figures have no 'characters' in any consistent sense (*pace* Cowden-Clarke, who believed them carefully discriminated); they act according to the immediate dramatic needs of the moment.

113. *passionate*] The Murderer means 'inclined to pity, compassionate' (OED 5b, citing this line), but the word has strong theological overtones, of Christ's passion, and hence also means 'holy', the very word found in Q. It is likely that the actor, aware of the second meaning, substituted the familiar term for the unfamiliar. See also Introduction, p. 112.

117. *Some*] See l. 120n.

120. *Zounds*] This oath was much misliked as an unnecessary profanity, and is surely missing from F in

1 M. Where's thy conscience now?

2 M. Oh, in the Duke of Gloucester's purse.

1 M. When he opens his purse to give us our reward, thy
conscience flies out?

2 M. 'Tis no matter; let it go. There's few, or none, will   125
entertain it.

1 M. What if it come to thee again?

2 M. I'll not meddle with it; it makes a man a coward.
A man cannot steal but it accuseth him; a man cannot swear but it checks him; a man cannot lie with   130
his neighbour's wife but it detects him. 'Tis a blush-
ing, shamefaced spirit, that mutinies in a man's
bosom. It fills a man full of obstacles; it made me
once restore a purse of gold that by chance I found.
It beggars any man that keeps it; it is turned out of   135
towns and cities for a dangerous thing; and every
man that means to live well endeavours to trust to
himself, and live without it.

---

121. Where's] *F;* Where is *Qq.*   122. Oh, in] *F;* In *Qq.*   123. When] *F;*
So when *Qq.*   125. 'Tis no matter] *F; not in Qq.*   126. it] *F,Q1,3–6;* vs
Q2.   127. What] *F;* How *Qq.*   128. it; it] *F;* it, it is a dangerous thing, /
It *Qq.*   129. a man] *F;* he *Qq.*   130. swear] *F,Q1–2;* steale *Q3–6.*   a
man] *F;* he *Qq.*   131. 'Tis] *F;* It is *Qq.*   133. a man] *F;* one *Qq.*
134. purse] *F,Q1–2;* piece *Q3–6 (subst.).*   by chance] *F; not in Qq.*   135.
cf] *F;* of all *Qq.*   137. trust to] *F,Q2–6;* trust to / To *Q1.*   138. live] *F;*
to liue *Qq.*

---

response to the statute of 1606, 3.
Jac. I. It is highly apposite and
ironical in context that the Murderer
should signal his return to depravity
and the intent to slay by appealing to
'God's wounds'. It is less certain that
the milder oath 'Faith' which prefixes
Q 1. 117 would have been expunged
for the same reason; it is thus more
likely to be gag.
128. *it; it*] The phrase found in Q
here is probably derived by anticipation of ll. 135–6 by the actor. NCS
remarks that it may be taken as a
general proposition, followed by
particular examples, but most modern
eds agree that the phrase is an
intrusion.

128 ff.] The material here, and
the style, are partly borrowed from
the Commination in the *BCP* (Noble,
p. 133).
129. *a man*] The Murderer here
(and at ll. 130 and 132) seems to be
attempting a fairly formal speech
characterized by the repetition of
parallel propositions, which evidently
became corroded by the actor's
memory in Q.
130. *swear*] Q3's 'steale' was
caught from l. 129.
137. *trust to*] The intrusive 'To' in
Q1 arises by dittography in a passage
which the compositor is valiantly
trying to force into verse.

1 M. Zounds, 'tis even now at my elbow, persuading me
    not to kill the Duke.   140

2 M. Take the devil in thy mind, and believe him not:
    he would insinuate with thee but to make thee sigh.

1 M. I am strong-framed; he cannot prevail with me.

2 M. Spoke like a tall man that respects thy reputation!
    Come, shall we fall to work?   145

1 M. Take him on the costard with the hilts of thy
    sword, and then throw him into the malmsey-butt
    in the next room.

2 M. Oh excellent device! and make a sop of him.

1 M. Soft, he wakes.   150

2 M. Strike!

139. Zounds *Qq; not in* F.   'tis] F; *it is* Qq.   142. but to] F; *to* Qq
143. I] F; *Tut, I* Qq.   strong-framed] F; *strong in fraud* Qq.   me.] F;
me, I warrant thee Qq.   144. Spoke] F,Q1–3; *Soode* Q4; *Stood* Q5–6.
man] F; *fellow* Qq.   thy] F; *his* Qq.   145. fall to work] F; *to this geere*
Qq.   146. on] F; *ouer* Qq.   thy] F,Q1–2; *my* Q3–6.   147. throw] F;
we wil chop Qq.   into] F; *in* Qq.   149. and make] F; *make* Qq.   sop]
F,Q1–2; *scoope* Q3; *soppe* Q4–6.   150–1. F; *1 Harke he stirs, shall I strike.*
Qq.

139. *Zounds*] See l. 120.

141. *Take the devil*] Eds have been
tempted to emend this obscure
phrase. The First Murderer says his
conscience is tempting him to mercy;
the Second rejoins, in words that
anticipate l. 146, with advice to
'take', that is to apprehend, or seize
(OED *v.*B.II.2) 'the devil', i.e. his
conscience: in this system of values,
mercy is a sinful failing and a
conscience a diabolical enemy to be
overcome.

143. *strong-framed*] Both this and
the Q reading 'strong in fraud' make
acceptable responses to the Second
Murderer's advice in the previous
speech; F implies a physical contest
between the Murderer and his
'diabolical' adversary, his conscience:
Q implies that he will vanquish it
thanks to his capacity for deceit.
Probably 'strong-framd' was misread as 'strong-fraud' and then
rationalized to 'strong in fraud'.

144. *tall*] brave, valiant (OED 1.3)

with raffish overtones, as a term used
by bravos. Cf. *Rom.*, II.iv.30.

146. *Take*] attack: OED *v.*B.II.5.

costard] OED 2: applied humor-
ously or derisively to the head.

147. *throw*] Q's 'chop' (see OED
v.[1] II.7) seems idiosyncratic with the
actors; it appears again as a substitute
at l. 259.

malmsey] Philip de Comines reported
that Clarence died 'en une pippe de
malvoysie': see Churchill, pp. 55–6.

149. *sop*] piece of bread, etc.,
soaked in wine or other liquid: OED
sb.[1] 2d, citing this line. The F spelling
is the same as that of Q1–2; for
whatever reason, the Q4–6 recovery
of the word (from Q3's error 'scoope')
in the longer form 'soppe' was not
followed by Compositor B: the only
other occasion in F when he set the
word (*Troil.*, I.iii.113) he used the
long form. A slight piece of evidence
against Q6 copy at this point, then.

150–1.] Q telescopes the two F
lines into one, and gives to the First

1 M. No, we'll reason with him.

Cla. Where art thou, Keeper? Give me a cup of wine.

2 M. You shall have wine enough, my lord, anon.

Cla. In God's name, what art thou?

2 M.   A man, as you are.   155

Cla. But not as I am, royal.

1 M. Nor you as we are, loyal.

Cla. Thy voice is thunder, but thy looks are humble.

1 M. My voice is now the King's, my looks mine own.

Cla. How darkly, and how deadly dost thou speak.   160
    Your eyes do menace me; why look you pale?
    Who sent you hither? Wherefore do you come?

Both. To—to—to—

Cla.   To murder me?

Both.   Ay, ay.

Cla. You scarcely have the hearts to tell me so,
    And therefore cannot have the hearts to do it.   165
    Wherein, my friends, have I offended you?

1 M. Offended us you have not, but the King.

Cla. I shall be reconcil'd to him again.

2 M. Never, my lord; therefore prepare to die.

152. *1 M.*] *F*; *2* | *Qq.*   we'll] *F*; first lets *Qq.*   him.] *F,Q 1–2*; him. *Cla.*
awaketh. *Q 3–6*.   154. *2 M.*] *F*; *1* | *Qq.*   155. *2 M.*] *Qq*; *1* | *F*.   157. *1*
M.] *F,Q 5–6*; *2* | *Q 1–4*.   159. *1 M.*] *F*; *2* | *Qq.*   161.] *F*; not in *Qq.*
162.] *F*; Tell me who are you, wherefore come you hither? *Qq.*   163. *Both.*
To] *As Qq (Am.); 2* To *F*.   *Both.* Ay, ay] *F*; *Am.* I *Qq.*   164. hearts]
F,Q 1–5; heart *Q 6*.

Murderer, thus initiating the confusion as to who speaks the ensuing
lines. Smidt's view (p. 49) that
Shakespeare intended the Second
Murderer to be more consistently
pitiful than the First is not in keeping
with the fact that the harsh speeches
of ll. 128–49 are unequivocally given
to the Second. On the whole it seems
best to follow F, with two exceptions
demanded by the sense of the action:
in l. 155 it ought to be the same
speaker who replies to Clarence as the
one who first broke into his awareness;
Clarence then becomes aware of the
pair of them and turns in l. 156 to the
other. Secondly, the confused res-

ponses in l. 163 clearly belong, as Q
has it, to both Murderers in mumbled
consort.

160. *darkly*] in a frowning, ominous
manner: OED 3, citing this line.

161.] Smidt holds (p. 109) that the
line was omitted from Q inadvertently,
but some (e.g. Vaughan) have
thought it contradicted l. 158 on the
grounds that 'looks' cannot mean
'general demeanour'. But that is
exactly what it does mean (OED
look *sb.*2b): Clarence is surprised that
a man of evidently low degree should
speak with such assurance.

162.] Cf. ll. 85 and 155. Actor-
confusion best accounts for Q.

Cla. Are you drawn forth among a world of men   170
  To slay the innocent? What is my offence?
  Where is the evidence that doth accuse me?
  What lawful quest have giv'n their verdict up
  Unto the frowning judge? Or who pronounc'd
  The bitter sentence of poor Clarence' death?   175
  Before I be convict by course of law,
  To threaten me with death is most unlawful.
  I charge you, as you hope to have redemption,
  By Christ's dear blood, shed for our grievous sins,
  That you depart and lay no hands on me: 180
  The deed you undertake is damnable.

1 M. What we will do, we do upon command.

2 M. And he that hath commanded is our King.

Cla. Erroneous vassals! The great King of kings
  Hath in the table of His law commanded   185
  That thou shalt do no murder. Will you then
  Spurn at His edict, and fulfil a man's?
  Take heed! For He holds vengeance in His hand
  To hurl upon their heads that break His law.

2 M. And that same vengeance doth He hurl on thee,   190
  For false forswearing, and for murder too:

---

170. drawn ... among] *F;* cald ... from out *Qq.* 172. is ... that doth] *F;* are ... that doe *Q 1–2;* are ... to *Q 3–6.* 177. threaten] *F,Q 1–2;* thteaten *Q 3;* thereaten *Q 4–6.* 178. to have redemption] *Qq;* for any goodness *F.* 179.] *Qq; not in F.* 183. our] *F;* the *Qq.* 184. vassals] *F;* vassaile *Qq.* 185. the] *F,Q 1–2;* his *Q 3–6.* table] *F;* tables *Qq.* 186. Will you] *F;* and wilt thou *Qq.* 188. hand] *F;* hands *Qq.* 190. hurl] *F;* throw *Qq.*

---

173. *quest*] See the extracts from 'Clarence' in the *Mirror,* in Appendix III, especially ll. 349–57, and Introduction, p. 88. Quest means an official or judicial inquiry: OED *sb.*[1] I. 1.

176. *convict*] i.e. convicted.

178–9.] Q's version of this, obviously right, fell victim to the 1606 Statute. Frye (p. 121) remarks on the parallel with the Atonement.

182–3.] Cf. Marlowe, *Edward II,* v.iv.103–4: '*Kent.* Art thou king, must I die at thy commaund? / *Mortimer.* At our commaund.'

184–9.] There are numerous scriptural and liturgical parallels for this imposing speech. Note, for instance, the *Sermon on Obedience* in the *Homilies,* F6ʳ, or the catechism. Specific Biblical sources include of course the Commandments: Exodus, xxxii. 15, and for ll. 188–9, Deuteronomy, xxxii. 35 and Romans, xii. 19. See Noble, pp. 133–4.

190–1.] See Leviticus, xxvii, Numbers, vi. 2, etc. The entire passage, to l. 199, is full of scriptural imagery.

Thou didst receive the sacrament to fight
In quarrel of the House of Lancaster.

1 M. And like a traitor to the name of God
Didst break that vow, and with thy treacherous blade
Unrip'st the bowels of thy sovereign's son.   196

2 M. Whom thou wast sworn to cherish and defend.

1 M. How canst thou urge God's dreadful law to us,
When thou hast broke it in such dear degree?

Cla. Alas, for whose sake did I that ill deed?   200
For Edward, for my brother, for his sake.
He sends you not to murder me for this,
For in that sin he is as deep as I.
If God will be avenged for the deed,
O know you yet, He doth it publicly;   205
Take not the quarrel from His powerful arm.
He needs no indirect or lawless course
To cut off those that have offended Him.

1 M. Who made thee then a bloody minister,
When gallant-springing, brave Plantagenet,   210
That princely novice, was struck dead by thee?

Cla. My brother's love, the devil, and my rage.

1 M. Thy brother's love, our duty, and thy faults

192-3. sacrament to fight / In] *F;* holy sacrament, / To fight in *Qq.*   197.
wast] *F;* wert *Qq.*   199. such] *F;* so *Qq.*   202. He] *F;* Why sirs, he *Qq.*
you] *F;* ye *Qq.*   203. that] *F;* this *Qq.*   204. avenged] *F;* reuenged *Qq.*
the] *F;* this *Qq.*   205.] *F; not in Qq.*   207. or] *F;* nor *Qq.*   lawless]
F,Q1; lawfull *Q2-6.*   210. gallant-springing] *F,Q1;* gallant-spring *Q2-6.*
211. That] *F,Q1-5;* The *Q6.*   213. our duty] *F;* the diuell *Qq.*   faults] *F;*
fault *Qq.*

192-3.] Cf. v. v. 18n.

204-8.] Also instinct with Biblical
references: 2 Samuel, xii. 12, Deuteronomy, xxxii. 35, 43, Romans, xii. 19,
Luke, xviii. 7, 8. Frye (p. 256) regards
the concepts expressed here as central
to the Christian doctrine concerning
vengeance, and quotes Calvin's *Commentary on Romans*: 'Paul . . . teaches
us that it belongs not to us to revenge,
except we would assume to ourselves
the office of God'. This is the source
of one aspect of the ethic of the
revenge play; it finds expression in

all sorts of Elizabethan documents.
Cf. the *Sermon on Obedience* in the
Homilies, G2r; also *2 Tamburlaine*,
II.i.56-8 and II.ii.42 for verbal
parallels.

210. *gallant-springing*] Cf. Spenser,
Shepheardes Calender, February, l. 52:
'That wouldest me, my springing
youngth to spil'.

213. *our duty*] Q's version is surely
attributable to the compositor's
catching the words from the previous
line.

Provoke us hither now to slaughter thee.

Cla. O, if you love my brother, hate not me: 215
I am his brother, and I love him well.
If you are hir'd for meed, go back again,
And I will send you to my brother Gloucester,
Who shall reward you better for my life
Than Edward will for tidings of my death.   220

2 M. You are deceiv'd: your brother Gloucester hates you.

Cla. O no, he loves me, and he holds me dear;
Go you to him from me.

1 M.   Ay, so we will.

Cla. Tell him, when that our princely father York
Bless'd his three sons with his victorious arm,   225
And charg'd us from his soul to love each other,
He little thought of this divided friendship:
Bid Gloucester think of this, and he will weep.

1 M. Ay, millstones, as he lesson'd us to weep.

Cla. O, do not slander him, for he is kind.   230

1 M. Right, as snow in harvest.
Come: you deceive yourself;

214. Provoke] *F;* Haue brought *Qq.*   slaughter] *F;* murder *Qq (subst.).*
215. O, if you love my brother] *Q1–3;* Oh, if you loue brother *Q4–6;* If you
do loue my Brother *F.*   217. are] *F;* be *Qq.*   meed] *F,Q1;* neede *Q2–6*
(subst.).   219. shall] *F;* will *Qq.*   221.] *As Qq;* deceiu'd / Your *F.*   223.]
As Steevens; me. | I *F,Qq.*   *1 M.*] *F;* Am. | *Qq.*   226.] *Qq; not in F.*
228. of] *Q1–5;* on *Q6,F.*   229. *1 M.*] *F;* Am. | *Qq.*   231–2. *One line in Qq.*
232. Come: you deceive yourself] *F;* thou deceiu'st thy selfe *Qq.*

215. *O, if you*] The omission of
'my' from the line in Q4 may have
influenced the F corrector, when he
restored the line's metre, to alter the
wording.

217. *meed*] unlawful or immoral
gain: OED *sb.*2. NCS's repunctua-
tion, 'If you are hired, for meed go
back again', obscures the contrast
Clarence is drawing between lawful
and unlawful rewards.

226.] Omitted from F perhaps by
compositorial oversight; it is essential
to the sense. The episode described
does not occur in the *Henry VI* cycle.

229. *millstones*] Cf. I.iii.353.

231. *snow . . . harvest*] Proverbial:
Tilley S590, from Proverbs, xxv.12.

232. *you*] Throughout the scene,
'thou' is used by Clarence (as master
to servant, or superior to inferior)
when addressing one specific murderer; when he uses 'you' he is
addressing both (e.g. ll. 164–6, and
the actor's confusion in l. 186). The
Murderers, however, fluctuate in
their usage. At first, they correctly
use 'you' to Clarence, but as the
debate takes wing from l. 190, they
both adopt the singular—without
incongruity, in view of the elevation
of moral and literary tone. When,
however, we return to the more
immediate issue of Clarence's life or
death, the plural reappears, at l. 221.
In F, both Murderers continue thus

'Tis he that sends us to destroy you here.

Cla. It cannot be: for he bewept my fortune,
And hugg'd me in his arms, and swore with sobs   235
That he would labour my delivery.

1 M. Why so he doth, when he delivers you
From this earth's thraldom to the joys of Heaven.

2 M. Make peace with God, for you must die, my lord.

Cla. Have you that holy feeling in your souls   240
To counsel me to make my peace with God,
And are you yet to your own souls so blind
That you will war with God by murd'ring me?
O sirs, consider: they that set you on
To do this deed will hate you for the deed.   245

2 M. What shall we do?

Cla.   Relent, and save your souls.

1 M. Relent? No, 'tis cowardly and womanish.

Cla. Not to relent is beastly, savage, devilish.
Which of you—if you were a prince's son,
Being pent from liberty as I am now—   250
If two such murderers as yourselves came to you,
Would not entreat for life? Ay, you would beg,
Were you in my distress.

233. that sends us to destroy you here] *F;* hath (that *Q 2–6*) sent vs hither now to
sl2ughter(murder *Q 2–5,* murther *Q 6*) thee *Qq.*   234–5. he bewept my fortune,
/ And] *F;* when I parted with him, / He *Qq.*   237. *1 M.*] *F;* *2 / Qq.*   when]
F; now *Qq.*   you] *F;* thee *Qq.*   238. earth's] *F;* worlds *Qq.*   239. *2 M.*]
F; *1 / Qq.*   Make] *F,Q 2–6;* Makes *Q 1.*   240. Have you . . . your souls]
F; Hast thou . . . thy soule *Qq.*   242. are you . . . your . . . souls] *F;* art
thou . . . thy . . . soule *Qq.*   243. you will] *F;* thou wilt *Qq.*   by] *F,Q 1–2;*
for *Q 3–6.*   244. O] *F;* Ah *Qq.*   they] *F;* he *Qq.*   245. the] *F;* this *Qq.*
246.] *As Steevens;* do? / Relent *F,Qq.*   247. No,] *F;* not in *Qq.*   248. devil-
ish] *F,Q 1;* and diuelish *Q 2–6 (subst.).*   249–53.] *F (after l. 246); not in Qq.*
252. Ay] *This edn;* as *F;* Ah! *Theobald;* Even so I beg / As *NCS.*

in ll. 232–58; in Q they revert to the
singular in ll. 232 ff., which rather
goes against the grain of the scene's
style and tone. The error probably
arose with the actors.

234–6.] A retrospective stage-
direction: see I.i.112 S.D. The
phrases in these lines have many
analogues: Atreus' hypocritical em-

brace of Thyestes, *Thyestes,* ll. 509–
22; *Spanish Tragedy,* III.vii.33; *Arden
of Faversham,* sc. xiv, 73 (probably an
echo of *Richard III*) or *Jew,* III.iii.57.
244–5.] Proverbial: Tilley K64.
247–57.] See Appendix II.
252. *Ay*] If the rearrangement of
ll. 247–57 printed here is adopted, this
line requires emendation to make it

[*To 2 Murderer*] My friend, I spy some pity in thy looks:
O, if thine eye be not a flatterer,   255
Come thou on my side, and entreat for me;
A begging prince, what beggar pities not?

2 M. Look behind you, my lord!

1 M. Take that! and that! (*Stabs him.*) If all this will not do,
I'll drown you in the malmsey-butt within.

Exit [*with body*].   260

2 M. A bloody deed, and desperately dispatch'd.
How fain, like Pilate, would I wash my hands
Of this most grievous murder.

Enter First Murderer.

1 M. How now? What mean'st thou that thou help'st me
not?
By heavens, the Duke shall know how slack you have
been.   265

2 M. I would he knew that I had sav'd his brother.
Take thou the fee, and tell him what I say,
For I repent me that the Duke is slain.   *Exit.*

1 M. So do not I: go, coward as thou art.

254. S.D.] *This edn; not in F,Qq.*   254. thy] *F,Q 1–5;* your *Q 6.*   255. thine]
F; thy *Qq.*   258.] *F; not in Qq.*   259.] *F;* I thus, and thus: if this wil not
serue *Qq.*   259. S.D. *Stabs] F; He stabs | Qq.*   260. drown . . . within] *F;*
chop . . . in the next roome *Qq*   260. S.D.] *As Steevens; Exit | F; not in Qq.*
261. dispatch'd] *F;* performd *Qq.*   262. hands] *F;* hand *Qq.*   263. grievous
murder] *F;* grieuous guilty murder done *Qq.*   263. S.D.] *F; not in Qq.*
264–5.] *F (as prose);* Why doest thou not helpe me, / By heauens the Duke
shall know how slack thou art *Qq (subst.).*   265. heavens] *Q 1–5;* heauen
Q 6,F.

grammatical. In view of the fact that
a similar problem occurred at
I.iii.155, it seemed plausible to adopt
the same solution. Theobald proposed
'Ah!', which would serve; NCS's
more elaborate solution follows a
conjecture by J. C. Maxwell; it
appears wordier than is necessary.

260. *drown . . . within*] Q's line is an
exact recollection of li. 147–8.

261. *desperately*] OED again fails to
identify the theological element in this
word: the Second Murderer is saying

that such a deed could be done only
in a state of despair, the mortal
theological sin of rejection of God
(cf. I.ii.85). This is important in
view of the association the Second
Murderer draws with Pilate in the
next line; see Introduction, p. 112.

263.] Q here is filled out to ten
syllables with superfluous adjectives,
doubtless by the actor.

265. *heavens*] The singular in F
enters via Q6.

Well, I'll go hide the body in some hole   270
Till that the Duke give order for his burial.
And when I have my meed, I will away:
For this will out, and then I must not stay.   *Exit.*

270. Well, I'll go] *F;* Now must I *Qq.*   271. Till that . . . give] *F;* Vntill . . .
take *Qq.*   272. will] *F;* must *Qq.*   273. then] *F;* here *Qq.*   273. S.D.
Exit] *F; Exeunt* / *Qq.*

273. *out*] Proverbial: Tilley M1315;   wil out' (*Mirror*, p. 220).
see also 'Clarence', l. 7: 'For truth

ACT II

SCENE I

Flourish. Enter KING EDWARD *sick*, QUEEN ELIZABETH,
DORSET, RIVERS, HASTINGS, BUCKINGHAM [*and* GREY].

King. Why, so: now have I done a good day's work:
You peers, continue this united league.
I every day expect an embassage
From my Redeemer, to redeem me hence;
And more in peace my soul shall part to Heaven   5
Since I have made my friends at peace on earth.
Rivers and Hastings, take each other's hand;
Dissemble not your hatred: swear your love.

ACT II

Scene 1

ACT II SCENE I] *Capell; Actus Secundus. Scæna Prima.* | *F; not in Qq.*   S.D.] *As
Capell; Flourish. Enter the King sicke, the Queene, Lord Marquesse Dorset, Riuers,
Hastings, Catesby, Buckingham, Wooduill.* | *F; Enter King, Queene, Hastings,
Ryuers, Dorset, &c.* | *Q1–2; Enter King, Queene, Hastings, Riuers, &c.* | *Q3–6.*
1. Why, so] *F;* So *Qq.*   have I] *F;* I haue *Qq.*   5. more in] *Rowe;* now
in *Qq;* more to *F;* more at *Capell.*   to] *F,Q1(Bodl., Yale, Folger copies), Q3–
6;* from *Q1(B.L., Hunt. copies),Q2.*   6. made] *F;* set *Qq.*   friends] *F,Q
1–5;* friend *Q6.*   7. Rivers and Hastings] *Qq; Dorset and Rivers F.*

S.D.] The F stage-direction per-
petuates the error that Rivers and
Woodeville are two persons: they are
not (see Introduction, pp. 17–18);
Catesby does not speak in the scene,
and though he was the messenger in
1.iii who fetched the group to the
King's presence, it would have been
out of place for him to remain. Grey,
though he is silent, is addressed at
l.67 and must be presumed to be
present throughout. The surprising
abbreviation of the Q S.D. is discussed
in the Introduction, pp. 27–8.

5. *more in*] Neither Q nor F can be

right; Rowe's emendation is satisfactory, though some eds prefer
Capell's.

7. *Rivers and Hastings*] F's variant is
inexplicable, since the following lines
are correctly assigned. Some compositorial aberration must be the
cause (though NCS blames the
author).

8. *Dissemble*] pass over or ignore:
OED 3. Edward is urging the nobles
to recognize and acknowledge their
hatreds, and to overcome them with
love.

Riv. By heaven, my soul is purg'd from grudging hate,
And with my hand I seal my true heart's love.   10
Hast. So thrive I, as I truly swear the like.
King. Take heed you dally not before your King,
Lest He that is the supreme King of kings
Confound your hidden falsehood, and award
Either of you to be the other's end.   15
Hast. So prosper I, as I swear perfect love.
Riv. And I, as I love Hastings with my heart.
King. Madam, yourself is not exempt from this;
Nor you, son Dorset; Buckingham, nor you:
You have been factious, one against the other.   20
Wife, love Lord Hastings, let him kiss your hand:
And what you do, do it unfeignedly.
Eliz. There, Hastings: I will never more remember
Our former hatred, so thrive I and mine.
King. Dorset, embrace him; Hastings, love lord Marquess.
Dors. This interchange of love, I here protest,   26
Upon my part shall be inviolable.
Hast. And so swear I.   [*They embrace.*]
King. Now, princely Buckingham, seal thou this league
With thy embracements to my wife's allies,   30
And make me happy in your unity.
Buck. Whenever Buckingham doth turn his hate
Upon your Grace, but with all duteous love

9. soul] *F*; heart *Qq.*   11. truly] *F,Q1–2*; not in *Q3–6.*   18. is . . . from]
F; are . . . in *Qq.*   19. you, son] *F* (*subst.*)*;* your son *Qq.*   23. There] *F*;
Here *Qq.*   25.] *As Rowe;* him: | *Hastings* | *F*; not in *Qq.*   26. This] *F,Q1*;
Thus *Q2–6.*   27. inviolable *F*; vnuiolable *Qq.*   28. I] *F*; I my Lord *Qq.*
28. S.D.] *Capell;* not in *F,Qq.*   30. embracements] *F,Q1–5*; embracement *Q6.*
33. Upon your Grace] *F*; On you or yours *Qq.*

9 ff.] Hypocritical professions of
'love' are a commonplace in the play
and in the sources. Cf. especially
Atreus in *Thyestes*, ll. 491–511; the
false reconciliation of Lorenzo and
Hieronymo in *Spanish Tragedy,*
III.xiv.139–64; Gloucester and Winchester in *1H6*, III.i.119–35.

9. *soul*] F is right, as the careful
contrast in the lines reveals; the
actor or the compositor could have
repeated 'heart' in Q by oversight.

12. *dally*] trifle with a person
under the guise of serious action:
OED 3.

19. *you, son*] The King is more
likely to address Dorset directly, as
he is present; the Q variant is thus
probably compositorial.

25.] Omitted from Q, no doubt by
compositor's oversight.

33. *Upon your Grace*] In Q Buckingham anticipates l. 40 to produce the
variant.

Doth cherish you and yours, God punish me
With hate in those where I expect most love.　　35
When I have most need to employ a friend,
And most assured that he is a friend,
Deep, hollow, treacherous, and full of guile
Be he unto me: this do I beg of God,
When I am cold in love to you or yours.　*Embrace.*　40
King. A pleasing cordial, princely Buckingham,
　　Is this thy vow unto my sickly heart.
　　There wanteth now our brother Gloucester here
　　To make the blessed period of this peace.

Enter RATCLIFFE *and* RICHARD.

Buck. And in good time,　　　　　　　　　45
　　Here comes Sir Richard Ratcliffe and the Duke.
Rich. Good morrow to my sovereign King and Queen;
　　And princely peers, a happy time of day.
King. Happy indeed, as we have spent the day;
　　Gloucester, we have done deeds of charity,　　50
　　Made peace of enmity, fair love of hate,
　　Between these swelling, wrong-incensed peers.
Rich. A blessed labour, my most sovereign lord.
　　Among this princely heap—if any here
　　By false intelligence or wrong surmise　　55
　　Hold me a foe—

39. God] *Qq*; heauen *F*.　　40. love] *F*; zeale *Qq*.　　40. S.D.] *F*; *not in Qq*.
44. blessed] *F*; perfect *Qq*.　　44. S.D.] *As F (after l. 46)*; *Enter Glocest.* | *Qq*
(after l. 44).　　45-6.] *F*; And in good time here comes the noble Duke. *Qq*.
50. Gloucester] *F*; Brother *Qq*.　　53. my most] *F,Q1-2*; most *Q3-6*.　　lord]
F; liege *Qq*.　　54. Among] *F*; Amongst *Qq*.　　56-7. *As Malone; one line*
F,Qq.

39. *God*] No doubt purged from F
in accordance with the 1606 Statute.
　41. *cordial*] restorative, stimulant
to the heart: OED *sb.*2b. *fig.*
　46. *Ratcliffe*] Ratcliffe does not
speak, and is not strictly necessary to
the scene. NCS observes that Q
probably gives us the original text,
and that Ratcliffe was 'thrust into
the F. as an afterthought . . . in order
to give Ric. an attendant'. This rather
goes against the grain of the scene,

which is not a public, ceremonial
affair, but a very private reconciliation of family and friends. A possible
need for Ratcliffe is suggested in
l. 135. S.D. n.
　52. *swelling*] haughty, arrogant:
OED *ppl.a.*7.
　54. *heap*] a great company or
multitude: OED 3. It is scarcely
possible to doubt the deflationary
overtones of the term applied to such
a group.

If I unwittingly, or in my rage,
Have aught committed that is hardly borne
By any in this presence, I desire
To reconcile me to his friendly peace: 60
'Tis death to me to be at enmity;
I hate it, and desire all good men's love.
First, madam, I entreat true peace of you,
Which I will purchase with my duteous service;
Of you, my noble cousin Buckingham,   65
If ever any grudge were lodg'd between us;
Of you, Lord Rivers, and Lord Grey, of you,
That all without desert have frown'd on me:
Dukes, earls, lords, gentlemen: indeed of all.
I do not know that Englishmen alive   70
With whom my soul is any jot at odds,
More than the infant that is born tonight—
I thank my God for my humility.

Eliz. A holy day shall this be kept hereafter;
I would to God all strifes were well compounded.   75
My sovereign lord, I do beseech your Highness
To take our brother Clarence to your grace.

Rich. Why, madam, have I offer'd love for this,
To be so flouted in this royal presence?
Who knows not that the gentle Duke is dead?   80
                              They all start.

---

57. unwittingly] *Qq*; vnwillingly *F*.   59. By] *Qq*; To *F*.   60. his] *F,Q 1,3–6*;
this *Q2*.   63. true peace] *F,Q 1–2*; peace *Q 3–6*.   67.] *As Qq*; Of you and
you, Lord *Riuers* and of *Dorset*, *F*.   68. me:] *Qq*; Me: / Of you Lord *Wooduill*,
and Lord *Scales* of you, *F*.   76. lord] *F*; liege *Qq*.   your] *F, Q 1–5*; you *Q 6*.
Highness] *F*; Maiesty *Qq*.   79. so flouted] *F*; thus scorned *Qq*.   80. gentle]
F; noble *Qq*.   80. S.D.] *F*; not in *Qq*.

57. *unwittingly*] F's variant is
merely a compositorial misreading.

59. *By*] F's 'To' was no doubt
caught from l. 60.

60. *his*] Q2's error 'this' makes
adequate sense, and it is distinctly
surprising that Q3 should have
corrected it.

67.] See Introduction, pp. 17–18.

73. *humility*] Note that Richard here
praises himself for the cardinal virtue
whose contrary deadly sin is Pride

—the characteristic most commentators remark upon in him. The
irony is elegant: to take pride in one's
humility.

75. *compounded*] settled or composed,
of a difference or strife: OED compound *v*. II. 6.

79. *flouted*] insulted, jeered at:
OED flout *v*. I. The verb 'scorn' was
in the actor's mind from l. 81, which
accounts for the Q variant.

You do him injury to scorn his corse!
Riv. Who knows not he is dead! Who knows he is?
Eliz. All-seeing heaven, what a world is this?
Buck. Look I so pale, Lord Dorset, as the rest?
Dors. Ay, my good lord, and no man in the presence   85
    But his red colour hath forsook his cheeks.
King. Is Clarence dead? The order was revers'd.
Rich. But he, poor man, by your first order died,
    And that a winged Mercury did bear;
    Some tardy cripple bore the countermand,   90
    That came too lag to see him buried.
    God grant that some, less noble and less loyal,
    Nearer in bloody thoughts, but not in blood,
    Deserve not worse than wretched Clarence did,
    And yet go current from suspicion.   95

Enter STANLEY *Earl of Derby.*

Stan. A boon, my sovereign, for my service done!
King. I prithee peace; my soul is full of sorrow.
Stan. I will not rise unless your Highness hear me.
King. Then say at once what is it thou demand'st.
Stan. The forfeit, Sovereign, of my servant's life   100

82. *Riv.*] *Qq; King.* / F.   *As Qq; ... dead?* / *Who* F.   85. no man] *F; no
one Qq.   the] *F; this Qq.*   88. man] *F; soule Qq.*   89. winged] *F, Q2–6;
wingled Q1.*   90. bore] *Qq; bare* F.   93. but] *Qq; and* F.   95. S.D.]
This edn; Enter Earle of Derby. / *F; Enter Darby.* / *Qq.*   97. prithee] *F; pray
thee Qq.*   98. hear me] *F; grant Qq (subst.).*   99. say] *F; speake Qq.*
demand'st] *Qq (subst.); requests* F.

82. *Riv.*] The tone of this query
seems wrong for the King, who might
have been shocked, but hardly
surprised in this way. His sense of
complicity is revealed by the muted
tone of l. 87, which in any event
would be inappropriate as a second
line if the same speaker had uttered
l. 82.

90. *tardy cripple*] One of Richard's
best jokes: he means himself, as
Laurence Olivier's film emphasized
—he had Richard almost give the
Murderer the wrong paper.

91. *lag*] Used adverbially: belatedly,
tardily: OED *sb.*[1] B.1.

92–4.] Proverbial: Tilley K38.

93. *but*] The Q variant has the
effect of strengthening the antithesis
between the two meanings of 'blood'
in the line.

95. *go current*] be received as
genuine: OED *a.*8.

96 ff.] This episode originates with
Polydore Vergil.

99. *demand'st*] The Q word here
has the look of an authorial variant,
rather than an actor's substitution.
It cannot be denied that Stanley's
importunity here is arrogant in tone.

100. *forfeit*] something to which the
right is lost by the commission of a

Who slew today a riotous gentleman
Lately attendant on the Duke of Norfolk.
King. Have I a tongue to doom my brother's death,
And shall that tongue give pardon to a slave?
My brother kill'd no man: his fault was thought,   105
And yet his punishment was bitter death.
Who sued to me for him? Who, in my wrath,
Kneel'd at my feet and bade me be advis'd?
Who spoke of brotherhood? Who spoke of love?
Who told me how the poor soul did forsake   110
The mighty Warwick, and did fight for me?
Who told me, in the field at Tewkesbury
When Oxford had me down, he rescued me
And said, 'Dear brother, live and be a king'?
Who told me, when we both lay in the field   115
Frozen almost to death, how he did lap me
Even in his garments, and did give himself,
All thin and naked, to the numb-cold night?
All this from my remembrance brutish wrath
Sinfully pluck'd, and not a man of you   120
Had so much grace to put it in my mind.
But when your carters or your waiting vassals
Have done a drunken slaughter, and defac'd
The precious image of our dear Redeemer,

104. that tongue] *F;* the same *Qq.*   105. kill'd] *F;* slew *Qq* (*subst.*).
106. bitter] *F;* cruell *Qq.*   107. wrath] *F;* rage *Qq.*   108. at] *Qq;* and *F.*
bade] *Qq;* bid *F.*   109. Who spoke . . . Who spoke] *F;* Who spake . . . who
Qq.   112. at] *F;* by *Qq.*   117. garments] *F;* owne garments *Q1–5;* owne
armes *Q6.*   did give] *F;* gaue *Qq.*   120. pluck'd] *F,Q2–6;* puckt *Q1.*

crime (OED *sb.*2): Stanley means his
servant's life is now due to the King,
and requests that this right be
transferred to himself.
103. ff] Edward's remorse for
Clarence, prompted by Stanley's
intercession for his man, resembles
in *Spanish Tragedy* the way Hieronimo's grief for Horatio is redoubled
by Bazulto's petition for his murdered
son: III.xiii.78 ff.
105–6.] Proverbial: Tilley T244.
108. *at . . . bade*] Q is certainly right
in the first word, and probably in the

second, though 'bid' is not incorrect
as a past tense.
113.] This incident Shakespeare
invented.
123–4.] Frye, pp. 199–200, notes
the importance of the image of God-
in-man in Christian theology, and
quotes Calvin's *Institutes* (2.8.40): 'If
we do not wish to violate the image
of God, we ought to hold our neighbour sacred. And if we do not wish
to renounce all humanity, we ought
to cherish his as our own flesh.'

You straight are on your knees for 'Pardon, pardon!' 125
And I, unjustly too, must grant it you.
But for my brother not a man would speak,
Nor I, ungracious, speak unto myself
For him, poor soul. The proudest of you all
Have been beholding to him in his life,   130
Yet none of you would once beg for his life.
O God, I fear Thy justice will take hold
On me, and you, and mine and yours for this.
Come, Hastings, help me to my closet.
Ah, poor Clarence!

                    Exeunt some with King and Queen. 135
Rich. This is the fruits of rashness: mark'd you not
How that the guilty kindred of the Queen
Look'd pale when they did hear of Clarence' death?
O, they did urge it still unto the King:
God will revenge it. Come, lords, will you go   140
To comfort Edward with our company.
Buck. We wait upon your Grace.   *Exeunt.*

127. man] *F,Q1–2,6;* mast *Q3–5.*   130. beholding] *F,Q1–3;* beholden *Q4–6.*
131. beg] *F;* pleade *Qq.*   133. yours] *F,Q1–5;* your *Q6.*   134–5. *As F; one*
line Qq.   135. Ah] *F;* oh *Qq.*   135. S.D.] *F; Exit. / Qq.*   136. fruits] *F;*
fruit *Qq.*   rashness] *F,Q1–2 (subst.);* rawnes *Q3–6 (Q6* rawnesse). 140.
Come, lords, will you go] *F;* But come lets in *Qq.*   142.] *F; not in Qq.*

135 S.D.] An unhelpful direction for
the prompter; see also Introduction,
pp. 11–13. It is plain that the
King, Queen, and Hastings leave,
and that Richard and Buckingham
stay. Who else is on stage? And to
whom is Richard speaking in ll. 136
ff.? Dorset, Rivers, Grey, Ratcliffe,
and Stanley have no exits marked
for them; in the note to l. 46 above
reasons are given why there probably
should not be any supernumeraries
on stage in this scene. The producer
must decide whether to leave any of

the Queen's party on stage to serve
as the objects of Richard's mendacious
diatribe. Certainly Richard cannot
be addressing them (though he might
include them in his change of tone
at l. 140); and to be convincing,
he needs more than Buckingham for
an audience. The best arrangement
would appear to be for Dorset,
Rivers, and Grey to leave with the
King, leaving Richard to press his
charges chiefly to Stanley, with
Buckingham and Ratcliffe as claque.
    140. *God . . . it*] Cf. I.iv.204–8.

SCENE II

Enter the old DUCHESS OF YORK, *with the two*
Children *of Clarence.*

Boy. Good grandam tell us, is our father dead?
Duch. No, boy.
Girl. Why do you weep so oft, and beat your breast?
And cry 'O Clarence, my unhappy son'?
Boy. Why do you look on us, and shake your head,   5
And call us orphans, wretches, castaways,
If that our noble father were alive?
Duch. My pretty cousins, you mistake me both:
I do lament the sickness of the King,
As loath to lose him; not your father's death: 10
It were lost sorrow to wail one that's lost.
Boy. Then you conclude, my grandam, he is dead:
The King mine uncle is to blame for it.
God will revenge it, whom I will importune
With earnest prayers, all to that effect.   15
Girl. And so will I.

Scene 11

SCENE II] F (*Scena Secunda.*); *not in Qq.*   S.D.] F; *Enter Dutches of Yorke, with*
Clarence Children. Qq.   1. Good grandam tell us] F; Tell me good Granam Qq.
3. *Girl*] F (*Daugh.*); *Boy* | Qq.   you weep so oft] F2; weep so oft F; you
wring your hands Qq.   5. *Boy*] F; *Gerl* | Qq.   6. orphans, wretches] F;
wretches, Orphanes Qq.   7. were] F; be Qq.   8. both] F; much Qq.
10. not . . . death] F,Q 1–5; now . . . dead Q6.   11. sorrow] F; labour Qq.
wail] F; weepe for Qq.   12. you conclude, my grandam] F; Granam you
conclude that Qq.   13. mine] F; my Qq.   15. earnest] F; daily Qq.
16.] F; not in Qq.

Scene 11

S.D. *Children*] Margaret and Edward Plantagenet, born 1473 and
1475 respectively. She married Sir
Richard Pole ('some mean poor
gentleman', IV. ii. 53; 'His daughter
meanly have I match'd in marriage',
IV. iii. 37), though Thompson believed Shakespeare confused her with
her first cousin, Princess Cicely,
whom (according to Holinshed)
Richard married 'to a man found in
a cloud, and of an unknowne linage
and familie' (p. 752/2). Edward, Earl
of Warwick ('the boy is foolish, and
I fear not him', IV. ii. 55) was 'pent
up' (IV. iii. 36) by both Richard and
Henry VII, and executed in 1499.

7.] For the grammar here, see
Abbott §§287 and 371.

10. *not . . . death*] A spectacular pair
of errors in Q6 here entirely reverses
the Duchess's meaning.

Duch. Peace, children, peace: the King doth love you well.
  Incapable and shallow innocents,
  You cannot guess who caus'd your father's death.

Boy. Grandam, we can: for my good uncle Gloucester   20
  Told me the King, provok'd to't by the Queen,
  Devis'd impeachments to imprison him;
  And when my uncle told me so he wept,
  And pitied me, and kindly kiss'd my cheek;
  Bade me rely on him as on my father,   25
  And he would love me dearly as a child.

Duch. Ah, that Deceit should steal such gentle shape,
  And with a virtuous vizor hide deep Vice!
  He is my son, ay, and herein my shame;
  Yet from my dugs he drew not this deceit.   30

Boy. Think you my uncle did dissemble, grandam?

Duch. Ay, boy.

Boy. I cannot think it. Hark, what noise is this?

---

21. provok'd to't] *F* (prouock'd to it); prouoked *Qq*.   23. my uncle] *F*; he *Qq*.
24. pitied me] *F*; hugd me in his arme *Qq*.   25. Bade] *F*; And bad *Qq*.
on my] *F,Q2–6*; in my *Q1*.   26. a] *F*; his *Qq*.   27. Ah] *F*; Oh *Qq*.
shape] *F*; shapes *Qq*.   28. vizor] *F*; visard *Qq* (*subst.*).   deep Vice] *F*;
foule guile *Qq*.   29. ay, and] *F* (I, and); yea, and *Q1–3*; and *Q4*; yea and
Q5–6.   33. S.D.] *F; Enter the Qucc. | Qq* (*subst.*).

---

18. *Incapable*] unable to comprehend, unaware: OED 2.

23. *wept*] Richard's Vice-like tears
again: see Spivack, p. 399.

24. *pitied me*] Patrick (pp. 51–2)
suggests the Q variant arose by
recollection of 1. iv. 234–5, 'an actor's
recollection of an earlier speech
delivered in a very similar context'.
Whatever the context, the plain fact
is that Clarence and the Boy could
not have been played by the same
actor, and so some special plead-
ing is needed to endorse Patrick's
view: see also Introduction, p. 47.
Spedding (quoted in Variorum,
p. 163) believed that Shakespeare
wrote 'hugged' in both places and
later revised the extra-metrical line·
Certainly, the earlier line, with the
image of Richard's characteristic
conduct, would have been in the
author's mind.

kindly] i.e. expressing his natural,
relative's feelings.

25. *on my*] An instance of Walton's
'coincidental correction': see Introduction, pp. 39–40 ff.

28. *deep Vice*] Q's 'foule guile' is
probably an actor's substitution of a
vague expression for the author's
precise one. Certainly F's use of the
word 'Vice' (capitalized here to
remind one of the association with
the theatrical role Richard is playing)
is more apt.

33. S.D.] For Q's omission of
Dorset and Rivers from the scene, see
Introduction, pp. 15–16. Elizabeth's
opening line sounds rather odd without them, but there are other
characters on stage to whom she can
address herself.

Enter QUEEN ELIZABETH *with her hair about her ears,*
RIVERS *and* DORSET *after her.*

Eliz. Ah! who shall hinder me to wail and weep,
    To chide my fortune, and torment myself?   35
    I'll join with black despair against my soul
    And to myself become an enemy.
Duch. What means this scene of rude impatience?
Eliz. To make an act of tragic violence:
    Edward, my lord, thy son, our King, is dead.   40
    Why grow the branches, when the root is gone?
    Why wither not the leaves that want their sap?
    If you will live, lament; if die, be brief,
    That our swift-winged souls may catch the King's
    Or like obedient subjects follow him   45
    To his new kingdom of ne'er-changing night.

34. Ah! who] *F;* Oh who *Q1–2,4;* Wh Who *Q3;* Whoy *Q5(Edinburgh U.,
Hunt., Folger 1 copies);* Who *Q5(all other copies),Q6.*   36. soul] *F,Q1–4;* selfe
Q5–6.   40. thy] *F;* your *Qq.*   41. when . . . gone] *F;* now . . . witherd *Qq.*
42. that want their sap] *F;* the sap being gone *Qq.*   46. ne'er-changing night]
F; perpetuall rest *Qq.*

34. *Ah! who*] The process of decay
in this phrase in the derivative Qq
is characteristic and instructive.

36. *despair*] Again, the theological
sense is wanted (cf. 1.ii.85 n.): Elizabeth is threatening suicide. The
phrase was proverbial: Tilley D126.

38. *impatience*] failure to bear
suffering with equanimity: OED 1;
hence, an opposite of the cardinal
virtue of fortitude.

39. *make*] Probably in the sense 'to
bring about' (OED 9) though some
of the more specialized senses are
possible.

41–2.] Probably proverbial, though
not listed by Tilley; a good parallel
exists in *Edward III*: 'No marvell
though the braunches be then
infected, / When poyson hath encompassed the roote' [D1ᵛ]. Patrick
rightly regards the Q version of these
lines as an actor's jumble of what in
F is clear and apt: Edward, the root,
is gone rather than merely withered;

Q's intrusive verb is an anticipation
of l. 42, and 'the sap being gone' a
paraphrase.

43. *brief*] expeditious or hasty:
OED *a*.1b.

46. *ne'er-changing night*] Compare
the Q variant with 1.iv.47: 'the
kingdom of perpetual night'. Rossiter
(in *DUJ*) suggests that the words
'rest' and 'night', 'ne'er-changing'
and 'perpetual' may all have been
present in one manuscript, 'which
was read in different ways at different
times'. This anticipates Honigmann's
attitude to such cruces (in his
Stability; see Introduction, pp. 45–8)
and is a plausible explanation,
especially in view of the Senecal
echoes in the phrase, more probable
than that the confusion originated
with the actors as Walker and
Patrick would have us believe: as in
l. 24 above, the relevant persons
were not on-stage to hear the other
line spoken.

Duch.　Ah, so much interest have I in thy sorrow
　　　As I had title in thy noble husband.
　　　I have bewept a worthy husband's death,
　　　And liv'd with looking on his images:　　　　　　　50
　　　But now two mirrors of his princely semblance
　　　Are crack'd in pieces by malignant death;
　　　And I, for comfort, have but one false glass,
　　　That grieves me when I see my shame in him.
　　　Thou art a widow—yet thou art a mother,　　　　55
　　　And hast the comfort of thy children left;
　　　But death hath snatch'd my husband from mine arms
　　　And pluck'd two crutches from my feeble hands:
　　　Clarence and Edward. O, what cause have I,
　　　Thine being but a moiety of my moan,　　　　　　60
　　　To overgo thy woes and drown thy cries.

Boy.　Ah, Aunt, you wept not for our father's death:
　　　How can we aid you with our kindred tears?

Girl.　Our fatherless distress was left unmoan'd:
　　　Your widow-dolour likewise be unwept.　　　　　65

Eliz.　Give me no help in lamentation:
　　　I am not barren to bring forth complaints:
　　　All springs reduce their currents to mine eyes,

---

47. I] *Qq; not in F.*　　50. with] *F;* by *Qq.*　　54. That] *F;* Which *Qq.*
56. left] *F;* left thee *Qq.*　　57. husband] *F;* children *Qq.*　　58. hands] *F;*
limmes *Qq.*　　59. Clarence and Edward] *F;* Edward and Clarence *Qq.*
60. Thine . . . a moiety] *F;* Then, . . . moity *Qq* (moitie *Q 3–5;* motitie *Q 6*).
moan] *F;* griefe *Q 1–5;* selfe *Q 6.*　　61. woes] *F,* plaints *Qq* (plants *Q 2*).
thy cries] *F, Q 1–4;* the cries *Q 5–6.*　　62. Ah] *F;* Good *Qq.*　　63. kindred]
F; kindreds *Qq.*　　65. widow-dolour] *F;* widdowes dolours *Qq (subst.).*
67. complaints] *F;* laments *Qq.*

---

57. *husband*] F is right, as the antithetical pattern reveals: 'children' may have been caught by actor or compositor from the preceding line.

60. *moiety*] A half.

　moan] Q6's 'selfe' is an example of a substitution by the compositor of a wrong, but not obviously impossible, word. In l. 80, 'griefs' appears in F, and 'mones' in Q. Patrick (p. 38) argues that the actor (for whom the lines are nearly consecutive) transposed the words to produce the Q readings, a very plausible

suggestion. The other Q variant in the line ('Then . . . but moity) obviously originated with the compositor.

61. *overgo*] surmount, rise higher than: OED I.3.

63. *kindred*] (1) belonging to relatives: OED B.1b; (2) similar, alike in quality: OED A.1b.

65. *be unwept*] Optative use of the subjunctive: Abbott §365.

67. *complaints*] Q's 'laments' is surely an actor's variant.

68. *reduce*] bring or lead back:

That I, being govern'd by the watery moon,
May send forth plenteous tears to drown the world.   70
Ah, for my husband, for my dear lord Edward!
Children. Ah, for our father, for our dear lord Clarence!
Duch. Alas for both, both mine Edward and Clarence!
Eliz. What stay had I but Edward, and he's gone.
Children. What stay had we but Clarence, and he's gone.   75
Duch. What stays had I but they, and they are gone.
Eliz. Was never widow had so dear a loss.
Children. Were never orphans had so dear a loss.
Duch. Was never mother had so dear a loss.
Alas, I am the mother of these griefs: 80
Their woes are parcell'd, mine is general.
She for an Edward weeps, and so do I;

69. moon] *F;* moane *Qq.*   71. Ah] *F;* Oh *Qq.*   dear] *F;* eire *Q1;* eyre
Q2; heire *Q3–6.*   72. *Children] F (Chil);* Ambo / *Qq.*   Ah] *F;* Oh *Qq.*
74. he's] *F;* he is *Q1–5;* is he *Q6.*   75. *Children] F (Chil);* Am / *Qq.*   he's
F; he is *Q1–5;* is he *Q6.*   76. stays] *F,Q1–5;* stay *Q6.*   77. never] *F,Q*
1–3,5–6; euer *Q4.*   78. *Children] F (Chil);* Ambo / *Qq (subst.).*   Were] *F;*
Was *Qq.*   never] *F,Q1;* euer *Q2–6.*   so dear a] *F;* a dearer *Qq.*   79.
never] *F,Q1;* euer *Q2–6.*   so dear a] *F;* a dearer *Qq.*   80. griefs] *F;*
mones *Qq (subst.).*   81. is] *F;* are *Qq.*   82. an Edward] *F;* Edward *Qq.*

OED 1.3. Elizabeth means that the
springs and streams bring their water
back to her eyes to provide her with
the tears to 'drown the world'.

69. *moon*] Astrologically, the moon
is the feminine (and queenly) planet
whose nature is moist: cf. the 'wat'ry
moon' in *MND* (II.i.162) which
'looks with a wat'ry eye' (III.i.198).
The tidal effect of the moon on the
oceans was well-understood. Thus
the Queen is under the influence of
the moon (astrologically, and by her
nature and rank) and so will become
the channel through which a new
watery Deluge will overwhelm the
world. The image is rather forced
(Johnson thought it unnatural) but
perfectly coherent. Q's reading,
'moane' must be compositorial.

71. *dear*] F's reading is obviously
right in view of the parallel in the
following line. Q's variant is technically possible, if the second half of

the line be taken as referring to
Edward V, but highly unlikely.

74–9.] This passage of antana-
clasis exists in F as a series of exclamations; in Qq these become progressively a series of rhetorical questions.
However as Q1 on the whole keeps
the F form the change cannot be
attributed to the actors but rather to
the frustrated rhetorician in the
compositors.

77–9.] For the ellipsis of 'there',
see Abbott §404. The phrasing is
Spenserian; cf. *Faerie Queene*, I.ii.23,
ll. 4–5: 'Was never Prince so faithfull
and so faire, / Was never Prince so
meeke and debonaire'.

80. *griefs*] See l. 60 n.

81. *parcell'd*] divided or distributed
into small portions: OED parcel *v.* 1
and *ppl.a.* (citing this line).

is] Collective noun takes the
singular verb, quite regularly.

I for a Clarence weep, so doth not she;
These babes for Clarence weep, and so do I;
I for an Edward weep, so do not they.   85
Alas, you three, on me, threefold distress'd,
Pour all your tears: I am your sorrow's nurse,
And I will pamper it with lamentation.
Dors. Comfort, dear mother: God is much displeas'd
That you take with unthankfulness His doing.   90
In common worldly things, 'tis call'd ungrateful
With dull unwillingness to repay a debt
Which with a bounteous hand was kindly lent:
Much more to be thus opposite with Heaven,
For it requires the royal debt it lent you.   95
Riv. Madam, bethink you, like a careful mother,
Of the young prince your son: send straight for him;
Let him be crown'd; in him your comfort lives.
Drown desperate sorrow in dead Edward's grave,
And plant your joys in living Edward's throne.   100

Enter RICHARD, BUCKINGHAM, STANLEY *Earl of Derby,*
HASTINGS *and* RATCLIFFE.

Rich. Sister, have comfort: all of us have cause
To wail the dimming of our shining star,

83. weep] *Qq;* weepes *F.*   84–5. and . . . Edward weep] *Q1–3,5–6;* and . . .
Edward *Q4; not in F.*   85. so do not] *F,Q1;* and so do *Q2–6.*   87. Pour]
F (Power), *Q1* (Poure), *Q3–6* (Powre); Proue *Q2.*   88. lamentation] *F;*
lamentations *Qq.*   89–100.] *F; not in Qq.*   100. S.D.] *F; Enter Glocest.
with others | Qq (subst.; after l. 88).*   101. Sister] *F;* Madame *Qq.*

84–5.] The lacuna in F is accounted
for by compositorial eye-skip.

85. *so do not*] Q2–6's error was likewise caused by the Q2 compositor's
eye skipping back a line.

87. *Pour*] The curious variants here
are all in spelling, with some transposed letters in Q2 as an added
complication.

89–100.] The omission of this
passage from Q is part of a deliberate
cut which eliminated Dorset and
Rivers from this scene. Smidt (p. 125)
complains that Dorset's comfort is
'cold and uncharitable . . . and just

as well omitted', thus missing the
dramatic point that Elizabeth has
indeed no grounds upon which to
console herself, and Dorset's speech
accurately reflects her bad prospects.
In any event, this can hardly have
been the reason for all the Q cuts in
this scene, which are patently inter-
related, and must have served some
specific theatrical purpose. See Introduction, pp. 15–16.

100. S.D.] See Introduction, pp.
11–13.

101. *Sister*] Once again, Richard
calls 'King Edward's widow "Sister"'.

But none can help our harms by wailing them.
Madam my mother, I do cry you mercy:
I did not see your Grace. Humbly on my knee   105
I crave your blessing.   [*Kneels.*]
Duch. God bless thee, and put meekness in thy breast;
Love, charity, obedience, and true duty.
Rich. Amen; [*Rises: aside*] and make me die a good old man—
That is the butt-end of a mother's blessing: 110
I marvel that her Grace did leave it out.
Buck. You cloudy princes and heart-sorrowing peers
That bear this heavy mutual load of moan,
Now cheer each other in each other's love.
Though we have spent our harvest of this king,   115
We are to reap the harvest of his son.
The broken rancour of your high-swoll'n hates,
But lately splinted, knit, and join'd together

103. help our] *F;* cure their *Qq.*   106. your] *F,Q 1–5;* you *Q 6.*   106. S.D.]
This edn; not in F,Qq.   107. breast] *F;* minde *Qq (subst.).*   109. S.D.] *This
edn; not in F,Qq.*   109. and] *F,Q 1–5; not in Q 6.*   110. That is] *F;* Thats
Qq.   a] *F,Q 1;* my *Q 2–6.*   111. that] *F;* why *Qq.*   112. and] *Qq; & F.*
113. heavy mutual] *F;* mutuall heauy *Qq.*   115. of] *F,Q 1;* for *Q 2–6.*
116. son] *F,Q 1–5* (sonne)*; soone Q 6.*   117. hates *F;* hearts *Qq.*   118.
splinted] *F,Qq* (splinter'd *F;* splinterd *Q 1*).

103.] Cf. *Jew,* I.ii.236–7: 'things
past recovery / Are hardly cur'd with
exclamations'.

109. S.D.] NCS rightly notes that
the 'Amen' is uttered aloud, and the
rest of the line is the aside. So most
modern eds print it.

110. *butt-end*] the mere concluding
part: OED 1b (from butt *sb.³*, the
lower end of a spear-shaft, etc.).

112. *cloudy*] darkened by misfor-
tune, hence gloomy, troubled: OED
*a.*6b. Cf. *Lucr.,* l. 1084. For Buckingham's 'rhetoric', see Introduction, p.
114.

and] F's ampersand is accounted
for by the fact that the line is full-
measure.

117.] Cf. *Edward III*: 'To shew the
rancor of their high swolne harts'
[E3ᵛ].

118. *splinted*] There can be no
question as to the meaning of the

word: the modern form used here
and in Q2–6 is identical with
'splinter' (OED *v.*2). It therefore
seems perverse of many modern eds
including NCS, NPS, Evans, and
Eccles (and Thompson) to prefer the
F/Q1 form which in modern English
has precisely the opposite meaning
to that Shakespeare intended, and
can only be confusing. Cf. *Oth.,*
II.iii.322–3, for a parallel usage. The
imagery of ll. 117–19 is compressed
and has caused confusion; many
commentators object that Buckingham appears to be urging the preservation of rancour, though Malone
understood the ellipsis. NCS's comment is singularly misleading: 'The
image is that of an ulcerated wound
swollen with the poison of hatred to
bursting point, and recently dressed.'
On the contrary, the image is of a
broken festered limb which has been

Must gently be preserv'd, cherish'd, and kept.
Meseemeth good, that with some little train,   120
Forthwith from Ludlow the young Prince be fet
Hither to London, to be crown'd our King.

Riv. Why with some little train, my lord of Buckingham?

Buck. Marry, my lord, lest by a multitude
The new-heal'd wound of malice should break out,   125
Which would be so much the more dangerous
By how much the estate is green and yet ungovern'd.
Where every horse bears his commanding rein,
And may direct his course as please himself,
As well the fear of harm, as harm apparent,   130
In my opinion, ought to be prevented.

Rich. I hope the King made peace with all of us,
And the compact is firm and true in me.

Riv. And so in me, and so, I think, in all:
Yet since it is but green, it should be put   135
To no apparent likelihood of breach,

119. gently] *F,Q1;* greatly *Q2–6.*   121. fet] *F;* fetcht *Qq.*   123–40.] *F;*
not in Qq.   123.] *As Pope; ...* Traine, / My *F.*

set and must now be treated gently
till it is strong.

121. *fet*] OED notes this as a
common obsolete alternative form of
'fetch'.

123–40.] See above, ll. 89–100 for
a note on this omission. The identity
of the speakers here has provoked
emendation, the most attractive being
that Rivers and Richard should
exchange speeches at ll. 132 and 134.
Rivers would thus continue to object
to Buckingham's argument, and
Richard would throw in the weight
of his authority, thus persuading
Hastings. Yet it is equally characteristic of Richard's devious style that he
should seem lukewarm to Buckingham, leaving Rivers to talk himself
into the arrangement. There seems
no imperative need to emend.

123. *little train*] The episode
received attention in the *Mirror*, in
'Rivers' (pp. 258, 264), 'Hastings'
(p. 273).

128–31.] Buckingham is, as usual
when he is being politic, rather
obscure. The drift of what he says is
something like: in the present
ungoverned state of things each man
takes whatever direction he pleases;
thus it is important not only to
prevent real trouble, but also to
prevent the possible causes of anxiety
(such as fetching the Prince with a
large train). There is, in point of
fact, no reason why such a train
should cause alarm, and Buckingham's
obscure language is a characteristic
politician's way of confusing the issue.

129. *please*] i.e. should please:
subjunctive used indefinitely: Abbott
§367.

135. *green*] In l. 127 applied to the
estate (i.e. the country under Edward's
minority) and here to the compact, it
means the same: not fully developed,
matured, or elaborated (OED *adj.*
II. 8a) with the implication of being
tender and easily damaged.

Which haply by much company might be urg'd.
Therefore I say with noble Buckingham
That it is meet so few should fetch the Prince.
Hast. And so say I.   140
Rich. Then be it so, and go we to determine
Who they shall be that straight shall post to Ludlow.
Madam, and you my sister, will you go
To give your censures in this business?
Eliz. and Duch. With all our hearts.   145
                    Exeunt all but Buckingham and Richard.
Buck. My lord, whoever journeys to the Prince,
For God's sake let not us two stay at home:
For by the way I'll sort occasion,
As index to the story we late talk'd of,
To part the Queen's proud kindred from the Prince. 150
Rich. My other self, my counsel's consistory,
My oracle, my prophet, my dear cousin:
I, as a child, will go by thy direction.
Toward Ludlow then, for we'll not stay behind.   *Exeunt.*

---

142. Ludlow] *Qq;* London *F.*   143. sister] *F;* mother *Qq.*   144. business]
F; waighty business *Qq (subst.).*   145.] *Qq (speech-prefix Ans.); not in F.*
145. S.D.] *F; Exeunt man. Glo. Buck. | Qq (subst.).*   146. whoever] *F,Q1–3,5–6*
(subst.); who *Q4.*   147. God's] *As Qq;* God *F.*   stay] *F,Q1;* be *Q2–6.*
at home] *F;* behinde *Qq (subst.).*   149. late] *F,Q1;* lately *Q2–6.*   of]
F,Q1–2; off *Q3–6.*   150. Prince] *F;* King *Qq.*   153. as] *F;* like *Qq.*
154. Toward] *F;* Towards *Qq.*   Ludlow] *Qq;* London *F.*   we'll] *F;* we
will *Qq.*   154. S.D.] *F; Exit. | Q3–6; not in Q1–2.*

---

142. *Ludlow*] Here and again in
l. 154 Compositor B makes this careless
misreading of his copy.

143. *sister*] As at l. 101, Richard
lives up to his hypocritical promise to
Clarence to call Elizabeth 'sister'.
The reading was probably changed
in Q for fear of misunderstanding.

144. *censures*] judgement or opinion:
OED *sb.3.*

145.] Patrick believes (p. 137) this
line was added to the text by the
prompter to smooth these characters'
exits. Or Shakespeare may have
added it: certainly it makes for a
better transition to give the ladies a
reply and most eds thus include it.

148. *sort occasion*] find an opportunity.

149. *index*] that which serves to
point to a particular fact or conclusion: OED *sb.4.* Buckingham means
that he will find an opportunity to
separate the Queen's kindred from
the Prince, as the guiding principle
of the plot (story) which is to ensue.

150. *Prince*] Q is technically right
that Prince Edward is now King, but
he is referred to throughout the play
as 'Prince', since he was never
crowned.

151. *other self*] A proverbial phrase
(Tilley F696) recently used in e.g.
Jew ('my second selfe': III. iv. 15).

SCENE III

Enter one Citizen *at one door, and* Another
at the other.

1 Cit. Good morrow, neighbour: whither away so fast?

2 Cit. I promise you, I scarcely know myself.
　　　　Hear you the news abroad?

1 Cit.　　　　　　　　　　　　Yes, that the King is dead.

2 Cit. Ill news, by'rlady; seldom comes the better.
　　　　I fear, I fear, 'twill prove a giddy world.　　　　　5

Enter another Citizen.

3 Cit. Neighbours, God speed.

1 Cit.　　　　　　　　　　　Give you good-morrow, sir.

3 Cit. Doth the news hold of good King Edward's death?

2 Cit. Ay, sir, it is too true, God help the while.

3 Cit. Then, masters, look to see a troublous world.

1 Cit. No, no; by God's good grace, his son shall reign.　　10

Scene III

SCENE III] F (*Scena Tertia*)*; not in Qq.*　　　S.D.] F; *Enter two Cittizens. | Qq*
(*Q 2–5 Citizens*).　　1. Good morrow, neighbour] F (*subst.*); Neighbour well
met *Qq.*　　3.] *As Steevens; . . .* abroad? / Yes *F.Qq* (*subst.*).　　Yes] F; I *Qq.*
4. Ill] F; Bad *Qq.*　　5. giddy] F; troublous *Q 2–6.* troublesome *Q 2–6.*　　6.]
As Steevens; . . . speed. / Giue F (*Q diff.*).　　Neighbours, God speed] F; Good
morrow neighbours *Qq.*　　*1 Cit.* Give you good-morrow, sir.] F; *not in Qq.*
7. the] F; this *Qq.*　　King] F,Q 1–2,4,6; Kings Q 3, 5.　　8.] F; It doth. Qq.
10. good grace] F,Q 1; grace Q 2–6.

consistory] a place where counsellors
meet: OED 1.1, quoting this line for
the figurative usage.

Scene III

4.] Proverbial: Tilley B332; for
'the' with comparatives to signify the
degree of excess, see Abbott §94.

6.] In Q the Third Citizen enters
with the phrase 'Good morrow
neighbours', a common enough salutation, but which, by anticipating the
First Citizen's greeting, leaves him
mumchance.

8.] Q renders the essence of F's line
in two brusque syllables. The compositor pulled the next line into the
space thus opened, and it is consequently extra-metrical. The relationship between the abridgement of the
line and the change of speaker
tempts speculation, but Smidt's view
(p. 49) that in the three citizens
Shakespeare intended to present an
optimist, a pessimist, and a shrewd
counsellor is far-fetched, since it
requires him to postulate that the
speech-prefixes were jumbled in both
F and Q versions.

3 Cit. Woe to that land that's govern'd by a child.

2 Cit. In him there is a hope of government,
    Which, in his nonage, council under him,
    And in his full and ripen'd years himself,
    No doubt shall then, and till then, govern well.   15

1 Cit. So stood the state when Henry the Sixth
    Was crown'd in Paris but at nine months old.

3 Cit. Stood the state so? No, no, good friends, God wot.
    For then this land was famously enrich'd
    With politic grave counsel; then the King   20
    Had virtuous uncles to protect his Grace.

1 Cit. Why, so hath this, both by his father and mother.

3 Cit. Better it were they all came by his father,
    Or by his father there were none at all:
    For emulation who shall now be nearest   25
    Will touch us all too near, if God prevent not.
    O, full of danger is the Duke of Gloucester,
    And the Queen's sons and brothers, haught and proud;
    And were they to be rul'd, and not to rule,
    This sickly land might solace as before.   30

1 Cit. Come, come: we fear the worst; all will be well.

13. Which] *F;* That *Qq.*   16. Henry] *F;* Harry *Qq.*   17. in] *F;* at *Qq.*
18. No, no, good friends, God wot] *F;* no good my friend not so *Qq.*   22.
1 Cit. Why so] *F;* 2 So *Qq.*   his] *F;* the *Qq.*   23. his] *F;* the *Qq.*   24.
his] *F;* the *Qq.*   25. who shall now] *F;* now, who shall *Qq.*   26. Will]
F,Q 1; Which *Q 2–6.*   28. sons and brothers, haught] *F;* kindred hauty *Qq*
(*subst.*).   29. not to] *F,Q 1–5;* not *Q6.*   31. *1 Cit.*] *F;* 2 / *Qq.*   will be]
F; shalbe *Q 1–2;* shall be *Q 3–6.*

11.] A very familiar phrase,
proverbial (Tilley W600) but deriving
originally from Ecclesiastes, x.15–16,
and thence to More in Buckingham's
oration: 'Vae regno, cuius Rex puer
est, woo to that realme whose king
is a child' (Hall, *Edward V*, fol. xxiiᵛ).

13. *nonage*] minority. The Citizen
argues that when Edward is of age
he will probably govern well; until
then, good counsel will preserve the
state.

21. *virtuous uncles*] Cf. 'Thomas,
Earl of Salisbury', ll. 104–5: 'Whose
wurthy uncles had the governaunce, /
The one at home, the other abrode in

Fraunce' (*Mirror*, p. 146). There were
actually three uncles: the Bishop of
Winchester, the Duke of Gloucester,
and the Duke of Bedford, whose
power-struggles are the subject of *1*
and *2 Henry VI.*

25. *emulation*] ambitious rivalry for
power or honours: OED 2.

30. *solace*] take comfort or consolation: OED *v.*3; here, specifically, to
recover health. If the Prince's uncles
were to control themselves, the sickly
land might become well. Cf. *Cym.*,
I.vi.86.

31. *we . . . well*] Proverbial: Tilley
W912.

3 Cit. When clouds are seen, wise men put on their cloaks;
        When great leaves fall, then winter is at hand;
        When the sun sets, who doth not look for night?
        Untimely storms makes men expect a dearth.   35
        All may be well; but if God sort it so
        'Tis more than we deserve, or I expect.

2 Cit. Truly, the hearts of men are full of fear:
        You cannot reason almost with a man
        That looks not heavily and full of dread.   40

3 Cit. Before the days of change still is it so:
        By a divine instinct men's minds mistrust
        Ensuing danger, as by proof we see
        The water swell before a boist'rous storm.
        But leave it all to God. Whither away?   45

2 Cit. Marry, we were sent for to the Justices.

3 Cit. And so was I : I'll bear you company.   *Exeunt.*

32. are seen] *F;* appeare *Qq.*   33. then] *F;* the *Qq.*   35. makes] *F;* make
Qq.   36. may] *F,Q 1–5;* men *Q 6.*   38. *2 Cit.*] *F; 1 / Qq.*   hearts] *F;*
soules *Qq.*   fear] *F;* bread *Q 1–2;* dread *Q 3–6.*   39. You] *F;* Yee *Q 1;*
Ye *Q 2–6.*   reason almost] *F;* almost reason *Qq.*   40. dread] *F;* feare *Qq.*
41. days] *F;* times *Qq.*   43. Ensuing] *Qq (F catchword);* Pursuing *F.*
danger] *F;* dangers *Qq.*   see] *F;* see. *Q 1–2;* see, *Q 3–6.*   44. water] *F;*
waters *Qq.*   46. Marry, we were] *F;* We are *Qq.*   Justices] *F;* Iustice *Qq.*

32–5.] Curiously, Tilley lists none
of this cascade of proverbial wisdom,
though all have analogues in common
sayings.

35. *makes*] 'Untimely storms' is a
collective singular.

36. *sort*] ordain or order events:
OED *v.*[1] 1.1b.

38. *fear*] The actor anticipated l.
40, transposing its 'dread' with this
line's 'fear', a not uncommon switch-
ing of synonyms. Q1's compositor
compounded the error with a foul-
case letter, thus producing one of the
most comical lines in 'Shakespeare'.

39. *almost*] Unusual word order:
the Citizen means it is almost
impossible to find a man who does
not look fearful.

41–4.] These lines are taken with
little change from More (in Hall,
Edward V, fol. xiii[r]). See also Tilley
M475, and in ll. 42–4 there is an
echo of the *Thyestes*, ll. 961–4.

46. *Justices*] A rather obscure
reference: NCS speculates on what
service is intended; NPS comments on
the apparent contradiction with l. 2.
Probably a sessions of the Justices of
Assize is meant.

SCENE IV

Enter ARCHBISHOP OF YORK, *the young* DUKE OF YORK,
QUEEN ELIZABETH, *and the* DUCHESS OF YORK.

Arch. Last night, I hear, they lay at Stony Stratford,
And at Northampton they do rest tonight:
Tomorrow, or next day, they will be here.
Duch. I long with all my heart to see the Prince;
I hope he is much grown since last I saw him.   5
Eliz. But I hear no: they say my son of York
Has almost overta'en him in his growth.
York. Ay, mother, but I would not have it so.
Duch. Why, my good cousin? It is good to grow.
York. Grandam, one night as we did sit at supper,   10
My uncle Rivers talk'd how I did grow
More than my brother. 'Ay,' quoth my uncle
    Gloucester,
'Small herbs have grace; great weeds do grow apace.'
And since, methinks I would not grow so fast,
Because sweet flowers are slow and weeds make haste. 15
Duch. Good faith, good faith, the saying did not hold

Scene IV

SCENE IV] F (*Scena Quarta*); *not in Qq.*   S.D.] *Camb.; Enter Arch-bishop, yong
Yorke, the Queene, and the Dutchesse.* | *F;Enter Cardinall, Dutches of Yorke. Quee.
young Yorke.* | *Qq* (*Q3–6 Qu.*).   1. *Arch.*] *F; Car.* | *Qq* [*throughout*].   hear]
Q1–2 (heare); *heard Q3–6,F.*   Stony Stratford] *F; Northampton Qq.*
2. And at Northampton they do rest] *F; At Stonistratford will they be Qq.*
7. Has] *F; Hath Qq.*   almost] *F,Q1–5; not in Q6.*   9. my good] *F; my
young Qq* (*subst.*).   12. uncle] *F,Q2–6* (*Q2 Vnckle*); *Nnckle Q1.*   13. do
grow] *F; grow Qq.*

Scene IV

S.D. *Archbishop of York*] See Introduction, p. 16.
Queen] See Introduction, p. 28,
for Q1's abbreviation.
1. *I hear*] Q1–2's reading is correct;
'heard' in F derives from Q3 and
introduces an unwanted ambiguity
into the line.
Stony Stratford] See Introduction,
p. 18.

13. *great*] J. C. Maxwell (NCS, p.
198) conjectured 'ill' for 'great' here,
declaring that the rhetorical pattern
was chiastic, and that 'great' must be
a 'reporter's antithesis to "small" '.
To this it may be replied that so
emending *makes* the line chiastic, but
it is not self-evident that the simpler
alliterative antithesis must be wrong.
It is true, however, that all Tilley's
examples (W238) read 'ill'.

In him that did object the same to thee!
He was the wretched'st thing when he was young,
So long a-growing, and so leisurely,
That if his rule were true, he should be gracious.   20
Arch. And so no doubt he is, my gracious madam.
Duch. I hope he is, but yet let mothers doubt.
York. Now by my troth, if I had been remember'd,
   I could have given my uncle's Grace a flout
   To touch his growth nearer than he touch'd mine.   25
Duch. How, my young York? I prithee let me hear it.
York. Marry, they say my uncle grew so fast
   That he could gnaw a crust at two hours old:
   'Twas full two years ere I could get a tooth.
   Grandam, this would have been a biting jest!   30
Duch. I prithee, pretty York, who told thee this?
York. Grandam, his nurse.
Duch. His nurse? Why she was dead ere thou wast born.
York. If 'twere not she, I cannot tell who told me.

20. his rule were true] *F;* this were a true rule *Q1–2;* this were a rule *Q3–6.*
21.] *F;* Why Madame, so no doubt he is. *Qq.*   22. he is] *F;* so too *Qq.*
25.] *F;* That should haue neerer toucht his growth then he did mine. *Qq.*
26.] *As Qq;* . . . Yorke, / I *F.*   young] *F;* prety *Qq (subst.).*   prithee] *F;*
pray thee *Qq.*   27. say] *F,Q1;* say that *Q2–6.*   28. old] *F,Q1–2,4,6;*
hold *Q3, 5.*   30. biting] *F,Q1;* pretie *Q2–6 (subst.).*   31. prithee] *F;* pray
thee *Qq.*   this] *F;* so *Qq.*   33. His nurse?] *F,Q1; not in Q2–6.*   wast]
F; wert *Qq.*

17. *object*] present in discourse or
argument: OED *v.* 3.

21, 25.] These lines are typical
actor's variants in Q where the
sense is preserved at the expense of
the metre. Synonyms and parallel
expressions are common in the scene,
e.g. ll. 22, 26.

24. *uncle's Grace*] Young York is
enjoying playing on the word 'grace'
and its derivatives: in l. 21 he uses
'gracious' in a merely complimentary
sense after the Duchess has just used
it theologically; now he 'moralizes
two meanings' in the word. A parlous
boy indeed.

27–8.] The tale of Richard's being
born with teeth originates in Rous's

Historia: 'tyrannus rex Ricardus, qui
natus est . . . biennio matris utero
tentus [a flat lie!], exiens cum
dentibus et capillis ad humeros'
(Churchill, p. 47). More reiterates it
(Hall, *Edward V*, fol. 1ᵛ) and Shakespeare gleefully adopts it.

30. *biting*] Young York is quite a
punster; though Richard later comments: 'He is all the mother's, from
the top to toe' (III.i.156), it rather
seems as if something of the family's
sardonic way with words, so vivid
in his uncle, has found its way into
the new generation. It should be
noted that Q2 introduced 'pretie'
here by repetition of l. 26 or anticipation of l. 31, thus missing the pun.

Eliz. A parlous boy: go to, you are too shrewd.   35
Duch. Good madam, be not angry with the child.
Eliz. Pitchers have ears.

Enter a Messenger.

Arch. Here comes a messenger. What news?
Mess. Such news, my lord, as grieves me to report.
Eliz. How doth the Prince?
Mess.   Well, madam, and in health. 40
Duch. What is thy news?
Mess.   Lord Rivers and Lord Grey
    Are sent to Pomfret, and with them
    Sir Thomas Vaughan, prisoners.
Duch. Who hath committed them?
Mess.   The mighty Dukes,
    Gloucester and Buckingham.
Arch.   For what offence?   45
Mess. The sum of all I can I have disclos'd:
    Why or for what the nobles were committed
    Is all unknown to me, my gracious lord.
Eliz. Ay me! I see the ruin of my House:
    The tiger now hath seiz'd the gentle hind;   50
    Insulting tyranny begins to jut

---

37. S.D.] *F; Enter Dorset. | Qq.*   38.] *F;* Here comes your sonne, Lo: M. Dorset. / What newes Lo: Marques? *Qq (subst.).*   39. *Mess.*] *F; Dor. Qq.* [*throughout*].   report] *F;* unfold *Qq (subst.).*   40.] *As Collier;* ... Prince? / Well *F,Qq.*   doth] *F;* fares *Qq.*   41.] *As Collier;* ... Newes? / Lord *F;* then? / Lo: *Qq (subst.).*   thy] *F,Q1;* the *Q2–6.*   news] *F;* news then *Qq* 41–3. Lord ... prisoners.] *As F;* Lo: Riuers ... Pomfret, / With them ... prisoners. *Qq.*   42. and with] *F;* With *Qq.*   44–5.] *As Steevens;* ... them? / The ... Buckingham. / For *F,Qq.*   47. or for what] *F,Q1,3–6;* or what *Q2.* the] *F;* these *Qq.*   48. lord] *F;* Lady *Qq.*   49. ruin ... my] *F;* downfall ... our *Qq.*   51. jut] *F;* iet *Qq.*

35. *parlous*] dangerously cunning or shrewd; mischievous: OED 3. See also III.i.154.

37. *Pitchers ... ears*] Tilley P363.

37. S.D.] For Q's use of Dorset here, see Introduction, pp. 15–16.

40–5.] The lineation is out in both Q and F, and the solutions retained here have been adopted by almost all eds. Even as rearranged, there are metrical defects in ll. 43, 44.

42. *Pomfret*] Pontefract castle, an ominous destination: see III.iii.10 n.

43. *Vaughan*] Throughout pronounced as a disyllable.

51. *jut*] 'Jet' is the same word, meaning to overhang: the jutting first floor of the typical half-timbered

Upon the innocent and aweless throne.
Welcome destruction, blood, and massacre;
I see, as in a map, the end of all.

Duch. Accursed and unquiet wrangling days,   55
How many of you have mine eyes beheld!
My husband lost his life to get the crown,
And often up and down my sons were toss'd
For me to joy and weep their gain and loss;
And being seated, and domestic broils   60
Clean over-blown, themselves, the conquerors,
Make war upon themselves, brother to brother,
Blood to blood, self against self. O preposterous
And frantic outrage, end thy damned spleen,
Or let me die, to look on earth no more.   65

Eliz. Come, come my boy: we will to sanctuary.
Madam, farewell.

Duch.   Stay, I will go with you.

Eliz. You have no cause.

Arch.   My gracious lady, go,
And thither bear your treasure and your goods.
For my part, I'll resign unto your Grace   70
The seal I keep; and so betide to me

---

52. aweless] *F;* lawlesse *Qq.*   53. blood] *F;* death *Qq.*   62. brother to
brother,] *F; not in Qq.*   63. Blood to blood] *F;* bloud against bloud *Qq (in
l. 62).*   65. earth] *F;* death *Qq.*   67.] *As Steevens;* . . . farwell. / Stay . . .
you. *F;* Ile go along with you. *Qq.*   Madam, farewell] *F; not in Qq.*
68.] *As Steevens;* . . . cause. / My *F,Qq.*

---

house is properly called the 'jet'. See
OED jet *v.*² 1.1b; jut *v.*² b.

52. *aweless*] that inspires no awe:
OED 3, citing this line. Q's 'lawlesse'
is probably compositorial error, possibly actor's vulgarization.

58–65.] Neither F nor (especially)
Q is correctly punctuated here, but
the sense is not in doubt. The
omission of 'brother to brother' from
Q perhaps originated with the actor.
The images of ll. 61–3, of self-
destructive combat, are highly characteristic of Shakespeare's representation of the final stages in civil disorder.

Cf. *Troil.,* 1.iii.121–4, and of course
the *Sir Thomas More* fragment, in
which More concludes his summary
of the evils of disorder with the
phrase 'men like ravenous fishes /
Would feed on one another'.

65. *earth*] See Appendix II.

71. *seal*] Rotherham was in possession of the Great Seal of England,
from the hands of Edward IV: his
delivery of it to Elizabeth was an
illegal and politically extreme act,
remarked on by More (Hall, *Edward
V*, fol. vii^r).

As well I tender you and all of yours.
Go; I'll conduct you to the sanctuary.   *Exeunt.*

73. Go] *F;* Come *Qq.*

73. *Go*] The Archbishop is repeating his command from l. 68 with further emphasis. The Q version is more commonplace, and thus likely to have crept into the actor's part.

ACT III

SCENE I

The trumpets sound. Enter young PRINCE EDWARD, *the Dukes of* GLOUCESTER *and* BUCKINGHAM, LORD CARDINAL [BOURCHIER], [CATESBY,] *with* Others.

Buck. Welcome, sweet Prince, to London, to your chamber.
Rich. Welcome, dear cousin, my thoughts' sovereign.
 The weary way hath made you melancholy.
Prince. No, uncle, but our crosses on the way
 Have made it tedious, wearisome, and heavy;   5
 I want more uncles here to welcome me.
Rich. Sweet Prince, the untainted virtue of your years
 Hath not yet div'd into the world's deceit,
 Nor more can you distinguish of a man
 Than of his outward show, which—God He knows— 10
 Seldom or never jumpeth with the heart:
 Those uncles which you want were dangerous;
 Your Grace attended to their sugar'd words,
 But look'd not on the poison of their hearts.

ACT III

Scene 1

ACT III SCENE I] F (*Actus Tertius, Scæna Prima*); *not in* Qq. S.D. *Dukes*] F,Q*1–5*; Duke | Q*6*. *Lord Cardinal . . . with others*] F; *Cardinall, &c* | Qq. 1.] As Qq; . . . London, | To F. 8. *Hath*] Q*1–5*,F; Haue Q*6*. 9. *Nor*] Qq; No F.

Note: as explained in the Introduction, p. 33, the copy-text for this scene until l. 165 is Q1, which accounts for the different order of the texts collated in the textual apparatus.

 1. *chamber*] capital or metropolis: OED *sb.*1.6. Cf. Introduction, p. 89.

 4. *crosses*] vexations, annoyances: OED cross *sb.*B.I.10b.

9–11.] Cf. 1 Samuel, xvi. 7: 'For man looketh on the outward appearance but the Lord looketh on the heart'; also Luke, xvi.15 (Noble, p. 135).

 11. *jumpeth*] agrees completely: OED jump *v.*1.5.

 12. *want*] lack, are deficient in: OED *v.*2.

God keep you from them, and from such false friends! 15
Prince. God keep me from false friends—but they were none.

Enter LORD MAYOR [*with* Attendants].

Rich. My Lord, the Mayor of London comes to greet you.
Mayor. God bless your Grace with health and happy days!
Prince. I thank you, good my lord, and thank you all.
I thought my mother and my brother York   20
Would long ere this have met us on the way.
Fie, what a slug is Hastings, that he comes not
To tell us whether they will come or no.

Enter LORD HASTINGS.

Buck. And in good time, here comes the sweating lord.
Prince. Welcome, my lord. What, will our mother come? 25
Hast. On what occasion God he knows, not I,
The Queen your mother and your brother York
Have taken sanctuary. The tender prince
Would fain have come with me to meet your Grace,
But by his mother was perforce withheld.   30
Buck. Fie, what an indirect and peevish course
Is this of hers! Lord Cardinal, will your Grace
Persuade the Queen to send the Duke of York
Unto his princely brother presently?
If she deny, Lord Hastings, go with him   35
And from her jealous arms pluck him perforce.
Card. My Lord of Buckingham, if my weak oratory
Can from his mother win the Duke of York,
Anon expect him here; but if she be obdurate
To mild entreaties, God in Heaven forbid   40
We should infringe the holy privilege

16.] *As Qq*; . . . friends, / But *F.*   from] *Q1–3,5–6,F*; frō such *Q4.*   16.
S.D.] *This edn*; *Enter Lord Maior*/ *Qq,F* (*after l. 17*).   29. have come] *Q1–
2,4,F*; come *Q3,5–6.*   33. to send] *Q1–2,4,6,F*; the send *Q3*; they send *Q5.*
35. him] *Q1–4,F*; them *Q5–6.*   38. the] *Q1–2,4–F*; to *Q6,3.*   40. in
Heaven] *Q1–2*; *not in Q3–6,F.*

16. S.D.] It appears evident that   31. *indirect*] not straightforward or
the Mayor ought to enter before   honest; deceitful: OED 1b.
Richard's line, rather than after it.   *peevish*] perverse, obstinate, ca-
22. *slug*] i.e. sluggard.   pricious: OED 4.

Of blessed sanctuary! Not for all this land
Would I be guilty of so deep a sin.
Buck. You are too senseless-obstinate, my lord,
Too ceremonious and traditional.   45
Weigh it but with the grossness of this age,
You break not sanctuary in seizing him;
The benefit thereof is always granted
To those whose dealings have deserv'd the place,
And those who have the wit to claim the place.   50
This prince hath neither claim'd it nor deserv'd it:
And therefore in mine opinion cannot have it;
Then taking him from thence that is not there,
You break no privilege nor charter there.
Oft have I heard of sanctuary men,   55
But sanctuary children, never till now.
Card. My lord, you shall o'er-rule my mind for once.
Come on, Lord Hastings, will you go with me?
Hast. I go my lord.
Prince. Good lords, make all the speedy haste you may.   60
                         Exeunt Cardinal and Hastings.
Say, uncle Gloucester, if our brother come,
Where shall we sojourn till our coronation?

---

43. deep] *Q 1–2;* great *Q 3–6,F.*   44. senseless-obstinate] *Theobald;* senselesse
obstinate *Q q,F.*   46. grossness] *Q 1–5,F;* greatnesse *Q 6.*   53. taking] *Q 1–*
5,F; take *Q 6.*   60. S.D.] *As Camb., after l. 59 F; Exit. Car. & Hast. | Q 3–6,*
after l. 59; not in Q 1–2.

---

44. *senseless-obstinate*] One of a
number of unusual compounds in the
play, it is not as impertinent as
Collier (Variorum, p. 195) imagined.
OED 3b cites this use alone of the
meaning 'unreasonably' for 'senseless';
'obstinate' should perhaps be taken
as 'unyielding' or 'reluctant' rather
than merely stubborn. So Buckingham
is saying that the Cardinal is not
using his rational faculties on the
issue, but rather relying on his
ingrained principles.

45. *ceremonious*] punctilious in obser-
vance of formalities: OED 5.

46. *grossness*] lack of refinement in
habits or ideas: OED 4b. The

general drift of Buckingham's objection is that the Archbishop is without
thinking clinging to forms which have
ceased to be relevant.

47–56.] This is a neat précis of the
lengthy argument More gives Buckingham: Hall, *Edward V*, fols. ix^r–x^v.

56. *never*] It is probable that words
such as 'never', 'ever' and so on were
automatically elided when the metre
required it; on the other hand the
unexpected emphasis made by pro-
nouncing the foot as a triplet adds
force to the line. Honigmann (p. 50)
remarks however that Q is in this
word closer to the source.

Rich. Where it seems best unto your royal self.
    If I may counsel you, some day or two
    Your Highness shall repose you at the Tower,   65
    Then where you please and shall be thought most fit
    For your best health and recreation.
Prince. I do not like the Tower, of any place.
    Did Julius Caesar build that place, my lord?
Buck. He did, my gracious lord, begin that place,   70
    Which since, succeeding ages have re-edified.
Prince. Is it upon record, or else reported
    Successively from age to age, he built it?
Buck. Upon record, my gracious lord.
Prince. But say, my lord, it were not register'd,   75
    Methinks the truth should live from age to age,
    As 'twere retail'd to all posterity,
    Even to the general all-ending day.
Rich. [*Aside*] So wise so young, they say, do never live long.

63. seems] *Q1-2;* thinkst *Q3-6,F.*   78. all-ending] *Q1;* ending *Q2-6,F.*
79. [*Aside*] *Johnson; not in Qq,F.*   never] *Qq,F;* ne'er *Pope.*

65. *the Tower*] The name has a
sinister resonance now which in part
was caused by the subsequent murder
of Prince Edward and young York
therein. However, it is worth noting
that the Tower was indeed one of the
royal palaces, and in the fifteenth and
sixteenth centuries it was less ominous
than some other castles, such as Pomfret
(III.iii.9-10). It had been recently the
site of Henry VI's and Clarence's
murders, which is enough to account
for the Prince's reluctance. Cf.
ll. 140-5.
    68-9.] It seems clear that l. 68 is
not exactly an answer to Richard
(who could hardly have ignored it
if it had been) but almost an aside,
while l. 69 is clearly addressed to
Buckingham.
    69-93.] This dialogue (for which
there is no precedent in the sources)
seems to serve three functions: (1) It
establishes the Prince's royal nature
and potential. (2) It also reveals his
critical intellect (far more construc-

tive and mature than his brother's
wit-sallies) in his concern for the
historical truth of traditions. (3) It
ironically ventilates the issue of
historical 'record', especially in the
key ll. 72-8. Caesar's building of the
Tower is 'upon record' (but we have
only Buckingham's unreliable word
for it); even were it not, 'the truth
should live from age to age'. Just so:
and this dialogue is part of another
historical structure which will live
from age to age—the play itself, also
founded upon 'record' which was
however based largely upon report
and rumour. A fascinating insight;
see also Introduction, pp. 74-9.
    71. *re-edified*] rebuilt.
    75. *register'd*] i.e. written down.
    78. *all-ending*] Q2's compositor
was misled by the preceding word
'generall' into omitting the repeated
letters 'all-', and was followed by all
subsequent compositors.
    79.] See Tilley L384.

Prince. What say you, uncle?   80
Rich. I say, without characters fame lives long.
    [*Aside*] Thus, like the formal Vice, Iniquity,
    I moralize two meanings in one word.
Prince. That Julius Caesar was a famous man:
    With what his valour did enrich his wit,   85
    His wit set down to make his valour live;
    Death makes no conquest of this conqueror,
    For now he lives in fame, though not in life.
    I'll tell you what, my cousin Buckingham.
Buck. What, my gracious lord?   90
Prince. And if I live until I be a man,
    I'll win our ancient right in France again,
    Or die a soldier, as I liv'd a king.
Rich. Short summers lightly have a forward spring.

    Enter young DUKE OF YORK, HASTINGS, CARDINAL.

Buck. Now in good time here comes the Duke of York.   95
Prince. Richard of York: how fares our loving brother?

82. [*Aside*] F2; *not in* Qq,F.   Thus] Q1–5,F; That Q6.   86. valour]
Q3–6,F; valure Q1–2.   87. this] Q1; his Q2–6,F.   94. S.D. *Hastings,
Cardinal*] Qq; *Hastings, and Cardinall* | F.   96. loving] Q1–2; noble Q3–6,F.

81. *characters*] written records. The
accent is on the second syllable.
    82. *formal Vice, Iniquity*] For the
importance of this comparison, see
Introduction, pp. 99–102. Iniquity
is the Vice's name in *Nice Wanton* and
Darius. The best explanation of
'formal' is Spivack's (p. 394); he
observes that the adjective 'carries
the burden of Richard's meaning':
in one of its Elizabethan senses it
means 'conventional' or 'regular'
(OED 3b). Richard uses it to explain
that though 'he appears something
different from the conventional and
obvious Vice of the popular stage,
he is imitating the method of that
role'; he is 'inviting the appreciation
of the audience for his dexterity in
deceit'.
    83. *moralize*] interpret morally or
symbolically: OED 1, no doubt with,

as secondary meaning, an awareness
of the nature of the 'moral play' and
the Vice's role therein.
    85. *what*] Abbott §252 remarks on
this curious use of 'what' to mean
'that with which'. The Prince means
'What his valour enriched his wit
with, his wit set down to make his
deeds immortal'.
    86. *valour*] Q1's spelling may have
stood in the copy, and suggests a play
on words (valour/value). But the
spelling is obscure, and on balance
Q3's modernization seemed preferable, in a pair of lines of unusual
difficulty anyway.
    88. *lives in fame*] Cf. *Tit.*, 1.i.158.
    94.] Proverbial: Tilley F774.
'Lightly' means 'As may easily
happen, probably': OED 6; cf.
German 'vielleicht'.
    96. *loving*] Q3's 'noble' perhaps

York. Well, my dread lord—so must I call you now.
Prince. Ay, brother, to our grief as it is yours;
        Too late he died that might have kept that title,
        Which by his death hath lost much majesty.   100
Rich. How fares our cousin, noble lord of York?
York. I thank you, gentle uncle. O my lord,
        You said that idle weeds are fast in growth:
        The Prince my brother hath outgrown me far!
Rich. He hath, my lord.
York.   And therefore is he idle?   105
Rich. O my fair cousin, I must not say so!
York. Then he is more beholding to you than I.
Rich. He may command me as my sovereign,
        But you have power in me as in a kinsman.
York. I pray you, uncle, give me this dagger.   110
Rich. My dagger, little cousin? With all my heart.
Prince. A beggar, brother?
York. Of my kind uncle, that I know will give,
        And being but a toy, which is no grief to give.
Rich. A greater gift than that I'll give my cousin.   115
York. A greater gift? O, that's the sword to it.
Rich. Ay, gentle cousin, were it light enough.
York. O, then I see you will part but with light gifts;
        In weightier things you'll say a beggar nay.
Rich. It is too heavy for your Grace to wear.   120
York. I weigh it lightly, were it heavier.

---

97. dread] *Q1–2*; deare *Q3–6,F*.   111. With all] *Q3–6,F*; withall *Q1–2*.
114. grief] *Q1–5,F*; gift *Q6*.   120. heavy] *Q1*; weightie *Q2–6,F* (*subst.*).
your] *Q1–5,F*; you *Q6*.

appeared by a jump of the eye from
l.101.
        99. *late*] i.e. lately; the Prince
refers of course to his father.
        103. *idle weeds*] Tilley W238
again.
        111. *With all*] One of Richard's
best jokes: he would, with all his
heart, love to give young York a
dagger—thrust into the child's vitals.
One could retain the Q1 reading,
and punctuate: 'My dagger, little
cousin?—withal my heart', meaning,

my heart in addition to the material
gift. Depending on how the line was
spoken, any shade of the triple
ambiguity could be expressed by the
actor. But the two primary meanings
are best expressed by Q3's modernization.
        114. *toy*] i.e. a trifle—Richard was
not wearing a toy dagger.
        115. *greater gift*] Probably the
same gift he gave his brother, and
others: Heaven.
        121. *I weigh*] 'I consider it as of no

Rich. What, would you have my weapon, little lord?

York. I would, that I might thank you as you call me.

Rich. How?

York. Little. 125

Prince. My lord of York will still be cross in talk;
Uncle, your Grace knows how to bear with him.

York. You mean to bear me, not to bear with me;
Uncle, my brother mocks both you and me:
Because that I am little like an ape, 130
He thinks that you should bear me on your shoulders!

Buck. With what a sharp-provided wit he reasons:
To mitigate the scorn he gives his uncle
He prettily and aptly taunts himself.
So cunning and so young is wonderful! 135

Rich. My lord, will't please you pass along?
Myself and my good cousin Buckingham
Will to your mother, to entreat of her
To meet you at the Tower and welcome you.

York. What, will you go unto the Tower, my lord? 140

---

123. as] *Q1–2,4–6;* as as *Q3;* as, as, *F.*   132. sharp-provided] *Theobald;* sharpe prouided *Qq,F.*   133. gives] *Q1–2,4,6,F;* giue *Q3,5.*

---

value, and would, even if it were heavier' (Honigmann, in NPS). Hanmer's proposed emendation 'I'd weigh' is unnecessary.

123. *as*] F's retention of the unique Q3 error here is the firmest evidence for Q3 copy in this scene. See Introduction, pp. 32–3.

125. *Little*] As seen in II.iv, young York is verbally very alert to the same kinds of meaningful ambiguity that Richard is master of. Here he takes Richard's word and invests it with derogatory meaning: paltry, mean, contemptible (OED *a*.A.I.9) but perhaps also as an opposite of the colloquial term 'tall' for a brave man, so: cowardly.

126. *cross*] perverse, contrarious: OED *a*.5a, citing this line. It is possible, as Noble suggests, that the Prince intends an allusion in this and the next line to Luke, xiv.27:

'Whosoever doth not bear his cross . . .'

131. *bear*] Two traditions come together in York's gibe: the first that, as Johnson observed, an ape was set on a bear's shoulder at country shows (and thus his uncle's deformity and ungainliness are bear-like), and secondly that (as Douce noted) there was a tradition of the Fool carrying a monkey, evidenced by Holbein's picture which shows Will Somers so encumbered. So Richard is also a Fool. See Variorum, p. 208, NCS, p. 203, for further details.

135. *cunning*] possessing keen intelligence or learning; no derogatory connotation is necessarily implied at this date. Buckingham of course intends one, but only for Richard's ears: his encomium is obviously delivered to the bystanders in ironical admiration.

Prince. My Lord Protector needs will have it so.
York. I shall not sleep in quiet at the Tower.
Rich. Why, what should you fear?
York. Marry, my uncle Clarence' angry ghost:
    My grandam told me he was murder'd there.   145
Prince. I fear no uncles dead.
Rich. Nor none that live, I hope?
Prince. And if they live, I hope I need not fear.
    But come, my lord: with a heavy heart,
    Thinking on them, go I unto the Tower.   150
    A Sennet. Exeunt Prince, York, Hastings, Dorset, [and all but]
        Richard, Buckingham, and Catesby.
Buck. Think you, my lord, this little prating York
    Was not incensed by his subtle mother
    To taunt and scorn you thus opprobriously?
Rich. No doubt, no doubt; O, 'tis a parlous boy,
    Bold, quick, ingenious, forward, capable: 155
    He is all the mother's, from the top to toe.
Buck. Well, let them rest. Come hither, Catesby:
    Thou art sworn as deeply to effect what we intend
    As closely to conceal what we impart;
    Thou know'st our reasons, urg'd upon the way: 160

---

141. needs] *Q1; not in Q2–6,F.*   149. with] *Qq; and with F.*   150. S.D. *A Sennet . . . and Catesby] F; not in Qq.   Prince, York, Hastings, Dorset] F; Prin. Yor. Hast. Dors. | Qq. (Hast. Hast Q3).   and all but] This edn; Manent | F2; Manet | F,Qq.   Richard, Buckingham] F; Rich. Buck. | Q1; Rich. Buc. | Q2–4; Bich. Buc. | Q5; Bish. Buc. | Q6.   154. parlous] Camb.; perillous Q1–2,F; perilous Q3–6; perlous Q7–8.   157–8.] Qq,F; Well . . . sworn / As . . . intend, | Pope (omitting hither).*

150. S.D.] F has been taken as copy-text for this direction on the grounds that Q's directions are regularly abbreviated and unreliable. The process by which a 'Bishop Buckingham' appeared in Q6 seemed characteristic enough to warrant recording.

152. *incensed*] incited or instigated: OED incense *v.*² 4.

153. *opprobriously*] in a way involving shame or disgrace: OED 2.

154. *parlous*] The same word as the QF versions: see OED perilous *a.*2.

To avoid confusion, the Camb. modernization has been adopted, but parlous also can mean perilous in the modern sense: OED *a.*1. Cf. II.iv.35.

155. *quick*] lively. 'Capable' means intelligent; none of Richard's adjectives save 'bold' have precisely their modern meaning.

156.] Proverbial; see Tilley T436. See also II.iv.30 n.

157–8.] Pope's tidying of the metre here has been adopted by NCS and in part by NPS.

What think'st thou? Is it not an easy ma\
To make William Lord Hastings of our m
For the instalment of this noble Duke
In the seat royal of this famous isle?
Cat. He for his father's sake so loves the Prince   165
That he will not be won to aught against him.
Buck. What think'st thou then of Stanley? Will not he?
Cat. He will do all in all as Hastings doth.
Buck. Well, then, no more but this: go, gentle Catesby,
And as it were afar off, sound thou Lord Hastings   170
How he doth stand affected to our purpose,
And summon him tomorrow to the Tower
To sit about the coronation.
If thou dost find him tractable to us,
Encourage him, and tell him all our reasons;   175
If he be leaden, icy, cold, unwilling,
Be thou so too, and so break off the talk,
And give us notice of his inclination:
For we tomorrow hold divided Councils,
Wherein thyself shalt highly be employ'd.   180
Rich. Commend me to Lord William; tell him, Catesby,

167. Will not] *F;* what will *Qq.*   169–71.] *As Pope;* ... this: / Goe ... off, / Sound ... *Hastings,* / How ... purpose, / *F;* ... this: / Go ... off, / Sound ... affected / Vnto ... *Qq.*   170. afar] *Qq* (a farre); farre *F.*   thou] *F,Q1–2; not in Q3–6.*   171. doth stand] *F;* stands *Qq.*   to] *F;* Vnto *Qq.*   our] *F,Q1–3,5–6;* your *Q4.*   172–3.] *F; not in Qq.*   174.] *F;* if he be willing, *Qq.*   175. tell] *F;* shew *Qq.*   177. the] *F;* your *Qq.*

165. *He for his father's sake*] i.e. Hastings, for Edward IV's sake, so loves the young Prince.

169–73.] Here there is no objection to the rearrangement of the lines as made by Pope, since no amendment is called for. The text is disturbed as far as l. 174; probably, incomplete correction from the MS. in F is the cause. As for the omissions from Q, Patrick (p. 111) explains that Buckingham anticipates 'unwilling' from l. 176, and thus substitutes 'willing' for 'tractable', following which ll. 172–3 simply slipped his mind. But Smidt (p. 112) points out the contradiction between what Catesby is told

to do in ll. 172–3 and what he actually does in the next scene. This inconsistency is not infrequent in Shakespeare, and the differences in question extend beyond the present lines to l. 177, and again in ll. 188–9 Catesby promises to do something which he fails to carry out. For these reasons it is hard to think the omission of these two lines here deliberate. See also IV.ii.81 n. 'Afar off', as Honigmann noted, is nearer the sources (p. 49) and has been accepted into this text for that reason.

173. *sit about*] sit in conference upon.

His ancient knot of dangerous adversaries
Tomorrow are let blood at Pomfret castle,
And bid my lord for joy of this good news
Give Mistress Shore one gentle kiss the more.   185
Buck. Good Catesby, go effect this business soundly.
Cat. My good lords both, with all the heed I can.
Rich. Shall we hear from you, Catesby, ere we sleep?
Cat. You shall, my lord.
Rich. At Crosby Place, there shall you find us both.   190
                                        Exit Catesby.
Buck. Now, my lord, what shall we do if we perceive
Lord Hastings will not yield to our complots?
Rich. Chop off his head, man; somewhat will we do.
And look when I am king, claim thou of me
The earldom of Hereford, and all the moveables   195

184. lord] *F;* friend *Q 1–5;* friends *Q2 (Hunt. copy 69352),Q 6.*   185. Mistress]
F,Q 1–2; gentle Mistresse *Q 3–6 (subst.).*   186. go] *F; not in Qq.*   187. can]
F; may *Qq.*   190. Place] *Qq;* House *F.*   190. S.D.] *F,Q 3–6; not in Q 1–2.*
191.] *As Qq; . . .* Lord, / What *F.*   Now, my] *F,Qq;* My *Pope.*   192. Lord]
F; William Lo: *Qq.*   193.] *As Qq;* Chop . . . Head: / Something . . . de-
termine; *F.*   man] *Qq; not in F.*   somewhat] *Qq;* something *F.*   do]
Qq; determine *F.*   195. Hereford] *F,Q 1–2;* Herford *Q 3–5;* Hertford *Q 6.*
all] *F; not in Qq.*

182. *knot*] a small group or cluster
of persons: OED *sb.*¹ III. 18.
183. *let blood*] The surgical pro-
cedure, used here euphemistically.
190. *Place*] As noted at 1.ii.216,
'Place' occurs in More, but 'House'
was a common alternative.
191.] This, and many other lines
on p. 187 of the Folio (r6ʳ, the last
sheet of the inner forme) show signs
of the copy's having been 'stretched'
to fill up the space: see the opening
lines of scene ii, for example. Line 191
adds complication by the intrusive
'Now' at the beginning of the line,
which renders an otherwise exact
pentameter extra-metrical. Pope omitted it on these grounds, and was
followed by NCS; it is a possible
actor's addition, however, and is in
the part of Buckingham, so that if it
occurred only in Q one would have

no hesitation in rejecting it. As it is,
conservative principles incline one,
hesitantly, to include.
192. *Lord*] Here there can be no
doubt that the full title in Q originated with the actor.
complots] designs of covert nature
planned in consort (OED).
193.] Q here surely preserves a
rewritten line, brisker, more pointed,
and with the characteristic touch of
Richard's hail-fellow-well-met tone
in the familiar 'man'. It seems
unlikely that anyone save Shakespeare
could have contrived so apt an
improvement; see also *R2,* II.ii.116,
'somewhat we must do'.
195. *Hereford*] The confusion between the counties in Qq reveals a
most characteristic train of corruption.
moveables] personal possessions, as
distinct from 'real' estate.

Whereof the King my brother was possess'd.

Buck. I'll claim that promise at your Grace's hand.

Rich. And look to have it yielded with all kindness.

Come, let us sup betimes, that afterwards

We may digest our complots in some form. *Exeunt.* 200

SCENE II

Enter a Messenger *to the Door of Lord Hastings.*

Mess. My lord, my lord!   [*Knocks.*]

Hast. [*Within*] Who knocks?

Mess. One from the Lord Stanley.

196. was] *F*; stood *Qq*.   198. all kindness] *F*; all willingness *Q1*; willingnesse *Q2–6*.

Scene II

SCENE II] *F* (*Scena Secunda*); not in *Qq*.   S.D. *the Door of*] *F*; not in *Qq*.
1.] *F*; What ho my Lord *Qq*.   1. S.D.] *NCS*; not in *F,Qq*.   2. S.D.]
Thompson; not in *F,Qq*.   2. knocks?] *F*; knockes at the dore. *Qq* (dore? *Q2*;
doore? *Q3–5*; coore? *Q6*).   3. One] *F*; A messenger *Qq*.   3. S.D.] *Qq*;
F after l. 4.

196. *possess'd*] 'Humphrey de Bohun, Earl of Hereford, Essex, and Northampton, left two daughters. (1) The elder, Eleanor, married the youngest son of Edward III, Thomas, Duke of Gloucester and Earl of Buckingham, who was styled Earl of Essex in right of his wife. They had a daughter Anne, who married Edmund, Earl of Stafford: her son Humphrey was created Duke of Buckingham by Henry VI; and his grandson, the second Duke of Buckingham, is the Buckingham of this play. (2) The lands of Hereford were conveyed by the younger co-heiress, Mary, to her husband Henry, Earl of Derby, son of John of Gaunt, afterwards Henry IV. In 1397, three years after his wife's death, he was created Duke of Hereford. The fief continued in his line, and passed, with the other possessions of the crown, to the House of York: at this time it was in the hands of the King. Buckingham's claim to the Earldom of Hereford was thus a claim to the moiety of the Bohun possessions which, by the marriage of a younger co-heiress, had passed to an elder branch of the royal family' (Thompson).

Scene II

1–4.] Q and F here differ revealingly. Note the greater specificity of Q in ll. 2 and 3: the messenger is described as knocking 'at the door', and he defines his role as messenger in the next line. It is possible that these changes indicate modifications introduced for provincial performance, where a suitable door might not have been available (note that it is specified in the F S.D.) and where the messenger's status might not have been so evident. The lineation is doubtful: with slight emendation

Enter HASTINGS.

Hast. What is't o'clock?

Mess.   Upon the stroke of four.

Hast. Cannot my Lord Stanley sleep these tedious nights?   5

Mess. So it appears by that I have to say.

First, he commends him to your noble self.

Hast. What then?

Mess. Then certifies your lordship that this night

, He dreamt the boar had razed off his helm;   10

Besides, he says there are two Councils kept,

And that may be determin'd at the one

Which may make you and him to rue at th'other.

Therefore he sends to know your lordship's pleasure,

If you will presently take horse with him   15

4.] *As Steevens; . . .* a Clocke? / Vpon *F,Qq.*   What is't] *F;* Whats *Qq.*
5. my Lord Stanley] *F;* thy Master *Qq (subst.).*   these] *F,Q1;* the *Q2–6.*
tedious] *F,Q1–2,4,6;* teditous *Q3,5.*   6. appears] *F;* should seeme *Qq.*
7. self] *F;* Lordship *Qq.*   8. What] *F;* And *Qq.*   9.] *F;* And then he
sends you word. *Qq (subst.).*   10. drcamt] *F;* dreamt to night *Qq.*   boar]
F,Q6; beare *Q1–5 (subst.).*   razed off] *F;* raste *Q1–4;* caste *Q5;* cast *Q6.*
11. kept] *F;* held *Qq.*   15. you will presently] *F;* presently you will *Qq.*

---

ll. 1–3 could make a single pentameter;
Singer and Keightley both in fact
printed them as a single line. On the
other hand, some pauses would be
natural as the sleepy Hastings rouses
himself to reply, and strict metre
would be unlikely to be maintained.
It is evident that Hastings ought to
enter before l. 4, since a break between it and l. 5 is awkward: the
connexion between the hour and
Stanley's sleeplessness is obvious, and
ought to follow directly.

    5. *my Lord Stanley*] F appears
metrically defective, but in such a
line 'my lord' was probably pronounced in the same way as the
modern legal monosyllable, 'mlud'.

    9.] Here, and elsewhere (ll. 55,
33, etc.) the Messenger seems to have
had trouble remembering his lines:
he substitutes freely, more frequently
than most.

    10. *boar*] It is surprising that it was
not until Q6 that the original Q1
typographical error was mended,
since even the vaguest proof-reading
might have been expected to note
the recurrence of the word in ll. 27–8.
The imagery in the line is of course
heraldic. The boar was Richard's
emblem; the helm Stanley's head-
piece. But he expects Hastings (and
us) to perceive that the emblems have
a realistic connotation. To raze off
is to scrape, or cut off, but is also to
rub out, erase: Stanley fears not only
his death but the obliteration of his
line. See OED rase *v.*[1]. Q5's 'caste'
may have been an accident, or a
deliberate attempt to mend what
seemed erroneous. It is hard to tell:
the omission of 'off' from Q1 was no
doubt made by the actor to regu-
larize the metre following his re-
writing of his lines.

And with all speed post with him toward the north,
To shun the danger that his soul divines.
Hast. Go, fellow, go: return unto thy lord;
Bid him not fear the separated Council:
His honour and myself are at the one,   20
And at the other is my good friend Catesby,
Where nothing can proceed that toucheth us
Whereof I shall not have intelligence.
Tell him his fears are shallow, without instance;
And for his dreams, I wonder he's so simple   25
To trust the mockery of unquiet slumbers.
To fly the boar before the boar pursues
Were to incense the boar to follow us,
And make pursuit where he did mean no chase.
Go, bid thy master rise, and come to me,   30
And we will both together to the Tower,
Where he shall see the boar will use us kindly.
Mess. I'll go, my lord, and tell him what you say.   *Exit.*

Enter CATESBY

16. with him toward] *F;* into *Qq.*   18. Go, fellow] *F,Q 1-2 (subst.);* Good
fellow *Q 3-6.*   19. Council] *F;* counsels *Q 1;* councels *Q2-6.*   21. good
friend] *F;* seruant *Qq.*   24. without] *F;* wanting *Qq.*   instance] *F,Q 1;*
instancie *Q 2-6 (subst.).*   25. he's so simple] *F;* he is so fond *Q 1-3,5-6;* he is
fond *Q 4.*   27. pursues] *F;* pursues vs *Q 1-2;* pursue vs *Q 3-6.*   29. no
chase] *F,Q 1-3,5-6;* to chase *Q 4.*   33. I'll go, my lord, and] *F;* My gracious
Lo: Ile *Qq (subst.).*   33. S.D. *Exit*] *F,Q 3-6; not in Q 1-2.*   Catesby]
F,Q 1-2; Catesby to L. Hastings | Q 3-6.

19. *Council*] F's correction makes
clear—as indeed is clear from the
sources—that the formal Council is
meant, here and in the previous
scene, rather than mere sessions of
advice.

21. *good friend*] Smidt (p. 100)
argues that the Q reading 'servant' is
a significant change. However,
Catesby was of course not a servant
in the modern sense: the son of a
knight, he was himself an 'esquire of
the royal body'. After Hastings's
death he succeeded to some of his
offices: chancellor of the exchequer,
chamberlain for receipt of the
exchequer; subsequently he was

Speaker in Richard's only parliament. See OED servant *sb*.2e and
4a for non-menial uses of the word.
See also Introduction, p. 17, and
J. S. Roskell, *Bulletin of the John
Rylands Library* 42 (1959), pp. 145-74
for a detailed account of Catesby's
career.

24. *instance*] The Q2 variant
'instancie' is the same word: see
OED instancy 4 = instance *sb*.6.

32. *kindly*] 'Hastings means that
Richard will use them kindly, i.e.
gently, courteously. But the audience
knows that he will use them kindly in
another sense, i.e. after his boarish
nature or kind' (Thompson).

Cat. Many good morrows to my noble lord.

Hast. Good morrow, Catesby; you are early stirring.   35
    What news, what news in this our tott'ring state?

Cat. It is a reeling world indeed, my lord,
    And I believe will never stand upright
    Till Richard wear the garland of the realm.

Hast. How, wear the garland? Dost thou mean the crown?

Cat. Ay, my good lord.   41

Hast. I'll have this crown of mine cut from my shoulders
    Before I'll see the crown so foul misplac'd.
    But canst thou guess that he doth aim at it?

Cat. Ay, on my life, and hopes to find you forward   45
    Upon his party for the gain thereof;
    And thereupon he sends you this good news
    That this same very day your enemies,
    The kindred of the Queen, must die at Pomfret.

Hast. Indeed, I am no mourner for that news,   50
    Because they have been still my adversaries:
    But that I'll give my voice on Richard's side
    To bar my master's heirs in true descent,
    God knows I will not do it, to the death.

Cat. God keep your lordship in that gracious mind.   55

Hast. But I shall laugh at this a twelve-month hence,
    That they which brought me in my master's hate,
    I live to look upon their tragedy.
    Well, Catesby, ere a fortnight make me older

38. will] *F*; it will *Q1–2*; twill *Q3–6*.   40.] *As Qq*; . . . Garland? / Doest *F.*
How] *F,Q1–2 (subst.);* Who *Q3–6.*   43. Before I'll] *F*; Ere I will *Qq.*
45. Ay, on my life] *F*; Vpon my life my Lo: *Qq (subst.).*   50. that] *F,Q1–3,5;*
this *Q4,6.*   51. my adversaries] *F*; mine enemies *Qq.*   56. twelve-month]
F; tweluemonth *Q1–5*; twelmonth *Q6.*   57. which] *F*; who *Qq.*   59.
Well, Catesby,] *F*; I tell thee Catesby. *Cat.* What my Lord? *Qq (subst.).*
older] *F*; elder *Qq.*

39. *garland*] More's term, in
Buckingham's oration (Hall, *Edward
V*, fol. xxiʳ), but also widely used
e.g. in 'Alurede' (*Parts Added*, p. 472),
or 'Richard' (*Mirror*, p. 369), or *2H4*,
IV.V.201.

53. *my master's*] Edward IV's.
57. *they*] The Queen's kindred.

58. *tragedy*] Hastings uses the term
precisely in the sense found in the
Mirror, and thus creates a dramatic
irony.

59.] The phrase for Catesby which
Q inserts in this line is probably
actor's gag.

I'll send some packing that yet think not on't. 60

Cat. 'Tis a vile thing to die, my gracious lord,
When men are unprepar'd and look not for't.

Hast. O, monstrous, monstrous! And so falls it out
With Rivers, Vaughan, Grey: and so 'twill do
With some men else that think themselves as safe 65
As thou and I, who as thou know'st are dear
To princely Richard and to Buckingham.

Cat. The Princes both make high account of you—
[*Aside*] For they account his head upon the Bridge.

Hast. I know they do, and I have well deserv'd it. 70

Enter STANLEY *Earl of Derby.*

Come on, come on: where is your boar-spear, man?
Fear you the boar, and go so unprovided?

Stan. My lord, good morrow; good morrow, Catesby.
You may jest on, but by the holy Rood,
I do not like these several Councils, I. 75

Hast. My lord, I hold my life as dear as you,

60. on't] *F;* on it *Qq.*   65. that] *F;* who *Qq.*   69. [*Aside*] *Rowe; not in F,Qq.*
70. deserv'd it] *F,Q1–2,4,6;* deserued i *Q3,5.*   71. Come on, come on] *F;*
What my Lo: *Qq.*   72. go] *F,Q1–5 (subst.);* goe you *Q6.*   76. My lord,
I . . . you] *This edn;* My Lord, I . . . yours *F;* My Lo: I . . . you doe yours *Qq*
(subst.); My Lord, / I . . . you do yours *Johnson;* I . . . you do yours *NCS.*

68. *high account*] A pleasant irony,
developed out of Hastings's 'dear' in
l. 66. In the next line Catesby takes
the play further: 'in their account, his
head is as good as exposed already on
London Bridge, with those of other
traitors' (Thompson). The irony of
advancement leading to the scaffold
is a common one; Queen Elizabeth
makes use of it in IV.iv.242–3. It
occurs in *Parts Added* ('Sigebert',
p. 462; 'Galba', p. 325, etc.) and in
Spanish Tragedy, III.ii.93: 'Then shalt
thou mount for this'.

76. *My lord, I . . . you*] The meaning of the line(s) is clear: Hastings
values his life as much as Stanley does
his. The problem is simply that the
expression of this idea is either
elliptical or extra-metrical. Johnson's

solution, which leaves an awkward
four-beat pause after 'My lord', was
however adopted by Thompson,
Evans, and Sisson among recent
eds, Capell, Malone, and Camb.
among the older. F has been followed
by Alexander, Eccles, and other
earlier eds; NPS follows Q, and
NCS regularizes the line by omitting
the opening apostrophe. The version
proposed here is colloquial, but not
ungrammatical, and has the advantage of being readily explicable:
namely that the corrector crossed out
'you' in Q by mistake for 'yours'. The
F reading as it stands is unaccept-
able, since it does not convey the
intended meaning: that Hastings
holds his and Stanley's lives in equal
care.

And never in my days, I do protest,
Was it so precious to me as 'tis now:
Think you, but that I know our state secure,
I would be so triumphant as I am?   80
Stan. The lords at Pomfret, when they rode from London,
Were jocund, and suppos'd their states were sure,
And they indeed had no cause to mistrust:
But yet you see how soon the day o'ercast.
This sudden stab of rancour I misdoubt;   85
Pray God, I say, I prove a needless coward.
What, shall we toward the Tower? The day is spent.
Hast. Come, come: have with you. Wot you what, my lord?
Today the lords you talk'd of are beheaded.
Stan. They, for their truth, might better wear their heads   90
Than some that have accus'd them wear their hats.
But come, my lord, let's away.

Enter HASTINGS, *a Pursuivant.*

Hast. Go on before; I'll talk with this good fellow.
Exeunt Stanley and Catesby.

77. days] *F;* life *Qq.*   78. so . . . as] *F;* more . . . then *Qq.*   'tis] *F;* it is *Qq.*
81. at] *F,Q 1–5;* of *Q6.*   82. were] *F;* was *Qq.*   83. they] *F,Q 1–2; not in*
Q 3–6.   85. stab] *F;* scab *Qq.*   87. What . . . toward] *F;* But come my
Lo: . . . to *Qq (subst.).*   The day is spent.] *F; not in Qq.*   88.] *As Pope;*
. . . you: / Wot *F;* I go: but stay, heare you not the newes, *Qq (subst.).*
89. Today the lords] *F;* This day those men *Qq.*   talk'd] *Q 1–2;* talke *Q 3–6,F.*
91. hats] *F,Q 1,6;* hat *Q 2–5.*   92. let's] *F;* let vs *Qq.*   92. S.D.] *As Qq*
(Enter Hastin. (a Purssuant) Q 1); Enter a Pursuiuant. / F.   93. on . . . talk with
this good fellow] *F;* you . . . follow presently *Qq.*   93. S.D.] *As F,Q 3–6; not in*
Q 1–2.

87. *spent*] The scene, as we know, is taking place at four a.m.; though OED (spent *pa.pple.*1.2) makes it clear that the word can mean 'well under way' as well as 'finished', only the broad-minded would concede that a day was well under way at four in the morning. Cf. *Ven.*, 717–19, for a parallel usage, where 'spent' means 'arrived'. Thus Stanley means 'day has come'; the various commentators who object to the phrase as 'mere padding' (Pickersgill, quoted in Variorum) have overlooked the parallel. Its omission from Q may have more than accidental significance. In this and other nearby scenes the hand of a corrector, perhaps the book-keeper, can be detected: see II.iv.1–2; III.iv.78 and 79 S.D., and Introduction, pp. 17–18. This literal-minded individual may have found the phrase as confusing as most critics, and altered the line with the unfortunate results evident in the metre.

92. S.D. *Hastings*] See Appendix II.

Well met, Hastings; how goes the world with thee?

H. Pur. The better that your lordship please to ask.   95

Hast. I tell thee, man, 'tis better with me now
　　Than when I met thee last, where now we meet:
　　Then was I going prisoner to the Tower,
　　By the suggestion of the Queen's allies:
　　But now I tell thee—keep it to thyself—   100
　　This day those enemies are put to death,
　　And I in better state than e'er I was!

H. Pur. God hold it to your honour's good content.

Hast. Gramercy, Hastings: there, drink that for me.

　　　　　　　　　　　　　　　　Throws him his purse.

H. Pur. I thank your honour.   *Exit.* 105

　　　　　　　　　Enter a Priest.

Priest. Well met, my lord; I am glad to see your honour.

Hast. I thank thee, good Sir John, with all my heart.
　　I am in your debt for your last exercise:
　　Come the next sabbath and I will content you.

　　　　　　　　　　　　　　He whispers in his ear.

94. Well met, Hastings] *Qq;* How now Sirrha *F.*   95. your lordship please]
F; it please your Lo: *Q 1-2;* it please your good Lordship *Q 3-6.*   96. man]
F; fellow *Qq.*   97. I met thee] *Qq;* thou met'st me *F.*   102. e'er] *F* (ere)*;*
euer *Qq.*   104. Hastings] *Qq;* fellow *F.*   there, drink that for me] *F;*
hold spend thou that *Qq.*   104. S.D. *Throws*] *F; He giues / Qq.*   105.] *F;*
God saue your Lordship. *Qq.*   105. S.D.] *This edn; Exit Pursuiuant. / Enter a*
Priest. / F,Q 3-6 (subst.); Enter a priest. Q 1-2.   106.] *F; not in Qq.*   107.] *F;*
What Sir John, you are wel met, *Qq (subst.).*   108. in your debt] *F;* beholding to you *Qq.*   last] *F;* last daies *Qq (subst.).*   109. S.D. *He whispers in his*
ear.] *Qq; not in F.*   *Enter Buckingham*] *F,Qq (after l. 110 F).*

97. *I met thee*] Q is here closer to
Hall: see Honigmann, p. 49.

99. *allies*] relatives: OED II.3.

104. *Gramercy*] thanks: OED 1.

106, 110.] The omission of these two
lines from Q saves a speaking part,
as Smidt remarked (p. 112). The
entire scene is marked by small, but
complex, restructuring of lines which
suggests the company found some
source of dissatisfaction with the
original drafting. There is no doubt
that in Shakespeare's primary version as represented by F, both the
Pursuivant Hastings and the Priest

were designed to talk with Hastings;
despite the clumsy repetition of l. 110
in l. 121 F ought to be retained. Q's
version of l. 107 assimilates some of
the Priest's deleted l. 106, which
suggests that the speaker had heard
the uncut version at some stage.

107. *Sir John*] 'A clergyman who
had taken his first degree was called
"Sir" as the English equivalent of
Dominus' (Craik, in Arden *T.N.*,
III.iv.276 n.).

108. *exercise*] a religious discourse:
OED *sb.*10c (citing this line).

109. *content*] remunerate: OED *v.*4.

Enter BUCKINGHAM.

Priest. I'll wait upon your lordship.   [*Exit Priest.*]   110
Buck. What, talking with a priest, Lord Chamberlain?
      Your friends at Pomfret, they do need the priest;
      Your honour hath no shriving work in hand!
Hast. Good faith, and when I met this holy man,
      The men you talk of came into my mind.   115
      What, go you toward the Tower?
Buck. I do, my lord, but long I cannot stay there:
      I shall return before your lordship thence.
Hast. Nay, like enough, for I stay dinner there.
Buck. [*Aside*] And supper too, although thou know'st it not.
      Come, will you go?   121
Hast.   I'll wait upon your lordship.   *Exeunt.*

110.] *F; not in Qq.*   110. S.D.] *This edn; not in F,Qq.*   111.] *F;* How now
Lo: Chamberlaine, what talking with a priest, *Qq* (*subst.*)   115. The] *F;*
Those *Qq.*   116. toward] *F;* to *Qq.*   Tower] *F;* tower my lord *Qq.*
117. do, my lord . . . cannot stay there] *F;* doe, . . . shall not stay *Qq.*
119. Nay] *F;* Tis *Qq.*   120. [*Aside*] *Rowe; not in F,Qq.*   120. know'st] *F;*
knowest *Q1-2;* knowst *Q3-5;* knowh *Q6.*   121. will you go] *F;* shall we go
along *Qq.*   I'll wait upon your lordship] *F; not in Qq.*

109. S.D.] The omission of the Q
part of the S.D. from F is surely
accidental. It is clear from l. 111
that Buckingham enters while Hastings is still in conversation with
the Priest, no doubt retailing to him
the news about the Queen's kin
at Pomfret. Upon Buckingham's
approach, the Priest withdraws with
his formal l. 110, and, it seems clear,
should exit at this point: the ensuing
conversation between Buckingham
and Hastings is plainly private, and
there is no need to keep the Priest
on-stage until the end of the scene;
'I'll wait upon your lordship' means
he will visit Hastings again, not that
he will attend him here and now. In
More the role given here to Buckingham is played by Sir Thomas
Haward, son of Lord John Haward,
whom Richard created Duke of
Norfolk.
      110.] See l. 106 above.

111.] The extra-metrical bungling
of the line in Q is presumably
Buckingham's mistake.
      113. *shriving*] making an act of
confession. Buckingham's indelicacy
at this point is quite unusual, though
he is impatient with religious scruple
generally (cf. III.i).
      121. *I'll wait upon your lordship*] The
fact that this phrase repeats exactly
l. 110 has caused it to be viewed with
suspicion. NCS feels that it is in
place here and wrongly inserted at
l. 110, which is not metrical (a minor
distinction in a scene characterized
by erratic metre). Reasons have been
given above (l. 106 n.) for retaining
l. 110, so doubt must focus upon its
appearance at l. 121. However, these
exit-phrases are wholly conventional,
and tend to be repetitious anyway,
and its re-use so near to l. 110 may
simply be authorial oversight.

SCENE III

Enter Sir Richard Ratcliffe, *with* Halberds, *carrying the nobles*, Rivers, Grey, *and* Vaughan, *to death at Pomfret.*

Rat. Come, bring forth the prisoners.

Riv. Sir Richard Ratcliffe, let me tell thee this:
Today shalt thou behold a subject die
For truth, for duty, and for loyalty.

Grey. God bless the Prince from all the pack of you!   5
A knot you are of damned bloodsuckers.

Vaugh. You live, that shall cry woe for this hereafter.

Rat. Dispatch: the limit of your lives is out.

Riv. O Pomfret, Pomfret! O thou bloody prison,
Fatal and ominous to noble peers!   10
Within the guilty closure of thy walls
Richard the Second here was hack'd to death;
And for more slander to thy dismal seat,

Scene III

Scene iii] *As F (Scena Tertia); not in Qq.*   S.D. *Richard Ratcliffe*] *F; Richard Ratliffe | Qq (subst.).*   Halberds, *carrying the nobles*] *F; the Lo: | Q 1; the Lord | Q 2–6.   Rivers, Grey, and Vaughan*] *As Qq; not in F.   to death at Pomfret*] *F; prisoners | Qq.*   1.] *Qq; not in F.*   2. Ratcliffe] *F; Ratliffe Qq.*   5. bless] *F; keepe Qq (subst.).*   7.] *F; not in Qq.*   8.] *F; not in Qq (see l. 24).*   10. ominous] *F,Q 1,6;* dominious *Q 2–3;* ominious *Q 4–5.*   13. seat] *F; soule Qq.*

Scene III

S.D. and 1.] See Introduction, p. 8.

6. *knot*] cluster of things or persons: OED *sb.*[1] ii.18, with implication perhaps of a nest of snakes.

7.] With ll. 8, 16, 24 this constitutes a surprising number of Q omissions in a short scene. By the omission of l. 7 a speaking part is saved (though Vaughan retains a line as a ghost in v. iii). The omission of l. 8 is explicable if we take it that Ratcliffe forgot one of his interventions, and wrongly spoke l. 8 in l. 24's place. For l. 16, see below.

10. *ominous*] 'Pontefract Castle had

been the scene of the execution of Thomas, Earl of Lancaster (19 June 1322) for rebellion against his cousin Edward II. Richard II died there, probably by murder, 14 February 1400. In 1405, Archbishop Scrope was imprisoned there before his execution; and in 1461, after Wakefield, Richard Nevill, Earl of Salisbury, father of the "Kingmaker", was murdered there by order of Margaret of Anjou' (Thompson).

11. *closure*] bound or limit: OED 1b, citing this line.

13. *seat*] location. Q's 'soul' is obviously wrong, but the error could equally well have originated with actor or compositor.

We give to thee our guiltless blood to drink.

Grey. Now Margaret's curse is fall'n upon our heads,   15
When she exclaim'd on Hastings, you, and I,
For standing by when Richard stabb'd her son.

Riv. Then curs'd she Richard, then curs'd she Buckingham,
Then curs'd she Hastings. O remember, God,
To hear her prayer for them, as now for us;   20
And for my sister and her princely sons,
Be satisfied, dear God, with our true blood,
Which—as thou know'st—unjustly must be spilt.

Rat. Make haste: the hour of death is expiate.

Riv. Come Grey, come Vaughan, let us here embrace.   25
Farewell, until we meet again in Heaven.   *Exeunt.*

14. to thee] *F;* thee vp *Qq.*   blood] *F;* blouds *Qq (subst.).*   16.] *F; not in*
Qq.   18.] *As Qq; . . . Richard,* / Then *F.*   18–19. Richard . . . Hastings]
F; Hastings . . . Richard *Qq.*   20. prayer] *F;* praiers *Qq (subst.).*   21. sons]
F; sonne *Qq.*   22. blood] *F;* blouds *Qq (subst.).*   24.] *F;* Come come
dispatch, the limit of your liues (linea *Q1;* lines *Q2*) is out. *Qq.*   25. here] *F;*
all *Qq.*   26. Farewell,] *F;* And take our leaue (leaues *Q6*) *Qq.*   again] *F;*
not in Qq.

16.] Daniel (p. xviii) suggests that
the line was omitted from Q because
none of the three was, in fact,
present at the relevant scene in *3H6*
(v. v); neither does the present scene
correspond very well with Margaret's
curses in i. iii. Patrick, however,
rejects this notion: 'If the greater
inconsistency did not deter the
author from writing the line, the
present minor one need not trouble a
hypothetical reviser' (p. 112). Smidt
believes that Grey's speech should
not include Hastings, since he is
named in Rivers's reply in l. 19: 'This
seems a clear example of revision in
the quarto copy to make it logically
and factually consistent' (p. 113).
These commentators consider it too
closely, and miss the dramatic point.
It is hardly likely that the actual
dramatis personae of *3H6*, v. v,
would be foremost in Shakespeare's
mind at this point; neither, perhaps,
would the precise details of Margaret's
curse. The Queen's allies serve in this
scene a choric function, in which they
express by their downfall a communal
sense of guilt and of participation in
wrongful action. In a sense, all of
England 'stood by' while Richard
and his brothers killed the Lancastrian
heir.

18–19.] Patrick observes that Margaret's speech in i. iii is of no use in
deciding between Q and F here; it is
usually remarked that she did not
curse Buckingham anyway. She certainly warned him, and in his final
scene he regards himself as having
fallen in accordance with her prophecies, so in general he is not to be
excluded from the group. Patrick's
further opinion that the variant arose
from an actor's transposition is not
self-evidently true, but as F order is
as valid as that of Q, it is retained
here.

19–23.] Rivers's prayer derives
from Hall exclusively: in More and
Holinshed it is not present. In Hall
it is spoken by Vaughan (*Edward V,*
fol. xvii[r-v]).

25.] Cf. *Edward II,* iv. vii. 80.

SCENE IV

Enter BUCKINGHAM, STANLEY *Earl of Derby*, HASTINGS, *the*
BISHOP OF ELY, NORFOLK, RATCLIFFE, LOVELL, *with* Others,
at a table.

Hast. Now, noble peers, the cause why we are met
    Is to determine of the coronation.
    In God's name speak: when is the royal day?
Buck. Is all things ready for the royal time?
Stan. It is, and wants but nomination.   5
Ely. Tomorrow, then, I judge a happy day.
Buck. Who knows the Lord Protector's mind herein?
    Who is most inward with the noble Duke?

Scene IV

SCENE IV] *As* F (*Scæna Quarta*); *not in* Qq.   S.D.] *As* F; *Enter the Lords to
Councell.* | Qq.   1. Now, noble peers,] F; My Lords at once Qq.   3. speak]
F; say Qq.   the] F; this Qq.   4. Is ... ready ... the] F; Are ... fitting
... that Qq.   5. wants but] F,Q1–2; let but Q3,5–6; lack but Q4.
6. Ely.] F; Ryu. | Q1; Riu. | Q2; Bish. | Q3–6.   judge ... day] F; guesse
... time Qq.

Scene IV

S.D.] The Q S.D. is one of the
vaguest in that text: see Introduction,
pp. 11–12. In the scene, Q replaces
Ratcliffe and Lovell with Catesby;
see Introduction, pp. 16–17. Patrick
(p. 26) remarks that Norfolk might
also be spared as he is mute. The F
stage-direction is also vague ('with
Others') but implies the useful
theatrical information that a table
was 'thrust out' for the scene. The
Bishop of Ely is the man who became
Cardinal Morton, Thomas More's
patron.

1 ff.] The degree of variation
between the two texts in the opening
lines of this scene is unusually high.

2. *determine of*] decide upon.

4. *Is*] A singular verb appropriately
used with a collective singular ('all
things'); it is shown to be correct,
despite Q1's improvised alteration,

by Stanley's response 'It is'.

6. *Ely*] Q1's erroneous prefix
'Ryu.' (for Rivers) is corrected to
'Bish.' evidently by inspiration in
Q3. A reasonable explanation is that
the part of the Bishop was doubled
by the actor who played Rivers. To
the objection, made by Smidt, that
Rivers had been led to execution
immediately before, it may be
returned that the costume of a
bishop merely entailed donning a
cope over the existing costume, and
wearing a mitre, a change which
could have been made in a few
seconds. There is no technical reason
why Rivers could not exit through
one door to his execution and appear
well-nigh immediately through the
other as the Bishop in the procession.
The only other possible explanation
of the error is that the compositor
misread 'By.' (for 'Byshop') as 'Ry.',
an unlikely, but not impossible error.

Ely. Your Grace, we think, should soonest know his mind.

Buck. We know each other's faces; for our hearts   10
    He knows no more of mine than I of yours,
    Or I of his, my lord, than you of mine.
    Lord Hastings, you and he are near in love.

Hast. I thank his Grace, I know he loves me well;
    But for his purpose in the coronation   15
    I have not sounded him, nor he deliver'd
    His gracious pleasure any way therein.
    But you, my honourable lords, may name the time,
    And in the Duke's behalf I'll give my voice,
    Which I presume he'll take in gentle part.   20

Enter RICHARD.

Ely. In happy time, here comes the Duke himself.

Rich. My noble lords and cousins all, good morrow:
    I have been long a sleeper, but I trust
    My absence doth neglect no great design
    Which by my presence might have been concluded.   25

9. Your Grace, we think] *F;* Why you my Lo: me thinks you *Qq* (*subst.*).
10–12. We . . . hearts / He . . . yours, / Or I of his, my lord, . . . mine.] *F;*
Who I my Lo? we . . . faces: / But for . . . mine, / Then . . . nor I no more
of his . . . mine: *Qq* (*subst.*).   17. gracious] *F;* Graces *Q 1–2;* graces *Q 3–6.*
18. honourable lords] *F;* noble Lo: *Q 1–2;* L. *Q 3–6.*   20. he'll] *F;* he will *Qq.*
gentle] *F,Q 1–5;* good *Q 6.*   20. S.D.] *As F;* after l. 22 *Q 1–2;* after l. 21 *Q 3–6.*
21. In happy time] *F;* Now in good time *Qq.*   23. a sleeper] *F,Q 1–5;* a
sleepe *Q 6.*   but] *F,Q 1;* but now *Q 2–6.*   trust] *F;* hope *Qq.*   24. design]
F; designes *Qq.*

9.] Q's version here must be
attributed to the actor; it is totally
unmetrical.

10–12.] This apparently complex
variant is readily accounted for:
Buckingham transposes, bringing 'my
lord' from l. 12 into l. 10, and
rearranges the text slightly (and the
lineation) to make the rest fit.

18. *honourable lords*] F is extra-
metrical unless 'honourable' was
slurred in speech as 'hon'ble' (which
is quite possible); Hastings was
perhaps unhappy with it and substituted 'noble', which in turn was
dropped by Q3's compositor, leaving

the line short.

19. *my voice*] Chambers, *Elizabethan
Stage*, 1.38, reminds us that the Lord
Chamberlain often served as the
royal mouthpiece, in Council and in
Parliament.

21. *In happy time*] Perhaps Ely
borrowed from Buckingham the
cliché 'Now in good time'.

22. *cousins*] OED *sb.*5a: used by a
sovereign in addressing . . . a noble-
man of the same country. In England
applied . . . to earls and peers of
higher rank.

24. *neglect*] cause something to be
neglected: OED *v.*5, citing this line.

Buck. Had you not come upon your cue, my lord,
　　William Lord Hastings had pronounc'd your part—
　　I mean your voice for crowning of the King.

Rich. Than my Lord Hastings no man might be bolder:
　　His lordship knows me well, and loves me well.　　30
　　My Lord of Ely, when I was last in Holborn
　　I saw good strawberries in your garden there;
　　I do beseech you, send for some of them.

Ely. Marry, and will, my lord, with all my heart.　　*Exit.*

Rich. Cousin of Buckingham, a word with you.　　35
　　Catesby hath sounded Hastings in our business,
　　And finds the testy gentleman so hot
　　That he will lose his head ere give consent
　　His master's child (as worshipfully he terms it)
　　Shall lose the royalty of England's throne.　　40

Buck. Withdraw yourself a while: I'll go with you.

　　　　　　　Exeunt [Richard and Buckingham].

Stan. We have not yet set down this day of triumph.
　　Tomorrow, in my judgement, is too sudden,
　　For I myself am not so well provided
　　As else I would be, were the day prolong'd.　　45

Enter BISHOP OF ELY.

Ely. Where is my lord the Duke of Gloucester?

26. you not] *F;* not you *Qq.* cue] *F* (Q), *Qq* (kew), *Rowe.* 27. had] *F;* had now *Qq.* your] *F,Q1–5;* you *Q6.* 30. well.] *F;* well. / *Hast.* I thanke your Grace. *Qq.* 31. Ely,] *F;* Elie, *Bish.* My Lo: / *Glo.* When *Q1–2;* Elie. / *Bish:* My Lord. / *Glo.* When *Q3–6.* 33. do] *F,Q1–3,5–6;* now *Q4.* 34.] *F;* I go my Lord. *Qq.* (*subst.*). 34. S.D.] *As F; not in Qq.* 35. Cousin of] *F;* Cosen *Qq* (*subst.*). 37. testy] *F,Q1–3,5–6;* resty *Q4.* 38. That] *F;* As *Qq.* ere] *F,Q2–4,6;* eare *Q1,Q2(B.L. & Hunt. 69352 copies);* are *Q5.* 39. child] *F;* sonne *Qq.* worshipfully] *F;* worshipfull *Qq.* 41. yourself a while: I'll go with] *F;* you hence my Lo: Ile follow *Qq* (*subst.*). 41. S.D.] *As F; Ex. Gl.* / *Qq* (*subst.*). 43. my judgement] *F;* mine opinion *Qq.* sudden] *F;* sodaine *Q1;* soone *Q2–6.* 46–7.] *As F;* one line *Qq.* 46. the Duke of Gloucester] *F;* protector *Qq* (*subst.*).

30–4.] Q here seems to be swollen by gag, showing itself in unmetrical commonplace responses: 'I thank your Grace'; 'My lord'; 'I go my lord'. There is no reason to think any of these Shakespearean, nor necessary to the scene.

32. *strawberries*] See Appendix II.

43. *sudden*] happening at an early date: OED 9, citing this example.

45. *prolong'd*] postponed: OED prolong *v.*3.

46–7.] Camb. prints as prose, which seems intrusive in an otherwise

I have sent for these strawberries.

Hast. His Grace looks cheerfully and smooth today:
There's some conceit or other likes him well
When that he bids good morrow with such spirit.   50
I think there's never a man in Christendom
Can lesser hide his love or hate than he,
For by his face straight shall you know his heart.

Stan. What of his heart perceive you in his face
By any livelihood he show'd today?   55

Hast. Marry, that with no man here he is offended,
For were he, he had shown it in his looks.

Stan. I pray God he be not, I say.

Enter RICHARD *and* BUCKINGHAM.

Rich. I pray you all, tell me what they deserve
That do conspire my death with devilish plots   60
Of damned witchcraft, and that have prevail'd
Upon my body with their hellish charms?

Hast. The tender love I bear your Grace, my lord,

48. today] *Qq;* this morning *F.*   50. that he bids] *F;* he doth bid *Qq.*
such] *F;* such a *Qq.*   51. there's] *F;* there is *Qq.*   52. Can] *F;* That can
Qq.   55. livelihood] *F;* likelihood *Qq.*   57. were he, he had] *F;* if he
were, he would haue *Qq.*   looks] *F,Q1;* face *Q2–6.*   58.] *Qq;* not in F.
58. S.D.] *F; Enter Glocester. / Qq (subst.).*   59. tell me what] *F;* what doe *Qq*
(subst.).

verse scene. Ely was inclined to extra-
metrical lines anyway (cf. l. 9, Q
version), and though neither of the
F lines is metrically correct either,
that is no distinction in this play.
    48. *smooth*] Ellipsis of adverb:
Abbott §397.
    today] Q is metrically preferable;
perhaps an authorial improvement.
    49. *conceit*] idea, thought: OED
*sb.*I. 1.
    55. *livelihood*] liveliness: OED liveli-
hood² ; Q's 'likelihood' is probably a
foul-case error.
    57. *were he, he had*] Q's version here
is less elegant, and extra-metrical; it
may be attributed to the actor.
    looks] See Introduction, pp. 100–1,
for Richard's dissembling appearance.

58.] This line, clearly an addition
to the Q text, is not to be classed with
the gag of ll. 30–4: though unmetrical,
it is plain and clear, perfectly in
character with the timorous Stanley,
and appropriate to the dramatic
irony of the scene. Even the repetition of 'I pray' in the next line
(objected to by Patrick, p. 28) is not
inappropriate in view of the contrasting use made of the words.
Among modern eds, NPS and Evans
include the line; NCS classes it as
'doubtful' and omits.
    58. S.D.] See Introduction, pp. 27–8.
    63. *love*] This is the word in both
More and Holinshed; Hall has
'familiaritie'. In the *Mirror*, Hastings
refers to 'acquayntaunce olld' (l. 564).

Makes me most forward in this princely presence,
To doom th'offenders, whatso'er they be: 65
I say, my lord, they have deserved death.
Rich. Then be your eyes the witness of their evil.
See how I am bewitch'd! Behold, mine arm
Is like a blasted sapling wither'd up!
And this is Edward's wife, that monstrous witch,   70
Consorted with that harlot, strumpet Shore,
That by their witchcraft thus have marked me.
Hast. If they have done this deed, my noble lord—
Rich. If? Thou protector of this damned strumpet,
Talk'st thou to me of ifs! Thou art a traitor: 75
Off with his head! Now by Saint Paul I swear
I will not dine until I see the same.
Lovell and Ratcliffe, look that it be done;
The rest that love me, rise and follow me.
        Exeunt all but Lovell and Ratcliffe and the Lord Hastings.
Hast. Woe, woe for England; not a whit for me—   80
For I, too fond, might have prevented this.

64. princely] *F;* noble *Qq.*   65. th'offenders] *F;* the offenders *Qq.*
whatso'er] *As Qq (whatsoeuer);* whosoe're *F.*   67. their evil] *F;* this ill *Qq.*
68. See] *Qq;* Looke *F.*   70. And this is] *F;* This is that *Qq.*   72. witch-
craft] *F,Q1;* witchcrafts *Q2–6.*   73. deed] *F;* thing *Qq.*   noble] *F;*
gratious *Qq (subst.).*   75. Talk'st thou to me] *F;* Telst thou me *Qq.*   76. I
swear] *F; not in Qq.*   77–8.] *F;* I will not dine to day, I sweare, / Vntill I
see the same, some see it done, *Qq (subst.).*   79. rise] *F;* come *Qq.*   79.
S.D.] *As F; Exeunt. manet Cat. with Ha. / Qq (subst.).*

65. *whatso'er*]. More, Hall, and
Holinshed agree on this reading.
Perhaps the compositor of F normalized the word.
    68. *See*] The reading is derived
from More/Holinshed (Hall phrases
differently). See also Honigmann,
p. 49.
    69. *wither'd up*] The sources make it
explicit that Richard's arm was
deformed from his birth: 'therupon,
every mannes mynde mysgave theim,
well perceyvyng that this matter was
but a quarell' (Hall, *Edward V* fol.
xiiii^r).
    75. *ifs*] Hall has 'with yf and with
and' (*Edward V*, fol. xiiii^v); Holinshed

'with ifs and with ands' (p. 722/2).
The phrase was proverbial: Tilley
I16.
    76–8.] The variants in ll. 76–7
seem to have originated with the
actor; that in l. 78 clearly arises
from the change of personnel (see
next n.). Lines 76–7 may be an allusion
to Acts, xxiii.12. Hall reads 'I will
not dyne till'; Holinshed has 'I will
not to dinner until'.
    79. S.D.] See Introduction,
pp. 16–17. Retaining F, as we do here,
leaves the awkwardness of Ratcliffe's
dual location in Pomfret and London
as a problem for the producer.
    81. *fond*] foolish.

Stanley did dream the boar did raze his helm,
And I did scorn it and disdain to fly;
Three times today my foot-cloth horse did stumble,
And started when he look'd upon the Tower,   85
As loath to bear me to the slaughter-house.
O, now I need the priest that spake to me;
I now repent I told the pursuivant,
As too triumphing, how mine enemies
Today at Pomfret bloodily were butcher'd,   90
And I myself secure in grace and favour.
O Margaret, Margaret, now thy heavy curse
Is lighted on poor Hastings' wretched head.

Rat. Come, come, dispatch: the Duke would be at dinner;
Make a short shrift: he longs to see your head.   95

Hast. O momentary grace of mortal men,
Which we more hunt for than the grace of God.

82. raze his helm] *Qq;* rowse our Helmes *F.*   83. And I did scorne it, and
disdain] *F;* But I disdaind it, and did scorne *Qq* (dsidaind, and *Q4*).
85. started] *F;* startled *Qq.*   87. need] *F;* want *Qq.*   89. too] *F;* twere *Qq.*
how] *F;* at *Qq.*   90. Today] *F;* How they *Qq.*   93. lighted] *F,Q1–5;*
lightened *Q6.*   94. *Rat.*] *F (Ra.); Cat. | Qq.* Come, come, dispatch] *F;* Dis-
patch my Lo: *Qq (subst.).*   96. grace of mortal] *F;* state of worldly *Qq.*
97. than] *F,Q1–2;* then for *Q3–6.* God] *F;* heauen *Qq.*

82. *raze his helm*] Q must be accepted
here. F's 'rowse' is an error, perhaps
derived from MS. misreading; both
versions are specific in III.ii that
Stanley had dreamed it was his own
helm that was razed (which, it is
worth noting, does not happen).

83. *And I did scorn it and disdain*] At
first glance Q seems much superior
here, but if 'did' is understood before
'disdain', the F reading becomes
perfectly acceptable.

84. *Three times*] Tilley T259.

foot-cloth horse] A horse 'equipped
with foot-cloths, i.e. trappings hang-
ing over the horse's sides and covering
the rider's feet' (Thompson): a sign
of gentility. James Riddill notes
(*Eng.S.*, 56 (1975), pp. 29–31) that
Florio and Nashe use the term to
refer to a special kind of horse.

94. *Come, come, dispatch*] The phrase
is repeated by Lovell in l. 102, and

perhaps before he was eliminated
from the Q text someone felt the
need to remove the repetition. It may
also have been an actor's variant.
There is a similar passage in *The
Wounds of Civil War*, where Scilla cries
'Dispatch! . . . For sore I long to see
the traitor's head.' (v.i. 110–15).

96–7.] See Jeremiah, xvii.5, Psalm
cxlvi.3; also the Commination in the
BCP. Q's reading in l. 96, 'state of
worldly', entirely misses the point of
the antithesis between divine and
human grace. See also next line.

97. *God*] A surprising survivor from
the anti-profanity law, the F reading
here (as in the previous line) is
undoubtedly right. Q does not elsewhere reveal tampering of this sort,
yet its reading is precisely characteristic of the kind of change made
in texts to avoid the charge of profanity.

Who builds his hope in air of your good looks
Lives like a drunken sailor on a mast,
Ready with every nod to tumble down   100
Into the fatal bowels of the deep.
Lov. Come, come, dispatch: 'tis bootless to exclaim.
Hast. O bloody Richard! Miserable England,
I prophesy the fearfull'st time to thee
That ever wretched age hath look'd upon.   105
Come, lead me to the block: bear him my head.
They smile at me who shortly shall be dead.   *Exeunt.*

[SCENE V]

Enter RICHARD *and* BUCKINGHAM *in rotten armour,
marvellous ill-favoured.*

Rich. Come, cousin, canst thou quake and change thy colour,
Murder thy breath in middle of a word,
And then again begin, and stop again,

98. hope] *F;* hopes *Qq.*   good] *F;* faire *Qq.*   looks] *F,Q 1–3,5–6;* looke
Q 4.   99. a . . . sailor] *F,Q 1–3,5–6;* Saylers *Q 4.*   101. the fatal] *F,Q 1–5;*
fatall *Q 6.*   102–5.] *F; not in Qq.*   107. who] *F;* that *Qq.*

Scene v

Scene v] *Capell; not in F,Qq.*   S.D. *rotten armour, marvellous ill-favoured] F;*
armour / *Qq.*   1.] *As Qq;* . . . Cousin, / Canst *F.*   3. again begin] *F;* be-
ginne againe *Qq (subst.).*

98–101.] See *Proverbs,* xxiii. 31–4,
for the source of this image. However,
it is worth recalling that 'the fatal
bowels of the deep' is an echo from
Clarence's nightmare, I.iv.20 and 32,
thus linking Hastings's and Clarence's
falls.
102–5.] Line 102 was sacrificed
when Lovell was eliminated from Q,
but it is not clear why Hastings's
effective reiteration of the curse-theme
should have been deleted.

Scene v

S.D.] Perhaps the most obviously
authorial direction in the play: the
F phrase comes from More, 'harnessed in olde evill-favoured briganders' (Hall, *Edward V,* fol. xvᵛ; a
brigander is body-armour for a foot-
soldier: OED 1). 'Rotten' means
rusted, 'ill-favoured', ugly. Hanham
(p. 173) believes the description in
More to have been invented by the
author, and based on Falgan's
description of the armour worn by
Richard's northern troops. Sidney,
in the *Arcadia,* describes a similar
stratagem (1.40). The omission from
Q of the phrase need not imply a
change in the Q MS.: we have seen
already that the compositor abridged
long directions.
2. *Murder*] spoil by bad execution,

As if thou were distraught and mad with terror?

Buck. Tut, I can counterfeit the deep tragedian,   5
Speak, and look back, and pry on every side,
Tremble and start at wagging of a straw,
Intending deep suspicion. Ghastly looks
Are at my service like enforced smiles,
And both are ready in their offices   10
At any time to grace my stratagems.
But what, is Catesby gone?

Enter the [LORD] MAYOR *and* CATESBY.

Rich. He is, and see, he brings the Mayor along.
Buck. Lord Mayor—
Rich. Look to the draw-bridge there!   15
Buck. Hark, a drum!
Rich. Catesby, o'erlook the walls!   [*Exit Catesby.*]

4. were] *F;* wert *Qq.*   5.] *F;* Tut feare not me. / I . . . Tragedian: *Qq.*
deep] *F,Q1–3,5–6;* deere *Q4.*   7.] *F; not in Qq.*   11. At any time] *F; not
in Qq.*   12.] *F; not in Qq.*   12. S.D.] *F (after l. 13);* Enter Maior. | *Qq
(after l. 11).*   13.] *F;* Here comes the Maior. *Qq.*   14.] *F;* Let me alone
to entertaine him. Lo: Maior, *Qq (subst.).*   16.] *F;* The reason we haue sent
for you. *Qq.*   17. S.D.] *This edn; not in F,Qq.*

representation, or pronunciation: OED *v.*2 (no example cited before 1644). Richard and Buckingham understand each other well in these first 11 lines, which are all borrowed from the theatre (cf. l. 5) and no doubt refer to specific aspects of the practice of acting. One can guess that the histrionic trick Richard refers to is to seem to run out of breath for fear in the middle of a word.

4. *were*] 'The subjunctive "thou were" is found in 16c (v. OED be 7.2) but not I think elsewhere in Shakespeare' (Dover Wilson, NCS, p. 212).

5.] The intrusive 'fear not me', like 'Let me alone to entertain him' in l. 14, characteristically shows Buckingham 'improving' his part—the scene is full of his memorial variants.

7.] Omitted from Q inadvertently: probably the actor rather than the compositor at fault. The phrase, 'wagging of a straw' is proverbial (Tilley W5).

8. *Intending*] pretending, or implying by behaviour. See OED intend *v.*VI.22 for a less specific definition, citing this line.

10. *offices*] function, appointed position; in this case, the proper action of an organ or faculty: OED *sb.*3b.

12.] Omitted from Q because Catesby in that text has the role of Hastings's executioner (but note l. 17).

16 and 18.] In Q, Buckingham simply reverses these lines.

17. S.D.] Either the entire scene must be imagined as occurring on the battlements, or Catesby must leave in order to 'o'erlook the walls'. The latter has been adopted here

Buck. Lord Mayor, the reason we have sent—

Enter LOVELL *and* RATCLIFFE, *with Hastings's Head.*

Rich. Look back! Defend thee, here are enemies!
Buck. God and our innocence defend and guard us!   20
Rich. Be patient, they are friends: Ratcliffe and Lovell.
Lov. Here is the head of that ignoble traitor,
    The dangerous and unsuspected Hastings.
Rich. So dear I lov'd the man that I must weep.
    I took him for the plainest harmless creature   25
    That breath'd upon the earth a Christian;
    Made him my book, wherein my soul recorded
    The history of all her secret thoughts.
    So smooth he daub'd his vice with show of virtue
    That, his apparent open guilt omitted—   30
    I mean his conversation with Shore's wife—
    He liv'd from all attainder of suspects.

18.] *F;* Harke, I heare a drumme. *Qq.*   18. S.D.] *As F (after l. 20); Enter*
Catesby with Hast. head. Qq (after l. 20).   20. innocence] *Q1;* innocencie
Q2–6,F.   defend and guard] *F;* defend *Qq.*   21.] *F;* O, O, be quiet, it is
Catesby. Qq.   25. creature] *F;* man *Qq.*   26. the] *F,Q4;* this *Q1–3,5–6.*
Christian.] *F;* christian, / Looke ye my Lo: Maior. *Qq (subst.).*   27. Made]
F,Q1–4; I made *Q5–6.*   32. liv'd] *F;* laid *Qq.*   suspects] *F;* suspect *Qq.*

(though previous eds have allowed Catesby to remain on-stage) as less perplexing for an audience.

18. S.D.] In Q Catesby now enters with Hastings's head (thus leaving l. 17 spoken to empty air). The entry, either way, must take place before l. 19 to motivate Richard's new burst of alarm.

20. *innocence*] F's 'innocency', though a perfectly respectable word, enters accidentally via Q2's variant, perhaps introduced by the compositor to make the line metrical.

25. *plainest harmless*] Ellipsis of superlatives: Abbott §398.

26.] The additional half-line in Q has generally been rejected as gag, though Smidt (p. 132) defends it on the grounds that its very irregularity may have been effective. The play indeed has more than its share of

irregular metre; yet the criterion should not be effectiveness, but authenticity, and in this passage of otherwise smooth blank verse the phrase looks intrusive. See also l. 33.

29.] Here Richard is accusing Hastings of his own Vice's behaviour, See also Spivack, p. 398.

31. *conversation*] Here (but not regularly so in Shakespeare), sexual intimacy: OED 3.

32. *liv'd*] Q's 'laid' makes no sense, and must be regarded as a compositor's guess in a line whose meaning he did not fathom—it is indeed difficult in its compression, and the punctuation is unhelpful in both Q and F. Paraphrased, it means that, apart from his association with Mistress Shore, Hastings lived free from all taint of suspicion.

Buck. Well, well, he was the covert'st shelter'd traitor.
　　Would you imagine, or almost believe,
　　Were't not that by great preservation　　　　　　35
　　We live to tell it, that the subtle traitor
　　This day had plotted, in the council-house,
　　To murder me and my good lord of Gloucester?
Mayor. Had he done so?
Rich. What, think you we are Turks or infidels?　　40
　　Or that we would, against the form of law,
　　Proceed thus rashly in the villain's death,
　　But that the extreme peril of the case,
　　The peace of England, and our persons' safety,
　　Enforc'd us to this execution.　　　　　　45
Mayor. Now fair befall you! He deserv'd his death,
　　And your good Graces both have well proceeded,
　　To warn false traitors from the like attempts.

33. traitor.] *As Pope, NCS;* Traytor / That euer liu'd. / *F;* traitor / That euer liu'd, would . . . *Qq.* 　　34–5. Would . . . believe, / Were't . . . preservation] *F;* That . . . imagined, / Or . . . preseruation *Qq.* 　　34. imagine] *F;* haue imagined *Qq.* 　　35. Were't] *F,Q1–5* (wert); were *Q6.* 　　36. it, that the] *F;* it you? The *Qq.* 　　37. This day had] *F;* Had this day *Qq.* 　　39.] *F;* What, had he so? *Qq.* 　　40. you] *F,Q1–2;* ye *Q3–6.* 　　41. form] *F,Q1–2;* course *Q3–6.* 　　42. in] *F;* to *Qq.* 　　43. extreme] *F,Q1–3,5–6;* very extreame *Q4.* 　　45. this] *F,Q1–3,5–6;* that *Q4.* 　　47. your good Graces] *F;* you my good Lords *Qq (subst.).*

33.] F prints 'That euer liu'd' as a separate half-line following l. 33; Q joins it to the next line, with consequent dislocation of the lineation until l. 36. Walker accounts for the mistake by declaring the phrase an expansion by the actor of the sense implicit in l. 33's 'was'. Presumably the F corrector properly indicated the right lineation and emendations in ll. 33–4, and then forgot to strike the intrusive phrase from the Q copy, which thus stands in F from Q. Some eds (e.g. Sisson), finding two redundant half-lines following ll. 26 and 33, glue them together to give Buckingham a metrical line following l. 33. However, it is not clear how l. 26+ could have migrated to its position in F, and it seems better to regard both as actors' additions.

33. *Well, well*] See Tilley W269.

covert'st shelter'd] Compounded adjectives: Abbott §2. See OED covert *a.*3 (deceitful, secretive), shelter *v.*1c (screened from punishment).

34. *almost*] Abbott §29; used for 'generally'.

35. *great preservation*] Buckingham means providential intervention for their protection.

40. *Turks or infidels*] Cf. *BCP*, 3rd Collect for Good Friday: 'Have mercy upon all Jews, Turks, Infidels, and Hereticks . . .'

41–5.] The dispensation with the law in Hastings's death, together with the specious reasons alleged in ll. 43–4 (the common coin of tyranny) was perhaps the most shocking of the many outrageous aspects of the affair. See also Introduction, p. 88.

Buck. I never look'd for better at his hands
       After he once fell in with Mistress Shore.   50
       Yet had we not determin'd he should die
       Until your lordship came to see his end—
       Which now the loving haste of these our friends,
       Something against our meanings, have prevented—
       Because, my lord, we would have had you heard   55
       The traitor speak, and timorously confess
       The manner and the purpose of his treasons,
       That you might well have signified the same
       Unto the citizens, who haply may
       Misconstrue us in him and wail his death.   60
Mayor. But, my good lord, your Graces' words shall serve
       As well as I had seen and heard him speak;

---

49. *Buck.*] *F; not in Qq.*   51. Yet] *F; Dut.* Yet *Q 1–2; Clo.* Yet *Q 3,5; Glo.* Yet *Q 4,6.*   we not] *F; not we Qq.*   52. end] *F; death Qq.*   53. loving] *F;* longing *Qq.*   54. Something] *F;* Somewhat *Qq.*   meanings] *F;* meaning *Qq.*   55. we] *Qq;* I *F.*   57. treasons] *F;* treason *Qq.*   61. But, my] *F,Q 1–2;* My *Q 3–6.*   words] *F;* word *Qq.*   62. and] *F;* or *Qq.*

49–50.] These lines are correctly assigned to Buckingham in F; as NCS remarks, l. 49 refers to the 'attempts' of l. 48 and so is properly spoken by one of those threatened. The displacement of the speech-prefix to l. 51 in Q, and its erroneous printing there, imply a damaged or illegible margin at this point. See note to l. 51.

51.] Q's speech-prefixes are highly confused. Q1 has '*Dut.*', presumably a misreading of '*Buc.*'; Q3, realizing that there was no Duchess on-stage, assigned the line to Richard but misspelled his prefix as '*Clo.*', which Q4 put right. The dependent Qq clearly have no authority in giving the lines to Richard beyond their attempt to put right Q1's impossible prefix.

53. *friends*] The plural stands in Q though in that version Catesby alone was responsible for Hastings's execution: another sign of the clumsy repair which followed the assigning

of Ratcliffe's and Lovell's parts to Catesby in III.iv–v.

54. *have*] 'The verb apparently has been attracted into the plural after "friends" in the previous line' (Thompson).

55. *we*] Buckingham has been speaking for himself and Richard since l. 51: it is odd he should change to the singular for this one verb. Q thus seems more correct; but Walker (p. 213, NCS) prefers to read 'hear'. It looks rather as if Shakespeare meant 'We would have wished you to have heard'.

61. *Graces'*] Most eds print 'your Grace's words', i.e. Buckingham's description of events. But neither F nor Q use the apostrophe, and the word can be punctuated as here to show the Mayor referring to the assurances of both the Dukes. As they are making a combined effort to impose on the Mayor, this seems the right choice.

And do not doubt, right noble princes both,
But I'll acquaint our duteous citizens
With all your just proceedings in this cause.   65
Rich. And to that end we wish'd your lordship here,
T'avoid the censures of the carping world.
Buck. Which, since you come too late of our intent,
Yet witness what you hear we did intend:
And so, my good Lord Mayor, we bid farewell.   70

Exit [Lord] Mayor.

Rich. Go after, after, cousin Buckingham:
The Mayor towards Guildhall hies him in all post.
There, at your meet'st advantage of the time,
Infer the bastardy of Edward's children;
Tell them how Edward put to death a citizen   75
Only for saying he would make his son
Heir to the Crown—meaning indeed his house,
Which by the sign thereof was termed so.
Moreover, urge his hateful luxury
And bestial appetite in change of lust,   80
Which stretch'd unto their servants, daughters, wives,
Even where his raging eye or savage heart

63. do not doubt] *F;* doubt you not *Qq.*   64. our] *F;* your *Qq.*   65. cause]
Q 1–5; ease *Q 6;* case *F.*   66. wish'd] *F;* wisht *Q 1–5;* wish *Q 6.*   67.
T'avoid] *F;* To auoyde *Qq (subst.).*   censures . . . carping world] *F;* carping
censures . . . world *Qq.*   world] *F,Q 1–2,4–6;* word *Q 3.*   68. Which] *F;*
But *Qq.*   come] *F,Q 1–2;* came *Q 3–6.*   intent] *F;* intents *Qq.*   69. you
hear we] *F;* we *Qq.*   intend:] *F;* intend, and so my Lord adue. *Qq.*
70.] *F; not in Qq.*   70. S.D.] *As F; after l. 71 Qq.*   71. Go after] *F;* After
Qq.   73. meet'st advantage] *Q 1–5;* meetest aduantage *Q 6;* meetest vantage
F.   81. stretch'd unto] *F;* stretched to *Qq.*   82. raging] *F;* lustfull *Qq.*

63. *As*] For 'as if': Abbott §107.
65. *cause*] See Introduction, p. 36.
68. *of*] Used with verbs and
adjectives implying motion, such as
'fail', 'want', or, here, 'come':
Abbott §166.
69–70.] See Introduction, pp. 4–5.
72. *in all post*] i.e. post-haste.
73. *meet'st advantage*] See Introduction, p. 36.
75. *put to death a citizen*] More tells
the story with some relish; see
Appendix III, p. 357.
79. *luxury*] lustfulness.

80. *change of lust*] i.e. his constant
search for sexual variety.
81. *their*] the citizens'. In his haste
Richard forgets there is no antecedent.
82–3. *raging . . . lusted*] At first the
Q alternatives seem attractive. But
the epithets in l. 82 connect with the
noun 'prey' in l. 83 to make a
coherent image of Edward as a wild
animal; this entails reading 'lusted' in
the sense 'chose' (OED lust *v.*3); this
sense is not available for the adjective
'lustful', which therefore disturbs the
image-pattern.

Without control lusted to make a prey.
Nay, for a need, thus far come near my person:
Tell them, when that my mother went with child   85
Of that insatiate Edward, noble York
My princely father then had wars in France,
And by true computation of the time
Found that the issue was not his-begot;
Which well appeared in his lineaments,   90
Being nothing like the noble Duke, my father—
Yet touch this sparingly, as 'twere far off;
Because, my lord, you know my mother lives.

Buck. Doubt not, my lord: I'll play the orator
As if the golden fee for which I plead   95
Were for myself; and so, my lord, adieu.

Rich. If you thrive well, bring them to Baynard's Castle,
Where you shall find me well accompanied
With reverend fathers and well-learned bishops.

Buck. I go, and towards three or four o'clock   100
Look for the news that the Guildhall affords.   *Exit.*

Rich. Go, Lovell, with all speed, to Doctor Shaa;
[*To Ratcliffe*] Go thou to Friar Penker; bid them both

83. lusted] *F;* listed *Qq.*   a] *F;* his *Qq.*   84. come] *F,Q 1–3,5–6;* comes *Q 4.*
86. insatiate] *F;* vnsatiate *Qq.*   88. true] *F;* iust *Qq.*   92. Yet] *F;* But *Qq.*
'twere far] *F;* it were farre *Q 1–3,5–6;* it were a farre *Q 4.*   93. my lord, you
know] *F;* you know, my Lord *Qq.*   my mother] *F,Q 1–4;* my brother *Q 5;*
me brother *Q 6.*   94. Doubt] *F;* Feare *Qq* (Faree *Q 3*).   96. and so, my
lord, adieu] *F; not in Qq.*   100–1.] *F;* About three or foure a clocke look to
heare / What news Guildhall affordeth, and so my Lord farewell. *Qq* (*subst.*).
102–4.] *F; not in Qq.*   103. S.D.] *This edn; not in F,Qq;* [*To Catesby*] *Capell.*
103. Penker] *Capell;* Peuker *F.*

84. *for a need*] if necessary.
95. *golden fee*] The crown.
96.] See Introduction, pp. 4–5.
97. *Baynard's Castle*] On the Thames, between Blackfriars and London Bridge.
100–1.] Buckingham manages to convey the sense of his lines, at very considerable cost to the metre. See also Introduction, pp. 4–5
102–4.] Omitted from Q no doubt because of the deletion of Lovell.
102. *Shaa*] John Shaa (a version of Shaw) was the Mayor's brother.

The tale of his sycophantic sermon in Richard's behalf is retailed by More with great enjoyment. An abridged version is in Appendix III, pp. 356–7.
103. *thou*] To whom is Richard speaking? Most eds supply Catesby, without offering any reason. This leaves Ratcliffe totally idle. If, as suggested at l. 17. S.D. n., Catesby leaves the stage early in the scene, Ratcliffe is the obvious choice for this errand. F's S.D. at l. 108 is thus a false plural, for Richard's ll. 105–8

Meet me within this hour at Baynard's Castle.

       Exeunt Ratcliffe and Lovell.

Now will I go to take some privy order   105
To draw the brats of Clarence out of sight,
And to give notice that no manner person
Have, any time, recourse unto the Princes.   *Exit.*

[SCENE VI]

Enter a Scrivener *with a paper in his hand.*

Scriv. Here is the indictment of the good Lord Hastings,
 Which in a set hand fairly is engross'd,
 That it may be today read o'er in Paul's.
 And mark how well the sequel hangs together:
 Eleven hours I have spent to write it over,   5
 For yesternight by Catesby was it sent me;
 The precedent was full as long a-doing
 And yet within these five hours Hastings liv'd,
 Untainted, unexamin'd, free, at liberty.

---

104. S.D.] *This edn; Exit | F; not in Qq.* 105. go] *F; in Qq.* 107. notice]
Qq; order F. manner] *F,Q 3–4; manner of Q 1–2,5–6.* 108. Have, any
time,] *F (no punctuation); At any tyme haue Qq (subst.).* 108. S.D. Exit] *Qq;
Exeunt | F.*

Scene VI

SCENE VI] *Capell; not in F,Qq.* S.D. with a paper in his hand] *Qq; not in F.*
1. Here] *F;* This *Qq.* 3. today] *F;* this day *Qq.* o'er] *F;* ouer *Qq.*
5. have spent] *F;* spent *Qq.* 6. sent] *F;* brought *Qq.* 8. Hastings liv'd]
F; liued Lord Hastings *Qq (subst.).*

---

is surely a soliloquy. Hence, F's
Exit at l. 104 is a wrong singular;
perhaps the two directions were
transposed by some accident of
transcription.

 Penker] Thus spelled in Holinshed;
Hall has Pynkie; according to More
he was Provincial of the Augustine
friars.

 107. *notice*] F, rather awkwardly,
repeats 'order' in ll. 105 and 107; Q's
'notice' is a clear improvement, and
may well be the author's.

manner] See Introduction, p. 37.

Scene VI

 2. *set hand*] a formal hand, suitable
for legal documents: OED set
*ppl.a.*5 and hand *sb.*B.I.16.

 engross'd] written out large (OED).

 7. *precedent*] the original from which
a copy is made: OED *sb.*1d.

 9. *Untainted*] i.e. no accusation
(attainter) had been brought against
him. OED has no other instance of
the word.

Here's a good world the while! Who is so gross   10
That cannot see this palpable device?
Yet who's so bold but says he sees it not?
Bad is the world, and all will come to naught
When such ill-dealing must be seen in thought.   *Exit.*

[SCENE VII]

Enter RICHARD *and* BUCKINGHAM *at several doors.*

Rich. How now, how now? What say the citizens?
Buck. Now by the holy Mother of our Lord,
      The citizens are mum, say not a word.
Rich. Touch'd you the bastardy of Edward's children?
Buck. I did, with his contract with Lady Lucy,   5
      And his contract by deputy in France;

10–11.] *As Qq;* . . . while. / Who *F.*   10. Who is] *F;* Why whoes *Qq* (who's
Q 3–6).   11. cannot see] *F;* sees not *Qq.*   12. who's] *Q 1–2;* who *Q 3–6,F.*
bold] *F;* blinde *Qq* (*subst.*).   13. naught *Q 1–2;* nought] *Q 3–6,F.*   14. ill]
F; bad *Qq.*   dealing] *F,Q 1–3,5–6;* dealings *Q 4.*

Scene VII

SCENE VII] *Pope; not in F,Qq.*   S.D.] *F; Enter Glocester at one doore, Buckingham
at another.* | *Qq* (*subst.*).   1. How now, how now] *F;* How now my Lord *Qq*
(*subst.*).   3. say] *F;* and speake *Qq.*   5–6. his . . . France;] *F; not in Qq.*

10–11.] Why F gets the lineation
here wrong is hard to say. Perhaps
some confusion was caused by the
correction of Q 'Why whoes'.

10. *Here's . . . while*] Cf. *John,*
IV.ii.100: 'bad world the while'; also
IV.iii.116: 'Here's a good world!'

11. *palpable device*] obvious trick.

13. *naught*] A synonym for evil:
OED A. *sb.*2.

14. *ill*] Q's 'bad' is picked up from
the previous line, probably by the
compositor.

in thought] The scrivener means that
a world in which men can only
think about such things, rather than
speak their minds, will come to
disaster.

Scene VII

S.D.] Both versions mean the same,

and are characteristic of texts of this
period. Neither direction implies
more than two doors (and I believe
there were in fact only two).

3. *mum*] silent (OED *sb.*1). See
Tilley W767.

5. *Lady Lucy*] More is the source of
these stories: that Edward had been
engaged to Elizabeth Lucy at the
time he married Elizabeth Grey, and
that at the same time a dynastic
marriage was being arranged in
France with Bona of Savoy. See
3H6, III.ii–iii and IV.i, for Shakespeare's version of the events.

5–6, 8, 11.] The omission of these
lines from Q is variously explained:
Marshall (Variorum, p. 256) believed them deleted in deference to
Elizabeth I's feelings, the charges
being similar to those brought

Th'unsatiate greediness of his desire,
And his enforcement of the city wives;
His tyranny for trifles; his own bastardy,
As being got, your father then in France,   10
And his resemblance, being not like the Duke.
Withal, I did infer your lineaments—
Being the right idea of your father,
Both in your form and nobleness of mind—
Laid open all your victories in Scotland,   15
Your discipline in war, wisdom in peace,
Your bounty, virtue, fair humility;
Indeed, left nothing fitting for your purpose
Untouch'd, or slightly handled in discourse.
And when mine oratory drew to an end,   20
I bid them that did love their country's good
Cry, 'God save Richard, England's royal King!'

Rich. And did they so?

Buck. No, so God help me: they spake not a word,
But like dumb statues or breathing stones   25
Star'd each on other, and look'd deadly pale.

7. unsatiate] *F;* insatiate *Qq.*   desire] *F;* desires *Qq.*   8.] *F; not in Qq.*
11.] *F; not in Qq.*   14. your] *F,Q1–2;* one *Q3–6.*   15. open] *F,Q1–5;*
vpon *Q6.*   victories] *F,Q1–3,5–6;* victorie *Q4.*   18. your] *F;* the *Qq.*
20. mine] *Q1–2;* my *Q3–6,F.*   drew] *F;* grew *Qq.*   to an] *Q1–2,4;* to
Q3,5–6; toward *F.*   21. bid] *F,Q1–4;* bad *Q5–6.*   did love] *F,Q1–2;*
loues *Q3–6.*   23. And] *F;* A and *Qq.*   24. they spake not a word,] *F; not
in Qq.*   25. breathing] *F,Q1–2;* breathlesse *Q3–6.*   26. Star'd] *F;* Gazde
Qq.

against her father—but Buckingham
is only repeating, in almost identical
words, Richard's instructions from
III.v. Smidt (p. 114–15) believes they
were cut for this very reason, excess
of repetition. This is possible, though
one cannot say if Shakespeare was
involved in the change.

7. *unsatiate*] The same meaning as
insatiate.

13. *idea*] a likeness or image:
OED *sb.*II.7; i.e. Richard (unlike
Edward) is a true likeness of his
father.

15. *victories in Scotland*] In 1482,
when Richard led the capture of
Berwick. Richard's military prowess

was a central aspect of his character
in *3H6*: in this play it is more fitfully
referred to.

19. *slightly handled*] passed lightly
over.

20. *mine . . . to an*] Two examples
of F accepting a reading from a
derivative quarto. The first is quite
plain; the second resembles the
'meet'st advantage' crux (III.v.73)
in that F's corrector appears to have
conjectured an emendation ('toward'), having found an irregular
line in his copy.

23. *And*] Q's 'A and' may be an
attempt to render something like
'Ah! and did they so?'

Which when I saw, I reprehended them,
And ask'd the Mayor what meant this wilful silence.
His answer was, the people were not us'd
To be spoke to but by the Recorder.   30
Then he was urg'd to tell my tale again:
'Thus saith the Duke; thus hath the Duke inferr'd'—
But nothing spake in warrant from himself.
When he had done, some followers of mine own
At lower end of the hall, hurl'd up their caps,   35
And some ten voices cried 'God save King Richard!'
And thus I took the vantage of those few:
'Thanks gentle citizens and friends,' quoth I;
'This general applause and cheerful shout
Argues your wisdoms and your love to Richard.'   40
And even here brake off, and came away.
Rich. What, tongueless blocks were they? Would they not
    speak!
Will not the Mayor then and his brethren come?
Buck. The Mayor is here at hand. Intend some fear;
    Be not you spoke with but by mighty suit.   45

28. meant] *F,Q 1–5;* meanes *Q 6.*   29. us'd] *F;* wont *Qq.*   33. spake]
Q 1–5; speake *Q 6;* spoke *F.*   35. lower] *F;* the lower *Qq.*   37.] *F; not in*
Qq.   38. gentle] *F;* louing *Qq.*   39. cheerful] *F;* louing *Qq.*   40. wis-
doms] *Q 1–2;* wisdome *Q 3–6,F.*   love] *F,Q 1–2;* loues *Q 3–6.*   41. even
here] *F;* so *Qq.*   42.] *As Qq (punct. as Alexander); . . .* were they, / Would *F.*
speak!] *F;* speake? / *Buc.* No by my troth my Lo: *Qq (subst.).*   44. *Buck.*]
F,Q 3–6; Glo. / *Q 1–2.*   at hand] *F,Q 1–2; not in Q 3–6.*   Intend] *F;* and
intend *Qq.*   45. you spoke with] *F;* spoken withall *Qq.*   but by] *F;* but
with *Qq.*

30. *Recorder*] The civil magistrate
for the city, at that time Thomas
Fitzwilliam. (The accent is on the
first syllable.)

33. *spake*] Another possible conjectural correction in F: Q6's 'speake'
being obviously wrong, the corrector
may have simply used his normal past
tense for the verb.

37.] Presumably an accidental
omission from Q.

38, 39, 40. *gentle*] Q's variants
'louing', 'louing', and 'loue' are
unimaginative by contrast with F's
careful ascension from 'gentle' (con-
ventionally used to flatter those

patently not of gentle birth), 'cheerful', 'love'.

40. *wisdoms*] F here seems to have
wrongly followed Q copy in keeping
the singular.

42.] Alexander's neat punctuation
of the first sentence is too good to
waste. The following line for Buckingham which appears in Q is
unmetrical, and is probably an
actor's intrusion.

44. *Buck.*] Q1's misattribution was
no doubt a compositor's error.

44. *Intend*] pretend, or represent.
See also III.v.8 n.

45. *mighty suit*] powerful entreaty.

And look you get a prayer-book in your hand,
And stand between two churchmen, good my lord:
For on that ground I'll build a holy descant.
And be not easily won to our requests:
Play the maid's part: still answer nay, and take it.   50
Rich. I go, and if you plead as well for them
As I can say nay to thee for myself,
No doubt we bring it to a happy issue.
Buck. Go, go up to the leads, the Lord Mayor knocks.
                                        Exit Richard.

Enter the [LORD] MAYOR *and* Citizens.

Welcome, my lord: I dance attendance here.   55
I think the Duke will not be spoke withal.

47. between] *F;* betwixt *Qq.*   48. build] *Qq;* make *F.*   49. And be] *F;*
Be *Qq.*   easily] *F,Q1;* easie *Q2–6.*   requests] *F;* request *Qq.*   50. still
answer nay, and] *F;* say no, but *Qq.*   51. I go, and if you] *F;* Feare not me,
if thou canst *Qq.*   53. we] *F;* weele *Qq.*   54.] *F;* You shal see what I can
do, get you vp to the leads. *Qq (subst.).*   54. S.D. *Exit] Qq; not in F.*
Enter . . . Citizens.] *F; not in Qq.*   55. Welcome, my lord] *F;* Now my L.
Maior *Qq (subst.).*   56. spoke] *F,Q1–2;* spoken *Q3–6.*

48. *build*] Q here conveys the two
intertwined images more exactly
than F. The primary image is
musical: to structure a descant on
the 'ground' (bass) of the theme
represented by Richard's pious appearance (cf. 1.i.27); the second
image is of the construction of a
fanciful house upon the ground
(foundation) of the same. A characteristic multiple image, it is better
served by Q's verb, which may be
presumed to be an authorial improvement. It is worth noting that Buckingham here presents as his scheme
the idea which had occurred to
Richard at III.v.98–9.

50.] Proverbial: Tilley M34; also
in Whetstone's *Promos* and elsewhere.

53.] Peter Short's printing of Q1
begins here: see Introduction, pp.
21–4.

54. *leads*] A flat roof covered with
lead (OED lead *sb.*[1] 7) here used
generally to mean 'in the upper

gallery': Richard plays the ensuing
part of the scene 'aloft', on the 'upper
stage'.

54. S.D.] The F corrector, in
adding the necessary entrance, obscured or deleted the exit marked
for Richard.

55. *dance attendance*] wait with
assiduous attention; originally to
stand 'kicking one's heels' in a
waiting-room: OED dance *v.*5. See
also Tilley A392.

56. S.D.] It is clear from the
context that two acting-areas are
involved: the main stage, upon
which Buckingham, the Mayor, and
the citizens appear, and the upper
stage, on which Richard appears
with his clergymen. In order to
emphasize the separation of the two,
it is preferable to have Catesby
located in Richard's area, appearing
and disappearing from the windows
at which Richard will make his
show.

Enter CATESBY [*above*].

Now, Catesby, what says your lord to my request?

Cat. He doth entreat your Grace, my noble lord,
To visit him tomorrow, or next day:
He is within, with two right reverend fathers,   60
Divinely bent to meditation;
And in no worldly suits would he be mov'd
To draw him from his holy exercise.

Buck. Return, good Catesby, to the gracious Duke;
Tell him myself, the Mayor and aldermen,   65
In deep designs, in matter of great moment,
No less importing than our general good,
Are come to have some conference with his Grace.

Cat. I'll signify so much unto him straight.   *Exit.*

Buck. Ah ha, my lord, this prince is not an Edward: 70
He is not lolling on a lewd love-bed,
But on his knees at meditation;
Not dallying with a brace of courtesans,
But meditating with two deep divines;
Not sleeping, to engross his idle body,   75
But praying, to enrich his watchful soul.
Happy were England, would this virtuous Prince
Take on his Grace the sovereignty thereof.

---

56. *above*] *This edn; not in* F,Qq.   57.] *F;* Here coms his seruant: how now
Catesby what saies he. *Qq (subst.).*   58. He . . . Grace, my noble lord] *F;* My
Lord, he . . . grace *Qq.*   60. right] *F,Q1–2; not in Q3–6.*   62. suits] *F;* suite *Qq*
(subst).   64. the gracious Duke] *F;* thy Lord againe *Qq.*   65. aldermen] *F;*
Cittizens *Qq (subst.).*   66. in matter] *F;* and matters *Qq.*   67. than] *F,Q1–5;*
them then *Q6.*   69.] *F;* Ile tell him what you say my Lord. *Qq* (subst.).
71. love-bed] *F;* day bed *Qq.*   77. virtuous] *F;* gracious *Qq.*   78. his Grace . . .
thereof] *F:* himselfe . . . thereon *Qq.*

63. *exercise*] Cf. III.ii.108.

65. *aldermen*] Patrick (p. 27) believes this was changed to 'citizens' in
Q to save costumes.

69.] Smidt (p. 84) thinks the F line
was found awkward on the stage (he
does not say why) and therefore
changed; a lapse of the actor's
memory is equally plausible.

71. *lolling . . . love-bed*] The grotesque alliteration is characteristic of

the style of oratory Shakespeare gives
Buckingham in the play. The word is
rare (OED records only this instance)
but perfectly clear. Q's 'day-bed' also
has connotations of sexual indulgence
(cf. *T.N.*, II.v.48 f.), but, as the
commoner term, may be an actor's
vulgarization. On balance F remains
preferable.

75. *engross*] Make gross or fat:
OED *v.*III.9a, citing this line.

But sure I fear we shall not win him to it.
Mayor. Marry, God defend his Grace should say us nay!   80
Buck. I fear he will.

Enter CATESBY.

Here Catesby comes again.
Now, Catesby, what says his Grace?
Cat. He wonders to what end you have assembled
Such troops of citizens to come to him,
His Grace not being warn'd thereof before.   85
He fears, my lord, you mean no good to him.
Buck. Sorry I am my noble cousin should
Suspect me that I mean no good to him.
By heaven, we come to him in perfect love:
And so once more return and tell his Grace. *Exit Catesby.*
When holy and devout religious men   91
Are at their beads, 'tis much to draw them thence,
So sweet is zealous contemplation.

Enter RICHARD *aloft, between two* Bishops [*with* CATESBY].

Mayor. See where his Grace stands, 'tween two clergymen!
Buck. Two props of virtue for a Christian Prince,   95
To stay him from the fall of vanity;
And see, a book of prayer in his hand—

79. not] *F;* neuer *Qq.*   80. defend] *F;* forbid *Qq.*   81. Here Catesby
comes again] *F;* how now Catesby *Qq.*   82.] *F;* What saies your Lord? *Qq*
(*subst.*).   83. He] *F;* My Lo. he *Qq* (*subst.*).   84. come to] *F;* speake with
Qq.   86. He fears, my lord] *F;* My Lord, he feares *Qq.*   89. we come to
him in perfect love] *F;* I come in perfect loue to him *Qq.*   92. their]
F,Q1–3,5–6; there *Q4*   much] *F;* hard *Qq.*   thence] *F,Q1–4;* hence
Q5–6.   93. S.D.] *F; Enter Rich. with two bishops a loste. | Qq (and two |
Q3–6; aloft | Q2–6).   [with Catesby] This edn; not in F,Qq.*   94. his Grace]
F; he *Qq.*   'tween] *F;* between *Qq.*   97–8.] *F; not in Qq.*

80. *God defend*] OED defend *v.*1.3e:
= 'God forbid'; the senses 'prohibit'
(3) and 'avert' (1) seem to unite.

93. S.D.] The odd misprint in Q1
only means an ſt ligature strayed into
the ſt box. The clergymen are, of
course, Shaa and Penker, mentioned
at III. v. 102–3.

96. *fall of vanity*] i.e. the danger of
falling into sin through vanity.

97–8.] Omitted from Q, probably
inadvertently. Buckingham is carefully underlining all the visual emblems of piety for the Mayor's benefit,
so they are not redundant description,
as Smidt thought (p. 115).

True ornaments to know a holy man.
Famous Plantagenet, most gracious Prince,
Lend favourable ear to our requests,　　　　　　　　100
And pardon us the interruption
Of thy devotion and right Christian zeal.

Rich. My lord, there needs no such apology;
I do beseech your Grace to pardon me,
Who—earnest in the service of my God—　　　　　105
Deferr'd the visitation of my friends.
But leaving this, what is your Grace's pleasure?

Buck. Even that, I hope, which pleaseth God above,
And all good men of this ungovern'd isle.

Rich. I do suspect I have done some offence　　　　110
That seems disgracious in the City's eye.
And that you come to reprehend my ignorance.

Buck. You have, my lord: would it might please your Grace
On our entreaties to emend your fault.

Rich. Else wherefore breathe I in a Christian land?　　115

Buck. Know then, it is your fault that you resign
The supreme seat, the throne majestical,
The sceptred office of your ancestors,
Your state of fortune, and your due of birth,
The lineal glory of your royal House,　　　　　　120
To the corruption of a blemish'd stock;
Whiles in the mildness of your sleepy thoughts—

---

100. ear] *F;* eares *Qq.*　　　our requests] *F;* our request *Q1;* my request *Q2–6.*
104. I do beseech your Grace to] *F;* I rather do beseech you *Qq.*　　106.
Deferr'd] *F;* Neglect *Qq.*　　111. seems] *F,Q1–4;* seeme *Q5–6.*　　eye] *F;*
eies *Q1–2;* eyes *Q3–6.*　　113.] *As Qq; . . .* Lord: / Would *F.*　　might] *F;*
not in Qq.　　114. On] *F;* At *Qq.*　　your] *F;* that *Qq.*　　115. Else where-
fore] *F,Q1–2,6;* Els wherefore *Q3(Hunt. copy),Q4;* Else wherfore *Q3(other copies),*
Q5.　　116. Know then] *F;* Then know *Qq.*　　119.] *F; not in Qq.*　　122.
Whiles] *F;* Whilst *Q1;* Whilest *Q2–6.*　　your] *F,Q1,3–6;* you *Q2.*

---

98. *ornaments*] The bishops, as well
as the prayer-book.

109. *ungovern'd*] As Richard is
Protector, the epithet is something
tactless. But Buckingham implies that
a Christian nation cannot thrive
without its proper head. See ll. 119–
20, 124–8.

111.] *disgracious* displeasing: OED
2.

119.] Omitted inadvertently from
Q, no doubt.

121. *corruption . . . blemish'd stock*]
Buckingham implies Edward's bastardy in this oratorical flourish. So
also in ll. 124–6.

Which here we waken to our country's good—
The noble isle doth want her proper limbs;
Her face defac'd with scars of infamy,   125
Her royal stock graft with ignoble plants,
And almost shoulder'd in the swallowing gulf
Of dark forgetfulness and deep oblivion;
Which to recure, we heartily solicit
Your gracious self to take on you the charge   130
And kingly government of this your land,
Not as Protector, steward, substitute,
Or lowly factor for another's gain,
But as successively from blood to blood,
Your right of birth, your empery, your own.   135
For this, consorted with the citizens—
Your very worshipful and loving friends,
And by their vehement instigation—
In this just cause come I to move your Grace.

Rich. I cannot tell if to depart in silence   140
Or bitterly to speak in your reproof
Best fitteth my degree or your condition.

123. our] *F,Q1–4;* your *Q5–6.*   124. The] *F;* This *Qq.*   her] *Q1–2;* his
Q3–6,F.   125. Her] *Qq;* His *F.*   scars] *F* (skarres), *Q1,5–6;* stars *Q2–4.*
126.] *F* (His Royall); *not in Qq.*   Her] *Pope;* His *F.*   127. the] *F,Q1–2;*
this *Q3–6.*   128. dark . . . deep] *F;* blind . . . darke *Qq.*   129. recure]
F,Q1–5; recouer *Q6.*   130–1. charge / And kingly government of this your
land] *F;* soueraingtie thereof *Qq* (soueraigntie *Q2–6*).   133. Or] *F,Q1–2;*
Nor *Q3–6.*   137. very] *F,Q1–2* (*subst.*); *not in Q3–6.*   loving] *F,Q1–2;*
very louing *Q3–6.*   friends] *F,Q2,4,6;* frinds *Q1;* friens *Q3* (*Hunt. copy*);
friends *Q3* (*other copies*); freinds *Q5.*   139. cause] *F;* suite *Q1;* sute *Q2–6.*
140. cannot tell] *F;* know not whether *Qq* (whither *Q5–6*).

124. *her*] See also ll. 125, 126. 'His'
in F l. 124 comes from Q 3, and no
doubt was overlooked by the corrector; either he or the compositor
changed the other two pronouns to
match.

126, 130–1.] These omissions (with
l. 119) led Smidt (p. 116) to declare
that Buckingham's speech is 'long,
and needs pruning': this may well be
so, but the omission of three lines is not
much help, and their absence is more
likely owing to the actor's failure to
recall all the phrases of his rhetoric.

127. *shoulder'd in*] rudely pushed
into. Buckingham's metaphors sound
impressive, but are fearfully mixed.

129. *recure*] remedy or repair:
OED *v.* 2b.

133. *factor*] agent or representative:
OED *sb.* 3.

135. *empery*] territory ruled by an
emperor: OED *sb.* 2.

142. *degree . . . condition*] Both mean
social rank: OED degree *sb.* 4b;
condition *sb.* 10.

142–54.] See Appendix 1.

If not to answer, you might haply think
Tongue-tied ambition, not replying, yielded
To bear the golden yoke of sovereignty   145
Which fondly you would here impose on me;
If to reprove you for this suit of yours,
So season'd with your faithful love to me,
Then, on the other side, I check'd my friends.
Therefore, to speak, and to avoid the first,   150
And then, in speaking, not to incur the last,
Definitively thus I answer you:
Your love deserves my thanks, but my desert
Unmeritable shuns your high request.
First, if all obstacles were cut away,   155
And that my path were even to the crown
As the ripe revenue and due of birth,
Yet so much is my poverty of spirit,
So mighty and so many my defects,
That I would rather hide me from my greatness—   160
Being a bark to brook no mighty sea—
Than in my greatness covet to be hid,
And in the vapour of my glory smother'd.
But, God be thank'd, there is no need of me—
And much I need, to help you, were there need.   165
The royal tree hath left us royal fruit,
Which, mellow'd by the stealing hours of time,
Will well become the seat of majesty,
And make, no doubt, us happy by his reign.

143–52.] *F; not in Qq.*   157. the ripe] *F;* my ripe *Q1;* my right *Q2–6.*
of] *F;* by *Qq.*   160. That I would] *F;* As I had *Qq.*   164. thank'd, there
is] *F;* thanked, there's *Qq (subst.).*   of] *F,Q1–2;* for *Q3–6.*   165. were
there need] *F;* if need were *Qq.*

143.] See Tilley S446.

144. *yielded*] i.e. yielded to your
entreaties.

149. *check'd*] 'You might haply
think' understood from l. 143.

153–4. *desert/Unmeritable*] unworthi-
ness (literally, meritless merit).

156. *even*] smooth.

157. *ripe revenue*] possession ready
to be inherited (Camb.): OED

revenue 3b. *fig.* The land seen as the
revenue or inheritance of the lawfully-
born owner.

165. *much I need*] Richard means he
lacks the ability to give help, if it were
needed, as Johnson explained.

169. *no doubt*] The effect of the
awkwardly placed intrusion of this
phrase into the sentence is to make
the hearers think there is a doubt.

On him I lay that you would lay on me: 170
The right and fortune of his happy stars,
Which God defend that I should wring from him.
Buck. My lord, this argues conscience in your Grace;
But the respects thereof are nice and trivial,
All circumstances well considered.   175
You say that Edward is your brother's son:
So say we too—but not by Edward's wife.
For first was he contract to Lady Lucy
(Your mother lives a witness to his vow),
And afterward by substitute betroth'd   180
To Bona, sister to the King of France.
These both put off, a poor petitioner,
A care-craz'd mother to a many sons,
A beauty-waning and distressed widow,
Even in the afternoon of her best days   185
Made prize and purchase of his wanton eye,
Seduc'd the pitch and height of his degree
To base declension and loath'd bigamy.
By her, in his unlawful bed, he got
This Edward, whom our manners call the Prince.   190
More bitterly could I expostulate,
Save that for reverence to some alive
I give a sparing limit to my tongue.

170. that] *F;* what *Qq.*   178. was he] *F;* he was *Qq.*   contract] *F,Q 1–5;*
contracted *Q6.*   179. his] *F;* that *Qq.*   180. afterward] *F,Q 1–5;* afterwards *Q6.*   182. off] *F;* by *Qq.*   183. to a many] *F;* of a many *Q 1;* of
many *Q 2–6.*   sons] *F;* children *Qq.*   186. wanton] *F;* lustfull *Qq.*
187. Seduc'd] *F;* Seduc t *Q 1,5;* Seduc't *Q 2–4;* Seduce *Q6.*   his degree] *F;*
al his thoughts *Qq (subst.).*   189. his] *F,Q 1–5;* this *Q6.*   190. call] *F;*
terme *Qq.*   191. could I] *F,Q 1–5;* could *Q6.*

174. *respects*] considerations, facts,
or motives leading to the formation of
a decision: OED *sb.*III. 14.
nice] unimportant, slight: OED 10b.
178–81.] See ll. 5–6.
183. *to a many*] For 'a many' see
Abbott §87; for a note on the Queen's
family see I. iii.67.
187. *pitch*] The height to which a
falcon soars before swooping down
(NCS), here used allegorically, the

falcon standing for the king.
188. *declension*] deviation from a
standard: OED 2.
bigamy] 'Alluding to his previous
contracts; but marriage with a widow
was bigamy according to canon law'
(NCS): the term originates in More.
192. *some alive*] The Duchess of
York: Buckingham alludes lightly to
the tale of Edward IV's being
illegitimate.

Then, good my lord, take to your royal self
This proffer'd benefit of dignity:　　　　　　　　195
If not to bless us and the land withal,
Yet to draw forth your noble ancestry
From the corruption of abusing times
Unto a lineal, true-derived course.

Mayor. Do, good my lord: your citizens entreat you.　　200
Buck. Refuse not, mighty lord, this proffer'd love.
Cat. O make them joyful; grant their lawful suit.
Rich. Alas, why would you heap this care on me?
I am unfit for state and majesty.
I do beseech you, take it not amiss;　　　　　　205
I cannot, nor I will not, yield to you.
Buck. If you refuse it, as in love and zeal
Loath to despose the child, your brother's son—
As well we know your tenderness of heart,
And gentle, kind, effeminate remorse,　　　　　210
Which we have noted in you to your kindred,
And equally indeed to all estates—
Yet know, whe'er you accept our suit or no,
Your brother's son shall never reign our king,
But we will plant some other in the throne　　　215
To the disgrace and downfall of your House;
And with this resolution here we leave you.
Come, citizens; zounds, I'll entreat no more.
Rich. O, do not swear, my lord of Buckingham!
　　　　　　Exeunt [Buckingham, Lord Mayor, and Citizens].

197. forth your noble ancestry] *F;* out your royall stocke *Qq.*　　198. times]
F; time *Qq.*　　201.] *F; not in Qq.*　　203. this] *F;* these *Q1;* those *Q2–6.*
care] *F;* cares *Qq.*　　204. majesty] *F;* dignitie *Qq.*　　211. kindred] *F;* kin
Qq.　　213. know, whe'er] *F* (where)*; whether Qq.*　　accept] *F,Q1–5;*
except *Q6.*　　218. zounds, I'll] *Qq;* we will *F.*　　219.] *Qq; not in F.*
219. S.D.] *As Eccles; Exeunt. | F; not in Qq.*

198. *abusing times*] i.e. the years
following Edward IV's marriage,
when the natural order in the
government of England suffered
abuse.

212. *estates*] all sorts of people:
OED *sb.*5, citing this line.

213. *whe'er*] A contraction of
'whether'.

218. *zounds*] See Introduction,
p. 43.

219. S.D., 225. S.D.] Neither
direction is entirely satisfactory. As
there is a large crowd on-stage
(presumably as many supers as were
available) it would take time for it to
empty and refill. What must happen
is that Buckingham, at l. 219,

Cat. Call him again, sweet Prince; accept their suit.   220
　　If you deny them, all the land will rue it.
Rich. Will you enforce me to a world of cares?
　　Call them again. I am not made of stones,
　　But penetrable to your kind entreaties,
　　Albeit against my conscience and my soul.   225

　　　　　Enter BUCKINGHAM *and* the rest.

　　Cousin of Buckingham, and sage grave men,
　　Since you will buckle fortune on my back
　　To bear her burden whe'er I will or no,
　　I must have patience to endure the load.
　　But if black scandal, or foul-fac'd reproach,   230
　　Attend the sequel of your imposition,
　　Your mere enforcement shall acquittance me
　　From all the impure blots and stains thereof:
　　For God doth know, and you may partly see,
　　How far I am from the desire of this.   235
Mayor. God bless your Grace: we see it, and will say it.
Rich. In saying so, you shall but say the truth.

220. him . . . sweet Prince; accept] *F;* them . . . my lord, and accept *Qq.*
221.] *F; Ano.* Do, good my lord, least all the land do rew it. *Qq.*   222. Will]
F; Would *Qq.* cares] *F;* care *Qq.*   223. Call] *F;* Well, call *Qq.*   224.
entreaties] *F;* intreates *Qq* (*subst.*).   225. S.D.] *F; not in Qq.*   226. sage]
F; you sage *Qq.*   227. you] *F,Q1–2,4–6;* your *Q3.*   228. her] *F,Q1–2;*
the *Q3–6.*   whe'er] *F* (where); whether *Qq.*   230. foul-fac'd] *F;* soule-
fac't *Q1–2;* so foule fac't *Q3–5;* so foulefac't *Q6.*   234. doth know] *F;* he
knowes *Qq.*   235. of this] *F;* thereof *Qq.*

sweeps for the exit, followed by the
citizens during Catesby's plea and
Richard's meditation; at l. 223
Catesby must make some gesture
(since he does not speak, and has not
time to exit and effect his task) which
reverses the general movement. Lines
223–5 are obviously not for Catesby's
or the bishops' benefit, but must be
spoken to some citizens who never
got as far as the exit. Buckingham
thus has time to make his reappearance by l. 226.
　221.] Q gives this line to an
anonymous speaker, perhaps a stooge
planted in the crowd. Perhaps this

arrangement was found effective on
stage, but there are no grounds for
thinking the alteration authorial.
　226. *grave men*] One of Richard's
jokes; cf. Mercutio's better-known
line in *Rom.*, iii.i.98.
　227. *back*] The image is developed,
another sardonic joke, out of Richard's
deformity.
　228. *whe'er*] whether, as at l. 213.
　231. *imposition*] Of the burden of
kingship.
　232.] i.e. 'your enforcing of the
matter shall acquit me'; mere: OED
*a.*2.

Buck. Then I salute you with this royal title:
          Long live Richard, England's worthy King!
All. Amen.   240
Buck. Tomorrow may it please you to be crown'd?
Rich. Even when you please, for you will have it so.
Buck. Tomorrow then we will attend your Grace;
          And so most joyfully we take our leave.
Rich. Come, let us to our holy work again.   245
          Farewell my cousin, farewell gentle friends.   *Exeunt.*

---

238. this royal] *F;* this kingly *Q1–3,5–6;* the kingly *Q4.*   239. Richard]
Q1–2; King Richard *Q3–6,F.*   worthy] *F;* royall *Qq.*   240. *All.*] *F;*
Mayor | Qq (subst.).   241. may] *F;* will *Qq.*   242. please, for] *F;* will,
since *Qq.*   244.] *F; not in Qq.*   245. work] *F;* task *Qq.*   246. my] *F;*
good *Qq.*   cousin] *Qq (subst.);* Cousins *F.*

238–9. *royal . . . Richard*] Q has far
too many 'kingly' words: the variant
in l. 238 is probably Buckingham
repeating himself; the 'King Richard'
which F takes from Q copy in l. 239
is compositor's dittography, so the
only necessary king is that at the end
of l. 239.

240. *All.*] No doubt the Mayor does
say 'Amen', but F is right to give it to
the entire cast.

246. *cousin*] It is possible Richard
means the plural found in F as a
courtesy term (cf. III.iv.22) but
more likely it is a compositor's slip
and he means Buckingham as Q
implies.

ACT IV

SCENE I

Enter QUEEN ELIZABETH, *the* DUCHESS OF YORK, MARQUESS
OF DORSET *at one door;* ANNE *Duchess of Gloucester at another
door* [*with Clarence's* Daughter].

Duch. Who meets us here? My niece Plantagenet
    Led in the hand of her kind aunt of Gloucester:
    Now, for my life, she's wandering to the Tower,
    On pure heart's love, to greet the tender Prince.
    Daughter, well met.

Anne.   God give your Graces both   5
    A happy and a joyful time of day.

ACT IV

Scene I

ACT IV SCENE I] *As F (Actus Quartus. Scena Prima.); not in Qq.*   S.D.] *As Qq*
(*Enter Quee. mother, Duchess of Yorke, Marques Dorset, at one doore, Duchess of
Glocest. at another doore.* | *Q1*); *Enter the Queene, Anne Duchess of Gloucester,
the Duchesse of Yorke, and Marquesse Dorset.* | *F.*   [*with Clarence's Daughter*] *As
Eccles; leading Lady Margaret Plantagenet, Clarence's young daughter.* | *Johnson.*
1.] *As Qq; ...* heere? | My *F.*   2–4.] *F; not in Qq.*   5. Daughter, well
met] *F;* Qu. Sister well met *Qq.*   5–6. *Anne.* God ... day.] *F; not in Qq.*
... both / A happy] *As Pope; ...* happie / And a *F.*

S.D.] Q form is followed here
because it specifies the entrance from
separate doors implied by the
Duchess's opening lines.

1–27.] The text of these lines in
Q is unusually disturbed besides the
usual synonym variation and poorly
recollected lines; some major alteration was botched involving the
'niece Plantagenet'. Theobald recognized that Clarence's daughter was
meant; 'niece' can be used of a
grand-child (cf. OED niece 1a),
though in Shakespeare it usually has
the modern meaning. Q, by omitting
the second line, makes the term refer

to Anne: niece by marriage and by
courtesy. Possibly the elimination of
the part led to some muddle in the
boys' minds, with consequent faulty
recollection of the rest of the material,
thus accounting for the omission of
ll. 2–4, 5–6, and part of 7. Brakenbury's memory was erratic, and his
carelessness must be added to the
errors of the boys and the cut to
remove Clarence's daughter. F is
wrongly lineated at ll. 1 and 5 which
adds to the air of confusion. See also
Introduction, p. 63.

    2. *aunt of Gloucester*] i.e. Lady
Anne.

Eliz. As much to you, good sister; whither away?

Anne. No farther than the Tower, and as I guess,
Upon the like devotion as yourselves:
To gratulate the gentle Princes there.   10

Eliz. Kind sister, thanks; we'll enter all together.

Enter BRAKENBURY.

And in good time, here the Lieutenant comes.
Master Lieutenant, pray you by your leave:
How doth the Prince and my young son of York?

Brak. Right well, dear madam. By your patience,   15
I may not suffer you to visit them:
The King hath strictly charg'd the contrary.

Eliz. The King! Who's that?

Brak.   I mean the Lord Protector.

Eliz. The Lord protect him from that kingly title!
Hath he set bounds between their love and me?   20
I am their mother; who shall bar me from them?

Duch. I am their father's mother: I will see them.

Anne. Their aunt I am in law, in love their mother;
Then bring me to their sights. I'll bear thy blame,
And take thy office from thee, on my peril.   25

7. As much to you, good sister;] *F; not in Qq.*   away] *F;* awaie so fast *Qq.*
(*subst.*).   8. *Anne.*] *F; Duch. | Q 1 ; Du. | Q 2 ; Dut. Glo. | Q 3–6.*   10. gentle]
F; tender *Qq.*   11. S.D. *Brakenbury*] *Capell; the Lieutenant | F,Qq (subst.).*
14.] *F;* How fares the Prince? *Qq* (feares *Q 6*).   15, 18, 26. *Brak.*] *Capell;*
Lieu. | F,Qq.   15.] *F;* Wel, Madam, and in health, but by your leaue, *Qq.*
16. them] *F;* him *Qq.*   17. strictly] *F;* straightlie *Qq (subst.).*   18. Who's]
F; whie whose *Qq (subst.).*   I mean] *F; (new line)* I crie you mercie, I meane
Qq (subst.).   20. between] *F;* betwixt *Qq.*   21. shall bar] *F;* should keep
Qq.   22. *Duch.*] *As F,Q 1 ; not in Q 2–6.*   father's mother: I] *As F* (Fathers)*;*
Fathers, Mother, I *Q 1 ;* father, Mother, and *Q 2–6.*   24. bring me to their
sights] *F;* feare not thou *Qq.*

10. *gratulate*] greet or salute: OED
1; NCS remarks this is a 'favourite
word' with Peele and Greene, and
compares *Tit.*, i.i.221.

11. S.D. *Brakenbury*] See Introduction, p. 5.

14.] Q inexplicably omits the Duke
of York despite the plural 'Princes' in
l. 10. Brakenbury emends his reply
into the singular to match.

17–18. *King . . . Protector*] Cf.

Edward III, ii.ii.35–7: '*Ken.* Ile looke
upon the Countesse minde anone, /
Dar. The Countesse minde, my liege /
Ken. I meane the Emperour'. An
example of the self-betraying slip of
the tongue, characteristic of the
morality heritage. See also Introduction, p. 10.1

20. *bounds*] boundary-lines: OED
sb.[1] 2.

Brak. No, madam, no: I may not leave it so.
  I am bound by oath; and therefore pardon me.   *Exit.*

Enter STANLEY *Earl of Derby.*

Stan. Let me but meet you, ladies, one hour hence,
  And I'll salute your Grace of York as mother
  And reverend looker-on of two fair queens.   30
  [*To Anne*] Come, madam, you must straight to
      Westminster,
  There to be crowned Richard's royal queen.
Eliz. Ah, cut my lace asunder
  That my pent heart may have some scope to beat,
  Or else I swoon with this dead-killing news.   35
Anne. Despiteful tidings! O unpleasing news!
Dors. Be of good cheer, mother: how fares your Grace?
Eliz. O Dorset, speak not to me; get thee gone.
  Death and destruction dogs thee at thy heels;
  Thy mother's name is ominous to children.   40
  If thou wilt outstrip death, go, cross the seas
  And live with Richmond, from the reach of hell.
  Go: hie thee, hie thee from this slaughter-house
  Lest thou increase the number of the dead,
  And make me die the thrall of Margaret's curse: 45

26.] *F; I doe beseech your graces all to pardon me: Qq (subst.).*   27. and
therefore pardon me] *F;* I may not doe it *Qq (subst.).*   27. S.D. *Exit
Brakenbury*] *As F (Lieutenant); not in Qq.*   *Stanley*] *F,Q4; Stanlie* / *Q1–2;
Standly* / *Q3,5–6.*   28. you] *F,Q1–5;* your *Q6.*   one] *F;* an *Q1–4;* at an
Q5–6.   30. reverend] *F;* reuerente *Qq (subst.).*   31. S.D.] *Capell; not in
F,Qq.*   straight] *F;* go with me *Qq.*   33–5.] *As F;* . . . heart, / May . . .
sound, / With *Qq.*   33. Ah] *F;* O *Qq.*   asunder] *F;* in sunder *Qq.*
35. else I] *F,Q1,3(all copies except Hunt.),5–6;* else *Q2,3(Hunt. copy),4.*   swoon]
F; sound *Qq.*   dead-killing] *F;* dead killing *Q1–4;* dead liking *Q5–6.*
36.] *F; not in Qq.*   37. Be of good cheer, mother] *F;* Madam, haue comfort
Qq.   38. gone] *F;* hence *Qq.*   39. dogs] *F (dogges);* dogge *Qq.*   thy]
F; the *Qq.*   40. ominous] *F,Q1–4,6;* ominious *Q5.*   41. outstrip] *F,Q1–5;*
ouerstrip *Q6.*   42. the reach] *F,Q1–5;* rhe race *Q6.*

26.] See Introduction, pp. 5–6.
  28. *one*] Q's 'an' may be a misprint
for 'on', a variant spelling of 'one'.
  35. *dead-killing*] Cf. *Lucr.*, l. 540.
  37. *Be of good cheer, mother*] The
phrase Q gives to Dorset recalls
Richard's 'Sister, have comfort' in

II.ii.101, as Smidt noted (p. 56);
Dorset was then on-stage, and may
have recollected the words here.
  39. *dogs*] 'Death and destruction' is
a collective singular.
  45. *thrall*] subject or slave: OED
sb.[1] 1.

Nor mother, wife, nor England's counted Queen.

Stan. Full of wise care is this your counsel, madam.

　　[*To Dorset*] Take all the swift advantage of the hours;

You shall have letters from me to my son

In your behalf, to meet you on the way.　　　　　　　　50

Be not ta'en tardy by unwise delay.

Duch. O ill-dispersing wind of misery!

O my accursed womb, the bed of death!

A cockatrice hast thou hatch'd to the world

Whose unavoided eye is murderous.　　　　　　　　55

Stan. Come madam, come: I in all haste was sent.

Anne. And I with all unwillingness will go.

O would to God that the inclusive verge

Of golden metal that must round my brow

Were red-hot steel, to sear me to the brains.　　　　60

Anointed let me be with deadly venom,

And die ere men can say 'God save the Queen'.

Eliz. Go, go, poor soul; I envy not thy glory.

To feed my humour, wish thyself no harm.

Anne. No? Why? When he that is my husband now　　65

Came to me as I follow'd Henry's corse,

---

48. S.D.] *NCS; not in F,Qq.*   48. hours] *F;* time *Qq.*   49. my son]
F,Q1–5; me sonne *Q6.*   50.] *F;* To meete you on the way, and welcome
you, *Qq.*   51. ta'en] *F,Q1 (subst.);* taken *Q2–6.*   54. hatch'd] *F,Q2–6;*
hatch *Q1.*   56. madam, come] *F;* Madam, *Qq.*   sent] *F,Q1–2;* sent for
Q3–6.   57. *Anne*] *F; Duch | Qq (subst.).*   with] *F;* in *Qq.*   58. O] *F;* I
Qq.   60. brains] *F;* braine *Qq.*   61. let me be] *F,Q1–2,4,6;* let me *Q3,5.*
venom] *F;* poyson *Qq (subst.).*   63. Go, go] *F;* Alas *Qq.*   thy] *F,Q1,3–6;*
the *Q2.*   65. Why?] *F; not in Qq.*   66. as I] *F,Q1–5;* I *Q6.*   corse] *F;*
course *Qq.*

---

49. *son*] George Stanley, who does
not appear in the play but is important to the plot in the Bosworth
scene.

51.] Proverbial in quality, the line
is not listed by Tilley.

52. *ill-dispersing*] i.e. spreading evil
abroad.

54. *cockatrice*] a serpent, identified
with the basilisk (see i. ii. 154): OED 1.
Cf. *Lucr.*, l. 540 (and l. 35 above).

55. *unavoided*] not avoided or
escaped: OED 1; cf. iv.iv.218 where

the word has the entirely different
second meaning.

58. *inclusive verge*] 'The hollow
crown / That rounds the mortal
temples of a king' (*R2*, iii.ii.161–2).

58–61.] Cf. Medea's murder of
Creusa, Seneca, *Medea*, ll. 573–4,
817–39.

65–9.] Cf. Seneca, *Hercules Furens*,
ll. 372–3.

66. *corse*] Q's 'course' may be a
variant spelling of 'corse' but might in
context mean 'track' or 'route'.

When scarce the blood was well wash'd from his hands
Which issued from my other angel-husband,
And that dear saint which then I weeping follow'd;
O when, I say, I look'd on Richard's face   70
This was my wish: 'Be thou', quoth I, 'accurs'd
For making me, so young, so old a widow;
And when thou wed'st, let sorrow haunt thy bed;
And be thy wife—if any be so mad—
More miserable by the life of thee   75
Than thou hast made me by my dear lord's death.'
Lo, ere I can repeat this curse again,
Within so small a time, my woman's heart
Grossly grew captive to his honey words,
And prov'd the subject of mine own soul's curse,   80
Which hitherto hath held my eyes from rest;
For never yet one hour in his bed
Did I enjoy the golden dew of sleep,
But with his timorous dreams was still awak'd.
Besides, he hates me for my father Warwick,   85
And will, no doubt, shortly be rid of me.

Eliz. Poor heart, adieu; I pity thy complaining.

Anne. No more than with my soul I mourn for yours.

---

69. dear] *F*; dead *Qq*.   74. mad] *F*; madde *Q1–2*; badde *Q3–6*.   75. More] *F*; As *Qq*.   life] *F*; death *Qq*.   76. Than] *F*; As *Qq*.   77. ere] *F*; eare *Q1*; euen *Q2–6*.   78. Within so small a time] *F*; Euen in so short a space *Qq*.   79. Grossly] *F,Q1*; Crosselie *Q2*; Crosly *Q3–6*.   80. subject] *F,Q1*; subiectes *Q2,4–6 (subst.)*; subsects *Q3*.   mine] *F*; my *Qq*.   81. hitherto] *F*; euer since *Qq*.   held] *F*; kept *Qq*.   my] *Q1–5*; mine *Q6,F.* rest] *F*; sleepe *Qq*.   83. Did I enjoy] *F*; Haue I enioyed *Qq*.   84.] *F*; But haue bene waked by his timerous dreames *Qq (subst.)*.   86. no doubt] *F,Q1*; not in *Q2–6*.   87. Poor heart, adieu] *F*; Alas poore soule *Qq*. complaining] *F*; complaints *Qq*.   88. with] *F*; from *Qq*.

---

68. *angel-husband*] Prince Edward, Henry VI's son. Cf. I. iv. 53.

69. *dear saint*] Henry VI.

74–6. *mad—* / *More . . . life . . . death*] See Appendix II.

77. *ere*] Q2 probably picked up 'euen' from the next line.

79. *Grossly*] stupidly: OED 6.

83. *golden . . . sleep*] Sleep is often described as golden: cf. *Tit.*, II. iii. 26, while in *Caes.*, II. i. 230, the 'dew of slumber' is referred to.

84. *timorous dreams*] Insomnia and evil dreams were hallmarks of the usurper; More/Hall is the source, but locates Richard's distress only after the death of the Princes (see Appendix III, p. 363). For the most famous example in Shakespeare, see of course *Macbeth*.

Dors. Farewell, thou woeful welcomer of glory.

Anne. Adieu, poor soul, that tak'st thy leave of it.   90

Duch. [*To Dorset*] Go thou to Richmond, and good fortune
  guide thee;
  [*To Anne*] Go thou to Richard, and good angels tend
    thee;
  [*To Elizabeth*] Go thou to sanctuary, and good thoughts
    possess thee;
  I to my grave, where peace and rest lie with me.
  Eighty odd years of sorrow have I seen,   95
  And each hour's joy wrack'd with a week of teen.

Eliz. Stay, yet look back with me unto the Tower.
  Pity, you ancient stones, those tender babes
  Whom envy hath immur'd within your walls—
  Rough cradle for such little pretty ones,   100
  Rude ragged nurse, old sullen playfellow
  For tender princes, use my babies well.
  So foolish sorrows bids your stones farewell.   *Exeunt.*

---

89. *Dors.*] *F,Q₁; Qu. | Q₂–6.*   90. that] *F;* thou *Qq.*   91. [*To Dorset*] *As F₄; not in F,Qq.*   92. [*To Anne*] *As F₄; not in F,Qq.* (*subst.*).   93. [*To Elizabeth*] *As F₄; not in F,Qq.*   tend] *F;* garde *Qq*   and] *F; not in Qq.*   95. odd] *F,Q₁–4;* olde *Q₅–6* (*subst.*).   96. of teen] *F;* ofteene *Qq.*   97–103.] *F; not in Qq.*   103. S.D.] *F; not in Qq.*

95. *eighty*] Actually 68 at the time.
96. *of teen*] Teen means misery or grief (OED *sb.*¹ 3); the compositor of   Q₁ left the space out between the words.
97–103.] See Appendix 1.

SCENE II

The trumpets sound a sennet. Enter RICHARD *in pomp, crowned;*
BUCKINGHAM, CATESBY, RATCLIFFE, LOVELL *with other* Nobles
[*and a* Page].

K. Rich. Stand all apart. Cousin of Buckingham!
Buck. My gracious sovereign!
K. Rich. Give me thy hand.

Here he ascendeth the throne. Sound [*trumpets*].

Thus high, by thy advice
And thy assistance is King Richard seated.
But shall we wear these glories for a day,   5
Or shall they last, and we rejoice in them?
Buck. Still live they, and for ever let them last!
K. Rich. Ah, Buckingham, now do I play the touch
To try if thou be current gold indeed.

Scene 11

SCENE 11] *As* F (*Scena Secunda*)*; not in* Qq.   S.D. *The trumpets sound*] Qq; *not
in* F.   *a sennet.*] F; *not in* Qq.   *in pomp*] F; *not in* Qq.   *crowned*] Qq; *not
in* F.   *Ratcliff, Lovell*] F; *not in* Qq.   *with other* Nobles] Qq; *not in* F.
[*and a* Page] *As Capell; not in* F,Qq.   2. Buck. My gracious sovereign!] F;
not in Qq.   3. S.D. *Here he ascendeth the throne*] Qq (*the throne* Q*1–2; throne*
Q*3; his throne* Q*4–6*)*; not in* F.   *Sound*] F; *not in* Qq.   *trumpets*] *As White;
not in* F,Qq.   3–4.] *As Rowe;* . . . hand. / Thus . . . assistance, / Is . . . seated:
F; . . . hand. / Thus . . . aduice / And . . . seated Qq.   5. glories] F; honours
Qq.   7. for ever] F,Q*1,3–6;* for for euer Q*2.*   let them] F; may they Qq.
8. Ah] F; O Qq.   do I] F,Q*1–2;* I do Q*3–6* (*subst.*).

S.D.] The direction printed here is
mainly a conflation of Q and F which
together provide most of the require-
ments for this 'state'-scene. Perhaps
'the throne thrust out' ought to be
added since it is clear from l. 3 and
the previous S.D. that Richard sits
on a formal throne. The Page is a
subsequent necessity, and we may
assume that the company put on the
stage as many hired men as could be
spared and for whom there were
costumes: perhaps eight. The omission of Lovell and Ratcliffe from Q
may be a deliberate economy measure; see Introduction, pp. 16–17.

1. *Stand all apart*] An order for his

followers to step back and clear a
space.

3. S.D.] This too conflates Q and
F. The action is clear: the procession
having entered comes to a halt;
Richard takes Buckingham's arm
and with him goes up the step or so
to the throne, thus effectively isolating
him and his protégé from the on-
lookers. The practice of private
scheming in the most public place is
thoroughly in Richard's character;
cf. i.ii.

8. *play the touch*] Play the part of a
touchstone to test Buckingham's
assay.

9. *current gold*] i.e. genuine coin.

Young Edward lives—think now what I would speak. 10
Buck. Say on, my loving lord.
K. Rich. Why, Buckingham, I say I would be King.
Buck. Why so you are, my thrice-renowned lord.
K. Rich. Ha, am I King? 'Tis so—but Edward lives.
Buck. True, noble Prince.
K. Rich.   O bitter consequence,   15
    That Edward still should live—true noble prince!
    Cousin, thou wast not wont to be so dull.
    Shall I be plain? I wish the bastards dead,
    And I would have it suddenly perform'd.
    What say'st thou now? Speak suddenly, be brief.   20
Buck. Your Grace may do your pleasure.
K. Rich. Tut, tut, thou art all ice; thy kindness freezes.
    Say, have I thy consent that they shall die?
Buck. Give me some little breath, some pause, dear lord,
    Before I positively speak in this;   25
    I will resolve you herein presently.   *Exit.*
Cat. The King is angry: see, he gnaws his lip.

10. speak] *F;* say *Qq.*   11. loving lord] *F;* gracious soueraigne *Qq.*   13.
lord] *F;* liege *Qq.*   15.] *As Steevens; . . .* Prince. / O . . . consequence! *F, Qq.*
17. wast] *F;* wert *Qq.*   20. say'st thou now] *F;* saist thou *Q1–5;* saiest thou
Q6.   22. freezes] *F;* freezeth *Qq.*   24. little breath, some pause] *F;* breath,
some little pause *Qq.*   dear] *F;* my *Qq.*   25. in this] *F;* herein *Qq.*
26. you herein presently] *F;* your grace immediatlie *Qq (subst.).*   26. S.D.]
F; Exit. | Q1; not in Q2–6.   27. gnaws his] *F;* bites the *Qq.*

11 and 24. *loving lord | dear lord*]
These are grouped together in case
they represent a considered change
in Q, whose more formal expressions
may be intended to reveal that by
l. 24 Buckingham is becoming aware
that Richard's is the smile on the
face of the tiger. However, in view of
the other substitutions Buckingham
is making hereabouts, it is more
likely that he is merely replacing his
words with the more commonplace
ones in Q, especially as 'gracious
sovereign' is the phrase he had
mislaid from l. 2; its reappearance in
l. 11 is perfectly characteristic of
Buckingham.
    12–13.] Cf. *Massacre at Paris,* sc.
xix: '*King:* I slew the *Guise,* because

I would be King. / *Queene Mother*:
King, why so thou wert before.'
(ll. 1066–7).
    15–16. *True . . . prince!*] There
seems to be no way to make Richard's
meaning clear by punctuation alone:
Alexander's has been adopted here,
though NCS calls it 'obscure'.
Richard picks up Buckingham's
vague reply, and turns its meaning,
to make it clear that Edward, while
he lives, is still the true Prince.
    19. *suddenly*] immediately, without
delay: OED 2. (Also l. 20.)
    27 ff.] Many eds give l. 28 as
'Aside to a bystander', after Capell,
and print Malone's direction to l.
28: 'He descends from the throne'.
Both of these are mistaken. Catesby

K. Rich. [*Aside*] I will converse with iron-witted fools
          And unrespective boys; none are for me
          That look into me with considerate eyes.   30
          High-reaching Buckingham grows circumspect.—
          Boy!
Page. My lord?
K. Rich. Know'st thou not any whom corrupting gold
          Will tempt unto a close exploit of death?   35
Page. I know a discontented gentleman,
          Whose humble means match not his haughty spirit;
          Gold were as good as twenty orators,
          And will, no doubt, tempt him to anything.
K. Rich. What is his name?
Page.   His name, my lord, is Tyrrel.   40
K. Rich. I partly know the man: go call him hither.

                                        Exit [*Page*].

28. *Aside*] *This edn; not in F,Qq.*   31. High] *F;* Boy, high *Q1–5; Boy,* high *Q6.*
32.] *F; not in Qq.*   33. My lord] *F,Q1–2;* Lord *Q3–6.*   34. Know'st] *F;*
Knowst *Q1,3–6;* Knowest *Q2.*   35. Will] *F;* Would *Qq.*   36. I] *F;* My
lord, I *Qq.*   37. spirit] *F;* mind *Qq.*   40.] *As Steevens; . . .* name? / His
. . . Tirrell. *F,Qq.*   41. I partly know the man:] *F; not in Qq.*   hither]
Pope; hither, / Boy. *F;* hither presentlie *Qq* (*subst.*).   41. S.D.] *As Camb.;*
Exit F; not in Qq.

is one of the group of courtiers on-
stage: he makes his remark to this
group generally; Richard is still
isolated on the throne, musing to
himself, then summoning the Page
from the main group to the throne
for private conversation. The old
tradition of simultaneous staging is
thus employed in this scene.

28. *iron-witted*] dull-witted or stu-
pid: OED iron *a*.3d and 4.

29. *unrespective*] heedless: OED 1,
citing this line.

30. *considerate*] careful, deliberate,
prudent: OED 1 and 2.

31. *High*] Q mistakenly prints
Richard's next line, the monosyllable
'Boy!', as the first word of this line,
perhaps an error of imposition. Q6
compounds the error by printing it
in italics, thus making it appear a
speech-prefix. The phrase 'high-

reaching' may have been suggested
by 'High reaching heades swimme
ofte in seas of smartes' (*Parts Added*,
p. 34, 'Fulgentius', l. 96).

35. *close*] secret.

41. *I partly know the man*] Evidently
means 'I have heard of the man' or 'I
have some idea who he is'.

hither] The F reading requires
explanation: 'Boy' is set alone on its
line save for the S.D. This page of F
(s3ᵛ) was set by Compositor A,
whose practice is to turn overlong
lines under to the left-hand margin.
He also regularly capitalizes 'Boy'
so the form found in F could be
merely a line too long for F measure.
The alternative, more likely explanation, is that the F corrector mistakenly
inserted the 'Boy' from l. 32 in the
wrong place, and failed to strike it
out.

[*Aside*] The deep-revolving, witty Buckingham
No more shall be the neighbour to my counsels.
Hath he so long held out with me, untir'd,
And stops he now for breath! Well, be it so.   45

Enter STANLEY *Earl of Derby.*

How now, Lord Stanley, what's the news?
Stan. Know, my loving lord,
The Marquess Dorset, as I hear, is fled
To Richmond in the parts where he abides.
K. Rich. Come hither, Catesby. Rumour it abroad   50
That Anne my wife is very grievous sick;
I will take order for her keeping close.
Enquire me out some mean poor gentleman,
Whom I will marry straight to Clarence' daughter—
The boy is foolish, and I fear not him.   55
Look how thou dream'st! I say again, give out
That Anne, my Queen, is sick and like to die.
About it, for it stands me much upon
To stop all hopes whose growth may damage me.
                                                      [*Exit Catesby.*]

---

42. *Aside*.] *This edn; not in F,Qq.*   43. counsels] *F;* counsell *Qq.*   45. Well, be it so.] *F; not in Qq.*   46. Lord Stanley, what's the news] *F;* what neewes vvith you *Qq* (*subst.*).   47–9.] *As Craig;* Know . . . Dorset / As . . . Richmond, / In . . . abides. *F;* My Lord, I heare the Marques Dorset / Is fled to Richmond, in those partes beyond the seas where he abides. *Qq* (*subst.*).   50. Come hither] *F; not in Qq.* Catesby.] *F;* Catesby. *Cat.* My Lord. *Qq.* Rumour it abroad] *As F;* new line, *Qq.*   51. very grievous sick] *F;* sicke and like to die. *Qq.*   53. poor] *F;* borne *Qq.*   57. Queen] *F;* wife *Qq.*   59. S.D.] *Capell; not in F, Qq.*

---

42. *revolving*] pondering: OED revolve *v.*4b.

witty] crafty, cunning: OED 2b.

47–9.] Neither F nor Q is metrical. The F corrector must have found 'Know, my loving lord' in the MS. while 'beyond the seas' was not; the lineation is less certain. Pope's neat solution cannot be accepted because it omits 'Know' and 'loving'. It seems best to retain F with some improvement of the lineation, after Craig (as do most modern eds).

50.] The reply given Catesby in Q is surely gag.

51. *very grievous sick*] The Q version of the phrase, 'sicke and like to die', is borrowed from l. 57, presumably by the actor.

52. *keeping close*] remaining in private.

53–5.] See II. ii. S.D. n.

58. *stands me much upon*] Transposition of preposition: Abbott §204; the meaning is 'it is imperative upon me'.

59. *stop*] Besides the obvious mean-

I must be married to my brother's daughter,   60
Or else my kingdom stands on brittle glass.
Murder her brothers, and then marry her—
Uncertain way of gain! But I am in
So far in blood that sin will pluck on sin;
Tear-falling pity dwells not in this eye.   65

Enter TYRREL.

Is thy name Tyrrel?
Tyr. James Tyrrel, and your most obedient subject.
K. Rich. Art thou indeed?
Tyr.   Prove me, my gracious lord.
K. Rich. Dar'st thou resolve to kill a friend of mine?
Tyr. Please you; but I had rather kill two enemies.   70
K. Rich. Why then thou hast it; two deep enemies,
Foes to my rest, and my sweet sleep's disturbers,
Are they that I would have thee deal upon.
Tyrrel, I mean those bastards in the Tower.
Tyr. Let me have open means to come to them,   75
And soon I'll rid you from the fear of them.
K. Rich. Thou sing'st sweet music. Hark, come hither,
        Tyrrel:

64. will pluck] *F,Q1*; plucke *Q2–5*; plucks *Q6*.   65. Tear] *F,Q1–5*; Teares
Q6.   68.] *As Steevens*; . . . indeed? / Proue *F,Qq*.   lord] *F*; soueraigne *Qq*.
70.] *As Qq*; . . . you: / But *F*.   Please you] *F*; I my Lord *Qq*.   enemies]
F,Q1; deepe enemies *Q2–6*.   71. then] *F*; there *Qq*.   72. disturbers] *F*;
disturbs *Qq*.   77.] *As Qq*; . . . Musique: / Hearke *F*.   Hark] *F*; *not in Qq*.

ing, it is worth noting that OED records (not till 1699, to be sure) a horticultural meaning: to pinch out the head of a plant (*v.* II. 29), which continues the metaphor of hopes which grow like plants.

61. *brittle glass*] A common image for the fragility of power; cf. *R2*, IV. i. 287–8; earlier instances occur in Lyly's *Sapho and Phao*, 1.i.4: 'Who climeth, standeth on glasse' or in the *Mirror*: 'I . . . sawe my state, as brittell as a glasse' ('Wolsey', ll. 466–7, p. 510) or 'brittle as the glas' ('Clarence', l. 88, p. 223).

63–4. *But . . . sin*] Another famous image; cf. *Mac.*, III. iv. 135–7. The original source is probably Seneca, *Agamemnon*, l. 115: 'per scelera semper sceleribus tutum est iter' ('through crime ever is the safe way for crime'). It had become proverbial in Shakespeare's time: Tilley C826; and is used in many works such as 'Buckingham' in the *Mirror* (see Introduction, p. 87).

70. *enemies*] Q's 'deep enemies' is picked up by the compositor from the next line.

72. *sweet sleep's disturbers*] Richard here acknowledges his guilty insomnia, while presenting a specious reason for it.

Go by this token. Rise, and lend thine ear.

He whispers in his ear.

There is no more but so: say it is done,

And I will love thee, and prefer thee for it.   80

Tyr. I will dispatch it straight.   *Exit.*

Enter BUCKINGHAM.

Buck. My lord, I have consider'd in my mind

The late request that you did sound me in.

K. Rich. Well, let that rest. Dorset is fled to Richmond.

Buck. I hear the news, my lord.   85

K. Rich. Stanley, he is your wife's son. Well, look unto it.

Buck. My lord, I claim the gift, my due by promise,

For which your honour and your faith is pawn'd:

Th'earldom of Hereford, and the moveables

Which you have promised I shall possess.   90

K. Rich. Stanley, look to your wife; if she convey

Letters to Richmond, you shall answer it.

Buck. What says your Highness to my just demand?

78. this] *F;* that *Qq.*   78. S.D.] *Qq; Whispers. F.*   79. There is] *F;* Tis *Qq.*
it is] *F,Q 3-5;* is it *Q 1-2,6.*   80. for it] *F;* too *Qq.*   81.] *F;* 'Tis done my
gracious lord. / *Rich.* Shal we heare from thee. *Tirrel* ere we sleep? / *Tir.* Ye
shall my lord, *Qq (subst.)* (Yea my good Lord *Q6*).   81. S.D. *Exit*] *F; not
in Qq.*   83. request] *F;* demand *Qq.*   84. rest] *F;* passe *Qq.*   85. the]
F; that *Qq.*   86. son] *F,Q 2-6;* sonnes *Q 1.*   unto] *F;* to *Qq.*   87. the]
F; your *Qq.*   89. Th'earldom] *F;* The Earledom *Qq.*   Hereford] *Q 1-3,
5-6* (Herford); Herfort *Q 4;* Hertford *F.*   90. Which] *F;* The which *Qq.*
you have] *F;* you *Q 1,3-6;* your *Q 2.*   shall] *F;* should *Qq.*   93. demand]
Qq; request *F.*

78. S.D.] The more explicit Q
form is used to show that Richard
whispers, not ll. 79–80, but rather
some secret instructions for the
Princes' murder, which may require
a short pause to be made.

79. *it is*] The form found in Q1–2,6
cannot be right; normally one would
regard a derivative Q/F reading as a
corruption, but here it must be a
coincidental correction (see Introduction, p. 39).

81.] The additional question and
answer in Q here are identical with
III.i.188–9, the exchange between
Richard and Catesby. Daniel believed

the lines were intended to be transferred from Act III to here by a
reviser who realized that Catesby
did not in fact report to Richard as
promised; the lines were then also
left standing in Act III by oversight.
Patrick observes that such a revision
would be 'one of the poorest jobs ever
done' (pp. 60–1), and proposes
instead a duplication by the actors—
a likelier explanation.

86. *he*] i.e. Richmond: see I.iii.20 n.

93. *demand*] Buckingham grows
more peremptory, and the Q reading
'demand' seems a definite reinforce-
ment of the tone.

K. Rich. I do remember me, Henry the Sixth
    Did prophesy that Richmond should be King,   95
    When Richmond was a little peevish boy.
    A king . . . perhaps . . . perhaps—
Buck.   My lord!
K. Rich. How chance the prophet could not, at that time,
    Have told me—I being by—that I should kill him?
Buck. My lord, your promise for the earldom—   100
K. Rich. Richmond! When last I was at Exeter,
    The Mayor in courtesy show'd me the castle,
    And call'd it Rougemont, at which name I started,
    Because a bard of Ireland told me once
    I should not live long after I saw 'Richmond'.   105
Buck. My lord—
K. Rich. Ay—what's o'clock?
Buck. I am thus bold to put your Grace in mind
    Of what you promis'd me.
K. Rich. Well, but what's o'clock?   110
Buck. Upon the stroke of ten.
K. Rich. Well, let it strike.
Buck. Why let it strike?
K. Rich. Because that like a jack thou keep'st the stroke
    Betwixt thy begging and my meditation.   115
    I am not in the giving vein today.
Buck. May it please you to resolve me in my suit?

---

94. I do . . . me] *F;* As I *Qq.*   97.] *As Q 1–3,5–6* (A king perhaps, perhaps);
A King perhaps. *F,Q4.*   My lord!] *Qq; not in F.*   98–116.] *As Qq; not in F.*
114. keep'st] *Q1,3,5–6* (keepst); keepest *Q2,4.*   117.] *F;* Whie then resolue
me whether you wil or no? *Qq (subst.).*

94–6.] See *3H6,* IV.vi.66–76.
98–116.] See Appendix I.
98. *prophet*] i.e. Henry VI.
101. *Exeter*] The story Richard
recounts here appears only in Holinshed (745/2–746/1); the source was
John Hooker (alias Vowell) of that
city (mentioned by Holinshed in a
shoulder-note) and the date of
Richard's visit was November 1483.
103. *Rougemont*] 'The popular pronunciation of "Rougemont" and
"Richmond" may have been so
nearly alike as to make the play on

words tolerable' (Thompson).
114. *jack*] the figure of a man which
strikes the bell on the outside of a
clock: OED *sb.*[1] 1.6; the word also
has overtones of OED *sb.*[1] 1.2: a low-
bred or ill-mannered fellow (as at
I.iii.53). John Hutchins, in his
*History and Antiquities of the County of
Dorset* (3rd edn, 1868, III. 207/2) has
an extended account of the 'Jackman'
at Wimborne Minster—the life-size
figure actuated by the clockwork to
strike the quarter-hours.

K. Rich. Thou troublest me; I am not in the vein.

Exit [followed by all save Buckingham].

Buck. And is it thus? Repays he my deep service
 With such contempt? Made I him King for this?   120
 O let me think on Hastings, and be gone
 To Brecknock while my fearful head is on.   *Exit.*

[SCENE III]

Enter TYRREL.

Tyr. The tyrannous and bloody act is done;
 The most arch deed of piteous massacre
 That ever yet this land was guilty of.
 Dighton and Forrest, who I did suborn
 To do this piece of ruthless butchery—   5
 Albeit they were flesh'd villains, bloody dogs—
 Melted with tenderness and mild compassion,
 Wept like two children, in their deaths' sad story.

---

118. Thou] *F; Tut, tut, thou Qq.*   118. S.D.] *This edn after Capell; Exit. | F,Qq.*   119. And is it thus] *F; Is it euen so Qq.*   Repays] *F; rewardst Q1; rewards Q2–6.*   deep] *F; true Qq.*   120. contempt] *F; deepe contempt Qq.*

Scene III

SCENE III] *Pope; not in F,Qq.*   S.D.] *F; Enter Sir Francis Tirrell. | Qq.* 1. act] *F; deed Qq.*   2. deed] *F; act Qq.*   4. who] *F; whom Qq.* 5. piece of ruthless] *Pope; ruthles peece of Q1–2 (subst.); ruthfull peece of Q3–6; peece of ruthfull F.*   6. Albeit] *F; Although Qq.*   7. Melted] *F; Melting Qq.*   mild] *F; kind Q1–5; not in Q6.*   8. two] *Qq; to F.* deaths'] *F,Q1–3,5–6 (deaths); death Q4.*   story] *F; stories Qq.*

---

122. *Brecknock*] Buckingham's family seat of Brecon, in Wales.

Scene III

1 ff.] The actor playing Tyrrel seems to have had a very indifferent memory, to judge by the number of variants in this short scene. For the source of Tyrrel's narration, see Introduction, pp. 96–7; also cf. the dumb-show of the smothering of the young Princes in bed in *Alcazar*.

4. *Dighton and Forrest*] Named in More; see Appendix III, p. 362

5. *piece of ruthless*] It seems clear here that the F corrector properly changed the Q word-order but neglected to correct the adjective.

6. *flesh'd*] inured to bloodshed, hardened (OED 2a); 'hounds were said to be fleshed when they ate of the first game which they killed' (Thompson).

8. *in . . . story*] i.e. in the telling of the story of their deaths.

'O thus', quoth Dighton, 'lay the gentle babes';
'Thus, thus', quoth Forrest, 'girdling one another   10
Within their alabaster innocent arms;
Their lips were four red roses on a stalk,
And in their summer beauty kiss'd each other.
A book of prayers on their pillow lay,
Which once', quoth Forrest, 'almost chang'd my mind.
But O, the Devil—' There the villain stopp'd,   16
When Dighton thus told on: 'We smothered
The most replenished sweet work of Nature,
That from the prime creation e'er she fram'd.'
Hence both are gone with conscience and remorse   20
They could not speak, and so I left them both
To bear this tidings to the bloody King;

Enter KING RICHARD.

And here he comes. All health, my sovereign lord.
K. Rich. Kind Tyrrel, am I happy in thy news?
Tyr. If to have done the thing you gave in charge   25
Beget your happiness, be happy then,
For it is done.
K. Rich.   But did'st thou see them dead?
Tyr. I did, my lord.
K. Rich.   And buried, gentle Tyrrel?

9. O] *F;* Lo *Qq.*   the] *F;* those *Q 1–5;* these *Q 6.*   gentle] *F;* tender *Qq.*
11. alabaster innocent] *F;* innocent alablaster *Qq.*   12. lips were] *F,Q 1;* lips
Q 2; lips like *Q 3–6.*   13. And] *F;* Which *Q 1–5;* When *Q 6.*   15. once]
Qq; one *F.*   16. There] *F,Q 3–6;* their *Q 1–2.*   17. When] *F;* Whilst *Qq.*
(*subst.*).   19. e'er she] *F;* euer he *Qq.*   20.] *F,Q 1–2; not in Q 3–6.*
Hence] *F;* Thus *Q 1–2.*   22. bear] *F;* bring *Qq.*   this] *F,Q 1–5;* these *Q 6.*
22. S.D. As *Qq* (*subst.*); *Enter Richard* | *F.*   23. comes. All] *F,Q 3–5;*
comes, all *Q 1–2;* come. All *Q 6.*   health] *F;* haile *Qq.* lord] *F;* leige *Qq*
24. am] *F,Q 1–5;* and *Q 6.* (*subst.*).   25. gave] *F,Q 3–6;* giue *Q 1–2.*   27.] *As*
Steevens; . . . done. | But F; . . . Lord. | But Qq.   done] *F;* done my Lord
Qq.   28.] As *Steevens; . . . Lord. | And F,Qq.*

11. *alabaster*] Shakespeare com-
monly associates the image, applied
to a sleeping victim before death,
with a recumbent figure upon a
tomb (Dover Wilson in NCS). Cf.
Lucr., l. 419.

18. *replenished*] Qualifies 'sweet'; it
means full or perfect: OED, citing

this line.

19. *e'er she*] Dame Nature is surely
feminine, and Q surely wrong.

20. *both*] i.e. Dighton and Forrest.

22. *tidings*] OED 2b (plural construed as singular). Cf. *John*, IV. ii. 115.

25. *gave*] Another coincidental
correction originating in Q 3.

Tyr. The chaplain of the Tower hath buried them,
  But where, to say the truth, I do not know.   30
K. Rich. Come to me, Tyrrel, soon at after-supper,
  When thou shalt tell the process of their death.
  Meantime, but think how I may do thee good,
  And be inheritor of thy desire.
  Farewell till then.
Tyr.   I humbly take my leave.   *Exit.*   35
K. Rich. The son of Clarence have I pent up close;
  His daughter meanly have I match'd in marriage;
  The sons of Edward sleep in Abraham's bosom,
  And Anne my wife hath bid this world good night.
  Now, for I know the Breton Richmond aims   40
  At young Elizabeth, my brother's daughter,
  And by that knot looks proudly on the crown—
  To her go I, a jolly thriving wooer.

Enter RATCLIFFE.

30. But where, to say the truth] *F;* But how or in what place *Qq.*   31. *K. Rich.*] *F; Tir. | Q1–2; King. | Q3–6.* And *Qq.*   35. then] *F;* soone *Qq.* in *Qq.*   35. S.D.] *Qq (l. 33); not in F. F,Qq* (Brittaine *F;* Britaine *Qq*), Capell. on] *F;* ore *Qq.*   43. go I] *F;* I go *Qq.*   31. *K. Rich.* at] *Qq;* and *F.*   32. When] *F; Tyr.* I humbly take my leave] *F; not* 39. this] *F;* the *Qq.*   40. Breton] 41. At] *F,Q1–5;* And *Q6.*   42. 43. S.D. *Ratcliffe*] *F; Catesby | Qq.*

31. *K. Rich.*] Q1's giving this to Tyrrel is mere accidental eye-skip, which Q3 rectified.
  at after-supper] Cf. *MND*, v.i.33–4: 'this long age of three hours / Between our after-supper and bed-time'; see n. in Arden edn, which makes it clear that Shakespeare means 'dessert' by the term, rather than 'rere-supper', the other available meaning.
  35 and S.D.] Perhaps in inserting the phrase for Tyrrel omitted in Q, the corrector overlooked or obscured the '*exit*' in the margin.
  36–7.] See II.ii.n.
  38. *sleep . . . bosom*] Tilley A8.
  40. *Breton*] The term or a derivative occurs six times in the play. There is no doubt that Shakespeare, like his compositors, spelled it in something

like the way it appears in Q and F. Except in *Cym.* the word 'Britain' almost exclusively means 'Breton' or 'Brittany' in Shakespeare; see OED Britain *sb.*2; *a* and *sb.*2. Richmond was not, of course, a Breton: the epithet is transferred as a term of abuse; he was in exile there.
  aims] i.e. at her hand in marriage.
  42. *knot*] i.e. prospective marriage.
  43. S.D. *Ratcliffe*] The roles of Catesby and Ratcliffe, which were interchanged in Q in Act III, are still at variance. Both texts require Catesby in IV.ii; Ratcliffe appears to be omitted from Q, and is deleted here thus keeping him off-stage until the latter part of IV.iv. See also Introduction, pp. 16–17.

Rat. My lord!

K. Rich. Good or bad news, that thou com'st in so bluntly?

Rat. Bad news, my lord. Morton is fled to Richmond,   46
  And Buckingham, back'd with the hardy Welshmen,
  Is in the field, and still his power increaseth.

K. Rich. Ely with Richmond troubles me more near
  Than Buckingham and his rash-levied strength.   50
  Come: I have learn'd that fearful commenting
  Is leaden servitor to dull delay;
  Delay leads impotent and snail-pac'd beggary:
  Then fiery expedition be my wing,
  Jove's Mercury, and herald for a king.   55
  Go muster men. My counsel is my shield.
  We must be brief, when traitors brave the field.   *Exeunt.*

SCENE IV

Enter old QUEEN MARGARET.

Marg. So now prosperity begins to mellow,
  And drop into the rotten mouth of death.
  Here in these confines slily have I lurk'd

44. *Rat.*] *F; Cat.* | *Qq.*   45. Good or bad news] *F;* Good newes or bad *Qq.*
com'st in] *F,Q 1* (comst); comest in *Q 2–6.*   46. *Rat.*] *F; Cates.* | *Qq* (subst.).
Morton] *F;* Ely *Qq.*   50. strength] *F;* armie *Qq* (subst.).   51. learn'd] *F;*
heard *Qq.*   54. wing] *F,Q 1–2;* wings *Q 3–6.*   55. Jove's] *F,Q 1–2* (Ioues);
Ioue *Q 3,5–6;* Loue *Q 4.*   56. Go] *F;* Come *Qq.*

Scene IV

SCENE IV] *Pope; Scena Tertia.* | *F; not in Qq.*   S.D.] *F; Enter Queene Margaret*
sola. Qq.

46. *Morton*] Q changes to 'Ely',
which may have been accidental: cf.
the Derby/Stanley variants (Introduction, p. 13).

51. *fearful commenting*] nervous
discussion.

53. *snail-pac'd beggary*] Tilley S579.

54. *expedition*] speed, promptness:
OED 5.

55. *Jove's Mercury*] '"Fiery expedition" is to herald Richard's entry into
the field, and be the Mercury to his

Jove' (Thompson).

56. *My . . . shield*] He has rejected
discussion in ll. 51–2; his counsel
therefore will be not his counsellors
but his weapons (shield).

57. *brief*] expeditious, hasty: OED
brief *a.*A.1 b.

Scene IV

1–2. *mellow . . . drop*] Cf. I. i. 1–2: the
'glorious summer' has changed to
decaying autumn.

To watch the waning of mine enemies.
A dire induction am I witness to,   5
And will to France, hoping the consequence
Will prove as bitter, black, and tragical.

Enter DUCHESS OF YORK *and* QUEEN ELIZABETH.

Withdraw thee, wretched Margaret: who comes here?
Eliz. Ah, my poor Princes! Ah, my tender babes,
    My unblow'd flowers, new-appearing sweets!   10
    If yet your gentle souls fly in the air,
    And be not fix'd in doom perpetual,
    Hover about me with your airy wings,
    And hear your mother's lamentation.
Marg. [*Aside*] Hover about her; say that right for right   15
    Hath dimm'd your infant morn to aged night.
Duch. So many miseries have craz'd my voice
    That my woe-wearied tongue is still and mute.
    Edward Plantagenet, why art thou dead?
Marg. [*Aside*] Plantagenet doth quit Plantagenet: 20
    Edward, for Edward, pays a dying debt.

4. enemies] *F;* aduersaries *Qq.*   7. S.D.] *As F (after l. 8); Enter the Qu. and
the Dutchesse of Yorke.* | *Qq (after l. 8).*   9. poor] *F;* young *Qq.*   10. un-
blow'd] *F;* vnblowne *Qq.*   flowers] *F,Q1–5;* flower *Q6.*   13. about]
F,Q1–5; aboue *Q6.*   15, 20, 25. [*Aside*] *NCS, conj. Abbott; not in F,Qq.*
17–19.] *As F; after l. 34 Qq.*   18. still and mute] *F;* mute and dumb *Qq.*
20–1.] *F; not in Qq.*

5. *induction*] prologue. Margaret
develops a theatrical metaphor, continued in l. 7.

7. *black*] The emblematic colour of
tragedy on the Elizabethan stage.

7. S.D.] Moved to this position
because the entrance must be made before the character on stage reacts to it.

8. *Withdraw*] i.e. stand apart, not
exit.

10. *unblow'd*] immature, cut before
they reached ripeness.

new-appearing sweets] flowers but
newly opened.

12. *doom*] judgement: OED *sb.*2; it
does not mean hostile judgement. In
other words, Elizabeth prays for the
souls of her children to 'hover about'

her unless they have already received
their final judgement.

15. *right for right*] 'Justice answering
to the claims of justice' (Johnson).

17–21.] Patrick (p. 45) suggests
either confusion of cues or the 'carelessness of a printer who first omitted
and later patched' to account for the
lacuna in Q. But no printer would
patch in such a way deliberately, so
the former alternative is probably
correct.

17. *craz'd*] broken, cracked: OED 1.
Cf. *Err.*, v.i. 308–11.

19. *Edward Plantagent*] The Duchess
could mean either Edward IV or
Edward V: probably, the latter.

21. *Edward, for Edward*] Probably

Eliz. Wilt thou, O God, fly from such gentle lambs,
      And throw them in the entrails of the wolf?
      When didst Thou sleep when such a deed was done?
Marg. [*Aside*] When holy Harry died, and my sweet son.   25
Duch. Dead life, blind sight, poor mortal living ghost;
      Woe's scene, world's shame, grave's due by life usurp'd;
      Brief abstract and record of tedious days,
      [*Sitting*] Rest thy unrest on England's lawful earth,
      Unlawfully made drunk with innocent blood.   30
Eliz. Ah, that thou wouldst as soon afford a grave
      As thou canst yield a melancholy seat,
      Then would I hide my bones, not rest them here.
      [*Sitting*] Ah, who hath any cause to mourn but we?
Marg. If ancient sorrow be most reverend   35
      Give mine the benefit of seigniory,
      And let my griefs frown on the upper hand.
      If sorrow can admit society,
      Tell o'er your woes again by viewing mine.

25. Harry] *F,Q 1–2;* Mary *Q 3–6.*   26. Dead life, blind sight] *F;* Blind sight, dead life *Qq.*   28.] *F; not in Qq.*   29. thy] *F,Q 1–4;* they *Q 5;* their *Q 6.*
29. S.D.] *As Capell; not in F,Qq.*   30. Unlawfully] *F,Q 1–5;* Vnlawfull *Q 6.*
innocent] *F;* innocents *Qq.*   31. Ah] *F;* O *Qq.*   as soon] *F;* aswel *Q 1;*
as well *Q 2–6.*   33. S.D.] *This edn; not in F,Qq.*   34. Ah] *F;* O *Qq.*
we] *F;* I *Qq.*   35. reverend] *Camb.;* reuerent *F,Qq.*   36. seigniory] *F,Qq*
(signeurie *F;* signorie *Q 1–5;* signiorie *Q 6); seniory *Camb.*   37. griefs] *F;*
woes *Qq.*   hand.] *Warb.;* hand *F;* hand, *Qq.*   39.] *Qq; not in F.*   o'er]
Warb.; ouer *Qq.*

Edward V, in exchange for Edward, Prince of Wales, Henry VI's son.

a dying debt] i.e. a debt paid by his death; probably echoing the proverb 'death pays all debts' (Tilley D148; see also M800).

22–3.] The image first occurs in Rous's Latin *Historia* (Churchill, p. 47) but there are Biblical connotations: cf. John, x.12.

25. *Harry*] Q3, faced with an unusual saint, produced a truly spectacular emendation.

28.] Omitted from Q probably by oversight.

29.] Cf. *Tit.*, iv.ii.31, probably echoing *Spanish Tragedy*, i.iii.5; iii.xiii.39.

29. S.D., 33. S.D.] Sitting on the ground was a traditional sign of extreme grief: cf. *R2*, iii.ii.155. Most eds since Capell have inserted directions to make the action explicit. Whether Margaret joins them is not clear from her dialogue; though her 'griefs frown on the upper hand' this phrase is probably meant figuratively. The director may decide.

36. *seigniory*] lordship, sovereignty: OED *sb.* 1.

37. *griefs*] Q's 'woes' appears by anticipation of l. 39. Cf. Tilley H95.

39.] Omitted from F, which rearranged the punctuation to suit. Perhaps this was the work of the compositor, following the omission of

I had an Edward, till a Richard kill'd him;　　　40
I had a husband, till a Richard kill'd him:
Thou hadst an Edward, till a Richard kill'd him;
Thou hadst a Richard, till a Richard kill'd him.
Duch. I had a Richard too, and thou didst kill him;
I had a Rutland too: thou holp'st to kill him.　　　45
Marg. Thou hadst a Clarence too, and Richard kill'd him.
From forth the kennel of thy womb hath crept
A hell-hound that doth hunt us all to death:
That dog, that had his teeth before his eyes,
To worry lambs, and lap their gentle blood;　　　50
That excellent grand tyrant of the earth,
That reigns in galled eyes of weeping souls;

41. husband] *F;* Richard *Qq;* Henry *Rann, conj. Capell;* Harry *Camb.*　　45.
too: thou holp'st] *F2;* too, thou hop'st *F;* to, thou hopst *Q1;* too, thou hopst
Q2; too, and thou holpst *Q3–6.*　　46.] *As Qq; . . .* too, / And *F.*　　and] *F,*
Q1; till *Q2–6.*　　50. blood] *F;* bloods *Qq.*　　51–3.] *This edn;* That foule . . .
handy worke: / That reignes . . . soules: / That excellent . . . earth, *F;* That
foul . . . handiwork, / That excellent . . . earth, / That reigns . . . souls,
Capell; That foule . . . handie worke, *Qq; ll. 51–2 not in Qq.*

the line (which is essential) by the F
corrector.

41. *husband*] Eds have been
reluctant to accept F here on the
grounds that the word interrupts a
formal series of proper names. It has
been suggested that the F corrector
misread his MS. which had either
'Henry' (Capell) or 'Harry' (Camb.).
The intrusive 'Richard' in Q then
could be compositor-error—not unlikely in a string of names beginning
so similarly. But this explanation
assumes the coincidence of a double
error; there seems to be no absolute
need to emend F.

42. *Edward*] Edward V.

43. *hadst a Richard*] The younger of
the two Princes, Richard Duke of
York.

44. *Richard*] The Duchess's husband,
the former Duke of York.

45. *Rutland*] The Duchess's second
son.

too: thou holp'st] All texts here mean
the same thing, but the accidentals

are unusually confusing, and so have
been spelled out in the apparatus.
The only error is the introduction of
'and' into Q3–6.

47. *kennel . . . womb*] Her womb is a
kennel because Richard, dog-like, was
born with teeth. See also Tilley T234.

51–3.] All eds concede that the
lines here printed as 51–2 (which are
not in Q) were so inserted into F
copy that they appeared in print in
the wrong order. 'Tyrant' must be
the subject of 'reigns', so l. 52 must
follow l. 51. If this is so, it is by no
means unlikely that the entire insertion was misplaced too, and that
l. 53 (which is usually given before
l. 51) should be half of the rhetorical
climax of Margaret's period. The
structure is much more coherent thus,
and the mechanism plausible.

51. *excellent*] unequalled, pre-
eminent (no favourable connotation):
OED *a.* B.1b.

52. *galled*] sore from chafing: OED
galled *ppl. a.*[2] 1b.

That foul defacer of God's handiwork
Thy womb let loose to chase us to our graves.
O upright, just, and true-disposing God!   55
How do I thank thee, that this carnal cur
Preys on the issue of his mother's body,
And makes her pew-fellow with others' moan.
Duch. O, Harry's wife, triumph not in my woes.
God witness with me, I have wept for thine.   60
Marg. Bear with me: I am hungry for revenge,
And now I cloy me with beholding it.
Thy Edward he is dead, that kill'd my Edward;
Thy other Edward dead, to quit my Edward;
Young York, he is but boot, because both they   65
Match'd not the high perfection of my loss.
Thy Clarence he is dead, that stabb'd my Edward;
And the beholders of this frantic play,
Th'adulterate Hastings, Rivers, Vaughan, Grey,
Untimely smother'd in their dusky graves.   70
Richard yet lives, hell's black intelligencer,

---

59. wife] *F,Q2–6;* wifes *Q1.*   60. thine] *F,Q1;* thee *Q2–6.*   63. kill'd] *F;*
stabd *Qq.*   64. Thy] *Qq;* The *F.*   quit] *F,Q2–5;* quitte *Q1;* quite *Q6.*
66. Match'd] *F;* Match *Qq.*   67. stabb'd] *F;* kild *Qq.*   68. frantic] *F;*
tragicke *Qq.*

---

58. *pew-fellow*] one who shares a
pew in church: Margaret envisages a
pew full of grieving women, and
rejoices that the Duchess must join
them.

63. *Thy Edward*] Edward IV.
Margaret here launches a second
fearful litany of vengeance: see
Introduction, pp. 109–10.

kill'd] Margaret normally prefers
this more neutral word in her
summary here except at l. 67 where
the physicality of the death of her son
remains acute in her memory. Q
inadvertently reverses the words.

64. *Thy other Edward*] Edward V.
F's 'The other' is an unwanted
ambiguity (there being three Edwards) in a situation already fraught
with potential perplexity. It was
probably a compositorial slip.

quit] make a return for an injury

received: OED quit *v.* II. 11; also in
l. 20. The spelling variants here do
not indicate different meanings.

65. *boot*] that which is 'thrown in',
or given in addition, to make up a
deficiency of value: OED boot
sb.[1] 1.2.

68. *frantic*] frenzied, insane. Q's
'tragicke' is by no means a synonym,
and has the advantage of retaining
the theatrical imagery Margaret is
developing in these speeches: but this
alone does not make it so manifest an
improvement we can be certain it
originated with Shakespeare.

69. *adulterate*] adulterous. Margaret
refers to the scandal with Mistress
Shore.

71–3. *Richard . . . thither*] One of the
strongest statements of Richard's
demonic function: see Introduction,
pp. 89 and 103. Intelligencer means

Only reserv'd their factor to buy souls
And send them thither. But at hand, at hand
Ensues his piteous and unpitied end.
Earth gapes, hell burns, fiends roar, saints pray,   75
To have him suddenly convey'd from hence.
Cancel his bond of life, dear God I pray,
That I may live and say 'The dog is dead.'
Eliz. O, thou didst prophesy the time would come
That I should wish for thee to help me curse   80
That bottled spider, that foul bunch-back'd toad.
Marg. I call'd thee then vain flourish of my fortune;
I call'd thee, then, poor shadow, painted queen,
The presentation of but what I was;
The flattering index of a direful pageant;   85
One heav'd a-high, to be hurl'd down below;
A mother only mock'd with two fair babes;
A dream of what thou wast; a garish flag
To be the aim of every dangerous shot;
A sign of dignity; a breath, a bubble;   90
A queen in jest, only to fill the scene.
Where is thy husband now? Where be thy brothers?

---

73. at hand, at hand] *F,Q2–6;* at hand at handes *Q1.*   75. hell] *F,Q1–5;*
hels *Q6.*   76. from hence] *F;* away *Qq.*   78. and] *F;* to *Qq.*   81. bunch-
back'd] *F,Q1;* hunch-backt *Q2–6.*   87. fair] *F;* sweet *Qq.*   88–90.] *F;* A
dreame of which thou wert a breath, a bubble, / A signe of dignitie, a garish
flagge, / To be the aime of euerie dangerous shot, *Qq. (subst.).*

---

agent or spy; 'their factor': the paid
agent of the powers of hell. Richard
'buys' souls with flattery and deceit.

76. *convey'd*] carried or taken
forcibly (OED *v.* 3) with the implication of 'dragged to death'. Cf.
'conveyance', l. 283.

77. *bond of life*] In view of the
Faustian overtones of ll. 71–6, perhaps
the implication is that the bond to
which Richard owes his survival and
his success is diabolical, and ought
therefore to be terminated.

81. *bottled . . . toad*] See I.iii.242–6.
82. *flourish*] See I.iii.241 n.
84. *presentation of but*] the representation (as in a theatre) only of. For

this position of 'but' see Abbott §129.

85. *flattering . . . pageant*] Also
theatrical; the index (flattering because puffing what follows) is the
prologue to the ensuing frightening
pageant. The index to many Renaissance books was at the beginning.

86.] A reference to the motion of
Fortune's wheel.

88–90] The order of Margaret's
attack in F progressively diminishes
Elizabeth to the negligible, ending
with a 'bubble'. It is patently preferable to Q's order.

90. *sign*] symbol or image (as
distinct from the real thing).

91.] Again, a theatrical image.

Where are thy two sons? Wherein dost thou joy?
Who sues, and kneels, and says 'God save the Queen'?
Where be the bending peers that flatter'd thee?   95
Where be the thronging troops that follow'd thee?
Decline all this, and see what now thou art:
For happy wife, a most distressed widow;
For joyful mother, one that wails the name;
For one being sued to, one that humbly sues;   100
For Queen, a very caitiff, crown'd with care;
For she that scorn'd at me, now scorn'd of me;
For she being fear'd of all, now fearing one;
For she commanding all, obey'd of none.
Thus hath the course of justice whirl'd about   105
And left thee but a very prey to time,
Having no more but thought of what thou wast
To torture thee the more, being what thou art.
Thou didst usurp my place, and dost thou not
Usurp the just proportion of my sorrow?   110
Now thy proud neck bears half my burden'd yoke,
From which even here I slip my weary head,
And leave the burden of it all on thee.
Farewell, York's wife, and Queen of sad mischance;

---

93. are] *Q1–2;* be *Q3–6,F.*   two sons] *F;* children *Qq.*   94. and kneels, and says] *F;* to thee, and cries *Qq.*   100–4.] *As F; ll. 101/100/104/102 Qq (l. 103 not in Qq).*   102. she] *F;* one *Qq.*   105. whirl'd] *F;* whe'eld *Q1;* wheel'd *Q2–6.*   107. wast] *F;* wert *Q1–2;* art *Q3–6.*   109. dost] *F;* doest *Qq.*   112. weary] *Q1–5;* wearied *Q6,F.*   head] *F;* necke *Qq.*

---

95. *bending*] bowing.

97. *Decline*] Figuratively; from the grammatical sense. See Baldwin, 1.567.

100–4] Another lineation tangle (compounded by a missing line in Q). Patrick, supported by Greg (*Ed. Prob.*, p. 82), observes that F order follows that of the questions just posed by Margaret (i.e. it is a declension): husband, sons, suitor, queen, and that Q's omission and confusion are characteristic actors' lapses.

101. *caitiff*] a poor wretch: OED 2.

105. *whirl'd*] NPS prefers Q's

'wheel'd', as an allusion to the Wheel of Fortune: but 'whirl'd' has the same implication of circular motion and besides suggests the giddy-making haste of the reversal of Elizabeth's condition. Cf. *Parts Added*, 'Vortiger', l. 225: 'lothsome Lucke did turne her whurling wheele' (p. 430).

106. *prey to time*] For the sense in which tragic figures are victims of time, see Northrop Frye's *Fools of Time* (Toronto, 1967).

111.] See Tilley N69.

112. *weary*] F obtains 'wearied' from Q6.

These English woes shall make me smile in France.   115

Eliz. O thou, well skill'd in curses, stay awhile
    And teach me how to curse mine enemies.

Marg. Forbear to sleep the nights, and fast the days;
    Compare dead happiness with living woe;
    Think that thy babes were sweeter than they were,   120
    And he that slew them fouler than he is:
    Bettering thy loss makes the bad-causer worse.
    Revolving this will teach thee how to curse.

Eliz. My words are dull: O quicken them with thine.

Marg. Thy woes will make them sharp and pierce like mine.

                                                    Exit.

Duch. Why should calamity be full of words?   126

Eliz. Windy attorneys to their clients' woes,
    Airy succeeders of intestate joys,
    Poor breathing orators of miseries:
    Let them have scope, though what they will impart   130
    Help nothing else, yet do they ease the heart.

Duch. If so, then be not tongue-tied; go with me
    And in the breath of bitter words let's smother
    My damned son, that thy two sweet sons smother'd.
    The trumpet sounds; be copious in exclaims.   135

Enter KING RICHARD *and his* Train [*including* CATESBY],
    marching with drums and trumpets.

115. woes] F,Q*1–3,5–6;* wars Q*q.*   shall] F; will Q*q.*   118. nights . . .
days] Q*1–2;* night . . . day Q*3–6,*F.   120. thy babes] F,Q*1–3,5–6;* babes Q*4.*
sweeter] F; fairer Q*q.*   122. causer] F,Q*1–3,5–6;* causes Q*4.*   125.] *As*
Q*q;* . . . sharpe, / And F.   127. their clients'] F (their Clients), *this edn;*
your Client Q*1–3,5–6;* your clients Q*4;* their client *Capell;* their client's *Eccles.*
128. intestate] Q*q;* intestine F.   130. will] F; do Q*q.*   131. nothing else]
F; not at al Q*q (subst.).*   134. that] F; which Q*q.*   135. The trumpet
sounds] F; I heare his drum Q*q.*   135. S.D. *and his* Train] F; *not in* Q*q.*
including Catesby] *This edn; not in* F,Q*q.* *marching with drums and trumpets*] Q*q; not
in* F.

118. *nights . . . days*] Q3's use of the
singular was followed accidentally by
F.

123.   *Revolving*]   pondering;   cf.
IV.i.42.

124. *quicken*] bring them to liveli-
ness.

127–8. See Appendix II.

135.   *trumpet*]   See   Introduction,
p. 18.

135. S.D.] As elsewhere, a conflation of F and Q gives a complete
direction; Catesby is needed, as he
must speak at l. 446.

K. Rich. Who intercepts me in my expedition?

Duch. O, she that might have intercepted thee—
   By strangling thee in her accursed womb—
   From all the slaughters, wretch, that thou hast done.

Eliz. Hid'st thou that forehead with a golden crown   140
   Where should be branded, if that right were right,
   The slaughter of the Prince that ow'd that crown,
   And the dire death of my poor sons and brothers?
   Tell me, thou villain-slave, where are my children?

Duch. Thou toad, thou toad, where is thy brother Clarence,
   And little Ned Plantagenet his son?   146

Eliz. Where is the gentle Rivers, Vaughan, Grey?

Duch. Where is kind Hastings?

K. Rich. A flourish, trumpets! Strike alarum, drums!
   Let not the heavens hear these tell-tale women   150
   Rail on the Lord's anointed. Strike, I say!

                                        Flourish; alarums.

   Either be patient and entreat me fair,
   Or with the clamorous report of war
   Thus will I drown your exclamations.

Duch. Art thou my son?   155

K. Rich. Ay, I thank God, my father, and yourself.

Duch. Then patiently hear my impatience.

K. Rich. Madam, I have a touch of your condition,
   That cannot brook the accent of reproof.

Duch. O let me speak.

K. Rich.   Do then, but I'll not hear.   160

136. me in] *F; not in Qq.*   137. O] *F; A Qq.*   141. Where] *Qq; Where't F.*
should] *F,Q1–3,5–6; would Q4.*   branded] *F; grauen Qq.*   right,] *Qq;*
right? *F.*   143. poor] *F; two Qq.*   145.] *As Qq; . . . Toade, / Where F.*
146. Plantagenet] *F,Q1–2,6; Plantaget Q3–5.*   147. the gentle] *F; kind*
Hastings *Qq.*   148.] *F; not in Qq.*   151. S.D.] *F; The trumpets / Q1; The*
trumpets sound. / Q2–6 (Q3–6 sounds).   153. clamorous] *F,Q1–3,5–6; clamour*
Q4.   159. That] *F; Which Qq.*   160.] *As Steevens; . . . speake. / Do F;*
not in Qq.

136. *expedition*] Here, probably, the
modern 'a setting forth with martial
intentions' (OED 2, as in *1H4*,
I.iii.150) rather than 'the quality of
haste or promptness' (OED 5, as at
IV.iii.54).

138. *accursed womb*] Cf. 'Seneca',

Octavia, ll. 371–2.
   142. *ow'd*] See OED *v.*B. 1: to
possess or own.
   148.] See Introduction, p. 18.
   151. S.D.] See Introduction, p. 18.
   153–60.] Cf. *John,* v.ii. 162–5.

Duch. I will be mild and gentle in my words.

K. Rich. And brief, good mother, for I am in haste.

Duch. Art thou so hasty? I have stay'd for thee,
God knows, in torment and in agony.

K. Rich. And came I not at last to comfort you?   165

Duch. No, by the holy Rood, thou know'st it well:
Thou cam'st on earth to make the earth my hell.
A grievous burden was thy birth to me;
Tetchy and wayward was thy infancy;
Thy school-days frightful, desp'rate, wild, and furious;
Thy prime of manhood daring, bold, and venturous; 171
Thy age confirm'd, proud, subtle, sly, and bloody:
More mild, but yet more harmful, kind in hatred.
What comfortable hour canst thou name
That ever grac'd me with thy company?   175

K. Rich. Faith, none but Humphrey Hower, that call'd your
Grace
To breakfast once, forth of my company.

---

161. words] *F;* speach *Qq* (subst.).   164. torment and in agony] *F;* anguish, paine and agonie *Qq.*   171.] *F,Q 1–2;* not in *Q 3–6.*   172. sly, and bloody] *F;* bloudie, trecherous *Qq.*   173.] *F; not in Qq.*   175. with] *F;* in *Qq.* 176.] *As Qq; . . .* Hower, / That *F.*   Humphrey] *Q 1–6;* Humfrey *F.* Hower] *F;* houre *Qq.*   177. my company] *F,Q 1–3,5–6;* companie *Q 4.*

---

164. *torment and in agony*] Surely the right reading; Q's version contains a tautology ('pain and agonie') more likely to have suggested itself to the actor than to the author.

166. *the holy Rood*] the Cross. More than an oath is intended, for in the ensuing lines (especially l. 167) the Duchess describes the birth and growth not of God Incarnate, but of the Anti-Christ. See Introduction, p. 103.

170. *frightful*] tending to cause fright: alarming (OED 2).

172. *age confirm'd*] 'The time of life at which early tendencies and character become fixed and settled' (Thompson).

173. *harmful, kind*] NCS reads 'harmful-kind', after S. Walker and Alexander. But 'mild' and 'harmful', 'kind' and 'hatred' balance each

other in apposition. Q omits the line.

176. *Humphrey Hower*] This is either the feeblest joke Richard ever makes, or an allusion to something of which we have no record. It is possible that a proper name is intended, for which reason this edn retains F's spelling 'Hower' (pronounced, of course, 'hour'). Speculation has ranged on possible meanings, with Rossiter (*DUJ*, 68) the most widely accepted. He develops the suggestion of Steevens and Malone that 'dining with Duke Humphrey' was an Elizabethan phrase for going hungry. So Humphrey's hour = mealtime, when Richard was born, and the Duchess could eat without him. See also Variorum, pp. 333–4; NCS suggests 'perhaps an obs. expression familiar to Elizabethan midwives'; Eccles 'apparently the name of a man,

If I be so disgracious in your eye,
Let me march on and not offend you, madam.
Strike up the drum!

Duch.   I prithee, hear me speak.   180
K. Rich. You speak too bitterly.
Duch.   Hear me a word,
For I shall never speak to thee again.
K. Rich. So!
Duch. Either thou wilt die by God's just ordinance
Ere from this war thou turn a conqueror,   185
Or I with grief and extreme age shall perish,
And nevermore behold thy face again.
Therefore, take with thee my most grievous curse,
Which in the day of battle tire thee more
Than all the complete armour that thou wear'st.   190
My prayers on the adverse party fight;
And there the little souls of Edward's children
Whisper the spirits of thine enemies
And promise them success and victory.
Bloody thou art; bloody will be thy end.   195

---

178. If I] *F,Q1;* If it *Q2–3,5–6;* If *Q4.*   disgracious] *F,Q1–2;* gratious *Q3–6.*
eye] *F;* sight *Qq.*   179. you, madam] *F;* your grace *Qq.*   180.] *As
Steevens; . . .* Drumme. / I *F (Q diff.).*   Strike up the drum!] *F; not in
Qq.*   I prithee, hear me speak.] *F; not in Qq (but see l. 181).*   181.] *As
Steevens; . . .* bitterly. / Heare *F (Q diff.).*   You speak too bitterly] *F;*
Come, come, you are (art *Q1*) too bitter *Qq.*   181–2. Hear me a word, /
For I shall never speak to thee again] *F;* O heare me speake for I shall neuer
see thee more *Qq. (subst., after l. 179).*   183.] *F; not in Qq.*   187. nevermore
behold] *F;* neuer looke vpon *Qq.*   188. grievous] *F;* heauy *Qq.*   193.
spirits] *F,Q1–3,5–6;* spirit *Q4.*   195. art;] *F,Q1–5;* art, and *Q6.*

---

chosen for the play on "comfortable
hour"'; NPS more honourably admits
'unexplained'. It is more likely that a
satirical reference to some unidenti-
fied contemporary individual is meant
than the desperately weak play on
words Rossiter suggests.
180–3.] The variation in Q is
accounted for by the actor's having
telescoped the Duchess's words in
ll. 180 and 181–2 into a single line.
The omission of l. 183 from Q is probably inadvertent; that of Richard's

phrase from l. 180 may have something to do with the sound-effects: see
Introduction, p. 18.
188. *grievous*] In this context, this
word and Q's 'heauy' are synonyms
(OED heavy *a.*[1] VI.23).
190. *complete armour*] Accent on
first syllable. Richard, as King,
would be wearing full body armour
('cap-a-pe' as in *Ham.,* I.ii.200)
unlike the foot-soldiers, who would
wear the less cumbersome mail-shirt
or the brigander (as at III.v.S.D.).

Shame serves thy life and doth thy death attend.   *Exit.*

Eliz. Though far more cause, yet much less spirit to curse
Abides in me, I say Amen to her.

K. Rich. Stay, madam: I must talk a word with you.

Eliz. I have no more sons of the royal blood   200
For thee to slaughter. For my daughters, Richard,
They shall be praying nuns, not weeping queens,
And therefore level not to hit their lives.

K. Rich. You have a daughter call'd Elizabeth,
Virtuous and fair, royal and gracious.   205

Eliz. And must she die for this? O let her live,
And I'll corrupt her manners, stain her beauty,
Slander myself as false to Edward's bed,
Throw over her the veil of infamy;
So she may live unscarr'd of bleeding slaughter   210
I will confess she was not Edward's daughter.

K. Rich. Wrong not her birth; she is a royal princess.

Eliz. To save her life I'll say she is not so.

K. Rich. Her life is safest only in her birth.

Eliz. And only in that safety died her brothers.   215

K. Rich. Lo, at their birth good stars were opposite.

Eliz. No, to their lives ill friends were contrary.

K. Rich. All unavoided is the doom of destiny.

Eliz. True, when avoided grace makes destiny.
My babes were destin'd to a fairer death,   220
If grace had blest thee with a fairer life.

K. Rich. You speak as if that I had slain my cousins.

---

198. her] *F;* all *Qq.*   199. talk] *F;* speake *Qq.*   200. more] *F,Q2–6;* moe
Qq.   201. slaughter. For] *F;* murther for *Q1;* murther, for *Q2–6.*   210.
unscarr'd of] *F;* vnskard from *Qq* (*subst.*).   212. a royal princess] *F;* of roiall
bloud *Qq.* (*subst.*).   214. safest only] *F;* onlie safest *Qq* (*subst.*).   216.
birth] *F;* births *Qq.*   217. ill] *F;* bad *Qq.*   222–35.] *F; not in Qq.*

---

197. *spirit*] Frequently, as here, a
monosyllable.

202. *nuns*] Law observes that
Bridget, Elizabeth's third daughter,
was in fact a nun (Holinshed, p. 711,
from More; not in Hall).

203. *level*] aim (as with a weapon).

214. *safest only*] i.e. her life is most
safe because of her high birth.

218.] Tilley F83; also 'Clarence',
l. 128: 'Thinges nedes must drive as
destiny decreeth' (*Mirror*, p. 225).
Unavoided = unavoidable.

219. *avoided grace*] 'i.e. one who has
rejected the grace of God' (NCS).

222–35.] See Appendix I.

222. *that*] As a conjunctional affix:
Abbott §287.

Eliz. Cousins indeed! And by their uncle cozen'd
Of comfort, kingdom, kindred, freedom, life:
Whose hand soever lanc'd their tender hearts,   225
Thy head, all indirectly, gave direction.
No doubt the murd'rous knife was dull and blunt
Till it was whetted on thy stone-hard heart
To revel in the entrails of my lambs.
But that still use of grief makes wild grief tame,   230
My tongue should to thy ears not name my boys
Till that my nails were anchor'd in thine eyes,
And I in such a desp'rate bay of death,
Like a poor bark of sails and tackling reft,
Rush all to pieces on thy rocky bosom.   235
K. Rich. Madam, so thrive I in my enterprise
And dangerous success of bloody wars,
As I intend more good to you and yours
Than ever you or yours by me were harm'd.
Eliz. What good is cover'd with the face of heaven,   240
To be discover'd, that can do me good?
K. Rich. Th'advancement of your children, gentle lady.
Eliz. Up to some scaffold, there to lose their heads.
K. Rich. Unto the dignity and height of fortune,
The high imperial type of this earth's glory!   245

---

225. lanc'd] *As Rowe*³ *;* lanch'd *F.*   236–7.] *F;* Madam, so thriue I in my
dangerous attempt of hostile armes *Qq.*   238. I intend] *F, Q1–5;* Intend *Q6.*
239. or yours] *Q1–5;* and yours *Q6,F.*   by me were harm'd] *F;* were by me
wrongd *Qq.*   242. Th'] *F;* The *Qq.*   gentle] *F;* mightie *Qq.*   244.
Unto] *F;* No to *Qq*   fortune] *F;* honor *Qq.*   245. high] *F,Q1;* height *Q2–6.*

223. *Cousins*] Cf. Tilley C739.

230. *still*] constant: see Abbott §69.
The gist of ll. 230–5 is that Elizabeth
is only talking about her sons' death
(rather than physically attacking
Richard and so rushing to her death)
because her lamentations have somewhat tamed the wildness of her
grief.

234. *bark ... tackling*] a ship, lacking
sails and tackle (ropes, etc.). The
imagery of ll. 233–5 is of a helpless
ship obliged to anchor on a shore
which must destroy it.

236–7.] Patrick, defending his interpretation of the omission of ll. 222–35
as a theatrical cut, points out the
disturbance in Q here: the sixteener
can hardly be right.

237. *dangerous success*] hazardous
consequence (OED success *sb.*1).

243.] See Introduction, pp. 77–8.

245. *type*] emblem or symbol:
OED 1. Not, as usually annotated,
badge or stamp (OED 3): Richard
means that the earth's glory is
emblemized by the 'high imperial'
condition of royalty.

Eliz. Flatter my sorrow with report of it.
         Tell me what state, what dignity, what honour,
         Canst thou demise to any child of mine?
K. Rich. Even all I have—ay, and myself and all
         Will I withal endow a child of thine;   250
         So in the Lethe of thy angry soul
         Thou drown the sad remembrance of those wrongs
         Which thou supposest I have done to thee.
Eliz. Be brief, lest that the process of thy kindness
         Last longer telling than thy kindness' date.   255
K. Rich. Then know that from my soul I love thy daughter.
Eliz. My daughter's mother thinks it with her soul.
K. Rich. What do you think?
Eliz. That thou dost love my daughter from thy soul:
         So from thy soul's love didst thou love her brothers,   260
         And from my heart's love I do thank thee for it.
K. Rich. Be not so hasty to confound my meaning:
         I mean that with my soul I love thy daughter,
         And do intend to make her Queen of England.
Eliz. Well then, who dost thou mean shall be her king?   265
K. Rich. Even he that makes her Queen. Who else should be?
Eliz. What, thou?
K. Rich.   Even so. How think you of it?
Eliz. How canst thou woo her?

246. sorrow] *F;* sorrowes *Qq.*   249. ay] *F* (I); yea *Qq.*   255. date] *F;*
doe *Qq.*   256.] *As Qq;* ... know, / That *F.*   260. soul's love] *F,Q1–5;*
soule *Q6.*   thou love] *F,Q1,6;* thou *Q2–5.*   264. do intend] *F;* meane *Qq.*
265. Well] *F;* Saie *Qq.*   266.] *As Qq;* ... Queene: / Who *F.*   else should
be] *F;* should be else *Q1;* who should else *Q2–4,6;* how should else *Q5.*
266–7.] *As Steevens;* ... thou? / Euen ... it? / How ... her? / That ... you,
F; ... thou? / I ... Maddame? / How ... her? / That ... you. *Qq.*   267.
Even so] *F;* I euen I *Qq.*   How] *F;* What *Qq.*   it] *F;* it Maddame *Qq*
(*subst.*).

248. *demise*] convey or transmit in
the legal sense: OED *v.*2, citing this
line.

255. *date*] F is right; the word
completes the legal metaphor begun
in 'process'; cf. *Rom.,* 1.iv.106–11.

259. *from thy soul*] Wright truly
calls this 'a poor quibble'; Elizabeth
takes 'from' in the sense 'apart from'
or 'at variance with' (Abbott §158);

i.e. that Richard's 'love' is something
separate from his soul. She continues
the play in the next two lines.

264. *do intend*] Q's 'meane' is
caught from the previous line.

266. *else should be*] The modern
phrase 'who else?' obscures the fact
that in the sixteenth century Q's version
was the commoner word-order.

K. Rich.   That would I learn of you,
  As one being best acquainted with her humour.
Eliz. And wilt thou learn of me?
K. Rich.   Madam, with all my heart!
Eliz. Send to her, by the man that slew her brothers,   271
  A pair of bleeding hearts; thereon engrave
  'Edward' and 'York'. Then haply will she weep;
  Therefore present to her—as sometimes Margaret
  Did to thy father, steep'd in Rutland's blood—   275
  A handkerchief: which, say to her, did drain
  The purple sap from her sweet brother's body,
  And bid her wipe her weeping eyes withal.
  If this inducement move her not to love,
  Send her a letter of thy noble deeds: 280
  Tell her thou mad'st away her uncle Clarence,
  Her uncle Rivers—ay, and for her sake
  Mad'st quick conveyance with her good aunt Anne.
K. Rich. You mock me, madam; this is not the way
  To win your daughter!
Eliz.   There is no other way—   285
  Unless thou couldst put on some other shape,
  And not be Richard, that hath done all this.
K. Rich. Say that I did all this for love of her?
Eliz. Nay, then indeed she cannot chose but hate thee,
  Having bought love with such a bloody spoil.   290
K. Rich. Look what is done cannot be now amended:

268. would I] *Q 1–2;* I would *Q 3–6,F.*   269. being] *F;* that are *Q 1–2;* that
were *Q 3–6.*   270.] *As Steevens;* . . . me? / Madam *F,Qq.*   273. will she]
F; she will *Qq.*   274. sometimes] *Q 1–2;* sometime *Q 3–6,F.*   275–7.] *F;*
Did to thy father, a hankercher steept in Rutlands bloud, *Qq.*   278. wipe]
F; drie *Qq.*   withal] *F;* therewith *Qq.*   279. move] *F;* force *Qq.*   280.
letter] *F;* storie *Qq*   deeds] *F;* acts *Qq.*   281. mad'st] *F,Q 3–6;* madst
Q 1; madest *Q 2.*   282. ay] *F* (I); yea *Qq.*   283. Mad'st] *F;* Madst *Qq;*
Madest *Q 2–6.*   284. You] *F;* Come, come, you *Q 1–2;* Come, come, ye *Q 3–6.*
me, madam] *F;* me *Qq.*   285.] *As Steevens;* . . . daughter. / There *F,Qq.*
288–342.] *F; not in Qq.*

269. *humour*] disposition or character: OED *sb.*II.5b.
  274. *sometimes*] In this instance =
'on one specific occasion in the past'
(OED: sometimes 2 = sometime 2a).
Q3's normalization was overlooked
by the F corrector.

275–7.] See Introduction, p. 8.
  283. *conveyance*] forcible removal;
cf. l. 76.
  288–342.] See Introduction, p. 14.
  291.] Tilley T200. 'Look what'
means 'whatever' (Eccles, *JEGP*
(1943), pp. 386–400.)

Men shall deal unadvisedly sometimes,
Which after-hours gives leisure to repent.
If I did take the kingdom from your sons,
To make amends I'll give it to your daughter;   295
If I have kill'd the issue of your womb,
To quicken your increase, I will beget
Mine issue of your blood upon your daughter.
A grandam's name is little less in love
Than is the doting title of a mother;   300
They are as children but one step below;
Even of your metal, of your very blood;
Of all one pain, save for a night of groans
Endur'd of her, for whom you bid like sorrow.
Your children were vexation to your youth,   305
But mine shall be a comfort to your age;
The loss you have is but a son being King;
And by that loss your daughter is made Queen.
I cannot make you what amends I would:
Therefore accept such kindness as I can.   310
Dorset your son, that with a fearful soul
Leads discontented steps in foreign soil,
This fair alliance quickly shall call home
To high promotions and great dignity.
The King that calls your beauteous daughter wife,   315
Familiarly shall call thy Dorset brother;
Again shall you be mother to a king,
And all the ruins of distressful times
Repair'd with double riches of content.
What! We have many goodly days to see.   320
The liquid drops of tears that you have shed
Shall come again, transform'd to orient pearl,
Advantaging their loan with interest

323. loan] *Theobald;* loue *F.*

293. *Which*] i.e. which dealing.

297. *quicken . . . increase*] bring your descendants to life: OED increase *sb.*2b.

303–4.] Obscurely expressed: 'pain' means 'solicitude, trouble, effort' (OED *sb.*[1] 5 and 6); 'bid' is the past tense of 'bide' meaning to undergo or

to suffer (OED 9). Richard thus means that children and grandchildren are equally objects of one's care or trouble, except for the actual pain of birth the daughter must suffer—but the mother had previously suffered the like for her.

323–4. *loan . . . Of ten times*]

Of ten times double gain of happiness.
Go then, my mother; to thy daughter go: 325
Make bold her bashful years with your experience;
Prepare her ears to hear a wooer's tale;
Put in her tender heart th'aspiring flame
Of golden sovereignty; acquaint the Princess
With the sweet, silent hours of marriage joys,   330
And when this arm of mine hath chastised
The petty rebel, dull-brain'd Buckingham,
Bound with triumphant garlands will I come
And lead thy daughter to a conqueror's bed;
To whom I will retail my conquest won,   335
And she shall be sole victoress, Caesar's Caesar.

Eliz. What were I best to say? Her father's brother
Would be her lord? Or shall I say her uncle?
Or he that slew her brothers and her uncles?
Under what title shall I woo for thee,   340
That God, the law, my honour, and her love
Can make seem pleasing to her tender years?

K. Rich. Infer fair England's peace by this alliance.

Eliz. Which she shall purchase with still-lasting war.

K. Rich. Tell her the King, that may command, entreats.   345

Eliz. That, at her hands, which the King's King forbids.

K. Rich. Say she shall be a high and mighty queen.

Eliz. To vail the title, as her mother doth.

---

324. Of ten times] *Theobald;* Often-times *F.*   343. this] *F,Q1–3,5;* tuis *Q4;* his *Q6.*   345. Tell her] *F;* Saie that *Qq (subst.).*   that may] *F;* which may *Qq.*   346. forbids] *F,Q1;* forbid *Q2–6.*   348. vail] *F;* waile *Qq.*

Theobald's emendation here is very attractive, and has on the whole stood the test of time (though Sisson, Evans, and NPS revert to the F reading 'love'). The mechanism is simple: the word was spelled 'lone' and a 'u' which had strayed into the 'n' box was set by accident (it is not a turned letter). The word is very rare in Shakespeare: apart from one use in *Sonnet 6*, its only other appearance is in *Hamlet*, where by a splendid coincidence the same mistake as here occurred: Q2 reads 'loue', F 'lone' (I.iii.73) and in this instance there can be no doubt that 'loan' is the intended reading. In the present passage, the legal image becomes much more intelligible if 'loan' is read.

346. *forbids*] Because the marriage would infringe the prohibited degrees (listed in the *BCP*'s Table of Kindred and Affinity).

348. *vail*] Q's variant arose either from the actor's substituting a more familiar word for an unusual one, or from compositor-error. Vail means submit, subject, or yield one thing to another: OED *v.*[2] I.4a

K. Rich. Say I will love her everlastingly.

Eliz. But how long shall that title 'ever' last?   350

K. Rich. Sweetly in force, until her fair life's end.

Eliz. But how long fairly shall her sweet life last?

K. Rich. As long as heaven and nature lengthens it.

Eliz. As long as hell and Richard likes of it.

K. Rich. Say I, her sovereign, am her subject low.   355

Eliz. But she, your subject, loathes such sovereignty.

K. Rich. Be eloquent in my behalf to her.

Eliz. An honest tale speeds best being plainly told.

K. Rich. Then plainly to her tell my loving tale.

Eliz. Plain and not honest is too harsh a style.   360

K. Rich. Your reasons are too shallow and too quick.

Eliz. O no, my reasons are too deep and dead:

    Too deep and dead, poor infants, in their graves.

K. Rich. Harp not on that string, madam; that is past.

Eliz. Harp on it still shall I, till heart-strings break.   365

K. Rich. Now by my George, my Garter, and my crown—

Eliz. Profan'd, dishonour'd, and the third usurp'd.

K. Rich. I swear—

Eliz.   By nothing, for this is no oath:

    Thy George, profan'd, hath lost his holy honour;

---

350. 'ever'] *F,Q1–4,6* (euer), *Dyce; not in Q5.*   352. her sweet life] *F,Q1–2;*
that title *Q3–6.*   353. As] *F;* So *Qq.*   354. As] *F;* So *Qq.*   355. low] *F;*
loue *Qq.*   359. plainly to her tell] *F;* in plaine termes tell her *Qq.*   361.
Your] *F;* Madame your *Qq.*   363. graves] *F;* graue *Qq.*   364.] *Q1; after*
l. 369 F; not in Q2–6.   on] *F;* one *Q1.*   365. *Eliz.*] As *F,Q1; King. | Q2;*
not in Q3–6.   368. I swear] *F;* I sweare by nothing *Qq.*   369. Thy] *F;*
The *Qq.*   holy] *Qq;* Lordly *F.*

358.] Tilley T593.

361. *quick*] Richard means 'hasty',
and Elizabeth makes a play by
taking the word in the sense 'living'.

364.] This line, omitted from the
corrector's quarto(s) was wrongly
inserted in F after Elizabeth's rejoinder (l. 365). The expression is in
Hall, in a different context: the
Archbishop bids Lord Haward 'that
he shoulde harpe no more upon that
stryng' (*Edward V*, fol. xi^r–v).

365. *heart-strings*] The tendons or
nerves supposed by early anatomists

to brace the heart; hence figuratively,
the most intense feelings or emotions:
OED 1 and 2.

366. *George, Garter*] Emblems of
chivalry; the Order of the Garter was
augmented by the pendant image of
St George in Tudor times.

368. *I swear*] Q's 'I swear by
nothing' is obviously a copyist's
mistake.

369. *holy*] Smidt (p. 92) rightly
remarks that 'holy' is much more
apt with the verb 'prophan'd' than is
F's 'lordly'.

Thy Garter, blemish'd, pawn'd his knightly virtue;   370
Thy crown, usurp'd, disgrac'd his kingly glory.
If something thou wouldst swear to be believ'd,
Swear then by something that thou hast not wrong'd.

K. Rich. Now, by the world—
Eliz.   'Tis full of thy foul wrongs.
K. Rich. My father's death—
Eliz.   Thy life hath it dishonour'd.   375
K. Rich. Then by my self—
Eliz.   Thy self is self-misus'd.
K. Rich. Why then, by God—
Eliz.   God's wrong is most of all:
If thou didst fear to break an oath with Him,
The unity the King my husband made
Thou hadst not broken, nor my brothers died;   380
If thou hadst fear'd to break an oath by Him,
Th'imperial metal circling now thy head
Had grac'd the tender temples of my child,
And both the Princes had been breathing here,
Which now—two tender bed-fellows for dust—   385

370. Thy] *F;* The *Qq.*   371. Thy] *F;* The *Qq.*   glory] *F;* dignitie *Qq.*
372. wouldst] *F;* wilt *Qq.*   374-7.] *As Qq* (. . . world. / . . . wrongs. / . . .
death. / . . . dishonord. / . . . selfe. / . . . misusest. / . . . God. / . . . all, /); . . .
Selfe. / . . . misvs'd. / . . . World. / . . . wrongs. / . . . death. / . . . dishonor'd. /
. . . Heauen. / . . . all: *F; arranged in 4 ll., Steevens.*   375. life] *F,Q1-2;* selfe
Q3-6.   it] *F;* that *Q1.*   376. is self-misus'd] *F;* thy selfe misusest *Qq.*
377. God] *Qq;* Heauen *F.*   God's] *Qq;* Heanens *F.*   378. didst fear] *F;*
hadst feard *Qq.*   with] *F;* by *Qq.*   379. my husband] *F;* my brother
Q1-5,6(BL C34 k.51, Bodl., Trin., Hunt. copies); thy brother *Q6(other copies).*
380. Thou hadst not] *F;* Had not bene *Qq (subst.).*   my brothers died] *F;*
my brother slaine *Qq.*   382. head] *F;* brow *Qq.*   385. bed-] *F;* plaie- *Qq*
(subst.).

374-7.] This passage is clearly in complete lines divided between the two speakers rather than in stychomythia in partial lines. Richard attempts four oaths, each time interrupted by Elizabeth's objection. The Q order of world/father's death/self/God forms a clear rhetorical hierarchy which F order lacks. It is more likely that Shakespeare noticed this possibility after he had drafted the lines in F order, and so rearranged them, than that the actor hit upon

Q order by chance. The substitution of 'heaven' for 'God' in F is in accord with 3 Jac. I.

376. *self-misus'd*] Elizabeth implies that Richard has ever but slenderly known himself: the suggestion of a duality in his personality is in accord with his Morality-play origins, and the fragmentation of the personality that occurs in Act v, especially sc. iii, ll. 178-207. See also Introduction, pp. 106-7.

385. *bed-fellows*] Delius (*Jahrbuch*

Thy broken faith hath made the prey for worms.
What can'st thou swear by now?
K. Rich.   The time to come!
Eliz. That thou hast wronged in the time o'erpast:
For I myself have many tears to wash
Hereafter time, for time past wrong'd by thee.   390
The children live whose fathers thou hast slaughter'd:
Ungovern'd youth, to wail it in their age;
The parents live whose children thou hast butcher'd:
Old barren plants, to wail it with their age.
Swear not by time to come, for that thou hast   395
Misus'd, ere us'd, by times ill-us'd o'erpast.
K. Rich. As I intend to prosper and repent,
So thrive I in my dangerous affairs

386. the] *F;* a *Qq.*   worms] *F,Q 1–5;* worme *Q6.*   387.] *As F* (. . . now. /
The)*; King.* By the time to come. *Qq.*   388. wronged in the] *F;* wrongd in
Qq.   390. past wrong'd by thee] *F;* by the past wrongd *Q 1–4;* by thee past
wrongd *Q 5–6.*   391. fathers] *F;* parents *Qq.*   392. in their] *Q 1–4;* with
their *Q 5,F;* with her *Q6.*   394. barren] *F;* withered *Qq.*   396. ere] *F,Q6;*
eare *Q 1–3,5;* nere *Q 4.*   times ill-us'd] *F;* time misused *Qq.*   o'erpast]
Qq (orepast)*;* repast *F.*   398. affairs] *F;* attempt *Qq.*

vii, p. 150) observes that the Q
reading 'play-fellows' recalls the
lines not in Q at IV.i.97–103, especially l. 101 in which the Tower is
called a sullen playfellow for the
Princes. See Appendix I. Carter notes
that in the Geneva Bible Job, xxi.26
reads 'They shall sleepe both in the
dust, and wormes shall cover them'.
See also Tilley, M253.

387. *What . . . now?*] The omission
of this phrase from Q is probably a
compositor's oversight.

390. *Hereafter time*] in time to
come.

391 and 392. *fathers/in*] F presents a
neat antithesis in ll. 391–4, but 'with'
in l. 392 enters via Q5, an error Q6
compounds by printing 'with her': F
corrects the pronoun but neglects the
preposition. 'Fathers' in l. 391 is
more accurate as (Anne excepted)
Richard did not war on women. He
does, of course, despise and degrade
them. For the loss of self-identity this

entails, see Madonne M. Miner,
'Neither mother, wife, nor England's
queen' in *The Woman's Part: Feminist
Criticism of Shakespeare,* ed. Carolyn
Ruth Swift Lenz, Gayle Greene and
Carol Thomas Neely (Urbana, 1980),
pp. 35–55.

394. *barren*] F is correct: it is the
infertile state of the aged parents,
unable to replace their children, that
Elizabeth has in mind. Patrick (p. 64)
plausibly suggests the Q reading is a
recollection of II.ii.42.

395–6. *that . . . o'erpast*] Means
something like: you have misused the
time to come before it happens by the
continuing effects of the dreadful
things you did in the past. The line
gave the compositors trouble; perhaps the odd word in F, 'repast', was
a missetting of 'orepast' (the spelling
of Qq).

397–9. *As . . . arms!*] i.e. let me
succeed in my war only if I intend to
repent.

Of hostile arms! Myself myself confound!
God and fortune, bar me happy hours!   400
Day, yield me not thy light, nor, night, thy rest!
Be opposite, all planets of good luck,
To my proceeding if with dear heart's love,
Immaculate devotion, holy thoughts,
I tender not thy beauteous, princely daughter.   405
In her consists my happiness and thine;
Without her follows to myself, and thee,
Herself, the land, and many a Christian soul,
Death, desolation, ruin, and decay.
It cannot be avoided but by this;   410
It will not be avoided but by this.
Therefore, dear mother—I must call you so—
Be the attorney of my love to her;
Plead what I will be, not what I have been;
Not my deserts, but what I will deserve.   415
Urge the necessity and state of times,
And be not peevish found in great designs.

400.] *F; not in Qq.*   God] *This edn;* Heauen *F.*   403. proceeding] *F;*
proceedings *Qq.*   dear] *F;* pure *Qq.*   404. Immaculate] *F,Q1;* Im-
maculatd *Q2;* Immaculated *Q3–6.*   405. tender] *F,Q1–2,4;* render *Q3,5–6.*
407–8. myself, and thee, / Herself, the land] *F;* this land and me, / To thee
her selfe *Qq.*   409. Death] *F;* Sad *Qq*   411. by this] *F,Q2–6;* this *Q1.*
412. dear] *F;* good *Qq.*   415. my] *F;* by *Qq.*   417. peevish found] *F;*
pieuish, fond *Q1;* peeuish, fond *Q2;* peeuish fond *Q3–6;* peevish-fond *Malone.*

399–405. *Myself . . . daughter*]
Richard wishes all these unpleasant
things to happen to him if he does
not love Elizabeth's daughter. It is
worth remarking that all of them
come true in the next Act: Margaret
would have been pleased. For
'Myself myself confound!' cf. *Lucr.*,
l. 160: 'When he himself himself
confounds'.

400. *God*] The line is omitted
(probably an oversight) from Qq;
it seems very likely that the F reading
'Heaven' was determined by the
statute 3 Jac. I (as was l. 377 above).
Richard is not usually mealy-mouthed
and the strong monosyllable gives the
line a firmer rhythm though admit-
tedly only nine syllables. It seems very

likely, then, that Shakespeare wrote
'God'.

bar] hinder or prevent: OED *v.*7.

404. *Immaculate*] free from spot or
stain, unblemished (OED 1) but
with strong (and blasphemous) theological overtones.

405. *tender*] have a tender regard
for: OED *v.*² 3a.

409. *Death*] The F line is to be read
as four separate impending calami-
ties; Q gives us rather a pair: sad
desolation; ruin-and-decay. F is more
in keeping with the rhetorical
prolixity Richard is employing in
this speech.

417. *peevish found*] Most eds prefer
Malone's attractive conjecture, a
compound along the lines of 'childish-

Eliz. Shall I be tempted of the devil thus?
K. Rich. Ay, if the devil tempt you to do good.
Eliz. Shall I forget myself to be myself?   420
K. Rich. Ay, if your self's remembrance wrong yourself.
Eliz. Yet thou didst kill my children.
K. Rich. But in your daughter's womb I bury them,
    Where, in that nest of spicery, they will breed
    Selves of themselves, to your recomforture.   425
Eliz. Shall I go win my daughter to thy will?
K. Rich. And be a happy mother by the deed.
Eliz. I go. Write to me very shortly,
    And you shall understand from me her mind.
K. Rich. Bear her my true love's kiss; [*Kisses her*] and so
    farewell.   *Exit Elizabeth*   430

---

419. you] *F;* thee *Qq.*   422. Yet] *F;* But *Qq.*   423. I bury] *F,Q 3;* I buried
Q 1–2; Ile burie *Q 4–6.*   424. they will] *F;* they shall *Q 1–2;* there shall *Q 3–6.*
429. *F; not in Qq.*   430. *Kisses her*] *As Johnson; not in F,Qq.*   and so fare-
well] *F;* farewell *Qq.*   *Exit Elizabeth*] *As Qq; after l. 433 F.*

foolish' (I.iii.142). But F makes
perfect sense: 'do not be found
peevish in great designs'. It is clear
from the spelling and punctuation
variants in the Qq that the compositors were not happy with their
copy: F's reading ought to be
regarded as a genuine correction and
retained.

419.] Theologically, the devil can
only tempt one to do good if evil will
ultimately come of it. Cf. Matthew,
IV.1–10, or Luke, IV.1–13, for the
Temptation of Our Lord in the
wilderness, where the devil tempted
Him to do things not necessarily evil
in themselves. Elizabeth, in her response, shows no overt awareness of
the theological pitfall, but this is of a
piece with her refusal to be drawn by
Richard throughout the entire scene.
No doubt Richard himself intends
this admission of his diabolic nature
only in an hypothetical sense, but it is
of course also a genuine, if subconscious, acknowledgement of his
true nature. See Introduction, p. 102.

423–5.] Judith H. Anderson points
out a parallel of these lines with
Spenser's description of the Garden of
Adonis (*F.Q.* III.vi) in which the Boar
is imprisoned, and Adonis lies 'Lapped
in flowres and pretious spycery'
(*Biographical Truth*, New Haven,
1984, p. 118 & n.). Richard's metaphor
may seem a little less gross if it
is thus located in a mythic context.
Steevens noted that 'nest of spicery'
refers also to the fabled nest of the
phoenix in Arabia, whence the new-
born bird arose from the ashes of the
old. The variants of 'I bury' do not
affect its meaning (see Introduction,
p. 37).

425. *recomforture*] consolation (OED
cites only this instance).

430. S.D.] The direction to kiss
Elizabeth, inserted by Johnson, is
necessary; it is worth recalling to the
reader at this point that the entire
enormous dialogue between Richard
and Elizabeth has taken place in
public while Richard's army was
halted waiting for its leader. There

Relenting fool, and shallow, changing woman!

Enter RATCLIFFE.

How now, what news?

Rat. Most mighty sovereign, on the western coast
Rideth a puissant navy; to our shores
Throng many doubtful, hollow-hearted friends,   435
Unarm'd, and unresolv'd to beat them back.
'Tis thought that Richmond is their admiral;
And there they hull, expecting but the aid
Of Buckingham to welcome them ashore.

K. Rich. Some light-foot friend post to the Duke of Norfolk.
Ratcliffe, thyself—or Catesby—where is he?   441

Cat. Here, my good lord.

K. Rich.   Catesby, fly to the Duke.

Cat. I will, my lord, with all convenient haste.

K. Rich. Ratcliffe, come hither. Post to Salisbury.
When thou com'st thither—[*To Catesby*] Dull unmindful
villain!   445

431. S.D. *Enter Ratcliffe*] *As Qq; after l. 436* F.   432.] F; *not in Qq.*   433.
Most mighty] F; My gracious Qq.   434. our shores] F; the shore Qq.
438. they] F,Q1,3-6; thy Q2.   442.] As Steevens; . . . Lord. / Catesby F;
. . . Lord. / Flie Qq.   good lord] F; lord Qq.   Catesby, fly] F; Flie Qq.
443-4. Cat. I will, my lord, with all convenient haste. / Rich. Ratcliffe, come
hither.] As F; not in Qq.   444. Ratcliffe] Rowe; Catesby F.   Post] F; post
thou Qq.   445. com'st thither] F; comst there Q1; comest there Q2-6.
To Catesby] Rowe; not in F,Qq.   villain] F,Q1-5; villanie Q6.

seems to have been some minor
disruption to the text hereabouts,
resulting in misplaced S.D.s in F and
omitted lines in Q.

431.] Cf. *Aeneid*, iv. 569-70, 'Vari-
um et mutabile semper femina'.
Commentators have laboured to
settle the impossible, whether Elizabeth's acceptance was real or feigned.
More (and the other sources) thought
it real, and were very hostile to
Elizabeth; by the time of Cibber, it
seemed patent that she was deceiving
Richard, and this was made clear in
his text. Shakespeare offers no un-
ambiguous clues: it is a point that the
reader, and the director, must settle
for himself, though we may guess that

Shakespeare would have instructed
his own actors how to play.

434. *puissant*] powerful.

438. *hull*] float with sails furled:
OED *v*.[2] 1.

441 ff.] Richard's uncertainty and
agitation here was suggested probably
by More: 'he fell again in to a great
feare and penciveness of mynde' (Hall,
Richard III, fol. xxix[v]).

443. *convenient*] suitable to the
conditions or circumstances: OED
a.4b.

444. *Ratcliffe*] There is no doubt
that Rowe is right here; 'Catesby'
in F is a compositor's error from
l. 442.

445. *villain*] Q6's 'villanie' is not a

Why stay'st thou here and go'st not to the Duke?

Cat. First, mighty liege, tell me your Highness' pleasure,
What from your Grace I shall deliver to him.

K. Rich. O, true, good Catesby! Bid him levy straight
The greatest strength and power that he can make,   450
And meet me suddenly at Salisbury.

Cat. I go.   *Exit.*

Rat. What, may it please you, shall I do at Salisbury?

K. Rich. Why, what wouldst thou do there before I go?

Rat. Your Highness told me I should post before.   455

K. Rich. My mind is chang'd.

Enter STANLEY *Earl of Derby.*

                                  Stanley, what news with you?

Stan. None good, my liege, to please you with the hearing;
Nor none so bad but well may be reported.

K. Rich. Hoyday, a riddle! Neither good nor bad—
What need'st thou run so many miles about   460
When thou mayst tell thy tale the nearest way?
Once more, what news?

Stan.   Richmond is on the seas.

K. Rich. There let him sink, and be the seas on him—
White-liver'd runagate! What doth he there?

446. stay'st] *F;* standst *Q 1–3,5–6;* stands *Q 4.*   here] *F;* still *Qq.*   447.
liege] *F;* Soueraigne *Qq.*   tell me your Highness' pleasure] *F;* let me know
your minde *Qq.*   448. to him] *F;* them *Q 1–2;* him *Q 3–6.*   450. that he]
F; he *Qq.*   451. suddenly] *F;* presentlie *Qq.*   452 & S.D.] *F; not in Qq.*
453. may it please you, shall I] *F;* is it (it is *Q 5;* is *Q 6)* your highnes pleasure,
I shall do *Qq (subst.).*   456.] *As Capell; . . .* chang'd: / Stanley *F,Qq (subst.).*
chang'd.] *F;* changd sir, my minde is changd. *Qq.*   456. S.D.] *As F; after
l. 460 Qq.*   456. Stanley] *F;* How now *Qq.*   457. liege] *F;* Lord *Qq.*
458. but well may] *F;* but it may well *Qq.*   reported] *F;* told *Qq.*   460.
What need'st] *F;* Why doest *Qq (subst.).*   miles] *F;* mile *Qq.*   461. the
nearest] *F;* a neerer *Qq.*

variant; just a misspelling of the usual
Q form 'villaine'.

456. *chang'd*] Richard here uncharacteristically repeats the phrase,
in Q. See also l. 466; it may have
been one of Burbage's (few) bad
habits.

459. *Hoyday*] An exclamation denoting ironical surprise = hey-day
(OED).

464. *White-liver'd runagate*] White-
livered means cowardly (see also
v.iii.105 n. for an explanation);
a runagate is a renegade or apostate
(OED 1); Richard (as ll. 469–72
make clear) is in an unusually imperial
mood, and regards Richmond as a
disloyal subject. For the phrase, see
Tilley F180.

Stan. I know not, mighty sovereign, but by guess.   465
K. Rich. Well, as you guess?
Stan. Stirr'd up by Dorset, Buckingham, and Morton,
　　He makes for England, here to claim the crown.
K. Rich. Is the chair empty? Is the sword unsway'd?
　　Is the King dead? The empire unpossess'd?   470
　　What heir of York is there alive but we?
　　And who is England's King but great York's heir?
　　Then tell me, what makes he upon the seas!
Stan. Unless for that, my liege, I cannot guess.
K. Rich. Unless for that he comes to be your liege,   475
　　You cannot guess wherefore the Welshman comes.
　　Thou wilt revolt and fly to him, I fear.
Stan. No, my good lord; therefore mistrust me not.
K. Rich. Where is thy power then to beat him back?
　　Where be thy tenants and thy followers?   480
　　Are they not now upon the western shore,
　　Safe-conducting the rebels from their ships?
Stan. No, my good lord, my friends are in the north.
K. Rich. Cold friends to me! What do they in the north,
　　When they should serve their sovereign in the west?   485
Stan. They have not been commanded, mighty King.
　　Pleaseth your Majesty to give me leave,
　　I'll muster up my friends, and meet your Grace
　　Where and what time your Majesty shall please.
K. Rich. Ay, ay, thou wouldst be gone, to join with
　　　　Richmond.
　　But I'll not trust thee.   490
Stan. 　·　　　　Most mighty sovereign,

466.] *F; King.* Well sir, as you guesse, as you guesse. *Qq (subst.).*   467.
Morton] *F;* Elie *Q1–5;* Ely *Q6.*   468. here] *F;* there *Qq.*   473. makes]
F; doeth *Q1–2;* doth *Q3–6.*   seas] *F;* sea *Qq.*   476. Welshman] *F,Q1–3,*
5–6 (subst.); Welchmen *Q4.*   478. my good lord] *F;* mightie liege *Qq.*
480. be] *F;* are *Qq.*   484. me] *F;* Richard *Qq.*   486. King] *F;* soueraigne
Qq.   487. Pleaseth] *F;* Please it *Qq.*   490. Ay] *F* (I); I,I *Qq.*   491.] *As*
Steevens; . . . thee. / Most F,Qq (subst.).   But I'll not trust thee] *F;* I will not
trust you Sir *Qq.*

469. *chair . . . sword*] The throne and
the sword of state, emblem of the
king's military authority.
477–8.] Richard is rightly sus-

picious of the time-serving Stanley,
but is now becoming uncertain in his
reactions. See Introduction, p. 113.

You have no cause to hold my friendship doubtful.
I never was, nor never will be, false.

K. Rich. Go then, and muster men—but leave behind
Your son George Stanley. Look your heart be firm,   495
Or else his head's assurance is but frail.

Stan. So deal with him as I prove true to you.   *Exit.*

Enter a Messenger.

Mess. My gracious sovereign, now in Devonshire—
As I by friends am well advertised--
Sir Edward Courtney and the haughty prelate,   500
Bishop of Exeter, his elder brother,
With many more confederates, are in arms.

Enter another Messenger.

2 Mess. In Kent, my liege, the Guilfords are in arms,
And every hour more competitors
Flock to the rebels, and their power grows strong.   505

Enter another Messenger.

3 Mess. My lord, the army of great Buckingham—

494. Go then, and] *F*; Well, go *Qq*.   leave] *F*; heare you, leaue *Qq*.
495. heart] *F*; faith *Qq*.   497. So deal] *F*,*Q 1-3,5-6*; Deale *Q 4*.   497. S.D.
Exit Stanley] *F*; *Exit. Dar.* | *Q 3-5*; *Exit.* | *Q 6*; *not in Q 1-2*.   500. Edward]
F; William *Qq*.   501. elder brother] *F*; brother there *Qq*.   503. *2 Mess.*]
Capell; *Mess.* | *F*,*Qq*.   In Kent, my liege] *F*; My Liege, in Kent *Qq*.
505. the rebels, and their power grows strong] *F*; their aide, and still their
power increaseth *Qq* (*subst.*).   506, 509, 517. *3 Mess.*] *Capell*; *Mess.* | *F*,*Qq*.
My lord] *F*,*Q 1-3,5-6*; Lord *Q 4*.   great] *F*; the Duke of *Qq*.

496. *assurance*] security.

499. *advertised*] Four syllables,
accent on the second.

500. *Edward Courtney*] F is correct:
Hall, *Richard III*, fol. xxxix^r.

501. *elder brother*] Actually his
cousin: Thompson describes the
genealogy of the Courtenays.

503. *Guilfords*] Or Guildfords; a
descendant was husband of Lady Jane
Grey.

505. *their power grows strong*] There
is a possibility that the Q version, 'and

still their power increaseth', is derived
from Hall (*Richard III*, fol. lii^r): 'and
thus his powre encreasynge'. This
does not necessarily mean Shakespeare
was responsible: the hand of another
man familiar with the Chronicles has
been noted elsewhere in the Q text
(see Introduction, pp. 17–18). Besides,
the F version also has a source in Hall:
on fol. liii^r we read that the disaffected
lords 'resorted to hym wyth all their
powre and strength'.

K. Rich. Out on you, owls! Nothing but songs of death?

He striketh him.

There, take thou that, till thou bring better news.

3 Mess. The news I have to tell your Majesty
Is, that by sudden floods and fall of waters,   510
Buckingham's army is dispers'd and scatter'd,
And he himself wander'd away alone,
No man knows whither.

K. Rich.   I cry thee mercy;
There is my purse, to cure that blow of thine.
Hath any well-advised friend proclaim'd   515
Reward to him that brings the traitor in?

3 Mess. Such proclamation hath been made, my lord.

Enter another Messenger.

4 Mess. Sir Thomas Lovel and Lord Marquess Dorset

507 you] *Q1–5;* ye *Q6,F.*   507. S.D.] *F; after l. 510 Qq.*   508. There.
take thou that, till thou bring] *F;* Take that vntill thou (you *Q6*) bring me *Qq,*
509.] *F; Mes.* Your grace mistakes, the newes I bring is good, *Qq.*   510. Is]
F; My newes is *Qq.*   floods] *F;* floud *Qq (subst.).*   waters] *F;* water *Qq*
(watter *Q3*).   511. Buckingham's] *F;* The Duke of Buckinghams *Qq.*
512. wander'd away alone] *F;* fled *Qq.*   513.] *As Steevens; . . .* whither. /
Rich. I F *(Q diff.).*   No man knows whither.] *F; in l. 516 Qq.*   I cry thee
mercy] *F;* O I crie you mercie, I did mistake *Qq (subst.).*   514.] *F;* Ratcliffe
reward him, for the blow I gaue him, *Qq.*   515. proclaim'd] *F;* giuen out *Qq.*
516. Reward] *F;* Rewardes *Q1;* Rewards *Q2–6.*   to] *F;* for *Qq.*   the
traitor in] *F;* in Buckingham *Qq.*   517. lord] *F;* liege *Qq.*

507. *owls . . . death*] The cry of the
screech-owl was popularly supposed to
foretell death or disaster. Cf. *Lucr.,*
l. 165, and of course *Macb.,* ii. ii. 3;
also *Faerie Queene,* ii. vii. 23 and
ii. xii. 86.

509.] This line in Q appears
perfectly normal, but in fact is an
improvisation of the actor's, as the
botch in the following line reveals.

512. *wander'd away alone*] Q here
simply reads 'fled', and brings the
half-line from l. 513 into this line.
Richard thus has to improvise a full
line in 513 to prevent further dislocation. As for the events described, the
attempted revolt and betrayal of

Buckingham form a very large part of
Hall's continuation of More; Shakespeare obviously did not wish to dwell
on it, and gives here the barest gist of
events, omitting altogether Buckingham's betrayal by Banaster.

514.] The Q version here undoubtedly reflects a change in business; that for some reason Richard
was not carrying a purse, and Ratcliffe
was made paymaster for the nonce.

515. *well-advised*] prudent, thought-
ful. Cf. ii. i. 108.

518. *Lovel*] Not to be confused with
Lord Francis Lovell, Richard's chamberlain, who has a small part to play
in Act iii.

'Tis said, my liege, in Yorkshire are in arms;
But this good comfort bring I to your Highness: 520
The Breton navy is dispers'd by tempest.
Richmond, in Dorsetshire, sent out a boat
Unto the shore, to ask those on the banks
If they were his assistants, yea or no?—
Who answer'd him they came from Buckingham   525
Upon his party. He, mistrusting them,
Hois'd sail, and made his course again for Bretagne.

K. Rich. March on, march on, since we are up in arms:
If not to fight with foreign enemies,
Yet to beat down these rebels here at home.   530

Enter CATESBY.

Cat. My liege, the Duke of Buckingham is taken:
That is the best news. That the Earl of Richmond
Is with a mighty power landed at Milford
Is colder tidings, yet they must be told.

K. Rich. Away towards Salisbury! While we reason here   535
A royal battle might be won and lost.
Someone take order Buckingham be brought
To Salisbury; the rest march on with me.

Flourish. Exeunt.

519. in Yorkshire are] *F;* are vp *Qq.*   520. But] *F;* Yet *Qq.*   Highness] *F;*
grace *Qq.*   521. Breton] *F,Qq* (Brittaine), *Capell.*   by tempest] *F; not in Qq.*
521–3.] *F;* The ... Dorshire / Sent ... shore. *Qq.*   522. Dorsetshire] *F,Q6;*
Dorshire *Q1–5.*   523. Unto the shore] *F; not in Qq.*   those] *F;* them *Qq.*
banks] *F;* shore *Qq.*   527. Hois'd] *F;* Hoist *Qq.*   his course again] *F;*
away *Qq.*   Bretagne] *F,Qq* (Brittaine), *Theobald.*   532. That is] *F;* Thats
Qq.   534. tidings, yet] *Q1–5* (tydings *Q3–5*); newes, yet *Q6;* Newes, but
yet *F.*   538. S.D. *Flourish.*] *F; not in Qq.*   Exeunt.] *F,Q1; not in Q2–6.*

521–3.] Q here by omitting two
phrases squeezes the three lines into
two (the first badly extra-metrical).
Perhaps the substitution of 'shore' for
'banks' began the process; this is
another instance of poor memoriz-
ation of a secondary role.
      524. *assistants*] supporters.
      527. *Hois'd*] hoisted. The form

occurs in *2H6*, I.i.169, and is very
common in *Parts Added* (e.g. 'Alban-
act', l. 181, p. 54).
      Bretagne] Pronounced 'Breton'.
      533. *Milford*] Milford Haven, in
Wales.
      534. *tidings, yet*] See Introduction
pp. 36–7.
      535. *reason*] debate, discuss.

SCENE V

Enter STANLEY *Earl of Derby and* SIR CHRISTOPHER
[URSWICK].

Stan. Sir Christopher, tell Richmond this from me:
That in the sty of the most deadly boar
My son George Stanley is frank'd up in hold;
If I revolt, off goes young George's head;
The fear of that holds off my present aid.   5
So get thee gone: commend me to thy lord;
Withal say that the Queen hath heartily consented
He should espouse Elizabeth her daughter.
But tell me, where is princely Richmond now?
Chris. At Pembroke, or at Ha'rfordwest in Wales.   10
Stan. What men of name resort to him?
Chris. Sir Walter Herbert, a renowned soldier;
Sir Gilbert Talbot, Sir William Stanley,
Oxford, redoubted Pembroke, Sir James Blunt,
And Rice ap Thomas, with a valiant crew,   15
And many other of great name and worth;
And towards London do they bend their power,

Scene v

SCENE v] *Capell; Scena Quarta. | F; not in Qq.*   S.D. *and Sir*] F; *Sir Qq.*
Urswick] *Theobald; not in F,Qq.*   2. the most] F; *this most Qq.*   deadly]
F; *bloudie Qq.*   5. holds off] F; *with holdes Qq (subst.).*   6.] F; *not in Qq.*
7–8.] *As F; after l. 19 Qq.*   7. Withal say that] F; *Tell him Qq.*   8. should]
F; *shall Qq.*   10. Ha'rfordwest] *As Capell;* Harford-west *Q 1;* Herford-west
Q 2,5; Hertford-west *Q 3–4,6;* Hertford West *F.*   15. And] F; *not in Qq.*
ap] *F,Q 6;* vp *Q 1–5.*   16. And] F; *With Qq.*   other] F; *moe Qq.*   great
name] F; *noble fame Qq.*   17. do they] F; *they do Qq.*   power] F;
course *Qq.*

S.D. *Urswick*] A priest, chaplain to
the Countess of Richmond. His title
('Sir Christopher') is a courtesy: cf.
III. ii. 107 n.

3. *frank'd up in hold*] See I. iii. 314 n.
6–8.] The tangle in Q may be
explained by supposing that Stanley
forgot l. 6, but transferred its second
half to l. 19, whence it cued ll. 7–8,
which consequently occur at that
place in Q. For the light that this
episode sheds on Elizabeth's be-

haviour to Richard, see IV. iv. 431 n.

10. *Ha'rfordwest*] Haverfordwest, in
Wales.

13. *Sir William Stanley*] Brother of
the Stanley of the play. See Introduction, p. 13.

14. *Blunt*] Sidney Shanker (*MLN*
63 (1948), pp. 540–1) notes that the
family was not knighted until 1588.
The Blunts owned land in Stratford,
and were related by marriage to the
Combes.

If by the way they be not fought withal.
Stan. Well, hie thee to thy lord; I kiss his hand.
My letter will resolve him of my mind.   20
Farewell.   *Exeunt.*

19. Well, hie thee to] *F;* Retourne vnto *Qq.*   thy] *F,Q1;* my *Q2–6.*   I kiss his hand] *F;* commend me to him *Qq.*   20. My letter] *F;* These letters *Qq.*

ACT V

SCENE I

Enter [Sheriff] *with* HALBERDS, [*and*] BUCKINGHAM
led to Execution.

Buck. Will not King Richard let me speak with him?
Sher. No, my good lord; therefore be patient.
Buck. Hastings, and Edward's children, Grey and Rivers,
    Holy King Henry, and thy fair son Edward,
    Vaughan, and all that have miscarried   5
    By underhand, corrupted foul injustice—
    If that your moody, discontented souls
    Do through the clouds behold this present hour,
    Even for revenge mock my destruction.
    This is All-Souls' day, fellow, is it not?   10
Sher. It is.
Buck. Why then, All-Souls' day is my body's doomsday.
    This is the day which, in King Edward's time,
    I wish'd might fall on me when I was found

ACT V

Scene 1

ACT V SCENE I] *As* F (*Actus Quintus. Scena Prima*); *not in* Q*q*.   S.D. Sheriff]
Malone; not in F,Q*q*.   *with* Halberds] F; *not in* Q*q*.   *led*] F; *not in* Q*q*.
2. *Sher.*] F; *Rat.* Q*q*.   good lord] F; lord Q*q*.   3. Grey and Rivers] F;
Riuers, Gray Q*q*.   10. fellow] F; fellowes Q*q*.   11.] F; *Rat.* It is my
Lord. Q*q*.   13. which] F; that Q*q*.

S.D.] F omits to name the Sheriff;
Q neglects to specify Ratcliffe, who
replaces the Sheriff in that text.

5. *miscarried*] perished: OED miscarry *v.*1.

10. *All-Soul's day*] Buckingham's
sequence of thought is souls—revenge
—All-Souls'—judgement. (The Mass
for All-Souls' day includes the 'Dies
Irae'.) A theological basis for

Buckingham's penitence is implied. See
also Jones, pp. 228–9 for other
implications. The date of All-Souls'
day is 2 November (1483). Although
Shakespeare represents the events
as being contemporaneous, the Battle
of Bosworth did not take place until
August 1485, over twenty-one months
after Buckingham's execution.

13. *This . . . day*] See II.i.32–9.

False to his children and his wife's allies.　　　15
This is the day wherein I wish'd to fall
By the false faith of him whom most I trusted.
This, this All-Souls' day to my fearful soul
Is the determin'd respite of my wrongs:
That high All-seer which I dallied with　　　20
Hath turn'd my feigned prayer on my head,
And given in earnest what I begg'd in jest.
Thus doth He force the swords of wicked men
To turn their own points in their masters' bosoms.
Thus Margaret's curse falls heavy on my neck:　　　25
'When he,' quoth she, 'shall split thy heart with sorrow,
Remember Margaret was a prophetess!'
Come, lead me, officers, to the block of shame;
Wrong hath but wrong, and blame the due of blame.

Exit with Officers.

SCENE II

Enter RICHMOND, OXFORD, BLUNT, HERBERT, *and* Others,
with drum and colours.

Richmond. Fellows in arms, and my most loving friends,

15. and] *F; or Qq.*　　　17. whom most I trusted] *F;* I trusted most *Qq.*
20. That]*F,Q 1,3–6;* What *Q 2.*　　which] *F;* that *Qq.*　　23. swords]*F,Q 1–2;*
sword *Q 3–6* (sowrd *Q 5*).　　24. own points in] *F;* owne pointes, on *Q 1–2;*
points on *Q 3–6.*　　bosoms] *F;* bosome *Qq.*　　25. Thus] *F;* Now *Qq.*
falls heavy on] *F;* is fallen vpon *Qq.*　　neck] *F;* head *Qq.*　　28. lead me,
officers] *F;* sirs, conuey me *Qq.*　　29. S.D.] *F; not in Qq.*

Scene 11

SCENE 11] *F (Scena Secunda); not in Qq.*　　S.D. *Oxford, Blunt, Herbert, and
Others] F; not in Qq.*　　*and colours] F;* and trumpets / *Qq.*　　1. Fellows]
F,Q 1–4,6; Fellowe *Q 5.*

19. *determin'd respite*] The ordained
time to which the punishment of his
evil behaviour has been deferred:
OED respite *sb.5.*
25. *Margaret's curse*] See 1.iii. 299–301.

Scene 11

Scene 11] Many eds follow Hanmer
in indicating that the 'location' of the
scene is Tamworth (mentioned by
Richmond in l. 13).
S.D.] The Q direction is very
vague for a prompt-book: perhaps the
actors doubling the three lords were
as uncertain of their identities as they
were of their lines. (Richmond's part
is unusually accurate.)

Bruis'd underneath the yoke of tyranny;
Thus far into the bowels of the land
Have we march'd on without impediment;
And here receive we from our father Stanley   5
Lines of fair comfort and encouragement.
The wretched, bloody, and usurping boar,
That spoil'd your summer fields and fruitful vines,
Swills your warm blood like wash, and makes his trough
In your embowell'd bosoms—this foul swine   10
Is now even in the centre of this isle,
Near to the town of Leicester, as we learn.
From Tamworth thither is but one day's march:
In God's name, cheerly on, courageous friends,
To reap the harvest of perpetual peace   15
By this one bloody trial of sharp war.
Oxf. Every man's conscience is a thousand men,
    To fight against this guilty homicide.
Herb. I doubt not but his friends will turn to us.
Blunt. He hath no friends but what are friends for fear,   20
    Which in his dearest need will fly from him.
Richmond. All for our vantage; then in God's name march.
    True hope is swift, and flies with swallow's wings:

8. summer fields] *F,Q 1–2 (subst.)* ; sommer-field *Q 3–6.*   10. embowell'd] *F;*
inboweld *Q 1–5;* imboweld *Q 6.*   11. Is] *F;* Lies *Qq.*   centre] *Qq;* Centry
F.   12. Near] *Q 1–5* (Neare); Neere *Q 6;* Ne're *F.*   14. cheerly] *F,Q 1;*
cheere *Q 2;* cheare *Q 3–6.*   17. *Oxf.*] *F; 1 Lo. | Qq.*   men] *F;* swordes *Qq.*
18. this guilty] *F;* that bloudie *Qq (subst.).*   19. *Herb.*] *As F; 2 Lo. | Qq.*
turn] *F;* flie *Qq.*   20. *Blunt.*] *F; 3 Lo. | Qq.*   what] *F;* who *Qq.*   21.
dearest] *F;* greatest *Qq.*   fly] *F;* shrinke *Qq.*

5. *father*] step-father.
7–11.] D. L. Higdon, in *The
Explicator* 33 (September 1974), suggests a reference is intended to the
Calydonian boar of *Metamorphoses*,
viii. 270–545, sent by Diana to ravage
the crops. A link is implied with the
Scourge of God motif.
9. *Swills . . . wash*] drinks . . . like
pig-swill.
10. *embowell'd*] i.e. disembowelled.
11. *Is . . . centre*] F is rather uncertain in this and the next line: 'Is'
makes a less forceful impression than

Q's 'Lies'; it is not obviously wrong,
but F's 'Centry' surely is, while in l.
12 F clumsily emends Q6's 'Neere'
to 'Ne're' instead of the required
'Near'. This is the first sign of
uneven correction which in the rest of
the Act is most significant—see
Introduction, pp. 40–1.
17.] Tilley C601; Cf. v.iii. 194.
Baldwin (1.713) proposed that
Shakespeare was translating from
Erasmus's Latin version of the proverb. It seems far-fetched.

Kings it makes gods, and meaner creatures kings. *Exeunt*.

[SCENE III]

Enter KING RICHARD *in Arms, with* NORFOLK, RATCLIFFE,
and the EARL OF SURREY, *with* Others.

K. Rich. Here pitch our tent, even here in Bosworth field.
　　　　[*Richard's tent is raised, on one side of the stage.*]
　　My lord of Surrey, why look you so sad?
Sur. My heart is ten times lighter than my looks.
K. Rich. My lord of Norfolk.
Nor.　　　　　　　　Here, most gracious liege.
K. Rich. Norfolk, we must have knocks—ha, must we not?　5
Nor. We must both give and take, my loving lord.
K. Rich. Up with my tent! Here will I lie tonight—
　　But where tomorrow? Well, all's one for that.
　　Who hath descried the number of the traitors?

24. makes] *F,Q6*; make *Q1–5*.　24. S.D.] *F*; *Exit.* | *Q1*; not in *Q2–6*.

Scene III

SCENE III] *Pope*; not in *F,Qq*.　S.D. *in Arms*] *F*; not in *Qq*.　*and the Earl of
Surrey*] *F*; *Catesbie* | *Qq*.　*with* Others] *Qq*; not in *F*.　1. tent] *F*; tentes *Q1*;
tents *Q2–6*.　1. S.D.] *This edn*; not in *F,Qq*.　2. My lord of Surrey] *F*;
Whie, how now Catesbie *Qq*.　look] *F*; lookst *Q1*; lookest *Q2–6*.　you]
F; thou *Qq*.　sad] *F,Q2–6*; bad *Q1*.　3. *Sur.*] *F*; *Cat*, | *Qq*.　4.] *As
Steevens*; . . . Norfolke. | *Nor.* Heere *F*; *Q different*.　My lord of Norfolk] *F*;
Norffolke, come hether *Qq* (*subst.*).　*Nor.* Here, most gracious liege.] *F*; not
in *Qq*.　5.] *As Qq*; . . . knockes: | Ha *F*.　6. loving] *F*; gracious *Qq*.
7. tent] *F*; tent there *Qq*.　8. all's] *F*; all is *Qq*.　9. traitors] *F*; foe *Qq*.
10. utmost] *F,Q1*; greatest *Q1(Hunt. copy)*, *Q2–6*.　power] *F*; number *Qq*.

S.D.] This, the famous and long-
awaited battle-scene, needs additional stage-directions to make the
implicit instructions clear to the
reader and director. The first appear-
ances of Richard and Richmond
(ll. 1 and 19) are in the context of
surveying-parties; the leaders, with
two or three selected nobles and a
few men-at-arms who are occupied
during the leaders' conversations
with the raising of the tents, which
no doubt took a few minutes (see
Introduction, pp. 65–6). Directions have been added to make this
explicit. The precise number of
supers need not be specified; note
that Ratcliffe is present (though
silent), but in Q Catesby substitutes
for the Earl of Surrey, presumably
for reasons of actor-economy.
　1. *tent*] Q's plural is impossible.
　1. S.D.] See above.
　2. *Surrey*] See above.
　10. *utmost power*] See Introduction,
p. 29.

Nor. Six or seven thousand is their utmost power.   10
K. Rich. Why, our battalia trebles that account!
　　Besides, the King's name is a tower of strength
　　Which they upon the adverse faction want.
　　Up with the tent! Come, noble gentlemen,
　　Let us survey the vantage of the ground.   15
　　Call for some men of sound direction;
　　Let's lack no discipline, make no delay:
　　For, lords, tomorrow is a busy day!
　　　　　[*The tent is now ready.*] *Exeunt* [*through one door*].

Enter [*through the other door*] RICHMOND, SIR WILLIAM BRANDON,
OXFORD, *and* HERBERT [, BLUNT, *and* Others, *who pitch
Richmond's tent on the other side of the stage*].

Richmond. The weary sun hath made a golden set,
　　And by the bright track of his fiery car   20
　　Gives token of a goodly day tomorrow.

11. battalia] *F;* battalion *Q1,4,6;* battailon *Q2–3,5.*   13. faction] *F;* partie
Qq.   14. the tent! Come, noble] *As F* (Tent: Come)*; my tent there, valiant
Qq.*   15. ground] *F;* field *Qq.*   17. lack] *F;* want *Qq.*   18. S.D. *The
tent is now ready*] *This edn; not in F,Qq.*   *through one door*] *This edn; not in F,Qq.*
through the other door] *This edn; not in F,Qq.*   *Sir William Brandon, Oxford, and
Herbert*] *As Capell; Sir William Brandon,   Oxford, and Dorset / F; with the Lordes,
&c. / Q1–2; with the Lords / Q3–6.   Blunt, and Others, who pitch Richmond's
tent on the other side of the stage*] *This edn; not in F,Qq.*   19. sun] *F,Q2–6;* sonne
Q1.   set] *F;* sete *Q1;* seate *Q2–5;* seat *Q6.*   20. track] *Qq;* tract *F.*
21. token] *F;* signall *Qq.*

11. *battalia*] body of men in battle
array: OED 2, citing this line.
　12.] See Proverbs, xviii. 10.
　18. S.D.] As Richard's thrice-
repeated order shows, the raising of
the tent occupied the first eighteen
lines. Probably the soldiers follow
Richard and the nobles out to survey
the field; Richmond's entrance would
be concurrent—the theatrical fiction
of course is that the two locations,
Richard's and Richmond's, are
widely separated. The erection of
Richmond's tent proceeds during his
speech. F's inclusion of Dorset
amongst Richmond's followers is a
copyist's error for Herbert. Richmond
speaks to Herbert but makes no

mention of Dorset, who appears
nowhere in the Act. Hall specifically
says he was not at Bosworth, having
been left behind in France as a
hostage (*Richard III*, fol. l[v]).
　19. *sun*] The sun that rose on
Richard's opening soliloquy now
sets in favourable omen for Richmond; later (ll. 277–80) it will not
rise for Richard (see Brooke, p. 59).
Q1 compounds the allusion to
i.i.2 by misspelling as 'sonne'! The
favourable omen of sunset is proverbial: Tilley S515.
　20. *track*] The F word 'tract' also
means 'track': OED tract *sb.*[3] iv.8.
So nearly does this equate with
'track' that the issue is one of mod-

Sir William Brandon, you shall bear my standard.
My lord of Oxford, you Sir William Brandon,
And you Sir Walter Herbert, stay with me;
The Earl of Pembroke keeps his regiment—   25
Good captain Blunt, bear my goodnight to him,
And by the second hour in the morning
Desire the Earl to see me in my tent.
Yet one thing more, good captain, do for me:
Where is Lord Stanley quarter'd, do you know?   30
Blunt. Unless I have mista'en his colours much,
Which well I am assur'd I have not done,
His regiment lies half a mile at least
South from the mighty power of the King.
Richmond. If without peril it be possible,   35
Sweet Blunt, make some good means to speak with him,
And give him from me this most needful note.
Blunt. Upon my life, my lord, I'll undertake it;
And so God give you quiet rest tonight.
Richmond. Good night, good captain Blunt. [*Exit Blunt.*]   40
Give me some ink and paper in my tent;
I'll draw the form and model of our battle;

22.] *F;* Where is Sir William Brandon, he shall beare my standard, *Qq.*
23–4.] *F; not in Qq.*   24. you] *F2;* your *F.*   25. keeps] *F;* keepe *Qq.*
29. captain, do for me] *F;* Blunt before thou goest *Qq.*   30. do you] *F:*
doest thou *Qq.*   33. lies] *F,Q1–2;* liet *Q3–5;* lieth *Q4,6.*   36.] *F;* Good
captaine Blunt beare my good night to him, *Qq.*   37. note] *F;* scrowle *Qq.*
39.] *F; not in Qq.*   40. Good night] *F;* Farewell *Qq.*   captain Blunt] *F;*
Blunt *Qq.*   41–4.] *As Qq; after l. 22 F.*

ernization, rather than of alternate
meanings. Hence the Q form is
preferred here.

22.] The Q version of this line is
to be explained as actor-economy:
see Introduction, p. 15.

23–4.] Also omitted from Q for
economy; see Introduction, p. 15.

25. *keeps*] F is right: Pembroke is
not on-stage, as l. 26 reveals; 'keeps'
means 'stays with'.

36.] Richmond's excellent memory
betrays him; in Q he here repeats
l. 26 verbatim, and forgets this.

41–4.] In view of the high general
standard of reporting of Richmond's

part, there is a case here to suppose
(with some earlier eds, but no recent
one) that a deliberate alteration was
made in the location of these lines,
rather than that the actor simply
misplaced them. Perhaps the tent
was not ready for occupancy at l. 22,
but besides, the lines seem more apt
and coherent as a conclusion to the
episode than in the midst of it. It
seems reasonable to assume that
Shakespeare approved the change;
the Q placing has thus been adopted
into this text.

42. *draw . . . model*] make a sketch-
plan of the battle arrangements.

Limit each leader to his several charge,
And part in just proportion our small power.
Come, gentlemen: 45
Let us consult upon tomorrow's business;
Into my tent: the dew is raw and cold.

    [Richmond, Brandon, Oxford and Herbert] withdraw
        into the tent. [The others exeunt.]

Enter KING RICHARD, RATCLIFFE, NORFOLK, *and* CATESBY
        [and attendant Soldiers].

K. Rich. What is't o'clock?
Cat. It's supper time, my lord: it's nine o'clock.
K. Rich. I will not sup tonight. Give me some ink and paper.
  What, is my beaver easier than it was,   51
  And all my armour laid into my tent?
Cat. It is, my liege, and all things are in readiness.

---

44. power] *F*; strength *Qq.*   45.] *F*; *not in Qq.*   46. Let] *F*; Come, let *Qq.*
47. my] *F*; our *Qq.*   dew] *F*; aire *Qq.*   47. S.D. *Richmond, Brandon, Oxford
and Herbert] This edn; They | F; not in Qq.*   withdraw into the tent] *F*; *not in Qq.*
The others exeunt] This edn; not in F,Qq.   Catesby.] *F,Q 3–6; Catesbie, &c. | Q 1–2.*
and attendant Soldiers] *This edn; not in F,Qq.*   48. is't] *F*; is *Qq.*   49.] *F*;
Cat. It is sixe of clocke (*Q 3–6* of the clocke), full supper time. *Qq.*   50.] *As
Qq;* . . . to night, | Giue *F.*

---

43. *Limit . . . several*] appoint or
prescribe to the leaders their personal
duties.

44. *part*] divide.

47. S.D.] It would hardly have
been possible for the five lords *and*
the supers to 'withdraw into the
tent' in view of its probable size; the
supers thus leave through Richmond's
door. The Q1 entrance-direction
'&c' implies attendants in addition
to the three named characters; these
are here specified. See also notes to
ll. 64 and 79 S.D.

49. *nine o'clock*] Debate has raged
amongst eds, more entertainingly
than usefully, on the appropriate
time for supper in the late fifteenth
century. As the month is August,
and we have just heard details of the
sunset, F's hour must be accepted,
and we may presume 'six' crept into

Q from the actor's normal custom.

49–50.] Lineation here is a problem.
Some eds prefer to line, after Pope,
'What . . . Lord, / It's . . . to night',
which gives two lines only of good pentameter only to leave l. 50 a mere
seven syllables. The version adopted
here leaves l. 48 a half-line and l. 50
overlong, but this amount of variation
is not unusual in the play. Besides,
it is here that F collation ceases to be
reliable, as correction of Q copy
declines to almost nothing (see
Introduction, p. 40) and lineation
is one of the first casualties. From l.
50, therefore, in the collation Q1 is
taken to be the copy-text and the
order of eds in the apparatus is
adjusted accordingly.

51. *beaver*] Strictly, the face-guard
of a helmet: here, probably, the
entire helmet.

K. Rich. Good Norfolk, hie thee to thy charge;
    Use careful watch; choose trusty sentinels.   55
Nor. I go, my lord.
K. Rich. Stir with the lark tomorrow, gentle Norfolk.
Nor. I warrant you, my lord.   *Exit.*
K. Rich. Catesby!
Cat. My lord?
K. Rich.   Send out a pursuivant-at-arms   60
    To Stanley's regiment. Bid him bring his power
    Before sun-rising, lest his son George fall
    Into the blind cave of eternal night.   [*Exit Catesby.*]
    Fill me a bowl of wine. Give me a watch.
    Saddle white Surrey for the field tomorrow;   65
    Look that my staves be sound, and not too heavy.
    Ratcliffe!
Rat. My lord?
K. Rich. Saw'st thou the melancholy Lord Northumberland?
Rat. Thomas the Earl of Surrey and himself,   70
    Much about cockshut time, from troop to troop
    Went through the army cheering up the soldiers.
K. Rich. So, I am satisfied. Give me a bowl of wine.
    I have not that alacrity of spirit

---

55. sentinels] *F;* centinell *Qq.*   58. *Exit.*] *F; not in Qq.*   59. Catesby] *Qq;*
Ratcliffe *F.*   60.] As Steevens; . . . lord. / *King.* Send *Qq,F.*   Cat.] As *Pope;*
Rat. / *Qq,F.*   63. S.D.] *Camb.; not in Qq,F.*   67.] As *Rowe³; in l.* 66 *Qq,F.*
Ratcliffe] *Q6,F;* Ratliffe *Q1–5.*   69. Saw'st thou] *Qq;* Saw'st *F.*   71.
about] *Q1–5,F;* like *Q6.*

55. *sentinels*] Q's singular must be
an error; F's correction may have
been a compositor's guess.
    58. S.D. *Exit*] Q's exit-directions
are very uneven; the F compositor
probably supplied this one.
    59. *Catesby*] F's 'Ratcliffe' is a
simple error, occasioned by the misprint in l. 60's speech-prefix of
'Rat.' for 'Cat.' in all Qq. The
compositor, seeing the inconsistency,
made the wrong guess at correction.
    60. *pursuivant-at-arms*] 'Junior officer
attendant on a herald' (NCS).
    63.] A recollection, perhaps delib-
erate, of I.iv.47 and II.ii.46.

64. *watch*] 'A watch-light or candle'
(Thompson). These commands in
this line must be addressed to the
anonymous attendants, as Catesby
has left on his errand and Ratcliffe's
attention is not claimed until l. 67.
    65. *white Surrey*] Suggested by the
'greate whyte courser' on which, Hall
reports (*Richard III*, fol. liiiᵛ), Richard
entered Leicester.
    66. *staves*] the wooden shafts of the
lances.
    71. *cockshut*] the time when poultry
were shut up for the night, i.e.
twilight (OED).
    74–5.] Tilley M475. Richard seems

Nor cheer of mind that I was wont to have.   75
Set it down. Is ink and paper ready?
Rat. It is, my lord.
K. Rich.   Bid my guard watch; leave me.
Ratcliffe, about the mid of night come to my tent
And help to arm me. Leave me, I say.
                    Exit Ratcliffe. [*Richard withdraws into his tent;*
                                        attendant soldiers guard it.]

Enter STANLEY *Earl of Derby to Richmond in his tent.*

Stan. Fortune and Victory sit on thy helm!   80
Richmond. All comfort that the dark night can afford
Be to thy person, noble father-in-law.
Tell me, how fares our loving mother?
Stan. I, by attorney, bless thee from thy mother,
Who prays continually for Richmond's good.   85
So much for that. The silent hours steal on,
And flaky darkness breaks within the East.
In brief, for so the season bids us be,
Prepare thy battle early in the morning,
And put thy fortune to the arbitrement   90
Of bloody strokes and mortal-staring war.
I, as I may—that which I would, I cannot—
With best advantage will deceive the time,

77.] *As Steevens; . . .* lord. | *King.* Bid *Qq,F.*   78. Ratcliffe] *Q3,5–6,F;*
Ratliffe *Q1–2,4.*   mid] *Q1–5,F.* midst *Q6.*   79. S.D. *Richard withdraws*
into his tent; attendant soldiers guard it] *This edn; not in Qq,F.*   80. sit] *Q2–6,F;*
set *Q1.*   83. loving] *Q1–2;* noble *Q3–6,F.*

---

to be using 'spirit' in the technical/
medical sense, namely the *tertium*
quid that mediates between the soul
and body. On this, see C. S. Lewis,
The Discarded Image, Cambridge,
1964, pp. 166–9.

79. S.D.] It seems that Richard,
who has conducted this episode from
the front of his tent, now lies down
on a pallet within it. Ratcliffe leaves
by Richard's door; the soldiers take
up the watch. There must have been
means of ingress and egress from the
tents during the speeches, as the
furniture for Richard's tent must

have been fetched in. The four lords
may still be in Richmond's tent.

80. *sit*] Q1's 'set' is the same word,
but could confuse the modern reader.
The entire line echoes *1 Tamburlaine*,
II. ii. 73.

83. *loving*] Q3 catches 'noble' from
the preceding line.

87.] Cf. *Rom.*, II. iii. 1–3. Thompson
explains: 'darkness breaks into flakes
of cloud, as the dawn rises'.

91. *mortal-staring*] deathly and
glaring.

92–4.] Stanley's habitual fence-
sitting leads him into some contorted

And aid thee in this doubtful shock of arms.
But on thy side I may not be too forward,   95
Lest, being seen, thy brother, tender George,
Be executed in his father's sight.
Farewell; the leisure and the fearful time
Cuts off the ceremonious vows of love
And ample interchange of sweet discourse   100
Which so long sunder'd friends should dwell upon.
God give us leisure for these rites of love.
Once more adieu: be valiant, and speed well.
Richmond. Good lords, conduct him to his regiment.
I'll strive, with troubled thoughts, to take a nap   105
Lest leaden slumber peise me down tomorrow
When I should mount with wings of victory.

96. brother, tender] *Q 1–5,F;* tender brother *Q 6.*   97. his . . . sight] *Q 1–3,*
5–6,F; thy . . . fight *Q 4.*   101. sunder'd] *As Q q,F* (sundried *Q 1–2;* sundired
Q 3–4; sundered *Q 5–6;* sundred *F*).   102. rites] *F;* rights *Q q.*   104. lords]
Q 1–3,5–6,F; Lord *Q 4.*   105. thoughts] *Q q;* noise *F;* ioise (= joys) *Musgrove*
conj.

expression here; he scarcely dares use a plain noun to say what he means: that the best he can do for Richmond is to try to deceive Richard into thinking he is still fighting on Richard's side, but he will actually be doing what he can to aid Richmond.

96. *tender*] As Aldis Wright noted, George Stanley was a grown man at the time. But it suits Shakespeare to represent him as a youth, and as the last innocent to be threatened by Richard.

98. *leisure*] i.e. lack of leisure.

101. *sunder'd*] The variants are recorded in the form above because they are all matters of spelling, yet they look sufficiently different to require a note.

102. *rites*] Q's 'rights' is again only a spelling difference.

104.] This line seems to have been employed by Shakespeare as a device to get the four attendant nobles out of Richmond's tent and off-stage.

105. *thoughts*] This line has bothered

eds, especially R. G. White (Variorum pp. 389–90), who remarked that, as Shakespeare had gone out of his way to present Richmond as being untroubled in his mind, he ought not to have troubled thoughts. However, Hall's account of Richmond shows him at first fearful and uncertain (*Richard III,* fol. liii^r), and a recollection of this may have lodged in Shakespeare's mind here; it may also account for the terms of opprobrium Richard selects for Richmond: 'white-liver'd runagate' (iv.iv.464) and 'milksop' (l. 326). The problem of the F variant remains: it cannot be a compositorial misreading. White read 'troubled with noise'; S. Musgrove (quoted by Walton, p. 115) proposed that the compositor misread 'joys' (spelled 'ioise') which still does not account for the variant. On the whole it seems best to follow Q, and declare the F reading unexplained.

106. *peise*] weight down or burden (OED *v.*4), in association with 'leaden slumber'.

Once more, good night, kind lords and gentlemen.
　　　　　Exeunt [Stanley with Brandon, Oxford, Herbert].
[*Kneels.*] O Thou, whose captain I account myself,
Look on my forces with a gracious eye;　　　　　　　110
Put in their hands Thy bruising irons of wrath
That they may crush down, with a heavy fall,
Th'usurping helmets of our adversaries;
Make us Thy ministers of chastisement,
That we may praise Thee in the victory.　　　　　　　115
To Thee I do commend my watchful soul
Ere I let fall the windows of mine eyes:
Sleeping and waking, O defend me still!
　　　　　[*Rises, withdraws into his tent, lies down and*] *sleeps.*

　　　　Enter the ghost of young PRINCE EDWARD,
　　　　　　son of Harry the Sixth.

108. S.D. *Exeunt*] *Q 3–6; Exunt | Q 1–2; Exeunt. Manet Richmond | F.　　Stanley
with Brandon, Oxford, Herbert*] *This edn; not in Qq,F.*　　109. *Kneels*] *As Capell;
not in Qq,F.*　　113. *Th'usurping*] *F; The vsurping Qq.*　　*helmets*] *Q 1–4,F;
helmet Q 5–6.*　　115. *the*] *Q 1–2,6; thy Q 3–5,F.*　　118. S.D. *Rises, withdraws
into his tent, lies down and*] *This edn; not in Qq,F.*　　*sleeps*] *F; not in Qq.*
young] *Q 1–2; not in Q 3–6,F.*　　*of*] *This edn; to | Q 2–6,F; not in Q 1.*　　*Harry*]
Q 1; Henry Q 2–6,F.

108. S.D.] The stage now contains:
Richard's tent, he sleeping therein,
guarded by a couple of men-at-arms;
Richmond's tent, into which he is
about to retire, perhaps (at the
producer's discretion) similarly
guarded. Otherwise the stage is clear
for the ghost-scene.

109.] Frye (p. 191) makes the
point that Richmond is not presump-
tuous here since his reliance is clearly
on God rather than on himself
alone

111. *bruising irons*] Obviously meta-
phorically meant: Richmond does
not imply that his forces lack weapons.
Cf. Psalm ii.9: 'Thou shalt krush
them with a scepter of yron . . .'

113. *Th'usurping*] Borrowed from
F to make the rhythm clear to a
modern reader; Q's form would
automatically have been elided.

117. *windows*] eyelids: OED *sb.*4;
unique to Shakespeare.

118. S.D. *ghost*] How represented?
Bradbrook notes in *The Atheist's
Tragedy* 'a sheet, a hair, and a beard'
(IV.iii.55); in Thomas Rawlins's *The
Rebellion* (v.i.I2ᵣ) three comic tailors,
discussing play-acting, say that the
one who will act the ghost does not
look the part, yet 'A little Players
deceite: flower will doe't'; that is, the
face would be whitened with flour.
(*Themes and Conventions of Elizabethan Tragedy*, Cambridge, 1935,
p. 15.) These examples are both late;
for reasons given in the Introduction
(pp. 64–5) it seems likely that the
ghosts here would have been shrouded,
perhaps masked, but they would
probably not have used make-up
since they had to double other parts
in the scene.

Ghost of Pr. Ed. to K. Rich. Let me sit heavy on thy soul
  tomorrow.
    Think how thou stab'st me in my prime of youth   120
    At Tewkesbury; despair therefore, and die.
  To Richmond. Be cheerful, Richmond, for the wronged
    souls
    Of butcher'd princes fight in thy behalf;
    King Henry's issue, Richmond, comforts thee.   [*Exit.*]

Enter the ghost of HENRY THE SIXTH.

Ghost of Hen. to K. Rich. When I was mortal, my anointed
    body   125
    By thee was punched full of deadly holes.
    Think on the Tower and me: despair and die;
    Harry the Sixth bids thee despair and die!
  To Richmond. Virtuous and holy, be thou conqueror:
    Harry, that prophesied thou shouldst be King,   130
    Doth comfort thee in thy sleep. Live and flourish! [*Exit.*]

Enter the ghost of CLARENCE.

Ghost of Cla. [*to K. Rich.*] Let me sit heavy in thy soul
    tomorrow—
    I, that was wash'd to death with fulsome wine,
    Poor Clarence, by thy guile betray'd to death—
    Tomorrow in the battle think on me,   135

119. to K. Rich.] *As* Q1–2; *not in* Q3–6,F.   122.] *As* Qq; . . . Richmond, /
For F.   124. Exit.] *As NCS; not in* Qq,F.   126. deadly] Q1; *not in* Q2–6, F.
131. thy] Qq; *not in* F.   131. S.D. Exit.] *As NCS; not in* Qq,F.   132.
to K. Rich.] *Thompson; not in* F.   in] Q1–4,F; on Q5–6.

121. *despair . . . die*] See I.ii.85;
also Introduction, p. 91.
124. S.D. *Exit*] NCS makes merry
with eds who follow Rowe's collective
'the Ghosts vanish' at l.177. Undoubtedly it would be difficult to
arrange a simultaneous exit for 11
ghosts. It seems most practical to
assume that each ghost appeared
from Richard's door, directed its
malediction to the mouth of his tent,
crossed to Richmond's, blessed him
and immediately exited through his
door as the next ghost was making its

appearance at Richard's door. It
seems most unlikely that a trap
would have been used (and of course
it could not have been used on tour)
since the simultaneous entrance of
Vaughan, Rivers, and Grey would
have hardly been possible via a trap,
and its operation would have meant
a heavy drain on the company's
manpower in a scene which makes
maximum demands thereon anyway.
133. *fulsome*] offensive to the
senses, physically disgusting: OED 5.

And fall thy edgeless sword; despair and die.
To Richmond. Thou offspring of the House of Lancaster,
The wronged heirs of York do pray for thee.
Good angels guard thy battle; live and flourish.   [*Exit.*]

Enter the ghosts of RIVERS, GREY, VAUGHAN.

Ghost of Riv. [*to K. Rich.*] Let me sit heavy in thy soul
    tomorrow,   140
Rivers that died at Pomfret: despair and die.
Ghost of Grey. [*to K. Rich.*] Think upon Grey, and let thy soul
    despair.
Ghost of Vaugh. [*to K. Rich.*] Think upon Vaughan, and with
    guilty fear
Let fall thy lance; despair and die.
All to Richmond. Awake, and think our wrongs in Richard's
    bosom   145
Will conquer him: awake, and win the day.   [*Exeunt.*]

Enter the ghost of HASTINGS.

Ghost of Hast. [*to K. Rich.*] Bloody and guilty, guiltily awake,
And in a bloody battle end thy days.
Think on Lord Hastings; despair and die.

139. Exit.] As *NCS;* not in *Qq,F.*   139. S.D. ghosts] *Q1–2,6,F;* Ghoast | *Q3;*
Ghost | *Q4–5.*   Vaughan] *Qq;* and Vaughan | *F.*   140. Riv.] *Q3–6,F;* King |
Q1–2.   to K. Rich.] *Thompson;* not in *Qq,F.*   in] *Q1–4,F;* on *Q5–6.*
142. to K. Rich.] *Thompson;* not in *Qq,F.*   143. to K. Rich.] *Thompson,* not in
Qq,F.   145.] As *Qq;* . . . Awake, | And *F.*   146. Will] *Q2–6,F;* Wel *Q1.*
Exeunt.] As *NCS;* not in *Qq,F.*   147–51.] As *Q3–6,F;* after l. 159 *Q1–2.*
146. S.D. Hastings] *Q1–2;* L. Hastings | *Q3–6;* Lord Hastings | *F.*   147. to K.
Rich.] *Thompson;* not in *Qq,F.*

136. *edgeless*] blunted; figuratively,
impotent, useless (this sense not in
OED). For 'fall' = 'let fall', cf.
I.ii.186 S.D.
140. *Riv.*] Q3 here corrects Q1's
error.
145.] The division of lines in F
here (and at ll. 150, 152, 156, 160,
165, 168) is caused simply by the
measure of the composing-stick's
being too short to accommodate the
long directions and prefixes.

146. *Will*] Q2's guess is surely
correct.
147–51.] In Q1–2 the ghosts of the
Princes appear before that of Hastings; the Q3 compositor, in a
positively inspired correction, saw
that we are watching a chronological
recapitulation of Richard's murders,
and that the Princes died after
Hastings. Q3's order must therefore
be adopted; no doubt the error in
Q1 arose through some confusion in
the reporting process.

To Richmond. Quiet, untroubled soul, awake, awake: 150
Arm, fight, and conquer for fair England's sake.   [*Exit.*]

Enter the ghosts of the two young PRINCES.

Ghosts to K. Rich. Dream on thy cousins, smother'd in the
        Tower:
Let us be lead within thy bosom, Richard,
And weigh thee down to ruin, shame, and death;
Thy nephews' souls bid thee despair and die.   155
To Richmond. Sleep, Richmond, sleep in peace, and
        wake in joy;
Good angels guard thee from the boar's annoy.
Live, and beget a happy race of kings;
Edward's unhappy sons do bid thee flourish.   [*Exeunt*].

Enter the ghost of LADY ANNE, *his wife.*

Ghost of Anne. to K. Rich. Richard, thy wife, that wretched
        Anne, thy wife,   160
That never slept a quiet hour with thee,
Now fills thy sleep with perturbations.
Tomorrow in the battle think on me,
And fall thy edgeless sword: despair and die.
To Richmond. Thou quiet soul, sleep thou a quiet sleep;
Dream of success and happy victory.   166
Thy adversary's wife doth pray for thee.   [*Exit.*]

Enter the ghost of BUCKINGHAM.

Ghost of Buck. to K. Rich. The first was I that help'd thee to the
        crown;

150.] *As Qq; . . .* soule, / Awake *F.*   151. *Exit.*] *As NCS; not in Qq,F.*
151. S.D. the two] *Q 1–5,F;* two / *Q 6.*   152–9.] *As Q 3–6,F; after l. 146 Q 1–2.*
152. Ghosts] *F;* Ghost / *Q 1–2,6;* Gho. / *Q 3–5.*   to K. Rich.] *Q 1–2;* to K.R. /
Q 3–6; not in F.   152.] *As Qq; . . .* Cousins / Smothered *F.*   153. lead]
Q 1; laid *Q 2–6,F.*   155. souls bid] *Qq;* soule bids *F.*   156.] *As Qq; . . .*
Richmond, / Sleepe *F.*   159. *Exeunt.*] *As NCS; not in Qq,F.*   159. S.D.
Lady Anne] *Q 1–2;* Queene Anne / *Q 3–6;* Anne / *F.*   160. Ghost of Anne, to K.
Rich.] *As F; not in Qq.*   160.] *As Qq; . . .* Wife, / That *F.*   162. perturb-
ations] *Q 2–6,F;* preturbations *Q 1.*   165.] *As Qq; . . .* soule, / Sleepe *F.*
167. *Exit.*] *As NCS; not in Qq,F.*   168.] *As Qq; . . .* I / That *F.*

153. *lead*] Here Q 1 is right (cf. the   guess at a correction mistaken.
same association in l. 106) and Q 2's

The last was I that felt thy tyranny.
O, in the battle think of Buckingham,   170
And die in terror of thy guiltiness.
Dream on, dream on of bloody deeds and death;
Fainting, despair: despairing, yield thy breath.
To Richmond. I died for hope ere I could lend thee aid,
But cheer thy heart, and be thou not dismay'd.   175
God and good angels fight on Richmond's side;
And Richard fall in height of all his pride.   [*Exit.*]
                              Richard starteth up out of a dream.
K. Rich. Give me another horse! Bind up my wounds!
Have mercy, Jesu!—Soft, I did but dream.
O coward conscience, how dost thou afflict me!   180
The lights burn blue; it is now dead midnight.
Cold fearful drops stand on my trembling flesh.
What do I fear? Myself? There's none else by;
Richard loves Richard, that is, I and I.
Is there a murderer here? No. Yes, I am!   185
Then fly. What, from myself? Great reason why,
Lest I revenge? What, myself upon myself?
Alack, I love myself. Wherefore? For any good
That I myself have done unto myself?

174.] *As Qq;* ... hope / Ere *F.*   177. fall] *F;* falls *Qq.*   177. S.D. *starteth up*] *Q1–2; starteth* / *Q3–6; starts* / *F.*   a] *Qq; his* / *F.*   181. now] *Q1;* not *Q2–6,F.*   182. stand] *Q1–4,6,F;* stands *Q5.*   184. and] *Q1;* am *Q2–6,F.*   189. I myself] *Q1–5,F;* my selfe *Q6.*

174. *for hope*] This phrase has attracted emendation, without much improvement. The Camb. interpretation is the most widely received; comparing *Mac.,* I. v. 36, 'almost dead for breath', it glosses 'as regards hope, and hence almost equivalent to for want of hope'. Dyce found 'when I am dead for hope' in *James IV* (v. vi. 11). Malone's elaboration of Steevens, 'he lost his life in consequence of the hope which led him to engage in the enterprise' is accepted by NPS among others, and is supported by l. 196 of 'Glendower' in the *Mirror:* 'Lo thus fond hope did both theyr lyues abridge' (p. 128). It is perhaps the best interpretation.

177. *fall*] The optative (i.e. 'let Richard fall'); cf. ll. 139, 165–6.

178–9. *Give . . . Jesu!*] These phrases clearly are spoken in sleep, or at least while Richard is still in the throes of his nightmare vision. He is not fully awake until 'Soft, I did but dream.' The call for Christ's mercy is thus not spoken from his conscious mind.

181. *burn blue*] Traditional sign of ghostly presence. Cf. *Caes.,* IV. iii. 275.

181. *now*] Obviously right, the word is worth noting in view of its proximity to the major crux at l. 184, where Q1 again stands alone against the others.

184. *and*] See Appendix II.

O no , alas, I rather hate myself   190
For hateful deeds committed by myself.
I am a villain—yet I lie, I am not!
Fool, of thyself speak well! Fool, do not flatter.
My conscience hath a thousand several tongues,
And every tongue brings in a several tale,   195
And every tale condemns me for a villain:
Perjury, perjury, in the highest degree;
Murder, stern murder, in the direst degree;
All several sins, all us'd in each degree,
Throng to the bar, crying all, 'Guilty, guilty!'   200
I shall despair. There is no creature loves me,
And if I die, no soul will pity me—
And wherefore should they, since that I myself
Find in myself no pity to myself?
Methought the souls of all that I had murder'd   205
Came to my tent, and every one did threat
Tomorrow's vengeance on the head of Richard.

Enter RATCLIFFE.

Rat. My lord!
K. Rich. Zounds! Who is there?
Rat. Ratcliffe, my lord; 'tis I. The early village cock   210
Hath twice done salutation to the morn;
Your friends are up and buckle on their armour.
K. Rich. O Ratcliffe, I have dream'd a fearful dream!
What thinkest thou—will our friends prove all true?
Rat. No doubt, my lord.
K. Rich.   O Ratcliffe, I fear, I fear!   215

197. Perjury, perjury] *Q 1–2; Periurie Q 3–6,F.*   200. Throng] *Q 1–2;* Throng
all *Q 3–6,F.*   to the bar] *Qq;* to'th'Barre *F.*   202. will] *Q 1–2;* shall
Q 3–6,F.   203. And] *Qq;* Nay, *F.*   205. had murder'd] *Q 1,F;* murtherd
Q 2–6 (subst.).   206. Came] *Q 1–2,F;* Came all *Q 3–6.*   209. Zounds! Who
is] *As Qq;* Who's *F.*   there] *Q 1–3,5–6,F;* heare *Q 4.*   213–14.] *Qq; not
in F.*   214. thinkest] *Capell;* thinkst *Qq.*   215. *Rat.* No doubt, my lord.]
Qq; not in F.   doubt] *Q 1–3,5–6;* dopt *Q 4.*

194.] Proverbial: Tilley C601.
Cf. v. ii. 17.
201. *despair*] As the ghosts urged.
(Cf. 1. ii. 85, and Introduction, pp.
106–7).
209. *Zounds*] Deleted from F in

accord with 3 Jac. I.
213–15. *O . . . lord*] Omitted from
F, the cause undoubtedly compositorial eye-skip: Richard has two consecutive speeches beginning 'O Ratcliffe'.

Rat. Nay, good my lord, be not afraid of shadows.

K. Rich. By the Apostle Paul, shadows tonight
  Have struck more terror to the soul of Richard
  Than can the substance of ten thousand soldiers,
  Armed in proof, and led by shallow Richmond.   220
  'Tis not yet near day; come, go with me:
  Under our tents I'll play the eavesdropper,
  To see if any mean to shrink from me.

                              Exeunt Richard and Ratcliffe.

Enter the Lords *to* RICHMOND *sitting in his tent.*

Lords. Good morrow, Richmond.

Richmond. Cry mercy, lords and watchful gentlemen,   225
  That you have ta'en a tardy sluggard here.

1 Lord. How have you slept, my lord?

Richmond. The sweetest sleep and fairest-boding dreams
  That ever enter'd in a drowsy head
  Have I, since your departure, had, my lords.   230

---

222. eavesdropper] *As F4;* ease dropper *Q1;* ewse dropper *Q2;* ewse-dropper
Q3; eawse-dropper *Q4;* ewese-dropper *Q5–6;* Ease-dropper *F.*   223. see]
Q1–2; heare *Q3–6F.*   mean] *Q1–3,5–6,F;* means *Q4.*   223. S.D. *Richard
and Ratcliffe*] *F; not in Qq.*   *sitting in his tent*] *F; not in Qq.*   224. *Lords*]
Q3–6; Lo. | Q1; Lor. | Q2; Richm. | F.   226. a tardy] *Q1–3,5–6,F;* tardie
Q4.   227. *1 Lord*] *This edn; Lo. | Q1; Lor. | Q2–6; Lords | F.*   228.] *As
Qq; . . . sleepe, | And F.*

---

220. *proof*] capable of withstanding
attack, impenetrable: OED *sb.* B.
II. 10..

shallow] wanting in depth of mind
or experience: OED *a.*6c.

222. *eavesdropper*] The spellings
pursue a curious path before returning unexpectedly to the Q1 form
in F.

223. *shrink from me*] The phrase is
in Hall, *Richard III*, fol. 1v.

223. S.D.] Obviously only Richard
and his henchman go on the snooping
expedition, so the guards remain at
the tent. The Q entrance-direction is
vague; F makes it clear that a
conference in the general's tent
occurs, but does not specify the
participants. Probably they should be

the same three who left the stage at
l. 108: Brandon, Oxford, and Herbert,
and perhaps Blunt as well.

224. *Lords*] The speech-prefix in
Q1–2 is ambiguous; Q3's plural is a
plausible guess: the phrase sounds
like a collective greeting. F's prefix is
simply someone's mistake.

225. *Cry mercy*] Simply 'I cry you
mercy' abridged.

227. 1 *Lord*] See also ll. 224 and
236; the prefix in Q1 is ambiguous.
All eds here follow F's 'Lords',
apparently without reflection: no
producer would dare risk the comic-
opera effect of having this and l. 236
spoken in mumbled chorus. Any of
the lords available will do, but not
all!

Methought their souls whose bodies Richard murder'd
Came to my tent and cried on victory.
I promise you my soul is very jocund
In the remembrance of so fair a dream.
How far into the morning is it, lords?   235
1 Lord. Upon the stroke of four.
Richmond. Why then 'tis time to arm and give direction.
    [Comes out from the tent.]

His oration to his soldiers.

More than I have said, loving countrymen,
The leisure and enforcement of the time
Forbids to dwell upon. Yet remember this: 240
God, and our good cause, fight upon our side;
The prayers of holy saints and wronged souls,
Like high-rear'd bulwarks, stand before our faces.
Richard except, those whom we fight against
Had rather have us win than him they follow.   245
For what is he they follow? Truly, gentlemen,
A bloody tyrant and a homicide;
One rais'd in blood, and one in blood establish'd;
One that made means to come by what he hath,
And slaughter'd those that were the means to help him;

233. soul] *Qq;* heart *F.*   236. *1 Lord*] *This edn; Lo. | Q1-2; Lor. | Q3-6,F.*
237. S.D. *Comes out from the tent;*] *This edn; not in Qq,F.*   243. rear'd]
Q1-3,5-6,F; read *Q4.*   250. slaughter'd] *Q1-3,5-6,F;* slandered *Q4.*

232. *cried on*] invoke or bring about by outcry: OED cry on.

233. *soul*] NCS and Smidt (p. 67) think this reading is a compositor's recollection of l. 231. It is not obviously wrong, however.

236. *1 Lord*] See l. 227 n.

237. S.D. *Comes out from the tent*] The oration, obviously, is not spoken in the tent, so a direction is needed. To whom is it spoken? 'To his Troops, who now gather about the Tent', says Capell, and many eds print some version of this. But the risks are of having an awkwardly crowded stage or alternatively a patent shortage of supers (which seems to have been Q's case). It would seem the

simplest and most effective expedient would be to direct the oration directly to the audience, with Richmond's lords and guards serving to lead the reactions.

239. *leisure*] Again, as at l. 98, this means 'lack of leisure'.

249-50. *means . . . means*] To make means is a harmless phrase meaning to take steps—unless it is applied, as here, to people, as the second use reveals. Richmond is, in the phrase, actually attacking Richard for his Machiavellianism; that people were mere things to be made use of in his illegal pursuit of the crown and dispatched callously when used.

A base foul stone, made precious by the foil   251
Of England's chair, where he is falsely set;
One that hath ever been God's enemy.
Then, if you fight against God's enemy,
God will, in justice, ward you as his soldiers;   255
If you do sweat to put a tyrant down,
You sleep in peace, the tyrant being slain;
If you do fight against your country's foes,
Your country's fat shall pay your pains the hire;
If you do fight in safeguard of your wives,   260
Your wives shall welcome home the conquerors;
If you do free your children from the sword,
Your children's children quits in it your age.
Then, in the name of God and all these rights,
Advance your standards, draw your willing swords! 265
For me, the ransom of my bold attempt
Shall be this cold corpse on the earth's cold face;
But if I thrive, the gain of my attempt
The least of you shall share his part thereof.
Sound, drums, and trumpets, boldly and cheerfully! 270
God, and Saint George! Richmond and victory!
                    [*Exeunt Richmond and his followers.*]

251. foil] *Q1-2;* soile *Q3-5;* soyle *Q6,F.*   256. do sweat] *Q1-2;* do sweare
Q3-5,F; sweare *Q6.*   271. S.D. *Exeunt Richmond and his followers*] *This edn;*
not in Qq,F.   Soldiers] *This edn; c./Qq;* Catesby / *F.*

251. stone . . . foil] Image from
jewellery: England is the foil, or
setting, which helplessly gives value
to the otherwise worthless stone that
is Richard. Cf. *R2,* i.iii.266–7.
    252. chair] throne.
    255. ward] protect.
    259. fat] wealth, surplus goods;
cf. Genesis, xlv.18, 'the fat of the
land'. Walker (p. 29) would read
'foes', calling 'fat' 'a common corruption', but it is not clear how the
defeated invaders could pay their
pains the hire.
    263. quits] requites, repays (OED
quit *v.* II.10); 'children' is a collective
singular.
    266. ransom] This word is not in the
sources; Shakespeare certainly added

it for its figural overtones: Richmond
offers himself if needed as redemption
for England's wrongs. See OED *sb.*2b
for the scriptural sense.
    269.] Again, a promise full of
theological overtones.
    271. S.D.] This is the likeliest
place for Richmond and his forces to
leave the stage (which could take
place simultaneously with the next
few lines for Richard's party).
Richmond however must arm for
combat, as he remarks at l. 237. It
would hardly be possible to arm and
to orate in a dignified manner at the
same time, so either he does so on-
stage after his oration, or, as seems
more likely, leaves the stage to do so.
M. R. Holmes (*Shakespeare and his*

Enter KING RICHARD, RATCLIFFE *and* [Soldiers].

K. Rich. What said Northumberland, as touching
    Richmond?
Rat. That he was never trained up in arms.
K. Rich. He said the truth. And what said Surrey then?
Rat. He smil'd and said, 'The better for our purpose.'   275
K. Rich. He was in the right, and so indeed it is.

                                     The clock striketh.

    Tell the clock there! Give me a calendar—
    Who saw the sun today?
Rat.   Not I, my lord.
K. Rich. Then he disdains to shine, for by the book
    He should have brav'd the east an hour ago.   280
    A black day will it be to somebody.
    Ratcliffe!
Rat. My lord?
K. Rich.   The sun will not be seen today!
    The sky doth frown and lour upon our army:
    I would these dewy tears were from the ground.   285
    Not shine today? Why, what is that to me

---

273. trained] *Q1–5,F;* train'd *Q6.*   276. S.D.] *Qq; Clocke strikes. | F.*
277–8.] *As Pope;* . . . there. | Giue . . . today? | *Rat.* Not . . . Lord. *Qq,F.*
280. hour] *Qq,F* (hower *Q1;* houre *Q2–6,F*).   282.] *As Johnson; in l. 281*
Qq,F (. . . some bodie Rat. | *Qq;* somebody. *Ratcliffe.* | *F.*)   283.] *As*
Steevens; . . . Lord. | *King.* The *Qq,F.*   not] *Q2–6,F;* nor *Q1.*

Players, 1972) has an amusing essay on the use of stage-armour, and the practical problems in donning it, which have a bearing on this question: pp. 150–67. The F entrance-direction includes Catesby, but he has nothing to do, and there is no need for his presence now. Q implies in its vague way that Richard had picked up some more attendants during his circuit of the camp, who will now serve to react to his oration: unlike Richmond's audience (l. 237 n.) they do not appear to be 'men of name'. The question of whether or not to strike the tents needs comment. There is no absolute need to remove

them unless they would interfere with the producer's planned military manœuvres, in which case Richmond's is best struck after l. 272, and Richard's during his giving of directions, ll. 290–314

276. S.D.] The clock, presumably, was off-stage. 'Tell' (l. 277) means count the strokes.

277. *calendar*] What we would call an almanac, including astronomical and other data.

280–1.] See l. 19n. Line 281 is proverbial: Tilley D88.

284.] Cf. 'And all the clouds that lour'd upon our House' (I.i.3); the wheel is turning full circle.

More than to Richmond? For the self-same heaven
That frowns on me looks sadly upon him.

Enter NORFOLK.

Nor. Arm, arm, my lord: the foe vaunts in the field!
K. Rich. Come, bustle, bustle! Caparison my horse.   290
                                        [*Richard arms.*]
Call up Lord Stanley; bid him bring his power.
I will lead forth my soldiers to the plain,
And thus my battle shall be ordered:
My foreward shall be drawn out all in length,
Consisting equally of horse and foot;   295
Our archers shall be placed in the midst.
John, Duke of Norfolk, Thomas, Earl of Surrey
Shall have the leading of this foot and horse;
They thus directed, we will follow
In the main battle, whose puissance on either side   300
Shall be well winged with our chiefest horse.
This, and Saint George to boot! What think'st thou,
     Norfolk?
Nor. A good direction, warlike sovereign.
                              He sheweth him a paper.
This I found on my tent this morning.
K. Rich. [*Reading*] 'Jockey of Norfolk, be not so bold: 305

288. looks] *Q1–5,F;* looke *Q6.*   290. S.D.] *This edn; not in Qq,F.*   294.
drawn out all] *Q1;* drawne *Q2–6,F.*   298. this] *Q1–2;* the *Q3–6,F.*
300. main] *Q2–6,F;* matne *Q1.*   302.] *As Qq; . . .* boote. / What *F.*
boot] *Q3–6,F;* bootes *Q1–2.*   Norfolk] *Q1,F; Nor. Q2–5; not Q6.*   303.
S.D.] *Qq; not in F.*   305. *K. Rich.* [*Reading*]] *As Capell; not in Qq,F.*
of] *Qq,F; to Alexander.*   so] *Q1–5,F; to Q6; too Capell.*

290. *Caparison*] 'The caparison of a
horse was, strictly speaking, the rich
covering or housing which was worn
by the spare horse at a battle or
tournament' (Thompson).

290. S.D.] Required in response to
Norfolk's exhortation.

293–301.] The battle-plan is based
on Hall's description; Appendix III,
p. 369.

299. *we*] i.e. Richard.

300–1. *puissance . . . well winged . . .
chiefest horse*] i.e. the main power of

the army will have the best of the
cavalry on its wings.

302. *boot*] OED *sb.*[1] 1.i. No instance
is given of the plural in this sense.

305. S.D. *Reading*] As printed in
QqF it looks as if Norfolk is supposed
to read the verse to Richard; NCS
rightly protests that it would be impossible for him to read such an
insult to his King; Capell's emendation is sound.

of . . . so] For an unexplained
reason, Alexander reads 'Jockey, to

          For Dickon thy master is bought and sold.'
A thing devised by the enemy.
Go, gentlemen: every man unto his charge!
Let not our babbling dreams affright our souls;
Conscience is but a word that cowards use,   310
Devis'd at first to keep the strong in awe.
Our strong arms be our conscience, swords our law.
March on! Join bravely. Let us to it pell-mell—
If not to Heaven, then hand in hand to hell!

His oration to his army.

What shall I say, more than I have inferr'd?   315
Remember whom you are to cope withal:
A sort of vagabonds, rascals, and runaways;
A scum of Bretons and base lackey peasants,
Whom their o'er-cloyed country vomits forth
To desperate adventures and assur'd destruction.   320
You sleeping safe, they bring to you unrest;

307. A] *Capell; King.* A *Qq,F.*   308. unto] *Qq;* to *F.*   310. Conscience]
Qq; For Conscience *F.*   but a] *Q1-2;* a *Q3-6,F.*   311. at] *Q1-4,F;* as
Q5-6.   313. to it] *Q1-2;* too it *Q3-6;* too't *F.*   314. S.D.] *Qq; not in F.*
318. Bretons] *Capell;* Brittains *Qq,F (subst.).*   321. to you] *Q1;* you to
Q2-6,F.

Norfolk'; who 'Jockey' is supposed to
be he does not say. Capell's emendation 'too bold' has attracted wide
support since it is the reading in both
Hall and Holinshed. It is not self-
evidently such an improvement as to
imagine that Q must be wrong, however. The phrase was proverbial:
Tilley B787.
  306. *Dickon*] A contemptuous dim-
inutive of 'Richard'.
  310–11.] Cf. *Jew*, Prol., ll. 20–1:
'Might first made Kings, and Lawes
were then most sure / When like the
Dracos they were writ in blood'; also
Promos, II.iii: 'And wantons sure to
keepe in awe these statutes first were
made' (Bullough, II.452). Other
parallels are to be found in *Selimus,*
ii. 326, 328, and *Troublesome Raigne,*
xii. 85. The sentiments are the common coin of the Machiavel.

  314. S.D.] A parallel with Richmond's direction at l. 237 (omitted
from F perhaps accidentally by the
compositor). NCS remarks on the
contradiction of Richard's starting
his oration just after he has urged his
followers pell-mell to battle. The
director must take this into account;
perhaps the intention was to provoke
some 'bustle' among Richard's followers on-stage in ll. 308–14; while
military business is then taking place,
Richard (like Richmond) addresses
his oration to the audience.
  315. *inferr'd*] alleged or reported:
OED 2.
  317. *sort*] a band or group: OED
sb.[2] II. 17c (with contemptuous connotation in this instance).
  318. *lackey*] hanger-on, camp-
follower: OED *sb.* 2.

You having lands, and bless'd with beauteous wives,
They would restrain the one, distain the other.
And who doth lead them but a paltry fellow,
Long kept in Bretagne at our brother's cost?   325
A milksop! One that never in his life
Felt so much cold as over-shoes in snow.
Let's whip these stragglers o'er the seas again,
Lash hence these overweening rags of France,
These famish'd beggars, weary of their lives—   330
Who, but for dreaming on this fond exploit,
For want of means, poor rats, had hang'd themselves.
If we be conquer'd, let men conquer us!
And not these bastard Bretons, whom our fathers
Have in their own land beaten, bobb'd, and thump'd,
And in record left them the heirs of shame.   336
Shall these enjoy our lands? Lie with our wives?
Ravish our daughters?   *Drum afar off.*
        Hark, I hear their drum.

---

323. restrain] *Qq,F;* distrain *Warburton.*   325. Bretagne] *Hanmer;* Brittaine
Qq,F (subst.).   brother's] *This edn; mothers Qq F (subst.).*   326. milksop]
As Q6,F; milkesopt *Q1–5.*   334. Bretons] *Qq,F* (Brittains, *subst.*), *Capell.*
336. in] *Q1–2;* on *Q3–6,F.*   338.] *As Qq;* . . . daughters? / Hearke *F.*
338. S.D.] *F; not in Qq.*

323. *restrain*] Warburton's emendation has won wide support, including
NCS, NPS, and Eccles among
modern eds. Malone objected that
'distrain' meant to seize goods for
the non-payment of rent, to which
S. Walker and others have replied
that Shakespeare uses the word to
mean to seize or confiscate, without
qualifications: cf. *R2,* II.iii.131; *1H6,*
I.iii.61. 'Restrain' can mean 'withold'
(OED 4a), and this is probably the
meaning intended.
        distain] defile or dishonour: OED
*v.*2.
        325. *brother's*] The person intended
is the Duke of Burgundy. Shakespeare,
misled by a misprint in his 1587 edn
of Holinshed, copied its reading,
'moother's'. This is so perplexing the
Duchess was not paying Richmond
money—as to justify the emendation.

For the principles involved, see G.
Thomas Tanselle, 'External Fact as an
Editorial Problem', *SB* 32 (1979),
pp. 1–47.
        326–7.] Proverbial: Tilley S380.
        329. *overweening rags*] presump-
tuous, arrogant beggars. 'Rags' is
transferred from the clothes Richard
alleges they wear to the wearers
themselves. The images in ll. 328–30
link the alleged beggary of the
Bretons with the usual punishment
for vagabonds of a whipping by the
beadle and dispatch to their own
parish.
        335. *bobb'd*] beaten with fists:
OED *v.*2 1.
        336.] Richard refers to the exploits
of the English under Henry V in
defeating French forces.
        338. S.D.] Perhaps a prompter's
direction.

Fight, gentlemen of England! Fight, bold yeomen!
Draw, archers, draw your arrows to the head!   340
Spur your proud horses hard, and ride in blood!
Amaze the welkin with your broken staves!

Enter a Messenger.

What says Lord Stanley? Will he bring his power?
Mess. My lord, he doth deny to come.
K. Rich. Off with his son George's head!   345
Nor. My lord, the enemy is past the marsh!
After the battle let George Stanley die.
K. Rich. A thousand hearts are great within my bosom.
Advance, our standards! Set upon our foes!
Our ancient word of courage, fair Saint George,   350
Inspire us with the spleen of fiery dragons!
Upon them! Victory sits on our helms.   *Exeunt.*

339. Fight] *Q1–2;* Right *Q3–6,F.*   bold] *Q1;* boldly *Q2–6,F.*   342. S.D.]
F; not in Qq.   352. helms] *Q1–2,4;* helpes *Q3,5–6,F.*   *Exeunt.*] *Q1–2; not
in Q3–6,F.*

342. *welkin*] the sky, or firmament: OED 2.

broken staves] As at l. 66, staves are the wooden part of the lances, broken in the fierceness of the combat. A parallel use occurs in the *Arcadia* ('our staves having bene broken at the encounter', p. 270).

342. S.D.] According to l. 60, a pursuivant-at-arms had been sent by Catesby to chivvy Stanley. F's supplied direction here may have no more authority than Compositor B's

sense of tidiness, but the speech-prefix at l. 344 suggests it is correct.

349. *standards*] i.e. standard-bearers: OED standard *sb.*3.

350–1. *Saint George . . . fiery dragons*] As Wilson Knight pointed out, Richard here appeals to both of the legendary antagonists, St George and the Dragon: *The Sovereign Flower* (1958), pp. 22–5.

352. *Victory . . . helms*] Cf. l. 80, and *1 Tamburlaine,* II. ii. 73.

[SCENE IV]

Alarum. Excursions. Enter [NORFOLK *and* Soldiers; *then at the other door*] CATESBY.

Cat. Rescue! My lord of Norfolk, rescue, rescue!
The King enacts more wonders than a man,
Daring an opposite to every danger.
His horse is slain, and all on foot he fights,
Seeking for Richmond in the throat of death. 5
Rescue, fair lord, or else the day is lost!
[Exeunt Norfolk and soldiers.]

Alarums. Enter KING RICHARD.

K. Rich. A horse! A horse! My kingdom for a horse!
Cat. Withdraw, my lord; I'll help you to a horse.
K. Rich. Slave! I have set my life upon a cast,
And I will stand the hazard of the die. 10
I think there be six Richmonds in the field:

Scene IV

SCENE IV] *Capell; not in Qq,F.* S.D. *Norfolk and* Soldiers] *As Capell; not in Qq,F.at the other door] This edn; not in Qq,F.* 1.] *As Qq;* . . . Norfolke, / Rescue F. 6. S.D. *Exeunt Norfolk and soldiers.] This edn; not in Qq,F. Alarums.] F; not in Qq.* 10. die] *Q1–2;* dye *Q3,5–6,F;* day *Q4.*

S.D.] The Duke of Norfolk must be present for Catesby to appeal to; it would seem from the tone of Catesby's speech that he has some troops with him. This implies that Norfolk and his men are engaged in the excursions (i.e. actors running out of the tiring-house and in again) while the trumpet sounds the alarums; this action is intended to stand for the entire battle in the audience's mind. Catesby then appears at the other side of the stage and makes his appeal.

3.] 'Wherever Richard meets an opposite [i.e. an enemy or adversary] on the field, he dares him *à l'outrance*' (Thompson). The phrase makes sense thus, but Tyrwhitt's proposal 'daring and opposite' (i.e. boldly opposing all dangers) is very attractive, and was adopted by NCS.

6. S.D.] Norfolk and his men leave, and there is no reason why they should delay after hearing Catesby's account. Richard's famous last speech is thus uttered with only Catesby on stage.

7.] For the sources of this line, see Introduction, pp. 82–3, and Appendix III, p. 373.

9–10. *cast . . . die*] Metaphor from gaming: Richard has 'cast' the dice, and will accept ('stand') the risk or chance (OED hazard *sb.*3) of the die (one of a pair of dice) showing a low number.

11–12.] This surprising information is Shakespeare's invention. In

Five have I slain today instead of him.
A horse! A horse! My kingdom for a horse!   [*Exeunt.*]

[SCENE V]

Alarum. Enter KING RICHARD *and* RICHMOND; *they fight.*
Richard is slain, then, retreat being sounded, [*exit Richmond;*
Richard's body is carried off]. *Flourish. Enter* RICHMOND, STANLEY
Earl of Derby bearing the crown, with other Lords [*and* Soldiers].

Richmond. God, and your arms, be prais'd, victorious friends:
The day is ours; the bloody dog is dead.

13. *Exeunt.*] *Theobald; not in Qq,F.*

Scene v

SCENE V] *Dyce; not in Qq,F.*   S.D. *then, retreat being sounded*] *Qq; Retreat | F.*
exit Richmond; Richard's body is carried off] *This edn; not in Qq,F.   Flourish*] *F;*
not in Qq.   other] *Qq; diuers other | F.   and soldiers*] *This edn; &c. | Q 1–2;*
not in Q 3–6,F.   1.] *As Qq; . . . Armes | Be F.*

Hall Richard actively seeks single
combat with Richmond who is
nothing loth to encounter him
(Appendix III, p. 372). The idea of
a king's thus protecting himself was
not uncommon (it occurs again in
1H4, v.iii). But the stratagem,
while suitable enough for the sly
Henry IV, hardly seems appropriate
in the heroic Richmond.

Scene v

S.D.] This, the most physically
exciting moment in the play, is
badly served by the Q stage-directions. The minimum to make it
actable has been added here, but
the director ought to feel free to
improvise to make this wordless
encounter between Good and Evil
as symbolically effective as possible.
Catesby and Richard must leave at
one door; trumpets maintain the
tension, then the antagonists appear
through separate doors. They fight,
Richard is killed, the retreat is

sounded (as Q says) and Richmond
exits. Richard's body is still on-stage,
and, as we learn from Stanley's
remarks and the direction (ll. 4–7),
the crown is removed from Richard's
head off-stage, it is necessary to
assume that the stage-keepers acted
their routine part as bearers-of-the-
dead, and carried him off. The stage
is thus clear for the triumphal return
of the victor with Stanley, no doubt
Oxford, Blunt, and Herbert, and as
many supers as available. It should
be emphasized that the only death
that occurs on-stage is that of Richard:
the list of the killed given in ll. 13–14
does not even include Catesby.
Richard's death is thus the single act
of destruction necessary to purge the
kingdom of its accumulated ills. See
Introduction, pp. 107–9.

2. *the bloody . . . dead*] Cf. Harvey, in
Greene's Memoriall, l. 5: 'dead is the
Dog of spite' (in *Foure Letters and
Certeine Sonnets*, 1592). Cf. also
IV.iv.78.

Stan. Courageous Richmond, well hast thou acquit thee!
     [*Presenting the crown*] Lo, here, this long-usurped royalty
     From the dead temples of this bloody wretch   5
     Have I pluck'd off to grace thy brows withal.
     Wear it, enjoy it, and make much of it.
Richmond. Great God of Heaven, say Amen to all!
     But tell me, is young George Stanley living?
Stan. He is, my lord, and safe in Leicester town,   10
     Whither, if it please you, we may now withdraw us.
Richmond. What men of name are slain on either side?
Stan. John, Duke of Norfolk; Walter, Lord Ferrers;
     Sir Robert Brakenbury, and Sir William Brandon.
Richmond. Inter their bodies as become their births.   15
     Proclaim a pardon to the soldiers fled
     That in submission will return to us;
     And then, as we have ta'en the sacrament,
     We will unite the white rose and the red.
     Smile, heaven, upon this fair conjunction,   20
     That long have frown'd upon their enmity.
     What traitor hears me and says not Amen?
     England hath long been mad, and scarr'd herself:
     The brother blindly shed the brother's blood;

3.] *As Qq; . . .* Richmond, / Well *F.*   3-4. thee! / Lo] As *Qq;* thee: Loe, /
Heere *F.*   4. S.D. *Presenting the crown*] *This edn; not in Qq,F.*   4. this . . .
royalty] *Q1;* this . . . roialties *Q2-6 (subst.);* these . . . Royalties *F.*   7. enjoy
it] *Q1-2; not in Q3-6,F.*   11. if it please you] *Qq;* if you please *F.*   may
now] *Qq;* may *F.*   13. *Stan.] F; not in Qq.*   Walter] *Q6,F;* Water *Q1-5.*
Ferrers; / Sir] *F;* Ferris, sir / Robert *Q1;* Ferris, sir Robert *Q2-6.*   17. to us]
Q1-5,F; vs *Q6.*   21. have] *Q1-5. F;* hath *Q6.*

---

3. *acquit*] Participle's -ed omitted
after d and t: Abbott §342.

4. *royalty*] i.e. the crown, symbol of
royalty (cf. *1H4,* IV.iii.55).

13-14.] This is a very peculiar pair
of lines of verse; F's attribution of
them to Stanley may have been only
a guess. Perhaps he or another handed
Richmond a paper, from which he
read (in prose) these four names. The
odd form, 'Water Lord Ferri[s]'
derives from Hall.

18. *as . . . sacrament*] as has been

sworn by solemn oath (in Rheims
cathedral, as Hall (*Richard III,* fol.
xiiv) reports, Richmond took his
'corporall othe' to marry the princess
Elizabeth, and so 'unite the white
rose and the red'). It was customary
to receive the Eucharist in guarantee
of a vow (cf. I.iv.192-3).

20. *conjunction*] In the astrological,
as well as the marital, sense.

22. *Amen*] Presumably the on-
lookers pronounce the word in
response.

The father rashly slaughter'd his own son;   25
The son, compell'd, been butcher to the sire.
All this divided York and Lancaster—
Divided, in their dire division.
O now let Richmond and Elizabeth,
The true succeeders of each royal House,   30
By God's fair ordinance conjoin together,
And let their heirs, God, if Thy will be so,
Enrich the time to come with smooth-fac'd peace,
With smiling plenty, and fair prosperous days.
Abate the edge of traitors, gracious Lord,   35
That would reduce these bloody days again,
And make poor England weep in streams of blood.
Let them not live to taste this land's increase,
That would with treason wound this fair land's peace.
Now civil wounds are stopp'd; peace lives again.   40
That she may long live here, God say Amen.   *Exeunt.*

FINIS

32. their] *Q1-2;* thy *Q3-6,F.*   Thy] *Q1-4,F;* they *Q5-6.*   41. here]
Q3,F; heare *Q1-2,4-6.*   41. S.D. *Exeunt.*] *F; not in Qq.*

25.] A recollection of the cele-brated scene in *3H6*, II. v.

27–8.] Various attempts have been made to punctuate and/or emend these lines. The version here is intended to convey: all this (re-counted in ll. 23–6) divided York and Lancaster—more, divided them internally by this war (the very point of ll. 23–6 is of the unnatural, intestine divisions the war has caused). See NCS and R. G. White (Variorum, p. 427) for the most interesting alternatives.

30. *true succeeders*] A conventional Tudor piety, but of course an untruth. The heir of York was indeed the Princess; the house of Lancaster was so devastated by war and murder it could hardly be said to exist, and certainly it no longer could claim to be near to the succession. After Richard's son (unmentioned in the play) died in 1484, Richard adopted his nephew John de la Pole as heir-

presumptive, an honour which cost him his life in the rebellion at Stoke in 1487; after Elizabeth the next in line of succession was the 'foolish' son of Clarence, Edward Earl of Warwick, whose tragi-comic history of imper-sonation by Lambert Simnel and Perkin Warbeck led eventually to his execution in 1499. Henry VII was in historical fact hardly less thorough in eliminating potential opponents than was Richard.

31. *ordinance*] That which is or-dained or decreed by God: OED *sb.* 5b.

35. *Abate*] Literally, to blunt or turn the edge (OED *v.*[1] III.8); so 'make blunt the edges of traitors' swords'; also figuratively to put an end to (OED *v.*[1] I.2) the sharpness of dissatisfaction which produces traitors.

36. *reduce*] bring back. Cf. II.ii.68.

40. *stopp'd*] staunched, prevented from bleeding.

APPENDIX I

LONGER PASSAGES UNIQUE TO F AND Q

I.ii. 159–70 (*F only*).] Patrick observed that as l. 171 seems to refer in summary to the events described in these lines, the passage must be original, and have been cut from Q to accelerate the scene (pp. 124–5). Smidt (pp. 123–4) believes that since neither York, Edward, nor Richard was present at the death of Rutland, the lines were removed for reasons of 'historical accuracy'. Neither of these views is very persuasive, especially Smidt's, which is based on a premiss (of the need for literal accuracy) which would not have occurred to Shakespeare or his colleagues in such a form. Although the passage was probably cut from Q (perhaps because the references were not very clear to the audience—yet Rutland's death is made much of in the next scene) it is a shame to lose it. It expands the implications of l. 171, thereby recalling some crucial events from the *H6* plays; it usefully emphasizes the abhorrence in which infanticide was held, and so points an ironical finger towards Richard's future commission of this crime; and it demonstrates Richard's Vice-like trick of weeping on demand (while he carefully fosters the belief that he never wept under any circumstances). If indeed it was a cut, it was not a fortunate one.

I.iv. 69–72 (*F only*).] Patrick believed these lines to be a late addition to F (p. 125); Smidt (p. 124) objected to them on the grounds that Clarence's wife was already dead (not perhaps the sort of fact Elizabethan theatregoers would have had in the forefront of their minds to quarrel over). A more likely objection is that the Christian imagery of the passage is at variance with the classical terminology of the Dream. Yet the objection is false; the lines introduce well the tone and the language of the ensuing scene with the Murderers. Again, a misguided cut.

III.vii. 143–52 (*F only*).] Undoubtedly a cut in Q. The omission of these lines is neatly made to shorten Richard's speech by eliminating its rhetoric without removing its substance. Patrick remarks that the parallelism between ll. 140–1 and 153–4 is not exact (p. 127), and this merely strengthens the case for regarding the F as original, from which the lines were cut.

IV.i. 97–103 (*F only*).] Patrick observes, 'this sentimental apostrophe to the Tower has every appearance of being an addition to the original text' (p. 127), following as it does upon a perfectly normal exit-couplet for the Duchess. Delius (*Jahrbuch* VII, p. 139) believed the lines were added so that Elizabeth would not depart without a final reference to the plight of her children. Johnson found the lines puzzling, and Malone objected to the pathetic fallacy, but no one has seriously suggested they are not by

Shakespeare. Despite Patrick's confidence, one must not generalize too
much upon the existence of a couplet for the Duchess at ll. 95–6; cf.
IV.iv.114–15, where Margaret has an exit-couplet, but stays for another
ten lines, ending with another couplet. Perhaps Malone was right; the
lines are not Shakespeare's best, and as Elizabeth borrows the concept of
them for her diatribe against Richard in IV.iv.385, someone decided these
could well be dispensed with. Again, then, a cut in Q is the likeliest
explanation.

IV.iv.222–35 (*F only*).] This, the shorter F-only passage in the scene, has been
variously explained. The issue seems to be one of tone: throughout her
conversation with Richard in this scene Elizabeth remains, in the modern
idiom, 'cool': collected, ironic, witty, Richard's match. These lines are
more in Queen Margaret's vein, and out of place tonally: the violent
imagery (e.g. l. 229) reminds one of the wilder flights in the *Henry VI*
plays. The question is then, whether Shakespeare deliberately *added* such
a passionate passage, or whether he, or another, cut it in Q for the sake
of consistency of tone. The second is the likelier alternative, but as we
cannot be sure who was responsible for its elimination, it must be retained
in a modern edition.

IV.iv.288–342 (*F only*).] See Introduction, p. 14. There can be no reasonable
doubt that Q cut these lines to shorten the scene.

IV.ii.98–116 (*Q only*).] This, the sole long Q-only passage in the play, has not
been satisfactorily explained. Spedding thought it was part of the original
play, subsequently cut; Pickersgill held it was omitted from F by the
corrector because of its metrical deficiencies; Daniel argued it was inserted for the actor; Schmidt thought it was inserted *by* the actor. (See
Variorum, pp. 300–1, for these and other views.) Alexander (Shakespeare's
Henry VI and Richard III, Cambridge, 1929, pp. 157 ff.) thought it part of
the original because it is in the source (the specific details about Ruge-
mount are in Holinshed, not Hall). Moriarty (*MP* 1913, p. 458) protests
that 'Shakespeare's maturer study of character would not allow him to
make the previously pictured, wary and resourceful Buckingham persist
so crudely under evidently unpropitious circumstances merely because his
doing so long enough would help strike off a figure of speech'. Patrick
(pp. 142–4) remarks that l. 118 is hardly intelligible without l. 116, a
strong point in favour of the passage's being integral; but his explanation
of how it came to be omitted from F is weak, being based on the good old
standby of a defective manuscript. The least attractive theory is that of
external influence: that the passage was cut in order to avoid giving
offence to the current Duke of Buckingham (a well-known scrounger) and
because King James had a palace at Richmond. It is amazing this absurd
notion should have proceeded from so wise heads as those of Griffin and
McKerrow (*RES* 1937, pp. 329–32) and that it should have convinced
NCS. Apart from the huge improbability that the Jacobean Buckingham
(in no way related to the Stafford family, the Buckingham of the play)
should feel himself affected by these lines or reflected upon by Richard's
waspish language, it must be pointed out that the *substance* of the scene is
present in the F version; only the manner is altered. The only circumstance
which would make the case plausible would be if the play had been

presented at court, when for tact in the presence of the King and his friend the passage might well have been omitted. But the signs of this would appear in the prompt-book, and F's copy was probably not prompt-book (see Introduction, pp. 42–4). The F corrector, faced with the passage in Q, either had it in his MS. or he did not. If he did not, that would have been an adequate reason to excise it, but if it was present, unless the corrector was making a transcript, rather than marking up Q copy (see Introduction pp. 41–2), it is less likely to have been omitted inadvertently. However, Patrick's argument is based on hindsight: l. 118 is certainly more effective if l. 116 is there, but it is not unintelligible on its own. And the fact that the details are unique to Holinshed suggests that Shakespeare had re-read Holinshed after making his first copy of the play, and decided on the hint of 'Ruge-mont' to expand the scene and deepen Buckingham's humiliation. This, then, is the best explanation for the passage that the data admit.

APPENDIX II

LONGER NOTES

1.ii.27–8. *More ... Than*] Q's tame 'As ... As' may be ascribed to the deficiency of the actor. The thought is clear in F: Anne, doubly bereaved of husband and monarch, prays that Richard's hypothetical wife may feel even sorrier than she now does, when Richard shall die. There the matter could rest, had not Walker and Wilson combined in NCS to elaborate: 'Any wife of such a monster would be happy, not miserable, at his death, while it is not Prince Edward and King Henry who make Anne miserable but *their* death' (p. 174). They refer to iv.i.74–6 where Anne, recalling this moment, says, 'And be thy wife—if any be so mad— / More miserable by the life of thee / Than thou hast made me by my dear lord's death'. Thus, they would have the lines here read: 'More miserable by the life of him / Than I am by my young lord's death and thee!', where 'thee' is Richard, not the dead Henry. The emendation is plausible and quite attractive. But it is not necessary. First, Q reads 'death' rather than 'life' in the Act iv passage—but this is probably an actor's slip (see below, p. 339). More importantly, Anne is an older, wiser woman in Act iv, and the realization that one may be more unhappy living with someone evil than grieving for someone dead reveals this growth in her character. To return to the present lines and the NCS objection to them; the insight needed to realize that life with a monster can be terrible has not yet dawned on Anne: she imagines a wife—who had, for whatever reason, loved Richard —mourning for him. She is very much alone at this time; she has no reason to assume her view of Richard's character is universally held (as indeed it is not). Anne is being made miserable by the dead bodies of her young lord and Henry, which latter she addresses as 'thee'—having it beside her, and making it the visual focus for her elegy and commination.

1.iv.26. *anchors*] [The following note contributed by Harold Brooks.] Retained on the authority of Q1; F may have followed suit simply in course of printing from the Q copy; though if it did so because the corrector found 'anchors' also in the MS. there would be twofold authority for the word. To emend, one would need to be confident that the QF line was corrupt; on the contrary, though 'anchors' is in contrast with the other items, it does not jar with its context; it may be meant to recall the wrecks among the treasure, and by its very incongruity to suggest disordered ruin. Nevertheless, the case for Kinnear's conjecture is exceptionally strong. (1) 'Anchors' *is* an 'odd man out'; (2) the proposal 'ingowes' is not conjured up by editorial ingenuity: it belongs to what is probably the source of Shakespeare's line: Spenser, *Faerie Queene*, ii.vii.5, l.6, where gold is 'distent' into ' . . . *great Ingowes* and to *wedges* square' (italics mine); the stanza has also 'heapes of gold'. (3) The claim that this is the source does not rest on mere observation of the parallel: it is clear that where

336

Clarence's dream depicts the voyage, the sea-floor, its wrecks and its treasure, Shakespeare is inspired by *Faerie Queene*, II. vii (Mammon's Cave), xii (Guyon's voyage), III. iv (the Rich Strond and Cymoent's bower, deep 'in the bottome of the sea'). Cf. Introduction, p. 80. (4) If Shakespeare (or a scribe) wrote 'ingowes' the process of corruption is easy to conjecture, with 'w' misread as a two-stemmed 'r', and 'g' as 'ch' (Secretary 'h' having a great hook below the line). The unfamiliarity of 'ingowes' would encourage misreading (though the familiar 'anchors', regularly associated with the sea bed, would not).

To Brooks's note the following is worth adding: Thomas H. Cain argues, with reference to the Belphoebe material in *Faerie Queene*, that there is a pattern of references to America in the poem, and that the word 'Ingoes' is probably a variant spelling of 'Incas', derived from Raleigh's habitual spelling 'Ingas' in his *Discoverie*. Spenser thus deliberately gives a false etymology for 'ingots' by this spelling, in what Cain describes as 'an ancient means of allegory to which the synthetically archaic language of *F.Q.* lends itself effortlessly' (*Praise in The Faerie Queene*, Lincoln, Nebraska, 1978, p.205, n.18). While these arguments effectively dispose of McKerrow's suggested reading 'ouches' or 'owches' for the spelling intended by Shakespeare, they of course have no bearing on the possibility that 'anchors' may be a compositorial error. However, Golding's Ovid, another source for the dream, includes the suggestive phrase 'And in the toppes of mountaynes high old Anchors have been found' (xv.291).

I. iv. 247–57.] The solution adopted here to this, the major textual crux of the first Act, was suggested by Harold Jenkins. It has long been recognized that the problem is caused by a botched insertion in F copy: ll. 249–53 were omitted from Q perhaps by a copyist's oversight, and were incorrectly marked for insertion in F by the corrector; they appear there between ll. 246 and 247, sundering the coherent argument on the merits of relenting. Jenkins comments: 'the over-riding consideration is that Clarence first appeals to both Murderers and then, when he sees one relenting, appeals to him alone. And it is when he has passed from speaking to both to concentrate on the Second that the First has the chance to get behind him. Hence the added passage addressed to both *must* precede the lines to the Second Murderer.'

The commonest previous solution to the difficulty was conjectured by Tyrwhitt, adopted by Steevens and followed by many eds including Camb., Thompson, Alexander, and Sisson among others. It reads (in Alexander's text):

> *Clar.*   Relent, and save your souls.
> *1 Murd.*   Relent! No, 'tis cowardly and womanish.
> *Clar.*   Not to relent is beastly, savage, devilish.
> Which of you, if you were a prince's son,
> Being pent from liberty as I am now,
> If two such murderers as yourselves came to you,
> Would not entreat for life?
> My friend, I spy some pity in thy looks;
> O, if thine eye be not a flatterer,
> Come thou on my side and entreat for me—
> As you would beg were you in my distress.
> A begging prince what beggar pities not?

The disadvantage of this, apart from its complication, is the inconsistency of pronouns in the last lines, which makes nonsense of the careful distinctions Shakespeare has been drawing between 'thou' and 'you' in this scene. Evans, in the Riverside and Pelican Shakespeares, retains F order but prints 'As you . . . distress' as a single line after 'Come thou . . . me', which exacerbates the pronoun difficulty. NCS retains F, except for the emendation it makes in ll. 252–3 (*q.v.*); NPS retains F unchanged. For other, earlier suggestions, see Variorum, pp. 144–6.

II. iv. 65. *earth*] Almost all eds prefer Q's striking image, 'let me die to look on death no more', though Rowe and Pope retained the F reading. Even the most conservative modern texts make the emendation, including Evans and Eccles. Walker (p. 30) remarks that it is hard 'to determine whether the Folio compositor or an editor was responsible for an occasional folly' like this. However, the F reading is not a folly: it is, to be sure, a thoroughly conventional expression, but by no stretch of the imagination an obvious blunder. Q's reading may rather be a sophistication: Theobald remarked, 'By the reading of the Quarto the thought is finely and properly improved', which is how most eds seem to feel. Yet we must feel certain that the improvement originated with Shakespeare and not with the compositor or the actor, and it is impossible, in this instance, to be certain. Textual critics who remember Matthiessen's famous 'soiled fish of the sea' and other choice examples of editorial endorsement of misprints, will see cause for caution. The F expression is wholly in accord with the formal character of the Duchess's lament; we need something stronger than mere critical preference to permit us to reject the F reading here.

III. ii. 92. S.D. *Hastings*] The absence of the pursuivant's name from F has caused much speculation. Among recent eds, Alexander and NPS keep the name; Evans includes the name in the S.D. but uses the F dialogue; Eccles and NCS retain F. NCS complains that the introduction of the name has no dramatic point, 'and merely puzzles the reader . . . as Shakespeare's audience would have been puzzled had they heard Hastings calling another man by his own name without any sort of explanation' (p. 154). But the entire episode as it appears in F seems pointless: it merely repeats what has already been said by Hastings, adds a superfluous character, and would probably be cut by an economy-minded producer. The fact that it was not cut in Q suggests that someone felt strongly enough about it to retain it, and that the identity of the pursuivant served to make an ironical point. Names, like other designations, are interchangeable and misleading in Richard's world (see Introduction, pp. 114–15.) How the name came to be omitted from F is easy to guess at: either the corrector or the compositor (as it is Compositor A, the corrector is more likely) couldn't believe that a mistake had not been made, and changed both the direction and the dialogue to avoid it. The name would not be as baffling on stage as NCS would have us believe, especially if Lord Hastings delivered his salutation with appropriate enjoyment of the coincidence.

III. iv. 32. *strawberries*] For the source of this celebrated episode, see Appendix III, p. 350. No doubt More, as a page in Cardinal Morton's household, heard the story from his patron. The dramatic importance of the episode in both More and Shakespeare is to build up the atmosphere of normality, so that Richard's infuriated entry at l. 58 becomes a significant peripeteia, and serves to enhance the importance of Hastings's fall as an emblem of the fate of England under Richard's rule (see also Introduction, pp. 97–8). Richard is role-playing too, trying to keep Hastings in his state of gulled complacency: the strawberries are a means to this end of dramatic characterization. Prior (p. 295) sees the episode as part of Richard's thespian dissimulation, 'the extraordinary performance . . . in which he fools Hastings with the disarming request to the bishop for strawberries and then suddenly changes to accusations of witchcraft and treason'.

Dover Wilson (*MLR* 52 (1957), pp. 565–6) refers to an article in the *British Medical Journal* by a Dr Joly in which the suggestion was made that Richard might have been allergic to strawberries, and intended to produce a rash by eating them, which would then serve as a sign of witchcraft. Lawrence J. Rose (*Studies in the Renaissance* 7 (1960), pp. 225–40) is rightly sceptical. He proposes instead that Shakespeare had in mind the proverbial association of strawberries and serpents: 'In gathering of flowers, and strawberries that grow low upon the ground, we must be verie carefull for the adder and snake that lieth lurking in the grass.' This is from Paradin's *Historicall Devises* (1591) and is illustrated with a cut of a serpent twining around a strawberry plant (reproduced by Ross, pp. 229–30). This emblem undoubtedly helps to add ironical depth to the entire episode, and it seems very likely that Shakespeare also had it in mind.

IV. i. 74–6. *mad—/More . . . life . . . death*] Cf. I. ii. 27–8 above. In both Acts Q has 'As . . . death . . . As'; in Act I F also reads 'death', and reasons were given in the note above for retaining it. Here Anne alters her original expression twice: first she says anyone would have to be mad to marry Richard; then she substitutes 'life' for 'death', having come to recognize that life with a monster is worse than any grief for a loved one. Her changed circumstances reflect themselves in the growth of awareness that leads to these unconscious substitutions. Other characters at the moment of their downfall frequently rephrase the curses they have brought down upon themselves: cf. III. iii. It can be argued, as Ferrers did (see the note on this passage in NCS) that l. 74 should read 'And be thy wife—if any be so—made', thus bringing her speech here into conformity with I. ii. 26; one can also read 'life' at I. ii. 27, and so make both speeches exactly parallel. NCS does so, remarking that Ferrers's conjecture is 'surely correct'. It may be intriguing (though it destroys the signs of growth in Anne's character) but it is by no means sure, since Q3's 'badde' is a simple error for Q1–2's 'madde', which is not how anyone would spell 'made'. This edition therefore retains F.

IV. iv. 127–8] Perhaps the single most difficult crux in the play. The complex variants are made more confusing by the obscure meaning; paraphrased, the lines mean something like: words are windy attorneys, who give expression to the grievances of their clients; like the inheritor of a person who has died intestate, they are without substance—if one's joy has provided no means for its continuance, it has (as it were) died intestate, and thus one's miserable words are all one's inheritance. Words (l. 129) are the vehicles whereby one's grief becomes publicly known.

Even the lawyer-scholars have been uncertain in their interpretation of these lines: see Variorum, p. 329, for a survey. The general drift of the images is not in doubt: words, as T. S. Eliot said, are the insubstantial, airy residue of reality: 'Dust in the air suspended / Marks the place where a story ended': they are a vent for grief, but are not the grief itself; they bear a resemblance to the legal relationship between the aggrieved clients and the lawyers who must express that grief, or the orator who, at second hand, addresses himself to others' problems.

The variants noted for 'their clients' will show how many changes have been rung on the possible meanings. This edn follows F, but punctuates to show that Elizabeth is expressing a general comparison: she does not mean a particular client. Otherwise this reading is the same as that adopted by Eccles and NPS. Most eds follow Capell, which reading makes the woes themselves the attorney's clients—rather too fancifully, perhaps. Q1 can hardly be right, and there are no sound grounds for thinking that Q4 influenced F. So both 'their' and 'Clients' must be corrections made to what the corrector found in Q copy (unless, as seems unlikely, they are held to be compositor's corruptions). A genuine compositor's error occurs in the next line, where F's 'intestine' *must* be a mistake. For somewhat similar images, see *Ven.*, ll. 333–6, and *Tit.*, III. i. 233–4.

v. iii. 184. *and*] Although the reading 'I am I' which originates in Q2 has been accepted by every editor since, Malone observed 'I am not sure that the reading of Q1 is not right'. Is a recollection intended of *3H6*, v. vi. 83, 'I am myself alone'? Perhaps, but the recollection need not be merely repetitive; perhaps Richard too, like others, has learned something. The drift of the present passage seems to be that Richard, in what we would now call schizophrenic vein, is distinguishing between aspects of his personality: the clever, witty, self-reliant villain, and the conscience-smitten coward he is just now discovering. He is Legion, devil-in-man; and now the fearful self (the self which Anne reported could never sleep soundly, the repressed moral being) surfaces and stands beside the wilful Vice-demon self that rules Richard's conscious mind. The anguish of the passage, expressed in its short, choppy rhetorical dialectic, is an attempt to represent verbally the mutual encounter and alternation of these two selves, I and I. On balance, it seems that Q1's reading satisfactorily expresses the dramatic point that is being made. Q2's alteration must be classed with the series of guesses, good and bad, that its compositor has been making hereabouts (cf. ll. 146, 153, 181), and is without authority. Blakemore Evans, in '*Shakespeare Restored*—Once again!' (*Editing Renaissance Dramatic Texts*, ed. Anne Lancashire, New York, Garland, 1976, p. 46) comments that as the next line ends 'I am', compositorial eye-skip could account for Q2's reading. In these circumstances we ought to emend only if the copy-text reading is demonstrably wrong, and this is not. The basic source for the concept of self recognizing self is probably the *Andria*, l. 635: 'proxumus sum egomet mihi', a line Barabas misquotes in *Jew*, I. i. 189. Other parallels occur in the *Hippolytus*, ll. 162–3, and in *Spanish Tragedy*, III. ii. 118, III. x. 96–8.

APPENDIX III

SOURCES

I. Hall's *Union*

A. From *The prosperous reigne of Kyng Edward the fourthe.*
[*The interment of Henry VI* (fol. ccxxiii^r)]

The ded corps of kyng Henry, with billes and gleves pompe-
ously (if you call that a funerall pompe) was conveighed from the
tower, to the Churche of saincte Paule . . . and the next daie,
without Prieste or Clarke, Torche or Taper, syngyng or saiyng,
it was conveighed to the Monasterie of Chertesey . . . and there
was buried, but after he was removed to Winsore, and there in a
new vawte newly intumilate.

[*Clarence's end* (fol. ccxxxix^v)]

. . . there fel a sparcle of privy malice, betwene the kyng & his
brother the duke of Clarence whether it rose of olde grudges
before tyme passed, or were it newly kyndled and set a fyre by the
Quene or her bloud which were ever mistrustyng and prively
barkynge at the kynges legnage, or were he desirous to reigne
after hys brother . . . The fame was that the kyng or the Quene,
or bothe, sore troubled with a folysh Prophesye, and by reason
therof began to stomacke & grevously to grudge agaynst the duke.
The effect of which was, after king Edward should reigne, one
whose first letter of hys name shoulde be a G. and because the
devel is wont with sych wytchcraftes, to wrappe and illaqueat
the myndes of men, which delyte in such develyshe fantasyes,
they sayd afterward that that Prophesie lost not hys effect, when
after kyng Edward, Glocester usurped hys kyngdome.

Other allege this to be the cause of his death: That of late, the
olde rancor betwene them beyng newly revived . . . The king
muche greved and troubled with hys brothers dayly querimonye
. . . caused hym to be aprehended, and cast into the Towre,
where he beyng taken, adjudged for a Traytor, was prively
drouned in a But of Malvesey.

But sure it is, that although kyng Edward were consentyng to

341

his death and destruccion, yet he muche dyd bothe lamente hys
infortunate chaunce, and repent hys sodayne execucion. In
asmuche, that when any person sued to hym for Pardon or
remission, of any malefactor condempned to the punyshment of
death, he woulde accustomably saye, & openly speke, O infortunate brother, for whose lyfe not one creatoure woulde make
intercession, openly spekyng, and apparently meanynge, that by
the meanes of some of the nobilitie, he was circumvented, and
brought to hys confusion.

B. From *The pitifull life of kyng Edward the .v.* and *The tragical
doynges of Kyng Richard the thirde.* (This section of Hall's *Union*
is in fact Sir Thomas More's *History of King Richard III.* See
Introduction, 'Sources', p. 79.) (fol. iᵛ–xxviiiʳ).

[fol. iᵛ]   George duke of Clarence was a goodly and well
feautered prince, in all thynges fortunate, if either his owne
ambicion had not set hym against his brother, or thenvy of his
enemies had not set his brother againste hym: for were it by the
quene or the nobles of her blud, whiche highly maligned the
kynges kynred . . . at the leaste wise, heinous treason was laied
to his charge, and finally were he in faulte or wer he fautelesse,
attainted was he by parliamente and judged to death, and there
upon hastely drowned in a butte of malmesey within the towre
of London. Whose death kynge Edwarde (although he commaunded it) when he wiste it was dooen, piteously he bewayled
and sorowfully repented it.

Richard duke of Gloucester the third sonne (of whiche I must
moste entreate) was in witte and courage egall with the other,
but in beautee and liniamentes of nature far underneth bothe,
for he was litle of stature eivill featured of limnes, croke backed,
the left shulder muche higher than the righte, harde favoured of
visage, such as in estates is called a warlike visage, and emonge
commen persones a crabbed face. He was malicious, wrothfull
and envious, and as it is reported, his mother the duches had
muche a dooe in her travaill, that she coulde not bee delivered
of hym uncut, and that he came into the worlde the fete forwarde,
as menne bee borne outwarde, and as the fame ranne, not un-
tothed: whether that menne of hatred reported above the truthe,
or that nature chaunged his course in his beginnynge, whiche in
his life many thynges unnaturally committed, this I leve to God
his judgemente. He was none evill capitan in warre, as to the
whyche, his disposicion was more enclined too, then too peace.

Sondry victories he had and some ouerthrowes, but never for defaute of his owne persone, either for lacke of hardinesse or politique order. Free he was of his dispences and somewhat above his power liberall, with large giftes he gatte hym unstedfaste frendship: for whiche cause he was fain to borowe, pill and extort in other places, whiche gat hym stedfaste hatred. He was close and secrete, a depe dissimuler, lowlye of countenaunce, arrogante of herte, outwardely familier where he inwardely hated, not lettynge to kisse whom he thought to kill, dispiteous and cruell, not alwaie for eivill will, but ofter for ambicion and too serve his purpose, frende and fooe were all indifferent, where his avauntage grewe, he spared no mannes deathe whose life withstode his purpose. He slewe in the towre kynge Henry the sixte, saiynge: now is there no heire male of kynge Edwarde the thirde, but wee of the house of Yorke: which murder was doen without kyng Edward his assente, whiche woulde have appointed that bocherly office too some other, rather then to his owne brother. Some wise menne also wene, that his drifte lacked not in helpynge [fol. ii^r] furth his owne brother of Clarence to his death, whiche thyng in all apparaunce he resisted, although he inwardly mynded it. And the cause thereof was, as menne notyng his doynges and procedynges did marke (because that he longe in kynge Edwarde his tyme thought too obtaine the crowne in case that the kynge his brother, whose life he loked that eivil diet woulde sone shorten) shoulde happen to diseace, as he did in dede, his chyldren beynge younge. And then if the duke of Clarence had lived, his pretensed purpose had been far hyndered: For if the duke of Clarence had kepte hym selfe trewe to his nephewe the younge kyng, or woulde have taken upon hym too bee kynge, every one of these castes had been a troumpe in the duke of Gloucesters waye: but when he was sure that his brother of Clarence was ded, then he knewe that he might worke without that jeoperdy . . . wherefore liynge on his deathe bed at westminster, he called to hym suche lordes as then were aboute hym, whome he knewe to bee at variaunce, in especiall the lorde Marques Dorset sonne to the quene, and the lorde Hastynges, againste whom the quene especially grudged for the favoure that the kyng bare hym, and also she thoughte hym familier with the kynge in wanton compaignie . . . [fol. iii^r] And there in his presence (as by their woordes apeared) eche forgave other, and joyned their handes together, when as it after appeared by their dedes their hartes were far a sunder. And so whithin a fewe daies, this noble prince disceased at westminster . . . [fol. iii^v] [Richard,

for asmuche as he well wiste, and had holpe to maintain, a long
continued grudge and harte burning betwene the quenes kynred
and the kynges bloude, either parte enviyng others autoritee, he
now thought, as it was in deede, a furtherly beginnynge to the
pursute of his entente, and a sure grounde and situacion of his
unnaturall buyldynge, if he mighte under the pretence of reven-
gynge of olde displeasures, abuse the ignoraunce and anger of the
one partie too the destruction of the other, and then to wyn to
his purpose as many as he coulde: and suche as coulde not bee
wonne, mighte bee loste or they loked therefore. But of one
thynge he was certain, that if his entent wer once perceived, he
should have made peace betwene bothe parties with his owne
bloud: but all his intente he kept secrete till he knewe his
frendes, of the whiche Henry the duke of Buckyngham was the
firste . . .

[fol. v^r] The younge kynge at the deathe of his father kepte
houshoulde at Ludlowe. The governaunce of this younge Prince
was committed too lord Antony Woodvile erle Ryvers and lorde
Scales, brother to the quene, a wise, hardy and honourable
personage, as valiaunte of handes as politique of counsaill, and
with hym were associate other of the same partie, and in effect
every one as he was nerer of kynne unto the quene, so was he
planted nexte aboute the prince. That drift by the quene semed
too bee divised, whereby her blouode mighte of righte in tender
youthe bee so planted in the princes favoure, that afterwarde it
should hardely bee eradicated out of the same.

The duke of Gloucester turned all this to their distruction, and
upon that grounde set the foundacion of his unhappy buyldyng:
For whom soever he perceived too bee at variaunce with theim,
or to beare toward hym selfe any favoure, he brake unto theim,
some by mouthe, some by writynge and secrete messengers, that
it was neither reason nor yet to be suffered that the younge kynge
their master and kynsman shoulde bee in the handes and custody
of his mothers kynrede, sequestered in maner from their compaignie and attendaunce, of whiche every one oughte hym as
faithefull service as they, and many of theim of farre more
honorable parte of kynne then his mothers side . . .

[fol. v^v] Where upon the duke of Gloucester beynge advertised
that the lordes aboute the kynge entended to brynge hym too
London too his coronacion, accompaigned with suche a number
of their frendes that it shoulde bee harde for hym too brynge
his purpose to passe without the assemblying and gatheryng of
people & in maner of open warre, wherof the ende he wyst

was doubtfull, and in the which the kyng beyng on the other syde, his parte shoulde have the name and face of rebellion.

He secretely therefore by diverse meanes caused the quene to be persuaded that it was neither nede & should also be jeoperdeous for the kyng to come up so strong, for as now every lord loved other and none other thyng studied for, but the triumphe of his coronation & honoure of the kyng. And the lordes about the kyng, should assemble in the kynges names muche people, thei should geve the lordes betwixt whom & them ther had bene some tyme debate, an occasion to feare and suspecte least they should gather this people, not for the kynges save gard, whom no man impugned, but for their destruction, havying more regarde to their olde variaunce then to their new attonement . . . [fol. vi^r] then all the world would put her & her kynred in the blame, saiyng that thei had unwysely and untruely broken the amytie and peace whiche the kynge her husband had so prudently made betwene her kynred and his, whiche amyte his kynne had alwaies observed.

The quene beyng thus persuaded, sent worde to the kyng and to her brother, that there was no cause nor nede to assemble any people, & also the duke of Gloucester and other lordes of his bend, wrote unto the kyng so reverently and to the quenes frendes there so lovyngly, that they nothynge yearthly mistrustyng, brought the young kynge towarde London with a sober compaignie in great hast (but not in good spede) til he came to Northampton, and from thence he removed to Stony stratford . . . [fol. vi^v] The duke of Gloucester sent the lorde Ryvers, the lord Richard and sir Thomas Vaugham and sir Richarde Hawte into the Northparties into diverse prisones, but at last, al came to Poumfret where they all foure were beheaded without judgement.

In this maner as you have hard, the duke of Gloucester toke on him the governaunce of the yonge kyng, whom with much reverence he conveied towardes London. These tidynges came hastely to the quene before mydnighte, by a very sore reporte that the kynge her sonne was taken and that her brother and her other sonne and other her frendes were arested and sent, no man wyste whether. With this heavy tidynges the quene bewayled her chyldes ruyne, her frendes mischaunce, and her owne infortune cursyng the tyme that ever she was persuaded to leave [fol. vii the gatherynge of people to brynge up the kynge with a gre powre, but that was passed, and therfore nowe she toke younger sonne the duke of Yorke and her doughters and

out of the palays of Westminster into the sanctuary, and there
lodged in the abbotes place, and she and all her chyldren and
compaignie were regestred for sanctuarye persons. The same night
there came to doctor Rotheram Archebyshop of Yorke and lorde
Chauncelour, a messenger from the lorde Chambrelayne to
Yorke place besyde Westminster: the messenger was broughte to
the bishoppes bedsyde and declared to him that the dukes were
gone backe with the young kyng to Northampton, and declared
further, that the lorde Hastynges his maister sent hym worde
that he shoulde feare nothyng for all should be well. (Wel quod
the Archebishop) be it as wel as it wyll, it wyll never be so wel as
we have sene it, and then the messenger departed. Whereupon
the bishop called up all his servauntes and toke with hym the
great seale and came before day to the quene . . . The quene sat
alone belowe on the rushes all desolate & dismayde, whom the
Archebishoppe conforted in the best maner that he coulde . . .
A wo worth hym quod the quene, for it is [Hastings] that goeth
about to destroy me and my blodde. Madame quod he, be of
good comforte and I assure you, if they crowne any other kynge
then your sonne whom they nowe have, we shal on the morow
croune his brother whom you have here with you. And here is
the great seale, which in likewyse as your noble husband delivered
it to me, so I deliver it to you to the use of your sonne and therwith delivered her the greate seale . . .

[fol. vii^v] When the kynge approched nere the cytee, Edmonde
Shawe Goldesmythe then Mayre of the cytie with the Aldermenne
and shreves in skarlet, and fyve hundreth commoners in murraye
receyved [fol. viii^r] his grace reverently at Harnesay Parke, and
so conveighed him to the cytee . . . the duke of Gloucester bare
him in open sight so reverently . . . that from the greate obloquy
that he was in so late before he was sodenly fallen in so greate
trust that at the councel next assembled, he was made the onely
chiefe ruler, and thought most mete to be protectoure of the
kynge and his realme: so that, were it desteny or were it foly, the
lambe was betaken to the wolfe to kepe . . . Wherfore incontinent
at the nexte metynge of the lordes in councel he purposed to
them that it was an heynous thyng of the quene, and procedyng
of great malice toward the kynges councelers that she should
kepe the kynges brother in sanctuarye from him whose speciall
pleasure and comforte were to have his brother with him, and
at to be done by her to none other intente, but to brynge all
lordes in an obloquy and murmoure of the people, as though
were not to be trusted with the kynges brother . . . [fol. viii^v]

Wherfore [he said] me thinketh it were not the worst to send to the quene some honourable and trustie personage, such as tendreth the kynges weale and the honour of his councell, and is also in credite and favour with her: for whiche consideracions none semeth more metely to me then the reverende father my lorde Cardinall archebishop of Cauntorbury . . . And yf she percase be so obstinate and so precisely set in her owne wyll and opinion, that neither his wyse and faithfull advertisemente can move her, nor any mans reason satisfye her, then shall we by myne advice by the kynges authorytee fetche hym oute of that prison and brynge hym to his noble presence, in whose continuall compaignye he shalbee so well cheryshed and so honorably intreated that all the worlde shall to our honour and her reproche perceive that it was onely malice, frowardnesse and foly, that caused her to kepe him there.

The Archebishop of Cauntorburye, whom they all agreed also to be moost convenient therunto, tooke upon hym to move her, and therto to do his uttermooste endevoure. Howebeit if she coulde in no wyse be intreated with her good wyll to delyver hym, then thought he and such of the spiritualtie as were present, that it were not in any wyse too bee attempted to take hym out againste her wyll, for it would be a thyng that should turne to the grudge of all men and highe displeasure of God, yf the pryvilege of that place shoulde be broken whiche had so many yeres bene kepte, whiche bothe Kynges and Popes had graunted and confirmed, which ground was sanctifyed by Saint Peter him selfe more then fyve hundreth yeres agone. And syth that tyme, was never so undevoute a kynge that ever enterprised that sacred privilege to violate, nor so holy a byshop that durste presume the church of the same to consecrate: and therefore quod the Archebishop, God forbyd that any manne shoulde for any yearthely enterprise breake the immunyte and [fol. ix^r] libertie of that sacred sanctuary that hath bene the safegard of so many a good mans life, but I trust quod he, we shall not nede it, but for any maner of nede I would we should not do it, I trust that she with reason shalbe contented and all thynge in good maner obteined. And yf it hap that I brynge it not to passe, yet shall I further it to my best power, so that you all shal perceyve my good wyll, diligence, and indevoure: But the mothers dreade and womannishe fears shalbe the let yf any be.

Naye womannishe frowardnesse quod the duke of Buckyngham, for I dare take it on my solle that she well knoweth tha[t] she nedeth no such thynge to feare, either for her sonne or for h[er]

self . . . for my mynde, I wyll rather maugre her stomacke fetche
hym awaye, then leave him there till her feare or fonde frowarde
feare convey him [fol. ix^v] awaye, and yet will I breake no
sanctuary, for verely sithe the privelege of that place and other
of that sorte have so long continued I would not goe aboute to
breake it . . . sithe it is so long a goo I wote not what pope and
what prince, more piteous then politique, hath graunted it, and
other menne sence of a religious feare have not broken it, lette
us take a paine with it, and lette it stande a Goddes name in his
force, as far furthe as reason will, [fol. x^r] whiche is not so
farfurthe as may serve too lette us of the fetchynge furthe of this
noble manne to his honoure and wealthe out of that place in the
whiche he nether is nor can bee a sanctuarye or privileged man
. . . verely I have harde of sanctuarye menne, but I never harde
before of sanctuary [fol. x^v] children, and therefore as for the
conclusion of my mynde, whosoever maie deserve to have nede
of it, if thei thynke it for their suretee let theim kepe it, but he
can be no sanctuary manne that hath nother discresion to desire
it, ner malice to deserve it, whose life ner libertie can by lawfull
processe stande in jeoperdye : and he that taketh one out of sanctuarye to dooe hym good I saie plainly he breaketh no sanctuary.
     [fol. xiii^r] [When the Duke of York was brought to them] the
protectoure toke him into his armes and kissed hym with these
wordes: now welcome my lorde with all my verie herte, & he
saied in that of likelihod even as he inwardely thought, and there
upon, furthwith brought him to the kyng his brother into the
bishoppes palace at Paules, and from thence through the cytee
honorably into the tower, out of which after that daie they never
came abrode. When the protectour had both the chyldren in his
possession, yea & that they were in a sure place, he then began to
thrist to se the ende of his enterprise. And to avoyde al suspicion,
he caused all the lordes whiche he knewe to bee faithfull to the
kyng, to assemble at Baynardes castle to commen of the ordre of
the coronacion, whyle he and other of his complices & of his
affinitee at Crosbies place contrived the contrary and to make the
protectour kyng: to which counsail there were adhibite very
fewe, and they very secrete. Then began here & there some maner
of mutterynge emongest the people, as though all thyng should not
long be well, though they they wyste not what they feared nor
wherefore: were it, that before suche greate thynges, mennes
hertes (of a secrete instinct of nature) misgeveth theim, as the
outhwynde sometyme swelleth of hym selfe before a tempeste :
were it that some one manne happely somewhat perceivyng,

filled many menn with suspicion, thoughe he shewed fewe menn
what he knewe: howbeit, the dealyng it selfe made men to muse
on the matter, though the counsaill were close, for litle and litle
all folke drewe from the tower where the kyng was, and drewe to
Crosbies place, so that the protectoure had all the resorte, and the
kyng in maner desolate . . .

Thus many thynges commyng together, partly by chaunce and
partly by purpose, caused at length, not common people onely,
whiche waver with the wynde, but wyse menne also and some
lordes, to marke the matter and muse ther upon: in so much as
the lorde Stanley whiche afterwarde was erle of Derby wysely
mistrusted it and saied to the lord Hastynges, that he muche
misliked these two severall counsailes, for while we quod he talke
of one matter at the one place, litle wote we whereof they talke
in the other: peace my lorde quod the lorde Hastynges, on my
lyfe never doubte you, for while one manne is there, which is
never thence, neither can ther be any thyng once mynded that
should sounde amisse [fol. xiii^v] towarde me, but it should be in
myne eares or it were well out their mouthes. This ment he by
Catesby whiche was nere of his secrete counsail, and whom he
familierly used in his most waightie matters . . . in whom if the
lorde Hastynges had not put so speciall truste, the lorde Stanley
and he with diverse other lordes had daparted into their countrees
and broken all the daunce, for many evill signes that he sawe,
which he nowe construed all for the beste, so surely thought he
that there could be no harme towarde hym in that counsaill
entended where Catesbye was. And of trueth the protectoure and
the duke of Bukyngham made very good sembleaunce unto the
lorde Hastynges and kept hym muche in their compaignye. And
undoubtedly, the protectour loved hym well, and lothe was to
have loste hym savyng for feare leste his lyfe should have quayled
their purpose, for the whiche cause he moved Catesby to prove
with some wordes cast out a farre of, whether he could thinke it
possible to wynne the lorde Hastynges to their parte. But Catesby,
whether he assayed him or assayed him not, reported unto hym
that he found him so fast, and herde him speake so terrible wordes
that he durst no farther breake . . . Where upon the lorde protectour caused a counsaill to be set at the tower on the fridaye
the thirtene daye of June, where was muche commonyng for the
honourable solemnitee of the coronacion, of the whiche the tyme
appoincted aproched so nere, that the pageauntes were makyng
day & night at Westminster, and vitaile killed whiche afterwarde
was caste awaye.

These lordes thus sittyng, commonyng of this matter, the protectour came in emong theim about nyne of the clocke salutyng theim curteously, excusyng him self that he had been from theim so long saiyng merely that he had been a sleper that daye. And after a litle talkyng with theim he sayed to the bishopp of Ely, my lorde you have verye good strawberries in youre garden at Holborne, I rquire you let us have a messe of theim. Gladly (my lord quod he) I would I had some better thing as redy [fol. xiiii^r] to your pleasure as that, and with that in all hast he sente his servaunt for a dishe of strawberries. The protectour set the lordes faste in commonyng and there upon prayed theim to spare him alitle, and so he departed and came agayn betwene .x. and eleven of the clocke into the chambre all chaunged with a sowre angry countenaunce knittyng the browes, frownyng and fretyng and gnawyng on his lips and so set hym doune in his place. All the lordes were dismaied and sore marveyled of this maner and sodeyne chaunge and what thyng should hym ayle. When he had sitten a whyle, thus he began: What were they worthy to have that compasse and ymagine the destruccion of me beyng so neare of bloud to the kyng & protectoure of this his royall realme? At which question, all the lordes sate sore astonyed, musyng muche by whom the question should be ment, of which every man knew him self clere.

Then the lorde Hastynges as he that for the familiaritie that was betwene theim, thought he might be boldest with hym, aunswered and sayd that they were worthy to be punished as heynous traytours what soever they were, and all the other affirmed the same, that is (quod he) yonder sorceres my brothers wife and other with her, menyng the quene, at these woordes many of the lordes were sore abashed whiche favoured her, but the lorde Hastynges was better content in hys mynde that it was moved by her then by any other that he loved better, albeit hys hart grudged that he was not afore made of counsail of this matter as well as he was of the takyng of her kynred and of their puttyng to death, whiche were by hys assent before devysed to be beheaded at Pomfrete, this selfe same daye, in the whiche he was not ware that it was by other devised that he hym selfe should the same daye be beheaded at London: then sayed the protectour in what wyse that sorceresse and other of her counsayle, as Shores wyfe with her affinitie have by their sorcery and witchecrafte this wasted my body, and therwith plucked up his doublet to his elbowe on hys lefte arme, where he shewed a weryshe wythered arme & small as it was never other. And therupon, every mannes mynde mysgave theim, well perceyvyng that this matter was but a quarell, for well they wist that the quene was both to wyse to go about any such folye, & also if she would, yet would she of al folke make Shores wyfe least of her counsaile whom of all women she most hated as that concubine whom the kyng her husband most loved.

Also, there was no manne there but knewe that hys arme was ever such sith the day of his birth, Neverthelesse the lorde Hastynges, which from the death of kyng Edward kept Shores wife . . . somewhat grudged to have her whom he loved so highly accused, and that as he knewe well untruely, therefore he aunswered and sayed, certaynly my lorde, yf they have so doone, they be worthy of heynous punishement, what quod the protectour, thou servest [fol. xiiiiᵛ] me I wene with yf and with and, I tell the they have done it, and that wyll I make good on thy bodye traytour. And therewith (as in a great anger) he clapped his fyste on the borde a great rappe, at whiche token geven, one cried treason without the chamber, and therwith a doore clapped, and in came rushyng men in harneyes as many as the chamber could hold. And anone the protectoure sayed to the lorde Hastynges, I arrest the traytoure, what me my lorde quod he? yea the traytoure quod the protectour. And one let flye at the lorde Stanley, which shroncke at the stroake and fell under the table, or els hys head had bene cleft to the teth, for as shortly as he shrancke, yet ranne the bloud aboute his eares. Then was the Archebishop of Yorke and doctour Morton bishopp of Ely & the lorde Stanley taken and divers other whiche were bestowed in dyvers chambers, save the lorde Hastynges (whom the protectour commaunded to spede and shryve hym apace) for by sainct Poule (quod he) I wyll not dyne tyll I se thy head of, it boted hym not to aske why but hevily he toke a priese [sic] at aventure and made a shorte shrift, for a lenger would not be suffered, the protectour made so muche hast to his dyner, which might not go to it tyll this murther were done, for savyng of hys ungracious othe. So was he brought furthe into the grene besyde the chapel within the towre, and his head layed doune on a logge of tymber that lay there for buildyng of the chapel, & there tyrannously striken of . . .

A merveilous case it is to heare, either the warnynges that he should have voyded, or the tokens of that he could not voyde. For the next nighte before his death, the lorde Stanley sent to him a trusty messenger at midnight in all the hast, requiryng hym to ryse and ryde awaye with hym, for he was disposed utterly no lenger for to abyde, for he had a fearfull dreame in the whiche he thought that a bore with his tuskes so rased them bothe by the heades that the bloud ran aboute bothe their shoulders, and for asmuch as the protectour gave the bore for his cognisaunce, he ymagined that it should be he. This dreame made suche a fearfull impression in hys harte, that he was throughly determyned no lenger to tary but had his horse redy, yf the lorde Hastynges would go with him. So that they would ryde so farre that night, that they should be out of daunger by the next day. A good lord (quod the lord Hastynges) to the messenger, leaneth my lorde thy maister so muche to suche tryfles, and hath suche faithe in dreams, which either his awne feare phantasieth, or do ryse in the nightes rest by reason of the dayes thought. Tell him it is playne wichcraft to beleve in such dreames, which if they were tokens of thinges to come, why thynketh he not that we might as likely make theim true by oure goyng yf we were caught and brought backe, (as frendes fayle fliers) for then had the bore a cause lykely to race us with his tuskes, as folkes that fled for some falshead, wherefore either is there peryll, nor none there is deede, or yf any be, it is rather ingoyng [fol. xv^r] then abidying. And if we should nedes fall in peril one way or other, yet had I leaver that men should se it were by other mens falshed, then thynke it were either our awne faute or faynte feble hart, and therfore go to thy maister and commende me to him and I praye him to be mery & have no feare, for I assure hym, I am assured of the man he wotteth of, as I am sure of myne awne hand. God send grace (quod the messenger) and so departed. Certeyn it is also that in redyng to- warde the towre the same mornyng in whiche he was beheaded, hys horsse that he accustomed to ryde on stombled with him twyse or thryse almost to the fallyng, which thyng although it happeth to them dayly to whom no mischaunce is towarde, yet hath it bene as an olde evyll token observed as a goyng toward mischiefe . . .

[Sir Thomas Haward] while the lord Hastynges stayed awhile commonyng with a priest whom he met in the Towrstrete, brake the lordes tale, saiyng to him merely, what my lord I pray you come on, wherfore talke you so long with that priest, you have no nede of a priest yet, & laughed upon hym, as though he would saye, you shall have neded of one sone: But lytle wyst the other what he ment (but or night these wordes were well re- membred by them that hard them) so the true lord Hastynges little mistrusted, & was never merier, nor thought his life in

more suretie in al his dayes, which thyng is often a signe of
chaunge: but I shall rather let any thyng passe me then the
vayne surety of mans mynde so neare hys death, for upon the
very towre wharffe, so neare the place where his head was of, so
sone after, as a man might wel cast a balle, a pursyvaunt of his
awne called Hastynges mette with hym, & of their metyng in
that place he was put in remembraunce of another tyme, in
which it happened them to mete before together in the place, at
which tyme the lorde Hastynges had bene accused to kyng
Edward by the lord Ryvers the quenes brother, insomuche that
he was for a while which lasted not long highly in the kynges
indignacion as he nowe mette the same pursivaunt in the same
place, the jeoperdy so well passed, it gave him great pleasure to
talke with him therof, with whom he had talked in the same place
of that matter, & therfore he sayed, Ah Hastynges, art thou
remembred when I mette the here once with an heavy hart?
Ye my lorde (quod he) that I remembre well, and thanked be to
God they gat no good ner you no harme therby, thou wouldest
saye so (quod he) yf thou knewest so muche as I do, whiche few
knowe yet, & mo shall shortly, that meant he that therle Ryvers
and the lord Richard & sir Thomas Vaughan should that day
be beheaded at Pomfrete, as thei were in dede, which acte he
wist wel should be done, [fol. xvᵛ] but nothyng ware that the
axe hong so nere his awne head. In faith, man (quod he) I was
never so sory ner never stode in so greate daunger of my lyfe as
I dyd when thou and I mette here, and lo the worlde is turned
nowe, nowe stand myne enemies in the daunger as thou maist
happe to hear more hereafter, and I never in my lyfe merier nor
never in so great surerye, I praye God it prove so (quod Hast-
tynges, prove quod he? doubtest thou that) nay nay I warraunte
the, and so in maner displeased he entered into the Towre, where
he was not long on lyve as you have heard. O lorde God the
blyndnesse of our mortal nature, when he most feared, he was in
moste surety, and when he reconed hym selfe moste surest, he
lost his lyfe, and that within two houres after. Thus ended this
honorable manne a good knight & gentle, of great aucthoritie
with his prince, of livyng somwhat dissolute, playne and open to
his enemy, and sure and secrete to hys frende, easy to begyle, as
he that of good harte and courage foresawe no perilles, a lovyng
man and passyng welbeloved, very faythfull and trustie ynogh,
but trustyng to muche was hys destruction as you may perceyve.

Nowe flewe the fame of thys lordes death through the cytie and
farther about, lyke a wynde in every mans eare, but the Pr

tectoure immediatly after dyner (entendyng to set some colour upon the matter) sent in all the haste for many substancial men out of the cytie into the Towre, and at their commyng him selfe with the duke of Buckyngham stode, harnessed in olde evill favoured briganders, such as no man would wene that they would have vouchesafed to have put on their backes, excepte some sodeyne necessitie had constraigned them. Then the lord protector shewed them, that the lord Hastynges & other of his conspiracy had contrived to have sodeynly destroyed hym and the duke of Buckyngham there the same daie in counsail and what they entended farther, was yet not well knowen, of whiche their treason he had never knowlege before x. of the clocke the same forenone, which sodeyn feare drave them to put on suche harnesse as came nexte to their hands for their defence, and so God holpe them, that the mischiefe turned upon them that woulde have done it, & thus he required them to report. Every man answered fayre, as though no man mistrusted the matter, which of trueth no man beleved. Yet for the further appeasyng of the peoples myndes, he sent immediately after dynner an Heralde of armes with a proclamacion through the cytie of London whiche was proclaymed in the kynges name, that the lord Hastynges with divers other of his trayterous purpose had before conspired, the same day to have slayne the protectour and the duke of Buckyngham sittyng in counsaill, & after to have taken upon them the rule of the kyng and the realme at their pleasure . . . [fol. xvi^r] Nowe was thys proclamacion made within twoo houres after he was beheaded, and it was so curiously endyted and so fayre writen in Parchement in a fayre sette hande, and therewith of it selfe so long a processe, that every chyld might perceyve that it was prepared and studyed before (and as some men thought, by Catesby) for all the tyme betwene hys death and the proclamacion proclaimyng, coulde skant have suffyced unto the bare wrytyng alone, albeit that it had bene in paper and scribeled furthe in haste at adventure. So that upon the proclaimyng thereof, one that was scolemayster at Paules standying by and comparyng the shortenesse of the tyme with the length of the matter sayed to theim that stoode about hym, here is a gaye goodly cast, foule cast awaye for hast . . .

[fol. xvii^r] Now was it devised by the protectoure & his counsaile, that the same day that the lord Chamberlayne was headed in the towre of London and about the same houre should be beheaded at Poumfrete the earle Ryvers and the lorde Richarde the quenes sonne, syr Thomas Vaughan and sir

Richard Haute, whiche as you heard were taken at Northampton and Stony stratfort by the consent of the lorde Hastynges, whiche execution was done by the ordre & in the presence of sir Richard Ratclif knight, whose service the protectoure specially used in the counsail, and in the execution of suche lawlesse enterprises . . .

This knight brought these foure persons to the scaffolde at the daye apoincted, & shewed to all the people that they were traitours, not sufferyng the lordes to speake, & to declare their innocency, least their wordes might have enclined men to pytie them and to hate the protectour & his part & so without judgement & processe of the lawe caused them to be beheaded without other yearthly gylt, but onely that they were good men and true to the kyng & to nye to the quene, insomuch as sir Thomas Vaughan goyng to his death sayed, A wo worthe them that toke the prophecie that G. should destroy kyng Edwardes children, meaning that by the duke of Clarence lord George which for that suspicion is now dead, but now remaineth Richard G. duke of Cloucester [sic], which now I se is he that shal and will accomplishe the prophecie & destroye kyng Edwardes children & all their alyes & frendes, as it appereth by us this day, whom I appele to the high tribunal of God for his wrongful murther & our true innocencye. [fol. xvii^v] And then Ratclyffe sayed, you have well apeled, lay doune youre head, ye quod syr Thomas, I dye in right, beware you dye not in wrong, and so that good knight was beheaded and the other three, and buryed naked in the monastery at Poumfret.

To this counsaile [Richard and Buckingham] toke diverse such as they thought mete to be trusted and likely to be enduced to that parte and hable to stand theim in steade, eyther by powre or by polycye. Emong whom, they made a counsaile Edmond Shaa then Mayre of London, whiche upon trust of hys awyne avauncement, where he was of a proude harte highly desirous, toke on hym to traine the cytie to their appetite. Of spirituall men they toke suche as had wytte, and were in aucthoritie emongest the people for opinion of their learnyng, and had no scrupulous conscience. Emongest these had, they toke Raffe Shaa clearke brother to the Mayre, & Freer, Pynkie provinciall of the Augustine Freers, bothe doctours in divinitie, bothe great preachers, bothe of more learnyng then vertue, of more fame then learnyng, & yet of more learnyng then trueth . . . [fol. xviii^r] But now was all the laboure and study in the devise of some convenient pretexte, for which the people should be content to depose the prince & accept the protectour for kyng. In which diverse thinges they devised, but the chief thyng, & the weight of all that invencion rested in this, that they shoulde allege bastardy in kyng Edwarde hym selfe, or in his chyldren, or bothe, so that he should seme disabled to enherite the croune by the duke of Yorke and the prince by him. To lay bastardy in kyng Edward sounded openly to the rebuke of the protectours awne mother, whiche was mother to theim bothe. For in that poinct could be none other coloure, but to pretende that his awne mother was an avoutresse, but neverthelesse he would that poinct should be lesse and more fynely & closely handled, not even fully playne and directely, but touched a slope craftely, as though menne spared in that poinct to speake all the trueth for feare of his displeasure . . .

[fol. xix^v] Nowe to returne where I left, as I beganne to shewe you, it was by the protector and his counsaill concluded that this doctor Shaa should in a sermon at Paules crosse signifie to the people that neither king Edwarde hym selfe nor the duke of Clarence wer lawefully begotten, nor wer the very children of the duke of Yorke, but begotten unlawfully by other persones by advoutry of the duches their mother. And that dame Elizabeth Lucy was the very wife of kynge Edward, and so prince Edward and all the children begotten on the quene wer bastardes . . . then [fol. xx^r] began he to discende to the praise of the lord Richard duke of Yorke, callyng hym father to the protectour and declared his title to the croune bi inheritaunce and also by entaile authorised by parliament after the death of kynge Henry the sixte. Then shewed he that the lorde protector, was onely the righte heire, of his body lawfully begotten. Then declared he that kyng Edward was never lawfully maried to the quene, but his wife before God was dame Elizabeth Lucy, and so his children wer bastardes. And besides that, that neither kyng Edward hym selfe nor the duke of Clarence (emongest them that wer secrete in the duke of Yorkes houshoulde) were never reconed surely to bee the children of the noble duke as those that by their favoures more resembled other knowen menne then hym, from whose verteous condicions he saied, also that kyng Edwarde was farre of. But the lorde protector (quod he) that veraye noble prince, the speciall patrone of knightly prowes, aswell in all princely behaveour as in the liniamentes and favour of his visage representeth the very face of the noble duke his father. This is (quod he) the fathers awne figure, this is his awne countenaunce, the verie printe of his visage, the sure undoubted ymage, the playne expresse likenesse of that noble duke . . . While these wordes

were in speakynge, the protectour accompaignied with the duke
of Buckyngham, wente through the people up into the place wher
the doctors stande where they harde oute the sermond: but the
people wer so far from criynge kynge Richarde that they stoode
as they had been turned into stoones for wonder of this shamefull
sermonde . . .

Then on the tuesday after next foloyng this sermond, beyng
the [fol. xxᵛ] xvii. daye of June, there came to the Guyld hall of
London the duke of Buckyngham and diverse lordes and knightes
mo then happely knewe the message that thei brought. And at
the east ende of the hal where the hoystynges be kepte, the duke
and the maire and the other lordes sat downe, and the aldermen
also, all the commons of the citee beeynge, assembled and
standynge before theim. After scilence commaunded upon
a greate pain in the protectoures name: The duke stode up and as
he was well learned and of nature merveilously well spoken, he
sayed to the people with a cleare and a lowde voyce: Frendes, for
the zeale and hertie favoure that we beare you, we bee come to
breke of a matter righte greate and weightie, and no lesse
weightie then pleasyng to God and profitable to all the realme,
nor to no parte of the realme, more profitable, them to you the
citezens of this noble citee . . . [Buckingham alleges Edward's
harshness, concluding:] as though Burdet were forgotten whiche
[fol. xxiʳ] was for a worde spoken, in hast cruelly behedded.
(This Burdet was a marchaunt dwellyng in Chepesyd at the signe
of the croune, which now is the signe of the flowre de luse over
against soper lane: This man merely in the rufflyng tyme of kyng
Edward the .iiii. his rage, saied to his awne some [*sic*] that he
would make him in heritor of the croune, meaning his awne
house: but these wordes kyng Edward made to be mysconstrued,
& interpreted that Burdet meante the croune of the realme:
wherfore within lesse space then iiii. houres, he was apprehended,
judged, drawen and quartered in Chepesyde) by the miscon-
struynge of the lawes of the realme for the princes pleasure . . .
[fol. xxiᵛ] [Now turning to Edward's lust, he declares:] no
women was there any where young or old, poore or riche,
whom he sette his yie upon, whom he any thynge liked either for
persone or beautie, speche, pace or countenaunce, but without
any feare of God, or respecte of his honour, murmure, or grudgyng
of the worlde, he would importunately pursue his appetite and
have her, to the greate distruction of many a good woman, and
greate doloure to their husbandes and frendes, whiche beyng
honest people of theim selves, so much regarded the clenenesse

of their houses, the chastitee of their wives and children, that theim were lever to lose all that thei have beside, then to have suche a vilanie dooen to theim . . . [fol. xxii^v] When the duke had saied and loked that the people whom he hoped that the Maire had framed before, shoulde after this flatterynge preposicion made, have cried kynge Richarde, kynge Richarde, all was still and mute and not one woorde answered to: wherwith the duke was marvelously abashed, and takynge the Maire nere to hym, with other that wer aboute hym privy to the matter, saied unto theim softely. What meaneth this, that the people be so still? Sir quod the Maire, percase thei perceive you not well, that shall wee amende quod he, if that wil helpe, and therwith somewhat lowder rehersed the same matter again, in other ordre and other woordes so well and ornately, and nevertheless so evidently and plaine, with voice, gesture, & countenaunce so comely and so convenient that every man muche marveiled that hard him and thought that they never harde in their lives so evill a tale so well tolde. But wer it for wonder or feare, or that eche loked that other shoulde speake firste, not one worde was there answered of all the people that stoode before . . . When the Maire sawe this, he with other parteners of the counsaill, drewe aboute the duke and saied that the people had not been accustomed there to be spoken too, but by the Recorder, whiche is the mouthe of the citee, and happely too hym they will answere. With that the Recorder . . . made rehersall to the commons of that whiche the duke had twise purposed hym self, but the recorder so tempered his tale, that he shewed every thyng as the duke his woordes were, and no parte of his owne, but all this no chaunge made in the people wiche alwaie after one stoode as they had been amased . . . [fol. xxiii^r] And at these wordes the people began to whisper emong them selfes secretely, that the voyce was neither loude or base, but like a swarme of bees, till at the laste, at the nether ende of the hal a hushement of the duke servauntes and one Nashfeelde and other belongynge to the protectoure with some prentices and laddes that thrusted into the hall emongest the preace, began sodainly at mennes backes to crye out as lowde as they could, kynge Richard, kyng Richard, and there threwe up their cappes in token of joye, and thei that stoode before cast backe their heddes marveilynge therat, but nothyng thei saied. And when the duke and the Maire saw this maner, thei wisely turned it to their purpose, and saied it was a goodly crie and a joyfull to here every manne with one voyce and no manne saying nay . . .

Then on the morowe the Maire and aldremen and chief commoners of the citee in their best maner appareled, assemblyng theim together at Paules, resorted to Baynardes castle where the protectoure laie, to whiche place also accordyng too the appoinctment repaired the duke of Buckyngham, and diverse nobles with hym, besides many knyghtes and gentlemen. And there upon the duke sente woorde to the lorde protectoure of the beyng there of a greate honourable compaignie to move a great matter to his grace. Where upon the protectoure made greate difficulte to come doune to theim, excepte he knewe some parte of their errande, as thoughe he doubted and partely mistrusted the commynge of suche a numbre to hym so sodainely, without any warnyng or knowlege, whether they came for good or harme. Then when the duke had shewed this too the Mayre and other, that thei mighte there by se how litle the protectour loked for this matter, they sente again by the messenger suche lovynge message, and there with so humble besoughte hym to vouchsafe that thei mighte resorte to his presence to purpose their entent of wich thei woulde to none other persone any parte disclose. At the [fol. xxiiiᵛ] last he came out of his chambre, and yet not doune to theim, but in a galary over theim with a bishop on every hande of hym, where thei beneth might se hym and speke to hym, as thoughe he woulde not yet come nere them til he wist what they meante. And there upon, the duke of Buckyngham firste made humble peticion to hym on the behalfe of theim all, that his grace woulde pardon theim and licence them to purpose unto his grace the entent of their commyng without his displeasure, without whiche pardon obteined, they durste not bee so bold to move hym of that matter. In whiche, albeit they meante as muche honoure to his grace as wealth to all the realme, yet were thei not sure how his grace would take it, whom they would in no wise offende. Then the protectour, as he was verie gentle of hym selfe and also longed sore apparantly to know what they meante, gave hym leave to purpose what hym liked, verely trustynge for the good minde that he bare them all, none of theim any thyng woulde entende to hym warde, wherewith he thought to bee greved. When the duke had this leave and pardon to speake, then wexed he bolde to shewe hym their entente and purpose, with all the causes movyng theun [sic] thereto, as ye before have harde. And finall, to beseche his grace that it would like hym of his accustomed goodnesse and zeale unto the realme now with his yie of pitie to beholde the long continued distresse and decaie of the same, & to set his gracious hande to the redresse and amendemente therof by takynge upon hym the crouned and governaunce of the realme accordyng to his right and title laufully distended unto hym . . .

When the protector had harde the proposicion, he loked very strangely therat and made answere, that albeit he knewe partely the thynges by theim alleged to bee true, yet suche entiere love he bare to kynge Edward and his children, and so muche more regarded his honour in other realmes aboute, then the crouned of any one, of whiche he was never desyrous, so that he could not fined in his harte in this poinct to incline to their desire, for in al other nacions where the truth were not wel knowen, it shoulde paraventure bee thoughte that it were his awne ambicious mynde and devise to depose the prince and to take hym selfe the croune, with which infamy he would in no wise have his honour steined for any croune, in whiche he had ever perchaunce perceyved muche more labour and pein, then pleasure to hym that so would use it as he that would not and were not worthy to have it. Notwithstandyng, he not onely pardoned them of the mocion that they made hym, but also thanked them for the love and harty favoure they bare hym, praiyng theim for his sake to beare the same to the prince under whom he was and would be contente to live and with his labour & counsaill as far as it should like the kyng too use it . . .

[fol. xxiiiiʳ] Upon this answer geven, the duke of Buckyngham . . . shewed aloude unto the protectour, for a finall conclusion that the realme was apointed that kynge Edwarde his line should no longer reigne upon them . . . Wherefore if it would like his grace to take the croune upon him they would humbly beseche him therunto, and yf he would geve theim a resolute answere to the contrarye (whiche thei would bee lothe to here) then must they seke and shoulde not faill to find some other noble manne that would. These wordes muche moved the protector, whiche as every man of small intelligence maie wit woulde never have enclined thereto: but when he sawe there was none other waye but that he muste take it, or els he and his bothe to go from it, he saied to the lordes and commons, sithe it is wee perceive well that all the realme is so sette (wherof we bee very sory) that they will not suffre in any wise kynge Edwarde his line to governe theim, whom no man earthely can governe against their willes: And we also perceive that no manne is there to whome the crowne can by so juste title appertaine as to our selfe as very righte heire laufully begotten of the body of our moste dread and dere father Richard late duke of Yorke to whiche title is now joyned your election, the nobles and commons of the realme, whiche we of all titles possible take for mooste effectuall, wee bee contente and agree favourably to encline to your peticion & request, and accordynge to the same, here we take upon us the royall estate of preheminence and kyngdome of the twoo noble realmes, Englande and Fraunce ... With this there was a greate cry and shoute, criyng kyng Richard, and so the lordes wente up to the kynge, and so he was after that daie called.

[fol. xxvii^r] [Richard, after his coronation] ... forasmuch as his mynd gave hym that his nephewes livynge, men would not recon that he coulde have righte to the realme: he thoughte therefore without delaie to rid theim, as thouh the killynge of his kynsmen mighte ende his cause, and make hym kyndely kyng. Where upon he sent Jhon Grene ... unto sir Robert Brakenbury constable of the tower ... that the same should put the two children to death. This John Grene dyd his errand to Brakenbury ... who plainly answered that he woulde never put them to death to dye therefore. With the which answere Grene returned, recomptying the same to kynge Richard ... wherewith he toke suche displeasure and thoughte that the same nighte he sayde to a secrete page of his: Ah, whom shall a man truste? they that I have brought up my selfe, they that I went would moost surely served me, even those fayle me, and at my commaundemente wyll do nothynge for me. Syr, quod the page, there lieth one in the palet chambre with out that I dare wel say, to do your grace pleasure the thing were right hard that he would refuse, meanyng this by James Tirel, whiche was a man of goodly personage, and for the giftes of nature worthy to have served a muche better prince, yf he had well served God, and by grace obteyned to have as muche trueth and good wyll, as he had strength and wytt. The man had an high harte and sore longed upwarde, not risyng yet so fast as he had hoped ... upon the pages woordes, kyng Richard arose ... and came out into the palet chambre, where he ... called up James Tyrell, & brake to him secretely his mynd in this mischevous matter, in the which he found him nothing straunge. Therefore on the morowe he sent him to Brakynbury with a letter by the whiche he was commaunded to delyver to the sayd James all the keyes of the Towre for a night, to thende that he might there accomplishe the kynges pleasure in suche thynges as he there had geven him in commaundement ... [fol. xxvii^v] The prince ... and his brother were both shut up, and all other removed from them, one called blac

Wyl, or Willyam Slaughter onely except which wer sette to
serve them, and iiii. other to see them sure . . .

For James Tirrell devised that they shoulde be murthered in
their beddes, and no bloud shed: to the execution whereof, he
appoincted Myles Forest one of the foure that before kepte them,
a felowe fleshe bred in murther before tyme: and to him he
joyned one John Dighton his awne horsekeper, a bygge broade
square and strong knave. Then al the other beyng removed
from them, this Miles Forest and John Dighton aboute mydnight,
the sely children liyng in their beddes, came into the chaumbre
and sodenli lapped them up amongest the clothes and so be-
wrapped them and entangled them, kepying doune by force
the fetherbed and pillowes harde unto their mouthes, that
within a while thei smored & stiyfled them, and their breathes
failyng, they gave up to God their innocent solles into the joyes
of heaven, leavyng to the tourmentours their bodies dead in the
bed, whiche after the wretches perceyved, firste by the strugglyng,
with the panges of death, and after long liyng styl to be throughly
dead, they layd the bodies out upon the bed and fetched James
Tirrell to see them, whiche when he sawe them perfightly dead,
he caused the murtherers to burye them at the stayre foote,
metely deepe in the grounde under a great heape of stones.

Then rode James Tirrel in great hast to kyng Richard, and
shewed him all the maner of the murther, who gave him great
thankes . . . Wherupon a priest of sir Robert Brakenburies toke
them up & buried them in such a place secretely as by the
occasion of his death (which was very shortely after) whiche
onely knewe it the very trueth could never yet be very wel and
perfightly knowen. For some saye that kynge Richard caused
the priest to take them up and close them in lead and to put
them in a coffyne full of holes hoked at the endes with .ii. hokes
of yron, [fol. xxviii^r] and so to cast them into a place called the
Blacke depes at the Themes mouth, so that they should never
rise up nor be sene agayn. This was the very trueth unknowen
by reason that the sayd priest died so shortly & disclosed it never
to any person that would utter it. And for a trueth, when sir
James Tirrel was in the Towre for treason committed to kynge
Henrye the seventhe: bothe he and Dighton were examined
together of this poincte, and both they confessed the murther
to be done in the same maner as you have hard, but whether
the bodies were removed, they bothe affirmed thei never knewe.
And thus as I have learned of them that muche knewe and litle
▪use had to lye, where these two noble princes, these innocente

tendre children . . . by trayterous tirannye taken and deprived
of their estate, shortely shut up in prison and prively slaine and
murthered by the cruel ambicion of their unnaturall uncle and
his dispiteous tourmentours . . . I have harde by credible
reporte of suche as were secrete with his chamberers that after
this abhominable deed done, he never was quiet in his mynde
he never thought him selfe sure where he wente abroade, his
body prively feinted, his eyen wherled aboute, his hande ever
on his dagger, his countenaunce and maner lyke alwaies to
stricke againe, he toke evill reste on nightes, laye long wakyng
and musyng, forweried with care and watche, rather slombred
then slept, troubled with fearefull dreames, sodeinly somtyme
stert up, leapte out of his bed and loked about the chambre, so
was his restless harte continually tossed and tombled with the
tedious impression and stormy remembraunce of his abhominable
murther and execrable tyrannye.

C. From *The tragical doynges of Kyng Richard the thirde*, in Hall's
   Union (fols. xxxʳ–lixʳ).

[Buckingham falls out with Richard:] he so highly turned from
him and so highly conspired against him, that a man woulde
marveill wherof the chaunge grewe in so shorte space. Some say
this occasyon was that a litle before the coronacion, the duke
required the kynge amongest other thynges to be restored to the
erle of Herfordes landes: And forasmuche as the tytle whiche he
claymed by inheritaunce, was somewhat interlaced, with the
tytle of Lancaster, whiche house made a title to the croune, and
enjoyed the same thre discentes, as al men knewe, tyll the house
of Yorke deprived the third kynge, whiche was Henry the sixte,
Kynge Richarde somewhat mistrusted and conceived such an
[fol. xxxᵛ] indignacion, that he reiected the dukes request, with
many spitefull, and minotary wordes, whiche so wounded the
dukes harte with hatred and mistrust, that he could never after
endure to loke right on king Richard but ever feared his awne
lyfe . . . [fol. xxxiiiiʳ] For when I my self [said Buckingham]
sued to him for my part of the Earle of Hartfordes landes whiche
his brother kynge Edwarde wrongefully deteyned and with helde
from me, and also required to have the office of the highe constable shyppe of Englande, as divers of my noble anunceters
before this tyme have had, and in longe discente continued. In
thys my fyrste suyte shewynge his good mynde towarde me, he
dyd not onely fyrste delaye me, and afterwarde denay me, but
gave me suche unkynde woordes, with suche tauntes and [fol.

xxxiiii^v] retauntes ye in maner checke and checke mate to the uttermooste profe of my pacience. As though I had never furthered him but hyndered him, as though I had put hym downe and not sett hym up: yet all these ungratitudes and undeserved unkyndnes I bare closlye & suffered pacientelie and covertly remembred, owtwardely dissimulynge that I inwardelie thoughte . . . But when I was credibly enformed of the death of the .ii. younge innocentes, his awne natural nephewes contrarie to his faith and promyse, to the whiche God by my judge I never agreed nor condiscended. O lord, how my veynes panted howe my body trembled, and my harte inwardely grudged, in so much that I so abhorred the sighte and muche more the compaignie of hym, that I coulde no lenger abyde in his courte, excepte I shoulde be openly revenged. The ende wherof was doutfull, and so I fayned a cause to departe, and with a mery countenaunce and a dispiteful harte I toke my leave humbly of hym (he thinkyng nothynge lesse then that I was displeased) and so returned to Brecknock . . .

[fol. xxxix^r] [The rebellions against Richard, including Buckingham's, begin.] Sir Edwarde Courtney and Peter his brother bishop of Exsetter, reised another army in devonshire and cornewall. In kente, Richarde Guylforde and other gentlemen, collected a great companye of souldyoures and openly beganne warre. But kynge Richarde whiche in the meane tyme had gotten together a greate strength and puissaunce . . . took his journey towarde Salsburie. The kynge was skace .ii. daies journey from Salsburie when the duke of Buckyngham accompanyed with a greate power of wilde Weleshmen . . . mershed through the forest of deane entendying to have passed the river of Severne at Gloucester, and therto have joyned in army with the courtneys and other Westernmen . . . But se the chaunce, before he could attayne to Severne side, by force of continuall rayne and moysture, the ryver rose so high that yt overflowed all the countrey adjoyning . . . By this innudacion the passages were so closed that neither the duke could come over Severne to his complices, nor they to hym, durynge the whiche tyme, the Welshemen lyngerynge ydely and without money, vitayle, or wages, sodaynely scaled and departed: and for all the dukes faire promyses, manaces and enforcementes, they woulde in no wise neither goo farther nor abide. The duke thus abandoned and left almost post alone was of necessite compelled to flye . . .

[fol. xxxix^v] kynge Rycharde, whyche usynge a vigilaunte iye and a quycke remembraunce, beynge newely come to Salsburye,

havyng perfight notice and knowlege howe the duke was fled
. . . sente men of warre to all the nexte portes and passages to
kepe streightely the see coast, so that no person shoulde passe
outwarde nor take lande in the realme withoute their assente
and knowlege. Secondarely, he made proclamacion, that what
person coulde shewe and revele where the duke of Buckyngham
was shoulde be highely rewarded, yf he were a bondman he
should be enfraunchised and set at libertie, yf he were of fre
blood he shoulde have a generall perdon and be remunerate
with a thousand poundes . . .

[fol. xl^r] While this Busy searche was diligentely applied and
put in execucion, Homfrey Banaster . . . bewrayed his gest and
master [Buckingham] to Jhon Mitton then shriefe of Shropshire,
whyche sodaynely with a stronge power of men in harnes apprehended the duke in a lytle grove adjoynynge to the mansion
of Homfrey Banaster, and in greate hast and evyll spede conveighed him appareled in a pilled blacke cloke to the cytie of
Salsburie where kynge Richarde then kepte his housholde . . .
But when [Buckingham] had confessed the whole facte and
conspiracye upon Allsoulen daie withoute arreignemente or
judgemente he was at Salsburye in the open merket place on a
newe skaffolde beheded and put to deathe.

[fol. xl^v] While these thynges were thus handeled and ordred
in Englande, Henry Earle of Richemond prepared an armye of
fyve thousande manly Brytons, and fortie well furnyshed shippes.
When all thinges were prepared in aredynes . . . the whole
armye wente on shipboorde and halsed up their sailes, and with
a prosperous wynde tooke the see: but towarde nyghte the
wynde chaunged and the wether tourned, and so houge and
terrible a tempeste sodaynely roase, that with the verie power
and strengthe of the storme, the shippes were disparcled, severed and
separate a sondre: some by force were dryven into Normandye,
some were compelled to retourne agayne into Britayne. The
shippe werein the Earle of Rychemonde was, associate onely
with one other barcke was all nyghte tossed and turmoyled. In
the mornynge after the rage of the furious tempeste was assuaged,
and the Ire of the blusterynge wynde was some deale appeased,
aboute the houre of none thesame daye, the Earle approched
to the southe parte of the realme of Englande even at the mouthe
of the haven of pole in the countie of dorcet, where he mighte
playnely perceave all these bankes and shores garnished and
furnyshed with men of warre and souldioners appoynted and
deputed there to defende his arryvall and landynge as before

mencioned. Wherefore . . . he sente oute a shippe bote towarde the lande side to knowe, whyther they whiche stoode there in suche a nombre and so well furnysshed in apparell defensyve were hys capitall foes and ennemyes or elles his frendes fautoures and comforters. They that were sente in exploracion and message were instantely desyred of the men of warre kepynge these coast (whiche therof were before instructed and admonished) to dissende and take lande, affirmynge that they were appoyncted by the duke of Buckyngham there to awayte and tarie for the arryvall and landyng of the erle of Rychemond . . . [fol. xli^r] [who] suspectynge their flatterynge requeste to be but a fraude (as yt was in dede) after that he perceaved none of his shippes to apere in sight, he weied up his ancors and halsed up his sayles havynge a prosperous and strenable wynde . . . arryved safe and in securitie in the duchy of Normandye . . . [fol. xlii^r] In this troubleous ceason, nothinge was more merveled at then that the lord Stanley had not bene taken and reputed as an enemy to the king, considerynge the workynge of the ladye Margarete his wife mother to the earle of Richemonde . . . yt was geven him in charge to kepe her in some secrete place at home, withoute havynge enie servaunte or companye, so that from thence foorthe she shoulde never sende letter nor messenger to her sonne nor any of his frendes or confederates . . .

[fol. xlvii^v] There came into [Richard's] ungracious mynde a thing not onely detestable to be spoken of in the remembraunce of man, but muche more cruell and abhominable to be put in execucion . . . [fol. xlviii^r] yf no ingenyous remedye coulde be otherwise invented to save the innumerable mischiefes whiche were even at hand and like to falle, yf yt shoulde happen quene Anne his wife to departe oute of this presente worlde, then he him selfe woulde rather take to wife his cousyn and nece the lady Elizabeth, then for lack of that affinite the whole realme should runne to ruyne . . . Wherfore he sent to the quene beynge in sanctuarie diverse and often messengers, whiche first shoulde excuse and purge him of all thinges before againste her attempted or procured, and after shoulde so largely promes promocions innumerable and benefites, not onely to her but also to her sonne lord Thomas Marques Dorcett, that they should brynge her yf yt were possible into some wanhope, or as men saie into a fooles paradise . . . she began somewhat to relent & to geve to theim no deffe eare, in somuche that she faithfully promised to submyt & yelde her selfe fully and frankely to the ~ynges will and pleasure. And so she putting in oblivion the murther of her innocente children, the infamy and dishonoure spoken by the kynge her husbande, the lyvynge in avoutrie leyed to her charge, the bastardyng of her daughters, forgettyng also the feithfull promes & open othe made to the countesse of Richmond mother to the erle Henry, blynded by avaricious affeccion and seduced by flatterynge wordes [she acquiesced.] . . . Surely the inconstancie of this woman were muche to be merveled at, yf all women had bene founde constante, but let men speake, yet wemen of the verie bonde of nature will folowe their awne kynde. After that kynge Rycharde had thus with glorious promyses and flatterynge woordes pleased and appeased the mutable mynde of quene Elyzabeth [fol. xlviiiᵛ] which knewe nothing lesse then that he moost entended . . . nothinge was contrariant and obstacle to his pernicious purpose, but that his mancion was not voide of his wife, whiche thynge he in anywise adjuged necessary to be done . . . After this he procured a common rumour (but he woulde not have the author knowen) to be published and spred abroade emonge the common people that the quene was ded, to thentent that she takyng some conceipte of this straung fame, should fall into some sodayne sicknes or grevous maladye, & to prove if afterward she should fortune by that or any other waies to lese her life, whyther the people would impute her death to the thought or sicknes, or therof would laie the blame to him . . . howsoever that it fortuned, either by inward thought and pensyvenes of hearte, or by intoxicacion of poyson [fol. xlixʳ] (which is affirmed to be moost likely) within a few daies after, the quene departed oute of this transitorie lyfe . . .

The kyng thus (accordyng to his long desire) losed oute of the bondes of matrimony, beganne to cast a foolyshe phantasie to Lady Elizabeth his nece, making much suite to have her joyned with him in lawfull matrimony . . . Emongest the noble men whome he moost mystrusted [was] the Lorde Stanley, because he was joyned in matrimony with the lady Margarete mother to the erle of Richmond, as afterward apparauntly ye maie perceave. For when thesayde lorde Stanley woulde have departed into his countrey to visite his familie, and to recreate and refreshe his spirites (as he openly sayde) but the truth was to thentent to be in a perfight readines to receave the erle of Richmond at his first arrivall in England: the kyng in no wise woulde suffre hym to departe before that he had left as an hostage in the courte George Stanley lorde straung his first begotten sonne and heire . . .

[fol. liiʳ] [Richmond's invasion.] Kynge Rycharde at this

ceason kepynge his howse in the Castell of Notyngham was infourmed that the Earle of Richemond with such bannysshed men as fled oute of Englande to hym were nowe arryved in Wales, and that all thynges necessarie to his entreprice were unprovided, unpurveyed and verie weake, nothynge mete to withstande the powre of suche as the kyng had apoynted to resiste him . . . [fol. liiᵛ] tydynges came that the Earle of Richemond was passed Severne and come to Shrewsbury withoute any detrymente or encombreaunce. At whiche message he was sore moved and broyled wyth Melancolye and doloure, and cried out, askynge vengeaunce of theim that contrarye to their othe and promes had fraudulently deceaved hym. For whyche cause he beganne to have diffidence in other, in so muche that he determined hym selfe oute of hand thesame daye to occurre and resyste hys adversaries . . . And kepyng this araye, he with greate pompe entred the toune of Lecester after the sonne set. The Earle of Rychmonde reised his campe and departed from Lychefelde to the towne of Tomwoorth therto nere adjoynynge . . . [fol. liiiʳ] Diverse other noble personages whiche inwardely hated kynge Richard worsse then a toade or a serpent, lykewyse resorted to hym wyth all their powre and strength . . . [fol. liiiᵛ] the Earle came firste to his fatherinlawe in a lytle close, where he saluted hym and Sir William his brother, and after diverse congratulacions and many frendely embracynges eache rejoysed of the state of the other . . .

In the mean ceason kyng Richard (whiche was appoynted nowe to finyshe his last laboure by the very devyne justice and providence of God, whiche called him to condigne punyshemente for his scelerate merites and myscheveous desertes) marshed to a place mete for twoo battayles to encountre by a village called Bosworth, not farre from Leycester, and there he pitched his felde, refreshed his souldioures and toke his rest. The fame went that he had thesame night a dreadfull & a terrible dreame, for yt semed to hym beynge a slepe that he sawe diverse ymages lyke terrible develles whiche pulled and haled hym, not sufferynge hym to take any quyet or rest. The whiche straunge vision not so sodeinly strake his heart with a sodeyne feare, but it stuffed his hed and troubled his mynde with many dreadfull and busy Imaginacions. For incontynent after, his heart beynge almost damped, he pronosticated before the doubtfull chaunce of the battaile to come, not usynge the alacrite and myrth of mynde and of countenaunce as he was accustomed to do before he came toward the battaile. And least that it might be suspected that he

was abasshed for feare of his enemyes, and for that cause looked
so piteously, he recyted and declared to hys famylyer frendes in
the morenynge hys wonderfull visyon and terrible dreame. But
I thynke this was no dreame, but a punccion and pricke of hys
synfull conscyence . . . the next daie after, kyng Richard beyng
furnished with men & all abilimentes of warr, bringyng al his
men out of there camp into the plaine, ordered his forward in
a marveylous length, in which he appointed both horsemen &
[fol. liiii^r] footmen to thentent to emprynte in the hartes of
them that loked a farre of, a sodeine terror & deadlie feare, for
the great multitude of the armed soldiours: & in the fore Frount
he placed the archers like a strong fortified trench or bulwarke:
over this battaile was captain Jhon duke of Norfolke with whome
was Thomas erle of Surrey his sonne. After this long vantgard
folowed king Richard himself, with a strong compaigny of
chosen & approved men of warr, havyng horsmen for wynges
on both the sides of his battail.

After that therle of Richmond was departed from the com-
municacion of his frends as you have harde before, he began to
be of a better stomake & of a more valiant courage, & with al
diligens pitchid his feld juste by the camp of his enemies, & there
he lodgid that night. In the mornyng be tyme he caused his men
to put on there armure & appareyl them selfes redy to fight &
geve battaill, & sent to the lord Stanley (which was now come
with his bande in a place indifferently betwene both the armies)
requiryng him with his men to approche nere to his army & to
help to set the souldiours in array, he answered that therle
should set his awne men in a good order of battaile while he
would array his compaigny, & comme to him in time convenient
. . . For all his hole nomber exceded not v. thousande men
beside the powr of the Stanleys, wherof .iii. thousands were in
the felde under the standard of sir William Stanley: The kynges
nomber was doble as muche & more. When bothe these armies
were thus ordered & al men redy to set forward, kyng Richard
called his Chevetains together & to them sayde . . . [fol. liiii^v] I
doubt not but you knowe, howe the devell continuall enemie to
humane nature, disturber of concorde and sower of sedicion,
hath entered into the harte of an unknowen welshman, (whose
father I never knew nor hym personally sawe) excitynge hym
to aspire and covet oure realme, crowne and dignitie, and therof
clerely to depryve and spoyle us and our posterite: ye se farther
how a compaigny of traytors, thefes, outlawes and ronneagates
of our awne nacion be ayders & partakers of his feate and

enterprise, redy at hand to overcome and oppresse us: You se also, what a nomber of beggerly Britons & faynt harted Frenchmen be with hym arrived to distroy us our wyfes and children. Which Imminent mischifes & apparaunt inconveniences, if we wil withstond & refel, we must live to gether like brethern, fight together like lions, & feare not to dye together lyke men. And observyng and kepyng this rule and precept, beleve me, the fearefull hare never fledde faster before the gredy greyhound, nor the sylye larke before the sparowhauke, nor the symple shepe before the ravenous wolfe, then your proud bragging adversaries astonned & amased with the only sight of your manly visages, wil flee, ronne & skyr out of the felde. For yf yow consider and wisely ponder althings in your mynde, you shall perceyve that we have manifest causes, and apparant tokens of triumph and victorie. And to begyn with the earle of Richmond Captaine of this rebellion, he is a Welsh mylkesoppe, a man of small courage and of lesse experience in marcyall actes and feates of warr, brought up by my brothers meanes and myne like a captive in a close cage in the court of Fraunces duke of Britaine, and never saw armie, nor was exercised in marcial affaires, by reason whereof he neyther can nor is able on his awne wit or experience to guyde or rule an hoste . . . [fol. lv^r] And as for the Frenshmen & Brytons there valiantnes ys suche, that our noble progenitors & your valiaunt parentes, have them oftener vanquished & overcome in one moneth, then thei in the beginnyug [*sic*] imagened possible to compasse & fynishe in a hole yere . . . Wherfore, consideryng al these avauntages, expell out of your thoughts al doutes & avoide out of your mindes al feare, & like valiaunt champions avaunce furth your standards, & assaye whither your enemies can decide & trie the title of battaile by dent of swerde, avaunce (I say againe) forward my captains, in whome lacketh neither pollicie wisdome nor puissaunce. Every one gyve but one suer stripe, & suerly the jorney is ours . . . Now sent George to borowe, let us set forwarde, & remember wel that I am he which shal with high avauncementes, rewarde & preferre the valiaunt & hardy champions, & punishe and turment the shameful cowardes & dreadfull dastardes . . .

When therle of Richmond knewe by his forriders that the kyng was so nere embattayled, he rode about his armye, from ranke to ranke, [fol. lv^v] from wyng to wyng, gevyng comfortable wordes to all men, and that finyshed . . . he pawsed a while, and after with a lowde voyce and bolde spirite spake to his compaignions these or lyke wordes folowyng . . .

No doubt my felowes and frendes, but he of hys bountefull goodnes wyll this daye sende us triumphaunt victorye and a luckey journey over our prowde enemyes, and arrogant adversaries: for yf you remember and consider the very cause of our just quarell, you shall apparantlye perceyve the same to be trewe, Godly, and vertuous. In the whiche I doubte not but GOD wyll rather ayde us (ye and fyght for us) then se us vanquished and profligate by suche as neyther feare hym nor his lawes, nor yet regarde justice or honestie. Our cause is so juste that no enterprice can be of more vertue, bothe by the lawes divine and civile, for what can be a more honest, goodly, or Godly quarell then to fight agaynste a Capitayne, beyng an homicide and murderer of hys awne bloude and progenye? An extreme destroyer of hys nobylytie, and to hys and oure countrey and the poore subjectes of the same, a deadly malle a fyrye brande and a burden untollerable? . . . Lykewyse, hys mates and frendes occupie your landes cutt downe your woddes and destroy your manners, lettynge your wifes and children range a brode for ther livyng . . . [fol. lvi^r] I assure you that there be yonder in that great battaill, men brought thyther for feare and not for love, souldiours by force compelled and not with good will assembled: persons which desyer rather the destruccion then salvacion of ther master and captayn: And fynally a multitude: wherof the most parte will be our frendes and the lest parte our enemies . . . he hath violated, and broken bothe the lawe of God & man . . . If this cause be not juste, and this quarel Godly, let God the gever of vyctorie judge and determine . . . yf we wyn this battaill, the hole riche realme of England with the lordes and rulers of the same shall be [fol. lvi^v] oures, the profit shall be oures and the honour shall be oures. Therfore labour for your gayne and swet for your right . . . now is the tyme come to gett abundaunce of riches and copie of profit which is the rewarde of your service and merite of your payne . . . And now avaunce forward trew men against traytors, pitifull persones against murtherers, trew inheritors against usurpers, the skorges of God against tirauntes, display my banner with a good courage, marche furth like stronge & robustious champions, & begyn the battaill like hardy conquerers, the battaill is at hande, & the victorie approcheth, & yf we shamfully recule or cowardly flye, we and all our sequele be destroyd & dishonored for ever. This is the daie of gayne, & this is the time of losse, get this daie victorie & be conquerers, & lese this daies battail & be villains & therfore in the name of god & sainct George let every man coragiously avaunce forth his standard.

[The battle is joined.] [fol. lvii^r] While the two forwardes thus mortallye fought, eche entendyng to vanquishe & convince that other, kyng Richard was admonished by his explorators and espialles, that therle of Richmond accompaignied with a small nomber of men of armes was not farre of, & as he approched and marched toward him, he perfitely knew his personage by certaine demonstracions & tokens whiche he had learned and knowen of other. And being inflamed with ire and vexed with outragious malice, he put his spurres to his horse & rode out of the syde of the range of his battaile, levyng the avantgardes fightyng, & lyke a hungery lion ran with spere in rest toward hym. Therle of Richmonde perceyved wel the kyng furiusly commyng towarde him, and by cause the hole hope of his welth and purpose was to be determined by battaill, he gladlye proferred to encountre with hym body to body and man to man. Kyng Rychard sett on so sharpely at the first Brount that he overthrew therles standarde, and slew Sir William Brandon his standarde bearer . . . and matched hand to hand with sir Jhon Cheinye, a man of great force & strength which would have resisted hym, & the saied Jhon was by hym manfully overthrowen, and so he makyng open passage by dent of swerde as he went forwarde, therle of Richmond with stode his violence and kept hym at the swerdes poinct without avauntage longer then his compaignions other though or judged, which beyng almost in dispaire of victorie, were sodainly recomforted by Sir William Stanley, whiche came to succours with .iii. thousande tall men, at whiche very instant kynge Richardes men were dryven backe and fledde, and he him selfe manfully fyghtynge in the mydell of his enemies was slayne [fol. lvii^v] and brought to his death as he worthely had deserved . . .

In this battaill died fewe above the number of a thousande persones: And of the nobilitie were slayne Jhon Duke of Norfolke, whiche was warned by dyvers to refrayne from the felde, in so muche that the nyghte before he shoulde set forwarde towarde the kynge, one wrote on his gate.

Jack of Norffolke be not to bolde
For Dykon thy maister is bought and solde.

Yet all this notwithstandynge he regarded more his othe his honour and promyse made to kynge Richarde, lyke a gentleman and a faythefull subjecte to his prynce absented not hym selfe from hys mayster, but as he faythefully lyved under hym, so he manfully dyed with hym to hys greate fame and lawde. There were slayne besyde hym water lorde Ferrers of Chartley, Sir

Rychard Ratclyffe, and Robert Brakenburie Leutenaunt of the Tower and not many gentlemen mo . . .

[fol. lviii^r] Kyng Richard as the fame wente might have escaped and gotten savegarde by fliynge. For when thei whiche were next about his person saw and perceyved at the first joynyng of the battaill the souldiours fayntly and nothyng couragiously to set on their enemies, and not only that, but also that some with drewe them selfes pryvely out of the prease and departed. They beganne to suspect fraude and to smell treason, and not only exhorted but determinatly advysed hym to save hym selfe by flyght: and when the losse of the battayle was imminent and apparante, they brought to hym a swyfte and a lyght horse to convey hym awaie. He which was not ignorant of the grudge & yll will that the common people bare towarde him, casting awaye all hope of fortunate successe & happy chaunce to come, answered (as men saye) that on that daye he woulde make an ende of all battailes or els ther finyshe his lyfe. Suche a great audacitie & such a stowte stomake reigned in his body, for suerly he knew that to be the day in the which it should be decided & determined whither he should peaseably obteyne & enjoye his kyngdom duryng his lyfe, or els utterly forgo & be depryved of thesame, with which to much hardines be beyng overcome hastely closed his helmett and entered fiercely in to the hard battail, to thentent to obteine that day a quiet reigne & regiment or els to finyshe there his unquiet life & unfortunate governaunce . . .

When therle had thus obteigned victorie and slaine his mortal enemie, he kneled doune and rendred to almightie God his harty thankes with devoute & Godly orisons . . . Which praier finyshed, he replenyshed with incomperable gladnes, ascended up to the topp of a littell mountaine, where he not only praysed & lawded his valiaunt souldiours, but also gave unto theim his harty thankes, with promyse of condigne recompence for their fidelite & valiaunt factes, willyng & commaundyng al the hurt & wounded persones to be cured, and the dead carcases to be delivered to the sepulture. Then the people rejoysed & clapped handes criyng up to heaven, king Henry, king Henry. When the lord Stanley sawe the good will and gratuite of the people [fol. lviii^v] he toke the crowne of kynge Richard whiche was founde amongest the spoyle in the felde, and sett it on therles hed, as though he had byne elected kyng by the voyce of the people . . . When kynge Rycharde was come to Boswoorth, he sent a pursevaunt to the lord Stanley, commaundyng hym to avaunce forward with hys compaignie and to come to his presence, whiche thynge yf he refused to do, he sware by Christes passion that he woulde stryke of his sonnes hedde before he dined. The lorde Stanley aunswered the pursivaunt that yf the kynge dyd so, he had more sonnes a lyve, and as to come to hym he was not then so determined: when kynge Richarde harde this aunswere he commaunded the lorde Straunge incontinent to be behedded, which was at that very same season when bothe the armyes had sight eche of other. The counsaillers of kyng Rycharde ponderyng the time and the cause, knowynge also the Lorde Straunge to be innocente of his fathers offence, perswaded the kynge that it was now tyme to fight and not tyme to execucion, advisynge hym to kepe the Lorde Straunge as a prisoner tyll the battayll were ended, and then at Leyser his pleasure myght be accomplished . . .

[fol. lix^r] As [Richard] was small and little of stature so was he of body grrately deformed, the one shoulder higher then the other, his face small but his contenaunce was cruel, and such, that a man at the first aspect would judge it to savor and smel of malice, fraude, and deceite: when he stode musyng he woulde byte and chaw besely his nether lippe, as who sayd, that hys fyerce nature in his cruell bodye alwaies chafed, sturred and was ever unquiete: beside that, the dagger that he ware he would when he studied with his hand plucke upp and downe in the shethe to the middes, never drawing it fully out, his wit was pregnaunt, quicke and redy, wyly to fayne and apte to dissimule, he had a proude mynde and an arrogant stomacke, the whiche accompaignied him to his death, whiche he rather desyrynge to suffer by dent of swerde, then beynge forsaken and destitute of his untrewe compaignions, woulde by cowarde flight preserve and save his uncertaine liffe: Whiche by malice, sickenes or condigne punishement might chaunce shortly after to comme to confusion.

II. *The Mirror for Magistrates*

From Tragedy 18, *George, Duke of Clarence* (Campbell, p. 219).

For though the king within a while had died,　　　　337
As nedes he must, he surfayted so oft,
I must have had his children in my gyde
So Richard should beside the crowne have coft:
This made him plye the while the waxe was soft,
To find a meane to bring me to an ende,
For realme rape spareth neither kin nor frend.

And whan he sawe how reason can asswage   344
Through length of time, my brother Edwardes yre,
With forged tales he set him new in rage,
Til at the last they did my death conspire.
And though my truth sore troubled their desire,
For all the world did know mine innocence,
Yet they agreed to charge me with offence.

And covertly within the tower they called,   351
A quest to geve such verdite as they should:
Who what with fear, and what with favour thralde,
Durst nought pronounce but as my brethern would
And though my false accusers never could
Prove ought they sayd, I giltles was condemned:
Such verdites passe where justice is contemned.

This feat atchieved, yet could they not for shame   358
Cause me to be kilde by any common way,
But like a wulfe the tirant Richard came,
(My brother, nay the butcher I may say)
Unto the tower, when all men wer away,
Save such as wer provided for the feate:
Who in this wise did straungely me entreate.

His purpose was, with a prepared string   365
To strangle me. but I bestird me so,
That by no force they could me therto bring,
Which caused him that purpose to forgo.
Howbeit they bound me whether I would or no.
And in a butte of Malmesey standing by,
Newe Christned me, because I should not crie.

From Tragedy 21, *Lord Hastynges* (Campbell, p. 267).

To true it is .ii. sondry assemblies kept,   313
At Crossbyes place, and Baynardes castell sett.
The Dukes at Crossebyes, but at Baynards we.
The one to crown a kyng, the other to be.
Suspicious is secession of foule frends,
When eythers dryft to others myschefe tendes.
I feared the end. My Catesbyes beyng there
Discharged all dowtes. Hym held I most entyre.

Whose great preferment by my meanes, I thought   321
Some spurre, to paye the thankfullnesse he ought.
The trust he ought me, made me trust him so:
That privye he was bothe to my weale and woe.
My harts one halfe, my chest of confydence,
My tresures trust, my joye dwelt in his presence.
I loved hym Baldwyn, as the apple of myne eye.
I lothed my lyfe when Catesby would me dye.

     *   *   *

The fatall skyes, roll on the blackest daye,   377
When doubled bloudshed, my bloud must repay.
Others none forceth. To me, Syr Thomas Haward
As spurre is buckled, to provoke me forward.
Darbie whoe feared he parted syttynges yore.
Whether, much more he knew by experyence hoare,
Or unaffected, Clearer truth could see:
At midnight darke this message sendes to me.

Hastynges away. in slepe the Gods foreshew   385
By dreadfull dreame, fell fates unto us two.
Me thought a Boare with tuske so rased our throate,
That both our shoulders of the bloud dyd smoake.
Aryse to horse, strayght homewarde let us hye.
And syth our foe we may not mate, o flye.
Of Chaunteclere you learne dreames sooth to know.
Thence wysemen conster, more then the Cock doth crow.

     *   *   *

And, is thy Lord (quoth I) a sorcerer?   401
A wyse man now becumme? a dreame reader?
What though so Chaunteclere crowed? I reke it not.
On my part pledeth as well dame Partelott.
Unjudgd hangth yet the case betwixt them twaye,
Ne was his dreame Cause of hys hap I saye.
Shall dremyng doutes from prynce my servyce slacke?
Naye, then mought Hastynges lyfe and lyvyng lacke.

He parteth. I sleepe. my mynde surcharged with synne,   409
As Phebus beames by mysty clowde kept in,
Ne could missegeve, ne dreame of my mysse happe.
As block I tumbled to myne enemyes trappe.

Securitye causelesse through my carelesse frende,
Reft me foresyght of my approchyng end.
So Catesby clawed me, as when the Catt doth playe
Dalieng with mouse, whom straight he mindes to slaye.

The morow come, the latest lyght to me,   417
On Palfray mounted, to the Tower I hye.
Accompanyed with that Haward my mortall foe,
To slaughter led. thou God wouldest have yt so.
(O depe dissemblers, Honouryng with your cheare,
Whome in hydd hart ye trayterouslye teare.)
Never had realme so open signes of wrack.
As I had shewed me of my heavy happ.

The vysyon fyrst of Stanley, late descryed.   425
Then myrth so extreme, that neare for joye I dyed.
Were hit, that Swannelyke I forsesong my death,
Or merye mynde foresaw the loose of breath
That long it coveyted, from thys earthes annoye.
But even as syker as thende of woe is joye,
And gloryous lyght to obscure night doth tend:
So extreame myrth in extreame moane doth ende.

*   *   *

But forward yet. In tower streete I stayed.   465
Where (could I have seene) loe Haward al bewrayde.
For as I commond with a pryest I mett:
Away my lord quoth he. your tyme ne is yet
To take a pryest. Loe, Synon myght be seene,
Had Troyans eares, as they had hares foole eyen.
But, whome thou God allotted hast to dye
Some grace it is to dye with wympled eye.

Ne was this all. For even at Towerwharfe,   473
Neare to those walles within whose syght I starfe,
Where erst, in sorowe sowst and depe distresse,
I emparted all my pynyng pensyfnesse
With Hastynges: (so my pursevaunt men call)
Even there, the same to meete hit did me fall.
Who gan to me most dolefully renewe,
The wofull conference had erst in that Lieu.

Hastinges (quoth I) accordyng now they fare,   481
At Pomfret this daye dyeng, whoe caused that care.

My self have all the world now at my will,
With pleasures cloyed, engorged with the fyll.
God graunt it so quoth he whye doutest thou tho
Quoth I? and all in chafe, to hym gan shewe
In ample wyse, our drift with tedious tale.
And entred so the tower to my bale.

*   *   *

To Councell chamber come, awhyle we stayd   537
For hym, without whom nought was done or sayd.
At last he came, and curteously excused,
For he so long our patience had abused.
And pleasantly began to paynt his cheare,
And sayd. My lord of Elye, would we had here
Some of the strawberyes, whereof you haue stoare.
The last delyghted me as nothyng more.

Would, what so ye wyshe, I mought as well commaund,   545
My lord (quoth he) as those. And out of hand.
His servant sendth to Elye place for them.
Out goeth from us the restlesse devyll agayne.
Belyke (I thynk) scarce yet perswaded full,
To worke the mischiefe that thus maddeth his scull.
At last determynd, of his bloudy thought
And force ordaynd, to worke the wyle he sought:

Frownyng he enters, with so chaunged cheare,   553
As for myld May had chopped fowle Januere.
And lowryng on me with the goggle eye,
The whetted tuske, and furrowed forhead hye,
His Crooked shoulder bristellyke set up,
With frothy Jawes, whose foame he chawed and suppd,
With angry lookes that flamed as the fyer:
Thus gan at last to grunt the grymest syre.

What earned they, whoe me, the kyngdomes staye,   561
Contryved have councell, trayterously to slaye?
Abashed all sate. I thought I mought be bolld,
For conscyence clearenesse, and acquayntaunce olld.
Theyr hyre is playne quoth I. Be death the least,
To whoe so seekth your grace so to molest.
Withouten staye: the Queene, and the whore shores wyfe,
By witchcraft (quoth he) seeke to wast my lyfe.

Loe here the wythered and bewytched arme,   569
That thus is spent by those .ii. Sorceresse charme.
And bared his arme and shewed his swynyshe skynne.
Suche cloakes they use, that seek to clowd theyr synne.
But out alas, hit serveth not for the rayne.
To all the howse the coloure was to playne.
Nature had gyven hym many a maymed marke,
And hit amonges, to note her monstrous warke.

My doubtfull hart distracted this replye.   577
For thone I cared not. Thother nypped so nye
That whyst I could not. But forthwith brake forth.
Yf so hit be, of death they are doutlesse worth.
Yf, traytour quod he? playest thou with yfs and ands?
Ile on thy body avowe it with these hands.
And therewithall he myghtely bounced the bord.
In rushd hys byll men. one hym selfe bestyrrd.

Layeng at lord Stanley. whose braine he had suerly cleft   585
Had he not downe beneath the table crept.
But Elye, Yorke, and I, were taken strayght.
Imprysoned they: I should no longar wayt,
But charged was to shryue me, and shyft with hast.
My lord must dyne, and now midday was past.
The boares first dyshe, not the boares head should be.
But Hastynges heade the boaryshe beast would see.

Whye staye I his dyner? unto the chapell joyneth   593
A greenish hyll, that body and sowle oft twyneth.
There on a block my head was stryken of.
John Baptists dishe, for Herode bloudy gnoffe.

*   *   *

In rousty armure as in extreame shyft,   689
They cladd them selves, to cloake theyr divelysh dryft.
And forthwith for substancyall cytezyns sent,
Declaryng to them, Hastynges forged entent
Was to have slayne the duke: and to have seysed
The kyngs yonge person, slayeng whom he had pleasd.
But god of Justyce had withturnd that fate,
Which where hit ought, lyght on hys proper pate.

Then fedd they fame by proclamation spredd,   69
Nought to forgett, that mought defame hym dead,

Which was so curyous, and so clerkly pennd,
So long with all: that when some dyd attend
Hys death so yonge: they saw, that longe afore
The Shroud was shaped, then babe to dye was boare.
So wonteth god to blynde the worldly wyse,
That not to see, that all the world espyes.

One hearyng hit, cryed out. A goodly cast,   705
And well contryved, fowle cast away for hast.
Whereto another gan in scoffe replye,
Fyrst pennd it was by enspyryng prophecye.
So can god reape up secrete mischiefes wrought,
To the confusyon of the workers thought.
My lords, the tubb, that drownd the Clarence duke,
Dround not his death, ne yet his deathes rebuke.

From Tragedy 22, *Henrye duke of Buckingham* (Campbell, p. 318).

These heavy burdens pressed us upon,   200
Tormenting us so by our selves alone,
Much like the felon that pursued by night,
Startes at eche bushe as his foe were in sight.

Nowe doubting state, nowe dreading losse of life,   204
In feare of wrecke at every blast of wynde,
Now start in dreames through dread of murdrers knyfe,
As though even then revengement were assynde.
With restles thought so is the guylty minde
Turmoyled, and never feeleth ease or stay,
But lives in feare of that which folowes aye.

*   *   *

So we diepe wounded with the bluddy thought,   239
And gnawing wurme that grieved our conscience so,
Never tooke ease, but as our hart furth brought
The strayned syghes in wytnes of our woe,
Such restles cares our fault did well beknowe:
Wherewith of our deserved fall the feares
In every place rang death within our eares.

*   *   *

Hated be thou, disdayned of every wyght,   666
And poynted at where ever that thou goe,
   trayterous wretche, unwurthy of the light,

Be thou estemed: and to encrease thy woe,
The sound be hateful of thy name also:
And in this sort with shame and sharpe reproche,
Leade thou thy life till greater grief approch.

Dole and despayer, let those by thy delight,   673
Wrapped in woes that can not be unfolde,
To wayle the daye, and wepe the weary night,
With rayny iyen and syghes can not be tolde,
And let no wyght thy woe seeke to witholde:
But coumpt thée wurthy (wretche) of sorrowes store,
That suffryng much, oughtest still to suffer more,

Deserve thou death, yea be thou demed to dye   680
A shamefull death, to ende thy shamefull lyfe:
A syght longed for, joyful to everye iye,
Whan thou shalt be arraygned as a thief,
Standing at bar, and pleadyng for thy lyef,
With trembling toung in dread and dolors rage,
Lade with white lockes, and fowerskore yeres of age.

From Tragedy 24, *Richard Plantagenet duke of Glocester* (Campbell,
    p.359).

What though he refused, yet be sure you maye,   92
That other were as ready to take in hand the thyng,
Which watched and wayted as duely for theyr pray,
As ever dyd the Cat for the Mouse taking,
And howe they might their purpose best to passe bryng:
Where Tyrryl he thought good to have no bloud shed,
Becast them to kyl by smothering in theyr bed.

The Wolves at hand were ready to devoure   99
The silly lambes in bed whereas they laye
Abiding death and looking for the hower,
For well they wyst, they could not scape awaye.
Ah, woe is me, that did them thus betraye,
In assigning this vile dede to be done,
By Myles Forrest, and wycked John Dyghton.

Who prively into theyr chamber stale,   106
In secrete wyse somewhat before midnyght,
And gan the bed together tug and hale,

Bewrapping them alas in rufull plyght,
Keping them downe, by force, by power, and might.
With haling, tugging, tormoyling, torne and tost,
Tyl they of force were forced to yeeld the ghost.

From Tragedy 25, *Shores wife* (Campbell, p. 373).

Among the rest by Fortune overthrowen,   1
I am not least, that most may wayle her fate:
My fame and brute abrode the world is blowen,
Who can forget a thing thus done so late?
My great mischaunce, my fall, and heavye state,
Is such a marke whereat eche tounge doth shoote,
That my good name is pluckt up by the roote.

*   *   *

Oh darke deceyt with paynted face for showe,   22
Oh poysoned baite that makes us egre styll,
Oh fayned frende deceyving people so,
Oh world of thée we can not speake to yll,
Yet fooles we are that bende so to thy skyll,
The plage and skourge that thousandes dayly feele,
Should warne the wise to shonne thy whyrling whele.